Progressions
Readings
for Writers

Progressions
Readings
for Writers

BETSY S. HILBERT
Miami-Dade Community College

W. W. Norton & Company
New York · London

Copyright © 1998 by W. W. Norton & Company, Inc.

The text of this book is composed in Meridien
with the display set in Stone Sans
Composition by ComCom
Manufacturing by Haddon Craftsmen
Book design by Charlotte Staub

Library of Congress Cataloging-in-Publication Data

Hilbert, Betsy S.
    Progressions, readings for writers / Betsy S. Hilbert.
        p.   cm.
    Includes index.

    ISBN 0-393-97197-X (pbk.)

    1. College readers. 2. English language—Rhetoric—Problems,
exercises, etc. 3. Report writing—Problems, exercises, etc.
I. Title.
PE1417.H49   1998
808´.0427—dc21   97-34649
                                                              CIP

W. W. Norton & Company, Inc., 500 Fifth Avenue, New York, N.Y. 10110
http://www.wwnorton.com

W. W. Norton & Company Ltd., 10 Coptic Street, London WC1A 1PU

1 2 3 4 5 6 7 8 9 0

Contents

3 . ORGANIZING PATTERNS 117
**Attention here focuses on rhetorical patterns
and other useful approaches to organization.**

5 . FROM EXPERIENCE TO ISSUES   315
**Extended personal essays move
from individual experience to
broader significance.**

Preface

Students arrive in my classes these days like the gods in Ralph Waldo Emerson's poem "Days," each one bearing different gifts. They represent in their diversity the student populations that colleges have come to know: a marvelous mix of people with a wide and fascinating range of cultural backgrounds, language abilities, ages, genders, political convictions, social attitudes, intentions, ambitions, academic preparations. Many of these students have had superb academic training; many more need quantities of help. Their backgrounds may be widely diverse, but their processes as learners are remarkably similar. They need to be accepted and feel acceptable; to be challenged and encouraged forward; to be safe from destructive criticism or unalloyed failure; and to be guided step-by-step toward greater growth. On the first day of class, they wonder: *Will it be easy? Will it be hard? Will it be interesting? Will I be able to do this?* The answer to each of those questions ought to be Yes.

Step-by-Step to Increasing Literacy

The plan of this book is to help students move progressively to greater successes and further challenges. It goes, in brief, from easy to hard—from short, straightforward pieces at the beginning to longer, more complex readings at the end. In the first few chapters readers will find punchy, rapid readings, beautiful examples of skillful short prose, and then they will move onward to the rich, complex essays at the end, intended to challenge the best readers in the classroom (instructor included). All along the continuum, the emphasis is on adult themes, and the emotional and intellectual content of each piece—wherever it is placed—should lead to lively class discussion.

Much of the challenge and interest of this book also comes from the wide variety of writing. Students will discover here many types and styles of essays, in addition to editorials, memoirs, short fiction, poetry, and biography. The idea is to honor the diversity of readers with a corresponding diversity of subjects, approaches, genres, themes, and authors.

Organization

The readings in this book are divided into seven groups, by length and reading level. "Short Prose and the Mini-Essay" is a collection of short pieces designed to intrigue a wide range of students and encourage active writing and class discussion. "Clarity, Economy, and Style" also consists of complete short works, demonstrating tight focus and economy as they stretch language and vocabulary skills. Second-language English students will easily apprehend the pieces in these first two sections, while expanding their vocabularies and usage, and even excellent readers will find the content compelling. The third section, "Organizing Patterns," shows students various structures and approaches, illustrating and explaining rhetorical organization. "Critical Thought" presents a somewhat more difficult intellectual challenge, including arguments to serve as models and sources for discussion and response. The essays in this section also have somewhat longer paragraphing than earlier selections, and increased vocabulary level. "From Experience to Issues" provides longer, more developed personal essays; and from those full-length biographical pieces students move on to the sixth level, "Textual Challenges," developing analytic and interpretive skills as they encounter unfamiliar vocabulary. Finally, "Eloquence and Expertise" provides philosophically and stylistically advanced readings, including modernist prose, each piece a rewarding workout for the intellect and spirit.

In Focus

The study questions, writing assignments, and In Focus discussions also move progressively from reading into writing. Study questions in the early chapters tend to focus on understanding and interpretation, while the later study questions and writing assignments move to critical thinking and in-depth analysis. The writing assignments are diverse by design, drawing heavily on personal experience in the early parts of the book and moving toward more-critical and argumentative prose, some involving research, at the end. Students will find a good deal to talk about, both in class and on paper, with the topics engendered by the study questions and writing ⸱ignments.

⸱ In Focus essays that follow most of the reading selections are brief, informative discussions on various points of reading and writing, distillations of what readers and writers ought to know. (A selection without its own In Focus essay further illustrates the previous discussion.) These selections are also designed to run progressively, going from "basic" discussions such as explanations of subject, theme, thesis, and purpose in the early sections to advanced literary perceptions and techniques in the later chapters. In no case, even with the earliest, shortest prose selections, does an In Focus discussion run longer than the piece itself. Students need plenty of information about literacy and composition, and we have provided plenty, but we also believe, from long experience on both sides of the teaching desk, that extended lecturing about writing can often create more inattention than education. The In Focus pieces are short, pithy, and packed with information on how to read and write effectively; they accomplish their purposes in as little space possible.

Wide-ranging Subject Matter

This book takes a different direction from the many composition texts that organize contents by topic or theme, even though alternative tables of contents organized by subjects and by rhetorical modes have been provided for instructors who prefer those approaches. The emphasis of this reading is on expressive and interpretive ability. It operates from the conviction that any subject can be made interesting when a competent writer interacts with an open-minded reader. It challenges the stereotype that only certain kinds of content will attract certain kinds of readers, and encourages students to become more open-minded about the subjects that might interest them.

Thus, the major criterion for inclusion in this book was simply *Is it wonderful writing?* The choices of contents followed Salman Rushdie's description of literature from *Imaginary Homelands,* his parable of a house with many rooms and with voices in every room: "The voices are talking about the house, about everyone in it, about everything that is happening and has happened and should happen."

Increasing Literacy in the Community of Readers and Writers

When the selections in this book were field-tested in composition classrooms, the student response was gratifying: "This is different," they said. "This is definitely *interesting.*" Readers were captured by the human interest and drama of many of the selections, fiction and nonfiction. They saw reflections of their own lives, even when the events described were far from their own experiences. They began (with a little help from their instructors) to recognize the various techniques involved in skillful writing of any kind. Reading and writing were improving together.

This book responds to—and celebrates—the differences and diversities of the contemporary college English classroom and of the literatures it teaches. Above all, the book is intended to convey the variety, importance, and pleasures of the written word.

Acknowledgments

Progressions was itself a collaborative writing assignment, and I am grateful beyond expression to all the members of the team. First thanks go to the staff at W. W. Norton: to Julia Reidhead, who first fostered the idea of the book; to Carol Hollar-Zwick, the editor of an author's dreams, whose perspicacity and persistence made it all seem almost possible; to Kurt Wildermuth, for his careful and skilled manuscript editing; to Kristin Sheerin, for her capable handling of the permissions; and to Marian Johnson and Diane O'Connor. Thanks go to my colleagues at Miami-Dade Community College and elsewhere, for their ideas and responses: to Thelma Altshuler, Eric Lichtman, and Stan Miron, and to Luisa Leon and the other members of the Independent Studies Department, for putting up with me while my mind and energies were on this book. Gratitude also to the reviewers and consultants across the country who helped me improve this, step by step: Rose-Ann Cecere, Broward Community College; Pat Gregory, Community College of Philadelphia; Gary Hoffman, Orange Coast College; Sylvia Holladay, St. Petersburg Community College; Elizabeth Leyson, Fullerton College; Barbara Wolf Pearce, Durham Technical Community College; Linda Palumbo, Cerritos College; Jane Paznik-Bondarin, Borough of Manhattan Community College; Nell Ann Pickett, Hinds Community College; Kathleen Tickner, Brevard Community College; and especially Linda Daigle, Houston Community College, whose thoughtful commentary and teacher's guide have increased the book's usefulness manifold.

Above all, the Hilbert/Sokolof/Cohen clan loved and supported me in this endeavor, as in everything else. This book comes out of a lifetime of joy in reading, and so it is dedicated in loving memory to the person who first taught me how to read: my sister, Muriel Cohen.

Thematic Table of Contents

Sex, Gender, and the Mating Dance

Personal Challenges

Cultural Diversity

SOCIAL CRITIQUES

POLITICS AND GOVERNMENT

SCIENCE, NATURE, AND THE ENVIRONMENT

Rhetorical Table of Contents

4   ARGUMENT/PERSUASION

Short Prose and the Mini-Essay

Short Prose in Focus

The authors in this first chapter have asked readers to join their worlds for only a very short time. This chapter contains short pieces of prose, all of them well under a thousand words. Their brevity, however, does not mean that the works were quickly or thoughtlessly written, for carelessness is the enemy of simplicity. At its best, an effective short essay is a small jewel, glowing from being cut and recut, polished and polished again, with careful attention paid to the importance of every word.

The In Focus essays in this chapter deal with some of the basic skills required by perceptive readers and writers. The terms *subject, theme, thesis,* and *purpose* are explained, and there are discussions of the ways that writers work to articulate their thoughts and experiences. The final In Focus essay explains how the short short story may be a useful writing exercise.

The Readings in Focus

Jan Wiener's "The Last Game," the first reading in this chapter, is a good example of how very simple language can contain weighty emotional content. The selection tells a story of love and suicide in a way that deals the reader a sudden blow to the gut. The spare vocabulary and straight declarative sentences of Wiener's piece increase this emotional impact by initially masking the horror of the story. A careful reader will notice how powerful the individual sentences are and how much meaning each one conveys—just as brief comments made by a nontalkative person may take on special significance.

In a lighter mode, Michelle Genz's "Getting Pucked," a story of the Date from Hell, demonstrates that irony and humor, too, can be expressed in a tale told simply. Genz's story and Leonard Pitts Jr.'s "Too Many Youths," both originally published as newspaper articles, are pungent pieces intended for readers who look for information and opinions that can be absorbed in the time it takes to drink a cup of coffee. The brevity of the Genz and Pitts pieces also allows for quick identification and analysis of three key elements in the study of effective writing: *subject, theme,* and *thesis.*

If there is a single key to writing effective short prose, it is in one directive: *focus.* There is space for only a single point, a single effect. The writer must be very clear about what that point is and not try to say everything at once, choosing examples and supporting material with care. *Purpose* is the key decision in determining how to write the piece. What is the purpose? What is the point? If the intended point or emotional impact can be summarized in one sentence, then the writer has done the vital work of effectively thinking out the purpose of the piece.

All the writing in this chapter demonstrates that single-mindedness of purpose necessary to good short prose. In "For Women Only," Ana Veciana-Suarez demonstrates the possibility of painting a detailed picture in fewer than eight hundred words, as she focuses on her family's rituals. Robb Walsh's essay on the church that isn't there, "Phantom Church of Cluny," shows how a narrow subject and a clear sense of purpose can create focus. Marcus Bleecker's "My Father's Black Pride" is another good example of clear purpose and focus. Bleecker wants to make a significant point about how his white father raised an African-American child, giving enough examples (and yet not too many) to show how it was done.

In an excerpt from *All I Really Need to Know I Learned in Kindergarten,* Robert Fulghum shows how *point of view* can be used to help readers imagine how other people—and other life-forms—see the same events we do. Two short poems by Carl Sandburg from the early years of the twentieth century display different points of view: that of the speaker, perhaps the poet, in "A Fence," and those of two contrasting characters in "Onion Days." Molly Ivins's "Get a Knife, Get a Dog, but Get Rid of Guns" demonstrates how a firm opinion can be firmly expressed. Rafe Martin demonstrates a classic blend of experience and idea in a short personal essay derived from his Buddhist philosophy, while Maya Angelou, in an excerpt from *The Heart of a Woman,* relates her own experiences during the 1950s to American history and historical figures.

The final section of this chapter is a series of very short personal stories selected from *The Sun,* one of contemporary America's best small literary magazines. Each issue of the magazine includes a "Readers Write" column, which invites submissions of short personal experiences having to do with a single topic. In this case, the announced topic was "Watching TV," and readers from all over the country sent in their short short stories. The variety of these five different pieces, none more than a few brief paragraphs long, demonstrates the diversity of approaches writers can take, even in the briefest of space, on a single subject.

The Last Game

JAN WIENER

I felt I had to return to Czechoslovakia. I felt I had to be there in the autumn of 1989 as freedom finally came. I had been there when the Nazis marched in. I had fought against them from Britain as a member of the Czechoslovak Air Force. And I had been there when the Communists took over in 1948. I had served five years in a labor camp for fighting with the British rather than the Russians during World War II.

And so I returned to my homeland, having always been there during times of crisis. I felt bound to help the people who toppled the Communist government in any way I could.

But before returning to Prague for patriotic reasons, I had to attend to a personal matter. I had to go back to Novo Mesto in northern Yugoslavia. Novo Mesto was where my father, chased from his native Czechoslovakia, had been forced to flee for his life. It is also where he had taken his life. Indeed, where I had watched him die.

It was April 1941, and I had fled with him. I was 20 years old. Now, almost 50 years later, I wanted to be near my father and talk to him. I felt guilty for having let him die alone. Sometimes I felt it would have been simpler if I had also decided to die, though now I feel some anger that my father deserted me.

The little house where it happened was near a cornfield. On the outside, the house seemed not to have changed at all. I knocked on the door, and the Bosnian worker who was living there with his wife and three children let me in. Yes, he said, he had heard about what once occurred in that house.

Looking down the entry hall, I saw the door to the room where my father died and, next to it, my old room. My mind began ricocheting between the past and the present. As I was led into the kitchen, I looked out the window and remembered jumping out of it when I left for the last time, so that no one would see me.

In the kitchen, there were the same wood-carved chair and unsteady table. My knees gave in and I sat down. I was trembling with the force of a memory I thought I had under control.

The Bosnian's wife saw me shaking and prepared Turkish coffee. The

3

sound and smell of the grinding beans evoked more memories. In the semidarkness of the approaching evening, the wife's graceful movements and slim build reminded me of my mother, a Jew who was not able to escape from Nazi-occupied Prague and perished in Theresienstadt concentration camp. The Bosnian brought me a glass of homemade slivovitz, a Slavic plum brandy. I drank hastily, one and then another. Warmth spread like a blanket over my shivering body. A wave of remembering washed out the present, and I heard my father's voice.

"*Gardez la dame!*" he said, and I protected my queen with a knight. But my hand was trembling. My father put his hand on mine. I did not look up.

"We are still free, and we still have choices. If we wait any longer, even that last freedom won't be ours." He looked at me with apprehension. "We must make a decision now."

We were sitting facing each other, the chessboard between us, our hands locked. I raised my eyes and looked into his face: the long gray hair combed back, the light blue eyes with the green specks and that bold hooked nose.

"What choices do we have?" I asked, finally.

"To die our own way or theirs. We are trapped and I cannot run any more."

I looked out the window into the falling dusk. This is not happening, I thought. My father is supposed to know a way out.

"Tonight," my father said in a low voice, "I will take my life."

I had been prepared for these words, and yet they came as a blow because he said them softly.

"What about me?" I asked. I would have liked to have begged my father not to leave me. To stay. But something in my father's face made me not plead. I knew he was right, and I knew his greatest concern was not the loss of his own life but the fate of his son.

"Jan," he said, "you would do best if you did the same. There is no chance. I am not afraid of death. I am afraid of humiliation."

"How will you do it?" I whispered.

"Poison. It is completely painless. You fall asleep."

After a long, dark silence he asked, "What is your decision?"

I wondered, Why is he so calm? Then I knew. There is no doubt in him. But for me, not to live seemed impossible. Finally I said, "I want to try to get away."

Two emotions simultaneously welled up inside of me: a burning hatred for the Nazis who forced people to make life-and-death decisions and a deep feeling of love for my father. I nearly said, "Let's try to escape together." But I knew the decision had been made.

We went to my father's bedroom. He opened a drawer and took out

10 gold pieces. They were on a string. Father put them around my neck. He gave me the little money he had. "Try to get to Ljubljana and go to the Bolaffios' house," he said, referring to friends of our family. "They might help you. Tell them what has happened." He smiled faintly. "Dying is easy. Leaving you is difficult. I love you, son."

We were standing, holding each other. Breaking the embrace, my father said, "Let's finish the game." And we sat down at the chessboard. I lost.

"Promise me that you will wait until I am dead. If I am still breathing when you come into the room in the morning, wait. If the Nazis find me still alive, they'll pump out my stomach and I would have lost the freedom to choose."

I went to my bedroom, undressed and tried to sleep. If it could be only a bad dream, I lay thinking. But it was not. The feeling of irreversibility drove me frantic. I ran to my father's room and opened the door. He was standing by a table, putting white powder on a wafer. He looked up and said firmly: "You must not disturb me any more! Take this"—he handed me two sleeping pills—"it will make you sleep. Goodbye, now. Goodbye."

When I awoke early the next morning, I jumped out of bed and ran into father's room. He was lying on his bed, breathing heavily and irregularly. I called him, but he was unconscious. I wanted to run, but I remembered my promise. So I sat watching my father die and wishing he would die quickly.

His breathing became loud and slow. Then it faded away. I took my father's wedding ring and put it in my pocket. I bent down and kissed his forehead. I kissed his hand, took the other hand and gently folded them over his chest.

The pain of memory ebbed away. I was back in the present. I put my hand gently on the head of the Bosnian's young son, the way my father did when I was a boy his age.

The mother got up to draw the curtain over the window, and it was as if the drawn curtain blocked out the remaining pain.

LITERACIES

What does it mean to say we are literate? Does literacy mean reading well enough to interpret traffic signs or instructions for taking pills—or does it mean we read for pleasure, read on trains and buses and into long nights of solitude, haunt bookstores for something other than coffee? Is literacy the ability to write one's name on checks and legal documents, or does the term imply an ability to write something more complicated with ease and competence?

Traditionally, the term *illiterate* meant a total inability to read or write at even the most basic level. For millennia, reading and writing were confined to small, elite groups, while other people used Xs as their signatures on the rare occasions they came in contact with the law. (That is one reason why marriages and legal contracts still, out of tradition, require public witnesses.) Over the past few hundred years, however, as more and more of the general population needed to learn basic reading and writing, a different kind of illiteracy became apparent—a vast illiteracy of people who have degrees but cannot read with thoughtfulness and pleasure, who never write letters, e-mail, or notes, who are afraid of the languages of math and computers. Moreover, this poverty of the mind is frequently tied to poverty of the pocket: Economists point out that good jobs these days require more and more the ability to speak intelligently and clearly, to read and interpret information, to write reports and memoranda, to manage computer technologies.

Thus, *literacy* is not a single skill but a pathway to better, more sensitive, and more intelligent processing of what other people—writers and speakers—are trying to tell us. This book is based on the idea that with the right techniques to promote such development, people can become more and more literate in every area of communication. Literacy is not something that one gets and holds forever; it is always a process of growth.

Study Questions

1. Why didn't the young man in the story do anything to prevent his father's suicide? Was there anything he could have done or said? What do you think his feelings were then, and are they any different now?
2. Is the person telling the story older or younger than his father was at the time of his father's death?
3. Some of the action in the story revolves around a game of chess. What is the significance of that game? Can you perceive other kinds of "games" being played in the story?

Writing Topics

1. Does your family play any games, such as chess, Monopoly, or Scrabble? How do different people's characters come out as they play the games?

Write a brief scene in which you describe a family game and some of the people playing it. See if you can show something about the characters of the players through the way they play and the things they say.

2. Have you ever gone back to a place you knew in your youth or childhood? How was the place different from the way you remembered it? What things seemed to have stayed the same? Is there anything that was very important in your younger years that you now view differently? Write an essay in which you describe the experience of returning.

3. Write a short essay in which you or someone you know returns to the scene of a painful time. What are the benefits and consequences of returning? Is it a good idea to go back and remember, or should some things just be covered up and forgotten? What can we learn by going back?

Getting Pucked

MICHELLE GENZ

What Allison Ward doesn't like about dating is the drill, she says, the whole routine: meeting the guy, then getting asked out, like, Good, you've measured up. Then the whole exercise of dressing up, waiting, making conversation. Besides, for her efforts, she has never had great results.

Fact is, at 37, she finds that whatever heartache might come from the occasional Saturday night alone is mild compared to the headache of dating.

And this headache topped them all.

They'd met at a party, he called her up, they went out once. The drill. And now, the second date. She made him dinner; the grilled dolphin was fine. But he didn't like asparagus. "Less than 4 percent of the world's population likes asparagus," he told her.

The couscous, he called "air-rice."

Allison kept an open mind. There are probably men who make excellent husbands, after all, who don't like asparagus. "Like George Bush and broccoli," Allison says. Then imagines a second date with George Bush.

"Anyway." The game would be fun. Her date, a college coach, was taking her to see the Panthers. She likes hockey. But an hour into the game, the success of the evening is still up in the air. And then something strikes her. At 75 miles per hour.

It is a two-inch-wide freezing-cold wad of hard rubber, a hockey puck, launched from the end of a player's stick directly into her forehead. It leaves a bloody dent midway between her hairline and her brow.

"We're talking gusher here," says Allison.

"Wow," says Allison's date flatly. "We have a problem here."

Allison is "stupefied." Someone from the crowd passes her a napkin to sop up the mess. She thinks later she should have checked it for mustard.

An usher escorts her out. Quickly. Allison, a publicist, understands:

The smack of the puck has transformed her from a cheering fan to a big PR problem.

"I was *not* a good visual," says Allison.

Her date follows her up the stairs. Someone she knew in the stands later told her he was rolling his eyes as he walked: "Here we go, a girlie thing," is the way Allison interpreted that.

At the arena's first-aid station, a guy hands her his card. He is the insurance adjuster for the Florida Panthers, here every night, says Allison, just for this. It was a bad night for getting pucked. After Allison, two other people were hit.

"Why didn't you duck?" her date asks her as he drives her to the hospital.

"Why weren't you sitting in my seat?" she asked him.

He delivers her to the automatic doors of Mount Sinai [Hospital] and waits in the lobby. Small comfort that there is a basketball game airing on the wall TV; the hockey game is going on without him. Clearly he expects things to roll along now. He is wrong. He will spend the next three hours waiting for a woman he hardly knows to be tended to. Nurses report to Allison that he is pacing the floor, flagging down staff, demanding to know what's taking so long. "I'm on the date from hell," she tells Jody, the triage nurse, as she finally starts to sob. He had told her at the outset: he doesn't like high-maintenance women. "I'm a successful businesswoman," insists Allison. "Normally, I don't *need* maintenance."

"We better call plastics," nurse Jody announces in a somber tone, washing off blood that has dripped down Allison's arms, splattered her Anne Klein pale blue knit top, soaked her expensive pants and permanently stained her Cole-Haan loafers. There is blood in her hair, and under her fingernails. She is minus an earring. Jody wipes the mascara off Allison's cheeks, all that is left of the pre-date optimism in the mirror.

It is nearly midnight by the time they stitch her up and turn her back over to her date.

"Can I have a drink when I get home?" she asks Jody. Jody recommends it highly.

Her date drives her to her Brickell Avenue townhouse, walks her in, decides to stay. He wants to make sure she's OK.

"On a scale of one to 10, you were an eight," he tells her proudly. As if she wanted someone keeping score. She pours a double Scotch, puts in a movie, Kevin Costner's *No Way Out*. He stays until 2 in the morning. It doesn't cross her mind that on any other date this might give a guy something to talk about.

But then, he had enough already. "Great bar talk," he told her later.

Allison got her own trophy. Three weeks later, a Fed Ex box arrived from the Florida Panthers. A wooden plaque, with a puck attached. "I was caught cat-napping by the Florida Panthers, 1995," it says.

"I don't want the goddamned puck," she says.

Meanwhile the "incident" didn't completely ice the potential romance. Since the hockey game, they've spoken several times on the phone and gone to a party on a boat. When he saw her scar he said, "Wow, it's really pink."

OK, so maybe this isn't the one who's going to make all the bells ring. Still, if he calls her again she's inclined to go out with him. What the heck. Beats getting hit in the head with a puck.

IN FOCUS

SUBJECT AND THEME

The *subject* of a piece of writing is what the piece is about on the surface. Usually, the subject is obvious; in this case, the story is about a woman on a date who gets hit in the head with a hockey puck. But most stories have meanings that go beyond the obvious. Perhaps the Genz story is also about the different ways that women and men react to different situations. Perhaps it is also about the difficulties of dating, of finding someone for a loving relationship. Perhaps it also says something about sports, and how men and women see sports differently. All of those ideas, and groups of ideas, constitute *themes.*

The *theme* of a piece of writing is the idea or concept of the work, sometimes hidden, sometimes easily visible. Subject is what an author is writing about; theme is what the author is saying about the subject. Subject is "who does what"; theme is idea. Subject is the outward shape; theme is the inner working.

In "The Last Game," the piece just before this one, the subject is the suicide of the author's father. But there are also themes of war, of courage, of the relationship between father and son. All of these meanings and reflections are woven into what is, on the surface, a simple tale. Beneath an apparent subject can lie many layers of themes.

Study Questions

1. Take a careful look at what Allison says throughout the essay. Is she really trying to keep an open mind about this man? In what ways does her attitude affect her responses to the situation?
2. Suppose Allison's date had been struck with the hockey puck. How would Allison have reacted?
3. Many of the paragraphs in this piece are extremely short; in some cases, one or two sentences. Relatively short paragraphs are necessary in newspapers and magazines, where the columns are narrow, so that paragraphs don't become long blocks of text. In college essays and academic writing, however, longer paragraphs, usually five to six sentences, are often required. Consider the differences between the styles of writing of journalists and academic authors.

   How does sentence and paragraph length contribute to a writer's style? What effect does the short, "punchy" paragraph have on the reader? (Note: for a related discussion of sentence fragments, see Study Question 3, p. 15, for the Pitts essay following.)

Writing Topics

1. Do men and women have different reactions to sports events? What are those differences? Write a short essay in which you describe a couple at a sports event (or watching one on TV). Tell what each person is thinking.
2. Using "Getting Pucked" as a model, tell your own story about a perfectly horrible date.

Too Many Youths Turn Life's "Speed Bumps" into Unscalable Peaks

LEONARD PITTS JR.

I was 20 years old when Jo dumped me. A blind person could have seen it coming. She had been dropping clues for weeks, like a trail of bread crumbs meant to lead me to reality.

Only, I chose not to see.

Which is how I wound up standing at her front door that day. I had come unannounced, and she faced me with a look both sheepish and exasperated. She was wearing the robe I had bought her for Christmas, and behind her, in the room she wouldn't let me enter, I could see some guy I didn't know sitting on the couch.

Oh. *Now I get it.*

I had never felt so crushed, so humiliated. I wanted to crawl into a sewer and pull it shut behind me.

I wanted to die.

Last week, some gerbil-brained punk finally heard what my oldest daughter had been telling him for months: that she doesn't want to be his girlfriend.

He wanted to kill.

Call it a sign of the times—and of the boy's brazen stupidity. After all, he made the threat loudly, repeatedly, to anyone who would listen. Called my house maybe a half-dozen times to launch obscenity-laced tirades.

Nothing we can do about it, said the police officer who initially responded to our call. Nothing we can do until he follows through on the threat. Besides, he's a juvenile.

Nothing I can do about it, said his mother when we complained to her. I've prayed for him, she said, taken him for counseling. Nothing seems to work. He's out of control.

I'll show him control, I thought, indulging myself with violent fantasies that always ended with me standing over his bloodied and unmoving carcass.

And I thought about that day when Jo dumped me. How long ago it seemed. And how innocent I was.

I don't remember much of what happened after I staggered away from her, my heart shredded. But I know that I healed—and relatively quickly, at that. The memory eventually lost the power to hurt me. Time robbed it of passion, hindsight drew away the heat. It came to seem a minor thing, a speed bump on the road to adulthood.

But for too many kids these days, the bump is a mountain they can't get over. I don't pretend to know why. Only that the world seems radically different now. That the children of the day seem ferociously impatient when their desires are denied. That they imbue every tiny setback with the full weight and passion of Shakespearean tragedy. And so, every glancing wound becomes mortal, every real or imagined insult worth killing or dying for.

Does a rosy tint steal across my glasses? Maybe. But I know, have seen, have read of, too many kids for whom it would be inconceivable to merely stumble away, disheveled, from Jo's door. Too many kids in whom some misplaced sense of honor demands blood and vengeance.

Too many kids who haven't the time for healing.

And so, you get these awful, screaming headlines about adolescents, *babies,* shooting, stabbing, beating one another to death. Killing and dying over a boyfriend or a girlfriend, patch of street or a strip of park. Or, sometimes just because.

And if I write only about children here, it's not because I'm unaware that adults also kill and die for foolish, misplaced passions.

No, it's because they *are* children and as such, I expect them to be . . . I don't know . . . *better.* I want them to learn the value of time and perspective so they can know that not all pain kills. Or is worth killing for.

These words go into the computer on a blustery afternoon when the wind whips the trees and the quiet is broken only by the occasional sound of debris hitting the front door. The world is a gray and ugly place and my kids are out there in it. My oldest son is on the road to [The University of Florida at] Gainesville; the two middle boys, 12 and 9, are still in school.

And my daughter sits in class under threat of death for having spurned some boy. I watch the door and wait with unaccustomed anxiety for them all to be home.

THESIS

The subject and primary theme of Pitts's newspaper column are fairly obvious. They concern the worries of a father about the safety of his children, brought on by threats against the daughter from a boyfriend she no longer wants to see. The author is concerned not only about one child but about all, so that the subject of his daughter's predicament ties directly into the general theme of how all parents worry about their children. Another general theme is the problems of young people today, as different from those of young people in the writer's generation. In addition, however, Pitts clearly states a specific point: "the children of the day seem ferociously impatient when their desires are denied." This stated point becomes the author's *thesis*.

In this essay, the thesis is placed in the middle, just after the writer's description of his daughter's situation as seen in the light of his own memories. The writer makes his main point—that too many children today turn disappointment into tragedy—and then goes on to close the piece with his fears about the safety of his other children. The thesis is *embedded* in the essay, a technique that is acceptable for a short piece such as this column but would make the thesis difficult to find in a longer piece.

Most frequently, the thesis is stated early in an essay, particularly an essay meant to argue a specific point. Rhetoric textbooks often tell beginning writers to place a sentence or two specifically stating the main point or thesis at the end of the introduction, often as the last sentence or sentences of the first paragraph. (Marcus Bleecker, in "My Father's Black Pride," later in this chapter, makes his main point at the end of his first paragraph.) A thesis might also be effectively placed at the end of a piece of writing as a summary of the point already made. (Ana Veciana-Suarez's essay, also in this chapter, states a thesis nearly at the end of the piece.)

Wherever it is placed, the thesis statement is a specific message to the reader, focusing the writing on that single point. While there may be many themes, a short piece of writing has room for only one thesis.

Study Questions

1. The writer is in conflict with himself: he understands the boy's reactions, yet he secretly wants to murder the "gerbil-brained punk." What

is the difference between his reactions and the young man's? How does a person gain the kind of balance and maturity to avoid the violence that Pitts says so many children fall into?

2. The scene at the end of the piece is of a windy day, with litter blowing and banging against the front door. What significance does this image have? How does it reflect the mood of the writer?

3. Notice the number of sentence fragments Pitts uses. There are sentences that begin with the words "and" and "or": "And how innocent I was"; "Or is worth killing for." There are sentences that lack appropriate verbs: "Too many kids in whom some misplaced sense of honor demands blood and vengeance." There are also one-word sentences: "Maybe." Any of these sentence errors would be a mistake in a classroom essay, although in newspaper writing, short sentence fragments are relatively common and accepted.

Why are there such different standards for what is "correct" English? Why should academic writing require more attention to formal mechanics, such as grammatical rules? As you consider this question, also consider the differences between "correctness" in written and spoken language.

Writing Topics

1. Describe an event in your childhood or youth during which you lost self-control and on which you now look back with some wisdom and perspective. What were the repercussions? Tell what you experienced then and what you think about it now.

2. Pitts seems convinced that young people today are much more prone to act out their frustrations and behave violently than those of his generation or earlier. Do you agree or disagree? Give your own explanation of why young people today are prone to violent actions. Alternately, explain why you think that youths today are *not* more violent than previous generations.

For Women Only

ANA VECIANA-SUAREZ

Just the other week I won a very important contest before a group of people who matter dearly to me. Blindfolded, dizzy from being twirled, and giddy with the pleasure of an exquisite Sunday afternoon, I managed to pin, to the surprise of all gathered, a paper bundle to the beak of a cardboard stork. The round of applause that followed was deafening.

But just as I was to accept the prize—a night light decorated with a doll-size crocheted hat—I was overcome with guilt. Taller than all the other women in my family, I had seen the stork board through a sliver at the bottom of the blindfold.

"I cheated," I blurted suddenly to the audience.

"Boo!" the women hissed. Some threw paper napkins. "Boo!"

Disqualified but not necessarily embarrassed, I had to surrender the prize to my 9-year-old niece.

Tis the season for baby showers and wedding parties, for a ritual of female bonding that is as much part of our lives as the proverbial shopping spree, yet no one ever seems to discuss these rites much. We organize them, we attend them, we buy presents for the guests of honor, we play the silly games, we let our hair down—with nary a thought of the whys or wherefores of our actions. And that, I think, is the best part of these gatherings.

At a baby or wedding shower, we discuss intimacies we dare not reveal otherwise, not even to the stranger next to us on the flight to Montreal. With longtime friends, we pick up the knitting of our lives, the last stitch in a story, as though we had never put down the needles. We debate female plumbing, career moves, our children's frustrating behaviors, the men in our lives, all those complicated, complex relationships that both shade and lighten our days. Depending on our age and the quality of beverages served, we also dispense advice with the easy wisdom borne of relaxation.

Precious and few, these are afternoons filched from busy schedules, *our* time with other women, doing women things, *silly* women things, and making no pretension about it. This is when I hear the latest on the long-lost cousin, the feud between the two brothers, the impending divorce, the possible marriage, the emotional rise and fall of almost everybody I have known for the past four decades. And it also is during these discussions on languid afternoons that I realize the intricate interweaving of all our lives, and how very important the resulting fabric is to my well-being.

Which is why I have been dismayed that recent years have seen an increase in co-ed showers. "This one," a hostess once told me, "is non-gender specific." I had to bite my tongue and hold back laughter. The requirement in these politically correct times is to be inclusive, but there are occasions when we must shout a resounding PHOOEY! to that. I like, and need, my time with the "girls," alone and uninhibited, free to play—and cheat—without male competition or distraction.

Because, after pin-the-stork and honeymoon scrabble, following the cake and *pastelitos* and the ceremonial opening of presents, I return home to the family, having discussed every possible emotional entanglement *ad nauseam,* the engine of my heart pumping once again with the rich blood of female companionship.

Study Questions

1. The subject of this essay is the ritual of the baby shower, and the theme is the joy of the experience, the bonding ritual of the women together. At the end, the author also states a point, or thesis, about her opposition to making these women's rituals co-ed: "I like, and need, my time with the 'girls,' alone and uninhibited, free to play— and cheat—without male competition or distraction." What other kind of thesis sentence might the author have written? Try writing a thesis sentence for this essay that could be placed near the beginning.

2. There is a general opposition to "men only" activities today because for so long women were kept out of exclusively male occupations and activities and thus prevented from advancing their careers or social status. Is there an acceptable level of "exclusiveness," as Veciana-Suarez describes it? Where is the line drawn? What about a party that would exclude her, a party with a "no Hispanics" rule? Would she feel different? Would you?

3. In your opinion, is the author writing from a particular angle as a woman or as a member of a particular culture? What about her argument is specific to her personal situation?

Writing Topics

1. *Collaborative writing activity.* In every culture, there are ceremonies and rites of "bonding." What such ceremonies and events have you experienced? Were they male to male, female to female, family, cultural? Were there "men only" and "women only" activities? (Can there be bonding with other species?)

   After listening to other people's descriptions, write an essay in which you consider the similarities and differences in bonding ceremonies across cultural and personal lines.

2. Describe a kind of "bonding ceremony" you have participated in. Include in your essay a description of the group activities and customs with which everyone is familiar, activities that serve to produce a common experience. What makes those kinds of events important?

3. Imagine you are the husband of the pregnant woman for whom the baby shower is being held. You wanted to come to the party—after all, it's *your* wife and *your* baby. Write a letter to Ana, telling her how much you resented being kept away, and why. State your thesis, your main point, somewhere in the beginning of the essay, and then repeat it in different words toward the end.

Phantom Church of Cluny

ROBB WALSH

There is an emptiness that hangs in the air over the old stone houses and tree-shaded courtyards of the tiny Burgundy village of Cluny. Its invisible shadow darkens my mood as I walk through the stone archway of the town gate. It is an emptiness so well-defined and so palpable that visitors stand and point at it.

The hole in the sky above the crooked cobblestone streets of the old village center is where the second largest church in Christendom once stood. Like an amputee who still feels sensations in his phantom limb, the ancient village of Cluny is still haunted by its phantom church.

Begun in the year 1088, the Abbey Church of St. Peter and St. Paul was, at the time, the world's largest church: two football fields long, with a vaulted ceiling almost 100 feet high; the exterior stonework was crowned with spires and bell towers and supported by buttresses. In 1804, after the end of the French Revolution, the spectacular Romanesque masterpiece was dynamited. All that's left of it now are the towers of the south transept and bases of the interior pillar, the great church's foundations exposed and left vacant.

A museum dedicated to the church stands a few feet away from the excavation. Inside, I look at an animated, three-dimensional computer re-creation on videotape that shows views of the structure from all angles while a Gregorian chant fills the background. Back outside, I stare again at the void. The computer model is still so fresh in my mind that an image of the enormous edifice seems to appear before me. I'm not alone in this optical illusion: Everyone leaving the museum seems to do the same double take outside. It's as if we're having a mass hallucination of a building that no longer exists.

Later, I run into the man in charge of Cluny's tourism office, Deputy Mayor Serge Filion, in a hotel bar. The unlikely town official immigrated here from Quebec, Canada, and opened a fast-food outlet called Quebec Burger on Cluny's main street. His success in the hamburger business catapulted him into public office.

"So what do you think of Cluny?" Serge asks. "It's nice," I reply weakly. Serge moves a little closer. "I mean, what do you really think?"

"Well, if you really want to know, I think it's a tragic place," I confess. "What happened to the church seems to haunt everybody. You can't help but feel sad in Cluny."

"I know," Serge says with a sigh. "Everybody in Cluny feels guilty about what we did to the church. I feel guilty about it myself, and I'm from Canada!"

"But how did it happen?" I want to know. "Why did it happen? Were they just rebellious revolutionaries? Were they mad at the Catholic Church? Or did they do it just to make money selling the stones?"

Serge sadly repeats a story he has told many times before. The Benedictine Order founded the community of Cluny in the year 910, he tells me. It became one of the largest monastic centers the world had ever known. At its highest point, 1,100 Clunaic Benedictine monasteries inhabited by 10,000 monks were spread over Europe. The center of it all was right here in the Abbey of Cluny.

But as religious zeal waned over the years, the population of monks dwindled. With the execution of the abbot and many of the remaining monks during the Reign of Terror, the abbey and church were finally abandoned. The tiny village had no use for its massive, empty church. They tried using it as a horse stable, but it was too drafty. And it sat right in front of the entrance to the village, cutting off one side from the other.

And so the village of Cluny sold the church to a merchant from Mâcon, who turned it into a stone quarry. For more than a decade, the church was blasted away and sold, stone by stone.

"It wasn't anger or rebellion that caused them to dynamite the church." Serge shrugs. "It was just that the church was too big."

In the late 1800s, the French government enacted legislation to protect its architectural treasures. The preservation movement forced the citizens of Cluny to realize what a horrible thing they had done. Over the years, the remaining buildings of the Abbey of Cluny and what was left of the Abbey Church of St. Peter and St. Paul were carefully excavated and preserved.

Last year, 700,000 tourists came to see Cluny and the church that isn't there.

PURPOSE

Purpose is the rhetorical term for the writer's aim or goal for the work. What is the point of writing the piece; what is the expected outcome? (And no, the statement "My purpose as a writer is to get this thing over with" will not suffice.) What is the audience supposed to get out of the reading? What kind of effect is the piece to have on its readers? Will readers at the end be saddened or happier, amused, informed, made angry or more thoughtful, be moved to action? The writer's sense of purpose focuses the process on what the writing, in the end, is intended to do for the reader.

Robb Walsh could have written a public-relations travel piece about how wonderful Cluny is as a tourist destination, intending to encourage people to visit. He could have explained the architecture of cathedrals, the history of France, the economy of the country, or the mentality of people who live in small towns and villages. He could have tried to get his readers to send in donations in order to rebuild the church. Instead, he creates a sense of sadness at the mistakes people make in not valuing the past. Perhaps he also wants his readers to remember the church of Cluny the next time people in their own towns want to tear down something beautiful.

Notice how in nearly every essay the thesis relates to the author's sense of purpose. The thesis is the writer's central point; a statement of purpose indicates what effect the writer wants to have on the reader. For example, "Too much agricultural land in our country is being lost to housing development" is a thesis. "To make readers understand and feel the loss of agricultural land so that they will want to take action" is a statement of purpose.

Study Questions

1. The subject of this piece is the church that has disappeared and how it was destroyed. One of the themes has to do with how people don't appreciate the past or don't appreciate what they have until it's gone (the way that so many tourists now come to Cluny and miss the wonderful building that is now gone). What kind of thesis statement could be written for this essay? Where would you place the thesis statement?

2. How long did the great church last? How long from the time it was dynamited did it take for people to regret what they had done? Can you compare those two time periods to reach a conclusion?

3. Did the local people have a right to destroy something that might be considered a great work of humanity, a possession of all? Was the church theirs to do with as they wanted, even if they wanted the church gone? Where do you stand in the argument between local prerogatives and broader needs? What if, for example, the people living near a great forest want jobs cutting down all the trees, but people elsewhere want the forest to stay beautiful? Whose wants, needs, and rights are more important?

4. Should we take down buildings when they're no longer useful? What if they're in the way, as the church was, or even dangerous? What if they're historically important but not beautiful, like many factories?

Writing Topics

1. Describe something in your community that ought to be preserved for future generations. What does it mean to you? Why should it be maintained? What could lead to its destruction? Write a short argument in the form of a letter to the editor of a newspaper, giving reasons why this thing or place should be preserved.

2. Choose one of the buildings on your campus. Write an essay giving three good reasons for replacing it with something else.

3. Choose a building in need of preserving, or one that is being preserved, and do some research into its background. Perhaps you can find material on the building in the library or historical archives in your area. You may also be able to interview someone who was familiar with that building in the past. Write an essay in which you bring in the history of the building as part of an argument for its preservation.

My Father's Black Pride

MARCUS BLEECKER

I am black. My mother is black. My father is white. This wouldn't necessarily be important, but we live in a country where conflict runs deep between blacks and whites. We live in a country where white male slaveholders casually disavowed the black children they had sired. We live in a country where the worst of human traits—laziness, violence and irrationality—are seen as defining characteristics of those of African descent. This makes my being a mixed-race person whose ethnic identity is black somewhat complicated. There is a dissonance between who I say I am—a proud black man trying to do something positive with his life—and who society says I am. Yet I feel strong, and I embrace my black heritage. I've often reflected on how I learned to keep my positive self-image. The answer is, my white father.

With my olive-colored skin, hazel eyes and curly hair, I've been taken for Hispanic or Middle Eastern. In fact, in addition to being black, I am Jewish. And my father taught me to be proud of that heritage as well. When bullies at school demanded, "Are you black or white?" there was no confusion. When I ran home and asked my father, he said, "Tell them you are African-American." That was in the early 1970's and it was a term I wouldn't hear until the Afrocentric movement of the 1990's made it fashionable again.

It wasn't that my father wanted me to deny my Jewish roots, it's just that he knew we live in a society where my African heritage would define me socially. He didn't want me to seem ashamed of my black roots. My father knew that love and hopes for an ideal world in the distant future would be no panacea for the bigotry and small-mindedness I would encounter in my lifetime. He didn't want me, my brother or my sister to be unprepared for racism.

And so, my father, a writer and avid reader, lined my shelves with books about black American culture, African culture and Jewish culture. He encouraged me to think, to come up with my own ideas. A simple question posed to him was sure to be followed by his search for a book on the subject, with articles and additional materials to follow. In this way he gave me not only his opinion, but also the keys to how he arrived at that opinion. Knowing that I had those keys, too, he thought that I could evaluate his opinion and come up with my own. He encouraged me to determine what being black meant to me.

In the predominantly white suburb near Princeton, N.J., where I grew up, my father knew that I needed to know black men. So when I started playing drums at age 14, my father took me to jazz clubs. He encouraged me to talk to the musicians and get their autographs. This introduction led to my decision to become a professional musician, and also filled my home with a black male presence. Jazz was more than a genre of music; it instructed me in the cool posture of black men—Max Roach's shades, Miles Davis's scowl and his always stylish threads. It also instructed me in a kind of heroism. These men were geniuses who created America's only enduring art form despite its best efforts to stifle and ignore them.

My father also hired James, a black 16-year-old, who became my favorite baby sitter. My father gave me book knowledge and taught me to have an open mind; James showed me how to deal with people on a practical level. My father was gentle, but James taught me that as a black man, you have to be ungentle sometimes. You have to speak up for yourself. James never let me walk away from a confrontation without speaking my mind.

During the summers, my parents sent me to my mother's family in Virginia. My cousins—especially Jeffrey, who is seven years older than I—helped me become a mature black man. Jeffrey taught me to treat women with respect, through his example as well as through his words. These are lessons my father had taught me also, but he hoped that my summer visits down South would reinforce those values by being transmitted by black men of my generation.

In college, I counseled children from mixed backgrounds. I could see the emptiness in some of the kids either who didn't have a black parent around—usually the father—or whose parents weren't in agreement about how much emphasis should be put on black culture. Often these children would grow up in a predominantly white environment with a negative view of their black fathers or of black culture in general. I realized how fortunate I was to have both parents and to have a father who encouraged me to develop as a black person while never making me feel that I was any less his son because of my blackness.

In many ways what my father taught me about manhood was not related to color. He taught me that, ultimately, I determined through my behavior what a black man is. My father taught me to be a gentle man, to use my mind and not my fists. He taught me the value of education and encouraged me to ask questions. My father exposed me to black men who lived up to these universal ideals of manhood, and thereby emphasized that blacks shared in that tradition. All these things have made me the man, the black man, I am today.

My father and I are now the closest we have ever been. Of course, there are race-related topics, things I feel, that he will never be able to understand. I know that there are probably people who meet my father and see just another white man. But I know that there are things he has learned from me and my brother that have given him an insight into black masculinity that most white men will never experience. In this way, we have taught each other. Our relationship epitomizes a reality that is so rarely seen—a black man and a white man who are not adversaries. Who are more than father and son. They are men who love each other very deeply.

PERSONAL AND ACADEMIC WRITING

"We live in an autobiographical age," notes Tracy Kidder, in his introduction to *The Best American Essays 1994* (Boston: Houghton Mifflin, 1994). "Almost everyone who reports for magazines and journals uses the first person. Even academics and book reviewers begin essays with personal anecdotes, like waiters introducing themselves before getting down to business."

Certainly, however, not every academic begins every academic paper with a personal anecdote. There is still an often-expressed objection to using the first person, "I," in a college essay; the reasoning is that college should be a place where students learn to move beyond their own particular experiences and into a broader world, a world of ideas and theories that goes beyond the personal. Kidder himself includes a warning about the "I" essay even while he is justifying it: "but the first person beguiles some writers, and the act of writing the word 'I' tends to make them forget that they have to do more than merely assert the interestingness of their experience. . . . The thoroughgoing first person is a demanding mode. It asks for the literary equivalent of perfect pitch."

Once the difficulties are understood, personal writing remains an important part of many college composition courses. For one thing, it's a useful mode. People are interested in their own experiences, and so there is more motivation to describe those experiences at greater length, allowing for more muscular stretch. For another thing, writing down one's thoughts and daily incidents, as in a journal or an autobiographical essay, helps one to analyze and evaluate the thinking around those opinions and activities. Thus, the general run of composition courses, like the general pattern of this book, is to begin with meaningful individual stories and then move on to more intellectual, evaluative kinds of writing. Students who want someday to write essays for publication will eventually, of course, continue working to develop their "perfect pitch" in the personal essay.

A word of warning: Though the word "I" is not only acceptable (check with your instructor, as always) but necessary for some assignments, it shouldn't be overused. One or two "I"s in a paragraph should be more than enough; if too many sprout up, revise the sentences to eliminate most repeat "I"s. In addition, even though the first person may be used in college essays, the second person, "you," is not acceptable, unless it is a direct address to the reader. "You" should not be used in a general sense, to replace "one." For example, the conversational "You can see deer in many state parks" might be recast as the more formal "Visitors to many state parks can see deer." A basic rule is to use the word "I" infrequently but try to avoid the word "you."

Study Questions

1. Bleecker states his thesis early in the essay, at the end of the first paragraph: "I feel strong, and I embrace my black heritage. I've often reflected on how I learned to keep my positive self-image. The answer is, my white father." Later in the essay, he restates that point. Where at the end of the essay is the thesis again stated, as a summary?
2. Bleecker not only tells the reader that his father attempted to instill in him an appreciation of black culture, but he also gives a series of examples, listing the things his father did to accomplish that aim. What were some of the different methods his father used?
3. What, in your opinion, is the primary reason that Bleecker can say "My father and I are now the closest we have ever been?"

Writing Topics

Note: For each of the topics below, try to state a general thesis somewhere in the beginning of your essay. Restate that point in different words somewhere toward the end (or at the end), as a concluding summary.

1. Write a description of how a significant older person (parent, relative, teacher, or close friend) helped you to learn and understand your own cultural background. What kinds of activities did you do together? How did those activities help you to understand who you were and what kind of people you belonged to?

2. Suppose you were to marry someone of a different race, culture, or background. What would be some of the worst difficulties? What would be the good parts? Write an essay in which you imagine what that kind of marriage would be like, including the challenges of raising "mixed" children.

From All I Really Need to Know I Learned in Kindergarten

ROBERT FULGHUM

This is my neighbor. Nice lady. Coming out her front door, on her way to work and in her "looking good" mode. She's locking the door now and picking up her daily luggage: purse, lunch bag, gym bag for aerobics, and the garbage bucket to take out. She turns, sees me, gives me the big, smiling Hello, takes three steps across her front porch. And goes "AAAAAAAGGGGGGGGGGHHHHHHHHHH!!!!" *(That's a direct quote.)* At about the level of a fire engine at full cry. Spider web! She has walked full force into a spider web. And the pressing question, of course: Just where is the spider *now?*

She flings her baggage in all directions. And at the same time does a high-kick, jitterbug sort of dance—like a mating stork in crazed heat. Clutches at her face and hair and goes "AAAAAAAGGGGGGGGGGHHHHHHHHHH!!!!" at a new level of intensity. Tries opening the front door without unlocking it. Tries again. Breaks key in the lock. Runs around the house headed for the back door. Doppler effect of

"A A A A A G G G H H H H H a a g g h . . ."

Now a different view of this scene. Here is the spider. Rather ordinary, medium gray, middle-aged lady spider. She's been up since before dawn working on her web, and all is well. Nice day, no wind, dew point just right to keep things sticky. She's out checking the moorings and thinking about the little gnats she'd like to have for breakfast. Feeling good. Ready for action. All of a sudden all hell breaks loose—earthquake, tornado, volcano. The web is torn loose and is wrapped around a frenzied moving haystack, and a huge piece of raw-but-painted meat is making a sound the spider never heard before: "AAAAAAAGGGGGGGGGGHHHHHHHHHH!!!!" It's too big to wrap up and eat later, and it's moving too much to hold down. Jump for it? Hang on and hope? Dig in?

Human being. She has caught a human being. And the pressing question is, of course: Where is it going and what will it do when it gets there?

The neighbor lady thinks the spider is about the size of a lobster and has big rubber lips and poisonous fangs. The neighbor lady will probably strip to the skin and take a full shower and shampoo just to make sure it's gone—and then put on a whole new outfit to make certain she is not inhabited.

The spider? Well, if she survives all this, she will really have something to talk about—the one that got away that was THIS BIG. "And you should have seen the JAWS on the thing!"

Spiders. Amazing creatures. Been around maybe 350 million years, so they can cope with about anything. Lots of them, too—sixty or seventy thousand per suburban acre. It's the web thing that I envy. Imagine what it would be like if people were equipped like spiders. If we had this little six-nozzled aperture right at the base of our spine and we could make yards of something like glass fiber with it. Wrapping packages would be a cinch! Mountain climbing would never be the same. Think of the Olympic events. And mating and child rearing would take on new dimensions. Well, you take it from there. It boggles the mind. Cleaning up human-sized webs would be a mess, on the other hand.

All this reminds me of a song I know. And you know, too. And your parents and your children, they know. About the eensy-weensy spider. Went up the waterspout. Down came the rain and washed the spider out. Out came the sun and dried up all the rain. And the eensy-weensy spider went up the spout again. You probably know the motions, too.

What's the deal here? Why do we all know that song? Why do we keep passing it on to our kids? Especially when it puts spiders in such a favorable light? Nobody goes "AAAAAAAGGGGGGGGGHHHHHH-HHH!!!!" when they sing it. Maybe because it puts the life adventure in such clear and simple terms. The small creature is alive and looks for adventure. Here's the drainpipe—a long tunnel going up toward some light. The spider doesn't even think about it—just goes. Disaster befalls it—rain, flood, powerful forces. And the spider is knocked down and out beyond where it started. Does the spider say, "To hell with that"? No. Sun comes out—clears things up—dries off the spider. And the small creature goes over to the drainpipe and looks up and thinks it *really* wants to know what is up there. It's a little wiser now—checks the sky first, looks for better toeholds, says a spider prayer, and heads up through mystery toward the light and wherever.

Living things have been doing just that for a long, long time. Through every kind of disaster and setback and catastrophe. We are survivors. And we teach our kids about that. And maybe spiders tell their kids about it, too, in their spider sort of way.

So the neighbor lady will survive and be a little wiser coming out the door on her way to work. And the spider, if it lives, will do likewise. And if not, well, there are lots more spiders, and the word gets around. Especially when the word is "AAAAAAAGGGGGGGGGHH-HHHHHHH!!!!"

IN FOCUS

POINT OF VIEW

Point of view in writing is similar to point of view in photography or art; it is the angle from which the observer sees things. A writer may use point of view to show how various characters in a story see the same events. In this essay, we see the experience from the points of view of three beings: the neighbor, the spider, and the narrator, who watches it all. By use of this technique, the author is able to help readers empathize, or feel with, everyone concerned.

The point of view in a work of literature can be as complex and subtle as the writer wants to make it. A story can be told using multiple points of view, with rapid shifts as different voices take up the tale. On the other hand, the reader can be shown only the limited view of one character; or the point of view may be that of an all-seeing, all-knowing—"omniscient"—narrator. When writers of fiction use the tricky technique of having the narrator be a liar or unreliable, readers have to figure out the puzzle of what really happened.

Fulghum, however, uses relatively simple shifts of point of view, showing in turn how the neighbor reacts, the spider reacts, and what the narrator thinks about it all. He becomes in the end a narrator-turned-essayist, discussing the meaning of survival. By the end of the essay the narrator's point of view is that of a thoughtful, amused observer of life.

Study Questions

1. Did the narrator do the right thing, seeing his neighbor in trouble? Should he at least have rushed over and helped her pick up her things?

What would happen if something like that happened to you—would anyone come to your aid? What would happen in your neighborhood if someone were in real trouble?

2. Try to remember a simple rhyme or story that you learned as a child— if there's a special one from your ethnic heritage, use that. Does your example have a subtle meaning or theme, like the one Fulghum finds in "the eensy-weensy spider"?

Writing Topics

1. The basic experience Fulghum describes—of someone all ready to go somewhere, when disturbance strikes—is very common. Briefly describe such an event and the frustration it creates.

2. Describe a common event from an uncommon point of view: for example, a fishing expedition as the fish would describe it, or a kitchen clean-up from the point of view of a cockroach hiding in the wall. What would a pair of in-line skates think about a morning ride?

A Fence

Now the stone house on the lake front is finished and the workmen
are beginning the fence.

The palings are made of iron bars with steel points that can stab the
life out of any man who falls on them.

As a fence, it is a masterpiece, and will shut off the rabble and all
vagabonds and hungry men and all wandering children looking for a place to play.

Passing through the bars and over the steel points will go nothing
except Death and the Rain and Tomorrow.

Onion Days

Mrs. Gabrielle Giovannitti comes along Peoria Street every morning
at nine o'clock

With kindling wood piled on top of her head, her eyes looking
straight ahead to find the way for her old feet.

Her daughter-in-law, Mrs. Pietro Giovannitti, whose husband was
killed in a tunnel explosion through the negligence of a fellow-
servant,

Works ten hours a day, sometimes twelve, picking onions for Jasper
on the Bowmanville road.

She takes a street car at half-past five in the morning, Mrs. Pietro
Giovannitti does,

And gets back from Jasper's with cash for her day's work, between
nine and ten o'clock at night.

Last week she got eight cents a box, Mrs. Pietro Giovannitti, picking onions for Jasper,

But this week Jasper dropped the pay to six cents a box because so
many women and girls were answering the ads in the *Daily
News.*

Jasper belongs to an Episcopal church in Ravenswood and on certain Sundays

He enjoys chanting the Nicene creed with his daughters on each side
of him joining their voices with his.

If the preacher repeats old sermons of a Sunday, Jasper's mind wanders to his 700-acre farm and how he can make it produce
more efficiently

And sometimes he speculates on whether he could word an ad in
the *Daily News* so it would bring more women and girls out to
his farm and reduce operating costs.

Mrs. Pietro Giovannitti is far from desperate about life; her joy is in
a child she knows will arrive to her in three months.

And now while these are the pictures for today there are other pictures of the Giovannitti people I could give you for tomorrow,

And how some of them go to the county agent on winter mornings
with their baskets for beans and cornmeal and molasses.

I listen to fellows saying here's good stuff for a novel or it might be
worked up into a good play.

I say there's no dramatist living can put old Mrs. Gabrielle Giovannitti into a play with that kindling wood piled on top of her
head coming along Peoria Street nine o'clock in the morning.

Study Questions

1. Details in "Onion Days" suggest it was written a long time ago. (It was
actually first published in 1914.) People who pick onions probably get
paid more than six cents a box now—but probably whatever they do get
paid buys about as little as the six cents the pregnant daughter-in-law
in the poem earned. Though the specifics have changed somewhat,
the themes, the ideas dealt with, in these poems have certainly not
changed much since 1914 or even before then. Rich and powerful people have probably been taking advantage of poor and helpless people
since society began. The feeling of joy about new life coming that the
daughter-in-law experiences, even though clearly that baby is going to
be a financial burden, is undoubtedly as old as human beings.

   A reader of the Sandburg poems today can see them within their *historical context*—"Onion Days" describes the oppression of poor Italian
immigrants—but can also understand their universal meanings. Are the
feelings Sandburg expresses about the differences between rich and

poor people still valid today? How do they compare to your own feelings? If you were to write the same type of poem, what group of people would you use in place of Italian immigrants?

2. Sandburg's technique in both poems is to set up opposites, using *contrasting images* to establish a sense of *irony.* Irony sets out the differences between two things: what is versus what ought to be, what one person thinks versus what another knows to be the truth, what a person says versus what he or she does. Mr. Jasper, for example, sits in his beautiful church thinking about how he can squeeze more money out of desperately poor people. The wealthy people who put up the iron fence think they can keep out everything they don't like, but they can't fence out the natural way of the world. Thus, instead of describing one image or the other, the writer uses contrast to give a clearer picture of both sides.

   There is also irony in the last two lines of "Onion Days," which state that a writer couldn't make a novel or play out of the life of Mrs. Giovannitti. After all, somehow Sandburg has managed to create a poem.

   Do you see any other examples of irony in these two poems?

Writing Topics

1. *Collaborative writing activity.* Rewrite "Onion Days" as it might be written today, using images of any group of poor people who would fit the idea of the poem. (Homeless people might fit, for example, or another group of immigrants.) Put in as many specific details as you can. What would a box of onions cost today? Where would the people work? Would Mr. Jasper still be in church?

2. Use the technique of setting up contrasting images to achieve a sense of irony in your own short poem. Imitate Sandburg's style, but provide different examples. Describe, for example, any short scene that demonstrates hypocrisy.

3. Suppose Mr. Jasper were the executive of a modern corporation responsible to its shareholders for increasing profits as much as possible. If it were then necessary to get the onions picked as cheaply as possible, would the Jasper Corporation's actions be defensible? On the other hand, could there be good economic reasons for paying Mrs. Giovannitti decent wages?

   Consider a comparable modern situation, such as shoe or clothing manufacturers who pay their workers in third-world countries starvation wages. If these workers were paid better, American clothing might cost more. Write an essay in which you analyze the situation Sandburg describes in terms of modern economics and/or ethics.

Get a Knife, Get a Dog, but Get Rid of Guns

Guns. Everywhere guns.

Let me start this discussion by pointing out that I am not antigun. I'm proknife. Consider the merits of the knife.

In the first place, you have to catch up with someone in order to stab him. A general substitution of knives for guns would promote physical fitness. We'd turn into a whole nation of great runners. Plus, knives don't ricochet. And people are seldom killed while cleaning their knives.

As a civil libertarian, I, of course, support the Second Amendment. And I believe it means exactly what it says:

A well-regulated militia being necessary to the security of a free state, the right of the people to keep and bear arms shall not be infringed. Fourteen-year-old boys are not part of a well-regulated militia. Members of wacky religious cults are not part of a well-regulated militia. Permitting unregulated citizens to have guns is destroying the security of this free state.

I am intrigued by the arguments of those who claim to follow the judicial doctrine of original intent. How do they know it was the dearest wish of Thomas Jefferson's heart that teenage drug dealers should cruise the cities of this nation perforating their fellow citizens with assault rifles? Channeling?

There is more hooey spread about the Second Amendment. It says quite clearly that guns are for those who form part of a well-regulated militia, that is, the armed forces, including the National Guard. The reasons for keeping them away from everyone else get clearer by the day.

The comparison most often used is that of the automobile, another lethal object that is regularly used to wreak great carnage. Obviously, this society is full of people who haven't enough common sense to use an automobile properly. But we haven't outlawed cars yet.

We do, however, license them and their owners, restrict their use to presumably sane and sober adults, and keep track of who sells them to whom. At a minimum, we should do the same with guns.

In truth, there is no rational argument for guns in this society. This is no longer a frontier nation in which people hunt their own food. It is a crowded, overwhelmingly urban country in which letting people have access to guns is a continuing disaster. Those who want guns—whether for target shooting, hunting, or potting rattlesnakes (get a hoe)—should be subject to the same restrictions placed on gun owners in England, a nation in which liberty has survived nicely without an armed populace.

The argument that "guns don't kill people" is patent nonsense. Anyone who has ever worked in a cop shop knows how many family arguments end in murder because there was a gun in the house. Did the gun kill someone? No. But if there had been no gun, no one would have died. At least not without a good foot race first. Guns do kill. Unlike cars, that is all they do.

Michael Crichton makes an interesting argument about technology in his thriller *Jurassic Park*. He points out that power without discipline is making this society into a wreckage. By the time someone who studies the martial arts becomes a master—literally able to kill with bare hands—that person has also undergone years of training and discipline. But any fool can pick up a gun and kill with it.

"A well-regulated militia" surely implies both long training and long discipline. That is the least, the very least, that should be required of those who are permitted to have guns, because a gun is literally the power to kill. For years I used to enjoy taunting my gun-nut friends about their psychosexual hang-ups—always in a spirit of good cheer, you understand. But letting the noisy minority in the NRA force us to allow this carnage to continue is just plain insane.

I do think gun nuts have a power hang-up. I don't know what is missing in their psyches that they need to feel they have the power to kill. But no sane society would allow this to continue.

Ban the damn things. Ban them all.

You want protection? Get a dog.

IN FOCUS

SPEAKING YOUR MIND

The title of Molly Ivins's first collection of newspaper columns, *Molly Ivins Can't Say That, Can She?* (1991), indicates her hard-hitting approach as a political writer. Outrageous, funny, unafraid, part of a journalistic tradition that includes Mark Twain and H. L. Mencken, she is a satirist and commentator who pulls no punches. One demonstration of her outspoken courage is that the essay above was first published in the Fort Worth, Texas, *Star-Telegram* (March 9, 1993), in a region of the United States where gun ownership is almost a religious issue. Through such outspoken columns, Ivins has become a model for writers who feel they have something to say about the world and want to say it with force.

It's important to note what Ivins does *not* do in the course of her essays: She doesn't employ unprovable assumptions, instead basing her points on facts and evidence. She doesn't use hurtful or abusive language. She doesn't call people names, and tends to avoid stereotyping. She attacks ideas and issues, not people personally. When she needs to expose a public figure's ineptitude, immorality, or just plain thievery, she focuses on the crime, rather than something personal she doesn't like about the criminal. She is forceful, but seldom vicious or mean. Just as Ivins follows a long tradition of outspoken journalism, she follows the guidelines that anyone who is learning to write persuasive essays must also learn.

Study Questions

1. Notice how much Ivins does in one short essay:
   A. She begins with a startling announcement, a little twist designed to catch the reader's interest: "I am not antigun. I'm proknife."
   B. She counters the opposition's basic argument, that gun ownership is guaranteed by the U.S. Constitution.
   C. She goes on to counter, one by one, other arguments for unlicensed gun ownership.
   D. She puts the issue into a wider context, discussing gun ownership as one way in which technology has overrun our ability to deal with it.
   E. She ends with a memorable phrase, as a strong conclusion.
   Reread the essay, marking A through E in the appropriate place.
2. In several places Ivins argues by analogy, or comparison, comparing guns to automobiles and the United States to Britain. Are these comparisons accurate? Are there other comparisons in the essay? What are some other comparisons she could have used?

Writing Topics

1. Imitation of a good model is one way of learning to write. Imitating Ivins's procedure as outlined in Study Question #1 above, write a short

column on another subject entirely. Open with a "twist," then counter opposing arguments, as she does.

2. Try using Ivins's process to argue against her. Write a humorous essay in which you facetiously argue that knife ownership should be licensed. Use some of Ivins's own points, but focus on knives instead of guns.

3. Write a serious essay either for or against gun ownership, bringing in your own experience or that of someone you know.

Zen Failure

RAFE MARTIN

For many years while practicing Zen, I thought I was a failure. But as more years went by, I began to realize that failure is the heart of Zen. Failure is what Zen is about. Perhaps it's what life is about. Successes never seem to last. Death, after all, comes in the end to take all successes away. If you want something abiding, something for the long run, look to failure.

When I say *failure,* I don't mean giving up, turning around, and walking away. I mean the failure that we work hard for, failure that we put everything into—bitter failure. Real failure requires real effort, and is its own reward.

In "The Four Ages of Man," William Butler Yeats speaks of failure as the essence of spiritual life:

> *He with body waged a fight*
> *But body won: it walks upright.*
> *Then he struggled with the heart;*
> *Innocence and peace depart.*
> *Then he struggled with the mind;*
> *His proud heart he left behind.*
> *Now his wars on God begin;*
> *At stroke of midnight, God shall win.*

There it is: Failure. The defeat of all one's hopes, fears, stratagems, efforts. The thing we fear the most.

In Yeats's poem there is also some glimmer that failure may not be as bad as we think. Is it so bad that God wins? And through the little doorway opened by that doubt, we come to Zen.

But failure is a two-edged sword. There's the failure that prevents us from living fully, the failure built of fears and expectations, patterns to which mind and body have long been habituated. There's the failure to hear the birds singing, failure to use the intricate senses with which we've all been so lavishly endowed. Then there's the failure to get what we want—perhaps that's the one we know best.

And then there's the failure that's open and pure—the failure that

Zen is all about. What could be more ridiculous, after all, than working hard, in retreat after retreat, facing fear after fear, letting go of desire after desire, hope after hope, only to find out that we have to fail completely in the end? We work so hard in this life—only to die. We must give up everything! And this discovery is exactly where "success" in Zen, in life, can begin.

During this last winter and early spring my wife's mother and my own mother died. With their deaths has come the heartfelt recognition that all efforts come to naught. Each of us will die, and everything we have gained, everything we have worked hard for, will be taken from us: thoughts, feelings, the singing of birds, the cool wind on our skin on a hot day, the sunrise and the sunset, the people we love—all gone. Our children will be gone, the children we worry about, whom we hover over in our minds day and night. They're going to die, no matter how hard we work protecting them, no matter how well they do growing up. And our grandchildren will die, and our great-grandchildren. So underneath all our success, even after a lifetime of successes, we still have to come face to face with this insurmountable failure.

Each of us starts off in life complete and whole. But after a while, trained by the world around us, we discover that we want *more*. We want to be handsome or beautiful, to be loved and respected. We want to be independent and strong, perhaps wise, and, certainly, eternal. But somehow few of these things work out. The failure becomes so bitter that we have to *do something*. Perhaps we begin practicing Zen. And for many years it's failure after failure, as if we're shooting at a target but keep missing. One day we find that failures are a kind of success.

I came to Zen through a number of failures, the pain of which was bitter enough to drive me onto a completely different path, the path of practice. And then, since I began practicing, there was the glorious failure of the bookshop I started. It took much effort to engineer that one. It all fell apart and then—great surprise!—something new emerged, something truly better.

After the closing of the bookshop I had an idea for a book. Much earlier, I'd lost a lot, and my wife and I were living in backwoods Pennsylvania. There had been an old quarry there, and I thought I might take a wish from my childhood and combine it with someof the feelings I'd had while walking through that quarry and make something new—as well as heal some old wounds. For three years I worked on the story of a boy and his imagination.

For three years I was turned down by my editor. A hundred rewrites on this one little story: turned down each time. Then suddenly, as I was about to drop the project, I saw how the whole thing could work. After three years of failure, it was essentially written in thirty seconds. And the book became a great success. That period of loss and pain from many years ago gave me the basis to create something new, something that pleased me greatly. How do we explain it? Can failure be a good thing?

One day when I was young, my father looked into my room, saw me drawing, and said, "Don't become an artist." I worried about what he'd said for a long time. Ultimately, I failed to follow his advice.

I had a talk with my father a couple of years ago as he was driving me to a storytelling performance I was giving. I said to him, "You know, the people I respected most when I was younger were not really successes. Van Gogh never sold a painting and died in poverty and madness. William Blake died in poverty, too, but at least in joy. And then there's Herman Melville: after writing perhaps the greatest American novel, he got terrible reviews and lived his life in obscurity and despair. During their lives, these people seemed to be failures.

"Then there are people who are successes. Perhaps they earn a lot of money, take lavish vacations, and wear expensive clothes. Maybe they make some product that pollutes the environment a bit. The legacy they leave doesn't last long, and if it does it's often something we don't want in the long run anyway. But Van Gogh, Blake, Melville: their works just get stronger and stronger. How do you explain this? Which is success, which failure?"

There's an old story from China called "The Green Pillow Dream": Once there was a farmer who was very dissatisfied with his life. He set out to seek his fortune. He walked for a day and came to an inn nestled in the foothills of some mountains. He was hungry, so he went inside. Because he didn't have much money, he ordered only a bowl of rice and some tea. He was very tired and was going to lie down until his meal was served. An old man who was staying at the inn said, "If you're going to lie down, why don't you take my pillow?" (Pillows in ancient China weren't soft cushions; they were ceramic, and shaped to your neck and shoulders.) The old man offered the farmer a beautiful, glazed green pillow.

The farmer had a conversation with the old man, who mentioned that it must be nice to be young and healthy. The farmer said that, although he was, indeed, young and healthy, he wasn't very happy. He worked all day in the fields and had nothing to show for it. Finally, the farmer put his head down and fell asleep. The next thing he knew he was walking through a tunnel, from which he emerged into an open field with mountains in the distance, waterfalls flowing like silver threads, horses and deer running, and tigers stalking. He walked down the road that ran through the field and came to a village. A beautiful young woman ran out of the biggest house and called him by name. She'd been waiting for him. They got married, and before long he was overseeing the estate of his father-in-law. He and his wife had children. In time, he became governor. When barbarians invaded, he was called to lead the armies. Just like that, he achieved a great victory, driving the invaders before him like dust before the wind. He was made prime minister. The land flourished as it never had before.

But some of the other ministers became jealous and set up a plot against him, producing forged letters to show that he'd been working with the barbarians to overthrow the empire. So he was banished and lost everything. He and his wife and children went to live in a hotel, where guards watched them day and night. He had no privacy, no peace of mind. He had nothing. He would have been happier, he realized, being an unknown farmer.

Eight years went by, then a rider arrived with a message from the emperor, who had discovered the plot and asked now for forgiveness. All the man's lands were restored. His sons became great generals and ministers, and again the land flourished. He became a very old man, and at last was lying in his deathbed. The emperor sent the best doctor in the world, but it was hopeless. Tears flowed—his sons and daughters, his grandsons and granddaughters, his daughters-in-law, and his old wife were crying and crying as he left this world. He found himself back in the tunnel, walked through, and opened his eyes: he was lying in the inn with his head on the pillow; the rice and tea were just being put down on the table. He had lived a whole life, yet hardly a moment had passed.

There's a line in Zen that goes: "The failure is wonderful indeed." We all come to know failure intimately, don't we? Is it wonderful? Another Zen line says: "When your bow is broken and your last arrow spent, then shoot, shoot with your whole heart." Failure comes as we try to succeed. It happens naturally; no special efforts are needed. So, my advice is, just forget all of this. In fact, don't fail to do so.

SPEAKING FROM THE CENTER

The great contemporary essayist Edward Hoagland defines the essay as a balance between the expression of personal experience and the statement of the implications or meaning of that experience. Essays, Hoagland writes, "hang somewhere on a line between two sturdy poles: this is what I think, and this is what I am. . . . A personal essay is like the human voice talking, its order the mind's natural flow, instead of a systematized outline of ideas. Though more wayward or informal than an article or treatise, somewhere it contains a point which is its real center, even if the point couldn't be uttered in fewer words than the essayist has used" ("What I Think, What I Am," from *The Tugman's Passage,* New York: Random House, 1982).

A fine personal essay such as "Zen Failure" thus includes "what I think" as it arises from "what I am," the writer's life. Every great personal essay comes from the center of the writer's being, as this one does. Martin is honest and open, has thought carefully about the meaning of his experiences, and clearly wants the reader to share his understandings. He is offering a difficult and, on the surface, seemingly contradictory idea—that failure can become a kind of success—which will only make sense as the reader joins the thought process.

Just as breathing, in Zen Buddhist meditation, comes consciously from the center of the body, so in the practice of writing a fine essay the content must come from the center of the writer. Honesty about what one has experienced, willingness to look inside and consider why things happened, and an intention to communicate what it all means are the tools of the essayist. Putting the words on paper is, of course, a necessary next step, but it is the *second* step. Thinking, a combination of contemplation, memory, and concentration, always comes first.

Study Questions

1. What is the meaning of the story of "The Green Pillow Dream"? What purpose does it serve in the essay? What does it tell us?
2. Martin asks, "Can failure be a good thing?" In your opinion, can it, or

does failure lead only to further failure and depression? How do people go from saying "I have failed" to saying "I am a failure"?

3. What is the meaning of the Zen line "When your bow is broken and your last arrow spent, then shoot, shoot with your whole heart"?

4. One of the factors identified on various psychological tests and personality profiles is the degree to which a person is "inner-directed" or "outer-directed." That is, does the person respond more to the dictates of the outer world, to "the rules" or to "what people will think," or does the person most often follow his or her individual "inner light"? Based on this essay, does Martin seem to be more "inner-" or "outer-" directed?

Writing Topics

1. *Collaborative writing activity* (or can be done alone). Make a list of three or four times that you failed at something you intended to do or failed to get something. These can be personal failures or group failures. Then, beside each item on the list, describe a way that the failure could be used, a way that it could be turned to "success."

2. Write an essay about a time in which you felt like a complete failure. What did you learn from the experience? What would you do, or not do, again?

From The Heart of a Woman

MAYA ANGELOU

*"The ole ark's a-moverin', a-moverin', a-moverin',
the ole ark's a-moverin' along"*

That ancient spiritual could have been the theme song of the United States in 1957. We were a-moverin' to, fro, up, down and often in concentric circles.

We created a maze of contradictions. Black and white Americans danced a fancy and often dangerous do-si-do. In our steps forward, abrupt turns, sharp spins and reverses, we became our own befuddlement. The country hailed Althea Gibson, the rangy tennis player who was the first black female to win the U.S. Women's Singles. President Dwight Eisenhower sent U.S. paratroopers to protect black school children in Little Rock, Arkansas, and South Carolina's Senator Strom Thurmond harangued for 24 hours and 18 minutes to prevent the passage in Congress of the Civil Rights Commission's Voting Rights Bill.

Sugar Ray Robinson, everybody's dandy, lost his middleweight title, won it back, then lost it again, all in a matter of months. The year's popular book was Jack Kerouac's *On the Road,* and its title was an apt description of our national psyche. We were indeed traveling, but no one knew our destination nor our arrival date.

I had returned to California from a year-long European tour as premier dancer with *Porgy and Bess.* I worked months singing in West Coast and Hawaiian night clubs and saved my money. I took my young son, Guy, and joined the beatnik brigade. To my mother's dismay, and Guy's great pleasure, we moved across the Golden Gate Bridge and into a houseboat commune in Sausalito where I went barefoot, wore jeans, and both of us wore rough-dried clothes. Although I took Guy to a San Francisco barber, I allowed my own hair to grow into a wide unstraightened hedge, which made me look, at a distance, like a tall brown tree whose branches had been clipped. My commune mates, an icthyologist, a musician, a wife,

45

and an inventor, were white, and had they been political (which they were not), would have occupied a place between the far left and revolution.

Strangely, the houseboat offered me respite from racial tensions, and gave my son an opportunity to be around whites who did not think of him as too exotic to need correction, nor so common as to be ignored.

During our stay in Sausalito, my mother struggled with her maternal instincts. On her monthly visits, dressed in stone marten furs, diamonds and spike heels, which constantly caught between loose floorboards, she forced smiles and held her tongue. Her eyes, however, were frightened for her baby, and her baby's baby. She left wads of money under my pillow or gave me checks as she kissed me goodbye. She could have relaxed had she remembered the Biblical assurance "Fruit does not fall far from the tree."

In less than a year, I began to yearn for privacy, wall-to-wall carpets and manicures. Guy was becoming rambunctious and young-animal wild. He was taking fewer baths than I thought healthy, and because my friends treated him like a young adult, he was forgetting his place in the scheme of our mother-son relationship.

I had to move on. I could go back to singing and make enough money to support myself and my son.

I had to trust life, since I was young enough to believe that life loved the person who dared to live it.

I packed our bags, said goodbye and got on the road.

Laurel Canyon was the official residential area of Hollywood, just ten minutes from Schwab's drugstore and fifteen minutes from the Sunset Strip.

Its most notable feature was its sensuality. Red-roofed, Moorish-style houses nestled seductively among madrone trees. The odor of eucalyptus was layered in the moist air. Flowers bloomed in a riot of crimsons, carnelian, pinks, fuchsia and sunburst gold. Jays and whip-poorwills, swallows and bluebirds, squeaked, whistled and sang on branches which faded from ominous dark green to a brackish yellow. Movie stars, movie starlets, producers and directors who lived in the neighborhood were as voluptuous as their natural and unnatural environment.

The few black people who lived in Laurel Canyon, including Billy Eckstein, Billy Daniels and Herb Jeffries, were rich, famous and light-skinned enough to pass, at least for Portuguese. I, on the other hand, was a little-known nightclub singer, who was said to have more determination than talent. I wanted desperately to live in the glamorous surroundings. I accepted as fictitious the tales of amateurs being discovered at lunch counters, yet I did believe it was important to be in the right place at the right time, and no place seemed so right to me in 1958 as Laurel Canyon.

When I answered a "For Rent" ad, the landlord told me the house had been taken that very morning. I asked Atara and Joe Morheim, a sympathetic white couple, to try to rent the house for me. They succeeded in doing so.

On moving day, the Morheims, Frederick "Wilkie" Wilkerson, my friend and voice coach, Guy, and I appeared on the steps of a modest, overpriced two-bedroom bungalow.

The landlord shook hands with Joe, welcomed him, then looked over Joe's shoulder and recognized me. Shock and revulsion made him recoil. He snatched his hand away from Joe. "You bastard. I know what you're doing. I ought to sue you."

Joe, who always seemed casual to the point of being totally disinterested, surprised me with his emotional response. "You fascist, you'd better not mention suing anybody. This lady here should sue you. If she wants to, I'll testify in court for her. Now, get the hell out of the way so we can move in."

The landlord brushed past us, throwing his anger into the perfumed air. "I should have known. You dirty Jew. You bastard, you."

We laughed nervously and carried my furniture into the house.

Weeks later I had painted the small house a sparkling white, enrolled Guy into the local school, received only a few threatening telephone calls, and bought myself a handsome dated automobile. The car, a sea-green, ten-year-old Chrysler, had a parquet dashboard, and splintery wooden doors. It could not compete with the new chrome of my neighbors' Cadillacs and Buicks, but it had an elderly elegance, and driving in it with the top down, I felt more like an eccentric artist than a poor black woman who was living above her means, out of her element, and removed from her people.

• • •

One June morning, Wilkie walked into my house and asked, "Do you want to meet Billie Holiday?"

"Of course. Who wouldn't? Is she working in town?"

"No, just passing through from Honolulu. I'm going down to her hotel. I'll bring her back here if you think you can handle it."

"What's to handle? She's a woman. I'm a woman."

Wilkie laughed, the chuckle rolling inside his chest and out of his mouth in billows of sound. "Pooh, you're sassy. Billie may like you. In that case, it'll be all right. She might not, and then that's your ass."

"That could work the other way around. I might not like her either."

Wilkie laughed again. "I said you're sassy. Have you got some gin?" There was one bottle, which had been gathering dust for months. Wilkie stood, "Give me the keys. She'll like riding in a convertible."

I didn't become nervous until he left. Then the reality of Lady Day coming to my house slammed into me and started my body to quaking. It was pretty well known that she used heavy drugs, and I hardly smoked grass anymore. How could I tell her she couldn't shoot up or sniff up in my house? It was also rumored that she had lesbian affairs. If she propositioned me, how could I reject her without making her think I was rejecting her? Her temper was legendary in show business, and I didn't want to arouse it. I vacuumed, emptied ashtrays and dusted, knowing that a clean house would in no way influence Billie Holiday.

Study Questions

1. The opening song establishes Angelou's theme of "moving on" (something she does a lot of in this short excerpt). What kinds of "moving" do you see—physical, emotional, mental? What is she searching for?
2. What contrasts do you see between the characters—between Angelou and her housemates, her mother, and the landlord?
3. What might Angelou mean by the statement "I had to trust life, since I was young enough to believe that life loved the person who dared to live it"?

Writing Topics

1. Consider Joe Morheim, the friend who helped Angelou rent her apartment. What kind of courage did it take to do what he did? Was there ever a time when you were asked to stand up for a friend? Write an essay in which you describe the circumstances and tell what you did, explaining your feelings at the time.
2. Moving on is one of the themes of the piece. Write an essay on "moving on," giving an example or examples from your own life or the lives of people you know.

Watching TV

My daughter's third-grade teacher asked her class not to watch television for five days. Anyone who completed the assignment would receive a gift certificate for a free pizza. With some encouragement from her dad and me, Elise decided to accept the challenge.

On Monday night, Elise and I went to the library and checked out a stack of books, then bought ice-cream cones. We came home and read together until her bedtime. *What a wonderful assignment,* I thought.

On Tuesday night, Elise was in tears. "Please, please," she begged. "I *have* to watch *Full House*. It's my favorite show. I'll *die* if I don't watch it!" This frightened me. Was I raising a television addict? I reminded her of her decision, and the TV remained off. After she went to sleep, I guiltily snapped on the set at the foot of my bed.

On Wednesday night, she tried to bargain: just one half-hour of TV and she'd do extra homework. "No, let's see this commitment through," I replied. We broke out the board games, but argued throughout the evening over who was cheating. Our nerves were frayed by all this togetherness.

On Thursday, Elise did not even ask about television. She played with her Barbies, and Dad and I joined her for a game of Parcheesi. Then I held her in my arms and read her to sleep. She drifted off, smiling and peaceful. I climbed into bed, annoyed by the sound of my husband watching television.

On Friday morning, I wrote a note confirming that Elise had completed the assignment. When she arrived home that night with her pizza coupon, we congratulated her. She felt proud and strong. I felt relieved that we weren't lost to TV addiction.

After dinner, we flipped on the TV and watched until bedtime.

Dee Endelman
Seattle, Washington

My husband, Tim, works all day in town at his plumbing job, then returns home and begins work around our pecan farm. During the summer, he is busy until dark cultivating, pruning, or fertilizing the trees. Once the sun sets, he comes inside, kicks off his shoes, and turns on the TV.

At first, I couldn't get used to this habit. I have always felt TV to be a complete waste of time. Finally, I asked him why he watched it every night. He explained that it was the only time in the day when he could truly relax. No matter that it was mindless drivel, he could sit back and rest.

Upon hearing this, I stopped complaining. After he'd worked a twelve- or thirteen-hour day, how could I deny him this simple pleasure?

Karen R. George
Las Cruces, New Mexico

As an American traveling abroad, I sometimes find it hard to avoid being stereotyped—especially when I am in a so-called Third World country. To people there, I am from the "land of milk and honey," where everyone has a house, a car, a job, vacations, and money to buy lots of things to keep them happy.

My friend and I recently visited a family who lived in a dilapidated one-room plywood house. The mother and children worked making embroidered bags and belts to sell to tourists. They had a hard time getting by, even compared to other people in the village, yet they owned a small TV. Sitting down with the family in front of the set, we watched beautifully manicured boys and girls play volleyball on a beach somewhere in California. They had expensive toys, nice clothes, and shiny cars; they looked so pretty, so happy, so perfect.

As I watched, I thought about the waterfall where we'd spent the day with a few of the children, eating oranges, baptizing each other with the juice, and diving into the pool to cleanse ourselves. They'd done flips off the rocks, fighting for our attention. It had been a moment of true paradise.

I was ashamed of the illusory American paradise on TV, uncomfortable with the children's envy of what they saw, and with my envy of what I thought they had right here.

Connie Holloway
Bellingham, Washington

In the twenty-six years I knew my grandpa, we never really talked. The TV was our only bond. Now that he is gone, I realize how little

I know about him. I know that he liked to eat pickled onions with rice, and could sketch chickens. I know he was a Nisei—a second-generation Japanese American—and had once worked on the railroads and picked grapes.

I grew up in Hilo, Hawaii, less than five minutes from my grandpa's house. Whenever he and my grandma came over to babysit me and my twin sister, Judi, we would watch TV and eat sweet rolls dripping with sugary glaze. I can name every show that played during those years, from *Gilligan's Island* to *My Three Sons*. Grandpa's favorites were *Cannon* and *The Streets of San Francisco*. During the summer, we'd watch *All My Children*, which he and Grandma followed for years. (I now find it amusing that my traditional grandparents enjoyed a show about young white people who wore lots of jewelry and had affairs all the time.)

Sometimes they'd watch the Japanese channel on cable: samurai shows, singing contests, family dramas. Rather than read the English subtitles, I'd try to understand the dialogue, hoping to learn the language. I was too shy to practice my Japanese with Grandpa.

My grandma died in 1983, and in 1991 Grandpa was diagnosed with kidney cancer. While home from college for Christmas, I accompanied my parents to Grandpa's house at five or six every afternoon. Judi and I would take turns sitting in the rocking recliner while Grandpa would lie on the sofa with his head propped up on a Japanese headrest, a hard vinyl cushion on a metal stand.

We watched the news, baseball, *Wheel of Fortune*, and *Murder, She Wrote*. Without the TV on, it would have been too quiet. An air of drowsy calmness permeated the creaky rooms: faded furniture still draped with my grandma's weblike yarn doilies; snapshots of Judi and me in grade school; a wind-up alarm clock with glow-in-the-dark hands; an old man in baggy pajamas.

I wonder what he was thinking in his last years. Was he lonely? Did he fear dying? Was life still worth living now that he had lost his wife and gotten cancer, now that he couldn't walk without a cane and needed his children's help to survive?

But I never asked him those questions. We only watched TV.

Luci Yamamoto
Berkeley, California

Sometimes, on soft summer nights, my children and I go for walks in the moonlight. In house after house, this is what we see: people staring, transfixed, at a glowing TV screen. If the shades are drawn, an eerie blue light emanates from behind them. There is no one but us out under the star-filled, moon-magic sky.

Kathye Fetsko Petrie
Swarthmore, Pennsylvania

BRIEF NARRATIVES

The brief stories in this section were selected from the "Readers Write" column of *The Sun,* a small literary magazine published and edited by Sy Safransky in Chapel Hill, NC. Each issue of *The Sun* includes an invitation for readers to submit personal stories on a given topic, such as "Nudity," "Moving Out," "The End of the Day," "Getting Caught," or "Vietnam." Though the common theme unites the stories in a particular issue, each writer approaches that theme differently. Each piece is a miniature character sketch or slice of experience.

The advantage of the short personal narrative as a writing exercise is that it forces a writer to pare down description to barest necessities. The short piece must have punch, and it must have just enough detail to allow the reader to create a mental picture. How to tell everything that needs saying, to give the reader a feel for the person or the experience, in just a few paragraphs? Only the most important information can be included, yet the point must be clear. This exercise is much more difficult than it appears on the surface, but—as with many simple exercises—the effort will pay off in the development of important skills.

Study Questions

1. What impression do you get of the personality of each author? How is each person different from the rest? Which details tell you about each writer's life? What is the dominant feeling or emotion expressed in each piece?

2. Just as each story has a different tone, each reader might respond to a piece differently. Examine your own feelings as a reader. How do you respond after reading each of the stories? What are your emotions?

Writing Topics

1. *Collaborative writing activity.* With the other members of your group or class, choose a common theme or subject and write brief narratives or mood pieces. The pieces should be from two to five paragraphs. Compare your work, noticing how each person takes a different approach to the topic.

2. In a very brief narrative, describe an incident involving your family during which you learned something, or during which something significant was revealed to you. Use dialogue and descriptions of actions to show what people felt, but do not directly tell the reader these feelings. For example, rather than writing "I felt sad," you might describe going to your room, closing the door, and crying.

Clarity, Economy, and Style

Economy and Style in Focus

The short pieces that make up this chapter were chosen not only because they are relatively easy reading but also because they demonstrate the characteristic of *economy,* a characteristic they share with the selections in chapter 1. Economy means that no word or phrase is extra or unnecessary. The writing says what needs to be said, gives just enough detail to set the scene, and lets readers come to their own conclusions. Such concise writing, from which anything that could be cut has been cut, can take as much work in editing as in composition.

Economy in writing doesn't necessarily mean short, any more than economy in shopping means cheap. The idea is to look for essential value, and necessity is the key: Does each word or phrase carry its own weight? Can anything be removed without damaging the meaning? Has the writer avoided long or meaningless phrases that distract from the point?

Moreover, conciseness doesn't necessarily equal simplicity or informality. Sometimes, particularly in formal writing, complex sentences and specialized language are required for the author to express a complicated point or idea. The writing in, for instance, a multilayered novel or diatribe can be as economical as the writing in an essay, a story, or a poem that takes less than fifteen minutes to read.

One of the most important skills in economical writing, and the basis for a writer's individual style, is close attention to the use of language, the kinds of words chosen and the meanings they convey. Most of the In Focus essays in this chapter, therefore, deal with language: word choice, word meanings, descriptive language, tone, and phrasing as the reflection of a consciousness of the audience. The readings in this chapter all illustrate such careful choice of exactly the kind of language necessary for a given effect. In addition, an In Focus essay discusses the writer's individual *stance,* as a factor in the decision about what to say and how to say it.

The Readings in Focus

The selections in this chapter are about the same length as those in chapter 1, in the range of a thousand words or slightly more, but here the language becomes a little more challenging. In the opening piece, "Back to School," Andrea Lee begins by presenting a memory and goes on to examine the personal cost of obtaining the education she now uses to such good effect in her writing. In the piece that follows, "Lines in the Mind, Not in the World," Donella H. Meadows conveys ideas through a thought-provoking near-poem written in prose. As the sentences grow somewhat longer, more effort at interpretation is needed, but the conciseness of the writing ensures that one or two read-throughs and a few minutes' careful consideration will allow the works to be understood.

Other selections illustrate different and equally distinctive uses of language and sentence structure. Robert Frost's "Mending Wall" is the deceptively simple product of one of the master stylists of American poetry. Abraham Lincoln's "Address at the Dedication of Gettysburg Cemetery as a War Memorial" and Aurora Levins Morales's "Kitchens" employ two different kinds of diction, each kind reflecting careful attention to precise and beautiful language.

A deciding factor in a writer's choice of wording and style is the sense of *audience,* of the people who will be listening or reading. Anatole Broyard, for example, writing the journal entries that make up this excerpt from *Intoxicated by My Illness,* might have thought of himself as the primary or even sole reader. William Faulkner, on the other hand, accepted his Nobel Prize, and delivered his "Award Speech," before a group of distinguished guests who would appreciate his characteristic style of seemingly endless, rolling, rhythmic sentences, a style that helped make his fictional works enduring classics.

Langston Hughes's "The Animals Must Wonder" and David James Duncan's "A Streetlamp in the Netherlands" are illustrations of how a writer maintains *tone,* a way of slanting or coloring a piece, reflecting the writer's attitude toward the subject. Following the Duncan essay are three excellent examples of using *descriptive detail* to give the reader a complete picture: William Bryant Logan's "Clyde's Pick-Up" shows a person by describing the contents of his truck rather than the person himself; Barry Lopez's vignettes from "The Log Jam" depict the scene and the action through descriptive nouns and active verbs; and William Maxwell's "What He Was Like" creates a character through the outward facts of his life, the secret notebooks he kept, and the responses of people who loved him.

Roger L. Welsch's "Send in the Clown," another superb example of using detail to describe an activity or incident, also demonstrates *stance,* the position of the writer. Following it is Ursula K. Le Guin's "The Creatures on My Mind," in which the writer's subtle unspoken stance forces the reader to discern her attitude toward the animals she describes. Finally, Abigail Zuger's "The Pain Game" combines outward description with internal thought processes to tell a story of intense self-questioning.

Back to School

ANDREA LEE

A couple of weeks ago, I paid a visit to the girls' preparatory school outside Philadelphia where, about thirty years ago, I enrolled as one of the first two black students. It wasn't my first return trip, but it was one that had a peculiarly definitive feeling: this time, I was going back to look at classes with my daughter, who is eleven—exactly the age I was when I first put on a blue-and-white uniform and walked in the front entrance of an institution where black people had always used the back door. My daughter, who was born in Europe, and who views the civil-rights struggles of the sixties as an antique heroic cycle not much removed in drama and time frame from the *Iliad,* sees her mother's experience as a singularly tame example of integration. There were, after all, no jeering mobs, no night riders, no police dogs or fire hoses—just a girl going to school and learning with quiet thoroughness the meaning of isolation.

The air inside the schoolhouse smelled exactly as it used to on rainy April days—that mysterious school essence of damp wood and ancient chalk dust and pent-up young flesh. For an instant, I relived precisely what it felt like to walk those halls with girls who never included me in a social event, with teachers and administrators who regarded me with bemused incomprehension—halls where the only other black faces I saw were those of maids and cooks, and where I never received the slightest hint that books had been written and discoveries made by people whose skin wasn't white. I remembered the defensive bravado that I once used as a cover for a constant and despairing sense of worthlessness, born and reinforced at school.

As I delivered my daughter to the sixth-grade classroom where she would spend the day, I saw that in the intervening time not only had the school sprouted a few glossy modern additions—an art wing, science and computer facilities, and a new lower school—but the faculty and the student body had also been transformed. Black and Asian girls mingled in the crowd of students rushing back and forth between classrooms and playing fields, giddy with excitement over the impending Easter and Passover weekend. A black teacher with braids strode out of the room where long ago I'd conjugated Latin verbs. Posters celebrating African-American artists and scientists hung on the walls, and the school's curriculum included dozens of works by black, Native American, and Hispanic writers. The director of the middle school was, miracle of miracles, a young black woman—a woman who combined an old-fashioned headmistress's unflappable good sense with a preternatural sensitivity to the psychology of culture and identity. She explained to me that she herself had once been a student at a mostly white East Coast prep school. When I asked who on her staff, in particular, was responsible for the self-esteem of minority students, she said firmly, "Every person who works here."

That day, I finally forgave my old school. I'd held a touchy rancor toward it through much of my adult life, like someone heaping blame on a negligent parent, and had taken the institution rather churlishly to task during a Commencement address I gave there some years ago. The changes I saw now disarmed and delighted me. Watching my daughter run by with a group of girls, I realized with envy how different her experience would be from mine if she were enrolled there. "Just think, I used to dream of burning the place down," I remarked to her, as we drove away, along the school's winding drive. She looked at me impatiently. "Can't you just forget all that?" she asked. The sound of her voice—half childish and half adolescent—made it clear to me that I wouldn't do any such thing. Wounds that have healed bring a responsibility to avoid repeating the past. The important thing is to pardon, even with joy, when the time comes—but never, I thought, driving on in silence, to forget.

IN FOCUS

DEFINING FROM CONTEXT

People who struggle with difficult readings often assume that other readers are fast because they know and understand all the words and the meaning immediately. Actually, rapid readers encounter many unknown words, but they skip over those words the way a professional musician skips over mistakes in a rapid sequence. Rapid readers have learned how to slide over unfamiliar words—making a note (mental or on the page) to look up the definitions later—meanwhile getting the general meaning from the surrounding information. The technique is called *defining from context*.

The method of defining from the context, or surrounding words, is relatively simple: Read as rapidly as possible to get the general meaning. Do not be distracted by words or phrases you don't understand. Most of the time, you will see the idea, the big picture, even if some of the details are unclear.

The point is to keep up speed, grasp as much of the *content* as you can, and reread later to clarify exactly what was meant.

Good readers often underline, highlight, or make a quick mark near something they don't understand, making it easy to find the mystery word later and look it up. When reading textbooks, they may write definitions in the margin, so the terms will be visible and handy for studying.

For example, a reader of "Back to School" might not know what a preparatory school is. (It's a private school, usually expensive and with high admissions standards, offering intensive preparation for ivy-league colleges.) The meaning of "preparatory" becomes clearer as Lee describes the school, but the reader still should note the word and define it precisely later.

Practice defining from context as you reread "Back to School." Mark any words you don't understand and guess at the meanings before looking up the definitions in a dictionary. Then go to one of the essays with an advanced vocabulary in chapter 6 or 7 of this book and practice defining from context in a few of the paragraphs.

Study Questions

1. Why did Lee feel so alienated as a student at that school? Was the prejudice she encountered blatant or subtle? How will her daughter feel while attending the same school?
2. The education that Lee received at the school seems to have helped her become a success. She has become an important public figure. Was all the suffering, then, worthwhile? Would you put a child of your own through the experience that Lee went through?

Writing Topics

1. The source of Andrea Lee's alienation was a very real social situation, one in which she was the only black person at an exclusive and exclusively white school. Other people, in different and sometimes less clearly defined situations, experience similar feelings. Was there ever a time, at

school or elsewhere, that you felt alone as an "outsider"? Write a short essay explaining your situation at that time and describing your feelings. How did you survive?

2. In "Back to School," Lee's adolescent daughter is not concerned with her mother's memories. "Can't you just forget all that?" she asks. Why can't Lee forget? *Should* Lee forget? Is it important to remember the past, even if the situation has changed or been improved? Why should we remember?

   Choose a specific situation in history or your own background. Imagine someone saying "Can't you just forget all that?" Write an essay in which you explain exactly why the situation should or should not be forgotten.

Lines in the Mind, Not in the World

DONELLA H. MEADOWS

The earth was formed whole and continuous in the universe, without lines.

The human mind arose in the universe needing lines, boundaries, distinctions. Here and not there. This and not that. Mine and not yours.

That is sea and this is land, and here is the line between them. See? It's very clear on the map.

But, as the linguists say, the map is not the territory. The line on the map is not to be found at the edge of the sea.

Humans build houses on the land beside the sea, and the sea comes and takes them away.

That is not land, says the sea. It is also not sea. Look at the territory, which God created, not the map, which you created. There is no place where land ends and sea begins.

The places that are not-land, not-sea, are beautiful, functional, fecund. Humans do not treasure them. In fact, they barely see them because those spaces do not fit the lines in the mind. Humans keep busy dredging, filling, building, diking, draining the places between land and sea, trying to make them either one or the other.

Here is the line, the mind says, between Poland and Russia, between France and Germany, between Jordan and Israel. Here is the Iron Curtain between East and West. Here is the line around the United States, separating us from not-us. It's very clear here, on the map.

The cosmonauts and astronauts in space (cosmonauts are theirs, astronauts are ours) look down and see no lines. They are created only by minds. They shift in history as minds change.

On the earth's time-scale, human-invented lines shift very quickly.

The maps of fifty years ago, of 100 years ago, of 1,000 years ago are very different from the maps of today. The planet is 4 billion years old. Human lines are ephemeral, though people kill one another over them.

Even during the fleeting moments of planetary time when the lines between nations are held still, immigrants cross them legally and illegally. Money and goods cross them legally and illegally. Migrating birds cross them, acid rain crosses them, radioactive debris from Chernobyl crosses them. Ideas cross them with the speed of sound and light. Even where Idea Police stand guard, ideas are not stopped by lines. How could they be? The lines are themselves only ideas.

Between me and not-me there is surely a line, a clear distinction, or so it seems. But now that I look, where is that line?

This fresh apple, still cold and crisp from the morning dew, is not-me only until I eat it. When I eat, I eat the soil that nourished the apple. When I drink, the waters of the earth become me. With every breath I take in I draw in not-me and make it me. With every breath out, I exhale me into not-me.

If the air and the waters and the soils are poisoned, I am poisoned. Only if I believe the fiction of the lines more than the truth of the lineless planet will I poison the earth, which is myself.

Between you and me, now there is certainly a line. No other line feels more certain than that one. Sometimes it seems not a line but a canyon, a yawning empty space across which I cannot reach.

Yet you keep appearing in my awareness. Even when you are far away, something of you surfaces constantly in my wandering thoughts. When you are nearby, I feel your presence, I sense your mood. Even when I try not to. Especially when I try not to.

If you are on the other side of the planet, if I don't know your name, if you speak a language I don't understand, even then, when I see a picture of your face, full of joy, I feel your joy. When your face shows suffering, I feel that too. Even when I try not to. Especially then.

I have to work hard not to pay attention to you. When I succeed, when I close my mind to you with walls of indifference, then the presence of those walls, which constrain my own aliveness, are reminders of the you to whom I would rather not pay attention.

When I do pay attention, very close attention, when I open myself fully to your humanity, your complexity, your reality, then I find, always, under every other feeling and judgment and emotion, that I love you.

Even between you and me, even there, the lines are only of our own making.

IN FOCUS

DENOTATION AND CONNOTATION

The word *line* has many meanings, some of them subtle. The lines that Meadows writes about begin as lines on a map, but they take on abstract significance. People go to war over these imaginary lines. Meadows doesn't like these artificial lines between people; she wants to cross these "borders." Thus, the lines here are real and made-up at the same time. They have meanings far beyond the simple figures drawn on paper.

The literal definition of a word, the thing it stands for, is termed *denotation*. The unspoken ideas and attitudes that a word carries—the emotional content of language—is called *connotation*. In the sentence "At the beach yesterday, I drew a line in the sand," the word *line* denotes an object; in the sentence "Biting your mother is going over the line," that same word connotes an uncrossable boundary. The word *snake* denotes an animal, but it also connotes danger and repulsion—except that for people who like snakes the same word carries a positive connotation.

The denotation of a word is given and apparent; its connotation is a personal and social construction. Think of the differences in denotation and connotation for words like *candy, thunder,* or *silence*. Notice the differences in connotation: my child is free, open, and creative, while your child is an unrestrained hyperactive monster. One person's cute doggy is another's mangy mutt, depending on what a person has stepped into that morning. (And in some cultures, *dog* carries the connotation of *food*.) Notice also that connotations change dramatically for different people and groups. The writer's job is to make the connotations explicit, and the reader's job is to understand the subtle meanings of the writer's language.

Study Questions

1. Find some words, phrases, or expressions in Meadows's piece that might have different connotations. For example, what is the connotative meaning of her phrase "walls of indifference"? Couldn't that phrase have a different connotation for someone else or in another context, a meaning such as "necessary privacy"? Explain the denotation, the connotation for Meadows, and the other possible connotations of each element you identify.
2. Meadows writes about four different divisions, or "lines"—the constructs by which humans separate nature, countries, and individuals—and gives an example of each: the line between land and sea, the line between one country and another, the line between humans and the environment, the line between "you and me." Can you name other kinds of constructed or imaginary lines and divisions involving nature, countries, or individuals?

Writing Topics

1. *Collaborative writing activity.* Try to imagine what the world would be like if the borders between countries were eliminated or the lines between groups of people were dissolved. Choose a particular border or line and write an essay in which you discuss the results of its being removed. Would all the results be advantageous?
2. Reflecting on Meadows's piece, describe a line (in history or your life) that once seemed permanent but now has shifted. What created the change? Did the elimination of the line have positive or negative results? Would Meadows have approved of the change?

Mending Wall

ROBERT FROST

Something there is that doesn't love a wall,
That sends the frozen-ground-swell under it,
And spills the upper boulders in the sun;
And makes gaps even two can pass abreast.
The work of hunters is another thing:
I have come after them and made repair
Where they have left not one stone on a stone,
But they would have the rabbit out of hiding,
To please the yelping dogs. The gaps I mean,
No one has seen them made or heard them made,
But at spring mending-time we find them there.
I let my neighbor know beyond the hill;
And on a day we meet to walk the line
And set the wall between us once again.
We keep the wall between us as we go.
To each the boulders that have fallen to each.
And some are loaves and some so nearly balls
We have to use a spell to make them balance:
"Stay where you are until our backs are turned!"
We wear our fingers rough with handling them.
Oh, just another kind of outdoor game,
One on a side. It comes to little more:
There where it is we do not need the wall:
He is all pine and I am apple orchard.
My apple trees will never get across
And eat the cones under his pines, I tell him.
He only says, "Good fences make good neighbors."
Spring is the mischief in me, and I wonder
If I could put a notion in his head:
"*Why* do they make good neighbors? Isn't it
Where there are cows? But here there are no cows.
Before I built a wall I'd ask to know
What I was walling in or walling out,
And to whom I was like to give offense.

Something there is that doesn't love a wall,
That wants it down." I could say "Elves" to him,
But it's not elves exactly, and I'd rather
He said it for himself. I see him there
Bringing a stone grasped firmly by the top
In each hand, like an old-stone savage armed.
He moves in darkness as it seems to me,
Not of woods only and the shade of trees.
He will not go behind his father's saying,
And he likes having thought of it so well
He says again, "Good fences make good neighbors."

Study Questions

1. The first line of "Mending Wall" is a key to the way the poem is written—deceptively simple on the surface, with deeper meanings underneath: "Something there is that doesn't love a wall." What is that something? Frost doesn't answer, leaving his readers to search for their own meanings. Why not just say "walls have a tendency to fall down" or "gravity doesn't like a wall"? Consider the reasons for Frost's precise word choice in the first line, then investigate his language through the poem.

2. Critics have argued passionately about whether the poet's real feelings are expressed in the poem. Certainly the speaker of the poem teases his neighbor, questioning the old folk wisdom of "good fences make good neighbors." Is the attitude of the speaker really the same as the attitude of the poet? Does Robert Frost himself want to say "good fences make good neighbors" to the readers of the poem? Describe the attitudes of the speaker, the neighbor, and the poet.

3. Compare "Mending Wall"—its surface simplicity and Frost's use of irony—to Carl Sandburg's "A Fence" (in chapter 1). Both poems are about kinds of fences, but they approach the subject very differently than does Donella H. Meadows's essay earlier in this chapter. How are the pieces alike? What are the thematic and stylistic differences?

Writing Topics

1. Write a short essay describing the fence-mending day from the point of view of the neighbor. Give your opinion of the man on the other side of the wall. How do you respond to him?

2. Describe two people performing a task together, only with different

attitudes toward the activity. Include information about how each person works, what they say to one another, and also what they think but do not say.

An interesting variation on this topic might be to work with a classmate, comparing the ways the two of you go about writing—or performing any other common task.

Address at the Dedication of Gettysburg Cemetery as a War Memorial

ABRAHAM LINCOLN

November 19, 1863

Four score and seven years ago our fathers brought forth on this continent, a new nation, conceived in liberty, and dedicated to the proposition that all men are created equal.

Now we are engaged in a great civil war, testing whether that nation, or any nation so conceived and so dedicated, can long endure. We are met on a great battlefield of that war. We have come to dedicate a portion of that field, as a final resting place for those who here gave their lives that that nation might live. It is altogether fitting and proper that we should do this.

But, in a larger sense, we cannot dedicate—we cannot consecrate—we cannot hallow—this ground. The brave men, living and dead, who struggled here, have consecrated it, far above our poor power to add or detract. The world will little note, nor long remember, what we say here, but it can never forget what they did here. It is for us the living, rather, to be dedicated here to the unfinished work which they who fought here have thus far so nobly advanced. It is rather for us to be here dedicated to the great task remaining before us—that from these honored dead we take increased devotion to that cause for which they gave the last full measure of devotion—that we here highly resolve that these dead shall not have died in vain—that this nation, under God, shall have a new birth of freedom—and that government of the people, by the people, for the people, shall not perish from the earth.

IN FOCUS

DICTION

Diction is the technical term for the way a writer or speaker uses certain kinds of words in particular kinds of sentences (short and clipped, long and flowing, very long and complex, and so on) in order to create a distinctive style. For example, Donella H. Meadows's diction in "Lines in the Mind, Not in the World" (p. 62) involves relatively simple words that echo one another, creating a poetic effect when read aloud. Abraham Lincoln's choice of wording and pattern also approaches poetry. His diction is rich and resonant, his sentences rolling. The opening phrase, "Four score and seven years ago," is a way of saying "eighty-seven years ago" that echoes the diction of the King James Bible, a language that was old-fashioned even in Lincoln's time, but one that Lincoln's listeners would have known well.

Diction is basically a choice of wording, and that choice depends on the writer's sense of the language his or her audience will best respond to. Just as a person, almost unconsciously, speaks differently at a family gathering than in a raucous nightclub, in a classroom, or at an interview, so a writer will find diction appropriate for the specific situation and purpose.

Study Questions

1. Notice that the three paragraphs progress from past to present to future. What words and phrases signal those time periods?
2. Lincoln delivered this address at a solemn ceremony in the middle of a terrible war. How do the sounds of the words and sentences carry forward the meaning of the piece?
3. Find a copy of the King James translation of the Bible, in the 1623 version. (Note that King James of England didn't do the translating—he commissioned it.) This was the version that Lincoln and most of his listeners would have been most familiar with. How much of that language is familiar to you? Try to write a sentence or two, copying the diction of that Bible.

Writing Topics

1. *Collaborative writing activity.* Imagine a formal, public situation in which a short speech is called for. Develop a three-part speech for the occasion that shows the same "past, present, future" pattern as the Lincoln address. If you are working in a group, one or two people can write each paragraph, and the group can join the paragraphs together.
2. Lincoln speaks of the resolution that "these dead shall not have died in vain . . . that from these honored dead we take increased devotion to that cause for which they gave the last full measure of devotion." Imagine that you were in the audience that day, possibly a relative of one of the dead soldiers. Write a letter to an imaginary family member, describing the President's speech and your reactions to it.

Kitchens

AURORA LEVINS MORALES

I went into the kitchen just now to stir the black beans and rice, the shiny black beans floating over the smooth brown grains of rice and the zucchini turning black, too, in the ink of the beans. Mine is a California kitchen, full of fresh vegetables and whole grains, bottled spring water and yogurt in plastic pints, but when I lift the lid from that big black pot, my kitchen fills with the hands of women who came before me, washing rice, washing beans, picking through them so deftly, so swiftly, that I could never see what the defects were in the beans they threw quickly over one shoulder out the window. Some instinct of the fingertips after years of sorting to feel the rottenness of the bean with a worm in it or a chewed-out side. Standing here, I see the smooth red and brown and white and speckled beans sliding through their fingers into bowls of water, the gentle clicking rush of them being poured into the pot, hear the hiss of escaping steam, smell the bean scum floating on the surface under the lid. I see grains of rice settling in a basin on the counter, turning the water milky with rice polish and the talc they use to make the grains so smooth; fingers dipping, swimming through the murky white water, feeling for the grain with the blackened tip, the brown stain.

From the corner of my eye, I see the knife blade flashing, reducing mounds of onions, garlic, cilantro, and green peppers into *sofrito* to be fried up and stored, and best of all is the pound and circular grind of the *pilón: pound, pound, thump, grind, pound, pound, thump, grind. Pound, pound* (the garlic and oregano mashed together), THUMP! (the mortar lifted and slammed down to loosen the crushed herbs and spices from the wooden bowl), *grind* (the slow rotation of the pestle smashing the oozing mash around and around, blending the juices, the green stain of cilantro and oregano, the sticky yellowing garlic, the grit of black pepper).

> It's the dance of the *cocinera:* to step outside
> fetch the bucket of water, turn,
> all muscular grace and striving,

pour the water, light dancing in the pot,
and set the pail down on the blackened wood.
The blue flame glitters in its dark corner,
and coffee steams in the small white pan.
Gnarled fingers, *mondando ajo,*
picando cebolla, cortando pan,
colando café,
stirring the rice with a big long spoon
filling ten bellies
out of one soot-black pot.

It's a magic, a power, a ritual of love and work that rises up in my kitchen, thousands of miles from those women in cotton dresses who twenty years ago taught the rules of its observance to me, the apprentice, the novice, the girl child: "Don't go out without wrapping your head, child, you've been roasting coffee, *y te va' a pa'mar!*" "This much coffee in the *colador,* girl, or you'll be serving brown water." "Dip the basin in the river, so, to leave the mud behind." "Always peel the green bananas under cold water, *mijita,* or you'll cut your fingers and get *mancha* on yourself and the stain never comes out: that black sap stain of *guineo verde* and *plátano,* the stain that marks you forever."

So I peel my bananas under running water from the faucet, but the stain won't come out, and the subtle earthy green smell of that sap follows me, down from the mountains, into the cities, to places where banana groves are like a green dream, unimaginable by daylight: Chicago, New Hampshire, Oakland. So I travel miles on the bus to the immigrant markets of other people, coming home laden with bundles, and even, now and then, on the plastic frilled tables of the supermarket, I find a small curved green bunch to rush home, quick, before it ripens, to peel and boil, bathing in the scent of its cooking, bringing the river to flow through my own kitchen now, the river of my place on earth, the green and musty river of my grandmothers, dripping, trickling, tumbling down from the mountain kitchens of my people.

IN FOCUS

REVISION

A really good professional often can make even the most amazing achievement look easy. Think of the deceptive simplicity of Robert Frost's "Mending Wall" (p. 66), a poem that looks almost casual but upon closer inspection is revealed to be a highly polished jewel. The basketball player turning in elegant balance; the horse and rider soaring over a fence; the chef preparing a perfect sauce—experts make it look as though anyone could do those things. Actually, almost anyone can—after hours upon hours of training and practice. Like every other skill, writing is a matter of training and practice. The rough spots don't appear in a piece of professional writing because they have been polished over in the author's most important ongoing activity: *revision.*

Talent without sweat goes nowhere. There are very few genius writers who are struck with insight as if by lightning and then pour out eloquent, nearly perfect prose. There are many more very competent writers—perhaps even geniuses—who struggle for hours in front of pages or computer screens, working to make their writing better. To achieve the seemingly easy flow and graceful structure of prose like that of Aurora Levins Morales, most writers will need to compose and read a first draft, make changes, write over, read again, and change again. In every revision, sentences and paragraphs may need to be restructured. Large chunks of material may be moved or even thrown out. Other readers—editors, friends, teachers, or fellow students—may look at the work and make comments and suggestions. Although this process will vary from writer to writer, and from one piece of writing to another, almost no one produces good work without some serious revising.

One thing students sometimes forget is that *recopying is not the same thing as revising.* Frequently, a beginning writer will attempt to go from rough first draft to submitted paper in one easy glide, just checking the spelling and making a neat final version. Good editing and revising requires much more awareness of structure and careful attention to how things might be better or more concisely said. Often, reading the paper aloud to oneself reveals awkward wording or twisted sentences. Trying the paper out on other readers shows the points that were clear to the writer but not adequately communicated to the audience. Editing can be a simple matter of cutting words, phrases, sentences, but revision takes time—the time required to put a piece away for a while, then go back to it with fresh insight and more effort.

Study Questions

1. Consider Morales's diction, the choice of words that makes "Kitchens" such an appealing piece. To lure the reader into her kitchen, she uses carefully chosen adjectives and descriptive verbs, appealing to the senses of sight, hearing, smell, and touch that fine cooking speaks to,

in addition to the sense of taste. In just one sentence, a host of sensory impressions are invoked: the feel and look of the beans, the hiss of steam, the smell of the bean scum in the pot.

Diction involves not only the choice of individual words, but the way the words fit together within the sentences. Notice the rhythmic way Morales's sentences flow, as a result of choosing words that connect in sound as well as meaning: "the green and musty river of my grandmothers, dripping, trickling, tumbling down from the mountain kitchens of my people."

Review Morales's description, reading sentences aloud to yourself. Notice the *feel* of the language, the choice of words that seem almost to run together. Point out sentences and passages where you find particularly effective diction.

2. Morales's cooking connects her to the kitchens of her mother, grandmothers, and ancestors. How does her language make that same connection? Why does she quote Spanish words that were spoken to her as a child? Why does she mix the two languages?

3. In the last paragraph, what does Morales mean by "the stain won't come out"? How is the green banana stain connected to "the green and musty river of my grandmothers"?

Writing Topics

1. Write an essay in which you describe cooking or creating something the way you learned it from a family member or friend. Bring your memories of learning this process into your description of doing it now. Pay attention to the ways that you shift from the present to the past and back to the present.

2. If you know another language, write a short essay imitating the way Morales mixes Spanish and English in her third paragraph. Use words from your other language, writing in such a way that a reader who does not speak the language can figure out what the words mean. The essay can be on any subject, but use the format of an older person speaking to a younger one.

From
Intoxicated by My Illness

ANATOLE BROYARD

So much of a writer's life consists of assumed suffering, rhetorical suffering, that I felt something like relief, even elation, when the doctor told me that I had cancer of the prostate. Suddenly there was in the air a rich sense of crisis—real crisis, yet one that also contained echoes of ideas like the crisis of language, the crisis of literature, or of personality. It seemed to me that my existence, whatever I thought, felt, or did, had taken on a kind of meter, as in poetry or in taxis.

When you learn that your life is threatened, you can turn toward this knowledge or away from it. I turned toward it. It was not a choice but an automatic shifting of gears, a tacit agreement between my body and my brain. I thought that time had tapped me on the shoulder, that I had been given a real deadline at last. It wasn't that I believed the cancer was going to kill me, even though it had spread beyond the prostate—it could probably be controlled, either by radiation or hormonal manipulation. No. What struck me was the startled awareness that one day something, whatever it might be, was going to interrupt my leisurely progress. It sounds trite, yet I can only say that I realized for the first time that I don't have forever.

Journal Notes

Being ill and dying is largely, to a great degree, a matter of style. My intention is to show people who are ill—and we will all be ill someday—that it's not the end of their world as they know it, that they can go on being themselves, perhaps even more so than before. They can make a game, a career, even an art form of opposing their illness. There are so many interesting and therapeutic things they can do. It's not enough to be "positive," brave, or stoical: These are too simple, like New Year's resolutions.

We should break down the idea of "the will to live" into more palatable components, into insights and tactics that appeal not only to the man of average sensibility but to skeptical, ironical people. In a sense, illness is a drug, and it's partly up to the patient to determine whether it will be a low or a high.

I would advise every sick person to evolve a style or develop a voice for his or her illness. In my own case I make fun of my illness. I disparage it. This wasn't a deliberate decision; the response simply came to me. Adopting a style for your illness is another way of meeting it on your own grounds, of making it a mere character in your narrative.

One of the things I think the patient has to avoid is developing a false self. If you try to seduce your doctor by being particularly nice, then you become untrue to yourself and you develop a false self with the doctor, which is very damaging. You must remain yourself. Of course, if you remain yourself with the doctor, he may not like it. Doctors are used to having patients offer them false selves, but I think that doctors have to be taught to recognize and accept the patient's true self.

When you're ill you instinctively fear a diminishment and disfigurement of yourself. It's that, more than dying, that frightens you. You're going to become a monster. I think you have to develop a style when you're ill to keep from falling out of love with yourself. It's important to stay in love with yourself. That's known as the will to live. And your style is the instrument of your vanity. If they can afford it, I think it would be good therapy, good body narcissism, for cancer patients to buy a whole new wardrobe, mostly elegant, casual clothes.

Anxiety is the cancer patient's worst enemy. It reminds me of a catheter, which all prostate cancers require at some point. Anxiety is like a catheter inserted in your soul, and if the patient can get on better terms with his anxiety, he'll feel something like the relief I felt when the doctor pulled the catheter out of my penis and urethral canal. I've been studying anxiety for many years—it's my hobby—and I've learned that it can sometimes be turned around and made into a kind of a pet, like a dog, or an amusing Kafkaesque companion.

The sick person's best medicine is desire—the desire to live, to be with other people, to do things, to get back to his life. When I was in the hospital, I was always gazing out of the window at the real world, which had never looked more desirable. I'd like to suggest, to invent or imagine or recall, ways of keeping one's desire alive as a way of keeping oneself alive.

I really think you have to have a style in which you finish your life. That's what I'm doing right now. I'm finishing my life. I think one ought to die at a kind of party, the way Socrates died. All of his disciples came to his bedside. When André Gide was dying, he was surrounded by friends and journalists. Gide was a very compulsive man. He used to play the piano without touching the keys because he was afraid that someone might hear him making a mistake. So, when he died, his last words were to the journalists: "Before you quote me, make sure I'm conscious." He wanted to die in his own style, and that seems to me quite reasonable. I think in the last stage of dying the doctor should be removed and so too the grisly Elisabeth Kübler-Ross, who actually wrote to the parents of a child who had died saying how much she had enjoyed participating in the event. I would like to die in my own way. It's my house, my life, my death, my friends. Why not?

A critically ill person ought to be entitled to anything that affords him relief. While Byron's Sardanapalus went too far in condemning his concubines, his slaves, his horses and dogs, to die with him, one can understand the impulse. A better way, I think, would be for the patient to write a last will and testament, summing up his satisfactions and regrets, describing his loves in lyrical, even pornographic, detail and his hatreds too in all their vehemence, as a kind of final settling of unfinished business. A last will and testament would be like a final disinhibiting, fuller than the one-sided deathbed confession to a priest. It would be a period to the long sentence of life. Cranked up in his bed like Sardanapalus, the patient could bestow symbolic life and death, in his own heart at least, among his intimates. He could leave the legacy of his true feelings.

There comes a point where it's pretty obvious that a patient is going to die, and I think to eke out a few more days by mechanical means is a mistake, and I think that the patient should be allowed to glide or skate or dance into death in the way that he chooses rather than be ministered to until the last minute, which I think is obscene. You know when a patient is moribund, and then you leave him alone. You let him die in his own way, and you let him make his final arrangements unimpeded by technology.

JOURNALS

On January 13, 1835, a young college student named Henry David Thoreau submitted to his composition instructor an essay titled "Of keeping a private journal or record of our thoughts, feelings, studies, and daily experience,—containing abstracts of books, and the opinions we formed of them on first reading them." His teacher had assigned the topic, but Thoreau, who was later to become one of America's most influential writers, already knew the value of keeping a personal journal:

> If each one would employ a certain portion of each day in looking back upon the time which has passed, and in writing down his thoughts and feelings, in reckoning up his daily gains, . . . not only would his daily experience be greatly increased, since his feelings and ideas would thus be more closely defined, but he would be ready to turn over a new leaf, having carefully perused the preceding one. . . .
>
> In fine [in the end], if we endeavoured more to improve ourselves by reflection, by making a business of thinking, and giving our thoughts form and expression, we should be led to "read not to contradict and confute, nor to believe and take for granted, nor to find talk and discourse, but to weigh and consider."

Thoreau thus identified the basic use of keeping a journal: making a record of one's thoughts, opinions, and readings, for the purpose of looking back later on. In years to come, he would use his extensive journals as a gold mine for his public writings.

In addition to being an aid for remembering one's earlier experiences and states of mind, and for later self-examination (Where was I emotionally a year ago? How far have I come?), the journal is a place to practice writing. Like any other skill, writing takes practice, and the daily exercise of writing in a journal brings the benefit of improvement.

Although the terms *diary* and *journal* are often used interchangeably, the general difference is that a diary records what one *does*, while a journal records what one *thinks*. Ideas go into a journal: thoughts, dreams, quotations and summaries from one's reading, the state of one's mind and heart. The regular practice of keeping a journal improves a person's ease and skill at writing, and the journal itself becomes a repository of the person's attitudes, ideas, emotional progress, and intellectual growth. "Every one can think," as Thoreau noted in his student essay, "but comparatively few can write, can express their thoughts. Indeed, how often do we hear one complain of his inability to express what he feels!"

Study Questions

1. In 1992, the author's widow wrote in the prologue to the posthumous *Intoxicated by My Illness* that "my husband, Anatole Broyard, was diagnosed with metastatic prostate cancer in August 1989, and this sudden confrontation with mortality inspired him to write about his experience." What, in your opinion, was unique and important about the way Broyard faced his approaching death? How did his approach differ from the reactions of other very sick people?

2. Do you think that writing about his illness in his journal helped Broyard, or was he just dwelling on his problems? If you think it might have helped, what benefit could it have been? What benefit can keeping a journal be for other people, sick or well? Could there be negative consequences?

   As you consider this question, think about the person described in the William Maxwell story "What He Was Like" (p. 99). What did keeping the diary do for the husband? Was it "healthy" or "sick" to include the things that so shocked his daughter later?

3. Broyard never had the chance to turn his journal entries into the finished book he wanted to write. Why did his wife think these unpolished, sketchy pieces were interesting enough to publish? In what way is reading the entries from someone's journal different from reading a completed book?

Writing Topics

1. This is an ongoing activity: Practice keeping a journal for a specific period of time, from a two-week minimum to a few months. Record your responses to things you read as well as your thoughts about what goes on in your life and the outer world. Treat your journal as if it were a body-building exercise program: Decide from the start when and how often you will make entries, then try to keep to the plan.

   Later, as you go back over the journal, see if you can discern "threads" or patterns of entries on a single topic, something that interested or disturbed you over the time period. Choose which entries on that subject you are willing to share, and combine them into a short essay.

2. *Collaborative writing activity* (with the group sharing experiences before writing individual essays). Think of a time that, like Broyard, you realized "I don't have forever." Did you recognize that *something was ending,* such as your childhood, a love affair, or your time in high school? Perhaps you or someone you know escaped a life-threatening situation. Write an essay in which you describe your feelings and responses.

Nobel Prize Award Speech

WILLIAM FAULKNER

I feel that this award was not made to me as a man, but to my work—a life's work in the agony and sweat of the human spirit, not for glory and least of all for profit, but to create out of the materials of the human spirit something which did not exist before. So this award is only mine in trust. It will not be difficult to find a dedication for the money part of it commensurate with the purpose and significance of its origin. But I would like to do the same with the acclaim too, by using this moment as a pinnacle from which I might be listened to by the young men and women already dedicated to the same anguish and travail, among whom is already that one who will some day stand here where I am standing.

Our tragedy today is a general and universal physical fear so long sustained by now that we can even bear it. There are no longer problems of the spirit. There is only the question: When will I be blown up? Because of this, the young man or woman writing today has forgotten the problems of the human heart in conflict with itself, which alone can make good writing because only that is worth writing about, worth the agony and the sweat.

He must learn them again. He must teach himself that the basest of all things is to be afraid; and, teaching himself that, forget it forever, leaving no room in his workshop for anything but the old verities and truths of the heart, the old universal truths lacking which any story is ephemeral and doomed—love and honor and pity and pride and compassion and sacrifice. Until he does so, he labors under a curse. He writes not of love but of lust, of defeats in which nobody loses anything of value, of victories without hope and, worst of all, without pity or compassion. His griefs grieve on no universal bones, leaving no scars. He writes not of the heart but of the glands.

Until he relearns these things, he will write as though he stood among and watched the end of man. I decline to accept the end of man. It is easy enough to say that man is immortal simply because he will endure: that when the last ding-dong of doom has clanged

and faded from the last worthless rock hanging tideless in the last red
and dying evening, that even then there will still be one more sound:
that of his puny inexhaustible voice, still talking. I refuse to accept
this. I believe that man will not merely endure: he will prevail. He is
immortal, not because he alone among creatures has an inexhaustible voice, but because he has a soul, a spirit capable of compassion and sacrifice and endurance. The poet's, the writer's, duty is
to write about these things. It is his privilege to help man endure by
lifting his heart, by reminding him of the courage and honor and
hope and pride and compassion and pity and sacrifice which have
been the glory of his past. The poet's voice need not merely be the
record of man, it can be one of the props, the pillars to help him endure and prevail.

IN FOCUS

Audience

Looking at Faulkner's language, one can guess the kind of people for whom he was writing this speech. It would take an educated audience to understand his language, with words such as
commensurate, significance, and *travail* in the first paragraph alone.
It would also take an educated audience to deal with his long,
complicated sentences as he spoke them. Most people have to
read this little speech two or three times to grasp the full meaning.

But Faulkner's audience was much wider than the group of dig-
nitaries and other invited guests who had traveled to Stockholm,
Sweden, in 1950 to view his acceptance. He was also speaking to
a wider audience of people who interested themselves in the
meaning and importance of modern literature. Moreover, he was
speaking to other writers, "the young man or woman writing
today."

The writer's sense of *audience,* a perception of the people who
will read or listen to the work, determines to a great degree what
will be said and the way it will be said, the diction as well as the
style of the writing. Faulkner certainly wouldn't have said the
same things in the same way in a bar, celebrating the award with
his friends. Audience is the writer's sense of the kind of person
who will read the work.

Any writer, including the beginning student writer, needs to
consider the intended audience. Is an essay being written solely
for the instructor? For others in the class? What will interest and

engage that particular audience? How can that audience be impressed with the writer's skills and intellect? What will best bring that audience to accept the writer's ideas?

Study Questions

1. Faulkner wrote at a time in which the word *he* was generally used to mean either a man or a woman, a practice that now is considered sexist. In more-recent years, language experts have pointed out that the exclusive use of *he* psychologically excluded women, even though it was supposed to include them. Today, *gender-neutral language* is the preferred usage. We use the term *police officer* instead of *policeman, firefighter* instead of *fireman,* to indicate that these occupations no longer exclude women. Of the modern alternatives to *he*—such as *he or she, he/she,* or using *he* and *she* interchangeably—that are now available, which do you prefer, and why?

   Examine Faulkner's use of *he.* Does it exclude women? Did Faulkner intend to indicate that most writers are men?

2. In 1950, Faulkner wrote that "our tragedy today is a general and universal fear." Does a similar generalized fear exist today? What are people afraid of? How does such fear affect everyday life? Is this situation, as Faulkner claims, a tragedy?

3. Is Faulkner saying that hope will drive out the fear? Does he refuse to be pessimistic about humanity? If so, do you think he's being naive and overoptimistic? Do you agree or disagree with his position?

Writing Topics

1. *Collaborative writing activity* (with the group discussing, researching, and comparing opinions).

   About "the money part" of the Nobel Prize, Faulkner wrote, "It will not be difficult to find a dedication . . . commensurate with the purpose and significance of its origin." According to his biographer Frederick Karl, Faulkner did use some of the prize money to establish college scholarships for African-American students. (Many of Faulkner's works dealt with racial injustice in the American South.)

   Imagine you have just won an award that carries with it a huge amount of money, but to receive the prize you must give at least half of it to some worthy cause—the money must be used to make the world a better place. Investigate one or more charities or organizations that seek to "do good" and choose one to receive your money. Or, make up your own charity and describe how it would serve a need. Finally, explain how the money would be spent and what you would hope to accomplish with that part of your prize.

2. What is it that Faulkner wanted young writers to do, to say, and to write about? In your opinion, what should young writers be saying and writing about now? What kind of audience is there now for literature?

As a preliminary to this writing assignment, visit a local bookstore. Draw some conclusions about what kinds of writing seem to be most popular these days.

Then write an essay in the form of a letter beginning "Dear Mr. Faulkner . . . " Tell him the results of your investigations and suggest what, if anything, should be done about the situation.

The Animals Must Wonder

LANGSTON HUGHES

February 3, 1945

Once I saw a man and a woman, who loved each other, quarrel. There were bitter words and the threat of blows. Bursts of anger punctuated minutes of silent defiance. It was sad for an outsider to see. But equally sad to observe was the hurt fright of their dog, his wonder, dumb fear, and terror at the strange loud violence of the two human beings he loved.

At first the animal trotted nervously about the house. He got under his master's feet and was shoved away. His mistress paid him no mind, being too busy yelling at her husband. Finally the dog sat trembling in a corner thinking, perhaps, that both were mad.

A recent dispatch from the European front reports how frightened and panic-stricken domestic animals in the war zones are, caught in the crosscurrent of battle between the Nazis and the Allied lines. As the armies of human beings go at each other with all the explosive weapons of death at our command, as the skies fill with the roar of bombers, the earth shakes with the bursts of shells, and the very air crackles with gun-fire—unprotected in their terror, the dogs, cats, horses, cows, and sheep must wonder if man, their superior and civilized master, has gone mad.

Panic of Animals

Newspaper men report lost and homeless dogs wandering cold and hungry through wrecked villages where the armies have passed. They report wild-eyed farm horses on stampede, crazed by tanks and planes, cows caught in an artillery barrage, dropping premature calves in snowy fields, sheep and pigs running in circles as if pursued by furies.

Animals, of course, do not know the difference between Nazis and Allies. To a gentle old plow horse deserted by his fleeing owners in the Aachen sector of the Western Front, the guns of both sides must sound like the very roar of hell itself. To a herd of sheep whose pasture is suddenly invaded by flame-throwing tanks, it must seem as if the world has gone mad. The animals in the war zones must be as puzzled as the precocious child whom one of the New York columnists reports as having written a most penetrating little verse to the effect that "in this world of ours wonders never cease! All the civilized peoples are at war—while the savages are at peace."

To the dogs, cats, parrots, and canaries of cities like Warsaw, Budapest, Bitche, or Manila, all human beings must suddenly seem like demons. As bad as life is for barnyard animals caught in the cross-fire of explosive warfare, things must be even worse for household pets accustomed to closer and more intimate contacts with mankind.

To suddenly be deserted in an empty house on a day when the very air explodes like thunder, aviation roars overhead, shells burst in the street, snipers' bullets shatter window panes, and steel tanks crush fences and gardens . . . on such a day, left-lonesome cats and dogs and birds in cages must think the end of time has come.

The S.P.C.A. Is Powerless

I have not read anywhere that the Society for the Prevention of Cruelty to Animals is taking up this current problem of animals and war. But then I suppose this estimable society would be just as impotent to deal with so vast a problem now as was the League of Nations to deal with the problem of human beings and war when Mussolini invaded Ethiopia.

If human beings do .not care enough about each other to work out ways of preventing wars before they happen, one could hardly expect them to be considerate of cats, dogs, parrots, canaries, horses, cows, pigs, or sheep. The human race has long claimed superiority over beasts. However, at the moment, from the Rhine to Burma, animals must wonder if this is true.

Given a chance, a cat might eat a canary, but he would not first bomb the canary's house, shell his cage, strafe his perch, snipe at him from ambush, shoot flames at him, then run him down with a tank . . . before slitting his gullet with a bayonet. Neither would a cat use a robot bomb to scare the birdseed out of him. If cats were ever to start doing such things, all vertebrates from canaries to Churchill would swear cats had gone mad. Not only would they be declared as crazy as loons . . . but as crazy as men! Then indeed would cats have lost their minds!

And if the canaries would suddenly start firing back at the cats, we would know the universe had gone mad!

TONE

Tone is the way a writer indicates his or her attitude toward the subject of a piece. The tone of writing is the author's subtle, unspoken message to the reader about how the piece is to be taken. The word *tone* is allied to speaking and singing and carries a sense of the spoken word; the tone of a voice tells whether someone is angry or happy, for example, usually better than the words themselves. In the same way, and even more subtly, a piece of writing can have a tone of sadness, romance, sarcasm, seriousness, exuberance, or irritation. The tone of a piece can be formal or folksy, solemn or childlike, enthusiastic or skeptical, disapproving or supportive. Evaluating the tone of a piece of writing is one of the keys to fully understanding its meaning.

The key to accurately conveying tone involves a careful choice of wording and approach. A person may, for example, be called stubborn, pigheaded, or an independent thinker—each way of putting it carries a different connotation and conveys a different tone. The content of the piece also indicates tone: is it so outrageous as to become humorous and ironic, or so factual that the tone is one of scientific objectivity?

One good way for a reader to perceive the tone of a piece is to imagine a picture of the writer's face as the work was being written. Is there a playful smile on Langston Hughes's face, as you imagine it, or a serious sadness? Were the faces of William Faulkner and Abraham Lincoln solemn as they delivered their famous speeches, and what did their voices sound like? Writing can carry a great deal of information that is not precisely in the piece itself, information about the way the writer felt and how the writer wanted the audience to respond. One good way to apprehend and convey this information is to learn to be sensitive to the tone of writing.

Study Questions

1. Where in the Hughes essay is the main point stated? Is it stated more than once? Express the main point in your own words and explain how the tone of the essay supports that point.
2. During World War II, as Hughes wrote this newspaper column, millions of human beings were suffering and dying. Should we care as much

about the terror and pain of the animals as we do about that of people? What about the farm animals that Hughes describes? They would
probably have been killed for their meat, whether there was war or
peace, so why do we feel sorry for them?

3. Langston Hughes was a great African-American writer whose newspaper columns from this period dealt largely with civil rights and social justice. How does knowing that give added insight into his essay?

Writing Topics

1. *Collaborative writing activity.* Consider Study Question #2 above. Have
   half the group choose the side of "people are more important" and
   half the group choose the side of "animals are just as important." Now
   consider some issue that will focus this debate: vegetarianism, testing
   drugs or medical procedures on animals, testing cosmetics on animals,
   replacing wilderness with housing projects, or some other issue that
   puts "animal rights" and "people rights" into conflict. Hold an informal
   debate in which each side presents its position.

2. Follow up on Study Question #2 by writing an essay in which you argue
   that even though the title of Hughes's essay mentions animals, his main
   point is about people. In the essay, explain what you see as Hughes's attitude toward human beings.

3. Describe an event in a household or outdoor setting from the point of
   view of an animal. Write the essay as though you were the animal,
   telling what happened in the way the animal could perceive and understand it.

A Streetlamp in the Netherlands

DAVID JAMES DUNCAN

Early August, 1969. I was standing on a sidewalk outside a delft-ware factory in Amsterdam, smoking an English Pall Mall. The sun was bright, the morning still, the neighborhood one of shops and old, stately houses. The dullness of the delftware lecture my American traveling companions were enduring indoors added pleasure to my smoke.

The sidewalk bordered a two-lane, one-way street evenly lined with broad-leaf trees and enormous old wrought-iron streetlamps. They were the sort of lamps—we'd seen them all over Europe—that had been converted, decades ago, from gas to electricity. They'd been standing for close to a century. They had survived two world wars. As I was staring up the empty street, my head equally empty but for a nicotine buzz, a lamp a hundred or so feet away let out a groan, then fell with a crash to the pavement.

I looked, at once, in every direction to see if anyone else witnessed its fall. The only person in sight was a silhouette in the backseat of a Fiat sedan, parked across the street from the delftware factory, and the Fiat's windows were closed; the silhouette seemed not to have noticed. I was disappointed. A fellow witness and I could have shared an amazed laugh. Alone, I was having trouble believing what I'd seen. Yet there the lamp lay, blocking half the street, its glass panes shattered, its post badly twisted. "Weird," I said aloud.

At the sound of a cartoonish buzzing I looked past the fallen lamp and saw a Vespa motor scooter far up the same street. As it came closer I made out a neatly dressed young man in front and a pair of bare knees just behind him. Closer yet the knees began to shine in the morning light. Closer yet I saw that they belonged to a pretty young woman, and that the miniskirt she was wearing had been forced, by the wind and her posture, clear up to her panties. Confused though I was by the streetlamp, I was riveted with lust by the way her beautiful bare legs embraced the young man.

They'd been using the right lane. When the man saw the fallen lamp he swerved, scarcely slowing, to the left lane. Neither he nor the woman showed any surprise at the sight of the lamp. As they passed me, doing perhaps twenty-five, I felt myself staring so carnivorously at her exposed legs that I attempted a friendly wave in hopes of softening, somewhat, my voracious staring. The young man, justifiably, ignored me. The woman didn't wave, either, but she flashed me a marvelous, and surprising, smile. Doubly smitten, I was still staring at her receding legs when the silhouette in the Fiat at the left curb suddenly opened the door. The couple on the Vespa had no time to react. The door missed the young man, but struck the woman in the center of the kneecap. Her leg snapped violently back, the scooter was thrown sideways, but the young man, using his left foot as a strut, somehow kept it upright and brought it to a stop. The woman slumped at once to the pavement and began to let out horrible, gasping groans. Her kneecap was as shattered as the lamp. The person in the Fiat remained frozen in the backseat, gaping at them both.

They were surrounded within seconds by people from the delftware factory. I tried to go help them, too. But when I got close enough to see the dent her knee had made in the metal edge of the car door, saw shattered bone knifing and blood spilling from the beautiful tan flesh for which I'd just lusted, I found myself veering like a drunk back to my original curb, the blood gone from my head. And as I hunched like a gargoyle on my curb there, trapped between the remembered gleam of her legs and animal agony of her groans, I kept looking up the street at the preposterously fallen lamp that started the chain reaction, trying, like a gargoyle, to work out a way to hate it; trying to find a way to make it stand back up and pay.

Study Questions

1. Before looking them up, try defining from the context, or surrounding sentences, the meanings of *delftware, stately, carnivorously, smitten, gargoyle,* and other words in this essay.
2. Who is at fault in the accident? Why is Duncan trying to find someone or something to blame? What does he mean by "trying to find a way to make it stand back up and pay"?
3. Duncan never tells outright what he is feeling at any given moment in the story, but his actions and reactions are revealing. Reread the essay, tracing the ways in which the author shows his feelings.

Writing Topics

1. Consider a time that you watched something happen to someone else and were unable to help or unwilling to become involved. Write an essay describing the scene and telling what happened. Describe your feelings at being an outside observer.

2. *Collaborative writing activity.* With your group or class, discuss the accident and the graphic description of the injury. For example, one reader of the story reported that it "made me sick." Should something that makes people sick be in a college textbook? Should it be required reading? How do you feel about descriptions of violence in newspapers or on television news? What about blood-and-guts-and-gore movies, where violence is included for its own sake?

   After the discussion, write an essay giving your own position on the depiction of violence in the media. Can or should anything be done about it? How much exposure do you personally choose to have? For example, do you view "action" movies or television programs?

Clyde's Pick-Up

A year ago, Clyde fell off a scaffold. He is a big, black Texan, who wears a worn straw cowboy hat and the same jeans every day, and boots that he seems to have been born in.

He had assembled the scaffold out in front of the Great Portal of the Cathedral of St. John the Divine in New York City. He was to check the mortar on some limestone blocks high overhead, lest they come down some Easter morn and clean the Bishop's clock while he stood waiting to enter church in the role of the Risen Christ. Somehow, Clyde fell more than forty feet onto grey limestone steps.

While he was in the hospital, and as he has convalesced at home, his Chevy pick-up truck has sat unused and unmoved in a space at the head of the driveway, under a maple tree. The Cathedral's urban pigeon corps has made great cloud-like white patches of droppings all over it. Inside the cab, between the dashboard and the windshield, are stuffed sheafs and wads of notes, instructions, registrations, a box of toothpicks, cassette tapes, catalogues, the tops of commuter coffee cups, stirrers, newspaper clippings, chopsticks, and saw blades. This is Clyde's filing system.

In the back of the pick-up lies a rough pile of pigeon-spattered, sawed logs, along with a generation of fallen leaves, a broken fanbelt, an empty yellow antifreeze container, numbers of styrofoam cups, a boasted stone, a rusting can of Super Stripe Traffic paint, a few discarded service leaflets and menus for Chinese food, a ticket that reads "admit one," and a vintage book of Diocesan records with advertisements for long-vanished vestment stores and Episcopal schools, their lettering now half eaten by mold.

Out of these leavings a forest is growing. Not on the ground. Not beside the truck. But right in the back of it. The lobes of maple leaves are sharpening as their seedlings sprout, a light and glossy green. The red-stemmed, three-leaved poison ivy is showing its amazing skill at growing out of *any* slightly shady bit of dead wood. (You would think that wood spawned the stuff.) Seeds of albizia have somehow blown from the one little understory specimen halfway down the street and taken hold in the back of the truck. All of this is happening in Manhattan, fifty yards from Amsterdam Avenue, where eighteen-wheel trucks whizz by.

Clyde's truck is a study of a closed system versus an open system. Inside the cab, its windows closed, the dust gathers, the rip in the upholstery creeps infinitesimally towards the back of the seat, the papers yellow and curl. Nothing grows. The "Fan" and the "Hot-Cold" levers remain where they have been for a year. Park-R-D-2-1. Nothing is happening, because the motor is not running.

But in the back of the truck, open to the air and the wet, Great Nature's motor is emphatically running. Left out in the rain, the Diocesan book has a sprout in it. The tilted coffee cup has filled with leaf compost, dots of pigeon shit, and wood mold, and albizia is growing in it. The old black Chevy is alive.

Wherever there are decay and repose, there begins to be soil. It would be hard to imagine a more improbable set of ingredients, but even a truck can become dirt.

How can I stand on the ground everyday and not feel its power? How can I live my life stepping on this stuff and not wondering at it? Science says that every gram of soil holds 2.3 horsepower worth of energy. But you could pour gasoline all over the ground forever and never see it sprout maple trees! Even a truck turns to soil. Even an old black pick-up.

Recently, I have been reading Exodus, thinking about Moses and the Burning Bush. Moses, it is written, "turns aside to see a wonder," a bush that burns but is not consumed. Throughout my life, I had thought this a ridiculous passage. Why should God get Moses' attention by such outlandish means? I mean, Why couldn't He just have boomed, "Hey, Moses!" the way He would later call to the great king, "Hey, Samuel!"

Now I know why. The truth, when really perceived (not simply described), is always a wonder. Moses does not see a technicolor fantasy. He sees the bush as it really is. He sees the bush as all bushes *actually* are.

There is in biology a formula called the equation of burning. It is half of the fundamental pair of equations by which all organic life subsists. The other half, the equation of photosynthesis, describes the way plants make foods out of sunlight, carbon dioxide and water. In the equation of burning, plants (and animals) unlock the stored sunlight and turn it into the heat energy that fuels their motion, their feeling, their thought, or whatever their living consists of.

All that is living burns. This is a fundamental fact of nature. And

Moses saw it with his two eyes, directly. That glimpse of the real world—of the world as it is known to God—is not a world of isolated things, but of processes in concert.

God tells Moses, "Take off your shoes, because the ground where you are standing is Holy Ground." He is asking Moses to experience in his own body what the burning bush experiences: a living connection between heaven and earth, the life that stretches out like taffy between our father the sun and our mother the earth. If you do not believe this, take off your shoes and stand in the grass or in the sand or in the dirt.

DESCRIPTIVE DETAIL

In the essay above, William Bryant Logan uses a key writing technique to describe a person's character without ever putting the person in the essay. The reader never actually sees Clyde, or is told what Clyde is like, but knows him from the contents of his truck. "This is Clyde's filing system" tells a lot about the man. The reader also knows that Clyde is a courageous and conscientious worker, without being told that in so many words. Logan shows, rather than tells, what kind of person Clyde is through the abundant use of *descriptive detail*.

The choice of details determines the effectiveness of any description. Too many details, or the wrong kind, and the writing gets long-winded and boring, like the speaker who insists on adding unnecessary specifics, going on and on about nothing. Too few details, on the other hand, and the reader will never get a clear picture of the subject. One rule of adding details and descriptions in writing is that generally speaking, the more specific the details, the better. The list of specific items in the back of the truck, the colors of the growing plants, the rip in the upholstery inside the truck all add to the picture. Another rule of writing description is to add as many specific details as possible in the first draft; the extra material can always be taken out.

Thus, the key to, and challenge of, good descriptive writing is *appropriate, significant* detail. Examine the details that are provided. What do they tell you? How do you know about Clyde from his truck? What do you learn about the biological process taking place in the back of the pick-up from the description of what is happening?

Study Questions

1. Make a list of some of the details in the essay. Which of them interest you, and why? What do they tell you about Clyde—for instance, why is there a collection of empty containers and styrofoam cups in the back of the truck?
2. Continue the practice of defining from context. What would you guess a boasted stone to be? What kind of thing is albizia? List the other words you did not know on first reading the essay, and attempt to define them from context before looking them up in a dictionary.
3. What does Logan mean by the statement "All that is living burns. This is a fundamental fact of nature." How does he combine biology and religion in the essay?
4. What did Moses do that was so special and unusual? In what way does Logan suggest that we imitate Moses's action to some degree? How, in writing the essay, does Logan use Moses's approach to experience?

Writing Topics

1. *Collaborative writing activity.* List the kinds of everyday objects that you and your classmates own or use frequently: briefcases, pencils, pens, watches, and so on. Find something that everyone in the group owns or uses. Ask each person to write a one-paragraph detailed description of his or her own object. Share your paragraphs and discuss the similarities and differences in the descriptions.
2. Choose something that represents you personally, something complex enough for you to write a full-length essay about it, such as your car, room, clothing, or jewelry. Write an essay in which you describe your subject in a way that reveals aspects of your life or character, the way that Clyde's pick-up tells a lot about Clyde.
3. Moses sees a strange bush, and he turns out of his way to examine it, which brings on a sudden revelation for him about the nature of the universe. Think about the experience of a sudden idea or concept, a time when you suddenly saw something or some point quite clearly, something you hadn't noticed before. Perhaps it was something you had seen frequently before, but now were able to view a different way. Write an essay in which you describe the incident.

From
The Log Jam

Cawley Besson and his family—a wife called June, two boys, and a mixed-breed dog—came to work for the Forest Service. There was timber then, timber uncruised in backcountry valleys. Douglas firs ten feet through at the base and straight-grained for two hundred and fifty feet. Dense, slow-grown wood. It was show-off timber and no need to spare it.

Cawley opened roads to it. He was tight-bellied, dedicated, and clipped in his manners. He left early for work and came home late, with a reputation, he said, to think about. He had places to go after this job he told his wife (lying next to him, listening to him, wondering when they would make love again), places to go.

On a hot Sunday in June, Cawley sat at the river's edge in a pair of shorts, eating a picnic lunch, thinking about Monday, drinking cold beer and watching his sons. The boys were throwing rocks into the river, which the dog chased until he felt the current at his legs and stepped back. Cawley liked the feel of this: he looked toward his wife, feeling the warmth of his own body. The boy swept past him, gesticulating silently, before the scream arrived in his ears, as the dog ran over him barking, and he looked to see the other son standing motionless at the river's edge with his hands over his mouth.

Cawley leaped to his feet, spilling food away, calling out, running to catch up, cursing jibberish. He could not swim, the boy either. He saw the small white face in the dark water, the sunlight bright in his short wet hair, and what lay ahead began to close in on him. The boy, wide-eyed and quiet, went with the river.

Cawley continued to run. The panic got into him like leeches. The beer was coming up acid in his mouth. The river bore the boy on and he calculated how fast, running harder to get ahead, yelling to the boy Hold on! Hold on! Jesus hold on. A little ahead now. He saw the vine maple coming at him, grabbed it, bent it, broke it so fast he felt hope, ran hard into the shallows ahead of the boy to throw the end of the long branch to him—who spun off its tip with his hands splayed, rigid. Cawley dropped the limb and churning high-legged and mad, chest deep and with a sudden plunge had the boy, had his shirt, and was flailing for shore, grabbing for rocks in the river bed that swept by under him. His feet touched ground and held. His fist was white with his grip twisted in the boy's tee-shirt—the boy could hardly breathe against his clutch.

The maple limb drifted downriver and came to rest among willows, near a log round on which dark stains were still visible.

*   *   *

A storm came this year, against which all other storms were to be measured, on a Saturday in October, a balmy afternoon. Men in the woods cutting firewood for winter, and children outside with melancholy thoughts lodged somewhere in the memory of summer. It built as it came up the valley as did every fall storm, but the steel-gray thunderheads, the first sign of it anyone saw, were higher, much higher, too high. In the stillness before it hit, men looked at each other as though a fast and wiry man had pulled a knife in a bar. They felt the trees falling before they heard the wind, and they dropped tools and scrambled to get out. The wind came up suddenly and like a scythe, like piranha after them, like seawater through a breach in a dike. The first blow bent trees half to the ground, the second caught them and snapped them like kindling, sending limbs raining down and twenty-foot splinters hurtling through the air like mortar shells to stick quivering in the ground. Bawling cattle running the fences, a loose lawnmower bumping across a lawn, a stray dog lunging for a child racing by. The big trees went down screaming, ripping open holes in the wind that were filled with the broken-china explosion of a house and the yawing screech of a pickup rubbed across asphalt, the rivet popping and twang of phone and electric wires.

It was over in three or four minutes. The eerie, sucking silence it left behind seemed palpably evil, something that would get into the standing timber, like insects, a memory.

No one was killed. Roads were cut off, a bridge buckled. No power. A few had to walk in from places far off in the steep wooded country, arriving home later than they'd ever been up. Some said it pulled the community together, others how they hated living in the trees with no light. No warning. The next day it rained and the woods smelled like ashes. It was four or five days before they got the roads opened and the phones working, electricity back. Three sent down to the hospital in Holterville. Among the dead, Cawley Besson's dog. And two deer, butchered and passed quietly in parts among neighbors.

Study Questions

1. How does Lopez's diction show the language of the people he describes? (For a review of diction, see p. 69.) Who are these people? What kind of language do they speak among themselves? How does Lopez present Cawley's thoughts as he runs to save his son?
2. Notice the descriptive details that Lopez uses. What kinds of words provide pictures? Point out examples of particularly effective phrases. Which action verbs add to the impact of the descriptions?

Writing Topics

1. *Collaborative writing activity* (usefully done with a computer). Choose a brief event that the entire group is willing to write about. Have each person write a one-paragraph description of the event. Put all the descriptions together, weaving the various sentences and phrases from different people's paragraphs into one two-page description. Then go through the description, cutting out all the duplication but keeping effective phrases and active verbs, until you have a one-page description that is a cumulative effort.
2. Write a short essay in which you describe a time that you or someone you care about was in danger. Describe the danger and your own internal feelings. Tell what happened and how the danger was or wasn't overcome. Then go back through the essay, trying to use as many descriptive verbs and phrases as possible.

What He Was Like

WILLIAM MAXWELL

He kept a diary, for his own pleasure. Because the days passed by so rapidly, and he found it interesting to go back and see how he had occupied his time, and with whom. He was aware that his remarks were sometimes far from kind, but the person they were about was never going to read them, so what difference did it make? The current diary was usually on his desk, the previous ones on a shelf in his clothes closet, where they were beginning to take up room.

His wife's uncle, in the bar of the Yale Club, said, "I am at the age of funerals." Now, thirty-five years later, it was his turn. In his address book the names of his three oldest friends had lines drawn through them. "Jack is dead," he wrote in his diary. "I didn't think that would happen. I thought he was immortal. . . . Louise is dead. In her sleep. . . . Richard has been dead for over a year and I still do not believe it. So impoverishing."

He himself got older. His wife got older. They advanced deeper into their seventies without any sense of large changes but only of one day's following another, and of the days being full, and pleasant, and worth recording. So he went on doing it. They all got put down in his diary, along with his feelings about old age, his fear of dying, his declining sexual powers, his envy of the children that he saw running down the street. To be able to run like that! He had to restrain himself from saying to young men in their thirties and forties, "You do appreciate, don't you, what you have?" In his diary he wrote, "If I had my life to live over again—but one doesn't. One goes forward instead, dragging a cart piled high with lost opportunities."

Though his wife had never felt the slightest desire to read his diary, she knew when he stopped leaving it around as carelessly as he did his opened mail. Moving the papers on his desk in order to dust it she saw where he had hidden the current volume, was tempted to open it and see what it was he didn't want her to know, and then thought better of it and replaced the papers, exactly as they were before.

"To be able to do in your mind," he wrote, "what it is probably not a good idea to do in actuality is a convenience not always sufficiently appreciated." Though in his daily life he was as cheerful as a cricket, the diaries were more and more given over to dark thoughts, anger, resentment, indecencies, regrets, remorse. And now and then the simple joy in being alive. "If I stopped recognizing that I want things that it is not appropriate for me to want," he wrote, "wouldn't this inevitably lead to my not wanting anything at all—which as people get older is a risk that must be avoided at all costs?" He wrote, "Human beings are not like a clock that is wound up at birth and runs until the mainspring is fully unwound. They live because they want to. And when they stop wanting to, the first thing they know they are in a doctor's office being shown an X-ray that puts a different face on everything."

After he died, when the funeral had been got through, and after the number of telephone calls had diminished to a point where it was possible to attend to other things, his wife and daughter together disposed of the clothes in his closet. His daughter folded and put in a suit box an old, worn corduroy coat that she remembered the feel of when her father had rocked her as a child. His wife kept a blue-green sweater that she was used to seeing him in. As for the rest, he was a common size, and so his shirts and suits were easily disposed of to people who were in straitened circumstances and grateful for a warm overcoat, a dark suit, a pair of pigskin gloves. His shoes were something else again, and his wife dropped them into the Goodwill box, hoping that somebody would turn up who wore size-9A shoes, though it didn't seem very likely. Then the two women were faced with the locked filing cabinet in his study, which contained business papers that they turned over to the executor, and most of the twenty-seven volumes of his diary.

"Those I don't know what to do with, exactly," his wife said. "They're private and he didn't mean anybody to read them."

"Did he say so?" his daughter said.

"No."

"Then how do you know he didn't want anybody to read them?"

"I just know."

"You're not curious?"

"I was married to your father for forty-six years and I know what he was like."

Which could only mean, the younger woman decided, that her mother had, at some time or other, looked into them. But she loved her father, and felt a very real desire to know what he was like as a person and not just as a father. So she put one of the diaries aside and took it home with her.

When her husband got home from his office that night, her eyes were red from weeping. First he made her tell him what the trouble was, and then he went out to the kitchen and made a drink for each of them, and then he sat down beside her on the sofa. Holding his free hand, she began to tell him about the shock of reading the diary.

"He wasn't the person I thought he was. He had all sorts of secret desires. A lot of it is very dirty. And some of it is more unkind than I would have believed possible. And just not like him—except that it *was* him. It makes me feel I can never trust anybody again."

"Not even me?" her husband said soberly.

"Least of all, you."

They sat in silence for a while. And then he said, "I was more comfortable with him than I was with my own father. And I think, though I could be mistaken, that he liked me."

"Of course he liked you. He often said so."

"So far as his life is concerned, if you were looking for a model to—"

"I don't see how you can say that."

"I do, actually. In his place, though, I think I would have left instructions that the diaries were to be disposed of unread. . . . We could burn it. Burn all twenty-seven volumes."

"No."

"Then put it back in the locked file where your mother found it," he said.

"And leave it there forever?"

"For a good long while. He may have been looking past our shoulders. It would be like him. If we have a son who doesn't seem to be very much like you or me, or like anybody in your family or mine, we can give him the key to the file—"

"If I had a son the *last* thing in the world I'd want would be for him to read this filth!"

"—and tell him he can read them if he wants to. And if he doesn't want to, he can decide what should be done with them. It might be a help to him to know that there was somebody two generations back who wasn't in every respect what he seemed to be."

"Who was, in fact—"

"Since he didn't know your father, he won't be shocked and upset. You stay right where you are while I make us another of these."

But she didn't. She didn't want to be separated from him, even for the length of time it would take him to go out to the kitchen and come back with a margarita suspended from the fingers of each hand, lest in that brief interval he turn into a stranger.

Study Questions

1. Anthropologists can often reconstruct a great deal about a civilization from just a few bits of evidence about the way people lived in that civilization—a pot, a piece of cloth, the outline in the ground of a long-vanished house. From those clues, scientists infer a way of life, the basic pattern of a disappeared culture. In the questioning manner of an anthropologist, examine "What He Was Like" for clues to who the dead father was. What are we told about him, and when do we know it? What do we know about his marriage and who his wife is? What don't we know?

2. Why is the man's daughter shocked at the contents of the diaries and the wife not? What is different about the relationship to a child from that to a spouse?

3. Journals and diaries written for personal use and then published provide fascinating insights into history and the lives of people in former eras, as well as being literary experiences in themselves. Two of the most famous published diaries in English literature, the journals of Samuel Pepys in the seventeenth century and of James Boswell in the eighteenth century, have become classics.

    A little library research will reveal other classic journal-keepers, as well as many more not so famous but well worth reading. What other journals can you find or do you remember from other courses? What do these books tell us about their authors and the periods in which they were written?

Writing Topics

1. Write a short essay about what you would have done with the diaries, and why you would have done that, if you were in the position of the man's daughter. Try to imagine and describe your feelings in that position.

2. Suppose that the man in the story was a famous or politically significant person and that journalists and historians want to see his diaries. Should the diaries be made public? Would the daughter be morally justified in destroying the diaries to protect her father's reputation?

    Write an essay in which you argue either for or against (or examine both sides of) making the private diaries of public figures available to the public. Under what circumstances or rules should such material be made available, if ever?

Send in the Clown

ROGER L. WELSCH

A FUNNY THING HAPPENED ON THE WAY TO THE POWWOW

I never miss the annual Omaha tribal powwow, always held the weekend before the August full moon. I use the occasion to stuff myself with fry bread and corn soup, talk with friends and relatives, catch up on tribal news, listen to good music, and watch stirring dances. Although I am by training a folklorist and anthropologist, at powwow time I try to avoid anything that smacks of professional observation. This is time off, and anyway, it would be a breach of the confidence of my Omaha friends to "observe" them. But it's hard to be in a Native American setting and stay stupid. Some things are too hard to ignore.

My favorite—and most uncomfortable—moments are when a clown dancer appears in the powwow arena. It doesn't happen every year. You never know when this fellow is going to show up, which probably says something about him right off the bat. But when he does show up, a roar of continuous laughter goes up from all the Native Americans. As always, laughter signals something serious, worth paying attention to.

The clown dancer bursts on the scene, usually stumbling into the dance arena not through the traditional, prescribed opening to the east but from among the dancers and viewers seated around the arena. Chaos reigns as he stumbles over benches, audience members, lawn chairs, and dancers on his way into the arena.

His dance is, er, distinctive. His sense of rhythm is horrid, but even worse, he dances counterclockwise around the central drum, directly against the flow of all the other dancers. This is not only disruptive and clumsy, it is unheard of: besides being bad manners, it is considered very bad luck for everyone in attendance.

Among the Omaha it is very important that everything end with the last beat of a song. I sat at the Omaha drum for many years learning songs, but finally gave up not only because the repertoire was clearly beyond my abilities but also because I became a nervous

103

wreck from the fear of striking the drum one beat after the final thump, a humiliation for which my German upbringing had not equipped me. In competition, an Omaha dancer, no matter how skillful, is eliminated from the contest if he or she dances one step after the final note of the song. The clown dancer dances not just one step after the last beat of the song, but four, five, ten steps. He is lost in the music in his own head and preoccupied with checking the time on a large alarm clock in his hand.

Between dances he talks loudly with others, even while tribal elders are addressing the crowd, a violation of tribal courtesy. Even worse, he throws his arms around the shoulders of visitors and tribal members, even women, a dreadful breach of ethics in a community where a woman trying to get through a clogged aisle will leave and find a male relative to tap the shoulder of the man obstructing her passage rather than touch him herself.

There is no convention or courtesy the clown dancer does not ignore, no taboo he doesn't breach. He finds ways of offending others and embarrassing himself that you'd have to go out of your way to think up. He does nothing right. Nothing.

There is no confusing the clown dancer with fancy dancers, jingle dancers, or traditional dancers in the arena. He is dressed in an ancient, oversize, double-breasted suit, clearly purchased at a Goodwill or Salvation Army clothing store or rescued from the back of some closet. He is wearing a garish necktie, oxford shoes, and a homburg. A white linen flour sack pulled over his head hides his face, and on the sack are painted bright blue eyes and red lips, a startling contrast with the dark skins of the dancers around him. (I use the male pronoun, but in keeping with his hopeless perversity, this "man" is often, I have learned, a woman.)

In his hand, instead of a staff or dance ax or feather fan, the clown dancer carries the alarm clock, attached to his waist or vest with a stout rope or chain. As he "dances," he refers again and again to his clock, meanwhile colliding with other dancers, bumping singers at the drum, and stepping on the feet of visitors and dancers seated around the arena.

The message is clear (except maybe to some European American visitors): the clown dancer is the white man. This is me and my people as Native American "anthropologists" see us. They are good at it because they have so many opportunities to see the white man at work and play. I have to travel 175 miles to visit my Omaha friends and relatives. I am on the reservation a few times a year, a day or two at a time. I witness and learn Omaha ways, but the process is slow and incomplete.

Omahas live constantly in contact with the white man's world. They can't escape it for long, even when they want to. They see mainstream American culture every day, every hour. They know it well enough to offer up a good imitation of it.

At community festivals—regional, ethnic, historical, whatever—people project an image of themselves as they wish to be seen, as they for the moment see themselves. Occasionally, as in the Omaha clown dancer, they also capture others as they see them, providing perhaps the ultimate lesson gained in anthropology—a chance for the observer to be the observed. In a valley of the Omaha reservation near the Missouri River north of the city of Omaha, far away from my own home, I learn not nearly as much about the Omahas as I learn about myself.

IN FOCUS

THE WRITER'S STANCE

Roger L. Welsch lives in two worlds at the same time: he is both an adopted Native American and a well-known, respected anthropologist. As such, he sees the events in this essay from both points of view, Native American and white observer, and he has authority on both counts. He writes this piece from a personal point of view rather than with the distanced objectivity of a scientist. Although Welsch could have identified himself at the beginning, he decided to present that information in bits and pieces throughout the story.

In contemporary writing, it is increasingly important and customary for the writer to tell who he or she is and to identify the background from which he or she speaks. The technical term for this is *stance,* from the same root word as *standing.* We mean much the same thing in informal speaking or writing when we explain "where he's coming from" about a person. It is particularly important in this case for the reader to know that Welsch has the background, on both sides, that enables him to appreciate all the ramifications of what is happening.

Study Questions

1. How—and where in the piece—does Welsch tell the reader who he is and what his responses are to the clown dancer? How does he get the reader to accept his *authority* as a writer? What is his stance?

2. Examine the Lee, Faulkner, and Logan essays earlier in this chapter. For each of those essays, what is the writer's stance? Who is the author, what is his or her background, from what point of view does he or she approach the subject?
3. What descriptive details does Welsch use to give the reader a full picture of what the clown dancer looks like and does? For example, why does the clown dancer carry an alarm clock and refer to it so often? What does the reader learn about Native American customs and traditions by seeing the dancer violate them?
4. The Omaha people in the story are turning the tables: just as they have been stereotyped by what Welsh calls "European Americans," the majority culture, they create a comic stereotype in revenge. Is that a good thing? Is it all right to make fun of people who have sneered at you? What about hate—is it all right to hate in return? What is your opinion of what these Native American people are doing?

Writing Topics

1. Oppressed minorities have various ways of "getting back" at their oppressors. Write an essay in which you describe one of those ways. Describe one or more incidents that you have seen, experienced, or read about, telling whether you agree or disagree with the method.
2. Write a brief description of an activity (a sport, a family party, a social or religious occasion) in which you are an "insider," perhaps a dual insider like Welsch. Somewhere in the piece identify yourself and your background in relation to that activity. Try to work that information into the writing itself, giving thought to what you want to tell about yourself at the beginning and what you want to tell along the way.

The Creatures on My Mind

URSULA K. LE GUIN

The Beetle

When I stayed for a week in New Orleans, out near Tulane, I had an apartment with a balcony. It wasn't one of those cast-iron-lace showpieces of the French Quarter, but a deep, wood-railed balcony made for sitting outside in privacy, just the kind of place I like. But when I first stepped out on it, the first thing I saw was a huge beetle. It lay on its back directly under the light fixture. I thought it was dead, then saw its legs twitch and twitch again. No doubt it had been attracted by the light the night before, and had flown into it, and damaged itself mortally.

Big insects horrify me. As a child I feared moths and spiders, but adolescence cured me, as if those fears evaporated in the stew of hormones. But I never got enough hormones to make me easy with the large, hard-shelled insects: wood roaches, june bugs, mantises, cicadas. This beetle was a couple of inches long; its abdomen was ribbed, its legs long and jointed; it was dull reddish-brown; it was dying. I felt a little sick seeing it lie there twitching, enough to keep me from sitting out on the balcony that first day.

Next morning, ashamed of my queasiness, I went out with the broom to sweep it away. But it was still twitching its legs and antennae, still dying. With the end of the broom handle I pushed it very gently a little farther towards the corner of the balcony, and then I sat to read and make notes in the wicker chair in the other corner, turned away from the beetle, because its movements drew my eyes. My intense consciousness of it seemed to have something to do with my strangeness in that strange city, New Orleans, and my sense of being on the edge of the tropics, a hot, damp, swarming, fetid, luxuriant existence, as if my unease took the beetle as its visible sign. Why else did I think of it so much? I weighed maybe two thousand times what it weighed, and lived in a perceptual world utterly alien from its world. My feelings were quite out of proportion.

And if I had any courage or common sense, I kept telling myself, I'd step on the poor damned creature and put it out of its misery. We don't know what a beetle may or may not suffer, but it was, in the proper sense of the word, in agony, and the agony had gone on two nights and two days now. I put on my leather-soled loafers; but then I couldn't step on it. It would crunch, ooze, squirt under my shoe. Could I hit it with the broom handle? No, I couldn't. I have had a cat with leukemia put down, and have stayed with a cat while he died; I think that if I was hungry, if I had reason to, I could kill for food, wring a chicken's neck, as my grandmothers did, with no more guilt and no less fellow-feeling than they. My inability to kill this creature had nothing ethical about it, and no kindness in it. It was mere squeamishness. It was a little rotten place in me, like the soft brown spots in fruit: a sympathy that came not from respect, but from loathing. It was a responsibility that would not act. It was guilt itself.

On the third morning the beetle was motionless, shrunken, dead. I got the broom again and swept it into the gutter of the balcony among dry leaves. And there it still is in the gutter of my mind among dry leaves, a tiny dry husk, a ghost.

The Sparrow

In the humid New England summer the little cooling plant ran all day, making a deep, loud noise. Around the throbbing machinery was a frame of coarse wire net. I thought the bird was outside that wire net, then I hoped it was, then I wished it was. It was moving back and forth with the regularity of the trapped, the zoo animal that paces twelve feet east and twelve feet west and twelve feet east and twelve feet west, hour after hour; the heartbeat of the prisoner in the cell before the torture; the unending recurrence, the silent, steady panic. Back and forth steadily fluttering between two wooden uprights just above a beam that supported the wire screen: a sparrow, an ordinary sparrow, dusty, scrappy. I've seen sparrows fighting over territory till the feathers fly, and fucking cheerfully on telephone wires, and in winter they gather in trees in crowds like dirty little Christmas ornaments and talk all together like noisy children, chirp, charp, chirp, charp! But this sparrow was alone, and back and forth it went in terrible silence, trapped in wire and fear. What could I do? There was a door to the wire cage, but it was padlocked. I went on. I tell you I felt that bird beat its wings right here, here under my breastbone in the hollow of my heart. I said in my mind, Is it my fault? Did I build the cage? Just because I happened to see it, is it my sparrow? But my heart was low already, and I knew now that I would be down, down like a bird whose wings won't bear it up, a starving bird.

Then on the path I saw the man, one of the campus managers. The bird's fear gave me courage to speak. "I'm so sorry to bother you," I said. "I'm just visiting here at the Librarians Conference, we met the other day in the office. I didn't know what to do, because there's a bird that got into the cooling plant there, inside the screen, and it can't get out." That was enough, too much, but I had to go on. "The noise of the machinery, I think the noise confuses it, and I didn't know what to do. I'm sorry." Why did I apologise? For what?

"Have a look," he said, not smiling not frowning.

He turned and came with me. He saw the bird beating back and forth, back and forth in silence. He unlocked the padlock. He had the key.

The bird didn't see the door open behind it. It kept beating back and forth along the screen. I found a little stick on the path and threw it against the outside of the screen to frighten the bird into breaking its pattern. It went the wrong way, deeper into the cage, towards the machinery. I threw another stick, hard, and the bird veered and then turned and flew out. I watched the open door, I saw it fly.

The man and I closed the door. He locked it. "Be getting on," he said, not smiling not frowning, and went on his way, a manager with a lot on his mind, a hardworking man. But did he have no joy of it? That's what I think about now. Did he have the key, the power to set free, the will to do it, but no joy in doing it? It is his soul I think about now, if that is the word for it, the spirit, that sparrow.

The Gull

They were winged, all the creatures on my mind.

This one is hard to tell about. It was a seagull. Gulls on Klatsand beach, on any North Pacific shore, are all alike in their two kinds: white adults with black wingtips and yellow bills, and young gulls, adult-sized but with delicately figured brown feathers. They soar and cry, swoop, glide, dive, squabble and grab; they stand in their multitudes at evening in the sunset shallows of the creek mouth before they rise in silence to fly out to sea, where they will sleep the night afloat on waves far out beyond the breakers, like a fleet of small white ships with sails furled and no riding lights. Gulls eat anything, gulls clean the beach, gulls eat dead gulls. There are no individual gulls. They are magnificent flyers, big, clean, strong birds, rapacious, suspicious, fearless. Sometimes as they ride the wind I have seen them as part of the wind and the sea exactly as the foam, the sand, the fog is part of it all, all one, and in such moments of vision I have truly seen the gulls.

But this was one gull, an individual, for it stood alone near the low-tide water's edge with a broken wing. I saw first that the left wing dragged, then saw the naked bone jutting like an ivory knife up from blood-rusted feathers. Something had attacked it, something that could half tear away a wing, maybe a shark when it dove to catch a fish. It stood there. As I came nearer, it saw me. It gave no sign. It did not sidle away, as gulls do when you walk towards them, and then fly if you keep coming on. I stopped. It stood, its flat red feet in the shallow water of a tidal lagoon above the breakers. The tide was on the turn, returning. It stood and waited for the sea.

The idea that worried me was that a dog might find it before the sea did. Dogs roam that long beach. A dog chases gulls, barking and rushing, excited; the gulls fly up in a rush of wings; the dog trots back, maybe a little hangdog, to its owner strolling far down the beach. But a gull that could not fly and the smell of blood would put a dog into a frenzy of barking, lunging, teasing, torturing. I imagined that. My imagination makes me human and makes me a fool, it gives me all the world and exiles me from it. The gull stood waiting for the dog, for the other gulls, for the tide, for what came, living its life completely until death. Its eyes look straight through me, seeing truly, seeing nothing but the sea, the sand, the wind.

Study Questions

1. Ursula K. Le Guin labeled "The Creatures on My Mind" as fiction. The piece was published as a short story, even though the incidents certainly seem to have (and might have) happened to her. By announcing that the work was fictional, made-up, the writer gave herself more freedom to deal less with outward facts (What year was it? What beach did she stand on?) than with the imagined inner facts of her own internal conflict, faced with the suffering of creatures she could not help.

   Does it matter to you whether the story is labeled "fiction" or "nonfiction"? Why or why not? Do you prefer to read "truth" (for instance, journalism) or "fiction"?

2. Why doesn't Le Guin (or, at any rate, the narrator) just step on the beetle and put it out of its misery? What could she do about the gull? Does it make any difference that she wants to do something but probably can't?

3. Sympathy is the emotional capacity to feel—for instance, to feel sad—for someone or something else, as if from a distance; empathy allows one person to identify with another, to imagine himself or herself in the same position. When is it better to feel sympathy with another person or creature, and when is it better to feel empathy? What do you think Le Guin (or her narrator) feels?

Writing Topics

1. Is there anything in the world to which you respond with an unexplainable, irrational horror, the way Le Guin (or her narrator) responds to big bugs? Explain. Write an essay in which you examine the source of your response, and consider what might be done to help you get over your fear.

2. Does it matter that one creature is a despised bug and the other is a bird? Is the degree of their pain, or the way you feel about it, different? If the "creatures" were human, would you feel more intense sympathy or empathy?

   Write an essay in which you examine different responses to different creatures, explaining why you think the responses change with the creatures observed. Consider cultural conditioning: why and how do different groups or cultures respond differently to the same creature? (For example, consider that some cultures regard snakes as ancestors, while others eat them.)

The Pain Game ABIGAIL ZUGER

Milton is tooling up and down the clinic corridor in his wheelchair, cursing under his breath and looking at his watch, waiting for me to write his morphine prescription.

I am sitting behind the closed door to my cubicle, leafing through Milton's chart, wondering why I ever got into this line of work.

The issue here is not really Milton's pain: X-rays show the cracks and strains in his bad hip clearly enough to convince anyone that he has pain. The issue is not really that once upon a time Milton refused to stay in a hospital long enough to get his hip properly treated and now it can't be treated at all.

The issue is not the identity of which licensed idiot in this clinic— I can't read the signature on the chart—gave up trying to get Milton back into the hospital a couple of years ago, and started giving him morphine instead.

The issue is not that one of our nurses has seen Milton wheeling into the Veterans Administration hospital across town and that he is conceivably obtaining morphine from one of their clinics as well. Or even that the clinic clerk swears she saw him get out of his wheelchair a couple of months ago, leave it parked outside a crowded deli and saunter in, limpless, to buy a snack.

In fact, I have come to realize that the issue is not Milton at all. He is not an issue; he is a done deed, a permanency, an event as regular as the full moon, as regular as the twice-daily morphine pills rolling out of a tipped bottle. The issue here is me.

I don't want to write Milton's prescription. And every month, after a brief discussion with a taciturn Milton confirms that he is in excellent health except for his *pain*, I sit with his chart and delay writing his prescription.

I believe that Milton has pain. But not as much as he says he has. I believe that he needs his morphine. But not as much as he says he does. I believe that he is permanently, firmly, hopelessly addicted to some of it, and that he is selling the rest on the street to make ends meet; I also believe that he is a struggling small-business owner and I am one of his suppliers, and that if I were, say, *not* to write his prescription, he would make life indescribably unpleasant for me and everyone else who works in this clinic.

This is the issue.

All doctors have their Miltons, patients spinning in a vortex of pain, addiction and free enterprise so fast that it is impossible to distinguish one from the other. I would be kidding myself to think that I in the inner city have more than my share—Miltons penetrate medical practices everywhere. But I've certainly had enough of my own to know every possible jab and feint in their management, and how futile all Miltons are.

I could sit Milton down for a heart-to-heart ("The jig is up!"), and cut his morphine dose by two-thirds. I am no longer brave, or stupid, or cruel enough to do this to him. I could reason with Milton, and plead with him, taper his morphine and send him to a methadone program; I could bargain with him and make contracts, signed and witnessed—tit for tat—keep his pills at the nurses' station and tell the nurses to dispense them daily, two in the fist. I am no longer energetic enough for these efforts.

I could banish Milton from this clinic, and walk home in terror for the rest of my life. I could refuse to see him myself and foist him off on one of my colleagues, announcing that he frightens me, or that perpetuating addiction is not something I feel comfortable with. I could call the police, I suppose, and have them tell me that I must be out of my mind, wasting their time with small potatoes like this.

I have tried most of these tactics with other Miltons, and at the end of my and everyone else's Herculean efforts, I know what we will have: an anguished figure doubled over at my feet, or at someone else's, in this clinic or in another one. "Doc, I got pain, I got *pain*, I got PAIN!!"

I know Milton has pain. I don't disbelieve his pain for a minute. Relieving pain is something I am generally in favor of. Relieving pain might be said to be the party line here.

Then why am I so loath to drag out my prescription pad and soothe Milton's pain, even at the price of a few extra pills? I am being absolutely true to type—studies repeatedly show that doctors are stingy with narcotic pain relievers. This fact appalls some members of the general public, but is immensely reassuring to others—how else to interpret a proposal for cigarettes to become controlled substances, to be judiciously dispensed by prescription? I feel these plans are undue punishment for those of us with pads. God save me from Milton when he wants a smoke.

Why do doctors dread the Miltons? Staring at his chart all these months, I've begun working on a theory of why I dread my Milton. When he and his pain show up in my room—*my* room—they take over. Ordinarily, I am in charge there. But when a pain enters the room, the balance of power immediately shifts. I hear about a pain I can't see or touch, and I ask in reply, *What do you want from me, you and your pain?* I don't know what's going to happen next—and I like to know what's going to happen next. I've become used to leading. When there's a pain in the room I have to follow.

And there's nothing like pain to expose a person's core. Saints become saintly. Miltons become Miltonish. Hence the professional caution with people in pain. We can never really predict which way they will trend when pursued by a pain, which way we'll have to follow. I like to think that every once in a while, just on waking from sleep, or deep in a dream, even Milton is surprised for a moment by the places to which he has been pursued by his pain.

"Hey! I don't got all day here." Milton is at my door, furious, hands in black leather gloves gripping the rubber wheels of his chair, pointedly staring at my prescription pad on the desk.

I write his prescription and hand it to him. He tucks it carefully into his jacket and wheels around.

"Next month, Doc."

"Next month, Milton."

Study Questions

1. Zuger's essay is a fine example of *internal questioning*. The author is caught in a bind: the outcome is known to her (and to the reader), and she will finally do what she does not want to do. So the reader's interest in this essay doesn't come from wondering what will happen but from the author's willingness to let us in on her reasoning process.

    Why does the ending feel like such a defeat?

2. What, really, would be wrong with Milton being able to go to a pharmacy and buy as much morphine as he wants without a prescription? As the author points out, people can already do that with cigarettes and alcohol. What are the reasons for controlling drugs like the one Milton wants?

3. How does Zuger depict the tension, even conflict, between the doctor and the patient?

Writing Topics

1. Imagine that Zuger had said no, and instead of writing the prescription had confronted Milton with all she's heard. Write an essay in which you describe the imagined dialogue with Milton and the outcome.
2. Write an essay like Zuger's in which you place yourself in some familiar area (she uses her office) and are having to decide something. Report the various ideas going through your mind, and include your decision.

Organizing Patterns

Organizing Patterns in Focus

There are different ways of accomplishing any journey, whether that journey is a physical trip or the mental process involved in writing an essay. One method proceeds from point to point without an overall picture, sometimes even without a specific goal: A leads the traveler to B, and then to C, and so forth, with no fixed schedule or organized plan. Wonderful discoveries, often happening by accident, get made in the "unplanned" mode. A second way of traveling is to plan first, create a "map" on paper, and follow that route. Planning is organized, methodical, and efficient, and usually produces a satisfactory result with the least expenditure. Careful planning trades the serendipity of creative discovery for the convenience of rapidly arriving at one's destination.

The practiced writer usually uses a combination of those methods—often beginning with "brainstorming," or unplanned writing, as a means of making discoveries and stimulating invention. After getting some material down, the experienced writer then creates a pattern to follow, as the work begins to take shape. Thus, an essay writer might begin with an idea or question, start to write, and—in the process of discovering what he or she thinks about the subject—develop outlines and patterns, "maps" for the work. At some point in the process, at least one of those maps will become a necessary tool, showing how the parts relate to one another.

The most basic such map simply identifies the introduction, the body, and the conclusion. This is the pattern that most people use for formal interchanges: say hello, say what you've come to say, then say good-bye. The essay structure most commonly taught in secondary and college composition courses elaborates on this pattern: say hello (the introduction); summarize your main point (the thesis); say your piece (the body, with supporting evidence divided into logical units); and end with a restatement of the central idea (the conclusion, with the thesis given again in different words). That pattern is so time-honored that it has almost become a cliché, but it is prevalent precisely because it is useful.

The In Focus essays in this chapter discuss the various methods of organization illustrated by the readings. Beginning with a discussion of the way a writer's vision determines the structure of a paper, the essays provide a full commentary on the basic map described above. The traditional *modes,* or categories, of writing are explained as they are illustrated: narration, description, exposition (with its subset, expository classification), and argument. The most common types of papers students are asked to write—process, comparison/contrast, and cause-and-effect—receive full discussion. Finally, methods are presented of achieving coherence other than through structure, namely through transitions and the repetition of key terms.

Many teachers no longer focus on the four traditional modes of writing (narration, description, exposition, and argument). Teachers may use a different set of categories, called *rhetorical aims,* and divide prose into explanatory, expressive, and persuasive writing, depending on the objective of the writer. Whatever classifying system is used, attention to the purpose of the writing helps the writer to focus on the primary intention and the reader to understand the writer's objective.

The Readings in Focus

The first selection in this chapter, David Quammen's "The Face of a Spider," has an opening that establishes the theme, followed by a clearly identifiable thesis posed as a question, a series of points that speak to the question, and a return to the original image at the conclusion. The essay illustrates how the focus of the writer helps the parts of an essay fall into place.

Following the Quammen essay, Margaret Mead and Rhoda Metraux's "Time to Reflect, Time to Feel" gives a clear example of the way a "five-paragraph theme" can be put together. Even though "Time to Reflect" is somewhat longer than five paragraphs (and considerably longer than five hundred words), it can easily be used as a model for basic college essays. Meg Laughlin's "The Test" next provides a compelling commentary on, as well as a demonstration of, the uses to which that five-paragraph structure can be put.

Balance is one of the prime characteristics of "More Dismal Math Scores for U.S. Students," by John Allen Paulos, who is, not surprisingly, a mathematician. Seen in outline, "More Dismal Math Scores" shows how clarity can be achieved by effective planning.

After the Paulos essay with its discussion of outlines, a group of essays illustrates the four traditional categories of writing. The selection from Richard Selzer's *Raising the Dead* tells a story, providing an example of the narrative approach. The selection from Ann H. Zwinger's "The Lake Rock" shows how dependent good description is on a sense of order. Two readings then illustrate exposition: Harold Klawans's "The Mind of a Neurologist" and an excerpt from John Ruskin's *Fors Clavigera,* published in 1871. "Representing the Poor," by bell hooks (who spells her name without capitals), presents a powerful argument for changing the ways that poor people are viewed in America. (Many more examples of argument follow in chapter 4, Critical Thought.)

A series of more closely defined essays follows. Jenny Lyn Bader's "Larger than Life" not only defines heroes but also classifies their different types. Mohammad Yunus's "Grameen Bank" demonstrates process exposition. Two humorous selections demonstrate the effectiveness of comparison/contrast: Andrei Codrescu's "Pizza Woes" is a consideration of two favorite pop foods, and a selection from Esmeralda Santiago's *The American Invasion of Macún* offers sarcastic commentary on the differences in point of view between social classes. Two selections then demonstrate the cause-and-effect approach: the prologue to Robert D. Richardson Jr.'s biography of Ralph Waldo Emerson, and "Why We Crave Horror Movies," an *apologia* from Stephen King. Finally, Melvin Konner's "Why the Reckless Survive" illustrates not only the cause-and-effect approach but also a variety of methods for achieving coherence within a piece of writing.

The Face of a Spider

DAVID QUAMMEN

EYEBALL TO EYEBALL WITH THE GOOD, THE BAD, AND THE UGLY

One evening a few years ago I walked back into my office after dinner and found roughly a hundred black widow spiders frolicking on my desk. I am not speaking metaphorically and I am not making this up: a hundred black widows. It was a vision of ghastly, breathtaking beauty, and it brought on me a wave of nausea. It also brought on a small moral crisis—one that I dealt with briskly, maybe rashly, in the dizziness of the moment, and that I've been turning back over in my mind ever since. I won't say I'm *haunted* by those hundred black widows, but I do remember them vividly. To me, they stand for something. They stand, in their small synecdochical way, for a large and important question.

The question is, How should a human behave toward the members of other living species?

A hundred black widows probably sounds like a lot. It is—even for Tucson, Arizona, where I was living then, a habitat in which black widows breed like rabbits and prosper like cockroaches, the females of the species growing plump as huckleberries and stringing their ragged webs in every free corner of every old shed and basement window. In Tucson, during the height of the season, a person can always on short notice round up eight or ten big, robust black widows, if that's what a person wants to do. But a hundred in one room? So all right, yes, there was a catch: These in my office were newborn babies.

A hundred scuttering bambinos, each one no bigger than a poppyseed. Too small still for red hourglasses, too small even for red egg timers. They had the aesthetic virtue of being so tiny that even a person of good eyesight and patient disposition could not make out their hideous little faces.

Their mother had sneaked in when the rains began and set up a web in the corner beside my desk. I knew she was there—I got a reminder every time I dropped a pencil and went groping for it, jerking my hand back at the first touch of that distinctive, dry, high-strength web. But I hadn't made the necessary decision about dealing with her. I knew she would have to be either murdered or else captured adroitly in a pickle jar for relocation to the wild, and I didn't especially want to do either. (I had already squashed scores of black widows during those Tucson years but by this time, I guess, I was going soft.) In the meantime, she had gotten pregnant. She had laid her eggs into a silken egg sac the size of a Milk Dud and then protected that sac vigilantly, keeping it warm, fending off any threats, as black widow mothers do. While she was waiting for the eggs to come to term, she would have been particularly edgy, particularly unforgiving, and my hand would have been in particular danger each time I reached for a fallen pencil. Then the great day arrived. The spiderlings hatched from their individual eggs, chewed their way out of the sac, and started crawling, brothers and sisters together, up toward the orange tensor lamp that was giving off heat and light on the desk of the nitwit who was their landlord.

By the time I stumbled in, fifty or sixty of them had reached the lampshade and rappelled back down on dainty silk lines, leaving a net of gossamer rigging between the lamp and the Darwin book (it happened to be an old edition of *Insectivorous Plants*, with marbled endpapers) that sat on the desk. Some dozen others had already managed dispersal flights, letting out strands of buoyant silk and ballooning away on rising air, as spiderlings do—in this case dispersing as far as the bookshelves. It was too late for one man to face one spider with just a pickle jar and an index card and his two shaky hands. By now I was proprietor of a highly successful black widow hatchery.

And the question was, How should a human behave toward the members of other living species?

The Jain religion of India has a strong teaching on that question. The Sanskrit word is *ahimsa*, generally rendered in English as "non-injury" or the imperative "do no harm." *Ahimsa* is the ethical centerpiece of Jainism, an absolute stricture against the killing of living beings—*any* living beings—and it led the traditional Jains to some extreme forms of observance. A rigorously devout Jain would burn no candles or lights, for instance, if there was danger a moth might fly into them. The Jain would light no fire for heating or cooking, again because it might cause the death of insects. He would cover his mouth and nose with a cloth mask, so as not to inhale any gnats. He would refrain from cutting his hair, on grounds that the lice hiding in there might be gruesomely injured by the scissors. He could not plow a field, for fear of mutilating worms. He could not work as a carpenter or a mason, with all that dangerous sawing and crunching, nor could he engage in most types of industrial production. Consequently the traditional Jains formed a distinct socioeconomic class, composed almost entirely of monks and merchants. Their ethical canon was not without what you and I might take to be glaring contradictions (vegetarianism was sanctioned, plants as usual getting dismissive treatment in the matter of rights to life), but at least they took it seriously. They lived by it. They tried their best to do no harm.

And this in a country, remember, where 10,000 humans died every year from snakebite, almost a million more from malaria carried in the bites of mosquitoes. The black widow spider, compared to those fellow creatures, seems a harmless and innocent beast.

But personally I hold no brief for *ahimsa*, because I don't delude myself that it's even theoretically (let alone practically) possible. The basic processes of animal life, human or otherwise, do necessarily entail a fair bit of ruthless squashing and gobbling. Plants can sustain themselves on no more than sunlight and beauty and a hydroponic diet—but not we animals. I've only mentioned this Jainist ideal to suggest the range of possible viewpoints.

Modern philosophers of the "animal liberation" movement, most notably Peter Singer and Tom Regan, have proposed some other interesting answers to the same question. So have writers like Barry Lopez and Eugene Linden, and (by their example, as well as by their work) scientists like Jane Goodall and John Lilly and Dian Fossey. Most of the attention of each of these thinkers, though, has been devoted to what is popularly (but not necessarily by the thinkers themselves) considered the "upper" end of the "ladder" of life. To my mind the question of appropriate relations is more tricky and intriguing—also more crucial in the long run, since this group accounts for most of the planet's species—as applied to the "lower" end, down there among the mosquitoes and worms and black widow spiders.

These are the extreme test cases. These are the alien species who experience human malice, or indifference, or tolerance, at its most automatic and elemental. To squash or not to squash? Mohandas Gandhi, whose own ethic of nonviolence owed much to *ahimsa*, was once asked about the propriety of an antimalaria campaign that involved killing mosquitoes with DDT, and he was careful to give no simple, presumptuous answer. These are the creatures whose treatment, by each of us, illuminates not just the strength of emotional affinity but the strength, if any, of principle.

But what is the principle? Pure *ahimsa,* as even Gandhi admitted, is unworkable. Vegetarianism is invidious. Anthropocentrism, conscious or otherwise, is smug and ruinously myopic. What else? Well, I have my own little notion of one measure that might usefully be applied in our relations with other species, and I offer it here seriously despite the fact that it will probably sound godawful stupid.

Eye contact.

Make eye contact with the beast, the Other, before you decide upon action. No kidding, now, I mean get down on your hands and knees right there in the vegetable garden, and look that snail in the face. Lock eyes with that bull snake. Trade stares with the carp. Gaze for a moment into the many-faceted eyes—the windows to its soul—of the house fly, as it licks its way innocently across your kitchen counter. Look for signs of embarrassment or rancor or guilt. Repeat the following formula silently, like a mantra: "This is some mother's darling, this is some mother's child." *Then* kill if you will, or if it seems you must.

I've been experimenting with the eye-contact approach for some time myself. I don't claim that it has made me gentle or holy or put me in tune with the cosmic hum, but definitely it has been interesting. The hardest cases—and therefore I think the most telling—are the spiders.

The face of a spider is unlike anything else a human will ever see. The word "ugly" doesn't even begin to serve. "Grotesque" and "menacing" are too mild. The only adequate way of communicating the effect of a spiderly countenance is to warn that it is "very different," and then offer a photograph. This trick should not be pulled on loved ones just before bedtime or when trying to persuade them to accompany you to the Amazon.

The special repugnant power of the spider physiognomy derives, I think, from fangs and eyes. The former are too big and the latter are too many. But the fangs (actually the fangs are only terminal barbs on the *chelicerae,* as the real jaw limbs are called) need to be large, because all spiders are predators yet they have no pincers like a lobster or a scorpion, no talons like an eagle, no social behavior like a pack of wolves. Large clasping fangs armed with poison glands are just their required equipment for earning a living. And what about those eight eyes—big ones and little ones, arranged in two rows, all bugged-out and pointing everywhichway? (My wife the biologist offers a theory here: "They have an eye for each leg, like us—so they don't *step* in anything.") Well, a predator does need good eyesight, binocular focus, peripheral vision. Sensory perception is crucial to any animal that lives by the hunt and, unlike insects, arachnids possess no antennae. Beyond that, I don't know. I don't *know* why a spider has eight eyes.

I only know that, when I make eye contact with one, I feel a deep physical shudder of revulsion, and of fear, and of fascination; and I am reminded that the human style of face is only one accidental pattern among many, some of the others being quite drastically different. I remember that we aren't alone. I remember that we are the norm of goodness and comeliness only to ourselves. I wonder about how ugly I look to the spider.

The hundred baby black widows on my desk were too tiny for eye contact. They were too numerous, it seemed, to be gathered one by one into a pickle jar and carried to freedom in the backyard. I killed them all with a can of Raid. I confess to that slaughter with more resignation than shame, the jostling struggle for life and space being what it is. I can't swear I would do differently today. But there is this lingering suspicion that I squandered an opportunity for some sort of moral growth.

I still keep their dead and dried mother, and their vacated egg sac, in a plastic vial on an office shelf. It is supposed to remind me of something or other.

And the question continues to puzzle me: How should a human behave toward the members of other living species?

Last week I tried to make eye contact with a tarantula. This was a huge specimen, all hairy and handsomely colored, with a body as big as a hamster and legs the size of Bic pens. I ogled it through a sheet of plate glass. I smiled and winked. But the animal hid its face in distrust.

IN FOCUS

VISION AND STRUCTURE

The glue that cements an essay into one sinuous line of thought is the author's concentration on the central idea being explored: in this case, Quammen's question "How should a human behave toward the members of other living species?" Learning to ask the right questions is the key to an education. Knowing what kinds of questions to ask can become an art form, for the basic skill of formulating a thesis is really the skill of asking oneself "What do I really want to discover?"

Sometimes, as in the Quammen essay, the issue is stated explicitly in question form; other times, the writer begins with a question to himself or herself, so that the writing process itself begins to provide an answer. "What did it mean to me when my family left our homeland for exile?" is the kind of self-question that can become the start of an essay. "What do I think about —————?" is a different self-exploratory question. Other kinds of questions are less personal but still require examination: "Why do we watch horror movies?" "How did we accomplish what we've done?" "What is a hero, and why don't we have them anymore?" Those and similar questions are inquiries that the authors in this section posed for themselves as they began to write. Often the questions themselves don't appear in the finished essay, but remain implicit as focus points for the writers' ideas.

What keeps an essay unified is not only its pattern or form, therefore, but the focus and vision of the writer. This is not to say that form is unimportant. The pattern of the writing enables a reader to follow the idea, knowing where he or she is at any given point. A clear pattern of organization is a well-marked trip itinerary; it gives the piece direction, helps the writer to move along without getting stuck in one place or another, and also gives the reader something to follow. Good writing needs both wandering—the thought and questioning that goes into the process of writing—and getting there. Organization creates a method for arriving at one's destination, after one has decided on the reason for the journey.

Study Questions

1. How many times does Quammen repeat the key question of his essay, "How should a human behave toward the members of other living species?"? Why put the thesis as a question? Why repeat it? Where in the essay are the repetitions placed, and what is significant about the placement?

   How does Quammen answer that key question in the light of his own behavior toward the spiders?

2. Quammen begins with a personal anecdote to "set the stage" or "frame" (a technical literary term) his essay. Notice how even in a fairly objective expository essay a personal narrative can be used for examples and evidence. How does the story of the baby spiders help to engage the reader? What kind of evidence does that story provide?

3. Quammen describes the *ahimsa* approach toward animals. Paraphrase Quammen's description in your own words as you describe that approach. How does it compare to the "animal liberation" movement?

Writing Topics

1. *Collaborative writing activity.* Have each member of the class or group make a short list of animals that are "good," "bad," and "ugly." Compare the lists, and have each person share his or her reasons. Each person should then write an essay about different attitudes, both personal and cultural, toward types of animals. (Alternately, make lists and share them about animals or plants that are "good to eat," "bad to eat," or "disgusting.")
2. Write an essay responding to Quammen's question about how human beings should behave toward other species. Give examples of other approaches to animals than the ones Quammen writes about. Give examples of your own behavior or behavior you approve of. Alternately, write an essay on how *not* to behave toward other species, with examples.
3. Write an essay in which you consider the arguments in favor of and/or opposed to vegetarianism. If you know vegetarians, or are one yourself, bring in information from interviews or personal experiences.

Time to Reflect, Time to Feel

MARGARET MEAD
AND RHODA METRAUX

August, 1964

What are people going to do with so much leisure time—when it comes? This is a question thoughtful Americans ask as they read about the shortened workday, the shortened workweek, the shortened work year, earlier retirement. Granted, they themselves may know exactly what they would like to do with an extra ten hours a week. It is other people they are thinking about. But the question still expresses a doubt. Don't most people lack the resources to use more leisure time? Isn't it better, safer, for their hours to be filled with pressing, necessary tasks?

Most people will agree that there is little leisure now. They don't ever have time to do the things they want to do. This is particularly true of busy mothers. But it is also true of the men who spend tiring hours driving to work and home again on a crowded highway, the men who work long into the evening on a second job to support their families. It is true of high-school students who are trying to study and keep up with extracurricular activities and of married college students who are trying to combine studying with family life and, often, paid work besides. People complain about having no time. People want more leisure. But is it leisure to *do* more things that we really want?

There is a perpetual sense of crowding in our daily lives. Events involving millions of people are reported in the headlines of newspapers or they are accorded two minutes on a television roundup of news from Washington, Rome, New Delhi. And the next day they are replaced by other headlines, other news reports. And personal life is crowded. Events follow upon one another so fast that there is little time to reflect on what has just happened or to daydream about events we are waiting for—a summer vacation, the day a child returns home from college, the day when the house will hold only two because the children will be away for a whole month. Yet life is meager if it is lived only by the moment. Events caught on the fly and cast away lose their meaning. Experience becomes flat and two-dimensional—like the snapshots that catch a baby's step but not his stumbling progress across the room, or the slides fixing forever the views seen in the ten European countries visited in one six-week holiday, or the picture of the bride smiling in her wedding dress, untouched and unsoftened by the memories that retrospectively give that moment its poignancy.

There are two expressions—"Give yourself time to . . ." and "Take time to . . ."—which suggest that people have a private store of time or a fund of time, like money in a savings bank, on which they can draw if they want to, which they can use in an emergency. And these expressions, like the folk wisdom lying back of the warnings people give one another—"Take it easy," "Keep your shirt on"—point to a need in American life, to a lack we dimly feel when we complain about the lack of leisure.

For what we lack is not so much leisure to *do* as time to reflect and time to feel. What we seldom "take" is time to experience the things that have happened, the things that are happening, the things that are still ahead of us: going away from home for the first time, moving, starting the first child off to school, working into a new job, having a baby, having another baby, living through an accident or an operation, going on a long journey, getting married, helping to plan a brother's or a sister's marriage, deciding to retire, taking a foreign student to live in the house, taking in the child of a sick friend or neighbor, recovering from a fire or a flood or a bereavement, resolving a quarrel, coming into an unexpected inheritance. These are the events out of which poetry is made and fiction is written, but even in fiction and in poetry they become meaningful to us to the extent that we ourselves have experienced some of them and have had a chance to absorb what we have experienced.

There are several areas of our personal lives today in which we fail to "take time." One of these is marriage. Increasingly, young people are marrying over a weekend and returning on Monday to school or work, with the promise of a "nice long trip" sometime—next summer or next year. There are many reasons for these hurried weddings, but the central fact is that honeymoons—trips away from the familiar, where the newly married pair can be relatively alone—are going out. Yet getting married is an extraordinarily important moment in life, a time to be savored, prolonged, deeply experienced. Honeymoons are not always blissful—but then, neither is marriage. And no matter how casual or intimate the premarital relation has been, the experience of sitting down to a first meal face-to-face with the man or woman with whom one's life is to be shared, the experience of arranging one's personal belongings side by side with a husband's or a wife's, the decision as to which bed—or which side of the bed—belongs to each, is dazzlingly new. Putting all these experiences together requires time, time that can be shared fully by the two who are living through all that is new.

Another set of occasions to which we give too little time clusters around the birth of a baby. Very often today the mother prides herself on working right up to the last day, giving herself no time to live with the image of what the awaited baby will be like. Then in just a few days she comes home from the hospital to plunge into life as usual—plus the baby—instead of growing slowly into a world that now includes three people, not two. Even more important are the succeeding births, each of which is different from the one before because each involves a different family group that waits for and then discovers and begins to live with the new baby.

By taking slowly and savoring fully the days before the arrival of the newcomer, mothers—and fathers too—help the older children to absorb the whole experience. And when the newest baby is brought home, if life is not immediately bounced back to normal but instead moves a little more slowly around the new mother and the new baby—a fascinating combination for the older children—this gives the older children a chance to discover and play at their new places in the family—no longer "the baby" but the middle one, no longer "the older" but the oldest one. It gives the whole family a chance to discover how *this* baby moves, and the children time to discover the unpleasing facts that a new baby has no teeth and can't talk and to watch how its small fingers and toes curl and uncurl. Too often even the mother who has taken time to enjoy the prospect and the reality of a first baby later just fits the others into a niche that is stretched to hold them, forgetting that the experience is new to the older child, that each arrival is different and deserving of as much time for daydreaming and feeling and reflecting.

Mourning is another area of our lives in which today we do not take time. Mourning has become unfashionable in the United States. The bereaved are supposed to pull themselves together as quickly as possible and to reweave the torn fabric of life. The reasons for this attitude are not hard to trace. We have lived through wars in which our young men went away hale and hearty and smart in their new uniforms; if they died, they died far away, and relatives and friends were cut off from the familiar, traditional rites of mourning. The age of death is constantly rising and few young children learn about death gradually, as an event that affects now one home and now another, closer at hand and farther away. And above all, with our general sense of optimism we prefer those who keep their chins up and do not burden others with their loss and grief. So we do not allow for quiet in the hours immediately following a bereavement, when time is needed to absorb the shock, free from the pressures of the world; nor do we allow for the weeks and months during which a loss is realized—a beautiful word that suggests the transmutation of the strange into something that is one's own.

The slow pace of national participation in President Kennedy's funeral rites moved and helped Americans partly because the ceremonies of parting did take time. Television viewers were taken step by step, literally, as they followed the solemn cortege to Arlington. And when that long weekend was over, people had moved in their grief as the events themselves had moved—slowly, with time on their side.

Snapshots and slides hastily made and hastily glanced at tend to overcondense experience. Home movies, like the television replication of a real event, come closer to pacing participation in life. A film of a child's first steps, rerun intermittently after the same child can walk and run and roller-skate and dance, keeps feeling alive. Parents watching these first steps again with a stalwart, seven-year-old, two-wheeler rider beside them feel differently from the way they did when the baby, crowing with delight, stumbled and fell with a thud and got to his feet again. And the child himself re-experiences in tranquillity what he was too young to assimilate as he tumbled and got up again a long six years ago. In home movies we do have one device to hold old experience close and to relive it in a new setting.

But while a film can keep the past alive, it cannot help us take time to think and daydream about events that have not yet happened. Nor can film give us a way of experiencing more fully events as they happen or of stretching out moments until feeling and action match. In old Russia, when people were going on a journey those who were ready to go, cloaked and booted, and those who were remaining behind sat together for a long, precious, silent and apprehending moment before they separated. And in the days when people crossed oceans only on ships, there was the long moment when the passengers on deck and their friends ashore were still linked by bright paper streamers until at last, with a slow movement out of its dockside berth, the ship swung away and the streamers snapped.

Leisure opens the door to many things. Most often Americans think of what they would *do* with freer hours, days or weeks. If we gave ourselves and our children and our friends more time to feel and reflect, we would worry less about how people will use their leisure. For part of that leisure would be filled with anticipating, part with experiencing, part with remembering the things we have done.

A Simple, Basic Pattern for the Short Essay

When essays originally developed as a form of writing in the eighteenth century, there was no particular format. The old meaning of the word *essay*, in fact, was to try, to experiment, to go forth, and to attempt, so the pieces were usually written without a preconceived order. An essay could consist of meditations or commentary on any given subject, in any order the writer chose. Essays written for publication even now seldom follow any specific format besides the most basic "introduction-body-conclusion" pattern; within those borders, the modern essayist can go anywhere he or she wishes, so long as the reader is able to follow the logic.

When large numbers of students in American schools and colleges began to be taught to write essays in order to develop writing and logic skills, however, teachers needed to develop a simple format that students could follow. The idea was to establish a specific pattern for essay writing, so that a student could practice putting ideas into place. Thus was born what is now called the *five-paragraph theme*, the *thesis-directed essay*, or the *five-hundred-word theme*. Most college composition classes today move well beyond this pattern into looser and more-creative formats for essay writing, but the thesis-directed essay (by whatever name) remains an enormously useful and usable format, especially for essay exams.

Basically, it's an easy pattern to follow. The writer opens with a paragraph that introduces the subject and establishes a *thesis statement*, a sentence or two that states the main point and major (usually three to five) supporting points of the essay. Sample thesis statements are:

> The job of the peer counselor in the Guidance Center is to listen carefully and show sympathy for the clients' problems, but not to take on the role of a psychologist.

> There are four basic arguments for retaining the existing library building instead of replacing it: the cost of tearing down

and rebuilding, the nuisance to students and faculty, the effect of construction on surrounding buildings, and the historic beauty of the old library.

Notice that the parts of the thesis statement are always *parallel*, that is, in the same grammatical form. The rest of the essay follows the thesis statement like train cars behind a locomotive, each point developed in order, in one or two paragraphs each. The whole thing is wrapped up in the conclusion, through a summary that repeats—in different wording—the thesis.

This isn't a particularly creative format, but it has the advantage of getting an essay written in short order, with a minimum of fuss. Meg Laughlin's "The Test," which follows this selection, is the ironic story of a teacher who reads one such thesis-directed essay and realizes how much human trauma can fit into such an apparently cold, rigid pattern. Mead and Metraux's "Time to Reflect, Time to Feel" follows the thesis-based format, though not as rigidly as many student papers. After the first five paragraphs of introduction, Mead and Metraux state their thesis at the beginning of paragraph six: "There are several areas of our personal lives today in which we fail to 'take time.' " Three such areas are then described and discussed, and the authors then conclude with a few paragraphs reemphasizing their main point. The result is a clear, focused argument in a pattern that is easy for both writer and reader to follow.

Study Questions

1. Margaret Mead and Rhonda Metraux published this essay in book form in 1970, when Mead was at the height of her renown as an anthropologist. Does the language and/or style of the essay seem old-fashioned? Why or why not? Do we face the same issues today? What has changed from the time the essay was written, and what hasn't?

2. The authors state that "most often Americans think of what they would *do* with freer hours, days, or weeks." Why is that kind of thinking self-defeating? What could people be thinking of instead?

3. What methods do people use to escape the "rat race" they find themselves in today? If possible, provide examples of people who seem to have escaped, and explain how they did it.

Writing Topics

1. Write an essay in which you give three reasons why you do or do not have enough "time to reflect, time to feel" in your own life. What could you do to counter each of those three forces?
2. Write an essay in which you describe three forces in contemporary society that make people rush and feel stress.

The Test

MEG LAUGHLIN

Read this, the teacher sitting next to me says, handing me a paper. Along with the rest of the English faculty at the downtown campus of the community college, we are grading final essay exams to decide which students will pass basic English composition.

It is no wonder that students refer to this as judgment day. Regardless of how well they've done in their composition classes during the semester, they must pass this final essay exam to pass the course. And, no matter how well they've done in all of their other courses, unless they pass basic composition they can't graduate. So, more than anything they do at the community college, their futures hang on this one test.

The paper I have been handed to read is another unforgettable event. It is one of three topics students can choose from, so, all morning, I have been reading unforgettable events: grad night at Disney World, the prom, winning the district championship. But this one is different. This student tells about the time she saw her uncle cut off her father's head, then her grandfather's and, finally, her grandmother's.

She has correctly indented the first paragraph. (I know it's a she, though there is an ID number instead of a name, because she says she got blood all over her shift.) She has set up the five-paragraph theme in proper order, starting with an introduction, followed by three developmental paragraphs, ending with a conclusive paragraph. Her introduction contains the all-important thesis statement: "I never will forget the time I saw my uncle behead my father, my grandfather, and my grandmother." And, after establishing the topic, she goes on to develop the main idea.

Her first developmental paragraph tells the reader that they were on the beach in Trinidad. She was 8 years old. Her uncle used a machete, striking her father across the neck. He fell back in the sand. His head was hanging by a thread. Blood was everywhere. She could see his windpipe sticking out. It was white with ridges.

In the second developmental paragraph, she explains how her

uncle murdered her grandfather. When her grandfather heard her screaming, he ran out of the house toward the beach. Her uncle ran to meet him, bringing the machete down on his head, again and again. When he finished and ran toward the house, she ran up to her grandfather who had fallen on a concrete drain cover. She held his head in her lap. It felt like shards of coral rock. It was broken and rough. Oh, Dada, she said, you've been chopped. She could see his brains.

While the sentences are simple and clear, they lack structural variety. The student, one might conclude, does not know how to coordinate and subordinate sentences on a college level.

The third developmental paragraph tells the reader that she found her grandmother at home, wrapped in a blanket, drenched in blood. Through the slits in her grandmother's cheeks, she could see the gold crowns on her molars. The conclusive paragraph correctly gives the reader a sense of finality: "My father, grandfather, and grandmother all died that morning, and my uncle was hanged soon after." She brings the topic sentence full circle, stating that "it certainly was an unforgettable event."

Despite the fact that the paper develops well and is correctly organized, the student may not pass. There is a dangling modifier in the fourth paragraph: "Filled with fear and panic, there was no one to tell. I was alone in the house, my whole family vanished in 20 minutes." Whether the student passes or not will depend on how heavily the English teachers grading the paper weigh the error. Misplaced parts can be deadly.

To make the grading as objective as possible, teachers do not grade their own students' papers, nor do they see the names. But a quick punch of the ID number into any campus computer reveals a student's name, address, and phone number.

The unforgettable event is true. It happened on Jan. 22, 1969, in Cedros, Trinidad. Uncle Lloyd simply went mad. (She pronounces mad so it rhymes with sod. It is one of the few traces of Trinidad still with her.)

She is 27 now. Black hair, black eyes. Round face, round body. She is pretty and dresses well. For her, life has been one test after another, and she prides herself on having made it this far. Composition has been her hardest subject.

She has always had trouble organizing her thoughts on essay tests. Maybe this is because when the murders occurred she was learning to write paragraphs in school. The day of the murders, her mother, who had moved to another town years before, came for her. It was strange riding in a car with her after all that time. They didn't have much to say to each other, so her mother kept the radio turned up. On the news, they heard about the murders. Her grandparents were pronounced dead on arrival at the hospital, and her uncle was taken to the main jail in Port au Spain. She asked her mother if they would go to the funerals, and her mother said they had too much to do.

Overnight, her life went from play to work.

The thought of having only one hour to write the composition really scared her. She usually struggles to develop her ideas and get something down on paper. But she was relieved when she saw the topic, "An Unforgettable Event." The incident was one she remembered clearly. And, she knows how important details are to an English teacher. The story just flowed out of her.

Uncle Lloyd stayed calm through the whole thing and didn't lose his head even when the police grabbed him. He told them he had done what he did every morning: slaughter turtles to sell the meat.

It was true. Uncle Lloyd did use his machete to cut the heads off sea turtles every morning, and if you've ever seen a sea turtle, you know how big their heads can get—as big as human heads. They have yellowish, brownish skin and black eyes. Uncle Lloyd had complained the day before about feeling weird.

Salome has since taken a psychology course and knows about psychosis.

After living with her mother for six years, she went into a convent at the age of 14. It was here she learned the significance of her name, Salome. She read about John the Baptist and took vows never to be frivolous. To this day, she has not danced.

At 19, she had had enough of the convent. She moved to Miami and took secretarial and data processing courses at Lindsey Hopkins. Now, she works at the new Metro building downtown, putting tests into a computer. The tests are designed to assess how firemen and policemen react to emergencies. She likes her job, but if she could get a college degree, she could make more money. She likes nice clothes and furniture and jewelry. It would be nice to have satin sheets and Oriental rugs some day.

Every once in a while, she dreams about the unforgettable event. Her dad is wearing the V-neck undershirt he wore that day. Her grandfather has the murky hazel eyes that she found so haunting as a small child. Her grandmother's hair is in a tight gray bun. She is wearing a caftan.

They are all in the kitchen. And Uncle Lloyd is there, too. He is wearing the gray felt fedora he had on that morning. It is Uncle Lloyd who speaks to her. He tells her he is coming to Miami. When he says it, she wakes up, sits up with a start, and fumbles for her rosary.

Sometimes, she thinks about the picture in the paper of Uncle Lloyd that her mother showed her. It was taken the day before he was hanged. The photo was in an article entitled "Man on Death Row." It said he murdered three family members over a land dispute. Lloyd is smiling wanly; he is handcuffed and his head is shaved. He looks like a sea turtle. She remembers that her mother cried when she saw the picture.

Until the exam, Salome had not thought about losing her family, but since writing about it, she has thought about it often. She has also lost sleep worrying about how she did on her essay. There was so much to remember. "The student must use edited American English, correct sentence structure, grammar, and punctuation and avoid common errors in writing sentences like sentence fragments, run-on sentences, wordiness, spelling, capitalization, and informal punctuation." And, this is only the beginning of what the handout refers to as course competencies. One little slip could do her in. "The introduction, supporting body, and conclusion must be appropriate." How she hopes they were. "Sometimes," she says, "they want your blood."

Salome just called. She got a borderline pass on her exam and a pass in the course. What a relief. Now, she can get on with her life. Next, she'll take the GED (General Education Degree) exam, which takes the place of a high-school diploma. It seems the convent in Trinidad couldn't come up with a transcript acceptable to the college. But Salome is not worried about this next exam. It's a general knowledge test, which makes studying difficult. She is philosophical about it: "There are some tests you can't prepare for."

Study Questions

1. The five-paragraph pattern of organizing a student essay becomes a *subject* of Meg Laughlin's short essay, even though the essay itself is not organized in that way. Why did Laughlin make her essay a kind of story, instead of following the pattern Salome used?

2. Much of the intensity of "The Test" comes from the ironic contrast between the horrors that the child endured and the cold, formal, academic requirements of the composition exam. How does Laughlin achieve this contrast? Where else in the essay does she employ irony?

3. Why is the last sentence an appropriate summary of and conclusion for the entire essay?

Writing Topics

Note: Although the following essay topics seem to call for "personal experience," that doesn't necessarily mean your own personal experience—it can simply be a situation you have knowledge of, perhaps something that happened to a friend or acquaintance.

1. "There are some tests you can't prepare for," says Salome. Write an essay in which you describe such a "life test." What happened as a result? How did the life test compare to an academic test?

2. "Overnight," says the author, "her life went from play to work." What happens when children have to face sudden life-changes? How do they make the adjustments? What happens when they don't fully recover? Write an essay on the psychology of having one's life suddenly take a different turn, basing your essay on personal experience but also putting the subject into a wider context. What is most damaging (or growth-inducing) about the experience?

More Dismal Math Scores for U.S. Students[1]

JOHN ALLEN PAULOS

X, Y, AND U

Such headlines remind me of the children's riddle about Pete and Repeat.

> FIRST CHILD: PETE AND REPEAT ARE WALKING DOWN THE STREET. PETE FALLS DOWN. WHO IS LEFT?
> SECOND CHILD: REPEAT.
> FIRST CHILD: PETE AND REPEAT ARE WALKING DOWN THE STREET. PETE FALLS DOWN. WHO IS LEFT?
> SECOND CHILD: REPEAT.
> FIRST CHILD: PETE AND REPEAT ARE WALKING . . .

Looked at in the right way, it might almost be humorous. Some eminent commission issues a warning that the mathematics (or science) performance of American students is dismal. Then the stylized expressions of alarm are voiced, after which the subject is quickly forgotten until the next, even more dismaying report is announced. Pete and Repeat.

Why should we really care? As a mathematician, I'm often challenged to come up with compelling reasons to study mathematics. If the questioner is serious, I reply that there are three reasons or, more accurately, three broad classes of reasons to study mathe-

---

1. A longer version of this piece appeared in the August 7, 1994, issue of the *Washington Post* [Author's note].

139

matics. Only the first and most basic class is practical. It pertains to job skills and the needs of science and technology. The second concerns the understandings that are essential to an informed and effective citizenry. The last class of reasons involves considerations of curiosity, beauty, playfulness, perhaps even transcendence and wisdom.

And what are the costs incurred if we as a society continue in our perversely innumerate ways?

The economic cost of mathematical ignorance is gauged, in part, by people who, though they can perform the basic arithmetical operations, don't know when to do one and when to do another: clerks who are perplexed by discounts and sales taxes, medical personnel who have difficulty reckoning correct dosages, quality control managers who don't understand simple statistical concepts. The supply of mathematically capable individuals is also a factor in the U.S.'s position in many new scientific technologies, among them fuel-efficient engines, precision bearings, optical glasses, industrial instrumentation, laser devices, and electronic consumer products.

As Labor Secretary Robert Reich and others have written, those jobs and job classifications requiring higher mathematics, language, and reasoning abilities are growing much more rapidly than those that do not. (It should be admitted, however, that although their rate of growth is higher, the number of such jobs still doesn't compare with the huge number that require lesser skills.) Nevertheless, enrollment in college-level mathematics is down, and fewer and fewer American students are majoring in math or in the growing number of fields that require it.

The social cost of our mathematical naïveté is harder to measure (although I try to in this book),[2] but gullible citizens are a demagogue's dream. Charlatans yearn for people who can't recognize trade-offs between contrary desiderata; who lack a visceral grasp of the difference between millions of dollars for the National Endowment for the Arts and hundreds of billions of dollars for the savings-and-loan bailout; or who insist on paralyzing regulation of rare and minuscule health risks, whose cumulative expense helps to ensure the incomparably greater health hazard of poverty. As this book shows, almost every political issue—health care, welfare reform,

---

2. Paulos's *A Mathematician Reads the Newspaper* (New York: HarperCollins, 1995) [Editor's note].

NAFTA, crime—has a quantitative aspect. And, as I mentioned earlier and as the FDA is just now recognizing, the worst drug problem in this country is not crack or cocaine but cigarette smoking, which kills 400,000 Americans annually, the equivalent of three fully loaded jumbo jets crashing each and every day of the year. Or consider Lani Guinier's mathematical suggestions regarding the Voting Rights Act, or the possible economic and ecological implications of chaos theory, or the statistical snares inherent in the interpreting of test results, whether they be for academic achievement or the presence of drugs.

Regarding the third class of reasons, I think it's only fair to say that the "cost" of the philosophical impoverishment resulting from mathematical illiteracy is one that millions of Americans gleefully assume. Still, there is evidence that people respond enthusiastically to mathematical topics as long as they are not labeled as such. People enjoy complicated numerical and mechanical puzzles (Rubik's Cube, for example, the number of whose possible states— 4×10^{19}—is greater than the distance in inches that light travels in a century); crossword puzzles and word play (including certain kinds of humor); board games; all sorts of gambling; paradoxes and brain teasers. Part of the enjoyment is traceable to their quasi-mathematical charm. We have an innate attraction to pattern, structure, and symmetry that mathematics and science develop and refine. Certainly Bertrand Russell is not alone in prizing the subject's "cold and austere beauty," and many are excited by Andrew Wiles's likely proof of Fermat's last theorem, even if it is of little earthly use.

With these reasons to study mathematics, why don't American students do better? Enough's been written about our many social problems, so rather than plunging into that dreary story let me end this segment with five misconceptions about mathematics. Cumulatively, they contribute significantly to poor pedagogy in school and needless handicaps on the job.

Probably the most harmful misconception is that mathematics is essentially a matter of computation. Believing this is roughly equivalent to believing that writing essays is the same as typing them. Or, to vary the analogy, imagine the interest in literature that would be engendered if every English class focused exclusively on punctuation. Of course, this is not to say that calculating mentally or with paper and pencil is not important. Nor is it meant to discourage the excellent habit of estimating quantities. It is merely to assert that in mathematics, as in other endeavors, the big picture is seldom presented.[3]

Another misconception about the subject is that it is strictly hierarchical; first comes arithmetic, followed in lockstep by algebra, calculus, and differential equations, after which arrive abstract algebra, complex analysis, and so on. There is undeniably a cumulative aspect to mathematics, but it is less significant than many think. A third misconception concerns what, for lack of a better term, I'll call storytelling. An effective educational strategy since ancient times, storytelling places a question into context, demonstrates its relation to other questions, and concisely lays out some seminal idea. The rigid view that draws a sharp distinction between formal math and narrative may explain why this plain means is too seldom employed in mathematics education and why the topic of this book will seem strange to many people.

Parental expectations can be effective in thwarting the effects of the next misconception, which is frequently signaled by comments such as "I'm a people person, not a numbers person" or "Math was always my worst subject." Although it is undoubtedly true that some people have considerably more mathematical talent than others, mathematics is not only for the few. There are also disparities in writing ability, but people rarely counsel students to give up on their English courses because they're not going to make it as novelists.

The last misconception is the romantic belief that a concern with mathematics is somehow numbing, making one unresponsive to, say, stone farmhouses in the late afternoon sun. Asking How Much, How Many, or How Likely is thought to make one a member of Napoleon's despised "nation of shopkeepers." Sentiments such as these are as potent as they are baseless.

I'll forgo discussing the curricular and pedagogical suggestions that follow from this discussion, except to note that the newspaper

3. Although details are very often critically important, an inability to stand back and "chunk" facts leads to a myopic favoring of minutiae over ideas in many contexts. As I've mentioned, computation is valued above conceptual understanding in mathematics; in politics, smart tactics bring greater rewards than wise policies; technical hocus-pocus in the stock market attracts more attention than does analysis of fundamentals; for those with a religious temperament, rules, rites, and rituals obscure wonder, awe, and mystery; in sex, lust and fetishism are mistaken for love. I grant that the first element in each of these oppositions does sometimes rightfully take precedence over the second, but generally too little stress is placed on the second. It's much easier to put the jigsaw puzzle together after you've seen the whole picture (assuming there's one to see) [Author's note].

is an undervalued source of examples and ideas for mathematics classes at various levels. Once an idea or notion is grounded in some real-life situation, it can later be generalized, idealized, and aestheticized.

Pete and Repeat . . . Let's not.

FORMAL OUTLINES

A *formal outline* follows a specific pattern that shows the skeleton of the piece: the basic contents and ideas, and the relationships among the points. Probably the greatest benefit of a formal outline is that it distinguishes clearly between the main ideas and the supporting evidence.

There are just three general rules about the construction of formal outlines. First, the standard format should be carefully followed with respect to spacing, kinds of letters and numerals, and placement of specific and general information. Second, entries should be fairly parallel, either all in sentences or, as in the example below, all in phrases. Third, each subsection must have more than one entry: If section I, for example, has a subheading A, it also needs a subheading B—otherwise there is no point in having an A.

Examine the outline below. It's a good start, but not perfect. How can you improve it? (*Note:* If you are really a perfectionist, you will write your outlines so that the periods line up perfectly.)

    I. Introduction
       A. The story of Pete and Repeat
       B. Three reasons to study mathematics
    II. Costs to society of poor mathematical abilities
       A. Economic costs
          1. Cost to consumers
          2. Cost to society in lost technology and jobs
       B. Social costs
       C. Intellectual poverty
    III. Why American students don't do better at math
       A. Misconception that mathematics is the same as arithmetic
       B. Idea that math must be learned in a specific order
       C. Narrative is not used as a means of teaching math

D. Expectations are low, and students encouraged
   to give up
E. The "nerd" factor
IV. Conclusion

Study Questions

1. What does Paulos mean by "the philosophical impoverishment resulting from mathematical illiteracy"?
2. Have you experienced any of the effects of Paulos's "five misconceptions
   concerning mathematics"? Did your experience affect your study of
   math?

Writing Topics

Note: For either of the two essays, create a formal outline. You may
want to write a first draft of the essay without an outline, reorganize
your thoughts by creating an outline, then rewrite the essay by following the outline.

1. Paulos states that parents often have low expectations of the math per-
   formances of their children, and thus the children give up too easily. Do
   you agree or disagree with him? Write an essay giving your opinion
   and offering as evidence examples from your life or the experiences of
   people you know.
2. Write a proposal to your local school board in which you describe three
   ways that students' mathematical abilities can be improved.

From Raising the Dead

RICHARD SELZER

It is now ten minutes since the doctor's pronouncement of death. Already the man has taken on that look of dignity that the newly dead have because of their possession of secrets. Or is it that they travel in a beyond that must be entered formally? Maureen is still writing an account of the last minutes of his life, her efforts to resuscitate him—the intracardiac injections of calcium and adrenaline, the jolts of electricity delivered to his chest, the failure of the electrocardiogram to respond. Glancing up, she has noted the characteristic "settling" of his body, the fixity that is incontrovertible; she has seen that so many times. Alone in the room, Maureen pauses in her charting to wipe her eyes with the back of her hand. Bleary with tears, she does not see what I see, that a subtle change is taking place in the contents of the bed, that the utter stillness of the body has been replaced by a calmness of the flesh, that beneath the closed eyelids his eyeballs roll slowly from side to side, then dart the way fish will move in a pond. Look! He shudders as if to shake off something which threatens to cling, and tightens those eyelids; minnows of light rising in the shallows. Then he hears a wingbeat, and feels something fugitive, immaterial, a beige veil being drawn from his face, slowly at first then faster, until the final whisk is like a slap. A moment later he draws the first breath. It is a deep sigh that might be interpreted as one either of sorrow or of satisfaction, as though one precious thing were being relinquished and another embraced. The nurse's incredulous stare! Her galvanic leap to his side! He, blinking in the explosion of light. When he opens his eyes, their color has gone from the ambivalence of hazel to the jubilation of blue.

Again, a breath is drawn, and another and another. A tracing has returned to the electrocardiograph, which the nurse had not yet detached from his arms and legs. The room, which had descended into a subaqueous silence emanating from the corpse, is now fiercely active. All the machinery is back in place, chugging, vibrating, clicking, ringing. Nurses scurry, calling out to one another. They bend over the bed, coaxing, noting and recording each sign of revivification. The intravenous chandelier sends light streaming through his body until he is something radiant and glowing in the bed. From time to time, the nurses turn to look at each other, their faces swept with wild surmise. It is true! After ten minutes of certified death, this man has . . . risen. Risen! Such a word does not belong in an intensive care unit.

Now the man is coughing against the endotracheal tube, he wrinkles his forehead, tears stream from his eyes, he shakes his head slowly from side to side. It is painful to observe the resurrection of a man, to behold a log of inert flesh trying to raise itself. But the pain is all ours. He feels nothing as yet. He is like the bulb of a tulip probing the earth in which it has lain all winter unaware of its potential, without memory or hope. As we do not ascribe pain to the tulip in its rebirth so ought we not to imagine that he, the man, is torn loose and abraded.

Then he who has performed no purposeful movement in three weeks reaches up one hand and pulls the tube from his throat and mouth. And that is not all: a smile breaks upon his face, but such a smile as has never been seen on the continent of North America. And in a hoarse whisper, but plainly enough, he utters the single word: Yes.

"Did he say yes?"

"What do you suppose he means?"

"I couldn't say. Perhaps he was just answering a question someone had asked him weeks ago before he went into coma."

"Does that happen?"

"More likely it is some odd form of seizure activity."

What he means, what the nurses cannot know, is that everything begins with a yes. That is how the first two bits of energy in the universe greeted each other, collided. Boom! And yes! There was life. So it is with the resurrected. Once again his throat fills with the word until the pressure of it is unbearable and he cries out in the hoarse voice that sticks to his jaws . . . Yes! Saying yes to life, accepting once again the burden and thrill of it.

It is the next day. He lies on his back, arms and legs splayed out so as not to disengage any of the needles or tubes. Now and then, he is propped on one side or the other. What he really wants is to curl up so as to give himself a hug, to accept his own warmth. Still, on his face is a strange, far-off look, as if to say, death is easy; it is the return to life that requires courage. When a nurse comes to take his temperature, he follows her solemnly with his eyes that seem to say: I have been to the land of the dead. Do not touch me. From that moment on, his vital signs—pulse, blood pressure, temperature—are normal. His oxygen saturation, 100 percent. There is no longer any doubt that he will recover.

About the consternation of the entire medical staff, there is little to be said. The joy at his reawakening is general, but in each person it is colored with uncertainty.

"You must have been mistaken," they tell the nurses at the weekly morbidity/mortality conference. "It cannot be as you told it . . ."

"The cardiogram was flat," the nurses reply. "The pulse and blood pressure were unobtainable. What else do you need? He was dead."

"Then how . . . ?" The nurses shrug and shake their heads.

Throughout the hospital they can think of nothing else. For weeks, in the laundry, at the coffee shop, in the X-ray file room as in the morgue, every conversation will begin with the words: Did you hear . . . ? On whatever flimsy pretext, orderlies and technicians and next-of-kin will walk past the doors of the intensive care unit just to draw near to the site, each of them taking away a dollop of hope to be saved up for a rainy day. If it happened to *him,* then perhaps . . . It is as if no one who worked at the hospital could go on living without specific knowledge of the event. Just so has it swollen into a legend that even I have come to believe in time. Such is the power of literature, be it written down on paper or passed on from mouth to ear.

It is twenty-four days since the night he was taken to the emergency room, well into April. A warm day, with the sun streaming in and lighting up the wall of his room. Torpor envelops him. He hears grasshoppers. They seem to be in the bed with him, all around him, inside his chest. Yes! The noise of the grasshoppers is coming from inside his chest! He gives a soft, flannel cough and the stridulation abates. The ceiling at which he is gazing is made of squares of corkboard. Here and there the expanse of it is interrupted by the handle of an opaque glass panel that can be pulled down. Storage space. Or a hidden compartment like those in the ceiling of a ship's cabin. On board a ship you have to make use of every inch of space. He feels beneath him the gentle rocking of the sea. A coziness comes over him. He is perfectly comfortable. *So!* He thinks, *I am aboard a ship. But where? Perhaps I am in the South?* Yes, he remembers, it is the South; he had been there recently, lecturing in Texas. That's it, Texas! Then he sees the intravenous attached to his arm and he thinks that while in Texas he must have fallen sick, that he is aboard a hospital ship in the Gulf of Mexico. Doubtless soon to be discharged, from the way he feels. So comfortable and drowsy.

From somewhere comes the music of a Strauss waltz. He lies utterly still, letting the light from the intravenous chandelier trickle onto his face and collect there in small glistening pools, while the mattress takes up the rhythm of the music, scooping, dipping, turning his all but transparent body. He has never felt so graceful, so comfortable in his own flesh. All at once he has an irresistible urge to laugh. Should you ask him the reason for his laughter he would not know, for it is unlike any laughter of his life but something with which he has been infested, a holdover from some almost forgotten glee, now become reflexive and without rhyme or reason. He hears a woman's voice calling.

"Wake up! Wake up, sleepyhead! What's so funny?" It is as though she were summoning him up from a great depth to the surface where he now floats between two sheets, his face visible only in the trough between the waves. He opens his eyes to see his wife, Janet, standing by the bed.

"For goodness' sake!" he says. "What are you doing in Texas, or off the coast of it?"

"This is not Texas," she informs him. "And this is no ship. You are in the intensive care unit of the Yale–New Haven Hospital."

"But the rocking of the waves . . ." He is not ready to give up.

"They have you on one of those newfangled mattresses that inflates here, deflates there. It's run by electricity. That way you won't get bedsores."

"How long have I been here?" It is the only thing he wants to know.

"About three weeks. Twenty-three days of coma to be exact." But he is already hurrying back to sleep.

IN FOCUS

NARRATION

What happened? How did it happen? Telling a story is one of the central means of human communication. A baby begins to talk, and people begin to tell him or her stories. That baby will spend the rest of his or her life hearing and telling stories, using stories to make sense of life experiences. Psychologists say that people tell themselves stories about experience in order to see life as somehow coherent, and that even dreams are, in a sense, stories. Some psychologists theorize that narrative may be the most basic means of human thought.

Here's a story: A man dies, and then rises from his deathbed. In this case the man is a doctor, the author himself, and he tells the story of his life-threatening and even, briefly, life-ending illness. This perspective gives the story an interesting twist, because a medical condition is being described by the doctor who is also the patient. The *narrator* tells the story not only from the inside, reporting his feelings and reactions, but from the outside as well, from what he has seen and learned about intensive-care wards.

Events being told in narrative form have to fit together, to flow. The technical term for creating a flow that carries the reader along is *profluence*. Notice how Selzer's narrative profluence makes the reader want to find out what happens, to read on, to turn the page.

Study the way that Selzer tells his story. Look at the order in which he describes how things happened, what and how much he chooses to describe, and what he reveals about himself. The details in any narrative have to be appropriate to the point of the story. Too little detail, and the writer has not done his or her job. Too much detail going on for too long will put the readers or listeners eventually to sleep.

Study Questions

1. How does the spoken dialogue add to the effect of the story? How does the language that the characters use reflect who they are? How is the way that the medical people speak to one another different from the way the nurses and the patient's wife speak to the patient?
2. Why is this narration written in the present tense? Why does Selzer refer to himself in the third person ("he") instead of in the first person ("I")? Are these effective storytelling techniques? When is it appropriate or inappropriate to use these techniques?
3. What makes Selzer's descriptive language so effective? Underline the verbs in any two paragraphs, then note how active and descriptive the verbs are. Take another paragraph, underline all the adjectives, and note any striking characteristics of the modifiers and adjectival phrases.

Writing Topics

1. *Collaborative writing activity* (with members of the group checking each other's use of third person and description). Remember a time that you were ill or in great danger and write a descriptive essay in imitation of

the first paragraph of Selzer's narration. Write about yourself as though you were an outside observer, telling the story in third person. Use adjectives and descriptive verbs to convey the scene, and try to make your reader care about what was happening to you. Remember to achieve a balance: make it detailed enough to stay interesting and informative, but make the details appropriate.

2. Imagine that you are Richard Selzer's nurse or doctor during this time, or any medical professional during a time of crisis. Tell a story from your own point of view. Include as much detail as possible, and express the feelings of your character.

3. The following is from John Gardner's *The Art of Fiction: Notes on Craft for Young Writers* (New York: Knopf, 1984), and it is an extraordinarily difficult writing assignment. If you want to try an unusual exercise, you might enjoy this challenge:

> Write the paragraph that would appear in a piece of fiction just *before* the discovery of a body. You might perhaps describe the character's approach to the body he will find, or the location, or both. The purpose of the exercise is to develop the technique of at once attracting the reader toward the paragraph to follow, making him want to skip ahead, and holding him on this paragraph by virtue of its interest. Without the ability to write such foreplay paragraphs, one can never achieve real suspense.

From The Lake Rock

ANN H. ZWINGER

When I need my sense of order restored, I sit on the lake rock. It sums up all I have learned about this mountain world. Connected to the shore by a narrow, somewhat unstable catwalk, the rock is just big enough to sit on comfortably. It is a pebble dropped into the water, the center of widening rings of montane life, beginning with the life of the lake itself and culminating in the evergreen forests, where the succession that is taking place is mapped in the communities that I can see. The rock is a place of order, reason, and bright mountain air.

Encircling the rock is the community of plants and animals which can survive only in the water. Small motes of existence, they float with its currents, cling to underwater supports, or burrow in the brown silt of the lake bottom. Some I can see as I sit here. Others have to be corralled under a microscope lens. I watch a fat trout lurking in the fringed shadows of the sedges. All around the edges of the lake, where water meets land, grow willows, sedges, and rushes, predicting a time when amber water will be green plant, the lapping sound of small waves the sly whisper of grass stems.

It is a busy place with a constant spin of insects, punctuated by the pursuing green arcs of leopard frogs. The south stream enters the lake through willows and cow parsnip and a pile of logs placed there when the lake was built to prevent silting. The north stream's entrance is hidden in elephant-foot-sized clumps of bulrush which change sheen in every breeze. Tangles of willows forecast spring in their catkins. Yellow or red branches identify them even in winter. The streams are the one constant in this landscape.

The circle widens. Behind the lake edge, to the north and west, the land rises into the lake meadow, drying as it slopes upward. Blue grass and brome grass crowd every square inch. I see chipmunk and ground-squirrel burrows, haloed with dandelions. Hundreds of wildflowers grow in this meadow, perennials whose coming I look for each year. A few aspens tentatively grow along its edge.

The established young aspen community between the two streams contains small slender trees, growing almost a foot a year. Still gangling and adolescent, they will in a short time obscure the view of the mature grove behind them. Leaves flicker celadon in spring, viridian in summer, clinquant in fall, tallying the sovereign seasons, graying and greening to reiterate the message of snow and sun.

Wider still, the north edge of the lake meadow steps upward over its granite base. Where it levels off, the ponderosas grow, big and sturdy and full of cones. They stand staunch, widely spaced, allowing sunlight to filter through for wild geranium and kinnikinnik and tiny wild candytuft that crosses the dusky duff.

The south slope of the lake curves away from the shore, becoming more spruce-shaded as it retreats. This area is the first to be snow-covered, the last to be clear. Shade-tolerant plants root in the precipitous hillside; from here I can see a few late orange-red Indian paintbrush and the stalks of monkshood and larkspur. Dark-red strawberry blite ties down an old log with the help of raspberry and rose bushes. A few last aspens mingle with the spruces, their trunks thin and pallid, most of their branches down from insufficient light. Above them the Douglas-firs and spruces grow close together, presenting a solid wall of black-green.

The ever-widening circles of montane life culminate in these evergreens which intrude visually into the lake. Even in winter, when the India-ink reflections are gone, the uncompromising contrast of black and white still commands the eye. In the spring, when the air is heavy and laden with late snows, the lake reflects their pendent spires, solid as a German Expressionist woodcut. In the summer the reflections shimmer in the breeze, slotted with blue sky, an animate Monet. In the fall they form a moving mosaic with the aspen when the wind fragments the surface to create tesserae of emerald and gold leaf—a Byzantine pavement.

It is impossible to look at the land and not be aware of the evergreens. In all seasons they dominate, unchanging in color, towering in size. Their spires crenelate the sky. Their opacity of color, depth, and density create a background against which are measured the brightness of aspen leaf, iridescence of dragonfly wing, scarlet of gilia, and gleam of lake. The ponderosa, spruce, and Douglasfir are the reminders of an end point of succession for this land, for there is no other vegetation that will replace them, short of catastrophic climate change.

These trees change the environment to fit their needs, making an acid soil which is inhospitable to other plants, attracting rain by the massiveness of their own transpiration. At the beginning of succession, moss and lichen grow a few centimeters above the ground and a few below. At the end of succession, for this land, trees tower many feet into the air and send their roots through the ground, demanding the most that the environment can give. These conifers will be there in decades, in centuries, to come. They will shade out other trees and brighter flowers, intrude into the deepening soil of the meadows. Succession is an inexorable progression which may be altered or disrupted but which will eternally begin again and again to achieve the same end. No emotional pleas or moral inducements will change it; to understand this is to accept the irrevocableness of nature.

DESCRIPTION

If the function of a narrative is to tell a story, the function of description is to put the reader into the scene. The reader needs to be able to imagine being a part of the scene. Appeals to the different senses (sight, smell, taste, touch, hearing) and the various specific aspects of sensory perception (color, tone, temperature, complexity) are enormously helpful in bringing the reader to visualize and even almost feel the place or object, person or action being described. In the midst of such expert description, the reader might look up from the page and be surprised to find himself or herself back in the "real" world.

Good descriptive writing requires not only careful attention to details but also a clear, well-marked trail for the reader to follow. Meandering, zigzagging—telling one thing and then another without a sense of how the two items fit together—will only confuse readers. The *order*, or pattern, of the writing provides the organizing principle. For example, consider the description of a bedroom. Are the contents presented haphazardly, first the bed and then the carpet and then the bureau, or does the description move around the room, from wall to wall? A description in *space order* (also known as *spatial organization*), telling where objects are situated in space, might go from left to right (or right to left) as a viewer stands in the doorway. A space-order description of this solar system might go from the sun outward or the outermost planet inward. *Time order* (also called *temporal organization*), as the name indicates, arranges the elements of the description as things happen, or happened. Time order might be used to tell how the bedroom furniture was acquired: first a mattress on the floor, then a proper bed, then a charming old bureau from a garage sale, and so forth. Time order used to describe the solar system might tell how the "big bang" happened, how the sun came to be, how the planets took their shapes over millions of years.

"The Lake Rock" uses both space and time orders in an unusual way. Zwinger places herself at the center of the scene and then goes outward, describing the scene in a series of concentric circles. As Zwinger moves outward, she also uses time order to show how one species of plants replaces another in biological succession. All in all, the pattern of organization in the piece also supports her theme about the existence of natural order and the ways that humans can perceive that order of Nature.

Study Questions

1. Notice the different ways that Zwinger perceives the scene, using different sense impressions, from the microscopic plants to the huge evergreens. Where are the descriptions of what she sees, feels, hears? What other kinds of impressions does she reveal?

2. How does Zwinger reveal her *feelings* about the place? What kind of emotional contact does she have with this landscape?

Writing Topics

1. *Collaborative writing activity* (with members of the group reading each other's descriptions and checking for order). In one paragraph, describe a familiar place on campus, using a clear pattern of space order. Then describe the same spot in a *different* space order. For example, if you used top to bottom the first time try left to right, edges to center, or another particular space order the second time.

2. Choose a photograph or painting of a landscape and describe it in some space order that seems appropriate to the picture: top to bottom, foreground to background, and so on. Then consider how the eye of the viewer travels around the picture: what would a viewer look at first, and where would his or her attention go next? (A good way to accomplish this is to ask a friend to describe the objects and places in the order that he or she sees them. Be sure to take notes when you do this.)

Now write an essay in which you compare the space-order pattern of the picture with the viewer's perceptions. How did the artist predict what a viewer would want to look at?

If you can, include a photocopy of the picture or a photograph of the painting with your essay, so that your instructor will have an image of what you are describing.

3. Choose a place indoors or outdoors with which you are familiar. In a few paragraphs, describe that place in space order, using whatever arrangement seems most appropriate. Then describe that same place in time order. For example, you might want to tell what it looks like over the course of a day; or, you could tell how it got there or grew. Any division of time you wish to choose (a day, a month, ten thousand years) is acceptable.

The Mind of a Neurologist

HAROLD KLAWANS

"It wouldn't hurt to be nice to your aunt, would it?" she asked. "That depends upon your threshold for pain," he replied.

—*Conversation reputed to have taken place between Mrs. Kaufman and her son, George S.*

It was 6:45 and I was right on schedule. I'd been up working and sipping coffee for close to an hour and a half, and now I was in the shower. All I had to do was shave and get dressed, and I'd be out of the house by 7:00, on my way to the hospital for my real day's work. It's not that what I do early in the day isn't real work. I do my writing then, but it doesn't feel like work at all. I shampooed what little hair I have left, rinsed out the shampoo, turned off the water, opened the shower door, reached for the towel, began to dry myself off, stepped out of the shower stall with my left foot, as I had done a hundred or more times, swinging my right foot over the ledge—and missed! Pain. Excruciating pain exploded in my head! My right great toe had not swung over the ledge. I had somehow managed to smash it into that inch-and-a-half-high ledge. My broken right big toe. My big toe that was just beginning to heal. Why? Why this morning? Why not some other morning? Why did I have to be so damn clumsy when I already had a broken toe? Why?

The pain was beyond belief. It flooded my brain. My entire foot was aflame. My whole leg. Why did this morning have to be different from all other mornings?

On all other mornings my foot had glided safely above that ledge. On all those mornings when a stubbed toe would have meant only a stubbed toe. Not reinjury to a healing fracture. Why? Why when I had a broken toe?

Precisely, I suddenly realized, because I had that broken toe. Eureka! I felt more like Archimedes in a bathtub than a mere neurologist hopping on one foot outside a shower stall. I had not been clumsy. Not in the least. I was not a klutz. I had been suckered by my own brain. By some primitive defensive system of my brain that I'd never even heard of. It wasn't my fault. And as my toe throbbed and jolted away, I recognized that I had learned something about the brain, something that explained events that happen to everyone, usually more than once, but that remained unmentioned in any neurology book or journal I had ever read. Eureka. Land ho!

I had broken my toe three weeks earlier when I tripped coming down the stairs at 5:00 A.M., a result of not turning on any lights and of my own clumsiness. It was a fracture of the great, or big, toe on my right foot, right at the joint. I diligently taped it to my second toe and went on with my business, including a whirlwind professional trip to Europe that featured four different countries in six days and a lot of walking through airports and various other places. All of that, I'm certain, delayed the healing process, but now, three weeks after my original fall, my toe had finally been improving. I didn't have to be a physician to realize that all I had to do was act like a patient and rest the toe. Not only could I now stand without discomfort, I could walk without pain. And then the tragedy struck. Why? Because, simply put, the toe had not healed completely and I could not actually walk without pain. Painlessness had been an illusion, a conjurer's trick perpetrated by my own brain. True, I had been walking without consciously feeling any pain. But there is a difference between absence of consciously perceived pain and freedom from pain. A big difference. Just ask my toe.

If a tree falls in a forest and there is no one there to hear it, does that crash make any noise?

You know darn well that it does.

And does a broken toe cause pain each time you slam your weight down on it, even though you feel no pain?

Hell, yes!

Then why don't you feel the pain? Why hadn't I, as I stood in the shower that fateful morning?

It's called tolerance. You put on a tie in the morning; the collar feels tight around your neck. Half an hour later you can't feel it at all. Or you put on your bra and the straps pull on your shoulders. Not for long. In a few minutes you don't feel them. It's as if the straps have disappeared.

Why?

Tolerance. The steady, ongoing stimulus of the collar or the bra no longer registers consciously in the brain. Why not? Teleologically, it is because that unchanging stimulus serves no purpose. If it were otherwise, our consciousness would consist entirely of myriad unchanging messages, the feel of our clothing, our shoes, our socks, our pants, our underwear. If you are not thinking about it, do you feel your underwear? No. Yet your underpants are touching your skin and stimulating nerve endings. As a result of that stimulation, those nerves send messages toward the spinal cord and then up to the brain. The messages are coming in—all you have to do to feel your underpants on your buttocks is to think about them.

So why don't you feel them all the time? Your brain adapts to a fixed steady input and no longer "feels" it. Adaptation. *Tolerance.* That's the preferred neurologic term. Your brain develops tolerance. The stimulus no longer reaches consciousness.

What does that have to do with my stubbing my broken toe?

Pain is just one of a number of primary sensations the nerves send up to the brain. Pain. Position sense—where a part of the body is in space. Touch. Temperature—hot or cold. Pressure. One of many sensations. And each of them is subject to tolerance. The hot water in my shower that morning, like every morning, felt a lot hotter when I stepped into the shower than when I got to the second chorus of "Our Love Is Here to Stay." I usually sing old Broadway show tunes in the shower: Gershwin, Porter, Rodgers and Hart. By the second song, I have to make the water hotter. Tolerance. The same tolerance that keeps me from being plagued all day long by that collar around my neck. And causes me to feel for my watch to know it's still there. And my wedding band.

The pain from my toe, my broken toe, had obviously not gone away. The toe was not healed. It couldn't heal that quickly. Not in a fifty-year-old. All I had to do was look at it. It was still enlarged. The soft tissue was swollen. The bone itself had thickened as new bone was being laid down. And if I tried to move the toe, I realized how far from back to normal it was. The joint was half-frozen, hardly capable of any movement at all. And any movement I forced it to make was painful. Not uncomfortable, but downright painful. If I palpated it, or gave it a firm push, the toe was tender. Palpation, pressure, caused discomfort that was on a continuum with frank pain.

If pushing down with my thumb caused pain, if standing up on my foot the first thing in the morning caused pain, didn't stomping around in the shower cause pain? Standing on one foot, my right foot, the foot with the broken toe, in order to wash my left foot, and thereby pushing down hard with my right big toe for balance—didn't that make my right toe and its sensory receptors, the raw nerve endings that feel and respond to pain, send pain messages to my brain?

It did. Obviously. It had to.

But I felt no pain as I stomped away in the shower. I went right on singing. Bernstein. Then Sondheim. "Ladies Who Lunch," I think. And I didn't feel the pain because my brain had adapted to the constant low-grade input from the raw nerve endings of my broken toe. My brain had become tolerant to the pain, as it had to the hot water.

But it wasn't just tolerance. It had to be more than that. Why?

Each of us knows precisely where each part of our body is at each and every moment. That is because each part of the body—or more precisely, the nerves of each part of the body, especially the nerves of the joints—send messages to the brain telling their location, their position in space. The brain keeps track of all of these unconsciously. Automatically. Reflexively. We do not become consciously aware of these facts unless we move a part of our body or ask ourselves a conscious question. If there is a preconscious part of our knowledge that can effortlessly be called into consciousness, this is it. When you move an arm, you know where it is—know consciously—but then you no longer know. Another example of the brain turning off those inputs it no longer needs. Diverting these sensations out of conscious awareness, out of mind. While all the time, the brain maintains a state of unconscious intolerance, awareness—better yet, constant vigilance. Both conscious tolerance and unconscious awareness are necessary for survival.

A few examples: each morning when I get into my car, I duck my head and miss the top of the door frame. I've never hit my head on the door frame of my own car. Not once. Have you? I don't think about hitting it. I don't worry about it. It's not something that can happen. Just like I don't think about smashing my foot into the ledge around our shower stall. I know where my head is without thinking about it. But if I put on a hat, that hat hits the door frame as I slide into my seat unless I direct my attention to it.

I'm writing at my desk. I'm completely absorbed. I reach up with my left hand and run my fingers through what remains of my hair. Once. Twice. Three times. I know what I want to write. I start writing. I write all first drafts longhand. Without thinking, I put my left elbow back down on the desk. Softly. A perfect landing. Lindbergh touching down outside of Paris at Le Bourget. I never hit the "crazy bone," the nerve running along my elbow and at risk for hitting the edge of any desk.

Why not?

Because I know where my elbow is in space, or more precisely, my brain knows. Unconsciously. It's called *unconscious proprioception*, the perception or knowledge of the position in space of each and every body part. Of my elbow as I rest it back on my desk, of my head as I slip into the car, of my right foot as I get out of the shower.

But I had smashed my right foot into the ledge. My right foot with its broken great, big toe, the toe that was now causing me such terrible pain. Ergo, I hadn't known where my right foot was in space. I hadn't known it consciously. Of course, I wasn't supposed to know it consciously. I was not thinking about it. I was too busy working my way through some Gershwin tune. The problem was that I didn't know my foot's location unconsciously. That was where my brain screwed up.

So why didn't I? Or more precisely, why didn't my brain know where the hell my toe was?

The answer was obvious, like all such simple truths. It was there to be seen if you just looked at it. All it took was getting hit by the right falling apple. It was a matter of tolerance, but a far different and far more pervasive form of tolerance than I had ever been taught about. Tolerance to feeling your underpants or brassiere or collar doesn't mean that you don't know where your buttocks, breasts, or neck are in space. Wearing a tight collar and a tie with a big knot does not increase the chances of my banging my forehead or scalp as I get into my car. But in the case of my toe, tolerance to pain had done just that. I had not only developed a conscious tolerance to pain, I had—or rather, my brain had—automatically developed tolerance to unconscious proprioception, the unconscious sense of where my right toe and right ankle were in space. The phenomenon had to include the right ankle, because you lift the ankle to get the foot and toe over that all important ledge.

My tolerance had crossed two separate borders. It had spread from one order of sensation (pain) to another (position sense, proprioception) and from consciousness to unconsciousness. As a neurologist and neuroscientist I hadn't known that could happen. As a typical human being I now knew that it did happen, and on reflection I realized that it always had and that everyone else knew that it did, even though those of us who study the nervous system as a way of life had yet to sanctify the observation. It has happened to all of us. You are working around the house, hammering away. You hit your thumb with the hammer. Accidents do happen. Your thumb hurts. It kills. Soon it feels better. Back to work. More hammering. Within no time, within half a dozen hammer blows, you've done it again, smashed the same thumb with the same hammer. Why? Because in dampening the original pain, the brain has also dampened its knowledge of where the pain is, of where your thumb is.

And *bang*.

You did it again.

Pain.

Worse pain than before.

Pain has a unique place among sensations. It is the most primitive. It may in fact be the primary, earliest, and purest of all sensations. This primitive form of sensation is an integral part of the nervous system serving to protect the organism. And it retains many of its primitive features, even in man. The nerve endings that feel pain are just that, the naked, thin, fine endings of the nerves. Other sensations require specialized receptors. Not pain. Just the nerves themselves. Most—in fact, all—other sensations reach consciousness in man in the cerebral cortex, the mantle of gray matter, of nerve cells on the surface of the brain. An area far more developed and sophisticated in man than in any other species. Destroy the cortex or anesthetize it, and the conscious recognition of most sensation is lost: hearing, vision, position, touch, smell, temperature. But not pain. Pain is felt unconsciously, deep in the brain, in the thalamus, which for all other sensations (all but smell) is a clearinghouse for input on its pathway to the cortex and conscious awareness. And of course, thalamic pain is devoid of all the trappings of cortical sophistication. The cortex is capable of a far greater degree of recognition of gradation and location. It can make complex judgments. The last joint of the great toe is bent up by three degrees. That's a cortical sensation. The thumb is being held just two millimeters away from the first finger, and between the thumb and the first finger there is a cool, round, hard, cylindrical object. It is the nail, two millimeters in diameter, being held between the thumb and the forefinger, as the hammer comes crashing onto the nail.

But the hammer misses. It hits the thumb instead. Instant havoc. Right on the thumbnail, of course. I should have hired a carpenter. A handyman. Someone without ten thumbs.

Throbbing pain.

Where?

My whole hand.

No, my whole thumb, up to my elbow.

Pain is, essentially, poorly localized. This is because it is a thalamic sensation. Only when I move or touch my smashed digit do I know precisely where the hammer made contact. Moving or touching my thumb adds cortical components and localizes the source of the pain.

Pain that in a few minutes recedes.

Slowly.

Surely.

Thank God for tolerance.

I start to work again.

And *bang.*

DISASTER.

The thalamus lacks sophistication. It has no judgment. It dampens pain, and as it does, it also blocks position sense, preventing that sensation from reaching consciousness and even aborting unconscious awareness. That is why I hit my thumb that second time and the third time, and why you have done the same thing. And why I hit my broken big toe on that ledge.

I finally knew why it had been on that morning that the accident had occurred. Why that morning had been different from all other mornings.

EXPOSITION

To expose is to show, to bring to light, to carry out into the open. Exposition in literature—in a play, poem, or work of fiction—is the part that introduces the audience to the characters and the conflict, that shows what's happening in the imaginary world the reader is about to enter. An expository essay shows, tells, explains, or clarifies. Essentially, exposition is what a good teacher does. Many of the papers students in college are assigned to write are expository, for this kind of writing clearly shows what a person has learned. In turn, the writer passes on this learning to the reader.

Klawans's essay qualifies as expository because its purpose is to explain—to offer a scientific explanation for a common phenomenon. Many people have experienced the pain of hurting a part of the body that is already damaged, but few have bothered to seriously question why it happens so often. The scientist—in this case, a physiologist—searches for answers and explanations, and publishes his or her findings in a professional paper (a research report for other scientists) or, as here, in an article for the general public. The purpose, either way, is to share knowledge, which is the basic purpose of every expository essay.

Expository essays are traditionally categorized by the methods, or approaches, they use: definition, classification, analysis, process, or comparison/contrast. To define something is to show how it is individual, to demonstrate the qualities that make it unique, to tell what it is. To classify is to divide the subject into groups or to place it among other groups in a larger whole. To analyze is to separate a thing into its parts, showing how the parts relate to one another. To show a process is to demonstrate a step-by-step procedure. To compare and contrast is to present the subject as it is similar to and different from other things, in order to clarify exactly what this thing is. All of these types of exposition use the method of illustration, giving details and examples.

For example, an expository essay on cats might be an extended definition: What exactly is a cat? What's *not* a cat? (A tiger? A painting of a kitten?) An essay on classifications of cats might describe the various breeds and their origins, or classify cats by temperament. An analysis might be conducted of the reasons human beings keep cats as pets, or cat behavior might be analyzed, as various types of behavior (stalking, grooming) are separated out and considered. A process essay could be written on carrying a cat to the veterinarian. An amusing comparison/contrast paper might show the differences in character between dog lovers and cat lovers.

Study Questions

1. In your own words, explain the concept of *tolerance*. What does Klawans mean at the end of the essay, when he writes, "The thalamus lacks sophistication. It has no judgment. It dampens pain, and as it does, it also blocks position sense"?
2. How does the simple, almost comedic style, with short sentences and expressive phrases ("And *bang*. DISASTER"), help the reader to approach the subject? In what other kinds of styles could this explanation of physiological tolerance be written?
3. In "Clyde's Pick-Up" (p. 92), William Bryant Logan makes the point that what was unique about Moses was his ability to turn aside and contemplate a strange phenomenon, the burning bush, seeing it as it was. There are many stories also about Albert Einstein, the great physicist, and the ways he constantly sought explanations for the things he saw.

   Does it take a neurologist like Klawans to wonder why we always seem to bang the hurt toe or finger? What other kinds of ordinary experiences have interesting explanations? How can we make our minds more open and exploratory, like those of great thinkers and scientists?

Writing Topics

1. *Collaborative writing activity.* Follow Study Question #3 above by considering the question "How can we become more open, scientific, and

inquiring in our thinking"? Think of some ways the educational system could increase this kind of thinking among children. Write an essay on the education of scientists, bringing in experiences from your own education as either good or bad examples, and telling what ought to happen in our schools.

2. Choose a phenomenon for which you have an explanation, something that other people might see but not understand. Write an expository essay that describes the phenomenon and then explains why it happens. You may use the humorous, simplistic style of Klawans or a more serious, academic style. (Note that it may be easier to take a more serious approach, since humor is often hard to write.)

From Fors Clavigera

JOHN RUSKIN

[1871]

There are three Material things, not only useful, but essential to Life. No one "knows how to live" till he has got them.

These are: Pure Air, Water, and Earth.

There are three Immaterial things, not only useful, but essential to Life. No one knows how to live till he has got them also.

These are: Admiration, Hope, and Love.

Admiration—the power of discerning and taking delight in what is beautiful in visible form, and lovely in human character; and, necessarily, striving to produce what is beautiful in form, and to become what is lovely in character.

Hope—the recognition, by true Foresight, if better things to be reached hereafter, whether by ourselves or others; necessarily issuing in the straightforward and undisappointable effort to advance, according to our proper power, the gaining of them.

Love, both of family and neighbor, faithful, and satisfied.

These are the six chiefly useful things to be got by Political Economy, when it *has* become a science. I will briefly tell you what modern Political Economy—the great *savoir mourir*—is doing with them.

The first three, I said, are Pure Air, Water, and Earth.

Heaven gives you the main elements of these. You can destroy them at your pleasure, or increase, almost without limit, the available quantities of them.

You can vitiate the air by your manner of life, and of death, to any extent. You might easily vitiate it so as to bring such a pestilence on the globe as would end all of you. You or your fellows, German and French, are at present busy in vitiating it to the best of your power in every direction—chiefly at this moment with corpses, and animal and vegetable ruin in war, changing men, horses, and garden-stuff into noxious gas. But everywhere, and all day long, you are vitiating it with foul chemical exhalations; and the horrible nests, which you call towns, are little more than laboratories for the distillation into heaven of venomous smokes and smells, mixed with effluvia from decaying animal matter, and infectious miasmata from purulent disease.

165

On the other hand, your power of purifying the air, by dealing properly and swiftly with all substances in corruption; by absolutely forbidding noxious manufactures; and by planting in all soils the trees which cleanse and invigorate earth and atmosphere—is literally infinite. You might make every breath of air you draw, food.

Secondly, your power over the rain and river-waters of the earth is infinite. You can bring rain where you will, by planting wisely and tending careful—drought, where you will, by ravage of woods and neglect of the soil. You might have the rivers of England as pure as the crystal of the rock—beautiful in falls, in lakes, in living pools—so full of fish that you might take them out with your hands instead of nets. Or you may do always as you have done now, turn every river of England into a common sewer, so that you cannot so much as baptize an English baby but with filth, unless you hold its face out in the rain; and even *that* falls dirty.

Then for the third, Earth—meant to be nourishing for you, and blossoming. You have learned about it, that there is no such thing as a flower; and as far as your scientific hands and scientific brains, inventive of explosive and deathful, instead of blossoming and life-giving, Dust, can contrive, you have turned the Mother-Earth, Demeter, into the Avenger-Earth, Tisiphone—with the voice of your brother's blood crying out of it, in one wild harmony round all its murderous sphere.

That is what you have done for the Three Material Useful Things.

Then for the Three Immaterial Useful Things. For Admiration, you have learned contempt and conceit. There is no lovely thing ever yet done by man that you care for, or can understand; but you are persuaded you are able to do much finer things yourselves. You gather, and exhibit together, as if equally instructive, what is infinitely bad, with what is infinitely good. You do not know which is which; you instinctively prefer the Bad, and do more of it. You instinctively hate the Good, and destroy it.

Then, secondly, for Hope. You have not so much spirit of it in you as to begin any plan which will not pay until ten years; nor so much intelligence of it in you (either politicians or workmen) as to be able to form one clear idea of what you would like your country to become.

Then, thirdly, for Love. You were ordered by the Founder of your religion to love your neighbor as yourselves.

You have founded an entire Science of Political Economy on what you have stated to be the constant instinct of man—the desire to defraud his neighbor.

And you have driven your women mad, so that they ask no more for Love, nor for fellowship with you; but stand against you, and ask for "justice."

Are there any of you who are tired of all this? Any of you, Landlords or Tenants? Employers or Workmen?

CLASSIFICATION

One of the natural patterns of human thinking is to divide the universe into sets and subsets: we think of plants and animals, sweet foods and salty, good and evil, insiders and outsiders. Scientists create entire taxonomies that divide and subdivide classes of objects and beings; humanities scholars divide their discipline into the "arts" and "humanities"; mathematicians create sets of numbers and classes of properties. Chemists analyze solutions to determine the kinds of compounds that make them up. Classification is an almost universal approach to contemplating experience. We analyze by dividing into categories: What is the ethnic make-up of a class of students? Does this sonnet break into an octave and a sestet or into three quatrains and a couplet? What breed of puppy will you buy? Is giving a quarter to a beggar a moral or immoral action? Do you see more clearly by sunlight, moonlight, or twilight? Experience comes at a newborn infant in a great, undistinguished glob, but even young infants rapidly learn to categorize their worlds: this is my mother, this is another person; this is a taste I like, this is a taste I don't like; here is my family, here are other people. As children learn to classify, they begin to make sense of their experiences. Twenty or thirty years later, we read and write about classes and subsections in a more complex way and better understand the construction of the worlds we hold up for examination.

An essay that lists or divides its subject matter is technically termed "analysis" or "classification." Process analysis divides an action or procedure into logical, progressive steps: for example, how to change transmission oil or deliver a baby. Subject analysis, such as the Ruskin essay above, divides a group of objects or actions. Thus, a process analysis would explain how to bake a cake, while a subject analysis would divide cakes into categories (special-occasion cakes or everyday; chocolate, pound, or angel; or different kinds of cakes one's mother used to bake). Obviously, something that is divided into one set of categories can just as easily, and just as interestingly, be divided into other kinds of groups. For example, the table of contents for this book divides the readings into categories of "short and easy" and "long and challenging" reading, while the rhetorical table of contents divides the readings by the various approaches of the authors and the thematic table divides the readings by subject. Most categorization is useful; the thing to remember is that almost no categorization should be counted as final.

[A note of caution: if you number your categories, avoid the temptation to end all the introductory number-words with "ly": first*ly*, second*ly*, third*ly*, and so forth. Since there isn't any such word as *firstly*, use the word *first*, followed by *second, third*, and so on. *Finally* is acceptable for the last item in your series, but only barely. While the number-words are useful, employ other kinds of transitions wherever possible.]

Study Questions

1. Ruskin organizes his classification into two sets of three items each. Make a brief outline or sketch of his six main points, showing their relationship. See if you can repeat the same basic pattern or outline with different ideas of your own, on any topic you choose.
2. What facets of this essay make it "dated," that is, heavily of its own historical period? (For example, consider the use of "he" and the assumption that the reader is male.) On the other hand, what elements in the essay still seem valid and perhaps even more important today?
3. Consider Ruskin's comment to the men of England that "you have driven your women mad, so that they ask no more for Love, nor for fellowship with you; but stand against you, and ask for 'justice.' " Do you think that comment could be relevant today? How would the "women's liberation" or feminist movement fit into Ruskin's ideas?

Writing Topics

1. Write a short essay in which you analyze the Ruskin piece itself. Divide the elements of Ruskin's essay into "modern" and "outdated." Write an essay in which you give two examples of Ruskin's "modernity"—two points that seem to be as pertinent now as they were in 1871—and also give two examples of points that seem "outmoded" or no longer valid. In your conclusion, offer your own opinion of whether Ruskin seems to

speak to a modern reader or is just an interesting historic example of his own time.

2. Rewrite the Ruskin essay, updating the content but using the same basic format. Change the audience from "men of England" to any specific group you choose, and keep your expected audience in mind as you write. Try to maintain Ruskin's firm, "preachy" tone in your own essay.

Representing the Poor

BELL HOOKS

Cultural critics rarely talk about the poor. Most of us use words such as "underclass" or "economically disenfranchised" when we speak about being poor. Poverty has not become one of the new hot topics of radical discourse. When contemporary Left intellectuals talk about capitalism, few if any attempts are made to relate that discourse to the reality of being poor in America. In his collection of essays *Prophetic Thought in Postmodern Times,* black philosopher Cornel West includes a piece entitled "The Black Underclass and Black Philosophers" wherein he suggests that black intellectuals within the "professional-managerial class in U.S. advanced capitalist society" must "engage in a kind of critical self-inventory, a historical situating and positioning of ourselves as persons who reflect on the situation of those more disadvantaged than us even though we may have relatives and friends in the black underclass." West does not speak of poverty or being poor in his essay. And I can remember once in conversation with him referring to my having come from a "poor" background; he corrected me and stated that my family was "working class." I told him that technically we *were* working class, because my father worked as a janitor at the post office, however the fact that there were seven children in our family meant that we often faced economic hardship in ways that made us children at least think of ourselves as poor. Indeed, in the segregated world of our small Kentucky town, we were all raised to think in terms of the haves and the have-nots, rather than in terms of class. We acknowledged the existence of four groups: the poor, who were destitute; the working folks, who were poor because they made just enough to make ends meet; those who worked and had extra money; and the rich. Even though our family was among the working folks, the economic struggle to make ends meet for such a large family always gave us a sense that there was not enough money to take care of the basics. In our house, water was a luxury and using too much could be a cause for punishment. We never talked about being poor. As children we knew we were not supposed to see ourselves as poor but we felt poor.

I began to *see* myself as poor when I went away to college. I never had any money. When I told my parents that I had scholarships and loans to attend Stanford University, they wanted to know how I would pay for getting there, for buying books, for emergencies. We were not poor, but there was no money for what was perceived to be an individualistic indulgent desire; there were cheaper colleges closer to family. When I went to college and could not afford to come home during breaks, I frequently spent my holidays with the black women who cleaned in the dormitories. Their world was my world. They, more than other folks at Stanford, knew where I was coming from. They supported and affirmed my efforts to be educated, to move past and beyond the world they lived in, the world I was coming from.

To this day, even though I am a well-paid member of what West calls the academic "professional-managerial class," in everyday life, outside the classroom, I rarely think of myself in relation to class. I mainly think about the world in terms of who has money to spend and who does not. Like many technically middle-class folks who are connected in economic responsibility to kinship structures where they provide varying material support for others, the issue is always one of money. Many middle-class black folks have no money because they regularly distribute their earnings among a larger kinship group where folks are poor and destitute, where elder parents and relatives who once were working class have retired and fallen into poverty.

Poverty was no disgrace in our household. We were socialized early on, by grandparents and parents, to assume that nobody's value could be measured by material standards. Value was connected to integrity, to being honest and hardworking. One could be hardworking and still be poor. My mother's mother Baba, who did not read or write, taught us—against the wishes of our parents—that it was better to be poor than to compromise one's dignity, that it was better to be poor than to allow another person to assert power over you in ways that were dehumanizing or cruel.

I went to college believing there was no connection between poverty and personal integrity. Entering a world of class privilege which compelled me to think critically about my economic background, I was shocked by representations of the poor learned in classrooms, as well as by the comments of professors and peers that painted an entirely different picture. They were almost always portrayed the poor as shiftless, mindless, lazy, dishonest, and unworthy.

Students in the dormitory were quick to assume that anything missing had been taken by the black and Filipina women who worked
there. Although I went through many periods of shame about my
economic background, even before I educated myself for critical consciousness about class by reading and studying Marx, Gramsci,
Memmi, and the like), I contested stereotypical negative representations of poverty. I was especially disturbed by the assumption that the
poor were without values. Indeed one crucial value that I had
learned from Baba, my grandmother, and other family members was
not to believe that "schooling made you smart." One could have degrees and still not be intelligent or honest. I had been taught in a culture of poverty to be intelligent, honest, to work hard, and always to
be a person of my word. I had been taught to stand up for what I believed was right, to be brave and courageous. These lessons were the
foundation that made it possible for me to succeed, to become the
writer I always wanted to be, and to make a living in my job as an
academic. They were taught to me by the poor, the disenfranchised,
the underclass.

Those lessons were reinforced by liberatory religious traditions
that affirmed identification with the poor. Taught to believe that
poverty could be the breeding ground of moral integrity, of a recognition of the significance of communion, of sharing resources with
others in the black church, I was prepared to embrace the teachings
of liberatory theology, which emphasized solidarity with the poor.
That solidarity was meant to be expressed not simply through charity, the sharing of privilege, but in the assertion of one's power to
change the world so that the poor would have their needs met,
would have access to resources, would have justice and beauty in
their lives.

Contemporary popular culture in the United States rarely represents the poor in ways that display integrity and dignity. Instead, the
poor are portrayed through negative stereotypes. When they are lazy
and dishonest, they are consumed with longing to be rich, a longing
so intense that it renders them dysfunctional. Willing to commit all
manner of dehumanizing and brutal acts in the name of material
gain, the poor are portrayed as seeing themselves as always and only
worthless. Worth is gained only by means of material success.

Television shows and films bring the message home that no one
can truly feel good about themselves if they are poor. In television sit-
coms the working poor are shown to have a healthy measure of self-
contempt; they dish it out to one another with a wit and humor that
we can all enjoy, irrespective of our class. Yet it is clear that humor

masks the longing to change their lot, the desire to "move on up" expressed in the theme song of the sitcom *The Jeffersons*. Films which portray the rags-to-riches tale continue to have major box-office appeal. Most contemporary films portraying black folks—*Harlem Nights, Boomerang, Menace II Society*, to name only a few—have as their primary theme the lust of the poor for material plenty and their willingness to do anything to satisfy that lust. *Pretty Woman* is a perfect example of a film that made huge sums of money portraying the poor in this light. Consumed and enjoyed by audiences of all races and classes, it highlights the drama of the benevolent, ruling-class person (in this case a white man, played by Richard Gere) willingly sharing his resources with a poor white prostitute (played by Julia Roberts). Indeed, many films and television shows portray the ruling class as generous, eager to share, as unattached to their wealth in their interactions with folks who are not materially privileged. These images contrast with the opportunistic avaricious longings of the poor.

Socialized by film and television to identify with the attitudes and values of privileged classes in this society, many people who are poor, or a few paychecks away from poverty, internalize fear and contempt for those who are poor. When materially deprived teenagers kill for tennis shoes or jackets they are not doing so just because they like these items so much. They also hope to escape the stigma of their class by appearing to have the trappings of more privileged classes. Poverty, in their minds and in our society as a whole, is seen as synonymous with depravity, lack, and worthlessness. No one wants to be identified as poor. Teaching literature by African American women writers at a major urban state university to predominantly black students from poor and working-class families, I was bombarded by their questioning as to why the poor black women who were abused in families in the novels we read did not "just leave." It was amazing to me that these students, many of whom were from materially disadvantaged backgrounds, had no realistic sense about the economics of housing or jobs in this society. When I asked that we identify our class backgrounds, only one student—a young single parent—was willing to identify herself as poor. We talked later about the reality that although she was not the only poor person in the class, no one else wanted to identify with being poor for fear this stigma would mark them, shame them in ways that would go beyond our class. Fear of shame-based humiliation is a primary factor leading no one to want to identify themselves as poor. I talked with young black women receiving state aid, who have not worked in years, about the issue of representation. They all agree that they do not want to be identified as poor. In their apartments they have the material possessions that indicate success (a VCR, a color television), even if it means that they do without necessities and plunge into debt to buy these items. Their self-esteem is linked to not being seen as poor.

If to be poor in this society is everywhere represented in the language we use to talk about the poor, in the mass media, as synonymous with being nothing, then it is understandable that the poor learn to be nihilistic. Society is telling them that poverty and nihilism are one and the same. If they cannot escape poverty, then they have no choice but to drown in the image of a life that is valueless. When intellectuals, journalists, or politicians speak about nihilism and the despair of the underclass, they do not link those states to representations of poverty in the mass media. And rarely do they suggest by their rhetoric that one can lead a meaningful, contented, and fulfilled life if one *is* poor. No one talks about our individual and collective accountability to the poor, a responsibility that begins with the politics of representation.

When white female anthropologist Carol Stack looked critically at the lives of black poor people more than twenty years ago and wrote her book *The Culture of Poverty,* she found a value system among them which emphasized the sharing of resources. That value system has long been eroded in most communities by an ethic of liberal individualism, which affirms that it is morally acceptable not to share. The mass media has been the primary teacher bringing into our lives and our homes the logic of liberal individualism, the idea that you make it by the privatized hoarding of resources, not by sharing them. Of course, liberal individualism works best for the privileged classes. But it has worsened the lot of the poor who once depended on an ethic of communalism to provide affirmation, aid, and support.

To change the devastating impact of poverty on the lives of masses of folks in our society we must change the way resources and wealth are distributed. But we must also change the way the poor are represented. Since many folks will be poor for a long time before those changes are put in place that address their economic needs, it is crucial to construct habits of seeing and being that restore an oppositional value system affirming that one can live a life of dignity and integrity in the midst of poverty. It is precisely this dignity Jonathan Freedman seeks to convey in his book *From Cradle to Grave: The Human Face of Poverty in America,* even though he does not critique capitalism or call for major changes in the distribution of wealth and resources. Yet any efforts to change the face of poverty in the United States must link a shift in representation to a demand for the redistribution of wealth and resources.

Progressive intellectuals from privileged classes who are themselves obsessed with gaining material wealth are uncomfortable with the insistence that one can be poor, yet lead a rich and meaningful life. They fear that any suggestion that poverty is acceptable may lead those who have to feel no accountability towards those who have not, even though it is unclear how they reconcile their pursuit with concern for and accountability towards the poor. Their conservative counterparts, who did much to put in place a system of representation that dehumanized the poor, fear that if poverty is seen as having no relation to value, the poor will not passively assume their role as exploited workers. That fear is masked by their insistence that the poor will not seek to work if poverty is deemed acceptable, and that the rest of us will have to support them. (Note the embedded assumption that to be poor means that one is not hardworking.) Of course, there are many more poor women and men refusing menial labor in low-paid jobs than ever before. This refusal is not rooted in laziness but in the assumption that it is not worth it to work a job where one is systematically dehumanized or exploited only to remain poor. Despite these individuals, the vast majority of poor people in our society want to work, even when jobs do not mean that they leave the ranks of the poor.

Witnessing that individuals can be poor and lead meaningful lives, I understand intimately the damage that has been done to the poor by a dehumanizing system of representation. I see the difference in self-esteem between my grandparents' and parents' generations and that of my siblings, relatives, friends and acquaintances who are poor, who suffer from a deep-seated, crippling lack of self-esteem. Ironically, despite the presence of more opportunity than that available to an older generation, low self-esteem makes it impossible for this younger generation to move forward even as it also makes their lives psychically unbearable. That psychic pain is most often relieved by some form of substance abuse. But to change the face of poverty so that it becomes, once again, a site for the formation of values, of dignity and integrity, as any other class positionality in this society, we would need to intervene in existing systems of representation.

Linking this progressive change to radical/revolutionary political movements (such as eco-feminism, for example) that urge all of us to live simply could also establish a point of connection and constructive interaction. The poor have many resources and skills for living. Those

folks who are interested in sharing individual plenty as well as working politically for redistribution of wealth can work in conjunction
with individuals who are materially disadvantaged to achieve this
end. Material plenty is only one resource. Literacy skills are another.
It would be exciting to see unemployed folks who lack reading and
writing skills have available to them community-based literacy programs. Progressive literacy programs connected to education for critical consciousness could use popular movies as a base to begin learning and discussion. Theaters all across the United States that are not
used in the day could be sites for this kind of program where college
students and professors could share skills. Since many individuals
who are poor, disadvantaged or destitute are already literate, reading
groups could be formed to educate for critical consciousness, to help
folks rethink how they can organize life both to live well in poverty
and to move out of such circumstances. Many of the young women
I encounter—black and white—who are poor and receiving state aid
(and some of whom are students or would-be students) are intelligent, critical thinkers struggling to transform their circumstances.
They are eager to work with folks who can offer guidance, know-
how, concrete strategies. Freedman concludes his book with the reminder that

> it takes money, organization, and laws to maintain a social
> structure but none of it works if there are not opportunities for
> people to meet and help each other along the way. Social re-
> sponsibility comes down to something simple—the ability to
> respond.

Constructively changing ways the poor are represented in every aspect of life is one progressive intervention that can challenge everyone to look at the face of poverty and not turn away.

IN FOCUS

ARGUMENT

Where there is no difference of opinion, there is little opportunity for intellectual growth. In the challenge of ideas, the rub of
opinions against one another, the mind develops its faculty for
independent thinking and questioning. That is why so many of
the assignments in college courses require that students write argumentative papers. Developing a strong argument requires not
only attacking opposing positions but also knowing enough about

those opposing ideas to question (and thereby strengthen) one's own ideas. Nothing beats a good argument for stretching intellectual skills.

As in any good exercise, there are rules that should be followed in an argument; otherwise, the exercise degenerates into name-calling, which does no one any good (except, occasionally, to get a politician elected), or silent unhappiness, which might do harm. The first, and probably most important, rule in any argument is to avoid *ad hominem* (Latin for "to the person") attacks: one may assault another person's ideas, facts, and reasoning, but not the person personally. A second major concern is to stay focused on the subject: people arguing one thing often have a tendency to attempt to discuss four other things simultaneously ("Are we discussing schools for the children here, or your need for another car?"). Finally, even though emotional arguments can be very powerful, an attitude of open-minded fairness, not presenting one's position too heavy-handedly, often goes a long way toward winning an audience's acceptance.

In constructing an argumentative essay, the first consideration is to make sure the thesis *can be argued.* If everybody generally agrees on something, or if the thesis is a simple statement of fact, there is no argument. No one, for example, would bother to write a paper arguing that trees produce oxygen (a statement of fact), or that flowering trees are beautiful (a general agreement)—those statements could better be used as evidence for an essay arguing that the city ought to spend part of its budget planting trees in privately owned vacant lots. Problems with simple or obvious solutions, or positions that nearly everyone agrees on, do not make for interesting essays.

Study Questions

1. bell hooks (who spells her name without capitals) spends the first part of her essay defining and describing poverty and only gets into her main point halfway through the piece. Why does she do this? Is this two-part balance of the essay as effective as if she had presented her thesis first?

2. Do you agree with hooks that "television shows and films bring the message home that no one can truly feel good about themselves if they are poor." What examples can you give from current television shows and films?

3. What differences do you see between the "professional-managerial" class, the "working class," and the "poor"? How have you arrived at your opinions about those classes? How has your background affected those opinions?

Writing Topics

1. Write an essay in which you describe an encounter in a public place between a "professional-managerial" person and a "working-class" or "poor" person. After describing the encounter, write two statements in first person, describing the encounter from each person's point of view.
2. Do you agree or disagree with hooks that "individuals can be poor and lead meaningful lives"? Write an essay in which you argue one side or another, supporting your points with evidence you have seen or experienced.

Larger
than Life

When my grandmother was young, she would sometimes spot the emperor Franz Josef riding down the cobbled roads of the Austro-Hungarian Empire.

She came of age so long ago that the few surviving photographs are colored cream and chestnut. Early on, she saw cars replace horses and carriages. When she got older, she marveled at the first televisions. Near the end of her life, she grew accustomed to remote control and could spot prime ministers on color TV. By the time she died, the world was freshly populated by gadgetry and myth. Her generation bore witness to the rise of new machinery created by visionaries. My generation has seen machinery break down and visionaries come under fire.

As children, we enjoyed collecting visionaries, the way we collected toys or baseball cards. When I was a kid, I first met Patrick Henry and Eleanor Roosevelt, Abraham Lincoln and Albert Einstein. They could always be summoned by the imagination and so were never late for play dates. I thought heroes figured in any decent childhood. I knew their stats.

Nathan Hale. Nelson Mandela. Heroes have guts.

Michelangelo. Shakespeare. Heroes have imagination.

They fight. Alexander the Great. Joan of Arc.

They fight for what they believe in. Susan B. Anthony. Martin Luther King.

Heroes overcome massive obstacles. Beethoven, while deaf, still managed to carry an unforgettable tune. Homer, while blind, never failed to give an excellent description. Helen Keller, both deaf and blind, still spoke to the world. FDR, despite his polio, became president. Moses, despite his speech impediment, held productive discussions with God.

They inspire three-hour movies. They make us weepy. They do the right thing while enduring attractive amounts of suffering. They tend to be self-employed. They are often killed off. They sense the future.

They lead lives that make us question our own. They are our ideals, but not our friends.

They don't have to be real. Some of them live in books and legends. They don't have to be famous. There are lower-profile heroes who get resurrected by ambitious biographers. There are collective heroes: firefighters and astronauts, unsung homemakers, persecuted peoples. There are those whose names we can't remember, only their deeds: "you know, that woman who swam the English Channel," "the guy who died running the first marathon," "the student who threw himself in front of the tank at Tiananmen Square." There are those whose names we'll never find out: the anonymous benefactor, the masked man, the undercover agent, the inventor of the wheel, the unknown soldier. The one who did the thing so gutsy and terrific that no one will ever know what it was.

Unlike icons (Marilyn, Elvis) heroes are not only sexy but noble, too. Unlike idols (Gretzky, Streisand), who vary from fan to fan, they are almost universally beloved. Unlike icons and idols, heroes lack irony. And unlike icons and idols, heroes are no longer in style.

As centuries end, so do visions of faith—maybe because the faithful get nervous as the double zeroes approach and question what they've been worshipping. Kings and queens got roughed up at the end of the eighteenth century; God took a beating at the end of the nineteenth; and as the twentieth century draws to a close, outstanding human beings are the casualties of the moment. In the 1970s and 1980s, Americans started feeling queasy about heroism. Those of us born in the sixties found ourselves on the cusp of that change. A sweep of new beliefs, priorities, and headlines has conspired to take our pantheon away from us.

Members of my generation believed in heroes when they were younger but now find themselves grasping for them. Even the word *hero* sounds awkward. I find myself embarrassed to ask people who their heroes are, because the word just doesn't trip off the tongue. My friend Katrin sounded irritated when I asked for hers. She said, "Oh, Jesus . . . Do people still have heroes?"

We don't. Certainly not in the traditional sense of adoring perfect people. Frequently not at all. "I'm sort of intrigued by the fact that I don't have heroes right off the top of my head," said a colleague, Peter. "Can I get back to you?"

Some of us are more upset about this than others. It's easy to tell which of us miss the heroic age. We are moved by schmaltzy political speeches, we warm up to stories of pets saving their owners, we even get misty-eyed watching the Olympics. We mope when model citizens fail us. My college roommate, Linda, remembers a seventh-grade class called "Heroes and She-roes." The first assignment was to write about a personal hero or she-ro. "I came home," Linda told me, "and cried and cried because I didn't have one. . . . Carter had screwed up in Iran and given the malaise speech. Gerald Ford was a nothing and Nixon was evil. My parents told me to write about Jane Fonda the political activist and I just kept crying."

Not everyone feels sentimental about it. A twentyish émigré raised in the former Soviet Union told me: "It's kind of anticlimactic to look for heroes when you've been brought up in a culture that insists on so many heroes. . . . What do you want me to say? Lenin? Trotsky?" Even though I grew up in the relatively propaganda-free United States, I understood. The America of my childhood insisted on heroes, too.

Of all the myths I happily ate for breakfast, the most powerful one was our story of revolution. I sang about it as early as kindergarten and read about it long after. The story goes, a few guys in wigs skipped town on some grumpy church leaders and spurned a loopy king to branch out on their own. The children who hear the story realize they don't have to believe in oldfangled clergy or a rusty crown—but they had better believe in those guys with the wigs.

I sure did. I loved a set of books known as the "Meet" series: *Meet George Washington, Meet Andrew Jackson, Meet the Men Who Sailed the Seas,* and many more. I remember one picture of an inspired Thomas Jefferson, his auburn ponytail tied in a black ribbon, penning words with a feather as a battle of banners and cannon fire raged behind him.

A favorite "Meet" book starred Christopher Columbus. His resistance to the flat-earth society of his day was engrossing, especially to a kid like me who had trouble trying new foods let alone seeking new land masses. I identified with his yearning for a new world and his difficulty with finding investors. Standing up to the king and queen of Spain was like convincing your parents to let you do stuff they thought was idiotic. Now, my allowance was only thirty-five cents a week, but that didn't mean I wasn't going to ask for three ships at some later date.

This is pretty embarrassing: I adored those guys. The ones in the white powder and ponytails, the voluptuous hats, the little breeches and cuffs. They were funny-looking, but lovable. They did outrageous things without asking for permission. They invented the pursuit of happiness.

I had a special fondness for Ben Franklin, statesman and eccentric inventor. Inventions, like heroes, made me feel as though I lived in a dull era. If I'd grown up at the end of the nineteenth century, I could have spoken on early telephones. A few decades later, I could have heard the new sounds of radio. In the sixties, I could have watched black-and-white TVs graduate to color.

Instead, I saw my colorful heroes demoted to black and white. Mostly white. By the time I finished high school, it was no longer hip to look up to the paternalistic dead white males who launched our country, kept slaves and mistresses, and massacred native peoples. Suddenly they weren't visionaries but oppressors, or worse—objects. Samuel Adams became a beer, John Hancock became a building, and the rest of the guys in wigs were knocked off one by one, in a whodunit that couldn't be explained away by the fact of growing up.

The flag-waving of my youth, epitomized by America's bicentennial, was a more loving homage than I know today. The year 1976 rolled in while Washington was still reeling from Saigon, but the irony was lost on me and my second-grade classmates. The idea of losing seemed miles away. We celebrated July fourth with wide eyes and patriotic parties. Grown-ups had yet to tell themselves (so why should they tell us?) that the young nation on its birthday had suffered a tragic defeat.

Historians soon filled us in about that loss, and of others. Discovering America was nothing compared to discovering the flaws of its discoverers, now cast as imperialist sleaze, racist and sexist and genocidal. All things heroic—human potential, spiritual fervor, moral resplendence—soon became suspect. With the possible exception of bodybuilding, epic qualities went out of fashion. Some will remember 1992 as the year Superman died. Literally, the writers and illustrators at D.C. Comics decided the guy was too old to keep leaping buildings and rescuing an aging damsel in distress. When rumors circulated that he would be resurrected, readers protested via calls to radio shows, letters to editors, and complaints to stores that they were in no mood for such an event.

A monster named Doomsday killed Superman, overcoming him not with Kryptonite but with brute force. Who killed the others? I blame improved modes of character assassination, media hype artists, and scholars. The experts told me that Columbus had destroyed cultures and ravaged the environment. They also broke the news that the cowboys had brazenly taken land that wasn't theirs. In a way, I'm glad I didn't know that earlier; dressing up as a cowgirl for Halloween wouldn't have felt right. In a more urgent way, I wish I had known it then so I wouldn't have had to learn it later.

Just fifteen years after America's bicentennial came Columbus's quincentennial, when several towns canceled their annual parades in protest of of his sins. Soon other festivities started to feel funny. When my aunt served corn pudding last Thanksgiving, my cousin took a spoonful, then said drily that the dish was made in honor of the Indians who taught us to use corn before we eliminated them. Uncomfortable chuckles followed. Actually, neither "we" nor my personal ancestors had come to America in time to kill any Native Americans. Yet the holiday put us in the same boat with the pilgrims and anchored us in the white man's domain.

I am fascinated by how we become "we" and "they." It's as if siding with the establishment is the Alka-Seltzer that helps us stomach the past. To swallow history lessons, we turn into "we": one nation under God of proud but remorseful Indian killers. We also identify with people who look like us. For example, white northerners studying the Civil War identify both with white slaveholders and with northern abolitionists, aligning with both race and place. Transsexuals empathize with men and women. Immigrants identify with their homeland and their adopted country. Historians proposing a black Athena and a black Jesus have inspired more of such bonding.

I'll admit that these empathies can be empowering. I always understood the idea of feeling stranded by unlikely role models but never emotionally grasped it until I watched Penny Marshall's movie *A League of Their Own.* For the first time, I appreciated why so many women complain that sports bore them. I had enjoyed baseball before but never as intensely as I enjoyed the games in that film. The players were people like me. Lori Petty, petite, chirpy, wearing a skirt, commanded the pitcher's mound with such aplomb that I was moved. There's something to be said for identifying with people who remind us of ourselves, though Thomas Jefferson and Lori Petty look more like each other than either of them looks like me. I'll never know if I would've read the "Meet" books with more zeal if they'd described our founding mothers. I liked them as they were.

Despite the thrill of dames batting something on the big screen besides their eyelashes, the fixation on look-alike idols is disturbing for those who get left out. In the movie *White Men Can't Jump,* Wesley Snipes tells Woody Harrelson not to listen to Jimi Hendrix, because "White people can't hear Jimi." Does this joke imply that black people can't hear Mozart? That I can admire Geena Davis's batting but never appreciate Carlton Fisk? Besides dividing us from one another, these emotional allegiances divide us from potential heroes too, causing us to empathize with, say, General Custer and his last stand instead of with Sitting Bull and the victorious Sioux.

Rejecting heroes for having the wrong ethnic credentials or sex organs says less about our multicultural vision than our lack of imagination. By focusing on what we are instead of who we can become, by typecasting and miscasting our ideals—that's how we become "we" and "they." If heroes are those we'd like to emulate, it does make sense that they resemble us. But the focus on physical resemblance seems limited and racist.

Heroes should be judged on their deeds, and there are those with plenty in common heroically but not much in terms of ethnicity, nationality, or gender. Just look at Harriet Tubman and Moses; George Washington and Simón Bolívar; Mahatma Gandhi and Martin Luther King; Murasaki and Milton; Cicero and Ann Richards. Real paragons transcend nationality. It didn't matter to me that Robin Hood was English—as long as he did good, he was as American as a barbecue. It didn't matter to Queen Isabella that Columbus was Italian as long as he sailed for Spain and sprinkled her flags about. The British epic warrior Beowulf was actually Swedish. Both the German hero Etzel and the Scandinavian hero Atli were really Attila, king of the Huns. With all this borrowing going on, we shouldn't have to check the passports of our luminaries; the idea that we can be like them not literally but spiritually is what's uplifting in the first place.

The idea that we can never be like them has led to what I call jealousy journalism. You know, we're not remotely heroic so let's tear down anyone who is. It's become hard to remember which papers are tabloids. Tell-all articles promise us the "real story"—implying that greatness can't be real. The safe thing about *Meet George Washington* was that you couldn't actually meet him. Today's stories and pictures bring us closer. And actually meeting your heroes isn't the best idea. Who wants to learn that a favorite saint is really just an egomaniac with a publicist?

Media maestros have not only knocked public figures off their pedestals, they've also lowered heroism standards by idealizing just about everyone. Oprah, Geraldo, and the rest turn their guests into heroes of the afternoon because they overcame abusive roommates, childhood disfigurement, deranged spouses, multiple genitalia, cheerleading practice, or zany sexual predilections. In under an hour, a studio audience can hear their epic sagas told.

While TV and magazine producers helped lead heroes to their graves, the academic community gave the final push. Just as my peers and I made our way through college, curriculum reformers were promoting "P.C." agendas at the expense of humanistic absolutes. Scholars invented their own tabloidism, investigating and maligning both dead professors and trusty historical figures. Even literary theory helped, when deconstructionists made it trendy to look for questions instead of answers, for circular logic instead of linear sense, for defects, contradictions, and the ironic instead of meaning, absolutes, and the heroic.

It was the generations that preceded ours who killed off our heroes. And like everyone who crucified a superstar, these people thought they were doing a good thing. The professors and journalists consciously moved in a positive direction—toward greater tolerance, openness, and realism—eliminating our inspirations in the process. The death of an era of hero worship was not the result of the cynical, clinical materialism too often identified with my generation. It was the side effect of a complicated cultural surgery, of an operation that may have been necessary and that many prescribed.

So with the best of intentions, these storytellers destroyed bedtime stories. Which is too bad for the kids, because stories make great teachers. Children glean by example. You can't tell a child "Be ingenious," or "Do productive things." You can tell them, "This Paul Revere person jumped on a horse at midnight, rode wildly through the dark, figured out where the mean British troops were coming to attack the warm, fuzzy, sweet, great-looking colonists, and sent messages by code, igniting our fight for freedom," and they'll get the idea. America's rugged values come gift wrapped in the frontier tales of Paul Bunyan, Daniel Boone, Davy Crockett—fables of independence and natural resources. Kids understand that Johnny Appleseed or Laura Ingalls Wilder would never need a Cuisinart. Pioneer and prairie stories convey the fun of roughing it, showing kids how to be self-reliant, or at least less spoiled.

Children catch on to the idea of imitating qualities, not literal feats. After returning his storybook to the shelf, little Billy doesn't look around for a dragon to slay. Far-off stories capture the imagination in an abstract but compelling way, different from, say, the more immediate action-adventure flick. After watching a James Bond film festival, I might fantasize about killing the five people in front of me on line at the supermarket, while legends are remote enough that Columbus might inspire one to be original, but not necessarily to study Portuguese or enlist in the navy. In tales about conquerors and cavaliers, I first flirted with the idea of ideas.

Even Saturday-morning cartoons served me as parables, when I woke up early enough to watch the classy Superfriends do good deeds. Sure, the gender ratio between Wonder Woman and the gaggle of men in capes seemed unfair, but I was rapt. I wonder whether

I glued myself to my television and my high expectations with too much trust, and helped to set my own heroes up for a fall.

Some heroes have literally been sentenced to death by their own followers. *Batman* subscribers, for example, were responsible for getting rid of Batman's sidekick, Robin. At the end of one issue, the Joker threatened to kill the Boy Wonder, and readers could decide whether Robin lived or died by calling one of two "900" numbers. The public voted overwhelmingly for his murder. I understand the impulse of those who dialed for death. At a certain point, eternal invincibility grows as dull and predictable as wearing a yellow cape and red tights every day of the year. It's not human. We get fed up.

My generation helped to kill off heroism as teenagers, with our language. We used heroic words that once described brave deeds—*excellent, amazing, awesome*—to describe a good slice of pizza or a sunny day. In our everyday speech, *bad* meant good. *Hot* meant cool. In the sarcastic slang of street gangs in Los Angeles, *hero* currently means traitor, specifically someone who snitches on a graffiti artist.

Even those of us who lived by them helped shatter our own myths, which wasn't all negative. We discovered that even the superhero meets his match. Every Achilles needs a podiatrist. Every rhapsodically handsome leader has a mistress or a moment of moral ambiguity. We injected a dose of reality into our expectations. We even saw a viable presidential candidate under a heap of slung mud, a few imperfections, an alleged tryst or two.

We're used to trysts in a way our elders aren't. Our parents and grandparents behave as if they miss the good old days when adulterers wore letter sweaters. They feign shock at the extramarital exploits of Thomas Jefferson, Frank Sinatra, JFK, Princess Di. Their hero worship is a romance that falters when beloved knights end up unfaithful to their own spouses. People my age aren't amazed by betrayal. We are suspicious of shining armor. Even so, tabloid sales escalate when a Lancelot gives in to temptation—maybe because the jerk who cheats on you somehow becomes more attractive. Other generations have gossiped many of our heroes into philanderers. The presumptuous hero who breaks your heart is the most compelling reason not to get involved in the first place.

Seeing your legends discredited is like ending a romance with someone you loved but ultimately didn't like. However much you longed to trust that person, it just makes more sense not to. Why pine away for an aloof godlet who proves unstable, erratic, and a rotten lover besides? It's sad to give up fantasies but mature to trade them in for healthier relationships grounded in reality.

We require a new pantheon: a set of heroes upon whom we can rely, who will not desert us when the winds change, and whom we will not desert. It's unsettling, if not downright depressing, to go through life embarrassed about the identity of one's childhood idols.

Maybe we should stick to role models instead. Heroes have become quaint, as old-fashioned as gas-guzzlers—and as unwieldy, requiring too much investment and energy. Role models are more like compact cars, less glam and roomy but easier to handle. They take up less parking space in the imagination. Role models have a certain degree of consciousness about their job. The cast members of "Beverly Hills 90210," for example, have acknowledged that they serve as role models for adolescents, and their characters behave accordingly: they refrain from committing major crimes; they overcome inclinations toward substance abuse; they see through adult hypocrisy; and any misdemeanors they do perpetrate are punished. For moral mediators we could do better, but at least the prime-time writing staff is aware of the burden of having teen groupies.

Heroes don't have the luxury of staff writers or the opportunity to endorse designer jeans. Hercules can't go on "Nightline" and pledge to stop taking steroids. Prometheus can't get a presidential pardon. Columbus won't have a chance to weep to Barbara Walters that he didn't mean to endanger leatherback turtles or monk seals or the tribes of the Lucayas. Elizabeth I never wrote a best-seller about how she did it her way.

Role models can go on talk shows, or even host them. Role models may live next door. While a hero might be a courageous head of state, a saint, a leader of armies, a role model might be someone who put in a three-day presidential bid, your local minister, your boss. They don't need their planes to go down in flames to earn respect. Role models have a job, accomplishment, or hairstyle worth emulating.

Rather than encompassing the vast kit and caboodle of ideals, role models can perform a little neat division of labor. One could wish to give orders like Norman Schwarzkopf but perform psychoanalysis like Lucy Van Pelt, to chair a round-table meeting as well as King Arthur but negotiate as well as Queen Esther, to eat like Orson Welles but look like Helen of Troy, and so forth. It was General Schwarzkopf, the most tangible military hero for anyone my age, who vied instead for role-model status by claiming on the cover of his book: *It Doesn't Take a Hero*. With this title he modestly implies that anyone with some smarts and élan could strategize and storm as well as he has.

Role models are admirable individuals who haven't given up their lives or livelihoods and may even have a few hangups. They don't have to be prone to excessive self-sacrifice. They don't go on hunger strikes; they diet. They are therefore more likely than heroes to be free for lunch, and they are oftener still alive.

Heroism is a living thing for many of my contemporaries. In my informal poll, I not only heard sob stories about the decline of heroes, I also discovered something surprising: the ascent of parents. While the founding fathers may be passé, actual mothers, fathers, grands, and great-grands are undeniably "in." An overwhelming number of those I polled named their household forebears as those they most admired. By choosing their own relatives as ideals, people in their twenties have replaced impersonal heroes with the most personal role models of all. Members of my purportedly lost generation have not only realized that it's time to stop believing in Santa Claus, they have chosen to believe instead in their families—the actual tooth fairy, the real Mr. and Mrs. Claus. They have stopped needing the folks from the North Pole, the guys with the wigs, the studs and studettes in tights and capes.

In a way it bodes well that Superman and the rest could be killed or reported missing. They were needed to quash the most villainous folks of all: insane communists bearing nuclear weapons, heinous war criminals, monsters named Doomsday. The good news about Superman bleeding to death was that Doomsday died in the struggle.

If the good guys are gone, so is the world that divides down the middle into good guys and bad guys. A world without heroes is a rigorous, demanding place, where things don't boil down to black and white but are rich with shades of gray; where faith in lofty, dead personages can be replaced by faith in ourselves and one another; where we must summon the strength to imagine a five-dimensional future in colors not yet invented. My generation grew up to see our world shift, so it's up to us to steer a course between naïveté and nihilism, to reshape vintage stories, to create stories of spirit without apologies.

I've heard a few. There was one about the woman who taught Shakespeare to inner-city fourth graders in Chicago who were previously thought to be retarded or hopeless. There was the college groundskeeper and night watchman, a black man with a seventh-grade education, who became a contracts expert, wrote poetry and memoirs, and invested his salary so wisely that he bequeathed 450 acres of mountainous parkland to the university when he died. There was the motorcyclist who slid under an eighteen-wheeler at full speed, survived his physical therapy only to wind up in a plane crash, recovered, and as a disfigured quadriplegic started a business, got happily married, and ran for public office; his campaign button bore a caption that said "Send me to Congress and I won't be just another pretty face. . . ."

When asked for her heroes, a colleague of mine spoke of her great-grandmother, a woman whose husband left her with three kids in Galicia, near Poland, and went to the United States. He meant to send for her, but the First World War broke out. When she made it to America, her husband soon died, and she supported her family; at one point she even ran a nightclub. According to the great-granddaughter, "When she was ninety she would tell me she was going to volunteer at the hospital. I would ask how and she'd say, 'Oh, I just go over there to read to the old folks.' The 'old folks' were probably seventy. She was a great lady."

My grandmother saved her family, too, in the next great war. She did not live to see the age of the fax, but she did see something remarkable in her time, more remarkable even than the emperor riding down the street: she saw him walking down the street. I used to ask her, "Did you really see the emperor Franz Josef walking down the street?"

She would say, "Ya. Walking down the street." I would laugh, and though she'd repeat it to amuse me, she did not see what was so funny. To me, the emperor was someone you met in history books, not on the streets of Vienna. He was larger than life, a surprising pedestrian. He was probably just getting some air, but he was also laying the ground work for my nostalgia of that time when it would be natural for him to take an evening stroll, when those who were larger than life roamed cobblestones.

Today, life is larger.

DEFINITION

To define is to specify—that is, to show a thing as specifically itself and not anything else. Defining means showing the borders or boundaries that separate one thing from another. We define a word, for example, by showing how it is used, and also by giving its opposites, or antonyms. We define an object by telling what it is and what it is not, its properties and uses. (Bagel: a kind of bread with the approximate shape and size of a doughnut, crunchy on the outside and soft on the inside.) To define is to give the characteristics of an object or idea and, frequently, the ways that people perceive those characteristics.

Notice that Bader does not begin by offering a dictionary definition of the word *hero*. She defines by telling what heroes do and giving examples of her heroes. She also draws boundaries, telling what heroes are not: they are different from role models. The essay becomes an *extended definition*, not of the word, but of the concept, and of course as Bader defines her idea she also tells a great deal about contemporary society.

Study Questions

1. Make an informal outline of the essay, listing the points that Bader makes in the order she presents them. How does the pattern of the piece work toward an effective definition?
2. What is the author's purpose in beginning with a mention of her grandmother?
3. What is the difference between a role model and a hero? Describe one of each of your own, explaining the difference.

Writing Topics

1. Do you agree with Bader that we have very few heroes today? Do you agree with her reasoning about why there are so few? Or, do you think we have heroes of different kinds? Are contemporary heroes more or less worthy of our admiration than historical heroes? Write an essay in which you compare your heroes today with those you had as a child.
2. Using Bader's example of the definition of *hero,* write an essay in which you give an extended definition of *one* of these role-concepts, showing by example what that kind of person should and should not be: friend, teacher, student, sister (brother), minister (priest, rabbi), teammate.

Grameen Bank

MOHAMMAD YUNUS

1

I went back and joined everybody else in the country, and I thought, now things will start moving and moving up. To my surprise and to the surprise of all of us, the country was sliding downwards very rapidly. And by 1974, we had a terrible famine. A lot of people were dying on the streets. So I got very frustrated with what I teach, development economics and all those theories where everything sounds so good and it all works out. Because when you walk out of the university campus, you see that the real world is very different from what you describe in the classroom. To me the classroom was like a movie house: you go to a movie, you see how everything is working, and you consider that the hero in the end will win and at the end he does win. You come out of the classroom just like you come out of the movie house: the real world is very suddenly different—everybody gets beaten, nobody wins. I thought, what's the use of teaching this economics if I don't have faith in it? How can I teach my students who are so credulous? When I'm disenchanted, how can I inspire my students? So I wanted to learn economics the way I feel it should be, the way the real world is, and I wanted to know from the people around. Chittagong University campus is located among villages, it's out of town. So I had the advantage that I could just walk out of the campus and into real Bangladesh villages. And I chose to talk to the very poor people in the village because that's where the problem is: Why can't they change their life? Why can't they improve their living conditions? And I kept on talking—not as an economist, not as a teacher, not as a researcher—just as a human being, as a neighbor. Why do things remain the way they are?

And I learned so many things. I started feeling that this was the real university I missed out all my life. And in my classroom, in my textbooks, I never learned all these things that they're saying now. So among the many things I learned, I came across a woman and she

191

makes only two pennies a day by making bamboo stools. And I couldn't accept why anybody should work so hard and make only two pennies. And she explained why she makes two pennies: she doesn't have the money to buy the bamboo from the bamboo store, so she has to borrow money from a trader, the same trader who buys the final product. So he lends her the money to buy the bamboo. When he buys the final product, he offers her a price that barely covers the cost of the raw materials. Her labor comes almost like free, so she works like a slave. So I said, look, this is so simple to solve. It doesn't need big theories to solve this.

If somebody could make this money available to her so that she can buy her own bamboo, she can sell the product wherever she gets a good price. And I took a student of mine, and went around the village for several days to find out if there are other people like her who are borrowing from traders and missing out on what they should earn. And in a week's time, we came up with a list of forty-two such people. The total amount needed by all forty-two of them was thirty dollars. I was so ashamed of myself because, despite all the big theories we were talking about in classroom, here's a situation where we have not organized our society in a way that well-bodied, well-trained, skilled, hardworking people could get even thirty dollars to do their job. So my first reaction was to take this thirty dollars out of my pocket, and I asked my student to distribute this money to them as loans, tell them that it's a loan and that they have to pay me back. They can sell their product wherever they want, wherever they get a good price.

Having done that, I thought I had found a solution to this problem. A couple of days later I started feeling down again. I saw that this was not a real solution, because when they needed money they wouldn't come to me because I'm not available to them. I'm a teacher in a university, I'm not in the money business. I thought there must be some institutional rather than personal way of handling this.

So I thought of the bank. The bank should do the distribution. When I went to the bank and talked to the manager, he gave me a big laugh. He thought it was such a funny idea even to talk about. I said "Why?" He said, "This little money is not even worth all the papers they have to fill in and so on, and the bank is not going to do that." I said, "Why not? To them this is really important." Then he said, "Well, we can't give loans to the poor people." "Why not?" "They don't have any collateral."

I said, "So what? You don't eat collateral, you want your money back." "Of course we want our money back, but at the same time we need collateral." "To me it doesn't make sense: if somebody can be sure that the money comes back, why do you need collateral?" He said, "That's our rule." He said, "I can't help you. Why don't you go and talk to the officials in a higher position than me to convince them."

And I tried. I moved around, ran around to different offices trying to persuade. And everybody said the same thing: "Look, this is the rule. We can't do anything else." Somebody suggested, if you could find a guarantor in the village for each loan, a well-to-do person, then we can give the loan. I said, "No, I can't do that because then the guarantor would treat the other person as a slave, because he became the guarantor of the loan." I said, "I won't do that." Then I had an idea. I said, "Why don't I become the guarantor? I'll sign everything you give me." Then they were put on the spot. They thought about it and asked me, "How much money are you talking about?" I said, "Oh, altogether probably three hundred dollars, not more than that." And they said, "Okay, we'll accept you as a three hundred dollar guarantor, but don't ask for more money. That's all we can give you." I said, "Okay, that will be enough for me." This was in 1976. But after all this discussion, when I really wanted the money, they said, "No, we need permission from the head office." It took six months of writing back and forth to get it formalized and finally, at the end of 1976, I succeeded in taking a few loans and lending the money to the poor people at the village. That was the beginning of what I'm doing today—but after a long struggle. And I wanted to make sure that people do pay back so that the bank does not stop this procedure, and people did pay back. So I gave more loans and it became wider and wider. I then told the bank, "Why don't you do it yourself? Why do you need me as a guarantor? It's working. You said people will not pay. Now they're paying." "No, no, you can do it in one village, you have your students with you, you yourself work very hard, but if we do it, it won't work." I said, "That's funny." They said, "If you do it in more than one village, it won't work." So I said, "Okay, let me try. So I did it over several villages. Still it worked, but still the bankers were not satisfied. They said, "No, this is not big enough." So I did more villages, to the extent that I was challenged to do it over a whole district. I did it over a whole district. And still it worked. But then bankers were not persuaded.

So I said, why am I running after these bankers? Why don't I set up my own bank and just settle the whole issue? Then I started running around the Central Bank and the government offices to get permission to set up a bank that will work only for the poor people. It took a long time. Finally in 1983, the government permitted us to set up a bank and we became an independent bank.

This bank, now called Grameen Bank, works only for lending money to the poorest people in Bangladesh—landless, assetless people. Today we have over two million borrowers in this bank. We work in thirty-five thousand villages. We have 1,048 branches. And this bank not only lends money to the poor people, it is owned by the poor people. The people that we lend money to, they also become the shareholders of the bank and own the bank. Out of the two million borrowers that we have today, 90% are women. Our average loan size is less than $150.

2

The fact is that all along the way, in the last nineteen years, at every point we were told that it could not be done, and there were very compelling reasons why it could not be done. Whenever we debated whether it could or could not be done, whoever was saying that it could not be done would always win.

But the reality of the situation is not only that it is being done, but it is being done in a way that in Bangladesh you would not expect such a thing to happen. I have been asked about bureaucratic corruption in Bangladesh, and how Grameen's staff can remain honest and deliver the services that it delivers. In a corrupt environment, a staff of over twelve thousand carries cash all the time on their own bodies. Each day we carry as much as one-and-a-half million dollars on our bodies, going miles to our borrowers distributing loans or getting repayments back to the bank every week. So each week our staff goes to 35,000 villages to physically meet—do business at the doorstep of—two million borrowers, and during this time not a single case ever happened that one of our staff came back to our office with torn clothes or a beaten face or something, saying, "I've been robbed." Not even anybody has faked it, even though it's very easy to fake it, and then get away with the money. No way you can prove or disprove that he is faking it, because along the way somebody might have attacked him and took the money. And we always promote the idea that if you are under attack, if somebody wanted to snatch that money, don't put up a struggle because your safety is much more important than the money that you carry, so just give the money and don't put up a fight. It's very easy to come and say, well, I was attacked, so I gave the money and walked on, as you said. But it didn't happen. It doesn't happen.

It is not easy to explain how, in somewhere like Bangladesh, where the law and order situation is not one of the best in the world, people are letting this money be carried in a situation where people kill each other for much less money than that. For a very petty sum people will attack. So this is something to understand, because it is not happening in one village, it is not happening in a couple of hundred villages, it is happening in thousands of villages in Bangladesh.

Why do the staff do it? Well, in official government transactions or business, whatever they do in the government banks, they don't appear in the office on time; they do not deliver the service the way you would like it. In Grameen, they start their daily work early in the morning and continue to work late in the evening non-stop and very hard. Salary wise, they get the same salary as the government bank staff would get.

So these are the things that one has to look at, and the only explanation I can come up with is saying that in helping people, and because of your own personal role, you change the life of another person. And you see it happening right before your own eyes. That is, I think, a very intoxicating experience. You just can't get over it.

If the same person is offered a job in town, in the urban area, with a lot more fringe benefits and higher salaries and so on, if you have worked in Grameen Bank just one year, it would be impossible for anybody to persuade you to leave the Grameen Bank job and accept another job.

Speculation was that if we were looking for staff, it would be very difficult to find staff to work in Grameen Bank, because if it is a university graduate, no university graduate worth the name would come to work in Grameen Bank because he would have to work in the villages. Nobody would like to work in the villages because amenities in the villages are not comparable to the amenities in urban areas. But when we went into it, the situation, we found out it was just the reverse. We got a lot more people than we needed, and they worked very hard. They not only stayed in the villages: one of the problems Grameen faces today, when we transfer anybody from any rural area to our head office, we get a lot of running around and lobbying by the staff to cancel that transfer.

One of the arguments is, What am I supposed to do in the head office? Sit behind a desk? And how can I do that? Here I work with people, and that's a very pleasing thing to me. I work and I see those smiling faces, and it makes me alive. So they don't want to get transferred to the head office. We were told right from the beginning that we could not attract university graduates to work with us to go and work in the rural areas. So at each point everything that people normally thought turned out to be just the reverse of what actually happened.

So what can you do with this small a loan? This was, again, a very usual question that we faced, both in Bangladesh and outside. This is a $10 loan, a $15 loan, a $30 loan. So what?

Again, if you see the magic of that $30 loan, for one who for the first time received a loan, an amount of cash held in their hand, and the tremendous amount of self-confidence that it brings that you are worth the trust of that kind of money, this is a very routine kind of experience for us when new groups start in a new village. When this loan is handed over to a person, she will hold it and start shaking, start trembling, unable to believe that she is really holding such a big treasure in her hand, because she has no experience in her life holding such a large amount of cash in her hand. And many of these women never touched money in their life, because money is a matter for the men to handle. Women don't get involved with money. But this is her money.

I'm sure many of them think in their mind that an organization who trusted her with such a large amount of money, she will never let them down. She will work very hard to make sure that the trust that they put in her is worth it, and they really work very hard to make sure that the trust is justified.

The women who take these loans repay in weekly installments, usually a very tiny amount. When you take a 1,000 taka loan, each installment would be about 20 taka. When you pay that 20 taka, a tremendous amount of feeling goes into it: "I made it." Because everybody, everybody in the village told her, "You will never make it. You are no good." Her friends told her so, and her own life experience told her so, because since the time she was born, everybody in the family was very upset because she was a girl. And the rest of her life she was told by her parents and everybody else in the family and the neighborhood that she brought misery to the family because she is a woman, she is a girl, and she is no good.

Going through that process, now for the first time having money in her hand, and having been told, don't join Grameen Bank because you will create more trouble for your family, you won't be able to pay back, and they will catch you and put you in jail, and your family will be running around to get you out of that jail, she defies everybody and takes that money and really earns money. Now, here is the 20 taka for the first installment.

She finds a new identity for herself. And imagine that woman when she completes the loan payment and pays the last installment to the bank. It's not only in the bank's book that the loan is complete, payment is completed, but so far as she is concerned, she is a completely transformed woman. Now she has started believing in herself and her ability to make it.

So this is the process that one goes through at each cycle of the loan. She will start looking at the world in a different way. So it's not simply the monetary calculations of how much money she took in and how much she paid back. It is the worth that she finds in herself and the fact that she can take care of herself and her family, and her life and the world look so different for her.

So when the staff shares these experiences, this rubs onto the staff, and that is what keeps Grameen Bank moving, and we get inspired to come up with newer loan products like we are doing recently, like we did in the past, the loans for housing. People didn't believe that the poor deserve to get a housing loan. And how can they pay back a housing loan? And we have gone through this cycle of arguments. We understand when you give a loan for a cow, the cow gives milk, she sells the milk and pays you back. But the house doesn't give milk. How does she pay back the loan for the housing?

So we had to go through lots of arguments. We kept saying that housing is very productive because it enhances the productive capacity of the person in a monsoon country where it rains at least four months a year very heavily and usually five months. She can't work in a thatched house or with leaves over her head for a roof. If she has a roof house, well, she can keep the floor dry, and she can work all the year. She can pay back the loan without any problem. Besides that productivity argument, the self-worth again, the dignity that she starts enjoying, living like a human being, brings a tremendous amount of strength to her.

These are the human aspects of the credit operation that we go through in Grameen Bank, and there are literally millions of such stories.

PROCESS

Yunus's story of how the bank was established is both a narrative and a *process analysis.* Narrative tells a story: one event happens, and then another event, and so on. Process analysis is the step-by-step description of how a procedure is (has been, will be) carried out. The key difference between narration and process analysis is that in a process each step depends on the step before it. The first step leads directly to the second step, which couldn't happen without the first step being completed, and so forth. *Analysis* means "separation into component parts," and a process analysis separates the different steps in their necessary sequence.

Process analysis is often identified by the word *how,* as in "How to Bake a Cake," "How to Disassemble an Atom Bomb," "How I Lost Fifty Pounds and Survived Anorexia." Sometimes, to help the reader stay on track, the steps are numbered or identified by transition words: *first, next, third, fourth, then, last.* (See p. 168.) Parallel sentence structure, appropriate time indicators, and unified verb tenses are also aids to the reader.

Study Questions

1. Why did the bankers that Yunus went to in the beginning refuse to loan the people money? Were they right to do so? Did they have a responsibility to their employers not to do something irresponsible, that might lose money?
2. What, in your opinion, were the most important factors in the success of Grameen Bank? Do these factors dictate the success of any small business, or even any enterprise at all?

Writing Topics

1. *Collaborative writing activity* (with group discussing ideas before writing essays). Yunus's description of how he came to start Grameen Bank in Bangladesh is a description of a process that has helped the lives of thousands of desperately poor people. Notice that the first step in his process was mental: he had to start thinking that something could be done and that in a small way he could do it.

    With the group, discuss situations that need improvement in your own society. What specific actions could one person take—perhaps donating money, participating in a community project, or writing a letter to the local newspaper. Discuss some of the activities people in the class are already involved in. Then write a description of a positive, useful community activity that you or someone you know is participating in. Describe this activity in such a way as to encourage other people to join in.
2. The bank succeeded because it filled a need. Think of a time when something you did was successful because it too filled a need. Then use

the process-analysis method to write an essay describing how you accomplished your goals.

3. Think of the reverse of success: Write an essay in which you describe a *failed* process, one that doesn't work or is even damaging. How do things go from okay to bad to worse to disaster? How does that process of failure contrast with those of successes such as Yunus's bank?

Pizza Woes

ANDREI CODRESCU

Congress and people are in a cutting-and-banning mood. You hear this all the time now. Today I thought I'd do my part and try to find something to ban and cut. I see in the paper that a boy in Miami shot a man for wanting an extra slice from the pizza the boy bought for some homeless people, including the greedy man. Charity was mixed up, in this kid, with a heightened sense of justice. I've always been leery of charity for that reason: it's just bait, usually.

I also see that in California a pizza thief got twenty-five-years-to-life. That's not quite getting killed but it's still pretty severe. That's about five years a slice. I bet the man's sorry he didn't go for the poached salmon in ginger sauce with the steamed vegetables instead.

Not so long ago, two Eskimo kids were banished to two remote islands for robbing a pizza delivery man. The price for pizza-snatching is going up and up.

There was a time, back in the old days, when the national food was hamburger, not pizza. Everything was better then. Nobody snatched anybody's burger because it was disgusting eating a burger with a bite taken out of it. It's not like detaching a slice. The burger was also made of just three things, brown meat, bun, and slop, not a hundred different layers of things that can vary. The burger was simple to grasp, unlike the pizza which is complex and multicultural. And while both burger and pizza are round, the burger is an individual sphere, while the pizza is a communal circle. It is astounding that after the collapse of Communism it should be the Communistic pizza and not the individualistic burger that's got a hold on the nation.

The answer is clear: ban pizza. It makes people insane. It is slicing through the moral fiber of the nation like a razor-edged Frisbee with pepperoni on it.

COMPARISON/CONTRAST

Comparison: a way to show what something is like. Contrast: a way to show how something is different from something else. The two approaches work together to demonstrate the nature of a thing or idea, giving a clear picture by showing examples of what it is like and what it is not. A piece of pita bread, for example, can be described as something like a flour burrito, but harder and thicker and with a pocket in the center. (Of course, one could describe a burrito in a similar way, making reference to pita.)

Psychologists tell us that we actually seldom perceive a thing directly, but normally experience a thing within a context, as part of but also separate from its surroundings. For example, a cup will be perceived both in relation to and as distinct from the table on which it sits, and the table is seen as an object unto itself—an object capable of supporting a cup. (Impressionist painters often incorporated this instinctive perception in their work by placing thin, barely perceptible lines around some of the objects and people they painted, forcefully separating those subjects from their backgrounds. Such images were visually defined by connection to the rest of the scene, but also distinctly separate.)

There are two basic ways to organize a comparison/contrast piece of writing. The first method is to describe one thing and then describe the other, with implied similarities and differences. Someone wanting to compare rail and airplane travel, for example, might describe a train trip (comfort, food, service, relations with other passengers, and so on) and then an airplane trip (comfort, food, service, relations with other passengers—in the same order as before). An outline of the first method would look like this:

> A. Trains
>   1. Comfort
>   2. Food
>   3. Service
> B. Planes
>   1. Comfort
>   2. Food
>   3. Service

A second method is the technique Codrescu uses in comparing pizza and hamburgers, showing the differences point by point.

The rail/air comparison might then be ordered this way:

> A. Comfort
> 1. Trains
> 2. Planes
> B. Food
> 1. Trains
> 2. Planes

and so forth. The appropriate type of organization depends on the subject and the specific assignment.

Study Questions

1. Codrescu uses humor and overstatement throughout the essay. Does he really want to ban pizza? What is his true central point?
2. How might you rewrite the paragraph about the pizza and hamburgers to show the superiority of pizza?
3. What does Codrescu mean about the pizza "slicing through the moral fiber of the nation"? (Notice the pun on the word "slicing.")

Writing Topics

1. Write a short essay in which you compare/contrast a typical meal that your mother cooked with the kind of meal you generally eat now. Indicate somehow whether you think your eating has improved or gotten worse.
2. Compare/contrast a hand-operated machine or acoustic musical instrument to a motorized machine or electronic instrument. For example, compare/contrast manual to electric can openers or typewriters (or pencils) to computers.

From The American Invasion of Macún

Lo que no mata, engorda.

What doesn't kill you, makes you fat.

Pollito, chicken
Gallina, hen
Lápiz, pencil
y Pluma, pen.
Ventana, window
Puerta, door
Maestra, teacher
y Piso, floor.

Miss Jiménez stood in front of the class as we sang and, with her ruler, pointed at the chicks scratching the dirt outside the classroom, at the hen leading them, at the pencil on Juanita's desk, at the pen on her own desk, at the window that looked out into the playground, at the door leading to the yard, at herself, and at the shiny tile floor. We sang along, pointing as she did with our sharpened pencils, rubber end out.

"*¡Muy bien!*" She pulled down the map rolled into a tube at the front of the room. In English she told us, "Now gwee estody about de Jun-ited Estates gee-o-graphee."

It was the daily English class. Miss Jiménez, the second- and third-grade teacher, was new to the school in Macún. She looked like a grown-up doll, with high rounded cheekbones, a freckled *café con leche* complexion, black lashes, black curly hair pulled into a bun at the nape of her neck, and the prettiest legs in the whole *barrio*. Doña Ana said Miss Jiménez had the most beautiful legs she'd ever seen,

203

and the next day, while Miss Jiménez wrote the multiplication table on the blackboard, I stared at them.

She wore skirts to just below the knees, but from there down, her legs were shaped like chicken drumsticks, rounded and full at the top, narrow at the bottom. She had long straight hair on her legs, which everyone said made them even prettier, and small feet encased in plain brown shoes with a low square heel. That night I wished on a star that someday my scrawny legs would fill out into that lovely shape and that the hair on them would be as long and straight and black.

Miss Jiménez came to Macún at the same time as the community center. She told us that starting the following week, we were all to go to the *centro comunal* before school to get breakfast, provided by the Estado Libre Asociado, or Free Associated State, which was the official name for Puerto Rico in the Estados Unidos, or in English, the Jun-ited Estates of America. Our parents, Miss Jiménez told us, should come to a meeting that Saturday, where experts from San Juan and the Jun-ited Estates would teach our mothers all about proper nutrition and hygiene, so that we would grow up as tall and strong as Dick, Jane, and Sally, the *Americanitos* in our primers.

"And Mami," I said as I sipped my afternoon *café con leche*, "Miss Jiménez said the experts will give us free food and toothbrushes and things . . . and we can get breakfast every day except Sunday . . ."

"Calm down," she told me. "We'll go, don't worry."

On Saturday morning the yard in front of the *centro comunal* filled with parents and their children. You could tell the experts from San Juan from the ones that came from the Junited Estates because the *Americanos* wore ties with their white shirts and tugged at their collars and wiped their foreheads with crumpled handkerchiefs. They hadn't planned for children, and the men from San Juan convinced a few older girls to watch the little ones outside so that the meeting could proceed with the least amount of disruption. Small children refused to leave their mothers' sides and screeched the minute one of the white-shirted men came near them. Some women sat on the folding chairs at the rear of the room nursing, a cloth draped over their baby's face so that the experts would not be upset at the sight of a bare breast. There were no fathers. Most of them worked seven days a week, and anyway, children and food were woman's work.

"Negi, take the kids outside and keep them busy until this is over."

"But Mami . . ."

"Do as I say."

She pressed her way to a chair in the middle of the room and sat facing the experts. I hoisted Edna on my shoulder and grabbed Alicia's hand. Delsa pushed Norma out in front of her. They ran into the yard and within minutes had blended into a group of children their age. Héctor found a boy to chase him around a tree, and Alicia crawled to a sand puddle where she and other toddlers smeared one another with the fine red dirt. I sat at the door, Edna on my lap, and tried to keep one eye on my sisters and brother and another on what went on inside.

The experts had colorful charts on portable easels. They introduced each other to the group, thanked the Estado Libre Asociado for the privilege of being there, and then took turns speaking. The first expert opened a large suitcase. Inside there was a huge set of teeth with pink gums.

"Ay Dios Santo, qué cosa tan fea," said a woman as she crossed herself. The mothers laughed and mumbled among themselves that yes, it was ugly. The expert stretched his lips into a smile and pulled a large toothbrush from under the table. He used ornate Spanish words that we assumed were scientific talk for teeth, gums, and tongue. With his giant brush, he polished each tooth on the model, pointing out the proper path of the bristles on the teeth.

"If I have to spend that much time on my teeth," a woman whispered loud enough for everyone to hear, "I won't get anything done around the house." The room buzzed with giggles, and the expert again spread his lips, took a breath, and continued his demonstration.

"At the conclusion of the meeting," he said, "you will each receive a toothbrush and a tube of paste for every member of your family."

"¿Hasta pa' los mellaos?" a woman in the back of the room asked, and everyone laughed.

"If they have no teeth, it's too late for them, isn't it," the expert said through his own clenched teeth. The mothers shrieked with laughter, and the expert sat down so that an *Americano* with red hair and thick glasses could tell us about food.

He wiped his forehead and upper lip as he pulled up the cloth covering one of the easels to reveal a colorful chart of the major food groups.

"La buena nutrition is *muy importante para los niños."* In heavily accented, hard to understand Castilian Spanish he described the necessity of eating portions of each of the foods on his chart every day. There were carrots and broccoli, iceberg lettuce, apples, pears, and peaches. The bread was sliced into a perfect square, unlike the long loaves Papi brought home from a bakery in San Juan, or the round *pan de manteca* Miami bought at Vitín's store. There was no rice on the

chart, no beans, no salted codfish. There were big white eggs, not at all like the small round ones our hens gave us. There was a tall glass of milk, but no coffee. There were wedges of yellow cheese, but no balls of cheese like the white *queso del país* wrapped in banana leaves sold in bakeries all over Puerto Rico. There were bananas but no plantains, potatoes but no *batatas,* cereal flakes but no oatmeal, bacon but no sausages.

"But, *señor,*" said Doña Lola from the back of the room, "none of the fruits or vegetables on your chart grow in Puerto Rico."

"Then you must substitute our recommendations with your native foods."

"Is an apple the same as a mango?" asked Cirila, whose yard was shaded by mango trees.

"*Sí,*" said the expert, "a mango can be substituted for an apple."

"What about breadfruit?"

"I'm not sure . . ." The *Americano* looked at an expert from San Juan who stood up, pulled the front of his *guayabera* down over his ample stomach, and spoke in a voice as deep and resonant as a radio announcer's.

"Breadfruit," he said, "would be equivalent to potatoes."

"Even the ones with seeds?" asked Doña Lola, who roasted them on the coals of her *fogón.*

"Well, I believe so," he said, "but it is best not to make substitutions for the recommended foods. That would throw the whole thing off."

He sat down and stared at the ceiling, his hands crossed under his belly as if he had to hold it up. The mothers asked each other where they could get carrots and broccoli, iceberg lettuce, apples, peaches, or pears.

"At the conclusion of the meeting," the *Americano* said, "you will all receive a sack full of groceries with samples from the major food groups." He flipped the chart closed and moved his chair near the window, amid the hum of women asking one another what he'd just said.

The next expert uncovered another easel on which there was a picture of a big black bug. A child screamed, and a woman got the hiccups.

"This," the expert said scratching the top of his head, "is the magnified image of a head louse."

Following him, another *Americano* who spoke good Spanish discussed intestinal parasites. He told all the mothers to boil their water several times and to wash their hands frequently.

"Children love to put their hands in their mouths," he said, making it sound like fun, "but each time they do, they run the risk of infection." He flipped the chart to show an enlargement of a dirty hand, the tips of the fingernails encrusted with dirt.

"Ugh! That's disgusting!" whispered Mami to the woman next to her. I curled my fingers inside my palms.

"When children play outside," the expert continued, "their hands pick up dirt, and with it, hundreds of microscopic parasites that enter their bodies through their mouths to live and thrive in their intestinal tract."

He flipped the chart again. A long flat snake curled from the corner at the top of the chart to the opposite corner at the bottom. Mami shivered and rubbed her arms to keep the goose bumps down.

"This," the *Americano* said, "is a tapeworm, and it is not uncommon in this part of the world."

Mami had joked many times that the reason I was so skinny was that I had a *solitaria,* a tapeworm, in my belly. But I don't think she ever knew what a tapeworm looked like, nor did I. I imagined something like the earthworms that crawled out of the ground when it rained, but never anything so ugly as the snake on the chart, its flat body like a deck of cards strung together.

"Tapeworms," the expert continued, "can reach lengths of nine feet." I rubbed my belly, trying to imagine how long nine feet was and whether I had that much room in me. Just thinking about it made my insides itchy.

When they finished their speeches, the experts had all the mothers line up and come to the side of the room, where each was given samples according to the number of people in their household. Mami got two sacks of groceries, so Delsa had to carry Edna all the way home while I dragged one of the bags full of cans, jars, and bright cartons.

At home Miami gave each of us a toothbrush and told us we were to clean our teeth every morning and every evening. She set a tube of paste and a cup by the door, next to Papi's shaving things. Then she emptied the bags.

"I don't understand why they didn't just give us a sack of rice and a bag of beans. It would keep this family fed for a month."

She took out a five-pound tin of peanut butter, two boxes of cornflakes, cans of fruit cocktail, peaches in heavy syrup, beets, and tuna fish, jars of grape jelly and pickles and put everything on a high shelf.

"We'll save this," she said, "so that we can eat like *Americanos cuando el hambre apriete."* She kept them there for a long time but took them down one by one so that, as she promised, we ate like Americans when hunger cramped our bellies.

• • •

Study Questions

1. Most of the humor in this story comes from the contrast between the points of view of the villagers and the "experts." Santiago pokes gentle fun while making a point about the differences between the worlds, but there is also a darker side to the humor. The villagers really are desperately poor, nearly starving, and the help being offered isn't what they need. Where in the essay do you see the greatest contrast between the villagers' ideas and the opinions of the lecturers?
2. Santiago's book about growing up is titled *When I Was Puerto Rican,* which makes the title of the chapter "The American Invasion of Macún" somewhat ironic. Puerto Rico is already part of the United States. Why does the author call this an "invasion"?
3. Would there have been a better way to teach the villagers about good nutrition? How would you recommend going about it?

Writing Topics

1. *Collaborative writing activity.* With the other members of the group, make a list of actions that would really help the villagers and a list of actions that—though well-meaning—would be useless. You may want to choose situations other than the one Santiago describes, but keep to the idea of "wanting to help someone." Then write individual essays contrasting "what to do" with "what not to do."
2. Think of an event, perhaps one you have experienced or heard about, in which an "expert" comes to tell another person or group—who actually know more about the subject than the expert—what to do or how to proceed. Describe the scene, showing what the "ignorant" group really thinks about the expert's advice. Try to write this scene without moralizing or stating your opinion directly, but show what people think by what they say to one another.

Prologue to Emerson: The Mind on Fire

ROBERT D. RICHARDSON JR.

On March 29, 1832, the twenty-eight-year-old Emerson visited the tomb of his young wife, Ellen, who had been buried a year and two months earlier. He was in the habit of walking from Boston out to her grave in Roxbury every day, but on this particular day he did more than commune with the spirit of the departed Ellen: he opened the coffin. Ellen had been young and pretty. She was seventeen when they were engaged, eighteen when married, and barely twenty when she died of advanced tuberculosis. They had made frantic efforts at a cure, including long open-air carriage rides and massive doses of country air. Their life together had been stained almost from the start by the bright blood of Ellen's coughing.

Opening the coffin was not a grisly gothic gesture, not just the wild aberration of an unhinged lover. What Emerson was doing was not unheard of. At least two of Emerson's contemporaries did the same thing. A Unitarian minister and good friend of Margaret Fuller's, James Freeman Clarke, once opened the coffin of the woman he had been in love with when he was an undergraduate. Edgar Allan Poe's literary executor, the anthologist Rufus Griswold, opened the coffin of his dead wife forty days after the funeral.

Emerson opened not only the tomb or family vault but the coffin itself. The act was essential Emerson. He had to see for himself. Some part of him was not able to believe she was dead. He was still writing to her in his journals as though she was alive. Perhaps the very deadness of the body would help a belief in the life of the spirit. A modern writer has said that "beside the corpse of the beloved were generated not only the idea of the soul, the belief in immortality, and a great part of man's deep-rooted sense of guilt, but also the earliest inkling of ethical law." We do not know exactly what moved Emerson on this occasion, but we do know that he had a powerful craving for direct, personal, unmediated experience. That is what he

meant when he insisted that one should strive for an original relation to the universe. Not a novel relation, just one's own. Emerson
is the great American champion of self-reliance, of the adequacy of
the individual, and of the importance of the active soul or spirit.
Never content with mere assertion, he looked always for the sources
of strength. Emerson's lifelong search, what he called his heart's inquiry, was "Whence is your power?" His reply was always the same:
"From my nonconformity. I never listened to your people's law, or to
what they call their gospel, and wasted my time. I was content with
the simple rural poverty of my own. Hence this sweetness."

Emerson's direct facing of death owed something to his aunt Mary
Moody Emerson, the brilliant and original sister of Emerson's father,
who deliberately lived with death every day of her life and drew
much of her own power from that grim helpmeet. Her jagged, com-
bative prose uses death and pain as probes for faith. "Did I not assure good Lincoln Ripley, long since," she wrote, "that I should be
willing to have limbs rot, and senses dug out, if I could perceive
more of God?"

Emerson had also by now learned to think of ideas not as abstrac-
tions, but as perceptions, laws, templates, patterns, and plans. Ideas
were not less real than the phenomenal world. If anything, ideas
were more important than phenomena because they lay behind
them, creating and explaining the visible world. Ideas for Emerson
were tangible and had force. "Believe in magnetism, not in needles,"
he wrote. Ideas, even the idea of death, could not be separated from
sense experience.

Emerson's own journal entry for this March day was terse: "I visited Ellen's tomb and opened the coffin." They had been utterly in
love, and for a moment, on September 30, 1829, their wedding day,
the future had seemed clear. Notes and letters flew back and forth.
They traveled and wrote verses together and laughed at the Shakers
who tried to woo them to celibacy. She intended to be a poet, he a
preacher. He had accepted a pulpit in Boston, and they had set up a
home that became at once the center of the Emerson family, as both
Waldo's mother and his younger brother Charles came to live with
them. Now, a little more than a year after Ellen's death, Emerson's
life was unraveling fast. He was so desolate and lonely that his
mother tried to persuade his invalid brother Edward to come back
from the West Indies to look after him. His professional life was also
going badly. Though he was a much-loved minister in an important
Boston church, he was having trouble believing in personal immor-

tality, trouble believing in the sacrament of Communion, and trouble accepting the authority and historical accuracy of the Bible. The truth was that Emerson was in a fast-deepening crisis of vocation. He could not accept his ministerial role, he was unsure of his faith, and he felt bereft and empty. He was directionless. His brother Charles wrote to Aunt Mary that "Waldo is sick . . . I never saw him so disheartened . . . things seem flying to pieces."

At Ellen's grave that day in Roxbury in 1832 Emerson was standing amidst the ruins of his own life. More than ten years had passed since he had left college. Love had died and his career was falling apart. He was not sure what he really believed, who he really was, or what he should be doing. He felt the "vanishing volatile froth of the present" turning into the fixed adamantine past. "We walk on molten lava," he wrote.

In the months immediately ahead he continued to walk to Ellen's grave every day, but now his concentration on death was broken and he wrote a sermon called "The God of the Living" and another on astronomy. He reached a major watershed in his long struggle with religion. "Astronomy irresistibly modifies all religion," he wrote. "The irresistible effect of Copernican astronomy has been to make the great scheme of the salvation of man absolutely incredible." He would live no longer with the dead. "Let us express our astonishment," he wrote in his journal in May, "before we are swallowed up in the yeast of the abyss. I will lift up my hands and say Kosmos."

Before the year was out, Emerson had resigned his pulpit, moved his mother, sold his household furniture, and taken ship for Europe. He set out on Christmas Day, 1832. A northeast storm was on its way as the ship sailed from Boston, plunging into the grey expanse of the North Atlantic.

CAUSE AND EFFECT

The beginning of this selection presents a startling action: Ralph Waldo Emerson, one of the greatest American writers and philosophers, lifting the lid of a coffin to view the corpse of his dead wife. How, why could he do this? Emerson's biographer explains that it was not such an unheard-of act in its period, and then tells about the events that led up to the act. The writer describes the *cause* of the action, the psychological necessity that drove Emerson, and makes clear the *effects* of that moment: a facing of reality, and a release.

The essay that deals with cause and effect establishes reasons that something has happened, often reasons that something has had to happen. This kind of writing consistently asks *why:* Why did World War I begin? Why did one particular American president get elected, instead of another candidate? Why did my parents divorce one another? Why do frogs sing in the summertime?

The cause-and-effect essay may begin with a description of the effect, and then go back to list and explain the causes. Or it may move step by step, in increment after increment, to the final effect at the end of the essay. The Richardson selection is a mixture of those two patterns, giving the action first, going back to analyze the basic causes, then moving forward to show a still further effect of that moment at the tomb of Ellen Emerson: Emerson's acceptance of his wife's death, and his movement toward new life and new thinking. Whatever pattern a writer chooses for a cause-and-effect essay—moving from causes to final effect, or showing the end first and then the reasons—there has to be enough substantiating evidence for the reader to accept the writer's rationale for the explanation being offered. The writer's *because* to the question of *why* must be both believable and grounded in evidence.

Study Questions

1. Why, in your opinion, did Emerson open the coffin? What might have been happening to him spiritually at the time? What were the results of the experience?

2. Emerson's action may seem extraordinary and even gruesome to modern readers, but, as the selection points out, it wasn't completely unusual for its time. Different cultures, and people of different time periods, have varied attitudes toward death and human remains. Consider your reaction to Emerson's action, then imagine what you might have thought if you were living in some other culture or during some other time.

Writing Topics

1. *Collaborative writing activity.* What were the causes and effects of your family or ethnic group (or any other group you can effectively describe)

coming to America? Write a cause-and-effect essay on "Coming to America."

2. Emerson went from deep depression and despair to a course of action. Can you identify with him, or have you seen this in someone you know well? If you have never experienced an awful event in your life, try to interview someone, a friend or family member, who has. Write an essay about how people recover from loss or misfortune. What helps? What doesn't help?

Why We Crave Horror Movies

STEPHEN KING

I think that we're all mentally ill; those of us outside the asylums only hide it a little better—and maybe not all that much better, after all. We've all known people who talk to themselves, people who sometimes squinch their faces into horrible grimaces when they believe no one is watching, people who have some hysterical fear—of snakes, the dark, the tight place, the long drop . . . and, of course, those final worms and grubs that are waiting so patiently underground.

When we pay our four or five bucks and seat ourselves at tenth-row center in a theater showing a horror movie, we are daring the nightmare.

Why? Some of the reasons are simple and obvious. To show that we can, that we are not afraid, that we can ride this roller coaster. Which is not to say that a really good horror movie may not surprise a scream out of us at some point, the way we may scream when the roller coaster twists through a complete 360 or plows through a lake at the bottom of the drop. And horror movies, like roller coasters, have always been the special province of the young; by the time one turns 40 or 50, one's appetite for double twists or 360-degree loops may be considerably depleted.

We also go to re-establish our feelings of essential normality; the horror movie is innately conservative, even reactionary. Freda Jackson as the horrible melting woman in *Die, Monster, Die!* confirms for us that no matter how far we may be removed from the beauty of a Robert Redford or a Diana Ross, we are still light-years from true ugliness.

And we go to have fun.

Ah, but this is where the ground starts to slope away, isn't it? Because this is a very peculiar sort of fun, indeed. The fun comes from seeing others menaced—sometimes killed. One critic has suggested that if pro football has become the voyeur's version of combat, then the horror film has become the modern version of the public lynching.

It is true that the mythic, "fairy-tale" horror film intends to take away the shades of gray. . . . It urges us to put away our more civilized and adult penchant for analysis and to become children again, seeing things in pure blacks and whites. It may be that horror movies provide psychic relief on this level because this invitation to lapse into simplicity, irrationality and even outright madness is extended so rarely. We are told we may allow our emotions a free rein . . . or no rein at all.

If we are all insane, then sanity becomes a matter of degree. If your insanity leads you to carve up women like Jack the Ripper or the Cleveland Torso Murderer, we clap you away in the funny farm (but neither of those two amateur-night surgeons was ever caught, heh-heh-heh); if, on the other hand, your insanity leads you only to talk to yourself when you're under stress or to pick your nose on your morning bus, then you are left alone to go about your business . . . though it is doubtful that you will ever be invited to the best parties.

The potential lyncher is in almost all of us (excluding saints, past and present; but then, most saints have been crazy in their own ways), and every now and then, he has to be let loose to scream and roll around in the grass. Our emotions and our fears form their own body, and we recognize that it demands its own exercise to maintain proper muscle tone. Certain of these emotional muscles are accepted—even exalted—in civilized society; they are, of course, the emotions that tend to maintain the status quo of civilization itself. Love, friendship, loyalty, kindness—these are all the emotions that we applaud, emotions that have been immortalized in the couplets of Hallmark cards and in the verses (I don't dare call it poetry) of Leonard Nimoy.

When we exhibit these emotions, society showers us with positive reinforcement; we learn this even before we get out of diapers. When, as children, we hug our rotten little puke of a sister and give her a kiss, all the aunts and uncles smile and twit and cry, "Isn't he the sweetest little thing?" Such coveted treats as chocolate-covered graham crackers often follow. But if we deliberately slam the rotten little puke of a sister's fingers in the door, sanctions follow—angry remonstrance from parents, aunts and uncles; instead of a chocolate-covered graham cracker, a spanking.

But anticivilization emotions don't go away, and they demand periodic exercise. We have such "sick" jokes as, "What's the difference between a truckload of bowling balls and a truckload of dead babies?" (You can't unload a truckload of bowling balls with a pitchfork . . . a joke, by the way, that I heard originally from a ten-year-old). Such a joke may surprise a laugh or a grin out of us even as we recoil, a possibility that confirms the thesis: If we share a brother-hood of man, then we also share an insanity of man. None of which is intended as a defense of either the sick joke or insanity but merely as an explanation of why the best horror films, like the best fairy tales, manage to be reactionary, anarchistic, and revolutionary all at the same time.

The mythic horror movie, like the sick joke, has a dirty job to do. It deliberately appeals to all that is worst in us. It is morbidity un-chained, our most base instincts let free, our nastiest fantasies real-ized . . . and it all happens, fittingly enough, in the dark. For those reasons, good liberals often shy away from horror films. For myself, I like to see the most aggressive of them—*Dawn of the Dead,* for in-stance—as lifting a trap door in the civilized forebrain and throwing a basket of raw meat to the hungry alligators swimming around in that subterranean river beneath.

Why bother? Because it keeps them from getting out, man. It keeps them down there and me up here. It was Lennon and McCartney who said that all you need is love, and I would agree with that.

As long as you keep the gators fed.

Study Questions

1. As a cause-and-effect essay, "Why We Crave Horror Movies" goes into the psychological reasons why people pay money to be terrified. What is the good effect, according to King, of horror movies?
2. Do you agree that "the potential lyncher is in almost all of us . . . and every now and then, he has to be let loose to scream and roll around in the grass"? On the other hand, why not put the same energy into re-pressing "evil" impulses?
3. The horror novels he has written, and the horror movies based on those novels, have made King a multimillionaire. Is he using this essay to jus-tify what some people might call a sleazy way of making money? De-cide whether King is simply rationalizing his activities. Then read the de-scription of an *ad hominem* attack, in the In Focus: Argument essay on pp. 176–77, and rethink your answer.

Writing Topics

1. *Collaborative writing activity.* Make a list of horror-related make-believe experiences you have had, such as viewings of horror movies, Halloween

frights, visits to theme-park haunted houses, and so on. Then try to categorize the "scary" qualities into three or four groups, such as blood, death, disfigurement, "getting eaten up," and so on. Write an essay in which you discuss the ways that entertainment speaks to basic human anxieties and fears.

2. King states that horror movies appeal largely to the young. Do you agree? If so, write a cause-and-effect essay in which you explain why adolescents enjoy horror and action films that may leave adults cold. If you don't agree with King, write an essay in which you give your own reasons for why such films are popular.

Why the Reckless Survive

MELVIN KONNER

In a recent election Massachusetts rescinded its seat-belt law. As a result some hundreds of citizens of that commonwealth have in the past year gone slamming into windshields instead of getting a pain in the neck from the shoulder belt. Quite a few are unnecessarily brain-damaged or dead. Such laws in fact make a difference. Americans in general use seat belts at a rate of about 20 percent; but in Texas, where failure to wear one can cost you not only your life but also fifty dollars, nearly seven people in ten wear them habitually—a fivefold increase since the law was passed in 1985. Having lived in Massachusetts for fifteen years, I considered it—wrongly, perhaps—the most sensible state in the union, so I was rather amazed by its recent collective decision.

But I shouldn't have been. All I needed to do was to look at my own behavior. I have, while coauthoring a book on health, sat at my word processor at three A.M. guzzling coffee and gobbling Oreo cookies by the dozen, pecking solemnly away about our need to take better care of ourselves. I could almost feel the fat from the cookies sinking into the arteries of my brain, the coffee laying the groundwork for future cardiac arrhythmias.

Why can't we follow our own advice, or others', even when we know it's right? Is it the heedless child in us, or the perverse, destructive teenager, or only the antiauthoritarian, freedom-loving adult that says, *I will do as I please, thank you*? Or could it be that there is something inevitable—even something good—about the taking of all these chances?

People don't think clearly about risk. This is no mere insult, but a conclusion that emerges from attempts by behavioral scientists to understand how people make decisions. In part these studies were sparked by the unprecedented demand for risk reduction that has emerged in recent years. How many cases of cancer do people consider acceptable nationally as a result of the widespread use of a food additive or an industrial chemical? None. How many accidents or near-accidents at nuclear power plants? None. How many airline crashes per decade? Basically, none.

We may consider the change good: doesn't it reflect a healthy increase in awareness of real risks? But consider that this is the same American public that, after years of education, wears seat belts at the rate of 20 percent and has reduced its cigarette smoking only somewhat. The widespread success of lotteries alone shows that people do not think or act rationally, even in their own self-interest.

So we ignore some risks and overestimate others. The conundrum for an evolutionist is simple. Natural selection should have relentlessly culled systematic biases in decision making, producing a rational organism that hews to the order of real cost-benefit analysis—an organism that behaves efficiently to minimize those ratios. How can evolution, with its supposedly relentless winnowing out of error, have preserved this bewildering array of dangerous habits?

We are highly sensitive to certain dangers. A Harris poll conducted in 1980 showed that 78 percent of the American public (as opposed to roughly half of business and government leaders) thought that risks in general were greater than they had been twenty years before. The greatest perceived risks were in the areas of crime and personal safety, international and domestic political stability, energy sources, and "the chemicals we use." Comfortable majorities of the general public (but only small minorities of the leadership groups) agreed with the statements "Society has only perceived the tip of the iceberg with regard to the risks associated with modern technology" and "Unless technological development is restrained, the overall safety of society will be jeopardized significantly in the next twenty years."

But the logic of our concerns is problematic. People are willing to pay indirectly large sums of money to reduce the risk of a nuclear accident or a cancer death from a chemical to levels they consider acceptably low. But they will not pay a much smaller amount for air bags in automobiles, that, inflating on impact, will save many more lives; and they will not stop smoking, although this risk-reducing measure would actually save money, both immediately and in the long term.

Apparently, irrational factors are at work. But before we consider them, and why we may be subject to them, it is worth looking at the realities of risk. John Urquhart and Klaus Heilmann, both physicians, have reviewed some of these realities in their book *Riskwatch: The Odds of Life*. There is a genuine hierarchy of danger. For example, the number of deaths linked to cigarette smoking in the United States is equivalent to three jumbo jets full of passengers crashing daily, day in and day out. We have fifty thousand traffic fatalities a year—almost the number of deaths we suffered during our entire involvement in Vietnam. Half involve drunk drivers, and a large proportion would be prevented by seat belts or air bags.

Yet neither of these sources of risk evokes the interest—indeed the fear—shown in response to possible nuclear accidents, or to toxic-shock syndrome caused by tampons, or even to homicide, all (for most of us) trivial risks by comparison to smoking or driving. If you tremble when you strap yourself into the seat of an airliner, you ought to really shudder when you climb onto your bicycle, since that is much more dangerous as a regular activity. As for homicide, the people most afraid of it are the ones least likely to be victimized. And the millions of women who stopped taking birth-control pills because of the risk of death from stroke did so in response to an annual probability of dying equal to about one fourth their routine risk of death in an automobile.

Urquhart and Heilmann deal with this quirkiness in our response to risk by developing a Safety-Degree Scale analogous to the Richter scale for earthquake severity. The units are logarithms of the cohort size necessary for one death to occur. Thus lightning, which kills fewer than one person per million exposed, has a safety degree of more than six, while motorcycling, which kills one in a thousand, has a safety degree of three; motorcycling is three orders of magnitude more dangerous. But they aren't perceived in that relation. In general, people will accept one to two orders of magnitude more danger in voluntary risks than they will in involuntary ones. And that is only one aspect of the quirkiness. Risks that result in many deaths at once will be perceived as worse than probabilistically equal risks that kill in a more distributed way. And any bad outcome that is reported unexpectedly—especially if its shock value is exploited—increases fear.

Chronic departures from rationality have been the subject of a major line of thought in economics, in which the most distinguished name is Herbert Simon's. Simon, a winner of the Nobel Memorial prize in economics, has for years criticized and occasionally ridiculed the economic decision theory known as subjective expected utility, or SEU. According to this classic approach, individuals face their life choices with full knowledge of the probability and value of all possible outcomes, and furthermore they possess an unambiguous value scale to measure utility—in plain English, they know a great deal, in advance, about the consequences of their choices, and, more important, they know what they want. In the real world, Simon points out, no such knowledge exists. Whether in the choices of executives or in those of consumers, knowledge is imperfect and values (at least to some extent) indeterminate and mercurial.

A similar point was demonstrated in laboratory experiments by psychologists Amos Tversky and Daniel Kahnemann, in which people are shown to be rather feeble in their abilities to choose among various outcomes. They are readily confused by differences in the language in which a problem is posed. In one study, Tversky and Kahnemann asked physicians to choose among possible programs to combat a hypothetical disease that was on the verge of killing six hundred people. The physicians favored a program guaranteed to save *two hundred lives* over one that had a one-third probability of saving everyone and a two-thirds probability of saving no one. Yet a second group of physicians favored the riskier program over one described as resulting in exactly *four hundred deaths*. They were, of course, rejecting the same alternative the previous group had chosen. The only difference was that it was now being described in terms of victims rather than survivors. Human decision making is rife with such framing errors, and analyzing them has become a cottage industry.

At least equally interesting is a new psychological view—advanced by Lola Lopes among others—that certain "errors" may not be errors at all. Lottery players can be shown to be irrational by multiplying the prize by the probability of winning, and comparing that number to the cost of the ticket. But that does not take into account the subjective value placed on becoming rich, or the fact that this may be someone's only chance for that outcome. Nor, of course, does it consider the thrill of playing.

But another aspect of this behavior clearly is irrational: people—especially, but not only, compulsive gamblers—have unrealistically high expectations of winning. On the average, in the larger game of life, they also have unrealistically high expectations of protection against losing. Linda Perloff and others have shown that people—average people—think that they will live longer than average, that they will have fewer diseases than average, and even that their marriages will last longer than average. Since average people are likely to have average rates of disease, death, and divorce, they are (in these studies) underestimating their risks—a tendency Lionel Tiger has summarized as a ubiquitous, biologically based human propensity to unwarranted optimism.

While these results fit well with the prevalence of risky behavior, they seem to contradict the findings about people's *over*estimate of the risk of violent crime, or terrorist attacks, or airline crashes, or nuclear-plant accidents. Part of this is resolvable by reference to the principle that risks beyond our control are more frightening than those we consider ourselves in charge of. So we drink and drive, and buckle the seat belt behind us, and light up another cigarette, on the strength of the illusion that to *these* risks at least, we are invulnerable; and we cancel the trip to Europe on the one-in-a-million chance of an Arab terrorist attack.

Three patterns, then, emerge in our misestimates. First, we prefer voluntary risks to involuntary ones—or, put another way, risks that we feel we have some control over to those that we feel we don't. By the way we drive and react to cues on the road, we think, we reduce our risk to such a low level that seat belts add little protection. But in the case of the terrorist attack or the nuclear-plant accident, we feel we have no handle on the risks. (We seem especially to resent and fear risks that are imposed on us by others, especially if for their own benefit. If I want to smoke myself to death, we seem to say, it's my own business; but if some company is trying to put something over on me with asbestos or nerve gas, I'll be furious.)

Second, we prefer familiar risks to strange ones. The homicide during a mugging, or the airliner hijacked in Athens, or the nerve gas leaking from an armed forces train, get our attention and so loom much larger in our calculations than they should in terms of real risk. Third, deaths that come in bunches—the jumbo-jet crash of the disaster movie—are more frightening than those that come in a steady trickle, even though the latter may add up to more risk when the counting is done. This principle may be related in some way to the common framing error in which people in Tversky and Kahnemann's studies will act more strongly to prevent two hundred deaths in six hundred people than they will to guarantee four hundred survivors from the same group. Framing the risk in terms of death rather than survival biases judgment.

But there is yet another, more interesting complication. "The general public," "average people," "human" rational or irrational behavior—these categories obscure the simple fact that people differ in these matters.

Average people knowingly push their cholesterol levels upward, but only a third pay essentially no attention to doctors' orders when it comes to modifying their behavior (smoking, or eating a risky diet) in the setting of an established illness worsened by that behavior. Average people leave their seat belts unbuckled, but only some people ride motorcycles, and fewer still race or do stunts with them. Average people play lotteries, friendly poker, and church bingo, but an estimated one to four million Americans are pathological gamblers, relentlessly destroying their lives and the lives of those close to them by compulsively taking outrageous financial risks.

Psychologists have only begun to address these individual differences, but several different lines of research suggest that there is such a thing as a risk-taking or sensation-seeking personality. For example, studies of alcohol, tobacco, and caffeine abuse have found these three forms of excess to be correlated, and also to be related to various other measures of risk taking.

For many years psychologist Marvin Zuckerman, of the University of Delaware, and his colleagues have been using the Sensation Seeking Scale, a questionnaire designed to address these issues directly. Empirically, the questions fall along four dimensions: *thrill and adventure seeking,* related to interest in physical risk taking, as in skydiving and mountain climbing; *experience seeking,* reflecting a wider disposition to try new things, in art, music, travel, friendship, or even drugs; *disinhibition,* the hedonistic pursuit of pleasure through activities like social drinking, partying, sex, and gambling; and *boredom susceptibility,* an aversion to routine work and dull people.

At least the first three of these factors have held up in many samples, of both sexes and various ages, in England and America, but there are systematic differences. Males always exceed females, and sensation seeking in general declines in both sexes with age. There is strongly suggestive evidence of a genetic predisposition: 233 pairs of identical twins had a correlation of 0.60 in sensation seeking, while 138 nonidentical twin pairs had a corresponding correlation of only 0.21.

More interesting than these conventional calculations is a series of studies showing that sensation seeking, as measured by the questionnaire, has significant physiological correlates. For example, heart-rate change in reaction to novelty is greater in sensation-seekers, as is brain-wave response to increasingly intense stimulation. The activity of monoamine oxidase (MAO), an enzyme that breaks down certain neurotransmitters (the chemicals that transmit signals between brain cells), is another correlate. Sensation seekers have less MAO activity, suggesting that neurotransmitters that might be viewed as stimulants may persist longer in their brains. Finally, the sex hormones, testosterone and estrogen, show higher levels in sensation seekers.

But in addition this paper-and-pencil test score correlates with real behavior. High scores engage in more frequent, more promiscuous, and more unusual sex; consume more drugs, alcohol, cigarettes, and even spicy food; volunteer more for experiments and other unusual activities; gamble more; and court more physical danger. In the realm of the abnormal, the measure is correlated with hypomania, and in the realm of the criminal, with psychopathy.

In other words, something measured by this test has both biological and practical significance. Furthermore, independent studies by Frank Farley and his colleagues at the University of Wisconsin, using a different instrument and a somewhat distinct measure they call thrill seeking, have confirmed and extended these findings. For example, in prison populations fighting and escape attempts are higher in those who score high on thrill seeking. But Farley also emphasizes positive outcomes—a well-established correlation between sensation seeking and the extraverted personality underscores the possibility that some such people are well primed for leadership.

We can now return to the main question: how could all this irrationality have been left untouched by natural selection? Herbert Simon, in an accessible, even lyrical, summary of his thought, the 1983 book *Reason in Human Affairs,* surprised some of us in anthropology and biology who are more or less constantly railing against the un-Darwinian musings of social scientists. He shows a quite incisive understanding of Darwin's theories and of very recent significant refinements of them.

But my own anthropological heart was most warmed by passages such as this one: "If this [situation] is not wholly descriptive of the world we live in today . . . it certainly describes the world in which human rationality evolved: the world of the cavemen's ancestors, and of the cavemen themselves. In that world . . . periodically action had to be taken to deal with hunger, or to flee danger, or to secure protection against the coming winter. Rationality could focus on dealing with one or a few problems at a time. . . ." The appeal to the world of our ancestors, the hunters and gatherers, is as explicit as I could wish. As Simon recognizes, this is the world in which our rationality, limited as it is, evolved. It could not be much better now than it needed to be then, because less perfect rationality would not have been selected against; and we, the descendants of those hunters and gatherers, would have inherited their imperfections.

The result is what Simon calls "bounded rationality"—a seat-of-the-pants, day-by-day sort of problem solving that, far from pretending to assess all possible outcomes against a clear spectrum of values, attempts no more than to get by. "Putting out fires" is another way of describing it; and it follows directly from the concept of economic behavior that made Simon famous: "satisficing," the notion that people are just trying to solve the problem at hand in a way that is "good enough"—his practical answer to those too-optimistic constructions of economists, "maximizing" and "optimizing."

Simon has perceived that the basic human environment did not call for optimal decision making, in the modern risk-benefit sense of the phrase; thus our imperfection, this "bounded rationality." But this does not explain the systematic departures from rationality—the preference for "controllable" or familiar rather than "uncontrollable" or strange risks, or the particular fear attached to large disasters. And it does not explain, especially, the sense of invulnerability of risk takers. Certain kinds of recklessness are easy to handle by looking at the specific evolutionary provenance of certain motives. Kristin Luker, a sociologist at the University of California at San Diego, studied contraceptive risk taking and uncovered what often seemed an unconscious desire for a baby. It is no challenge to reconcile this with evolutionary theory; a Darwinian couple ought to take such risks right and left. Sexual indiscretions in general could be covered by a similar line of argument: sexy sensation seekers perpetuate their genes. Slightly more interesting are the specific risks involved in certain human culinary preferences. We overdo it on fats and sweets because our ancestors were rewarded for such excesses with that inch of insulation needed to carry them through shortages. Death by atherosclerosis may be a pervasive threat today, but for most of the past three million years it was a consummation devoutly to be wished.

But we are still far from the comprehensive explanation of recklessness we need. For this we must look to the darker side of human nature, as expressed in that same ancestral environment. Martin Daly and Margo Wilson, both psychologists at McMaster University in Ontario, explore this matter directly in a book called *Homicide*. Although their analysis is restricted to only one highly dramatic form of risk taking, it is paradigmatic of the problem.

Homicides occur in all human societies, and a frequent cause is a quarrel over something seemingly trivial—an insult, a misunderstanding, a disagreement about a fact neither combatant cares about. Of course, these conflicts are never *really* trivial; they are about status and honor—which in practical terms means whether and how much you can be pushed around. And on this will depend your access to food, land, women (the participants are almost always male)—in short, most of what matters in life and in natural selection. In societies where heads are hunted or coups counted, the process is more formalized, but the principle is similar.

If you simulate, as Daly and Wilson do, a series of fights in which individuals with different risk propensities—low, medium, and high—encounter each other, the high-risk individuals invariably have the highest mortality. But any assumption that winning increases Darwinian fitness—virtually certain to be correct in most environments—leads to predominance of high- or medium-risk individuals. Their candles burn at both ends, but they leave more genes.

The underlying assumption is that the environment is a dangerous one, but this assumption is sensible. The environments of our ancestors must have been full of danger. "Nothing ventured, nothing gained" must have been a cardinal rule; and yet venturing meant exposure to grave risk: fire, heights, cold, hunger, predators, human enemies. And all this risk has to be seen against a background of mortality from causes outside of human control—especially disease. With an average life expectancy at birth of thirty years, with a constant high probability of dying from pneumonia or malaria—the marginal utility, in economic terms, of strict avoidance of danger would have been much lower than it is now, perhaps negligible. In Oscar Lewis's studies of the Mexican "culture of poverty" and in Eliot Liebow's studies of poor black street-corner men, the point is clearly made: the failure of such people to plan for the future is not irrational—they live for the day because they know that they have no future.

To die, in Darwinian terms, is not to lose the game. Individuals risk or sacrifice their lives for their kin. Sacrifice for offspring is ubiquitous in the animal world, and the examples of maternal defense of the young in mammals and male death in the act of copulation in insects have become familiar. But great risks are taken and sacrifices made for other relatives as well. Consider the evisceration of the worker honeybee in the act of stinging an intruder and the alarm call of a bird or ground squirrel, calling the predator's attention to itself while warning its relatives. During our own evolution small, kin-based groups might have gained much from having a minority of reckless sensation seekers in the ranks—people who wouldn't hesitate to snatch a child from a pack of wild dogs or to fight an approaching grass fire with a counterfire.

In any case, both sensation seekers and people in general should have taken their risks selectively. They may have found it advantageous to take risks with the seemingly controllable and familiar, even while exaggerating the risk of the unknown, and hedging it around with all sorts of taboo and ritual. It is difficult to imagine a success-ful encounter with a volcano, but an early human would have had at least a fighting chance against a lion. And we, their descendants, fear toxic nuclear waste but leave our seat belts unbuckled.

Why can't we adjust our personal behavior to our modern middle-class spectrum of risks? Because we are just not built to cut it that finely. We are not designed for perfectly rational calculations, or to calibrate such relatively unimpressive risks. For many of us, life seems compromised by such calculations; they too have a cost—in ef-fort, in freedom, in self-image, in fun. And the fun is not incidental. It is evolution's way of telling us what we were designed for.

Sensation seeking fulfills two of the three cardinal criteria for evo-lution by natural selection: it varies in the population, and the vari-eties are to some extent inheritable. In any situation in which the va-rieties give rise in addition to different numbers of offspring, evolution will occur. The notion that riskier types, because they suf-fer higher mortality, must slowly disappear is certainly wrong for many environments, and it may still be wrong even for ours.

Ideally, of course, one would want a human organism that could take the risks that—despite the dangers—enhance fitness, and leave aside the risks that don't. But life and evolution are not that perfect. The result of the vastly long evolutionary balancing act is a most im-perfect organism. The various forms of personal risk taking often hang together; you probably can't be the sort of person who makes sure to maintain perfectly safe and healthy habits, and yet reflexively take the risks needed to ensure survival and reproductive success in the basic human environment. If you are designed, emotionally, for survival and reproduction, then you are not designed for perfect safety.

So when my father buckles his seat belt behind him, and my brother keeps on smoking, and my friend rides her motorcycle to work every day, it isn't because, or only because, they somewhat underestimate the risks. My father wants the full sense of compe-tence and freedom that he has always had in driving, since long be-fore seat belts were dreamed of. My brother wants the sense of calm that comes out of the cigarette. My friend wants to hear the roar of the Harley and feel the wind in her hair. And they want the risk, be-cause risk taking, for them, is part of being alive.

As for me, when I avoid those risks, I feel safe and virtuous but perhaps a little cramped. And I suspect that, like many people who watch their diet carefully—despite the lapses—and exercise more or less scrupulously and buckle up religiously, I am a little obsessed with immortality, with the prospect of controlling that which cannot be controlled. I know I am doing the sensible thing—my behavior matches, most of the time, the spectrum of real probabilities. But against what scale of value? I sometimes think that the more reckless among us may have something to teach the careful about the sort of immortality that comes from living fully every day.

COHERENCE

IN FOCUS

Coherence is the quality that holds an essay together and provides connections between and among the various elements, hooking up concepts so that the reader can follow the winding, moving train of the writer's thought. Coherence ensures that the reader doesn't get lost in the turns.

The pattern of organization of the essay is one important means of achieving coherence, for when ideas and points are all in their proper places the reader can follow easily from one to another. Organization provides the overall map of what is coming and helps the reader distinguish more-important points from lesser. A second way to achieve coherence is to clue the reader by the use of transition words and phrases, such as *next, finally, afterward, in addition, however,* and *furthermore.* Numbering major points also keeps them clear and separate—words such as *first, second, third,* and *last* provide helpful transitions. (A complete list of transition words is available in any grammar handbook.)

Another means of keeping the reader on track by keeping the essay coherent is to repeat key ideas, usually phrasing them slightly differently each time. For example, notice how often Konner repeats the word *risk* in his essay, reminding the readers of the subject. (Remember that too much repetition of the same word or phrase is counterproductive; repetition has to be used judiciously.) Notice how the first sentence in the eleventh paragraph repeats the point the author has made in the paragraphs just before: "Urquhart and Heilmann deal with this *quirkiness in our response to risk*" (italics added).

One way of understanding coherence is to examine what happens when it is absent, when a person is called "incoherent." For one reason or another, the incoherent person (often ill or under severe mental or emotional stress) expresses thoughts in disjointed, unrelated ways. Listeners cannot follow what he or she is saying, or understand a story he or she is telling, because of the great leaps between points. Although the story may seem clear to the speaker, who is mentally filling in the gaps, because the speaker is not communicating that same information the listeners are at a loss. To prevent such a breakdown in the coherence of your essay, place yourself in the position of your reader. Reconsider the organization, check that points are placed in their proper order, and use transition words and phrases as aids to the reader.

Study Questions

1. Examine the ways that Konner achieves coherence in his essay. How does the organization help the reader move through the essay? Where are the transition words and phrases? Where are points numbered in order? How are key words and phrases repeated in the topic sentences of following paragraphs?
2. What, according to Konner, explains people's being afraid of risks that aren't really very frequent (such as airplane crashes), while apparently ignoring proven dangers (cancer from smoking)? What is the general rule about how people perceive risks?
3. The basic paradox that Konner mulls over is that, in evolutionary terms, risk-taking behavior should not exist in human beings, as risk takers should have died early and therefore not passed on this trait. However, humans still exhibit this behavior. Why has it been retained? What positive things does risk-taking behavior offer human beings?

Writing Topics

1. *Collaborative writing activity* (with members of the group sharing their interviews). Interview people about their fears and their attitudes toward those fears, then compare your results with Konner's. Write an essay in which you present your results and relate them to why people develop certain fears and ignore other dangers.
2. Examine the paradoxes in your own life or that of someone you know well. Do you drink diet soda and eat potato chips at the same time? Do you fear flying but neglect to wear seat belts in cars? Proceed from those personal contradictions to paradoxes you perceive in society at large: for example, some states currently spend more money building jails than they do building schools. Write an essay on the paradoxes and contradictions in modern life.

Critical Thought

Critical Thinking in Focus

The key mind-sets of an advanced thinker are independence of thought and respect for evidence. These are the attributes of the scientist and the creative spirit, the critic and the good citizen. The cultivation of these two mental attitudes is probably the most basic, crucial function of a college education.

Independence of thought requires not only challenging other people's opinions but also questioning one's own conclusions. It demands that one face each experience with an open mind rather than relying on what has gone before—either the beliefs of others or the answers one has already reached and now clings to. The selections in this chapter all demonstrate such critical, independent thinking on the parts of the writers and demand it of readers as well.

The In Focus essays address the skills employed by critical, thoughtful writers and readers. Following a general discussion of the process of critical analysis are discussions of its particulars: ways of identifying the problem, of moving back and forth between specific points and general ideas, of citing evidence and authorities, of developing an argument in the classical manner, of dealing with satire, and of using deductive and inductive patterns of thought. Each In Focus essay explains how the writer of the selection employs a particular aspect of critical thinking to develop an effective argument.

The Readings in Focus

Independence of thought often requires an ability to become mentally unstuck, to reexamine the ideas one has previously held and to change what is no longer useful. For example, David Ehrenfeld's "Adaptation" examines a view that thousands of people drive past every day, working from his own personal experience to a broader picture, and shows how a critical approach can have positive effects. His essay is followed by Umberto Eco's "How to Speak of Animals" and Lani Guinier's "The Tyranny of the Majority," essays that present and defend ideas that are different from the ordinary, accepted views.

Jeremy Iggers's "Innocence Lost: Our Complicated Relationship with Food" challenges the reader to reconsider myths, habits, and lifelong patterns. Both the Iggers essay and Harry Stein's "Ah, Sweet Vengeance!", which follows it, are examples of looking at an issue in a different light, of looking to the real heart of a problem and finding the challenge it presents. Stein, in particular, demonstrates how a specific incident presented at the start can serve to illustrate a general conclusion; he also shows how thinking critically about an issue, in this case revenge, allows people to explore the possible solutions.

After independence of thought, the second most important critical faculty is a willingness to search for the facts. Respect for evidence begins by separating fact from opinion, information from attitude. When the critical mind is not in operation, a person tends to think his or her ideas are universal and operates on prejudgments, prejudices, without investigation. Each small conclusion becomes a rock, a mountain, a world—unassailable. Such a person is likely to deliver opinions without investigating first, without listening carefully to the other side.

In order to really respect a particular bit of evidence, of course, one might first need to find it and then use it. Do the facts obtained fit this particular case? What is the source—that is, where are the facts from? Is the expert really an expert? What is the expert's motivation? (Is this authority really an objective searcher for truth, or is there a hidden motive, as when an athlete or movie star is paid to advertise a product?) The next three essays model ways to deal with evidence: where to get it, how to apply it, how to get expert advice on an issue, and then how to use and quote those experts in writing. David C. Anderson's "The Crime Funnel" demonstrates the use of statistical figures and numbers, while Gina Kolata's "Should Children Be Told If Genes Predict Illness?" uses the varying opinions of experts in the fields of psychology and medicine. Anna Quindlen's "The Great White Myth" demonstrates how factual evidence and emotional appeal can be combined into an effective argument, thus challenging readers to separate opinion from evidence.

Much of critical analysis consists of considering how a problem came into being, so that effective solutions can be developed. Michael Nelson's "Politics as a Vital, Sometimes Noble, Human Activity" and Marty Klein's "Erotophobia: The Cruelest Abuse of All" both demonstrate how a damaging situation can be approached by analyzing the causes that brought it about.

To demonstrate how nearly universal effective forms of critical thinking can be, an In Focus essay on the patterns of classical argument derived from ancient Roman orators is paired with " 'Friend and Brother . . . ,' " an oration presented in 1805 by Otetiani, the great Native American known as "Chief Red Jacket." The selection that follows, Jonathan Swift's "A Modest Proposal," of 1729, satirically copies the classical pattern of argument while kicking its readers into critical thought.

As "A Modest Proposal" illustrates, sometimes the shock of an outrageous approach—or even just the power of a compelling thesis—is enough to break through a wall of solidified attitudes. Barbara Ehrenreich's "Kiss Me, I'm Gay" manages—she hopes—to offend practically everybody, and by offending, to get people thinking. Pattiann Rogers's "Animals and People: 'The Human Heart in Conflict with Itself' " also aims to provoke thought, in this case through a long, critical look at things people tend to take for granted.

Adaptation

DAVID EHRENFELD

> **adapt** (ə`dæpt) v. **2.** *intr. & refl.* [to]
> become adjusted to new conditions.
> —*The Oxford Modern
> English Dictionary*

When my wife Joan and I were newly married, we lived in a north Jersey suburb not far from the New York state line. Every weekday morning we drove down the Palisades Interstate Parkway to the George Washington Bridge and crossed the Hudson River to Manhattan, where we worked. The parkway runs along the Palisades, a magnificent, igneous bluff that flanks the west bank of the Hudson, facing, on the far shore, Yonkers, the Riverdale section of the Bronx, and Manhattan. Wooded parkland extends on either side of the road for its entire length until just before the approach to the bridge, where many lanes of superhighway converge on the toll booths. We loved the woods along the parkway—they calmed us before our immersion in the chaotic city, and soothed us when we left it at the end of the day.

That was before we went on our honeymoon, a three-week hike on the Appalachian Trail (interspersed with some hitchhiking on country roads), from Springer Mountain, Georgia, to the border of the Great Smokies, in North Carolina. The forest we walked through was a mixture of tall pines and an incredible variety of native hardwoods—an experience of natural diversity that was overwhelming. Nearly every tree we saw was new to us, yet we could feel the pattern and cohesiveness of the forest as a whole. Rhododendrons formed a closed canopy over our heads, fragmenting the June sunshine into a softly shifting mosaic of dappled patches. We stepped on a carpet of rhododendron petals.

The trip was over all too quickly. The plane carrying us back descended through a dense inversion layer of black smog before touching down on the runway at Newark. Home. We were depressed and silent. The ride from Newark Airport to our house took us on the Palisades Parkway. For the first time, we noticed that the woods along the parkway were dominated by thin, ungainly *Ailanthus,* with their coarse (and, we knew, rank-smelling) foliage, and by other weedy species such as the lanky *Paulownia.* Suddenly, these exotic species seemed very much out of place. The second-growth forest looked raw, monotonous, and badly assembled. We grew more depressed. It took about a month before the Appalachian memory faded and we became adapted once again to the Palisades parkland. Then the *Ailanthus* disappeared into the leafy background, the flowers of the *Paulownia* gave a welcome splash of purple against the green, and the disrupted state of the forest strip was all but invisible to us after the days in Manhattan.

I have described a very conservative, even beneficial example of adaptation. Although I drive the Palisades Parkway infrequently now, I'm glad it's there and grateful to those who created it and maintain it. But what about our other adaptations, the majority of them, the thousands of small and large adjustments that we make to the changes that technology and crowding are imposing on us and our surroundings?

My teacher, the great naturalist Archie Carr, once remarked (I think that he was quoting someone, perhaps Aldo Leopold) "Someday we will all learn to love gas stations." In a similar vein, while musing about the question "What will be pleasant in [the year] 3000?" he wrote in 1964 in the preface to his book *Ulendo:*

> Our race is frighteningly malleable. *Adaptable* we would rather call it. Already masses of people have been conditioned to processed cheese, to bread that I think is made of plastic foam, and to gaudy fruits from which all taste has been jettisoned. . . . People can be made not just to live shoulder-to-shoulder in tiers, but to enjoy living that way.

Orwell said pretty much the same thing in the final pages of *The Road to Wigan Pier,* first published in 1937. He attributed the worst adaptations in modern life to "the decay of taste" caused by our acceptance of and demand for more machine-made articles, and by our consequent distancing of ourselves from nature. "Mechanization," said Orwell, whatever its advantages, "is out of control." If we extend Orwell's thoughts, taste—that outdated notion of an absolute standard of quality—may well have been our last cultural barrier against indiscriminate adaptation.

Adaptation is a healthy and necessary process, as the apostles of progress frequently observe, but passive, heedless adaptation is dangerous. Surely some adaptation is needed if we are to preserve our sanity in this rapidly changing chaos of our own making. People who live in large cities, for instance, have to make many behavioral adaptations, such as suppressing their natural eye contact with strangers, if they want to survive. There comes a point, however, when the hidden cost of adaptation gets too high. I can give some examples:

We are adapting to enforced helplessness. We used to be able to fix things ourselves; now working parts are often sealed and can only be thrown away when broken, or require specialized tools to repair. At the same time, there has been a marked decrease in the durability of many products. Yet we have adapted to this rapid, planned obsolescence with hardly a whimper.

We are adapting to less personal contact with others. Synthetic voice answering systems, optical scanners in high-speed checkout lines, automatic tellers, self-service gas pumps, and computer-assisted work done in the isolation of home all take the flesh and blood people out of our daily lives. We are getting used to doing without them.

We have become adapted to the television screen as the source of much of our news, entertainment, and companionship. In other words, we have replaced two-way communications involving our full participation with one-way reception that allows no effective response. Moreover, we have become adapted to the steady substitution of commercials for content in the programs we watch.

We are adapting to less courtesy and consideration from others. This is partly because we are adapting to the imposed pressure of time on all our actions. Efficiency has become the only criterion of excellence. Courtesy takes time without yielding immediate benefits. Similarly, we are adapting to the constant demand for quick decisions. No longer is there time for reflection when we are faced with complex issues. Communities cannot survive without courtesy and time for reflection.

We are adapting to a relentless erosion of our privacy, the contraction of the boundaries of personal space in our business and social relations.

We have become adapted to an indoor climate regulated so that it is the same during winter and summer.

We are adapting to the headlines that tell us that business executives are making many millions of dollars a year even as their companies lay off tens of thousands of workers.

We have adapted nicely to the conventional modern wisdom that there is no special reason for people to live near the place where they were raised and where the bulk of their family resides.

And we are adapting to the removal of nature from our lives and its replacement with symbolic substitutes. The nature special on television replaces the walk in the woods; the voyeurism of ecotourism replaces the joy and toil of the garden. The change of seasons, the migration of swallows, the shower of the Perseids, and the lamentable decline of the dung beetles go by unnoticed.

Although our easy adaptability is not a primary cause of our troubles, it is allowing damaging forces to do their worst with little hindrance. Our passivity to the manipulation of our culture by short-term, anti-social, economic interests is making us pushovers for destructive change. More serious, our children are growing up to accept our adaptations as baseline, natural behaviors. They have internalized them.

What can we do to stop ourselves from adapting to conditions that should not be tolerated? There is a Human Rights Watch that reports on rights abuses around the world. Maybe we need an Adaptation Watch to warn us of dangerous lapses of taste and to remind us of truly self-interested, community-fostering behaviors that we are losing. We will have to speak out loudly, publicly, and often to point out the lethal changes in our environment and rouse the sleeping memory of what we were and the awareness of what we are fast becoming.

In the end, however, the war against foolish adaptation is a personal struggle. Each of us must set his or her own limits of the tolerable—which changes in our world we will accept and which ones we will resist. I drive a car; I don't watch television. I occasionally send a fax; I don't use e-mail. These choices are not arbitrary, although they may be disputed. What matters is that they are *my* choices. I am free to select my own battlefields, to change my mind at will, even to be inconsistent if I so choose.

Becoming the arbiters of our own adaptations often means selecting a less popular and more inconvenient way of doing things. Enormous forces backed by vast resources push at us to adapt. But in resisting we are not without power. We have the power of knowing that we can fight successfully without having to win the whole war, and the power of knowing that nature and community are on our side.

CRITICAL ANALYSIS

Critical analysis requires a willingness to stand back from an argument, to distance oneself emotionally in order to apply logic and reason to the issue. The common use of the word *critical* is in a negative sense, as in "Don't be so critical of your parents!", but true criticism—the kind presented in this chapter—is rational and objective and usually finds as much to praise as to condemn. The professional critic in any of the arts (dance, movies, literature, and so on) often condemns, but far more often finds something to praise, something to add to viewers' or readers' appreciation of the performance or work. Evaluation can be, and should be, a positive process.

The second word in the term *critical analysis* also deserves careful consideration. To *analyze* is to separate things and arguments into their separate parts so that the contents can be looked at carefully. A chemist who analyzes a solution tells what elements, in what proportions, are in the mixture. In logic, analysis is the process of drawing out the arguments and different methodologies in order to take a careful look at what is really being said. To analyze a piece of writing is to separate its various parts: theme, meanings, logical patterns, and so forth. The good critic will look at an argument carefully for examples of poor logic or for attacks on the opponent rather than on the opponent's ideas. Analysis requires the ability to separate logical appeals from emotional appeals, to judge the worth of a statement on whether its parts are valid and whether they hold together in a coherent way.

In "Adaptations," Ehrenfeld makes clear that sometimes it is necessary to get away from a situation in order to see it in a different light. The ability to step back and distance oneself from what is happening in order to see it objectively from the outside is a technique that requires practice and self-discipline. Sometimes distancing requires a trip like the one the author describes, while other times it requires a "cooling-off" period (say, after a fight); an opinion by a respected, uninvolved judge; or even the ability to say "Well, let's take another look." The true critic, the critical analyst, is one able to take a step back, see and evaluate the separate parts, judge the logical pattern, and then come to a conclusion about the whole.

Study Questions

1. What discoveries do Ehrenfeld and his wife make when they return from their trip? What would it take for people to recognize that there are choices in society other than the ones the author says we have unconsciously adapted to?

2. Notice the force of the *series* of examples that Ehrenfeld places in the middle of his essay: "We are adapting . . . We have become adapted

to . . . We are adapting . . . We are adapting . . ." and so forth. Repeating words and similar phrases in a series, or a list, can help the reader to follow, by making the connections clear. It is one of the methods of achieving coherence, making all the parts fit together in the reader's mind (see also pp. 228–29).

Remember that the items in any list must be parallel in structure, phrased in the same general way or form so that the balances are obvious. Once this parallel balance is achieved, the list takes on more force through the combination of its elements.

Can you add to Ehrenfeld's list? Write one or two new sentences that begin "We are adapting" or "We have become adapted to."

3. Ehrenfeld implies that there are different choices for each of the items on his list. We can decide, in each instance, to go another way. For each item on that list, what other choices could we make?

Writing Topics

1. *Collaborative writing activity.* Create a series of examples like Ehrenfeld's irritating or damaging things in our society to which people, especially the people making up the list, have adapted. Each member of the group should then write a short essay on one of those problems, discussing why we tolerate it, what we have done or how we have compromised in order to adapt to it, and what could be done to change it.
2. Examine Ehrenfeld's argument about the danger of human beings learning to tolerate environmental destruction. Do you agree with him? Is there a point or section in his essay you disagree with? Write an essay in the form of a letter to David Ehrenfeld, responding to his ideas.
3. A recurrent theme in travel writing is that the most important things you learn from traveling are the things you see after getting home. Write an essay about a time that you came home from a trip and recognized a truth you hadn't realized was there before. As you plan the essay, decide whether you want to describe the trip first and then tell what happened when you came home, or whether you want to describe the discovery first and then tell how the traveling prepared you for it.

How to Speak of Animals

UMBERTO ECO

Central Park. The zoo. Some kids are playing near the polar bear tank. One dares the others to dive into the tank and swim alongside the bears; to force them to dive in, the challenger hides the others' clothes; the boys enter the water, splashing past a big male bear, peaceful and drowsy; they tease him, he becomes annoyed, extends a paw, and eats, or rather chomps on, two kids, leaving some bits lying around. The police come quickly, even the mayor arrives, there is some argument about whether or not the bear has to be killed, all admit it's not his fault; some sensational articles appear in the press. It so happens that the boys have Hispanic names: Puerto Ricans, perhaps black, perhaps newcomers to the city, in any event accustomed to feats of daring, like all slum kids who hang out in packs.

Various interpretations ensue, all fairly severe. The cynical reaction is fairly widespread, at least in conversation: natural selection, if they were stupid enough to mess with a bear, they got what they deserved; even when I was five, I had enough sense not to jump into a bear tank. Social interpretation: areas of poverty, insufficient education, alas, the subproletariat has a tendency to act on impulse, without thinking. But, I ask you, what's all this talk about insufficient education? Even the poorest child watches TV, or has read a schoolbook in which bears devour humans and hunters therefore kill bears.

At this point I began to wonder if the boys didn't venture into the pool precisely because they do watch TV and go to school. These children were probably victims of our guilty conscience, as reflected in the schools and the mass media.

Human beings have always been merciless with animals, but when humans became aware of their own cruelty, they began, if not to love all animals (because, with only sporadic hesitation, they continue eating them), at least to speak well of them. As the media, the schools, public institutions in general, have to explain away so many acts performed against humans by humans, it seems finally a good idea, psychologically and ethically, to insist on the goodness of animals. We allow children of the Third World to die, but we urge children of the First to respect not only butterflies and bunny rabbits but also whales, crocodiles, snakes.

Mind you, this educational approach is per se correct. What is excessive is the persuasive technique chosen: to render animals worthy of rescue they are humanized, toyified. No one says they are entitled to survive *even* if, as a rule, they are savage and carnivorous. No, they are made respectable by becoming cuddly, comic, good-natured, benevolent, wise, and prudent.

No one is more thoughtless than a lemming, more deceitful than a cat, more slobbering than a dog in August, more smelly than a piglet, more hysterical than a horse, more idiotic than a moth, more slimy than a snail, more poisonous than a viper, less imaginative than an ant, and less musically creative than a nightingale. Simply put, we must love—or, if that is downright impossible, at least respect—these and other animals for what they are. The tales of earlier times overdid the wicked wolf, the tales of today exaggerate the good wolves. We must save the whales, not because they are good, but because they are a part of nature's inventory and they contribute to the ecological equilibrium. Instead, our children are raised with whales that talk, wolves that join the Third Order of St. Francis, and, above all, an endless array of teddy bears.

Advertising, cartoons, illustrated books are full of bears with hearts of gold, law-abiding, cozy, and protective—although in fact it's insulting for a bear to be told he has a right to live because he's only a dumb but inoffensive brute. So I suspect that the poor children in Central Park died not through lack of education but through too much of it. They are the victims of our unhappy conscience.

To make them forget how bad human beings are, they were taught too insistently that bears are good. Instead of being told honestly what humans are and what bears are.

IN FOCUS

PAUSE AND CONSIDER

In a wonderful book on learning to write called *Style: An Anti-Textbook* (New Haven: Yale UP, 1974), Richard Lanham suggests that "every course in composition ought to be a course in Slow Reading. . . . Before prose rhythm can be sensibly considered, one must redefine reading," he points out. "It cannot be a jet flight coast-to-coast. It must be a slow walk in the country, taken, as all such walks should be, partly for the walking itself."

A thoughtful essay such as Eco's "How to Speak of Animals" demands that the reader slow down and stop occasionally to pause and think. We seldom think about the skill of knowing when to stop reading, when to take a moment to review and consider. Although this essay can be read at one sitting, it requires concentration and a willingness to question the status quo.

Essays worth reading need time for thought, and time is precious; it leaks out of lives in a thousand ways. Action tends take the place of thought in daily life, and constant movement leaves little space for consideration. A student assigned to read "How to Think of Animals" may fall into rushing through the reading, hoping to get a quick sense of the meaning, in order to get by. But while newspapers can be roughly scanned over a morning cup of coffee, a literary essay or developed argument demands the time necessary to consider and digest.

Plan ahead. Slow down. Take pleasure as you ingest.

One method that readers use to slow themselves down in order to relish and understand good writing of this sort is to read with a pencil or pen in one hand, pausing every now and then to mark particularly interesting passages or to make comments in the margins. For suggestions on how to mark up a text, see "In Focus: Active Reading," p. 416. As you read Eco with a pencil in hand, you might consider the following questions:

- Where, in reading the Eco essay, was it useful to pause and think about what was being said? Go through the essay a second time, marking the pauses.
- What sentences so impressed you that you underlined them to find later?
- What passages so confused you that you had to stop for a few moments to figure them out?
- How did the meaning of the piece slowly evolve out of the cumulative effects of the language and the play of ideas?

Study Questions

1. In his classic *Walden* (see p. 523), Henry David Thoreau definitively describes an independent thinker: "If a man does not keep pace with his companions, perhaps it is because he hears a different drummer. Let him step to the music which he hears, however measured or far

away." (Thoreau was writing in an era when "man" could be generally taken to mean man or woman; today he might use "person.") Umberto Eco is clearly willing to listen to a "different drummer," instead of to prevailing opinion. Where in this essay does he indicate what most people think? Why is his analysis different from the rest? What is unusual about his idea?

2. Where is the thesis of Eco's essay placed? What is effective about its placement?

3. What is your own opinion as to why the children got hurt? Do you agree with Eco that the way animals are portrayed in the media is frequently wrong and even damaging?

Writing Topics

1. Write an essay in which you follow Eco's pattern of organization: Begin by describing a situation currently in the news. Tell what most people seem to think about it (note the paragraph that begins "various interpretations ensue"), then give your own opinion. Try to find a view different from those you think most people hold, and in the final section of your essay support your view, just as Eco ends with our error in giving animals human qualities.

2. Write an essay in which you disagree with Eco's thesis. Explain the good that can come of personalizing and humanizing animals. For example, *Bambi* helped the movement to prevent forest fires, and looking at "cute" animals in zoos might make people more committed to environmental preservation. Find other instances where "anthropomorphizing" animals is helpful.

The Tyranny of the Majority

LANI GUINIER

I have always wanted to be a civil rights lawyer. This lifelong ambition is based on a deep-seated commitment to democratic fair play—to playing by the rules as long as the rules are fair. When the rules seem unfair, I have worked to change them, not subvert them. When I was eight years old, I was a Brownie. I was especially proud of my uniform, which represented a commitment to good citizenship and good deeds. But one day, when my Brownie group staged a hat-making contest, I realized that uniforms are only as honorable as the people who wear them. The contest was rigged. The winner was assisted by her milliner mother, who actually made the winning entry in full view of all the participants. At the time, I was too young to be able to change the rules, but I was old enough to resign, which I promptly did.

To me, fair play means that the rules encourage everyone to play. They should reward those who win, but they must be acceptable to those who lose. The central theme of my academic writing is that not all rules lead to elemental fair play. Some even commonplace rules work against it.

The professional milliner competing with amateur Brownies stands as an example of rules that are patently rigged or patently subverted. Yet, sometimes, even when rules are perfectly fair in form, they serve in practice to exclude particular groups from meaningful participation. When they do not encourage everyone to play, or when, over the long haul, they do not make the losers feel as good about the outcomes as the winners, they can seem as unfair as the milliner who makes the winning hat for her daughter.

Sometimes, too, we construct rules that force us to be divided into winners and losers when we might have otherwise joined together. This idea was cogently expressed by my son, Nikolas, when he was four years old, far exceeding the thoughtfulness of his mother when she was an eight-year-old Brownie. While I was writing one of my law journal articles, Nikolas and I had a conversation about voting prompted by a *Sesame Street Magazine* exercise. The magazine pictured six children: four children had raised their hands because they wanted to play tag; two had their hands down because they wanted to play hide-and-seek. The magazine asked its readers to count the number of children whose hands were raised and then decide what game the children would play.

Nikolas quite realistically replied, "They will play both. First they will play tag. Then they will play hide-and-seek." Despite the magazine's "rules," he was right. To children, it is natural to take turns. The winner may get to play first or more often, but even the "loser" gets something. His was a positive-sum solution that many adult rulemakers ignore.

The traditional answer to the magazine's problem would have been a zero-sum solution: "The children—all the children—will play tag, and only tag." As a zero-sum solution, everything is seen in terms of "I win; you lose." The conventional answer relies on winner-take-all majority rule, in which the tag players, as the majority, win the right to decide for all the children what game to play. The hide-and-seek preference becomes irrelevant. The numerically more powerful majority choice simply subsumes minority preferences.

In the conventional case, the majority that rules gains all the power and the minority that loses gets none. For example, two years ago Brother Rice High School in Chicago held two senior proms. It was not planned that way. The prom committee at Brother Rice, a boys' Catholic high school, expected just one prom when it hired a disc jockey, picked a rock band, and selected music for the prom by consulting student preferences. Each senior was asked to list his three favorite songs, and the band would play the songs that appeared most frequently on the lists.

Seems attractively democratic. But Brother Rice is predominantly white, and the prom committee was all white. That's how they got two proms. The black seniors at Brother Rice felt so shut out by the "democratic process" that they organized their own prom. As one black student put it: "For every vote we had, there were eight votes for what they wanted. . . . [W]ith us being in the minority we're always outvoted. It's as if we don't count."

Some embittered white seniors saw things differently. They complained that the black students should have gone along with the majority: "The majority makes a decision. That's the way it works."

In a way, both groups were right. From the white students' perspective, this was ordinary decisionmaking. To the black students, majority rule sent the message: "we don't count" is the "way it works" for minorities. In a racially divided society, majority rule may be perceived as majority tyranny.

That is a large claim, and I do not rest my case for it solely on the actions of the prom committee in one Chicago high school. To expand the range of the argument, I first consider the ideal of majority rule itself, particularly as reflected in the writings of James Madison and other founding members of our Republic. These early democrats explored the relationship between majority rule and democracy. James Madison warned, "If a majority be united by a common interest, the rights of the minority will be insecure." The tyranny of the majority, according to Madison, requires safeguards to protect "one part of the society against the injustice of the other part."

For Madison, majority tyranny represented the great danger to our early constitutional democracy. Although the American revolution was fought against the tyranny of the British monarch, it soon became clear that there was another tyranny to be avoided. The accumulations of all powers in the same hands, Madison warned, "whether of one, a few, or many, and whether hereditary, self-appointed, or elective, may justly be pronounced the very definition of tyranny."

As another colonist suggested in papers published in Philadelphia, "We have been so long habituated to a jealousy of tyranny from monarchy and aristocracy, that we have yet to learn the dangers of it from democracy." Despotism had to be opposed "whether it came from Kings, Lords or the people."

The debate about majority tyranny reflected Madison's concern that the majority may not represent the whole. In a homogeneous society, the interest of the majority would likely be that of the minority also. But in a heterogeneous community, the majority may not represent all competing interests. The majority is likely to be self-interested and ignorant or indifferent to the concerns of the minority. In such case, Madison observed, the assumption that the majority represents the minority is "altogether fictitious."

Yet even a self-interested majority can govern fairly if it cooperates with the minority. One reason for such cooperation is that the self-interested majority values the principle of reciprocity. The self-interested majority worries that the minority may attract defectors from the majority and become the next governing majority. The Golden Rule principle of reciprocity functions to check the tendency of a self-interested majority to act tyrannically.

So the argument for the majority principle connects it with the value of reciprocity: You cooperate when you lose in part because members of the current majority will cooperate when they lose. The conventional case for the fairness of majority rule is that it is not really the rule of a fixed group—The Majority—on all issues; instead it is the rule of shifting majorities, as the losers at one time or on one issue join with others and become part of the governing coalition at another time or on another issue. The result will be a fair system of mutually beneficial cooperation. I call a majority that rules but does not dominate a Madisonian Majority.

The problem of majority tyranny arises, however, when the self-interested majority does not need to worry about defections. When the majority is fixed and permanent, there are no checks on its ability to be overbearing. A majority that does not worry about defectors is a majority with total power.

In such a case, Madison's concern about majority tyranny arises. In a heterogeneous community, any faction with total power might subject "the minority to the caprice and arbitrary decisions of the majority, who instead of consulting the interest of the whole community collectively, attend sometimes to partial and local advantages."

"What remedy can be found in a republican Government, where the majority must ultimately decide," argued Madison, but to ensure "that no one common interest or passion will be likely to unite a majority of the whole number in an unjust pursuit." The answer was to disaggregate the majority to ensure checks and balances or fluid, rotating interests. The minority needed protection against an overbearing majority, so that "a common sentiment is less likely to be felt, and the requisite concert less likely to be formed, by a majority of the whole."

Political struggles would not be simply a contest between rulers and people; the political struggles would be among the people themselves. The work of government was not to transcend different interests but to reconcile them. In an ideal democracy, the people would rule, but the minorities would also be protected against the power of majorities. Again, where the rules of decisionmaking protect the minority, the Madisonian Majority rules without dominating.

But if a group is unfairly treated, for example, when it forms a racial minority, *and* if the problems of unfairness are not cured by conventional assumptions about majority rule, then what is to be done? The answer is that we may need an *alternative* to winner-take-all majoritarianism. In this book, a collection of my law review articles, I describe the alternative, which, with Nikolas's help, I now call the "principle of taking turns." In a racially divided society, this principle does better than simple majority rule if it accommodates the values of self-government, fairness, deliberation, compromise, and consensus that lie at the heart of the democratic ideal.

In my legal writing, I follow the caveat of James Madison and other early American democrats. I explore decisionmaking rules that might work in a multi-racial society to ensure that majority rule does not become majority tyranny. I pursue voting systems that might disaggregate The Majority so that it does not exercise power unfairly or tyrannically. I aspire to a more cooperative political style of decisionmaking to enable all of the students at Brother Rice to feel comfortable attending the same prom. In looking to create Madisonian Majorities, I pursue a positive-sum, taking-turns solution.

Structuring decisionmaking to allow the minority "a turn" may be necessary to restore the reciprocity ideal when a fixed majority refuses to cooperate with the minority. If the fixed majority loses its incentive to follow the Golden Rule principle of shifting majorities, the minority never gets to take a turn. Giving the minority a turn does not mean the minority gets to rule; what it does mean is that the minority gets to influence decision making and the majority rules more legitimately.

Instead of automatically rewarding the preferences of the monolithic majority, a taking-turns approach anticipates that the majority rules, but is not overbearing. Because those with 51 percent of the votes are not assured 100 percent of the power, the majority cooperates with, or at least does not tyrannize, the minority.

The sports analogy of "I win; you lose" competition within a political hierarchy makes sense when only one team can win; Nikolas's intuition that it is often possible to take turns suggests an alternative approach. Take family decisionmaking, for example. It utilizes a taking-turns approach. When parents sit around the kitchen table deciding on a vacation destination or activities for a rainy day, often they do not simply rely on a show of hands, especially if that means that the older children always prevail or if affinity groups among the children (those who prefer movies to video games, or those who prefer baseball to playing cards) never get to play their activity of choice. Instead of allowing the majority simply to rule, the parents may propose that everyone take turns, going to the movies one night and playing video games the next. Or as Nikolas proposes, they might do both on a given night.

Taking turns attempts to build consensus while recognizing political or social differences, and it encourages everyone to play. The taking-turns approach gives those with the most support more turns, but it also legitimates the outcome from each individual's perspective, including those whose views are shared only by a minority.

In the end, I do not believe that democracy should encourage rule by the powerful—even a powerful majority. Instead, the idea of democracy promises a fair discussion among self-defined equals about how to achieve our common aspirations. To redeem that promise, we need to put the idea of taking turns and disaggregating the majority at the center of our conception of representation. Particularly as we move into the twenty-first century as a more highly diversified citizenry, it is essential that we consider the ways in which voting and representational systems succeed or fail at encouraging Madisonian Majorities.

To use Nikolas's terminology, "it is no fair" if a fixed, tyrannical majority excludes or alienates the minority. It is no fair if a fixed, tyrannical majority monopolizes all the power all the time. It is no fair if we engage in the periodic ritual of elections, but only the permanent majority gets to choose who is elected. Where we have tyranny by The Majority, we do not have genuine democracy.

Study Questions

1. Guinier writes that "we construct rules that force us to be divided into winners and losers when we might have otherwise joined together." List some examples of rules that enforce a "winner take all" philosophy, and consider alternatives to that procedure (such as rule by consensus, or a division of proceeds).
2. Notice that Guinier brings in two kinds of support for her argument: the contemporary example of the high school prom and the opinion of James Madison, one of the founders of the United States. What other forms of support might she have used for her essay?
3. Does Guinier want to replace "the tyranny of majority rule" with a "tyranny of the minority"? What might she say when one member of a jury insists on acquittal even though the other eleven people are convinced the person is guilty? Are there instances when minority rights must be protected no matter what and other times when the majority should have its way? What, for example, about a highly religious community making all the children in a public school say the prayers of the prevailing religion? What about the one person on a family vacation who refuses to go along with the desires of everybody else?
4. Notice the way that Guinier establishes her stance. (See "In Focus: The Writer's Stance" on p. 105.) How does she indicate the ways that her opinion derives from her work and her personal life?

Writing Topics

1. Write an essay in which you describe a real or imagined example of the "tyranny of the majority." Explain the causes of the unfairness resulting from simple majority rule and offer alternatives that would allow everyone to be "winners."

2. After considering Study Question #2 above, write an essay in which you argue against Guinier's ideas. Discuss Guinier's point and then counter with an argument in support of majority rule as the best means of effective democracy. Try to use supporting evidence as she does, with at least one example from contemporary life and one quotation from a classic thinker. A good place to start looking for the latter would be one of the many books of quotations in your library or a political-science or history textbook.

Innocence Lost: Our Complicated Relationship with Food

JEREMY IGGERS

Consider just how guilt-ridden our relationship with food has become. Today, there is hardly an element in the American diet that doesn't carry some moral stain.

Bumper stickers remind us that meat is murder, and magazine ads confront us with gruesome pictures of anemic penned-up calves, brood sows chained to concrete slabs, hens stuffed in wire mesh cages, downed cattle in slaughterhouses. We turn away but the images remain. The pride we once felt in producing the cheapest food in the world has given way to guilt over how it is produced: over the exploitation of farmworkers; the profligate use of pesticides and synthetic fertilizers; the destruction of family farms, rural economies, and the natural environment.

We feel guilty, too, about eating foods that contain too much fat and too much cholesterol. This goes far beyond a prudent concern for our health and appearance; it takes on strong overtones of guilt and moral judgment as we wrestle with our own weakness, with our inability to keep our bodies under control. And this isn't a moral judgment we impose exclusively on ourselves; it is also a judgment that we make on others, and they on us. To paraphrase Will Rogers, it's no sin to be fat, but it might as well be.

For parents, these feelings are amplified: The Natural Resource Defense Council didn't choose a white-coated scientist to spread the message about Alar, the suspected carcinogen used as a ripening agent for apples; it chose celebrity mother Meryl Streep, to link the issue of toxic chemicals to parents' deep feelings of responsibility.

We also feel guilty for enjoying such plenty on a planet where so many are hungry. As our diet becomes more exotic—mangoes imported from Haiti, basmati rice from India, gourmet coffees from Ethiopia and Tanzania—it drives into sharper focus the contrast between how we comfortable Americans eat and live and how the billions of hungry people on the planet struggle to survive.

It wasn't always this way. There was a time, or so it seems in retrospect, when eating was a simple pleasure, and Americans tackled
it with less sophistication, and more gusto, than anyone else in the
world. Steak was king of the table, but there was always room for
Jell-O. We'd open the lunch box to find a baloney sandwich and a
couple of Oreos, and we were satisfied. If we weren't really living in
a Garden of Eating, we at least had our innocence.

Something happened, rather abruptly, in the early '60s, right
around the time that Julia Child published *Mastering the Art of French
Cooking.* Before Child, food was simply something we ate. Since then,
it has become a core element of our identity. The serpent offered
Adam and Eve a bite of the apple and, having bitten into it, they be-
held their nakedness and felt shame. Child offered us a bite of tarte
Tatin, coq au vin, and *blanquette de veau,* and our innocence came to
an end. We looked at our Jell-O molds and tuna casseroles and Hostess Twinkies and recoiled in shame.

Once this new self-consciousness about food took hold, the rest
was only a matter of time. Food today has become eroticized, politicized, fetishized, and invested with symbolism and moral power as
never before in American society. Only after this climate was established could Cesar Chavez seize hold of the nation's moral imagination, showing us how the purchase of table grapes or iceberg lettuce
could be a moral choice, or Frances Moore Lappé make the same
connection a few years later between our appetite for beef and the
issues of hunger and environmental destruction.

It was also in the early '60s that the eroticization of food took hold
of mass culture in unprecedented ways. When Tony Richardson's
film *Tom Jones* appeared in 1963, its erotic feasting scenes were regarded as a breakthrough. Today, it's hard to turn on the television
or open a magazine without encountering sensuous, glistening images of food—often enlisted in the marketing of such mundane mer-
chandise as fast food burgers and bottled salad dressings. A mound
of whipped cream, a dewy bunch of grapes, a tawny turkey—food
has become sexy, while sex has become problematic.

The increasingly stringent ideal body type promoted by the media
is, of course, closely correlated to our guilt over eating. It's hard for
most of us to eat three squares a day and still look like Cindy Craw-
ford or Patrick Swayze. It's no coincidence that increasingly emaci-
ated models appeared in fashion ads simultaneously with the explosion in reported cases of bulimia and anorexia, and a big boom in the
diet book and diet food industries.

But if it is remarkable how riddled with guilt our relationship with food has become, it is even more noteworthy how much our morality has become centered on food. The word *sinful* is hardly ever used today except in connection with dessert. It would be wrong to dismiss this as mere metaphor: According to one recent study, single women who have affairs with married men are generally untroubled by feelings of guilt; by contrast, many dieters feel powerful guilt and self-loathing after succumbing to a pint of Häagen-Dazs.

It's not unusual at all to hear a woman wail, "I was so *bad* today," only to follow this dramatic statement with a seemingly tame admission like "I ate two doughnuts and a bag of Cheetos." And most waiters today describe dessert trays with the same lascivious smirk a sex show barker might use to describe the delights within.

In part, guilt about food represents a shrinking of the realm of morality from a once-majestic kingdom to a beleaguered enclave. Psychologists have carved out much of the territory, persuading us that conduct we once called good or evil is better understood in terms of psychopathology. And though the war is still being fought, there has been a large popular uprising aimed at overthrowing the dominion of morality over our sexual lives.

So why, at a time when morality is in retreat in almost every other sphere, has food become so morally problematic?

Let me offer a theory: At the heart of this new food guilt is a migration of both our eroticism and our moral focus from our groins to our guts. There is, I'll grant, still plenty of moral anxiety about sexuality, but not nearly as much as there once was. Is it mere coincidence that while participation in the Catholic sacrament of confession has declined dramatically, millions of Americans now pay to participate in that commercialized ritual of self-disclosure, the weekly Weight Watchers weigh-in?

In the Victorian era, when there was still a vibrant public world, the core of personal identity was thought to be found in how one connected to the social world—thus the tremendous emphasis on honor, duty, and, above all, sex, that most intimate and defining connection.

Sex was therefore fraught with moral perils, and immeasurable passion; a sexual transgression was a threat against the social order. Today, it's increasingly regarded as a private matter, largely because there is no social order in the old sense. It's of considerably less interest to everyone, including, often, the participants.

As society has become more individualistic and private, we have learned to express and understand ourselves mostly in terms of what we consume. We take the fact that we avoid red meat or can distinguish a cabernet sauvignon from a pinot noir to be important indicators of who we are, and of how we are different from or better than others. And in a culture in which consuming rather than connecting is the central motivating force, it is only natural that eating has more erotic potential than sex. Small wonder, then, that eating has also become more morally troublesome.

Our first impulse in dealing with food guilt, as with any other type, is to run away from it, and there are certainly plenty of books and self-help gurus who will teach us how to eliminate guilt from our lives. But those techniques of the est variety rarely work, and when they do, the result is a sort of moral lobotomy, a loss of connection to our innermost selves. The Vietnamese Buddhist monk and teacher Thich Nhat Hanh cautions against the Western tendency to try to cut away those parts of the self that we find painful: "Therapists want to help us throw out what is unwanted and keep only what is wanted. But what is left may not be very much. If we try to throw away what we don't want, we may throw away most of ourselves."

A better approach, argues Rabbi Harlan J. Wechsler, author of *What's So Bad About Guilt*, is to develop a discriminating conscience that recognizes when guilt is appropriate and when it is not. Rather than becoming slaves to guilt, we can listen to it, make peace with it, and try to understand its meaning. Some of its messages—like those that condemn us for not being slender enough or pure enough in what we eat—we can weigh and reject. But others may have real meaning for us: Deep down, most of us really don't want to cause suffering to other sentient beings, don't want our standard of living to come at the expense of people we exploit, and do want to live in a way that is sustainable for future generations. And it's no surprise, nor is it wrong, to feel troubled when we feel one way and live another.

It's a powerful act of self-affirmation to take these concerns seriously, to ask how your food choices can reflect your values. This can be a purely negative screening: You can choose not to eat veal, to buy only "free-range" chickens or "dolphin-free" tuna, to eat no meat at all, to eat grapes or lettuce only if they are picked by unionized farm workers, to buy no food from tobacco company subsidiaries. But living your food values can also mean taking positive steps: choosing vegetarian and organic foods, shopping at food co-ops and farmers' markets, supporting food shelves and meal programs, becoming a partner in community-supported agriculture. All of these acts are more than ways to avoid guilt; they are constructive moves toward creating a better world.

But making careful choices as a consumer, although this is important, may not be enough to assuage food guilt if its true source lies in a deeper kind of hunger: the hunger for meaning. In a society in which public life is in decay, we have come to expect that this hunger for meaning will be satisfied in private choices; indeed, the constant message of consumerism is that we can find that meaning in buying. If something is missing, we must be making the wrong choices. Maybe it's the meat. So we try vegetarianism for a while, but something is still missing. Maybe it's the boring casseroles, so we switch to Indian curries, buy gourmetware, and enroll in cooking classes—but that doesn't work either. So maybe it was really the car, all along. Let's buy a new car.

But maybe the whole premise is mistaken. Maybe the key to food guilt, and to our hunger for meaning (and to healing and repairing the world, for that matter) lies beyond the realm of making the right consumer choices. Maybe it lies in rebuilding a public world.

Where the institutions of community are strong, individual contributions to the common good can be rich sources of meaning in our lives: "I know him—he's the guy who organized our block club." "She's the one who got the new playground built." That's what it *really* means to be somebody.

Within the context of a strong spirit of community, even eating and its pleasures can be transformed. Whether it's at a Lutheran church supper or a Jewish Sabbath dinner, at a block party or a family reunion, when we gather together to celebrate, when we linger in the moment, even the simplest fare can seem rich in our mouths and our memories—without tasting the least bit sinful.

IN FOCUS

IDENTIFYING AND DEFINING THE PROBLEM

Iggers demonstrates a process essential to all critical thinking and especially to persuasive writing: *identifying and defining the problem*. The process requires reaching beyond the surface difficulties to find the underlying complication. The real problem with our current relationship to food, says Iggers, is not that we eat too much but that we attach moral values, especially guilt, to eating.

Locating the real problem is the first step to finding any real solution. Many people, when faced with a difficulty, tend to worry endlessly without considering the true problem. For example, is my problem that I can't afford a car, or is the issue really one of finding transportation? Are husband and wife arguing bitterly over the color to paint their house, or are they expressing dissatisfaction with each other? Do we need more jails, or do we need less crime? Do we need more income to pay off the credit cards, or do we need to use less credit? Once the problem is stated in a different way, possibilities for solutions can become apparent.

The process of defining the problem means going deeper into the issues. Questions such as "Why is this happening?" or "What's behind this problem?" are useful. The effects of a difficulty can be apparent, but often the underlying causes need careful consideration.

Study Questions

1. Iggers writes that "food today has become eroticized, politicized, fetishized, and invested with symbolism and moral power as never before in American society." Give some examples from the mass media of how food has been eroticized, politicized, fetishized, and invested with symbolism and moral power.

2. Consider Iggers's statement that "guilt about food represents a shrinking of the realm of morality from a once-majestic kingdom to a beleaguered enclave." Explain what he means by that sentence within the context of his discussion. (*Note:* Do not attempt to simply translate the sentence into your own words—use the context, the surrounding material in the essay, to restate Iggers's point.) What do people feel guilty about today? In your opinion, is the guilt that most people feel justified?

Writing Topics

1. Write an essay describing a wonderful experience you have had with a meal. Describe the food in as much delicious detail as possible. In your writing, be completely without guilt. Write as though you are inviting the reader to join you in an ecstatic experience.

2. In the last paragraph, Iggers recommends that we transform our eating patterns by restoring a sense of community to meals. Write an essay in which you begin by comparing the eating patterns of your family while you were growing up to the patterns you experience now. Then give your essay wider scope: how might shared meals improve families and communities? How could you and your family have more meals that are shared experiences?

Ah, Sweet Vengeance!

HARRY STEIN

Martha had a plan. In circumstances like these, Martha always had a plan. Her friend Jake, a minor executive at the New York office of a film studio, had been maneuvered out of a promotion by an ambition-consumed rival, and Martha damn well wasn't about to take it sitting down.

"Here's what we do," she said, leaning forward conspiratorially, though the restaurant was empty except for the five of us at the table. "We're gonna make a total fool out of the guy. We're gonna make him the laughingstock of the industry."

Jake grinned. "I could go for that," he said.

"How?" I asked.

Martha drummed her fingers on the table. "It's complicated," she said. "We're going to need some help out on the Coast, but I think I know where to get it." And then she presented the plan, a caper rivaling that of *The Sting* in scope. A few days hence, the rival would receive a call from an actor friend of Martha's posing as an important executive at Twentieth Century–Fox in California. The friend would hint at a job offer and urge him to drop everything in New York and come to California the next day. This important executive would add, casually, that the rival should fly out first class, register at the Beverly Hills Hotel, and drop the receipts off with his secretary when he arrived for the meeting. Then—this was the beauty part—another pal of Martha's, who worked as a secretary at the studio, would make sure there would be a pass in the rival's name waiting at the gate, insuring that he would actually make his way up to the executive's office—to face the humiliation of learning that no one there had the slightest idea who he was.

"Who knows?" concluded Martha triumphantly. "With luck, his current boss will find out about it. He might even get fired!"

There followed such an eruption of good cheer around the table that a waitress was drawn over to inquire whether we might be interested in a bottle of champagne. Only one of us—Jake's wife, Susan—remained aloof from the bonhomie.

"I'd just like to ask one thing," she ventured finally. "What is all of this going to accomplish?"

The rest of us looked at her in bald astonishment. "What will it accomplish?" repeated Martha. "It will accomplish *revenge.*"

In the end, thanks to Susan's considerable powers of dissuasion, Jake refused to give the plan his go-ahead, and Martha was left more than a little disappointed. But I don't mean to convey the wrong impression about Martha. She is, in general, a lovely woman—thoughtful, courteous, and as loyal as anyone I have ever known. Indeed, that is why she lashes out with such energy at those who cross her or hers.

That impulse is understandable because it is so terribly human. Most of us have felt surges of hostility so violent, so compelling, that we have literally fantasized murder. There was a period five or six years ago—it lasted a month—when I used to lie awake at night wondering how I might do away (inconspicuously yet very, very painfully) with a particularly loathsome agent who had double-crossed me. I still have to swallow hard when I think about the creep.

Indeed, what I personally find far less comprehensible than any imagined act of violence is utter calm in the face of terrible provocation. The "don't get mad, get even" mentality, that, to my mind, is the reaction that truly runs counter to every healthy human impulse. The fact that it has become embraced as a philosophy, not only by the efficiency experts who direct organized crime but by legions of political leaders and chamber-of-commerce types as well, has, the case can surely be made, a very great deal to do with the unhappy state in which this society finds itself. It is not for nothing that "J.R." rings true to so many millions of us.

But, of course, Jake's wife was right. Retribution for its own sake is hardly a reasonable alternative. Almost all of Martha's small acts of revenge would appear to have been justly motivated, and some of them have even worked, but not one has succeeded in righting the initial wrong. Nor, for that matter, have they served to make Martha or her friends feel better for more than a few minutes. For, of course, they have never touched the source of the pain.

With depressing frequency, the traveler along the low road actually ends up feeling a lot worse. For starters, we *look so* irredeemably small when we're caught being vindictive. I shudder to imagine how Jake would have reacted if the California scheme had gone through and his rival or—Jesus!—his boss had chanced upon its origin.

But detection is almost beside the point. The fact is, vindictive behavior and meanness of spirit finally make us as small as those we despise. Even when we do manage to hurt others as we have been hurt, we succeed, in a real sense, only in further victimizing ourselves.

That, obviously, is not an easy thing for one fixated on vengeance to recognize, for the impulse itself tends not only to obscure better impulses but to stymie logic. Not long ago I received a letter from a very articulate fellow who indicated that he would not rest until he saw an old girlfriend demolished as she had, two years earlier, demolished him. What, he queried in all earnestness, was the best way to achieve the goal? A confrontation of some kind? A carefully crafted series of hate letters? A public pie in the face?

There was a terrible poignancy to this note, not only because it was quite apparent that the girlfriend had, in fact, done him considerable dirt, but because he was clearly letting himself in for a great deal more pain. But vindictive behavior can be even more destructive than that, for, of course, it often wounds those wholly apart from the initial dispute. A friend of mine tells of arriving at her office one morning to find her boss, a prominent magazine editor, in tears. "She'd recently been dumped by her husband," said my friend, "and she was absolutely shattered. But suddenly she stopped crying. 'I'm going to get even,' she announced. 'I'm going to tell our daughter how her father screwed around when I was pregnant.' And I swear to God, she meant it!"

Relatively few people would be quite that candid about their vindictive intentions, but it is a pretty good bet that the editor would not be the first on her block to have adopted such a tactic.

"I tried to get her to calm down," continued my friend. "I explained to her how sorry she'd be later."

" 'Okay,' she replied, 'then what do you suggest I do to him?

" 'Nothing. Just go along as best you can, and eventually you'll get past this. The best way to get back at him is to show him how well you can do without him.' "

My friend, as you might surmise, is a soul of staggering sweetness, and she continues to express dismay at her boss's reaction. The editor ordered her from the room forthwith. Like most of us, my friend's boss was so used to operating the other way—to getting slammed and getting even—that she was incapable of recognizing the elementary truth of that famous maxim: Living well *is* the best revenge.

At this juncture another, more recent, adage springs to mind: What goes around comes around. It is, all in all, a terrific sentiment, and I know a lot of people who would turn handsprings if only they could be assured it was true.

Well, I'm here to do some assuring. The fact is, the editor's husband (if he is as vicious a bastard as she maintains) will almost certainly get his, and so will Jake's rival and all of Martha's many nemeses. They might be successful professionally—might even, conceivably, seem to lead placid domestic lives—but it is almost a sure thing that all of those people are in knots inside. People at peace with themselves simply don't act cruelly toward others. When the rest of us finally accept that law of human behavior, we'll be a hell of a lot better off ourselves.

I am all too well aware that such a view of the world is easier to set down on paper than to apply to one's own experience. Just a couple of weeks ago, I laid aside the beginnings of this essay to thumb through a local magazine of some repute, and there, to my astonishment, I found a vicious attack on the character of a very close friend of mine, whose much-acclaimed first novel had recently been published. Now, I care immensely about this fellow and am familiar with the fragility of his ego, and I found myself irate on his behalf. Not only had the attack—by a supposedly reputable journalist—been needlessly vituperative, it was also, I knew, completely without foundation. When I called my friend, I discovered that he had moved from deep depression to rage and was now ready to sling a little mud himself. "What do you think," he asked, "of my getting a friend in the press to blast the son of a bitch? Or would it be better just to call his editor myself? *I want the bastard to pay.*"

So, as it happened, did I, but for the moment we decided to do nothing more dramatic than discuss it over dinner. As I was leaving for this rendezvous I got a call from another old friend, a guy just back from a long business trip, and I suggested that he join us.

This other fellow made it to the restaurant just as the novelist and I were warming to the unpleasant subject at hand. When he'd gotten an earful, he broke into a broad grin.

"What's so funny?" I demanded. "Did you read what that guy wrote?"

"Yeah, I read it."

"So what's so funny?" I asked.

He laughed. "That you two are taking it so seriously." He turned to our friend. "Don't you know about that guy?" he asked. "For years he's been trying to get someone to pay attention to his own fiction. He's the most bitter guy in town."

This last, I understood, was hyperbole—the town in question was, after all, New York—but the revelation was more than enough to restore our friend's good humor. After eliciting a few more details about his adversary's ugly disposition, he settled back to enjoy his meal.

And enjoy it he did. By dessert he was in better spirits than I'd seen him in for months.

"No more plotting?" I inquired.

He laughed. "Nah. His private demons seem to be handling him just fine."

CONCRETE DETAILS AND ABSTRACT THOUGHT

All good writing balances specific details and general ideas. Without the general point, stated or unstated, emphasized or not, a story or essay has no meaning. We respond to pointless stories as we do to people who bore us with rambling, one-sided babbling that seems to go nowhere. On the other hand, without good detail the story never comes alive, or the argument is unsupported. There needs to be enough detail to evoke the scene within our imaginations, enough point that we can fix onto and remember why we are listening or reading.

The balance of specific and general changes with each piece of writing. Does the writer want rich and evocative descriptions, or will one or two small details—the light on a woman's hair, the dead dog at the side of the road—convey the scene? Or does the writer want to argue the point without resorting to images or anecdotes?

In his essay, Stein explores the concept of revenge and its dangers by presenting specific details of the ways a group of people, in this case sophisticated New Yorkers, think and plan vengeance. A different group of people, such as Viking warriors or members of a bowling club, might think about revenge in different terms—but Stein's points, such as the idea that the satisfaction of revenge would be only temporary, could apply equally to anyone he might choose to describe. Thus, the *details* of the essay could change, but the *idea* would be just as valid.

Notice the kinds of details and supporting material for the general points made in the previous essays. "Adaptation" uses scientific evidence and theory, as well as personal experience, while "How to Speak of Animals" refers to an incident reported in the news. "The Tyranny of the Majority" uses anecdotes as well as quotations, and "Innocence Lost" gives several kinds of evidence. In each case, the author balances general ideas with different kinds of specific support.

Study Questions

1. Where in the essay is the general point—"the fact is, vindictive behavior and meanness of spirit finally make us as small as those we despise"— supported by specific details?
2. Consider the eleventh paragraph (it begins "That impulse"). Which sentence carries the general point, or topic, of the paragraph? Which are the supporting details?
3. What would be wrong with the practical joke that Martha planned? What would be wrong with the deserted wife's telling her daughter nasty truths about the ex-husband? Can you think of other revenge plots that might backfire?

Writing Topics

1. Think of a situation in which you might have been treated badly by someone and then describe the situation and a plan for revenge. Explain what Harry Stein would say about your plan. (If you did, in fact, put the plan into action, tell what happened. How do you feel about it now?)
2. Stein's point is that revenge is something that makes for a good fantasy, but if carried out it will ultimately be worse for the person seeking vengeance. Can you think of any other activities in the same category, activities that may make us feel good momentarily but are ultimately not such a good idea? Describe one. Then, using Stein's essay as a model, give evidence and details to support your claim that the activity is not a good idea.

The Crime Funnel

People in California will not soon forget Polly Klaas and Kimber Reynolds.

A man abducted 12-year-old Polly from a slumber party in her own house, as her mother slept. He drove her away, strangled her and dumped her body at an abandoned lumber mill. Kimber, 18, was leaving a restaurant with a friend when two men on motorcycles roared up beside them. One grabbed her purse, and when she struggled he shot her in the head.

The men arrested for these murders turned out to have had long criminal records, and Polly and Kimber came to symbolize a specific response to public fury: life in prison for repeat offenders, or three strikes and you're out. The idea has swept the country and has been embraced by President Clinton, members of Congress, governors and legislators of several states. To most Americans, it seems like common sense: keeping dangerous criminals in prison longer will reduce crime and make life safer.

But does it make sense? However horrifying the individual cases may be, the use of sentencing laws to control crime can never have more than a marginal effect. The reason is clear from the arithmetic of criminal justice.

The numbers, published regularly by Federal agencies, constitute a big funnel. The 35 million crimes committed each year pour in at the top—everything from shoplifting, auto theft and drunken fights to rapes and murders. Of these, about 25 million are serious, since they involve violence or sizable property loss. But millions of these crimes go unpunished because the victims never report them. Only 15 million serious crimes come to the attention of the police.

The disparity between crimes suffered and crimes reported was a stunning revelation in the 1970's, after the Census Bureau began polling the general public to come up with estimates of crimes committed. Year after year, the number of crimes people said they had experienced far exceeded the crimes they reported to the police.

A subsequent survey for the National Institute of Justice explained the discrepancy. Victims told researchers they didn't consider the crimes important enough to report or they involved matters to settle privately. Many saw little chance the culprits would be arrested or lost property recovered, so why hassle with the cops?

That's the first narrowing of the funnel. The next comes at the point of apprehension. Each year, the police make arrests in only 21 percent of the 15 million most serious crimes—homicides, rapes, robberies, aggravated assaults, burglaries, larcenies and auto thefts. As a result, 3.2 million criminals are turned over to the courts for prosecution.

Why does only one serious reported crime out of five lead to an arrest? In millions of cases, arrests are made but disposed of as misdemeanors. Hundreds of thousands of other cases are turned over to the juvenile-justice system. In many urban neighborhoods, the police are simply overwhelmed by the volume of crime and can't hope to investigate each case aggressively. Millions of burglaries and auto thefts are reported for insurance purposes—not because anyone expects the police to make an arrest.

Further winnowing takes place in courthouses, as cases are dismissed for lack of evidence, because witnesses disappear or refuse to cooperate or for other technical reasons. Of the 3.2 million criminals arrested, 81 percent are actually prosecuted; prosecutors obtain convictions of 59 percent, or 1.9 million.

Now their fate is up to judges, who follow sentencing laws that vary considerably from state to state. Nearly everywhere, judges consider prison space a precious commodity to be used only when it makes obvious sense. Younger criminals convicted of their first or second offenses commonly get off with probation or suspended sentences. In the end, about 500,000 of the 1.9 million convicts are sent behind bars, a trickle from the funnel's stem compared with the flood of 35 million at its mouth.

The process that reduces flood to trickle costs taxpayers some $74 billion annually. The part that has changed most dramatically over the years is the number of people actually locked up. In 1980, the figure was about 200,000. During the next decade, states and the Federal Government embarked on a historic prison expansion binge. They spent more than $90 billion to triple the total amount of prison space. That boosted the annual operating cost to about $25 billion— a third of all the money spent to deal with crime.

Americans may think that the crime rate is worse than ever, but it actually fell somewhat during the 1980's. Violent offenses per

1,000 people declined from 33.3 in 1980 to 31.3 in 1991. Was that because of the big prison buildup? That's hard to believe, considering the difference in magnitude between a few hundred thousand criminals and tens of millions of crimes. Even after the prison buildup, only 1.4 percent of crimes result in imprisonment, only 2 percent of serious crimes. More likely, crime has fallen because of change in the structure of the population. During the 1980's, the number of young people—who commit the most crimes—declined as the median age of Americans rose from 30 to 33.

Even so, when frustrated, fearful Americans hear about Polly Klaas and Kimber Reynolds, they like the sound of prison as a way to give criminals what they deserve. Tough sentencing sounds like strong medicine, even if its effects are often illusory.

Three strikes and you're out? In truth, such a law will probably have no more than a slight effect on public safety. For one thing, the plea bargaining that dominates criminal justice eats deeply into the certainty the law seems to promise. And even if it should be widely applied, a three-strike law offers no hope for immediate relief. It could not be applied retroactively to the existing population of convicted felons sentenced to terms far shorter than life and likely to be paroled over the next several years.

Still, state legislators and members of Congress, reactive as ever, are desperate to appease public fear and outrage. They have little patience with troublesome facts and reach for comforting illusions. But to what end?

Suppose the current political mood generates a new round of sentencing laws tough enough to boost the number locked up each year to more than 1 million. That might cost taxpayers about $150 billion over a decade, or $15 billion a year. But it is very unlikely that an expansion of that magnitude would be enough to change the shape of the crime funnel. Even if crime continued its gradual decline to, say, 30 million a year, the new prison construction would raise the number incarcerated to only about 3 percent of the number of offenses.

These numbers are often seized upon by old liberals who never liked the idea of building prisons. Why pour more money into steel and concrete that don't do much for crime control, they say, when schools, health care and other social programs go begging? Yet politicians know that the public wants a more direct response to crime. For now, three strikes looks as good as any. And that is where the discussion usually ends.

But take another look at the funnel. Its sharply angled shape raises an obvious question: Why just tinker with the stem? Why not see what might be done at earlier levels of the process? For the sake of argument, consider different ways to spend the $15 billion a year now likely to be spent on new prisons. It could, for instance, be divided among three practical measures that are widely accepted as sound ways to reduce crime:

Spend $5 Billion to Hire More Officers for Community Policing

Most police work is reactive—responding to calls for help. Not surprisingly, that hardly serves as a deterrent to criminals. Studies show remarkably little connection between levels of crime and levels of traditional police activity. So why spend money for more cops?

Community policing provides an answer. Gaining popularity with police managers across America, this approach sends officers out to work together with communities to attack crime problems. Are landlords profiteering, for example, by renting to drug dealers? Dispatching cops to arrest the dealers, the traditional response, doesn't work. More dealers quickly move in. To get landlords to evict the dealers and to stop renting to other dealers, community police might help the neighbors challenge the landlords in court, or lodge complaints with a city housing agency or fire department, or even picket the landlords' homes in the suburbs.

Many communities attest to the success of this approach. But implementing it well requires more officers than most departments have to spare. The police still must respond to 911 calls even as they do more creative work with neighborhoods. And some tradition-bound cops resist the idea. But a big infusion of Federal money—$5 billion would pay for 100,000 police—might change that in a hurry.

Spend $5 Billion on Drug Treatment

Surveys of people arrested show phenomenal rates of drug use. In 1990, more than 66 percent of men charged with robbery and 68 percent of those charged with burglary tested positive for drugs. Those who undergo treatment and recover from their addictions are likely to commit fewer crimes. The long-term prognosis for them is better than for those who spend a few years in prison without drug treatment.

Americans have known for years how to treat drug addiction effectively. Yet addicts seeking treatment are often put on waiting lists. A 1989 study found that 79,072 people appeared on such lists nationwide. The figure understates the unmet demand, since treatment programs rarely market their services.

Five billion dollars would pay for about two million new treatment slots a year, nearly quadrupling the existing capacity. With the number of people needing treatment now estimated at three to four times the number receiving it, that could make a dent in the problem. Expanded capacity might also give more judges the option of sentencing drug-related offenders to treatment programs, on pain of imprisonment if they fail to participate.

Invest $5 Billion to Improve Probation

There are more than twice as many convicts on probation—released to the community under court supervision—as in prison. Yet for the majority, supervision is a joke. Probation departments are so understaffed that a probation officer may have more than 100 cases at a time. A few states and cities have spent money to reduce individual caseloads to 25 or so and establish a number of "intermediate sanctions"—electronic monitoring, drug testing and treatment, boot camps—that combine social services with various levels of control. The concept permits courts to intervene at an early stage with younger offenders, creating the real possibility, now all but nonexistent, that criminal justice could actually turn their lives around.

Community police, drug treatment and probation are not the only possibilities. Some of the $15 billion might be invested in continued research and evaluation of other crime reduction measures. But there is no arguing with the basic shape of the crime funnel—or the idea that a shift in emphasis from bottom to top would gain much and risk losing very little. The point of such a strategy would be to stop crimes by the million, rather than lock up criminals by the thousand—to shrink the mouth of the funnel instead of spending mindlessly to slightly widen its stem.

STATISTICAL EVIDENCE

David Anderson is not afraid of numbers, and his use of *numeric and statistical evidence* creates an almost irrefutable argument. The presentation of the figures is clear and impressive, leading directly to his point. Assuming that the figures are correct—and *The New York Times*, which first published this essay, has a reputation for making sure that its figures are correct—his conclusions seem inescapable.

The question of where and how to present statistics is a challenge for any writer of argument. Notice that Anderson moves slowly into the numbers, beginning with the human-interest stories of Klaas and Reynolds to capture the reader's interest. Had he opened with, say, the eleventh paragraph, the beginning would have been too daunting for most readers. Instead, he uses the numbers not for their own sake but to support the point on which his essay is focused: why our solutions to the crime problem have not been working and what alternate methods we could try. The key to this essay is not the numbers but the focused thesis that the numbers support.

Study Questions

1. Draw a picture or graph of "the crime funnel," placing the numbers Anderson gives in places where you think they belong on the funnel. Does the picture aid your understanding of the essay?
2. Evaluate your own ability to understand mathematical concepts and statistics. Why is this important? What loss is there to people who cannot conceptualize what Anderson is talking about? (See John Allen Paulos, "More Dismal Math Scores for U.S. Students," p. 139.)
3. What does Anderson mean, on p. 265, by "comforting illusions"? What are some of those illusions? What are some other such illusions that we apply to areas of society besides crime?

Writing Topics

1. *Collaborative writing activity* (with the members of the group sharing the research). Choose a social problem other than crime, such as illiteracy, alcoholism, or "deadbeat dads," and research some figures associated with the problem. Write an essay explaining the problem, in which you present those numbers, taking care to credit your sources. Create graphs or other visual aids where appropriate. If possible, use the numbers to support a solution or solutions to the problem, especially different solutions than the ones being tried.
2. Write an essay in which you respond to the Anderson essay but disagree with one or more of his solutions. Why do you think that solution won't work? What should be done instead? If possible, find some statistical evidence—or use Anderson's figures—to support your own argument. (Remember that when reporting figures, you must always give the source of the statistics.)
3. Interview two people about solutions to the problems of crime and analyze the reasons they have the opinions they do. What kinds of crime

are they most afraid of? What kinds most affect them? What kinds of promises and solutions do they want to hear from politicians? Try to include in your essay some statistics from the Anderson essay or statistics you find elsewhere. (Remember that when reporting figures, you must always give the source of the statistics.)

4. Write an essay in which you use figures to demonstrate why you cannot live on your present income. This problem can be real or imaginary. Make the essay in the format of a letter to someone (your parents, your boss, some other authority, yourself) explaining why you need more money. Be sure you include statistical evidence and graphs as appropriate.

Should Children Be Told If Genes Predict Illness?

GINA KOLATA

In their fevered race to isolate the breast cancer gene, researchers often discovered, through indirect tests, which relative of affected women also had the gene—and an 85 percent chance of developing the disease. Many of those relatives were children.

The researchers faced a troubling question: should they tell the parents and children what they knew? To the families' shock and dismay, some decided not to.

Many parents argued, to no avail, that it was their right to have medical information about their children. But many of the geneticists felt that the families should not be told because nothing could be done to prevent the disease. Increasingly, the geneticists are asking, Whose right is it to make that decision?

That question is becoming pressing as researchers find more ways to identify who is at risk of developing painful, deadly diseases. The problem, scientists and ethicists say, is that far more is known about predicting these ailments than preventing or treating them. And they worry that the knowledge of future illness could be too great a burden for some children and parents to bear.

"There are many more children that are going to face this issue, and many more conditions," said Dr. Arthur Caplan, director of the Center for Bioethics at the University of Pennsylvania. "I think there will be tremendous pressure" on parents to have their children tested.

So far, about 900 genes have been found that can cause genetic diseases, and the heated race to identify even more continues as part of the Human Genome Project to map genes. A few of the genes—including the breast cancer gene whose discovery was announced this month—have been found so recently that no commercial tests are available. But it is generally no more than a year or two between the discovery of a gene and the development of a test that can foretell whether someone is likely to develop a serious disease.

Dr. Barbara Weber of the University of Pennsylvania School of Medicine, who was one of those involved in the search for the breast cancer gene, said she and her colleagues decided that they would tell only those 18 or older who had asked whether the gene was present. Dr. Weber said she was afraid to give children and teen-agers information that might lead them to believe that "they were sick, that their breasts were somehow or other going to kill them."

But Dr. Mary Z. Pelias, a professor of genetics and a lawyer at Louisiana State University, said it should not be for ethicists and geneticists to decide what information would be available. "The final decisions should rest with the parents," she said.

As further evidence of the turmoil among experts, the American Society of Human Genetics is trying to put together a position paper on whether there should be restrictions on the genetic testing of children but has been unable to reach a consensus. The Human Genome Project, sponsored by the Federal government, is surveying adults in families where at least one person has an inherited genetic disease, and advocacy groups for people with genetic disorders are staking out positions.

"This is what I call the ragged edge of the genetics and moral community," said Dr. Charles R. Scriver, a geneticist at Montreal Children's Hospital. "There are no clear guidelines."

Some researchers have distinct opinions on the subject. Dr. Dorothy C. Wertz, a senior scientist at the Shriver Center for Mental Retardation in Waltham, Mass., and a member of the genetics society committee that is trying to come up with a statement, argues that children must be protected from the information. In a paper in the current issue of the *Journal of the American Medical Association,* she proposed that testing be readily available only when a direct medical benefit to the child could result. Conditions that could be prevented or treated if detected in childhood include familial hypercholesterolemia, which causes high cholesterol levels.

Dr. Wertz said in an interview that she was distressed by the cavalier attitude of many doctors and families toward the notion of testing children and adolescents.

"A lot of people think that knowledge is good in itself, and they also think that medicine is benign," Dr. Wertz said. "They are not aware of the dangers to a child's self-esteem, and dangers that they may view the child differently."

And, in fact, there are many instances where children have been psychologically harmed by testing. Mary Ann Wilson, the administrative director of a support group in Lanham, Md., for sufferers of a disfiguring disease, neurofibromatosis, told of a 9-year-old boy in Baltimore who tested positive for the gene for the disease. That meant that he would develop tumors along his nerves, some of which could be malignant. His family, Ms. Wilson said, "ostracized" the boy to such an extent that he was put in a foster home.

Dr. Joanna H. Famos, a research psychologist at the California Pacific Medical Center in San Francisco and author with Dr. Wertz of the article in the medical association journal, has also seen psychological harm to children from genetic tests. "There is a potential for parents not to be able to explain what's going on because of their own fears and guilt," she said. "Often communication in families is shut down, and children know better than to ask."

But many parents disagree, contending that it is better for children to know their prospects of developing a disease. In a pilot study, Dr. Wertz asked people visiting prenatal testing clinics how they felt about testing children for genetic disorders.

"We said right in the question that genetic testing might lower the child's self-esteem or cause emotional harm to the child," she said. Nonetheless, as many as 61 percent said that parents should be permitted to have their children tested for a disease like Alzheimer's, and 47 percent said parents should tell children the results of the tests.

Families already afflicted with a genetic disease seem to be more cautious. Joan Weiss, the executive director of the Alliance of Genetic Support Groups in Washington, and Dr. E. Virginia Lapham, the director of social work at Georgetown University's Child Development Center, are conducting the Human Genome Project survey. Although the survey is not complete, Ms. Weiss said that the participants seemed to feel strongly that parents should be allowed to have children tested for diseases that are treatable or preventable. But most think that such testing should be prohibited for diseases, like Alzheimer's, that can be neither treated nor prevented.

But Dr. Pelias, who is also a member of the genetics society, said geneticists should not try to influence parents' decisions about testing.

"I view the parents as the primary decision makers for their children, and there is a lot of constitutional law and family law to support that," she said. "We can counsel parents about the possible implications this information can have; we can even try to ascertain how much they understand. But after we have done that, we have done our professional best, and then we should step back."

Dr. Scriver said he also opposed prohibiting parents from having certain genetic tests done on their children. "Disclosure of information if people ask for it is the right thing," he said. "I have encountered families where a physician withheld information from the family. The family said: 'Your ethical values are one thing. Mine are different. It is my privilege to use the information.' "

Nonetheless, some parents say, it is not easy to decide to have children tested, even in situations where it is important to know whether a child has a deleterious gene.

Ann Fagan, a paralegal who lives in Cunningham, Pa., said that she had her two daughters tested when they were 11 and 13 years old for the gene that causes familial polyposis, which leads to colon cancer. She does not regret the decision, she said, but she understands why others might have chosen not to test.

Ms. Fagan herself has familial polyposis, as she discovered 10 years ago, when she was 26 and became very ill. Tiny polyps covered the lining of her colon and rectum, and some of them were malignant. She had to have her colon and rectum removed. "Then, about six or eight weeks later, I realized my daughters were at risk," she said. At that time, the girls were 1 1/2 and 3 years old.

Each girl had a 50 percent chance of inheriting the familial polyposis gene, and each has been examined regularly for signs of the disease. Nearly two years ago, when the gene was newly isolated, the girls agreed to be tested for it.

And when the results came back in March of 1993, the girls asked just one question: were both of them the same—did they both have or both not have the gene? The answer was that they were the same. Both had it.

"Horrible as it was, I was glad they both had the same outcome," Ms. Fagan said. "I am hoping they will be a comfort to each other as they grow older."

The girls have been told that eventually they will have to have their colons and rectums removed, Ms. Fagan said. But, she added, "I don't think the total impact of this disease has really hit."

"I know this is a controversial issue," Ms. Fagan said. "There are parents out there who have chosen not to have their children tested." But, she added, "it is of more benefit for us to know."

CITING AUTHORITIES

When Gina Kolata interviews experts in the field and identifies them as such in her essay, she is *citing authorities.* Notice how careful she has been to establish that the experts are real experts. One common error in logic is that of *false authority:* the famous basketball player in a commercial for orange juice (is he or she really an expert on taste and nutrition?), or the movie star hawking automobiles (ask him or her a question about the suspension system). Just because someone is famous or respected in one field does not make that person an authority in other fields.

Another issue at stake in citing authority is the objectivity of the person being interviewed. Every day on televised advertisements, for example, athletes wear and recommend athletic equipment and clothing. These famous people are presumably experts on the use of such products, but does the fact that they are paid to endorse these products compromise their integrity? Should that fact influence one's response enough to undermine their reliability?

Study Questions

1. Examine the credentials of the people Kolata quotes as experts. What gives them the right to speak on this issue? What makes Ms. Fagan an authority? See if you can find examples from current media in which people are quoted or referred to who probably could not give an educated, or an objective, opinion on the subject.
2. There is a body of law (and opinion in response to the law) regarding people's rights to the truth about their medical conditions, but most of that law deals with adults. An adult, generally speaking, has the right to know the truth about his or her condition. Why does the fact that the subjects here are children make such a difference?
3. After reading the essay, what is your opinion on a child's or a family's right to know? Should children be told when they have life-threatening diseases? What if they do not have the diseases, but have only the genes that give them a strong probability of contracting the diseases?

Writing Topics

1. *Collaborative writing activity.* Find an issue about which you can interview at least two authorities. This doesn't have to be a monumental, earthshaking question: perhaps your teachers have opinions on devel-

opments in education, or your mother and grandmother have ideas about the family vacation. Or perhaps you can locate two authorites who have ideas about a current local or political issue. Write an essay on the issue in which you identify and quote at least two authorities. Be sure to identify your sources as true authorities in the area.

2. Write an essay in which you discuss the kinds of choices you would make for yourself and your family if you were in the situation Kolata describes. Would you tell the researchers that you wanted to know the truth? What would you do if they refused?

The Great White Myth

ANNA QUINDLEN

In a college classroom a young white man rises and asks about the future. What, he wants to know, can it possibly hold for him when most of the jobs, most of the good positions, most of the spots in professional schools are being given to women and, most especially, to blacks?

The temptation to be short, sarcastic, incredulous in reply is powerful. But you have to remember that kids learn their lessons from adults. That's what the mother of two black children who were sprayed with white paint in the Bronx said last week about the assailants, teenagers who called her son and daughter "nigger" and vowed they would turn them white. "Can you imagine what they are being taught at home?" she asked.

A nation based on laws, we like to believe that when they are changed, attitudes will change along with them. This is naive. America continues to be a country whose people are obsessed with maintaining some spurious pecking order. At the bottom are African-Americans, taught at age twelve and fourteen through the utter humiliation of having their faces cleaned with paint thinner that there are those who think that even becoming white from a bottle is better than not being white at all.

Each generation finds its own reasons to hate. The worried young white men I've met on college campuses in the last year have internalized the newest myth of American race relations, and it has made them bitter. It is called affirmative action, a.k.a. the systematic oppression of white men. All good things in life, they've learned, from college admission to executive position, are being given to black citizens. The verb is ubiquitous: given.

Never mind that you can walk through the offices of almost any big company and see a sea of white faces. Never mind that with all that has been written about preferential treatment for minority law students, only about 7,500 of the 127,000 students enrolled in law school last year were African-American. Never mind that only 3 percent of the doctors in this country are black.

Never mind that in the good old days preferential treatment was routinely given to brothers and sons of workers in certain lines of work. Perceptions of programs to educate and hire more black citizens as, in part, an antidote to decades of systematic exclusion have been inflated to enormous proportions in the public mind. Like hot-air balloons, they fill up the blue sky of the American landscape with the gaudy stripes of hyperbole. Listen and you will believe that the construction sites, the precinct houses, the investment banks are filled with African-Americans.

Unless you actually visit them.

The opponents of affirmative action programs say they are opposing the rank unfairness of preferential treatment. But there was no great hue and cry when colleges were candid about wanting to have geographic diversity, perhaps giving the kid from Montana an edge. There has been no national outcry when legacy applicants whose transcripts were supplemented by Dad's alumnus status—and cash contributions to the college—were admitted over more qualified comers. We somehow discovered that life was not fair only when the beneficiaries happened to be black.

And so the chasm widens. The old myth was the black American incapable of prosperity. It was common knowledge that welfare was purely a benefits program for blacks; it was common knowledge although it was false. The percentage of whites on public assistance is almost identical with the percentage of blacks.

The new myth is that the world is full of black Americans prospering unfairly at white expense, and anecdotal evidence abounds. The stories about the incompetent black co-worker always leave out two things: the incompetent white co-workers and the talented black ones. They also leave out the tendency of so many managers to hire those who seem most like themselves when young.

"It seems like if you're a white male you don't have a chance," said another young man on a campus where a scant 5 percent of his classmates were black. What the kid really means is that he no longer has the edge, that the rules of a system that may have served his father well have changed. It is one of those good-old-days constructs to believe it was a system based purely on merit, but we know that's not true. It is a system that once favored him, and others like him. Now sometimes—just sometimes—it favors someone different.

EMOTIONAL APPEAL

The reference to the incident of the two African-American children being attacked is clearly an *emotional appeal*. There's nothing wrong with appealing to the emotions in persuasive writing, as long as the intellectual side is given equal weight.

Accepted and understood, emotions give power to the personality just as they do to arguments; but let run wild, without the balance of objective thought, emotional arguments are things that other people tend to regard as untamed wildfires, viewed with some apprehension but no real application. Emotional context gives strength and power to a rational argument, just as the feeling self, as long as it does not overcome the thinking self, is a source of great strength and weight. In this essay, Quindlen attempts a balance between emotional argument and the facts and history of the issue.

Study Questions

1. What kinds of emotional arguments could be presented on the other side? What kinds of rational arguments, including facts and figures, could be presented on the other side?
2. What does Quindlen mean by "the verb is ubiquitous: given"?

Writing Topics

1. "You have to remember that kids learn their lessons from adults," writes Quindlen. Where, when you were a young child, did you learn your attitudes about other races and cultures, and who taught you? Did people say things that contradicted what they actually did? Write an essay that discusses how you learned about racial and cultural differences as a child.
2. Construct an imaginary dialogue between two people who are on opposite sides of a currently controversial issue, perhaps something about which you feel strongly. Each person should present his or her side as clearly and rationally as possible. Write the dialogue in such away that your reader cannot tell which side you are on.

   (*Note:* Remember that when writing dialogue, it is customary to start a new paragraph each time a different person speaks. Identify each speaker each time, then follow the name with a colon.)

Politics as a Vital, and Sometimes Noble, Human Activity

MICHAEL NELSON

On the first day of class this fall, I plan to play a little word-association game with the students in my introductory American-government course. Here is what I'm going to say and (based on long experience) how they are going to respond:

Me: "Politics."

Students: "Corrupt," "dirty," "a waste." (The nicest thing I heard the last time I did this was "boring.")

Me: "Politician."

Students: "Selfish," "ambitious," "mediocre," "unprincipled."

The teacher in me despairs when students associate words like these with politics. I know, as did Aristotle, that politics is a vital and sometimes noble human activity. I know that our political system protects the freedoms that allow my students to criticize politics.

The teacher in me hopes that as the semester wears on, the more students learn about the American political system—warts and all—the less cynical they will become. A democracy can accommodate many things in its people—passion, ambition, selfishness, even corruption. But cynicism, especially when it is widespread, eats away at democracy's fundamental assumption—namely, that what the people want shapes what the government does.

To have half a chance of breaking down my students' cynicism, however, means stepping back to analyze, as a political scientist, their attitudes—in the same way I would analyze any other political phenomenon. What I find is that my students' cynicism is seldom born of experience. The worst encounter many college freshmen have had with government has been waiting in line to get a driver's license. Instead, they have breathed in their cynicism from the world—from parents, friends, rock lyrics, late-night comedians, the Zeitgeist. Students arrive in my classrooms politically cynical because American society is politically cynical.

Why do Americans disdain politics and politicians? Columnists and scholars have offered many answers: the spate of assassinations in the 1960s; the lies the government seems to have told about Vietnam and Watergate; network evening-news programs that treat politics with a sneer; radio talk shows overtly hostile to government; careerist politicians; negative campaign ads.

All of these explanations, meritorious though they may be, share a common failing: They are ahistorical, grounded entirely in recent events and development. Although the widespread presence and importance of government in modern America make contemporary cynicism a more serious problem that it was in the past, when government was smaller, as a political scientist I also know that there never has been a time when Americans were pro-politics. The Progressive movement at the turn of the 20th century, for example, was an all-out effort to strip power from politicians because they were perceived as corrupt.

If we who study politics genuinely want to do something about today's cynicism, we need a fuller explanation of its origins than we get from the present-centered theories offered by pundits. We need to find the historical piece of the jigsaw puzzle that will form a picture not just of this generation, but also of all its predecessors. The label on the new pice could read: "American political culture."

American political culture consists, in part, of long-standing, widely shared, and deeply felt values about how the American political process ought to work—what I call our "process" values.

One such fundamental value holds that government ought to work in accordance with a *higher law,* some ultimate standard of right. That's why Americans don't blink when they hear the bold assertion on which the Declaration of Independence is based: "We hold these truths to be self-evident." Even Ice T, the gangsta rapper, bespeaks that ideal in his book *The Ice Opinion:* "I have the right under *God* to say anything I want to say from my heart that comes out of my mouth."

Throughout history, Americans have revered the Constitution as the embodiment of higher law. Ask a random sample of Europeans (as political scientists have done) what they are proudest of about their country, and they are likely to mention its physical beauty or cultural achievements. Ask Americans, and they will describe their form of government—democracy, freedom, equality. When Americans travel to Washington with their families or high-school classes (as most of my students have done), they see themselves as making a pilgrimage of a sort. Their attitude is serious, even reverential.

If higher law were the only process value in our political culture, cynicism about politics and government might not be so widespread. But Americans also believe that our political system should operate in accordance with *popular sovereignty.* This value rests on two related beliefs: that the only legitimate basis of political authority is the consent of the governed ("government of the people"), and that government is supposed to work in accordance with what the public wants ("government by the people"). Belief in popular sovereignty underlies Americans' expectation, for example, that elected officials should vote in accordance with their constituents' wishes, not according to their own considered judgments as to what is best.

But which value—higher law or popular sovereignty—is supposed to prevail when what higher law seems to require and what the people want are not the same?

Americans may tell themselves that such conflicts will not arise because, as President Andrew Jackson put it, "the voice of the people is the voice of God." But, in reality, the conflicts between the values of higher law and popular sovereignty are what erode our confidence in politics. When things go wrong, as most people think has been the case in our political system, we cannot blame the Constitution: we revere it as the embodiment of higher law. Our belief in popular sovereignty makes us reluctant to blame ourselves. And so we blame the only people left—the politicians. And they, wanting to please us, confirm us in our belief that politicans are at fault by pointing their fingers at each other.

What happens on the second day of the fall semester? My students will discover that the Constitution, which they revere, was the product of politics at its best—that is, excellent but not perfect. They are going to learn that the Framers were politicians who, although not inattentive to their own well-being, cared about the public interest and, to advance it, used many of the same political strategies and tactics that politicians use today. They mobilized political pressure to bring about the calling of the Constitutional convention and to insure their own selection as delegates. They found a leader (George Washington) whose reputation brought credit to their cause, and arranged the rules of the game in their own favor by, for example, declaring that ratification of the Constitution would require the votes of only nine of the 13 states.

Then my students will move into the present, as they read and discuss books such as the journalist Steven Waldman's *The Bill* (Viking, 1995), which shows that modern politics, for all its imperfections, is still largely the work of people who really do care about making their country better. Mr. Waldman's book is wonderfully subtitled *How the Adventures of Clinton's National Service Bill Reveal What Is Corrupt, Comic, Cynical—and Noble—About Washington.* The noble strand emerges from the author's realization that partisans on all sides of the national-service debate in 1993 were sincerely committed to doing the right thing.

Students also will read *The Washington Post* or *The New York Times* all semester long, forming a habit that I hope will not end on the last day of class. No one would accuse the *Post* and *Times* of being starry-eyed in their coverage of politics. But many students are impressed when they find that reasonably balanced reporting of what politicians do creates less cause for cynicism that they initially had assumed.

I know I have a tough sell ahead of me, in part because intellectual honesty demands that I also describe the darker side of politics, such as the untoward influence of large campaign contributors and the desire of many politicians to be reelected at almost any cost. But mostly I will have to struggle because the idea that politics can be— and often is—a noble human activity is a hard one for Americans steeped in our political culture to accept. Teaching students about the inconsistencies in the values that form our political culture will help them to understand some of the roots of their cynicism. Telling them that embracing politics is not the same as embracing the political *status quo* also will help. Indeed, as was the case for the Framers of the Constitution, embracing politics is the best strategy for those who seek change.

Some students will catch my passion for politics. If the past is any guide, several will become active in the 1996 Presidential campaign, enlist in a local political cause, or enter student government. Others will endure the course—not even the best evangelists convert everyone. A few will actively resist—a splendidly political act that may even become habit-forming.

But consider the alternative to presenting politics as a vehicle for human betterment and as a noble calling. The more we continue to dishonor politics, the more we will discourage this generation's honorable people—my students included—from becoming politicians. And whom does that leave?

CAUSE AND EFFECT IN A PERSUASIVE ESSAY

Nelson's answer to the problem of political cynicism is not to preach to his students. He does not simply say "It's your responsibility to stay involved, or democracy has not much chance in America." After all, few people will actually listen to preaching about what they ought to do. Instead, Nelson asks his students to analyze the reasons for the current wave of political cynicism and to look at the history behind present-day attitudes. By taking a *cause-and-effect* approach, he involves his students in considering the issues; and this step should lead them them to evaluate their own actions. In asking how the country got to its present situation, he encourages critical thinking and application.

The cause-and-effect approach attempts to get behind present appearances. What happened in the past to make the present happen? The approach can be historical (event *A* is followed by event *B*, event *C*, and so forth), or the writer can set out a series of possible causes as equal logical elements, without any time sequence (*A*, *B*, and *C* are the reasons that something happened). Nelson uses that second pattern, laying out reasons as though the essay were a class lecture. In the second half of the essay, he uses a process approach to describe, step by step, what the class studies.

One good thing about a cause-and-effect approach is that it resists the tendency to see things simplistically, as though there were ever any one reason for something or as if a problem were any one person's fault. The critical thinker always looks for several possible causes. Even if he or she decides that one main reason is most important, other ideas have been proposed and considered. That willingness to consider many different ideas and causes is the key to critical thought.

Study Questions

1. Can you think of a reason for present-day political cynicism that Nelson has not named? What other factors, beyond cynicism, might account for people's lack of involvement or interest in government?
2. Nelson says that while Europeans are proudest about their countries' beauty or culture, Americans are proudest of their country's form of gov-

ernment. Do you believe that is true? Why or why not? What about
countries other than those in Europe? What causes you to believe this?
3. What kind of teacher is Michael Nelson? What are his class discussions
like? How can you tell? Would you enroll in his course? Why or why not?

Writing Topics

1. *Collaborative writing activity* (with members of the group sharing their
opinions). Begin a discussion based on Study Question #2 above. What
are the group members proudest of about America? Do people from immigrant families differ in their opinions from those whose families mi-
grated here a long time ago? Following the group discussion, write individual essays in which each person defines the aspect of this country
that is most important to him or her, giving reasons for that opinion.
2. Has a teacher ever changed your mind about something? (If not, you
need a different education.) Describe the incident and tell how the
teacher accomplished his or her aim.
3. In what area or areas do you disagree with what most people seem to
think? Is there a common opinion about sports, education, or family life
that strikes you as wrong? In the same way that Nelson explains why
Americans dislike politics, explain why people hold the opinion you
think is in error. A good way to prepare for this assignment is to try the
sentence: "Many people think ——————— because ———
——————, but I believe ———————."

Erotophobia: The Cruelest Abuse of All

MARTY KLEIN

Eroticism is an energy considered outlaw in this culture. Maybe that's because it's a reminder of the goddess, or because it's energy needed for civilization, or because of some obscure reason that made sense thousands of years ago. Three centuries of Puritanism certainly have taken their toll. Whatever the reason, eroticism is taboo energy—and our society spends vast amounts of its precious resources every minute of every year to undermine, co-opt, channel, ridicule, and distort it.

Each of us pays a price for this. We pay it in forfeited pleasure and foregone peace of mind, in the agonies of sexual and relationship dysfunction, and in the rage, guilt, and powerlessness we feel as we torment ourselves and others. Those others—lovers, children, our communities—pay stiff prices as well. Some people even go to jail because of it. We're all erotically crippled in this culture. We're erotophobic: afraid of our sexuality.

Virtually everyone grows up learning that sex is bad. We are taught this in the simplest, most effective ways. Parents do not discuss sexual topics with their children; if they do mention sex, they inevitably say "don't do it." They misname (or refuse to name) our sexual body parts. As children, we are prevented from and punished for masturbating. We are also punished for certain words because they have sexual connotations. We are deliberately told lies about sex.

But as children we also know that we are sexual. We are, for example, titillated by certain smells, curious about bodies (our own, our friends', our parents'), and delighted by genital stimulation. So we inevitably conclude: if sex is bad, *we* are bad. And if we are bad, that means we could be abandoned by our parents, literally or emotionally. We know we could be annihilated simply for experiencing or expressing our natural eroticism.

Since no one tells us why sex is bad, we have no way to test this terrible premise; our life experiences can never prove it wrong. *My sexuality and I are bad* becomes an untestable religious belief.

As we learn that sex is bad, we learn that there is no aspect of eroticism that we can safely reveal to others. We learn that it is *all* impolite, lewd, and dangerous. It must all be hidden. Eroticism is problematic by definition.

We learn to feel sleazy when experiencing our sexuality, and to feel an uncomfortable combination of embarrassment and prurience when we see or hear other people expressing theirs. We soon abandon the truth of our own experience (that sex can be wholesome, playful, and pleasant) in favor of the negative interpretation that is all around us. Eventually we come to believe that this distorted overlay *is* our experience. We are then poised to join the ranks of the erotic oppressors, enforcing this belief on others, continuing the cycle.

The first victims are ourselves. Freud believed that eroticism, active in infancy, lay dormant between early childhood and puberty—the so-called *latency period.* But children's sexuality only *seems* to disappear, as five or six years of constant negative programming teaches them to hide their sexual feelings and experiences from adults.

Our culture strongly believes that exposing children to any expressions of sexuality, such as pictures or words, will harm them, even if the activity being depicted is not itself harmful. Many people believe, for example, that a child will be hurt by seeing a photo of a couple making love, even though the lovemaking itself is in no way hurtful.

There is no other harmless activity that children (or adults) are similarly barred from seeing or hearing about. In no other arena does our society fear that depictions of activities are in themselves harmful. Our society even allows children to see depictions of activities that *are* harmful to those involved. The average American child, for example, sees one hundred murders every month on TV. That's called family entertainment.

One consequence of the social belief that children must be protected from sex is that children are denied accurate sexual information. This systematically-created ignorance is the single biggest influence shaping childhood sexual development. Lack of sexual information makes the normal sexual events of childhood terrifying. These include the onset of menstruation, wet dreams, the desire to masturbate, and unintentionally observing sexual activity.

Withholding sexual knowledge could even be seen as a deliberate engineering of early sexual experiences to make them scary, disgusting, guilt-ridden, and burdensome—that is, anti-erotic. This is, after all, how an anti-erotic culture instills its values in successive generations.

Sexual ignorance is then reinforced by culturally-generated misinformation. Distorted beliefs about masturbation, "nice" girls, fertility, "performance," female orgasm, and homosexuality alienate us from our bodies, from the other gender, and from our own desires.

Society maintains sexual illiteracy in both youth and adults through designated gatekeepers of sexual information. The people who teach about sexuality in our culture are typically anti-sexual, ill-informed, and committed to particular agendas for manipulating sexual thought and behavior. Thus, for example, while people are encouraged to direct sexual questions to their physicians, sexuality is typically excluded from most American medical training.

Most other people with the legitimacy to educate about sex are similarly ignorant and untrained: TV talk show hosts who are uncomfortable with sex and interested primarily in sexual extremes and distortions; clergy who are frightened of sex, often sexually abstinent, and committed to limited sexual choices such as monogamy and reproductive sex; newspaper columnists who are superficial, limited to "family" language, and committed to narrow definitions of sexual normalcy; parents who are often uncomfortable about sex and convinced that good parenting means protecting their children from sexual stimuli; mental health professionals whose training often includes only "abnormal" sexuality, and whose agenda regarding sex is generally to help people adjust and conform to anti-sexual societal norms.

Learning to question our sexual normalcy is a key step in internalizing society's repression of our eroticism. Since real sex is neither honestly discussed nor observed, no one really knows what most other people feel and do. Children grow up in families with sexual secrets, where it is impossible to feel secure with one's sexual thoughts and feelings. Advertisers continuously encourage consumers to doubt their sexuality (always ready to fix the resulting insecurities by selling a product). Further money is to be made from the various institutions set up to define or repair what becomes considered as abnormal sexuality.

Normalcy-anxiety is a form of social control; the power to decide who is sexually normal is the power to validate and invalidate individuals in a powerfully basic way. Fears about not being normal keep us from expressing our eroticism freely and joyfully. Trying to become normal, instead of trying to discover who we are, we act out our anxiety both sexually and nonsexually.

Thus, American culture frightens teenage boys about not being sufficiently masculine. As a result, teenage boys typically project their anxiety by running around deriding each other as *fags*. Of course these boys also then emphatically deny and repress any erotic impulse that could possibly be considered homosexual, such as tenderness, surrender, or any feeling of real emotional warmth toward other males. Boys learn that sexuality is about proving you're a man. How can a boy then be anything but intensely homophobic?

We need to grieve for the loss of our innate sense of gender adequacy, which our culture reduces to a reward tossed us if we perform well, an anchovy thrown to a circus seal. How frightening to have something that should be our birthright culturally transformed into something that must be earned over and over again. With so much at stake psychologically, it's no wonder that sex feels like a matter of life and death. This makes the outcome of sex more important than the process—an ironic tragedy, since sex is in fact one of the premier process-oriented opportunities in life.

Focused on sex's outcome, we become invested in the aspects of sexual expression that are easily measurable, such as erection and orgasm. Aspects of sex that are more diffuse, that are focused on dimensions such as sensuality, powerplay, or intimacy, seem less important and less interesting.

Another way we are taught to distrust our sexuality concerns the fear that our sexual feelings will get out of control. Children of both genders are taught that boys cannot be trusted to control their sexual impulses. We learn that masturbation is bad, and then feel in danger of losing control when our bodies yearn for that forbidden touch. We learn that not only sexual behavior, but sexual thoughts and feelings as well can be bad, and we are painfully aware of the difficulty of continually sanitizing our sexual desires and fantasies.

In a culture that at once fears and magnifies sexuality, we all feel terribly vulnerable to the temptation of the sexually forbidden. This is confirmed by religious attitudes that link eroticism to lust, encouraging us to think of sexual desire as a state which bypasses our usual, responsible decision-making. This attitude is now further confirmed as the Recovery movement asks us to believe that seventeen million Americans are "sex addicts," people who are unable to control their rampant sexual appetites.

We're taught that if our sexuality gets out of control we are likely to damage ourselves, our loved ones, innocent people, even our communities. We will offend God. We will be permanently stained. Since our sexuality is potentially uncontrollable under even the most conventional circumstances, the only way to safely regulate it is to repress it in all its guises, every minute of our lives. This becomes our erotic burden. Sex becomes the most dangerous, most powerful force on earth, *evil* in the classic sense. Controlling such a demonic force requires that we repress not only our own sexuality but the sexuality of others as well. Thus the censor, the crusading rescuer of women and children, is born.

How can we overcome our society's erotophobic heritage and encourage proper respect for both sex and eroticism? While this is a complex question, some directions are clear: we must recognize the existence and validity of childhood sexuality, recognize that pleasure is a need and a right, not a privilege or luxury, and recognize that eroticism can be expressed in many diverse ways without causing problems of any kind. We must also challenge the concept of *normal sex.*

In terms of social consequences, we need to recognize the devastating effects of the suppression of eros, including violence, relationship dysfunction, and poor health; help people understand that feeling anxiety within a sexual context doesn't mean they are inadequate; confront and resolve our core negative feelings about the body; expand the social definition of *sexy* so that everyone is eligible for this confirmation; and see the link between anti-eroticism and consumerism, the belief that the way to enjoy sex is to acquire and consume rather than simply be who you are.

On a policy level, we must take school sex education seriously, as preparation for adulthood and for sexual decision-making; make accurate information about all aspects of sexuality easily available to adults, adolescents, and interested children; and challenge seemingly rational social policies that are actually anti-sexual.

Ultimately, we must change the language of public debate to recognize the various guises of the suppression of eros, such as *pro-life* (anti-choice) and *anti-smut* (anti-sexual), and we must educate opinion and language leaders on all these issues, including medical students, journalists, clergy, and mental health professionals.

The fear of sexuality has been so strongly bred into us by custom and tradition that we think fear is a necessary part of sex. This is simply not true. Eroticism can, in fact, transform us precisely because it can provide the exquisite experience of fearlessness. Erotophobia is not inevitable. It is the result of cultural, social, and political forces, and is fueled by those who benefit from it.

For centuries, erotic energy has been considered a fundamental problem. The time has come to acknowledge it as a fundamental solution.

Study Questions

1. Find the dictionary definition of *eros.* Where does the term come from? What does *erotophobia* mean, as the author uses the term? What does he say accounts for our *erotophobia?*
2. Klein establishes his thesis in the first sentence of the essay. Where else does he state the main point? Where and how does he move from demonstrating the damage that erotophobia does to making suggestions for improving the situation?
3. How, according to the author, does society use fear to prevent people from developing a healthy sexuality? What do you think the author regards as a healthy sexual sense? What kinds of warnings about sex are appropriate and inappropriate, in your opinion?
4. Klein discusses some of the misinformation children are given, myths and fears that can hinder their healthy development. What other such myths and fears given to children—such as myths about Santa Claus, fears of the "boogie man" or similar monsters—can you think of? Are these useful, harmless white lies, or do they have serious consequences?

Writing Topics

1. In your opinion, should children never be lied to? Occasionally? If occasionally, under what circumstances? Write an essay in which you contrast an acceptable story with an unacceptable story and explain the differences. Or, if you believe that children should never be lied to, write an essay in which you explain why not.
2. The author suggests several potential cures for *erotophobia.* Respond to one of those suggestions in an essay. Why would it work, or not work? Establish your opinion in your thesis statement and then give three or four reasons why you approve or disapprove of the solution.

"Friend and Brother . . ."

Friend and Brother, it was the will of the Great Spirit that we should meet together this day. . . .

Brother, this council fire was kindled by you. It was at your request that we came together at this time. We have listened with attention to what you have said. You requested us to speak our minds freely. This gives us great joy; for we now consider that we stand upright before you and can speak what we think. All have heard your voice, and all speak to you now as one man. Our minds are agreed. . . .

Brother, listen to what we say.

There was a time when our forefathers owned this great island. Their seats extended from the rising to the setting sun. The Great Spirit had made it for the use of Indians. He had created the buffalo, the deer, and other animals for food. He had made the bear and the beaver. Their skins served us for clothing. He had scattered them over the country and taught us how to take them. He had caused the earth to produce corn for bread. All this he had done for his red children because he loved them. If we had some disputes about our hunting ground, they were generally settled without the shedding of much blood.

But an evil day came upon us. Your forefathers crossed the great water and landed on this island. Their numbers were small. They found friends and not enemies. They told us they had fled from their own country for fear of wicked men and had come here to enjoy their religion. They asked for a small seat. We took pity on them, granted their request, and they sat down among us. We gave them corn and meat; they gave us poison in return.

Brother, our seats were once large and yours were small. You have now become a great people, and we have scarcely a place left to spread our blankets. You have got our country, but are not satisfied; you want to force your religion upon us.

Brother, continue to listen.

You say that you are sent to instruct us how to worship the Great

Spirit agreeably to his mind; and, if we do not take hold of the religion which you white people teach, we shall be unhappy hereafter. You say that you are right and we are lost. How do we know this to be true?

We understand that your religion is written in a book. If it was intended for us, as well as you, why has not the Great Spirit given to us, and not only to us, but why did he not give to our forefathers the knowledge of that book, with the means of understanding it rightly. We only know what you tell us about it. How shall we know when to believe, being so often deceived by the white people?

Brother, you say there is but one way to worship and serve the Great Spirit. If there is but one religion, why do you white people differ so much about it? Why do not all agree, as you can all read the book?

Brother, we do not understand these things. We are told that your religion was given to your forefathers and has been handed down from father to son. We also have a religion which was given to our forefathers and has been handed down to us, their children. We worship in that way. It teaches us to be thankful for all the favors we receive, to love each other, and to be united. We never quarrel about religion. . . .

Brother, we do not wish to destroy your religion or take it from you. We only want to enjoy our own.

IN FOCUS

CLASSICAL ARGUMENT

Rhetoric, now meaning the effective use of language in all writing and speaking, began as the art of persuasion. Long before writing existed, speakers stood up before audiences and tried to move groups to action. In ancient Greece, the Sophists studied the ways that listeners—particularly listeners who were going to vote on an issue—could best be moved in one direction or another by emotional and rational appeals. Building on the techniques described by Greek theorists such as Aristotle (384–322 B.C.E.), Roman orators and rhetoricians such as Cicero (106–43 B.C.E.) studied the arts of appeal. They divided the process of creating a speech into five basic stages: invention (deciding what to present and how to present it), arrangement (organizing), style (using the best language for the occasion), memory (learning and practicing the speech), and delivery. The first three of those stages are still emphasized today in nearly every college composition class.

The classical rhetoricians in that Greco-Roman tradition, particularly Cicero, also developed a useful pattern for organizing an argument. They felt that the most effective beginning would be an introduction that interested the listener and appealed to the emotions. Then the logical, rational part of the argument would come forth, in the "statement of argument," which is most closely related to our concept of the thesis statement. Then came the argument, stating the writer's key points with supporting evidence, followed by a negation of the opponent's key points—refuting the opposing side would prove that the speaker had considered all aspects of the issue and come to the best position. That argument, with its counterattack on the opposition, constituted the part that we today call the body of the work. Finally, according to the classical rhetoricians, the conclusion should again make an emotional appeal, in order to leave the audience agreeing with the speaker.

Those essential elements of classical speech, studied and practiced for over two thousand years, are taught today as they were in medieval monasteries and nineteenth-century universities. The ways we describe these elements have changed, but the structure is so effective that it is nearly universal:

1. Introduce the subject, gaining the audience's interest and sympathy. (Introduction)
2. State the point. (Thesis, or Statement of Argument)
3. Argue the issue. (Body, Argument)
4. Show how the other side is wrong. (Refutation)
5. Say "good-bye," with a final call for action. (Conclusion)

Whenever a writer seeks action or a change of ideology from an audience of listeners or readers, the Ciceronian pattern provides a useful guide.

Study Questions

1. Otetiani, later known as Sagoyewatha and "Chief Red Jacket," was chief of the Seneca tribe during the American Revolution and a friend of George Washington. He came from a long tradition of tribal democracy, one that valued logic and effective oratory, and his 1805 speech in

response to the Christian missionaries who were trying to convert the Seneca people is a powerful example of argumentative prose.

Clearly, both Otetiani and Cicero had considered the best ways of constructing an argument so that it would appeal most effectively to its audience. Consider the ways that "Friend and Brother . . ." matches the pattern of a classical Roman oration, as outlined above. What similarities do you see?

2. Otetiani was probably aware that his speech would be reported to a wider audience than the people in the room at the moment. Ultimately, who was he speaking to? In one or two sentences, write a statement of purpose for his speech, explaining what he wanted the audience to do. Where in his speech is his thesis expressed?

Writing Topics

1. *Collaborative writing activity.* Choose an issue that is acceptable to everyone in the class. For the purposes of this exercise, avoid huge, emotion-laden topics such as abortion or capital punishment—choose a small, local or campus issue that everyone can write about rationally and comfortably. Then break up into pairs or groups of three. Half of the teams should construct a list of four arguments to support one position; the other half should support the other side. After two opposing teams trade lists, each side should write short refutations of the other team's arguments.

2. Consider Otetiani's argument. Now consider the opposing side. If you were a well-meaning Christian missionary—and most of the missionaries truly felt they were helping—what arguments could you present in opposition to the chief's? What could you say to convince him and his people to convert?

3. Pretend you are in the audience for Otetiani's speech. Write an essay in the form of a letter to an imaginary friend or family member who was not with you, describing the scene and the speaker. Tell how you felt on hearing the speech and describe the responses of the people around you. What did people say or do after the speech was over?

A Modest Proposal

JONATHAN SWIFT

FOR PREVENTING THE CHILDREN OF POOR PEOPLE
IN IRELAND FROM BEING A BURDEN TO THEIR
PARENTS OR COUNTRY, AND FOR MAKING THEM
BENEFICIAL TO THE PUBLIC

It is a melancholy object to those who walk through this great town or travel in the country, when they see the streets, the roads, and cabin doors, crowded with beggars of the female-sex, followed by three, four, or six children, all in rags and importuning every passenger for an alms. These mothers, instead of being able to work for their honest livelihood, are forced to employ all their time in strolling to beg sustenance for their helpless infants, who, as they grow up, either turn thieves for want of work, or leave their dear native country to fight for the Pretender in Spain, or sell themselves to the Barbadoes.

I think it is agreed by all parties that this prodigious number of children in the arms, or on the backs, or at the heels of their mothers, and frequently of their fathers, is in the present deplorable state of the kingdom a very great additional grievance; and therefore whoever could find out a fair, cheap, and easy method of making these children sound, useful members of the commonwealth would deserve so well of the public as to have his statue set up for a preserver of the nation.

But my intention is very far from being confined to provide only for the children of professed beggars; it is of a much greater extent, and shall take in the whole number of infants at a certain age who are born of parents in effect as little able to support them as those who demand our charity in the streets.

As to my own part, having turned my thoughts for many years upon this important subject, and maturely weighed the several schemes of other projectors, I have always found them grossly mistaken in their computation. It is true, a child just dropped from its dam may be supported by her milk for a solar year, with little other nourishment; at most not above the value of two shillings, which the mother may certainly get, or the value in scraps, by her lawful occupation of begging; and it is exactly at one year old that I propose to provide for them in such a manner as instead of being a charge upon their parents or the parish, or wanting food and raiment for the rest of their lives, they shall on the contrary contribute to the feeding, and partly to the clothing, of many thousands.

There is likewise another great advantage in my scheme, that it will prevent those voluntary abortions, and that horrid practice of women murdering their bastard children, alas, too frequent among us, sacrificing the poor innocent babes, I doubt, more to avoid the expense than the shame, which would move tears and pity in the most savage and inhuman breast.

The number of souls in this kingdom being usually reckoned one million and a half, of these I calculate there may be about two hundred thousand couple whose wives are breeders; from which number I subtract thirty thousand couples who are able to maintain their own children, although I apprehend there cannot be so many under the present distresses of the kingdom; but this being granted, there will remain an hundred and seventy thousand breeders. I again subtract fifty thousand for those women who miscarry, or whose children die by accident or disease within the year. There only remain an hundred and twenty thousand children of poor parents annually born. The question therefore is, how this number shall be reared and provided for, which, as I have already said, under the present situation of affairs, is utterly impossible by all the methods hitherto proposed. For we can neither employ them in handicraft or agriculture; we neither build houses (I mean in the country) nor cultivate land. They can very seldom pick up a livelihood by stealing till they arrive at six years old, except where they are of towardly parts; although I confess they learn the rudiments much earlier, during which time they can however be looked upon only as probationers, as I have been informed by a principal gentleman in the county of Cavan, who protested to me that he never knew above one or two instances under the age of six, even in a part of the kingdom so renowned for the quickest proficiency in that art.

I am assured by our merchants that a boy or a girl before twelve years old is no salable commodity; and even when they come to this age they will not yield above three pounds, or three pounds and half a crown at most on the Exchange; which cannot turn to account either to the parents or the kingdom, the charge of nutriment and rags having been at least four times that value.

I shall now therefore humbly propose my own thoughts, which I hope will not be liable to the least objection.

I have been assured by a very knowing American of my acquaintance in London, that a young healthy child well nursed is at a year old a most delicious, nourishing, and wholesome food, whether stewed, roasted, baked, or boiled; and I make no doubt that it will equally serve in a fricassee or a ragout.

I do therefore humbly offer it to public consideration that of the hundred and twenty thousand children, already computed, twenty thousand may be reserved for breed, whereof only one fourth part to be males, which is more than we allow to sheep, black cattle, or swine; and my reason is that these children are seldom the fruits of marriage, a circumstance not much regarded by our savages, therefore one male will be sufficient to serve four females. That the remaining hundred thousand may at a year old be offered in sale to the persons of quality and fortune through the kingdom, always advising the mother to let them suck plentifully in the last month, so as to render them plump and fat for a good table. A child will make two dishes at an entertainment for friends; and when the family dines alone, the fore or hind quarter will make a reasonable dish, and seasoned with a little pepper or salt will be very good boiled on the fourth day, especially in winter.

I have reckoned upon a medium that a child just born will weigh twelve pounds, and in a solar year if tolerably nursed increaseth to twenty-eight pounds.

I grant this food will be somewhat dear, and therefore very proper for landlords, who, as they have already devoured most of the parents, seem to have the best title to the children.

Infant's flesh will be in season throughout the year, but more plentiful in March, and a little before and after. For we are told by a grave author, an eminent French physician, that fish being a prolific diet, there are more children born in Roman Catholic countries about nine months after Lent than at any other season; therefore, reckoning a year after Lent, the markets will be more glutted than usual, because the number of popish infants is at least three to one in this kingdom; and therefore it will have one other collateral advantage, by lessening the number of Papists among us.

I have already computed the charge of nursing a beggar's child (in which list I reckon all cottagers, laborers, and four fifths of the farmers) to be about two shillings per annum, rags included; and I believe no gentleman would repine to give ten shillings for the carcass of a good fat child, which, as I have said, will make four dishes of excellent nutritive meat, when he hath only some particular friend or his own family to dine with him. Thus the squire will learn to be a good landlord, and grow popular among the tenants; the mother will have eight shillings net profit, and be fit for work till she produces another child.

Those who are more thrifty (as I must confess the times require) may flay the carcass; the skin of which artificially dressed will make admirable gloves for ladies, and summer boots for fine gentlemen.

As to our city of Dublin, shambles may be appointed for this purpose in the most convenient parts of it, and butchers we may be assured will not be wanting; although I rather recommend buying the children alive, and dressing them hot from the knife as we do roasting pigs.

A very worthy person, a true lover of his country, and whose virtues I highly esteem, was lately pleased in discoursing on this matter to offer a refinement upon my scheme. He said that many gentlemen of this kingdom, having of late destroyed their deer, he conceived that the want of venison might be well supplied by the bodies of young lads and maidens, not exceeding fourteen years of age nor under twelve, so great a number of both sexes in every county being now ready to starve for want of work and service; and these to be disposed of by their parents, if alive, or otherwise by their nearest relations. But with due deference to so excellent a friend and so deserving a patriot, I cannot be altogether in his sentiments; for as to the males, my American acquaintance assured me from frequent experience that their flesh was generally tough and lean, like that of our schoolboys, by continual exercise, and their taste disagreeable; and to fatten them would not answer the charge. Then as to the females, it would, I think with humble submission, be a loss to the public, because they soon would become breeders themselves: and besides, it is not improbable that some scrupulous people might be apt to censure such a practice (although indeed very unjustly) as a little bordering upon cruelty; which, I confess, hath always been with me the strongest objection against any project, how well soever intended.

But in order to justify my friend, he confessed that this expedient was put into his head by the famous Psalmanazar, a native of the island Formosa, who came from thence to London above twenty years ago, and in conversation told my friend that in his country when any young person happened to be put to death, the executioner sold the carcass to persons of quality as a prime dainty; and that in his time the body of a plump girl of fifteen, who was crucified for an attempt to poison the emperor, was sold to his Imperial Majesty's prime minister of state, and other great mandarins of the court, in joints from the gibbet, at four hundred crowns. Neither indeed can I deny that if the same use were made of several plump young girls in this town, who without one single groat to their fortunes cannot stir abroad without a chair, and appear at the playhouse and assemblies in foreign fineries which they never will pay for, the kingdom would not be the worse.

Some persons of a desponding spirit are in great concern about that vast number of poor people who are aged, diseased, or maimed, and I have been desired to employ my thoughts what course may be taken to ease the nation of so grievous an encumbrance. But I am not in the least pain upon that matter, because it is very well known that they are every day dying and rotting by cold and famine, and filth and vermin, as fast as can be reasonably expected. And as to the younger laborers, they are now in almost as hopeful a condition. They cannot get work, and consequently pine away for want of nourishment to a degree that if at any time they are accidentally hired to common labor, they have not strength to perform it; and thus the country and themselves are happily delivered from the evils to come.

I have too long digressed, and therefore shall return to my subject. I think the advantages by the proposal which I have made are obvious and many, as well as of the highest importance.

For first, as I have already observed, it would greatly lessen the number of Papists, with whom we are yearly overrun, being the principal breeders of the nation as well as our most dangerous enemies; and who stay at home on purpose to deliver the kingdom to the Pretender, hoping to take their advantage by the absence of so many good Protestants, who have chosen rather to leave their country than to stay at home and pay tithes against their conscience to an Episcopal curate.

Secondly, the poorer tenants will have something valuable of their own, which by law may be made liable to distress, and help to pay their landlord's rent, their corn and cattle being already seized and money a thing unknown.

Thirdly, whereas the maintenance of a hundred thousand children, from two years old and upwards, cannot be computed at less than ten shillings a piece per annum, the nation's stock will be thereby increased fifty thousand pounds per annum, besides the profit of a new dish introduced to the tables of all gentlemen of fortune in the kingdom who have any refinement in taste. And the money will circulate among ourselves, the goods being entirely of our own growth and manufacture.

Fourthly, the constant breeders, besides the gain of eight shillings sterling per annum by the sale of their children, will be rid of the charge of maintaining them after the first year.

Fifthly, this food would likewise bring great custom to taverns, where the vintners will certainly be so prudent as to procure the best receipts for dressing it to perfection, and consequently have their houses frequented by all the fine gentlemen, who justly value themselves upon their knowledge in good eating; and a skillful cook, who understands how to oblige his guests, will contrive to make it as expensive as they please.

Sixthly, this would be a great inducement to marriage, which all wise nations have either encouraged by rewards or enforced by laws and penalties. It would increase the care and tenderness of mothers toward their children, when they were sure of a settlement for life to the poor babes, provided in some sort by the public, to their annual profit instead of expense. We should see an honest emulation among the married women, which of them could bring the fattest child to the market. Men would become as fond of their wives during the time of their pregnancy as they are now of their mares in foal, their cows in calf, or sows when they are ready to farrow; nor offer to beat or kick them (as is too frequent a practice) for fear of a miscarriage.

Many other advantages might be enumerated. For instance, the addition of some thousand carcasses in our exportation of barreled beef, the propagation of swine's flesh, and improvement in the art of making good bacon, so much wanted among us by the great destruction of pigs, too frequent at our tables, which are no way comparable in taste or magnificence to a well-grown, fat, yearling child, which roasted whole will make a considerable figure at a lord mayor's feast or any other public entertainment. But this and many others I omit, being studious of brevity.

Supposing that one thousand families in this city would be constant customers for infants' flesh, besides others who might have it at merry meetings, particularly weddings and christenings, I compute that Dublin would take off annually about twenty thousand carcasses, and the rest of the kingdom (where probably they will be sold somewhat cheaper) the remaining eighty thousand.

I can think of no one objection that will possibly be raised against this proposal, unless it should be urged that the number of people will be thereby much lessened in the kingdom. This I freely own, and it was indeed one principal design in offering it to the world. I desire the reader will observe, that I calculate my remedy for this one individual kingdom of Ireland and for no other that ever was, is, or I think ever can be upon earth. Therefore let no man talk to me of other expedients: of taxing our absentees at five shillings a pound: of using neither clothes nor household furniture except what is of our own growth and manufacture: of utterly rejecting the materials and instruments that promote foreign luxury: of curing the expensiveness of pride, vanity, idleness, and gaming in our women: of introducing a vein of parsimony, prudence, and temperance: of learning to love our country, in the want of which we differ even from Laplanders and the inhabitants of Topinamboo: of quitting our animosities and factions, nor acting any longer like the Jews, who were murdering one another at the very moment their city was taken: of being a little cautious not to sell our country and conscience for nothing: of teaching landlords to have at least one degree of mercy toward their tenants: lastly, of putting a spirit of honesty, industry, and skill into our shopkeepers; who, if a resolution could now be taken to buy only our native goods, would immediately unite to cheat and exact upon us in the price, the measure, and the goodness, nor could ever yet be brought to make one fair proposal of just dealing, though often and earnestly invited to it.

Therefore I repeat, let no man talk to me of these and the like expedients, till he hath at least some glimpse of hope that there will ever be some hearty and sincere attempt to put them in practice.

But as to myself, having been wearied out for many years with offering vain, idle, visionary thoughts, and at length utterly despairing of success, I fortunately fell upon this proposal, which, as it is wholly new, so it hath something solid and real, of no expense and little trouble, full in our own power, and whereby we can incur no danger in disobliging England. For this kind of commodity will not bear exportation, the flesh being of too tender a consistence to admit a long continuance in salt, although perhaps I could name a country which would be glad to eat up our whole nation without it.

After all, I am not so violently bent upon my own opinion as to reject any offer proposed by wise men, which shall be found equally innocent, cheap, easy, and effectual. But before something of that kind shall be advanced in contradiction to my scheme, and offering a better, I desire the author or authors will be pleased maturely to consider two points. First, as things now stand, how they will be able to find food and raiment for an hundred thousand useless mouths and backs. And secondly, there being a round million of creatures in human figure throughout this kingdom, whose sole subsistence put into a common stock would leave them in debt two millions of pounds sterling, adding those who are beggars by profession to the bulk of farmers, cottagers, and laborers, with their wives and children who are beggars in effect; I desire those politicians who dislike my overture, and may perhaps be so bold to attempt an answer, that they will first ask the parents of these mortals whether they would not at this day think it a great happiness to have been sold for food at a year old in the manner I prescribe, and thereby have avoided such a perpetual scene of misfortunes as they have since gone through by the oppression of landlords, the impossibility of paying rent without money or trade, the want of common sustenance, with neither house nor clothes to cover them from the inclemencies of the weather, and the most inevitable prospect of entailing the like or greater miseries upon their breed forever.

I profess, in the sincerity of my heart, that I have not the least personal interest in endeavoring to promote this necessary work, having no other motive than the public good of my country, by advancing our trade, providing for infants, relieving the poor, and giving some pleasure to the rich. I have no children by which I can propose to get a single penny; the youngest being nine years old, and my wife past childbearing.

IN FOCUS

SATIRE

Satire is the art of saying what you do not mean in a way so outrageous, so sarcastic, that the reader will apprehend and accept what you actually do mean. Satire holds up to ridicule the thing it portrays. In "A Modest Proposal," for example, Swift suggests that a cure for the desperate poverty of the Irish people, who had been conquered and colonized by the more powerful British, would be to have Irish babies sold as meat in British markets.

Yeech! thinks the reader, making a noise of disgust deep in his or her esophagus. But why not? persists Swift, with a sly smirk behind his serious face. Are not Irish babies already dying of hunger, disease, and poverty? Are those deaths not the result of severe oppression and vicious economic policies? Why does the reader's stomach turn at one thing but not the other?

Thus, as we examine our own reactions, satire teaches us to criticize our ideologies. That is the difference between comedy and satire: comedy's intention is to make us laugh, to lighten our worlds for a bit; satire's intention is to produce change. Satire wants a better world. Jonathan Swift wants a better, more equal society—not, of course, a recipe for roast infant.

Study Questions

1. Note the points at which Swift uses subtle sarcasm and takes "digs" at the wealthy ruling classes. (For example, see the paragraph on p. 298 that begins "A very worthy person.")
2. Note the number of times Swift uses mathematical figures, as though he were writing a government document or economic report. How does this use of figures add to the satire?
3. Why does Swift include a "disclaimer," in the last paragraph, saying that he has no personal gain to be gotten from the proposal?

Writing Topics

1. Satire, though it looks easy, is extraordinarily hard to write because it requires the writer to strike a balance between being funny and being simply vicious. Fall too far in the direction of being mean and nasty, and the piece loses its effect or may even create backlash. For all that, however, satire can be fun to write.

   Choose a problem in society (this can be a little, annoying problem, rather than a great issue) that you think needs to be corrected. Then propose a completely outrageous solution, but one that might make your readers think seriously about the problem. Write a "modest proposal" in which you describe the problem and then propose your solution.
2. Swift was moved to write "A Modest Proposal" by the poverty he saw all around him. He also wrote seriously about the situation, although "A Modest Proposal" survives as his most famous work on the subject.) Write a serious essay describing some of the problems of the poor and homeless in society today, as you see them, and proposing one serious solution.

Kiss Me, I'm Gay

BARBARA EHRENREICH

A strange, unspoken assumption about human sexuality runs through the current debate on gay rights. Both sides agree, without saying so explicitly, that the human race consists of two types of people: heterosexuals and—on the other side of a great sexual dividing line—homosexuals. Heterosexuals are assumed to be the majority, while gays are thought to be a "minority," analogous to African Americans, Latinos, or any other ethnic group. Thus there is "gay pride" just as there is "black pride." We have Gay Pride marches just as we have Saint Patrick's Day or Puerto Rican Day parades. Gay militants even rallied, briefly, around the idea of a "queer nation."

There are ways in which this tribalistic view of human sexuality is useful and even progressive. Before the gay rights movement, homosexuality was conceived as a diffuse menace, attached to no particular group and potentially threatening every man, at least in its "latent" form. So, naturally, as gays came out, they insisted on a unique and prideful group identity: We're queer and we're here! How else do you get ahead in America except by banding together and hoisting a flag?

Some studies seem to indicate that homosexuality is genetically based, more or less like left-handedness or being Irish. Heterosexuals, whether out of tolerance or spite, have been only too happy to concede to gays a special and probably congenital identity of their own. It's a way of saying: We're on this side of the great sexual divide—and you're on that.

There's only one problem with the theory of gays-as-ethnic-group: it denies the true plasticity of human sexuality and, in so doing, helps heterosexual evade that which they really fear. And what heterosexuals really fear is not that "they"—an alien subgroup with perverse tastes in bedfellows—are getting an undue share of power and attention but that "they" might well be us.

Yes, certainly there are people who have always felt themselves to be gay—or straight—since the first unruly fifth-grade crush or tickle in the groin. But for every study suggesting that homosexuality is innate, there are plenty of others that suggest human sexuality is far more versatile—or capricious, if you like. In his pioneering study, Alfred Kinsey reported that 37 percent of the men and 19 percent of the women he surveyed acknowledged having had at least one orgasm with a partner of the same sex. William Masters and Virginia Johnson found that, among the people they studied, fantasies about sex with same-sex partners were the norm.

In some cultures, it is more or less accepted that "straight" men will nonetheless have sex with other men. The rapid spread of AIDS in Brazil, for example, is attributed to bisexual behavior on the part of ostensibly heterosexual males. In the British upper class, homosexual experience used to be a not uncommon feature of male adolescence. Young Robert Graves went off to World War I pining desperately for his schoolboy lover, but returned and eventually married. And, no, he did not spend his time in the trenches buggering his comrades-in-arms.

So being gay is not quite the same as being Irish. There are shadings; there are changes in the course of a lifetime. I know people who were once brazenly "out" and are now happily, heterosexually married—as well as people who have gone in the opposite direction. Or, to generalize beyond genital sexuality to the realm of affection and loyalty: we all know men who are militantly straight yet who reserve their deepest feelings for the male-bonded group— the team, the volunteer fire department, the men they went to war with.

The problem for the military is not that discipline will be undermined by a sudden influx of stereotypically swishy gays. The problem is that the military is still a largely unisexual institution—with all that that implies about the possibility of homosexual encounters. The traditionalists keep bringing up the "crowded showers," much like the dread unisex toilets of the ERA debate. But, from somewhere deep in the sexual imagination, the question inevitably arises: Why do they have such tiny, crowded showers anyway?

By saying that gays are a definite, distinguishable minority that can easily be excluded, the military may feel better about its own presumptive heterosexuality. But can "gays" really be excluded? Do eighteen-year-old recruits really have a firm idea what their sexuality is? The military could deal with its sexuality crisis much more simply, and justly, by ceasing to be such a unisexual institution and letting women in on an equal basis.

Perhaps we have all, "gays" and "straights," gotten as far as we can with the metaphor of gays as a quasi-ethnic group, entitled to its own "rights." Perhaps it is time to acknowledge that the potential to fall in love with, or just be attracted to, a person of the same sex is widespread among otherwise perfectly conventional people. There would still be enormous struggle over what is right and wrong, "normal" and "abnormal." But at least this would be a struggle that everyone—gay or straight—would have a stake in: gays because of who they are; straights because of who they might be, and sometimes actually are. All men, for example, would surely be better off in a world where simple acts of affection between men occasioned no great commentary or suspicion. Where a hug would be a hug and not a "statement."

IN FOCUS

INDUCTIVE AND DEDUCTIVE REASONING

It takes work to be offensive to everyone in sight, but Barbara Ehrenreich manages. Her kind of assertive writing, designed in this case for a newspaper column, requires the courage of a writer who rejects "correctness" on any side in order to present her vision of what is happening in the world. Her wit is sharp and pointed, with a good deal of sarcasm, and she effortlessly takes swipes all around.

Using humor to help readers see the point, the essay moves assertively, idea by idea, to the conclusion. This is an example of *inductive reasoning*, in which a piece of writing moves from specific ideas and examples through the piece to the large generalized thesis in the conclusion. Point *A* is given, and then point *B*, then *C*, and so forth, until they are all combined at the end into a single main point.

The contrasting pattern is called *deductive reasoning*, which involves moving from the general to the specific. The sixth paragraph of "Kiss Me, I'm Gay," beginning with "In some cultures," is an example of a deductive pattern. In this case the topic sentence of the paragraph is a general statement, which is then supported with specific examples.

A large general point may be in the form of a topic sentence for a paragraph or a thesis statement for an essay. Whether the entire piece is short or long, the topic or thesis may be placed at the beginning (deductive pattern) or the end (inductive pattern)—or, very rarely, in the middle. The choice between inductive and deductive logical patterns is the decision about whether to start with a large statement and then fill in the support, or to begin with the small stuff and work slowly up to the main point.

Thus, deductive reasoning starts with an accepted or given idea, derives its reasoning from that idea, and constantly refers back. Inductive reasoning works from the evidence first, to arrive at a large general theory or main point based on that evidence. Sherlock Holmes was an inductive thinker, not, as is commonly assumed, a deductive investigator. By and large, science (which places evidence first) works inductively, while religion (which usually places an important text or revelation first) works deductively. The thought process behind the statement "The Joneses' car is in their driveway, and the house lights are on; therefore, they must be home" is inductive. The thought process behind "Let's see whether the Joneses are home, and maybe they will lend us some money" is deductive.

Study Questions

1. Find other examples of inductive and deductive patterns in this essay and in other readings in the collection. Look at the way individual paragraphs work. Is the topic sentence first in the paragraph or at the end? Is the reader given a generalization first and then detail, or evidence first and then conclusion?

2. Explain what Ehrenreich thinks is really true about human sexuality and gender. Where in the essay is the thesis statement? What makes this essay an example of an inductive pattern?

Writing Topics

1. *Collaborative writing activity* (with group members checking each other's patterns of presentation). Write two paragraphs about human gender, giving whatever opinion you choose. Make the first paragraph identifiably inductive by putting your topic sentence first and then supporting that point. Then, using different examples and/or supporting material, write another paragraph on the same subject that is deductive, giving examples that lead to a conclusion. Underline the topic sentence in each paragraph.

2. Do you come from a culture in which expressions of affection between men (or women) are different from general American customs? Write an essay in which you describe the differences in customs. After you have written your first draft, make sure you have included in the essay at least one example of an inductive paragraph and one example of a deductive paragraph. Mark or identify those paragraphs before you turn in the assignment.

Animals and People: "The Human Heart in Conflict with Itself"

PATTIANN ROGERS

Some of us like to photograph them. Some
of us like to paint pictures of them. Some of us
like to sculpt them and make statues and carvings
of them. Some of us like to compose music
about them and sing about them. And some of us
like to write about them.

Some of us like to go out
and catch them and kill them and eat them. Some
of us like to hunt them and shoot them and eat them.
Some of us like to raise them, care for them and eat
them. Some of us just like to eat them.

And some of us
name them and name their seasons and name their hours,
and some of us, in our curiosity, open them up
and study them with our tools and name their parts.
We capture them, mark them and release them,
and then we track them and spy on them and enter
their lives and affect their lives and abandon
their lives. We breed them and manipulate them
and alter them. Some of us experiment
upon them.

We put them on tethers and leashes,
in shackles and harnesses, in cages and boxes,
inside fences and walls. We put them in yokes
and muzzles. We want them to carry us and pull us
and haul for us.

And we want some of them
to be our companions, some of them to ride on our fingers

and some to ride sitting on our wrists or on our shoulders
and some to ride in our arms, ride clutching our necks.
We want them to walk at our heels.

We want them to trust
us and come to us, take our offerings, eat from our hands.
We want to participate in their beauty. We want to assume
their beauty and so possess them. We want to be kind
to them and so possess them with our kindness and so
partake of their beauty in that way.

And we want them
to learn our language. We try to teach them our language.
We speak to them. We put *our* words in *their* mouths.
We want *them* to speak. We want to know what they see
when they look at us.

We use their heads and their bladders
for balls, their guts and their hides and their bones
to make music. We skin them and wear them for coats,
their scalps for hats. We rob them, their milk
and their honey, their feathers and their eggs.
We make money from them.

We construct icons of them.
We make images of them and put their images on our clothes
and on our necklaces and rings and on our walls
and in our religious places. We preserve their dead
bodies and parts of their dead bodies and display
them in our homes and buildings.

We name mountains
and rivers and cities and streets and organizations
and gangs and causes after them. We name years and time
and constellations of stars after them. We make mascots
of them, naming our athletic teams after them. Sometimes
we name ourselves after them.

We make toys of them
and rhymes of them for our children. We mold them
and shape them and distort them to fit our myths
and our stories and our dramas. We like to dress up
like them and masquerade as them. We like to imitate them
and try to move as they move and make the sounds they make,
hoping, by these means, to enter and become the black
mysteries of their being.

Sometimes we dress them
in our clothes and teach them tricks and laugh at them
and marvel at them. And we make parades of them
and festivals of them. We want them to entertain us
and amaze us and frighten us and reassure us
and calm us and rescue us from boredom.

We pit them
against one another and watch them fight one another,
and we gamble on them. We want to compete with them
ourselves, challenging them, testing our wits and talents
against their wits and talents, in forests and on plains,
in the ring. We want to be able to run like them and leap
like them and swim like them and fly like them and fight
like them and endure like them.

We want their total
absorption in the moment. We want their unwavering devotion
to life. We want their oblivion.

Some of us give thanks
and bless those we kill and eat, and ask for pardon,
and this is beautiful as long as they are the ones dying
and we are the ones eating.

And as long as we are not
seriously threatened, as long as we and our children
aren't hungry and aren't cold, we say, with a certain
degree of superiority, that we are no better
than any of them, that any of them deserve to live
just as much as we do.

And after we have proclaimed
this thought, and by so doing subtly pointed out
that we are allowing them to live, we direct them
and manage them and herd them and train them and follow
them and map them and collect them and make specimens
of them and butcher them and move them here and move
them there and we place them on lists and we take
them off of lists and we stare at them and stare
at them and stare at them.

We track them in our sleep.
They become the form of our sleep. We dream of them.
We seek them with accusation. We seek them
with supplication.

And in the ultimate imposition,
as Thoreau said, we make them bear the burden
of our thoughts. We make them carry the burden
of our metaphors and the burden of our desires and our guilt
and carry the equal burden of our curiosity and concern.
We make them bear our signs and our prayers and our hopes
into the desert, into the sky, into the stars.
We say we kill them for God.

We adore them and we curse
them. We caress them and we ravish them. We want them
to acknowledge us and be with us. We want them to disappear
and be autonomous. We abhor their viciousness and lack
of pity, as we abhor our own viciousness and lack of pity.
We love them and we reproach them, just as we love
and reproach ourselves.

We will never, we cannot,
leave them alone, even the tiniest one, ever, because we know
we are one with them. Their blood is our blood. Their breath
is our breath, their beginning our beginning, their fate
our fate.

Thus we deny them. Thus we yearn
for them. They are among us and within us and of us,
inextricably woven with the form and manner of our being,
with our understanding and our imaginations.
They are the grit and the salt and the lullaby
of our language.

We have a need to believe they are there,
and always will be, whether we witness them or not.
We need to know they are there, a vigorous life maintaining
itself without our presence, without our assistance,
without our attention. We need to know, we *must* know,
that we come from such stock so continuously and tenaciously
and religiously devoted to life.

We know we are one with them,
and we are frantic to understand how to actualize that union.
We attempt to actualize that union in our many stumbling,
ignorant and destructive ways, in our many confused
and noble and praiseworthy ways.

For how can we possess dignity
if we allow them no dignity? Who will recognize our beauty

if we do not revel in their beauty? How can we hope
to receive honor if we give no honor? How can we believe
in grace if we cannot bestow grace?

We want what we cannot
have. We want to give life at the same moment
we are taking it, nurture life at the same moment we light
the fire and raise the knife. We want to live, to provide,
and not be instruments of destruction, instruments
of death. We want to reconcile our "egoistic concerns"
with our "universal compassion." We want the lion
and the lamb to be one, the lion and the lamb *within*
finally to dwell together, to lie down together
in peace and praise at last.

Study Questions

1. In "The Face of a Spider," which leads off chapter 3 (p. 120), David Quammen asks the question "How should a human behave toward the members of other living species?" Rogers takes a different slant, analyzing the various ways humans do, in fact, behave, as she seeks to understand the reasons for our behavior. What, in Rogers's opinion, do we deeply want from "them"? Do you agree with her analysis?
2. Much of the power of Rogers's poem comes from the seemingly endless chain of repetitive short sentences and phrases. How does the style of the poem reflect its meaning? How do the repetitions of "we," "us," and "them" enforce the impact of the poem?
3. Consider the irony of the first stanza. "And some of us like to write about them," writes Rogers, who is, of course, writing about "them." What other examples of irony do you find in the poem?
4. "The human heart in conflict with itself" is a quotation from William Faulkner's Nobel Prize acceptance speech (see p. 81). Why did Rogers use this quotation in her title?

Writing Topics

1. Write an essay in which you describe your reactions to the format of the piece. Did you identify it as a poem, a prose poem, or an essay? Did the way you approached it influence your response?
2. Choose one example of human behavior toward animals that you think is wrong. Write an essay in which you explain why this type of action is wrong, giving suggestions for ways of preventing it from happening. Try to begin your essay with a quotation from "Animals and People."

From Experience to Issues

The Contemplative Autobiography in Focus

Who I am, how I feel—what I know, what I think—what is happening in the world. The writer of the type of essay in this chapter works from the inside outward. In a fully developed autobiographical essay (here running from two thousand to three thousand words) a writer has space to build from personal examples to ideas. The reader, who on average will probably spend about half an hour on each piece, has the time to become familiar with the author's style and content and will have been immersed in the topic long enough to have gained a fairly thorough understanding.

The In Focus essays show how each of the autobiographies in this group draws from the writer's personal experiences in order to say something significant about the larger world. That function is what gives an autobiography meaning. No one but the writer's family and best friend wants to know "What I Did on My Summer Vacation" (even with accompanying photographs), unless the vacation activities were in some way important for the reader. Was it a place that other people might want to visit? Did the vacation lead to some special learning that others might benefit from knowing about? Did the activities lead to a thoughtful consideration of some wider social, historical, or psychological meaning? If you write about what is meaningful to you, the subject must transcend the personal, must somehow become meaningful to other people.

At the beginning of this chapter, the focus is on the reading process, with discussions of the reader's background and speed. Another discussion presents empathy as a reading skill, while "In Focus: From the Self to Society" shows how both reader and writer move from the story to the meaning and the larger significance of the story. Toward the end of the chapter, the In Focus essays analyze some of the skills involved in writing effective essays of this kind: using sensory images, developing effective openings, and establishing the scene. Each of these skills makes it possible to write about oneself in a broader context.

The Readings in Focus

This chapter begins with some thoughts about reading: in "Making Up for Lost Time: The Rewards of Reading at Last," Richard Wolkomir writes about his experience as a volunteer reading tutor in a way that concentrates not on himself but on his student, a sixty-four-year-old man who, it turns out, has a few things to teach his teacher. The Wolkomir piece also goes beyond a description of the relationship between the two men to become a meaningful picture of adult illiteracy. Barbara Kingsolver begins "Stone Soup" with a Little League game, then moves into an extended discussion of what "family" means in the present era.

As the chapter continues, George Orwell—in "Shooting an Elephant," a classic essay about an incident from his life in Lower Burma (now Myanmar)—makes a point about psychological pressure while also making a historical point about colonialism and oppression. In "Claiming the Self: The Cripple as American Man," Leonard Kriegel speaks not only for himself but for all people with physical disabilities. In "Once More to the Lake," E. B. White looks at the connection between generations and at how the past is woven into the present.

In "The Looking-Glass Shame," Judith Ortiz Cofer remembers not only what it was like as she entered womanhood but also what it was like entering womanhood as a member of a minority, while in a selection from *Notes of a Native Son,* James Baldwin moves from his relationship with his father to the larger society that shaped that relationship. Finally, in "Where I Am," Kathleen Norris tells the reader about the people she lives with—who they are, and how they relate to the land and to one another.

Each of these writers understands that his or her own experiences are meaningful to others mainly as those experiences relate to a wider issue or social problem. Each writer is willing to see himself or herself as part of a larger social order, an individual within a wider context. An autobiography succeeds when it manages to make the reader feel as though any of the events could have happened to him or her, as though each person were capable of thoughts and experiences that affirm and at the same time transcend individuality. The self is important, and the society to which the self relates is equally important.

Making Up for Lost Time: The Rewards of Reading at Last

RICHARD WOLKOMIR

I decide simply to blurt it out. "Ken?" I ask. "Why didn't you learn to read?" Through the Marshfield community center's window, I see snowy fields and the Vermont village's clapboard houses. Beyond, mountains bulge. "I was a slow learner," Ken says. "In school they just passed me along, and my folks told me I wasn't worth anything and wouldn't amount to anything."

Ken Adams is 64, his hair white. He speaks Vermontese, turning "I" into "Oy," and "ice" into "oyce." His green Buckeye Feeds cap is blackened with engine grease from fixing his truck's transmission, and pitch from chain-sawing pine logs. It is 2 degrees below zero outside on this December afternoon; he wears a green flannel shirt over a purple flannel shirt. He is unshaven, weather reddened. He is not a tall man, but a lifetime of hoisting hay bales has thickened his shoulders.

Through bifocals, Ken frowns at a children's picture book, *Pole Dog*. He is studying a drawing: an old dog waits patiently by a telephone pole, where its owners abandoned it. He glares at the next pictures. Cars whizzing by. Cruel people tormenting the dog. "Looks like they're shootin' at him, to me!" he announces. "Nobody wants an old dog," he says.

Ken turns the page. "He's still by the pole," he says. "But there's that red car that went by with those kids, ain't it?" He turns the page again. The red car has stopped to take the old dog in, to take him home. "*Somebody* wants an old dog!" Ken says. "Look at that!"

This is my first meeting with Ken. It is also my first meeting with an adult who cannot read.

I decided to volunteer as a tutor after a librarian told me that every day, on the sidewalks of our prim little Vermont town, I walk by illiterate men and women. We are unaware of them because they can be clever at hiding their inability to read. At a post office counter, for instance, when given forms to fill out, they say, "Could you help me with this? I left my glasses home."

Ken Adams is not alone in his plight. A 1993 U.S. Department of Education report on illiteracy said 21–23 percent of U.S. adults—about 40 million—read minimally, enough to decipher an uncomplicated meeting announcement. Another 25–28 percent read and write only slightly better. For instance, they can fill out a simple form. That means about *half* of all U.S. adults read haltingly. Millions, like Ken Adams, hardly read at all.

I wanted to meet nonreaders because I could not imagine being unable to decipher a street sign, or words printed on supermarket jars, or stories in a book. In fact, my own earliest memory is about reading. In this memory, in our little Hudson River town, my father is home for the evening from the wartime lifeboat factory where he is a foreman. And he has opened a book.

"Do you want to hear about Peter Churchmouse?" my father asks. Of course! It is my favorite, from the little library down the street. My father reads me stories about children lost in forests. Cabbage-stealing hares. A fisherman who catches a talking perch. But my favorite is Peter Churchmouse, a small but plucky cheese addict who befriends the rectory cat. Peter is also a poet, given to reciting original verse to his feline friend during their escapades. I cannot hear it enough.

My father begins to read. I settle back. I am taking a first step toward becoming literate—I am being read to. And although I am only 2, I know that words can be woven into tales.

Now, helping Ken Adams learn to read, I am re-entering that child's land of chatty dogs and spats-wearing frogs. Children's books—simply worded, the sentences short—are perfect primers, even for 60-year-olds who turn the pages with labor-thickened fingers and who never had such books read to them when they were children.

"Do you remember what happened from last time?" asks Sherry Olson, of Central Vermont Adult Basic Education, who tutors Ken an hour and a half each week.

I have volunteered as Sherry's aide. My work requires too much travel for me to be a full-fledged tutor. But I am actually relieved, not having sole responsibility for teaching an adult to read. That is because—when I think about it—I don't know how I read myself. I scan a printed page; the letters magically reveal meaning. It is effortless. I don't know how I do it. As for teaching a man to read from scratch, how would I even begin?

Sherry, a former third-grade teacher, gives me hints, like helping Ken to learn words by sight so that he doesn't have to sound out each letter. Also, we read stories so Ken can pick out words in context. Ken reads Dr. Seuss rhyming books and tales about young hippopotamuses helping on the family farm. At the moment, we are reading a picture book about Central American farmers who experience disaster when a volcano erupts.

"The people had to move out, and put handkerchiefs over their noses!" Ken says, staring at the pages. He starts to read: "They . . . prayed? . . . for the . . . fire? . . ." "Yes, that's right, fire," Sherry says. "They prayed for the fire to . . . go out?" "That word is 'stop,' " Sherry says.

I listen carefully. A few sessions ahead, it will be my turn to try teaching. "They prayed for the fire to *stop*," Ken says, placing a thick forefinger under each word. "They watched from the s . . ." "Remember we talked about those?" Sherry says. "When a word ends in a silent *e*, what does that silent *e* do to the vowel?" "It makes it say itself," Ken says. "So what's the vowel in *s-i-d-e?*" she asks. "It's *i*, and it would say its own name, *i*," Ken says, pronouncing it "oy." "So that would be 'side.' " "Good," Sherry says.

Ken reads the sentence: "They watched from the side of the hill!" He sounds quietly triumphant. "They-uh," he says, in backcountry Vermontese. "That's done it."

After the session, I stand a few minutes with Ken in the frozen driveway. He has one foot on the running board of his ancient truck, which he somehow keeps going. He tells me he was born in 1931 into a family eking out an existence on a hardscrabble farm. His trouble in school with reading is puzzling, because Ken is intelligent.

For instance, he says he was late today because he had to fix his truck. And now he launches into a detailed analysis of the transmission mechanisms of various species of trucks. Also, during the tutoring session, we played a game that required strewing word cards upside down on a table and remembering their locations. Ken easily outscored both Sherry and me in this exercise.

Ken described himself as a "slow learner," but clearly he is not slow. Sherry has told me he probably suffers from a learning disability. People with these perceptual disorders experience difficulties such as seeing letters reversed. Although their intelligence may actually be above average, learning to read is difficult for them. They need individual tutoring.

"It was a one-room school, with eight grades, so I didn't get much

attention there," Ken tells me. "It was just the same as the folks at
home were doing when they kicked me along through the grades,
and when you got to be 16, that's when they kicked you out."

After he left school, he left home. "Then you knock around, one
farm to another," he says. "I'd get $15 a week, and room and board."
Besides farming, he worked in bobbin mills and sawmills and granite quarries. "Then I was at a veneer mill in Bradford," he says. "After
that I was caretaker at a farm for six years until I had to give it up because I had heart attacks."

Now he subsists on a $400-a-month Social Security disability pen-
sion plus $90 a month in food stamps. He lives alone in a farmhouse
he built himself more than 25 years ago, five miles up a mountain
dirt road. He earns money for his medicines by cutting firewood,
haying, digging postholes with his tractor, snowplowing and cutting
brush. "I'm doing odds-and-ends jobs where you can take your time,
because the doctor told me I have to stop whenever I feel I need to
rest," he says.

He cannot afford electricity from the power company, but he gets
what current he needs, mostly for lights, by—ingeniously—drawing
it from car batteries. To recharge the batteries, he hooks them up in
his truck for a day. He also can charge them with a diesel generator.
He waits until prices dip to buy fuel for his generator and tractor.
"I've got a few maples around my house," he tells me. "I'll find a
rusted-out evaporator, fix it up and make syrup—there's always a
few things I can do, I guess."

I ask how he's managed all these years, not reading. He says his
bosses did the reading for him. And now a Marshfield couple, lifelong
friends, help him read his mail and bills and notices. But they are entering their 80s. "Now I've got to learn to read myself, as a backup,"
Ken says.

To find out more about what illiteracy does to people like Ken, I
telephoned the U.S. Department of Education and spoke with the
Deputy Secretary, Madeleine Kunin. She told me that only 3–5 percent of adult Americans cannot read at all. "But literacy is a moving target," she said. "We figure the 40 million who do read, but at
the lowest proficiency levels, have difficulty handling some of the
tasks they need to hold a job today." Kunin, a former Vermont governor, cited that state's snowplow drivers: "Now they have computers attached, and they need a high school degree just to drive a
snowplow."

Ken arrives for his next session in a dark mood. It turns out his
tape recorder, used for vocabulary practice, is broken. "I can't fix it

because the money's all gone for this month," he says. "I had to go to the doctor, and that's $30, and it was $80 for the pills, and they keep going up." He says one of his prescriptions jumped from $6.99 to $13 in two months. "I don't know if I'll keep taking them," he says. Illiteracy has condemned Ken to a lifetime of minimum-wage poverty.

He brightens reading a story. It is about a dog, John Brown, who deeply resents his mistress's new cat. Ken stumbles over a word. "Milk?" Sherry and I nod. "Go and give her some milk," Ken reads, then pauses to give us a dispatch from the literacy front: "I was trying to figure that out, and then I see it has an *i,*" he says.

My own first attempt at solo tutoring finally comes, and I am edgy. Sherry has wryly admonished Ken, "You help Richard out." I show him file cards, each imprinted with a word for Ken to learn by sight. He is supposed to decipher each word, then incorporate it in a sentence. I write his sentence on the card to help him when he reviews at home. Ken peers at the first word. "All," he says, getting it easily. He makes up a sentence: "We all went away."

"That's right," I say. Maybe this won't be so hard after all. I write Ken's sentence on the card for him. Then I flip another card. Ken peers at it, his face working as he struggles with the sounds. "As," he says.

During out last session, he confused "as" and "at." Now he has it right. So he has been doing his homework.

"As we went down the road, we saw a moose," Ken says, composing a sentence. That reminds him that the state recently allowed moose hunting, game officials arguing that moose have become so plentiful they cause highway accidents. "Yesterday, I come around a turn and there was *ten* moose, a big male and females and young ones," Ken says. "They shouldn't be shooting those moose—they ain't hurting anyone, and it ain't the moose's fault if people don't use their brakes."

I flip another card. "At!" Ken says, triumphing over another of our last session's troublemakers. "We are at the school." But the next word stumps him. It is "be." I put my finger under the first letter. "What's that sound?" I ask. When he stares in consternation, I make the sound "buh." But Ken is blocked. He can't sound out the next letter, even though he has often done it before. "Eeeee," I say, trying to help. "Now put the two sounds together."

Ken stares helplessly at the word. I am beginning to understand the deep patience needed to tutor a man like Ken, who began these sessions a year before, knowing the alphabet but able to sound out only a few words. "Buh . . . eeee," I say, enunciating as carefully as I can. "Buh . . . eeee," Ken repeats. Abruptly, his forehead unfurrows. "Oh, that's 'be,' " he says. "Be—We should be splitting wood!"

"Was that what you were doing before the tutoring session?" I ask, to give us both a break. "Nope, plowing snow with my tractor for my friend who broke off his ankle," Ken says.

That is arresting information. When I ask what happened, Ken says his octogenarian friend was chain-sawing cherry trees when a bent-back branch lashed out, smashing his lower leg. Ken, haying a field, saw his friend ease his tractor down from the mountainside woodlot, grimacing in agony, working the tractor's pedals with his one good foot.

Ken himself once lost his grip on a hay bale he was hoisting. A twig poking from the bale blinded his right eye. Now learning to read is doubly difficult because his remaining eye often tires and blurs. These grim country stories of Ken's make my worries—delayed flights, missed appointments—seem trivial. I flip another card: "But." "Bat," Ken says, cautiously. "Buh . . . uh . . . tuh," I prompt. "But," he finally says. "I would do it, but I have to go somewhere else."

I write Ken's sentence on the card and he reads it back. But he stumbles over his own words, unable to sound out "would." I push down rising impatience by remembering the old man in the woods, crawling toward his tractor, dragging that smashed leg.

Finally, I put away the cards, glad to be done with them. Tutoring can be frustrating. Why are even easy words sometimes so hard to get? Now we look at a puzzle. On one side it has pictures of various automobile parts. On the other side are printed the parts' names. The idea is to match the pictures and the names. Before I can start asking Ken to try sounding out big terms like "connecting rod," he points to one of the drawings. It looks to me like deer antlers. "Carburetor?" I guess. "Exhaust manifold," Ken says.

"What's this one?" I inquire. For all I know, it might be something Han Solo is piloting through hyperspace. "Starter," Ken says. It seems to me he is gloating a little. He points again. "Camshaft?" I ask. Ken corrects me. "Crankshaft," he says, dryly.

It is a standoff. I know the printed words. Ken knows the actual objects to which the words refer. "When I was a kid," he tells me, "I bought an old '35 truck. Sometimes it had brakes and sometimes it didn't. I was probably 17. It made lots of smoke, so mosquitoes never bothered me. But one day I got sick of it. I put it under a pine tree and I hoisted the engine up into the tree to look at it. The pressure plate weren't no good. And the fellow showed me how to fix it."

That reminds Ken of a later episode. "One time we had to get the hay in, but the baler was jammed. We had the guys from the tractor place, but they could not fix it. Finally I asked the old guy for some wrenches and I adjusted it, and I kept on adjusting, and after that it worked perfectly. I just kept adjusting it a hair until I had it. And then we were baling hay!" No wonder Ken's bosses were happy to do his reading for him. Even so, in our late 20th-century wordscape, illiteracy stymies people like him. And working with Ken has me puzzled: Why do so many people fail to learn to read?

I telephoned an expert, Bob Caswell, head of Laubach Literacy International, a nonprofit organization that trains tutors worldwide. He told me many nonreaders, like Ken Adams, suffer from perceptual reading disorders. But there are other reasons for illiteracy, and it is by no means confined to any one part of the population.

"People think adult nonreaders are mainly poor, urban minorities, but 41 percent are English-speaking whites," Caswell said, adding that 22 percent are English-speaking blacks, 22 percent are Spanish-speaking, and 15 percent are other non-English speakers. More than half of nonreading adults live in small towns and suburbs. Caswell cited U.S. Department of Labor figures that put illiteracy's annual national cost at $225 billion in workplace accidents, lost productivity, unrealized tax revenues, welfare and crime. One big reason for this whopping problem is *parents* who read poorly.

Well over a third of all kids now entering public schools have parents who read inadequately, he said. "Everywhere we find parents who *want* to read to their kids, but can't," he added. "And a child with functionally illiterate parents is twice as likely to grow up to be functionally illiterate."

But as I met some of Ken Adams' fellow students, I discovered all sorts of causes for being unable to decipher an English sentence. For instance, I met a woman who had escaped from Laos to Connecticut knowing only Laotian. She learned enough English watching *Sesame Street* ("Big Bird and all that," she told me), and later from being tutored, to become a citizen.

I also met a man in his 30s who worked on a newspaper's printing press. He could not spell the simplest words. He said it was because, at age 10, he had begun bringing alcohol to school in peanut-butter jars. After his son was born, he turned to Alcoholics Anonymous and mustered the courage to seek tutoring.

I met another man who had dropped out of school in frustration. Not until he tried to enlist in the military did he discover he was nearly deaf. The operator of a creamery's cheese-cutting machine told me he never learned to read because his family had been in a perpetual uproar, his mother leaving his father seven times in one year. And I met a farm wife, 59, who rarely left her mountaintop. But now, with tutoring, she was finally learning to read, devouring novels—"enjoyment books," she called them.

In central Vermont, these struggling readers receive free tutoring from nonprofit Adult Basic Education offices, each employing a few professionals, like Sherry Olson, but relying heavily on armies of volunteers, like me. Other states have their own systems. Usually, the funding is a combination of federal and state money, sometimes augmented with donations. Mostly, budgets are bare bones.

Many states also rely on nonprofit national organizations, like Laubach Literacy Action (Laubach International's U.S. division) and Literacy Volunteers of America, both headquartered in Syracuse, New York, to train volunteers. Laubach's Bob Caswell told me that, nationwide, literacy services reach only 10 percent of adult non-readers. "Any effort is a help," he said.

Help has come late for Ken Adams. Reviewing his portfolio, I found the goals he set for himself when he began: "To read and write better. And to get out and meet people and develop more trust." Asked by Sherry to cite things that he does well, he had mentioned "fixing equipment, going to school and learning to read, trying new things, telling stories, farming." He remembered being in a Christmas play in second grade and feeling good about that. And he remembered playing football in school: "They would pass it to me and I'd run across the goal to make a score." He mentioned no fond family memories. But he had some good moments. "I remember the first time I learned to drive a tractor," he had said. "We were working in the cornfields. I was proud of that." And a later notation, after he had several months of tutoring, made me think of Ken living alone in his hand-built farmhouse on ten acres atop the mountain. "I like to use recipes," he said. "I use them more as I learn to read and write better. I made Jell-O with fruit, and I make bean salad. I feel good I can do that."

In our tutoring sessions, between bouts with the vocabulary cards, Ken tells me he was the oldest of four children. When he was small, his father forced him to come along to roadside bars, and then made Ken sit alone in the car for hours. Ken remembers shivering on subzero nights. "He always said I'd never amount to nothing," Ken says.

I ask Ken, one day, if his inability to read has made life difficult. He tells me, "My father said I'd never get a driver's license, and he said nobody would ever help me." Ken had to walk five miles down his mountain and then miles along highways to get to work. "And," he recalls, "I was five years in the quarries in Graniteville—that was a long way." Sometimes he paid neighbors to drive him down the mountain. "They said the same as my father, that I'd never get a license," he says. "They wanted the money."

It was not until he was 40 years old that he applied for a license. He had memorized sign shapes and driving rules, and he passed easily. "After I got my license I'd give people a ride down myself," he says. "And they'd ask, 'How much?' And I'd always say, 'Nothing, not a danged thing!'"

To review the words he has learned, Ken maintains a notebook. On each page, in large block letters, he writes the new word, along with a sentence using the word. He also tapes to each page a picture illustrating the sentence, as a memory aid. To keep him supplied with pictures to snip, I bring him my old magazines. He is partial to animals. He points to one photograph, a black bear cub standing upright and looking back winsomely over its shoulder. "That one there's my favorite," Ken says. And then he tells me, glowering, that he has seen drivers swerve to intentionally hit animals crossing the road. "That rabbit or raccoon ain't hurting anyone," he says.

We start a new book, *The Strawberry Dog.* Ken picks out the word "dog" in the title. "That dog must eat strawberries," he says. "I used to have a dog like that. I was picking blackberries. Hey, where were those berries going? Into my dog!"

We read these books to help Ken learn words by sight and context. But it seems odd, a white-haired man mesmerized by stories about talkative beavers and foppish toads. Yet, I find myself mesmerized, too. The sessions are reteaching me the exhilaration I found in narrative as a child, listening to my father read about Peter Churchmouse. Our classes glide by, a succession of vocabulary words—"house," would," "see"—interwoven with stories about agrarian hippopotamuses and lost dogs befriended.

One afternoon it is my last session with Ken. We have wrestled with words through a Christmas and a March sugaring, a midsummer haying, an October when Ken's flannel shirts were specked with sawdust from chain-sawing stove logs. Now the fields outside are snowy; it is Christmas again.

My wife and I give Ken a present that she picked out. It is bottles of jam and honey and watermelon pickles, nicely wrapped. Ken quickly slides the package into his canvas tote bag with his homework. "Aren't you going to open it?" Sherry asks. "I'll open it Christmas day," Ken says. "It's the only present I'll get." "No it isn't," she says, and she hands him a present she has brought.

And so we begin our last session with Ken looking pleased. I start with a vocabulary review. "Ignition coil," Ken says, getting the first card right off. He gets "oil filter," too. He peers at the next card. "Have," he says. And he reads the review sentence: "Have you gone away?"

He is cruising today. When I flip the next card, he says, "There's that 'for.' " It is a word that used to stump him. I turn another card. He gets it instantly. "But." He gets "at," then another old nemesis, "are." I ask him to read the card's review sentence. "Are we going down . . . street?" he says. He catches himself. "Nope. That's down*town!*"

I am amazed at Ken's proficiency. A while ago, I had complained to my wife that Ken's progress seemed slow. She did some math: one and a half hours of tutoring a week, with time off for vacations and snowstorms and truck breakdowns, comes to about 70 hours a year. "That's like sending a first grader to school for only 12 days a year," she said. And so I am doubly amazed at how well Ken is reading today. Besides, Sherry Olson has told me that he now sounds out—or just knows—words that he never could have deciphered when he began. And this reticent man has recently read his own poems to a group of fellow tutees—his new friends—and their neighbors at a library get-together.

But now we try something new, a real-world test: reading the supermarket advertising inserts from a local newspaper. Each insert is a hodgepodge of food pictures, product names and prices. I point to a word and Ken ponders. "*C,*" he says finally. "And it's got those two *e*'s—so that would be 'coffee'!" I point again. He gets "Pepsi." Silently, he sounds out the letters on a can's label. "So that's 'corn,' " he announces. He picks out "brownies." This is great. And then, even better, he successfully sounds out the modifier: "Fudge," he says. "They-uh!"

We're on a roll. But now I point to the page's most tortuous word. Ken starts in the middle again, "ta?" I point my finger at the first letters. "Po," he says, unsure. As always when he reads, Ken seems like a beginning swimmer. He goes a few strokes. Flounders.

"Po-ta . . . ," Ken says. He's swum another stroke. "To," he says, sounding out the last syllable. "Po-to-to, po-ta-to—Hey, that's potato!" He's crossed the pond. "Ken!" I say. "Terrific!" He sticks out his chin. He almost smiles. "Well, I done better this time," he says. "Yup, I did good."

IN FOCUS

THE READER IN THE PROCESS

Who are you, reader—there on the other side of the page? How old are you, what does the chair you're sitting in feel like (or are you under a tree, at the beach, in a library?), do you own a TV set, did your mother take you to the library when you were four? Are you reading this book because you're required to, as a way of getting through college, or because you're interested in reading? What are the conditions of your life, what background do you bring to this act of reading, what do you think about what you're doing? What do you think the author wants to tell you?

All of the questions above relate to what current theorists call the *situation* of reading. Reading is an activity affected by many factors: who the reader is, and what the reader both brings to and expects from the experience; who the author is, and what the author both intended and actually created; what the work itself is, and what its form, genre (kind), difficulty, and type of language are. All of these factors affect the reading experience. This activity is currently being studied in great detail by scholars who engage in reader-response criticism, as well as poststructuralist or deconstructionist critics, but basically they are contemplating an old question: what does the reader bring to and take away from the experience?

Reading builds a relationship among the writer, the writing, and the reader. As with most relationships, the more you know about yourself, the better the quality of relationship you can construct. The more you know, the better you will read, and—of course—the more you read, the more you know.

Study Questions

1. If it is possible to say that reading creates a relationship between the reader and the text, then Ken missed out on that relationship, just as he

never married and does not seem to have much of a family. How did his early experiences influence his future, in comparison to Richard Wolkomir's early experiences? Can you compare the two kinds of relationships, that of reading and that of human connections?

2. This piece contains a nice touch of irony when Volkomir cannot correctly name the parts of an engine. What does that situation tell us?

3. Consider how you and other children in your family learned to read. Were you read to by adults? How do you, or how do you plan to, help your own children learn to read?

Writing Topics

1. *Collaborative writing activity* (with members of the group sharing their experiences before writing individual essays. The group can then help edit the members' essays). Have you ever taught something to someone else? Write an essay in which you tell about the pleasures and frustrations of teaching. What kinds of things did you as the teacher learn from the experience?

2. Describe your own reading situation as you read this article or another selection in this book. Notice how, in doing so, you are describing yourself as a reader. Write an essay in which you describe the kind of reader you are and the kinds of relationships you enter into with what you read.

Stone Soup   BARBARA KINGSOLVER

In the catalog of family values, where do we rank an occasion like this? A curly-haired boy who wanted to run before he walked, age seven now, a soccer player scoring a winning goal. He turns to the bleachers with his fists in the air and a smile wide as a gap-toothed galaxy. His own cheering section of grown-ups and kids all leap to their feet and hug each other, delirious with love for this boy. He's Andy, my best friend's son. The cheering section includes his mother and her friends, his brother, his father and stepmother, a stepbrother and stepsister, and a grandparent. Lucky is the child with this many relatives on hand to hail a proud accomplishment. I'm there too, witnessing a family fortune. But in spite of myself, defensive words take shape in my head. I am thinking: I dare *anybody* to call this a broken home.

Families change, and remain the same. Why are our names for home so slow to catch up to the truth of where we live?

When I was a child, I had two parents who loved me without cease. One of them attended every excuse for attention I ever contrived, and the other made it to the ones with higher production values, like piano recitals and appendicitis. So I was a lucky child too. I played with a set of paper dolls called "The Family of Dolls," four in number, who came with the factory-assigned names of Dad, Mom, Sis, and Junior. I think you know what they looked like, at least before I loved them to death and their heads fell off.

Now I've replaced the dolls with a life. I knit my days around my daughter's survival and happiness, and am proud to say her head is still on. But we aren't the Family of Dolls. Maybe you're not, either. And if not, even though you are statistically no oddity, it's probably been suggested to you in a hundred ways that yours isn't exactly a real family, but an impostor family, a harbinger of cultural ruin, a slapdash substitute—something like counterfeit money. Here at the tail end of our century, most of us are up to our ears in the noisy business of trying to support and love a thing called family. But there's a current in the air with ferocious moral force that finds its way even into political campaigns, claiming there is only one right way to do it, the Way It Has Always Been.

In the face of a thriving, particolored world, this narrow view is so pickled and absurd I'm astonished that it gets airplay. And I'm astonished that it still stings.

Every parent has endured the arrogance of a child-unfriendly grump sitting in judgment, explaining what those kids of ours really need (for example, "a good licking"). If we're polite, we move our crew to another bench in the park. If we're forthright (as I am in my mind, only, for the rest of the day), we fix them with a sweet imperious stare and say, "Come back and let's talk about it after you've changed a thousand diapers."

But it's harder somehow to shrug off the Family-of-Dolls Family Values crew when they judge (from their safe distance) that divorced people, blended families, gay families, and single parents are failures. That our children are at risk, and the whole arrangement is messy and embarrassing. A marriage that ends is not called "finished," it's called *failed*. The children of this family may have been born to a happy union, but now they are called *the children of divorce*.

I had no idea how thoroughly these assumptions overlaid my culture until I went through divorce myself. I wrote to a friend: "This might be worse than being widowed. Overnight I've suffered the same losses—companionship, financial and practical support, my identity as a wife and partner, the future I'd taken for granted. I am lonely, grieving, and hard-pressed to take care of my household alone. But instead of bringing casseroles, people are acting like I had a fit and broke up the family china."

Once upon a time I held these beliefs about divorce: that everyone who does it could have chosen not to do it. That it's a lazy way out of marital problems. That it selfishly puts personal happiness ahead of family integrity. Now I tremble for my ignorance. It's easy, in fortunate times, to forget about the ambush that could leave your head reeling: serious mental or physical illness, death in the family, abandonment, financial calamity, humiliation, violence, despair.

I started out like any child, intent on being the Family of Dolls. I set upon young womanhood believing in most of the doctrines of my generation: I wore my skirts four inches above the knee. I had that Barbie with her zebra-striped swimsuit and a figure unlike anything found in nature. And I understood the Prince Charming Theory of Marriage, a quest for Mr. Right that ends smack dab where you find him. I did not completely understand that another whole story *begins* there, and no fairy tale prepared me for the combination of bad luck and persistent hope that would interrupt my dream and lead me to other arrangements. Like a cancer diagnosis, a dying marriage is a thing to fight, to deny, and finally, when there's no choice left, to dig in and survive. Casseroles would help. Likewise, I imagine it must be a painful reckoning in adolescence (or later on) to realize one's own true love will never look like the soft-focus fragrance ads because Prince Charming (surprise!) is a princess. Or vice versa. Or has skin the color your parents didn't want you messing with, except in the Crayola box.

It's awfully easy to hold in contempt the straw broken home, and that mythical category of persons who toss away nuclear family for the sheer fun of it. Even the legal terms we use have a suggestion of caprice. I resent the phrase, "irreconcilable differences," which suggests a stubborn refusal to accept a spouse's little quirks. This is specious. Every happily married couple I know has loads of irreconcilable differences. Negotiating where to set the thermostat is not the point. A nonfunctioning marriage is a slow asphyxiation. It is waking up despised each morning, listening to the pulse of your own loneliness before the radio begins to blare its raucous gospel that you're nothing if you aren't loved. It is sharing your airless house with the threat of suicide or other kinds of violence, while the ghost that whispers, "Leave here and destroy your children," has passed over every door and nailed it shut. Disassembling a marriage in these circumstances is as much *fun* as amputating your own gangrenous leg. You do it, if you can, to save a life—or two, or more.

I know of no one who really went looking to hoe the harder row, especially the daunting one of single parenthood. Yet it seems to be the most American of customs to blame the burdened for their destiny. We'd like so desperately to believe in freedom and justice for all, we can hardly name that rogue bad luck, even when he's a close enough snake to bite us. In the wake of my divorce, some friends (even a few close ones) chose to vanish, rather than linger within striking distance of misfortune.

But most stuck around, bless their hearts, and if I'm any the wiser for my trials, it's from having learned the worth of steadfast friendship. And also, what not to say. The least helpful question is: "Did you want the divorce, or didn't you?" Did I want to keep that gangrenous leg, or not? How to explain, in a culture that venerates choice: two terrifying options are much worse than none at all. Give me any day the quick hand of cruel fate that will leave me scarred but blameless. As it was, I kept thinking of that wicked third-grade joke in which some boy comes up behind you and grabs your ear, starts in with a prolonged tug, and asks, "Do you want this ear any longer?"

Still, the friend who holds your hand and says the wrong thing is made of dearer stuff than the one who stays away. And generally, through all of it, you live. My favorite fictional character, Kate Vaiden (in the novel by Reynolds Price), advises: "Strength just comes in one brand—you stand up at sunrise and meet what they send you and keep your hair combed."

Once you've weathered the straits, you get to cross the tricky juncture from casualty to survivor. If you're on your feet at the end of a year or two, and have begun putting together a happy new existence, those friends who were kind enough to feel sorry for you when you needed it must now accept you back to the ranks of the living. If you're truly blessed, they will dance at your second wedding. Everybody else, for heaven's sake, should stop throwing stones.

Arguing about whether nontraditional families deserve pity or tolerance is a little like the medieval debate about left-handedness as a mark of the devil. Divorce, remarriage, single parenthood, gay parents, and blended families simply are. They're facts of our time. Some of the reasons listed by sociologists for these family reconstructions are: the idea of marriage as a romantic partnership rather than a pragmatic one; a shift in women's expectations, from servility to self-respect and independence; and longevity (prior to antibiotics no marriage was expected to last many decades—in Colonial days the average couple lived to be married less than twelve years). Add to all this, our growing sense of entitlement to happiness and safety from abuse. Most would agree these are all good things. Yet their result—a culture in which serial monogamy and the consequent reshaping of families are the norm—gets diagnosed as "failing."

For many of us, once we have put ourselves Humpty-Dumpty-wise back together again, the main problem with our reorganized family is that other people think we have a problem. My daughter tells me the only time she's uncomfortable about being the child of divorced parents is when her friends say they feel sorry for her. It's a bizarre sympathy, given that half the kids in her school and nation are in the same boat, pursuing childish happiness with the same energy as their married-parent peers. When anyone asks how *she* feels about it, she spontaneously lists the benefits: our house is in the country and we have a dog, but she can go to her dad's neighborhood for the urban thrills of a pool and sidewalks for roller-skating. What's more, she has three sets of grandparents!

Why is it surprising that a child would revel in a widened family and the right to feel at home in more than one house? Isn't it the opposite that should worry us—a child with no home at all, or too few resources to feel safe? The child at risk is the one whose parents are too immature themselves to guide wisely; too diminished by poverty to nurture; too far from opportunity to offer hope. The number of children in the U.S. living in poverty at this moment is almost unfathomably large: twenty percent. There are families among us that need help all right, and by no means are they new on the landscape. The rate at which teenage girls had babies in 1957 (ninety-six per thousand) was twice what it is now. That remarkable statistic is ignored by the religious right—probably because the teen birth rate was cut in half mainly by legalized abortion. In fact, the policy gatekeepers who coined the phrase "family values" have steadfastly ignored the desperation of too-small families, and since 1979 have steadily reduced the amount of financial support available to a single parent. But, this camp's most outspoken attacks seem aimed at the notion of families getting too complex, with add-ons and extras such as a gay parent's partner, or a remarried mother's new husband and his children.

To judge a family's value by its tidy symmetry is to purchase a book for its cover. There's no moral authority there. The famous family comprised of Dad, Mom, Sis, and Junior living as an isolated economic unit is not built on historical bedrock. In *The Way We Never Were*, Stephanie Coontz writes, "Whenever people propose that we go back to the traditional family, I always suggest that they pick a ballpark date for the family they have in mind." Colonial families were tidily disciplined, but their members (meaning everyone but infants) labored incessantly and died young. Then the Victorian family adopted a new division of labor, in which women's role was domestic and children were allowed time for study and play, but this was an upper-class construct supported by myriad slaves. Coontz writes, "For every nineteenth-century middle-class family that protected its wife and child within the family circle, there was an Irish or German girl scrubbing floors . . . a Welsh boy mining coal to keep the home-baked goodies warm, a black girl doing the family laundry, a black mother and child picking cotton to be made into clothes for the family, and a Jewish or an Italian daughter in a sweatshop making 'ladies' dresses or artificial flowers for the family to purchase."

The abolition of slavery brought slightly more democratic arrangements, in which extended families were harnessed together in cottage industries; at the turn of the century came a steep rise in child labor in mines and sweatshops. Twenty percent of American children lived in orphanages at the time; their parents were not necessarily dead, but couldn't afford to keep them.

During the Depression and up to the end of World War II, many millions of U.S. households were more multigenerational than nuclear. Women my grandmother's age were likely to live with a fluid assortment of elderly relatives, in-laws, siblings, and children. In many cases they spent virtually every waking hour working in the company of other women—a companionable scenario in which it would be easier, I imagine, to tolerate an estranged or difficult spouse. I'm reluctant to idealize a life of so much hard work and so little spousal intimacy, but its advantage may have been resilience. A family so large and varied would not easily be brought down by a single blow: it could absorb a death, long illness, an abandonment here or there, and any number of irreconcilable differences.

The Family of Dolls came along midcentury as a great American experiment. A booming economy required a mobile labor force and demanded that women surrender jobs to returning soldiers. Families came to be defined by a single breadwinner. They struck out for single-family homes at an earlier age than ever before, and in unprecedented numbers they raised children in suburban isolation. The nuclear family was launched to sink or swim.

More than a few sank. Social historians corroborate that the suburban family of the postwar economic boom, which we have recently selected as our definition of "traditional," was no panacea. Twenty-five percent of Americans were poor in the mid-1950s, and as yet there were no food stamps. Sixty percent of the elderly lived on less than $1,000 a year, and most had no medical insurance. In the sequestered suburbs, alcoholism and sexual abuse of children were far more widespread than anyone imagined.

Expectations soared, and the economy sagged. It's hard to depend on one other adult for everything, come what may. In the last three decades, that amorphous, adaptable structure we call "family" has been reshaped once more by economic tides. Compared with fifties families, mothers are far more likely now to be employed. We are statistically more likely to divorce, and to live in blended families or other extranuclear arrangements. We are also more likely to plan and space our children, and to rate our marriages as "happy." We are less likely to suffer abuse without recourse, or to stare out at our lives through a glaze of prescription tranquilizers. Our aged parents are less likely to be destitute, and we're half as likely to have a teenage daughter turn up a mother herself. All in all, I would say that if "intact" in modern family-values jargon means living quietly desperate in the bell jar, then hip-hip-hooray for "broken." A neat family model constructed to service the Baby Boom economy seems to be returning gradually to a grand, lumpy shape that human families apparently have tended toward since they first took root in the Olduvai Gorge. We're social animals, deeply fond of companionship, and children love best to run in packs. If there is a *normal* for humans, at all, I expect it looks like two or three Families of Dolls, connected variously by kinship and passion, shuffled like cards and strewn over several shoeboxes.

The sooner we can let go the fairy tale of families functioning perfectly in isolation, the better we might embrace the relief of community. Even the admirable parents who've stayed married through thick and thin are very likely, at present, to incorporate other adults into their families—household help and baby-sitters if they can afford them, or neighbors and grandparents if they can't. For single parents, this support is the rock-bottom definition of family. And most parents who have split apart, however painfully, still manage to maintain family continuity for their children, creating in many cases a boisterous phenomenon that Constance Ahrons in her book *The Good Divorce* calls the "binuclear family." Call it what you will—when ex-spouses beat swords into plowshares and jump up and down at a soccer game together, it makes for happy kids.

Cinderella, look, who needs her? All those evil stepsisters? That story always seemed like too much cotton-picking fuss over clothes. A childhood tale that fascinated me more was the one called "Stone Soup," and the gist of it is this: Once upon a time, a pair of beleaguered soldiers straggled home to a village empty-handed, in a land ruined by war. They were famished, but the villagers had so little they shouted evil words and slammed their doors. So the soldiers dragged out a big kettle, filled it with water, and put it on a fire to boil. They rolled a clean round stone into the pot, while the villagers peered through their curtains in amazement.

"What kind of soup is that?" they hooted.

"Stone soup," the soldiers replied. "Everybody can have some when it's done."

"Well, thanks," one matron grumbled, coming out with a shriveled carrot. "But it'd be better if you threw this in."

And so on, of course, a vegetable at a time, until the whole suspicious village managed to feed itself grandly.

Any family is a big empty pot, save for what gets thrown in. Each stew turns out different. Generosity, a resolve to turn bad luck into good, and respect for variety—these things will nourish a nation of children. Name-calling and suspicion will not. My soup contains a rock or two of hard times, and maybe yours does too. I expect it's a heck of a bouillabaise.

IN FOCUS

How to Measure Your Reading Speed

It's usually a mistake to put too much emphasis on the speed with which something is done. Timed tests, for example, are everywhere in contemporary education—yet what possible reason can there be to add the stress of time pressure when we are trying to measure a person's thinking and retention of information? Why should a testing situation ever focus on the time it takes to take the test?

On the other hand, knowledge about how fast one works in comparison to other people can be useful personal information. If reading and studying take too long, less can be accomplished. There are exercises and techniques to help slow readers increase both their speed and their comprehension, for times when efficiency is necessary. On the other hand, when reading for pleasure, one may be choosing to read slowly and deliberately. Why gulp down a feast? Thus, the method of determining reading speed described below is intended purely as personal information, for those times when knowing one's average reading rate can be useful.

To measure your reading speed, time yourself while reading the Kingsolver essay. Make sure you are reading at your normal speed and slowly enough to fully understand what she says. Try not to rush in an attempt to "win the race."

Then divide 3,500 (the approximate number of words in the essay) by the number of minutes it took you to read the essay, in order to obtain your average word-per-minute (wpm) speed. The average careful reader of this kind of writing will read between 100 and 250 words per minute. (Those reading casually for entertainment, not feeling responsible for a thorough understanding, will on average read at about 250 to 400 wpm.) Thus, the average student, reading the Kingsolver essay in order to discuss or write about it, will probably take between twenty minutes and half an hour for one read-through. Studying textbooks, or reading an essay for close analysis, might take double that time. It's usually advisable to read any assignment twice, scanning the first time and underlining or marking the margins during the second reading for later reference.

For a further discussion of reading speed, see "In Focus: Pause and Consider" (p. 241).

Study Questions

1. Kingsolver begins with an event at which she is present, then goes on to make her point about current families. What experiences of her own does she describe in order to make her point?
2. The information in the essay does not depend solely on Kingsolver's own experiences or the lives of people she knows; she also brings in information from a book by Stephanie Coontz about the history of American families. How does she introduce the material from this book? Why is the quotation effective?
3. What does Kingsolver think of the "traditional" family as it is commonly conceived? What does she think is wrong with "The Family of Dolls"?
4. How did Kingsolver's own experience with divorce affect her beliefs on the subject?

Writing Topics

1. Look at the pattern of the paragraph that begins "Once upon a time I held these beliefs about divorce." Notice how the author in a few sort sentences develops a three-part structure: *Once I thought this way— then I experienced more—now I have a wider view.*

   Choose any subject on which you have changed your mind as a result of an experience. Write a brief essay of about three to five paragraphs in which you follow the pattern *once I thought, then I learned, now I know.*
2. Write an essay on divorce and the "new family" as you have seen or experienced it. Use the Kingsolver essay as a reference, just as Kingsolver uses Stephanie Coontz's book as a reference. Include a quotation from the Kingsolver essay in your own essay and remember to cite the essay as your source.

Shooting an Elephant

GEORGE ORWELL

In Moulmein, in lower Burma, I was hated by large numbers of people—the only time in my life that I have been important enough for this to happen to me. I was sub-divisional police officer of the town, and in an aimless, petty kind of way anti-European feeling was very bitter. No one had the guts to raise a riot, but if a European woman went through the bazaars alone somebody would probably spit betel juice over her dress. As a police officer I was an obvious target and was baited whenever it seemed safe to do so. When a nimble Burman tripped me up on the football field and the referee (another Burman) looked the other way, the crowd yelled with hideous laughter. This happened more than once. In the end the sneering yellow faces of young men that met me everywhere, the insults hooted after me when I was at a safe distance, got badly on my nerves. The young Buddhist priests were the worst of all. There were several thousands of them in the town and none of them seemed to have anything to do except stand on street corners and jeer at Europeans.

All this was perplexing and upsetting. For at that time I had already made up my mind that imperialism was an evil thing and the sooner I chucked up my job and got out of it the better. Theoretically—and secretly, of course—I was all for the Burmese and all against their oppressors, the British. As for the job I was doing, I hated it more bitterly than I can perhaps make clear. In a job like that you see the dirty work of Empire at close quarters. The wretched prisoners huddling in the stinking cages of the lock-ups, the grey, cowed faces of the long-term convicts, the scarred buttocks of the men who had been flogged with bamboos—all these oppressed me with an intolerable sense of guilt. But I could get nothing into perspective. I was young and ill-educated and I had had to think out my problems in the utter silence that is imposed on every Englishman in the East. I did not even know that the British Empire is dying, still less did I know that it is a great deal better than the younger empires that are going to supplant it. All I knew was that I was stuck between my hatred of the empire I served and my rage against the evil-spirited little beasts who tried to make my job impossible. With one part of my mind I thought of the British Raj as an unbreakable tyranny, as something clamped down, in *saecula saeculorum,* upon the will of prostrate peoples; with another part I thought that the greatest joy in the world would be to drive a bayonet into a Buddhist priest's guts. Feelings like these are the normal by-products of imperialism; ask any Anglo-Indian official, if you can catch him off duty.

One day something happened which in a roundabout way was enlightening. It was a tiny incident in itself, but it gave me a better glimpse than I had had before of the real nature of imperialism—the real motives for which despotic governments act. Early one morning the sub-inspector at a police station the other end of the town rang me up on the phone and said that an elephant was ravaging the bazaar. Would I please come and do something about it? I did not know what I could do, but I wanted to see what was happening and I got on to a pony and started out. I took my rifle, an old .44 Winchester and much too small to kill an elephant, but I thought the noise might be useful *in terrorem.* Various Burmans stopped me on the way and told me about the elephant's doings. It was not, of course, a wild elephant, but a tame one which had gone "must." It had been chained up, as tame elephants always are when their attack of "must" is due, but on the previous night it had broken its chain and escaped. Its mahout, the only person who could manage it when it was in that state, had set out in pursuit, but had taken the wrong direction and was now twelve hours' journey away, and in the morning the elephant had suddenly reappeared in the town. The Burmese population had no weapons and were quite helpless against it. It had already destroyed somebody's bamboo hut, killed a cow and raided some fruit-stalls and devoured the stock; also it had met the municipal rubbish van and, when the driver jumped out and took to his heels, had turned the van over and inflicted violences upon it.

The Burmese sub-inspector and some Indian constables were waiting for me in the quarter where the elephant had been seen. It was a very poor quarter, a labyrinth of squalid bamboo huts, thatched with palm-leaf, winding all over a steep hillside. I remember that it was a cloudy, stuffy morning at the beginning of the rains. We began questioning the people as to where the elephant had gone and, as usual, failed to get any definite information. That is invariably the case in the East; a story always sounds clear enough at a distance, but the nearer you get to the scene of events the vaguer it becomes.

Some of the people said that the elephant had gone in one direction, some said that he had gone in another, some professed not even to have heard of any elephant. I had almost made up my mind that the whole story was a pack of lies, when we heard yells a little distance away. There was a loud, scandalized cry of "Go away, child! Go away this instant!" and an old woman with a switch in her hand came round the corner of a hut, violently shooing away a crowd of naked children. Some more women followed, clicking their tongues and exclaiming; evidently there was something that the children ought not to have seen. I rounded the hut and saw a man's dead body sprawling in the mud. He was an Indian, a black Dravidian coolie, almost naked, and he could not have been dead many minutes. The people said that the elephant had come suddenly upon him round the corner of the hut, caught him with its trunk, put its foot on his back and ground him into the earth. This was the rainy season and the ground was soft, and his face had scored a trench a foot deep and a couple of yards long. He was lying on his belly with arms crucified and head sharply twisted to one side. His face was coated with mud, the eyes wide open, the teeth bared and grinning with an expression of unendurable agony. (Never tell me, by the way, that the dead look peaceful. Most of the corpses I have seen looked devilish.) The friction of the great beast's foot had stripped the skin from his back as neatly as one skins a rabbit. As soon as I saw the dead man I sent an orderly to a friend's house nearby to borrow an elephant rifle. I had already sent back the pony, not wanting it to go mad with fright and throw me if it smelt the elephant.

The orderly came back in a few minutes with a rifle and five cartridges, and meanwhile some Burmans had arrived and told us that the elephant was in the paddy fields below, only a few hundred yards away. As I started forward practically the whole population of the quarter flocked out of the houses and followed me. They had seen the rifle and were all shouting excitedly that I was going to shoot the elephant. They had not shown much interest in the elephant when he was merely ravaging their homes, but it was different now that he was going to be shot. It was a bit of fun to them, as it would be to an English crowd; besides they wanted the meat. It made me vaguely uneasy. I had no intention of shooting the elephant—I had merely sent for the rifle to defend myself if necessary—and it is always unnerving to have a crowd following you. I marched down the hill, looking and feeling a fool, with the rifle over my shoulder and an ever-growing army of people jostling at my heels. At the bottom, when you got away from the huts, there was a metalled road and beyond that a miry waste of paddy fields a thousand yards across, not yet ploughed but soggy from the first rains and dotted with coarse grass. The elephant was standing eight yards from the road, his left side towards us. He took not the slightest notice of the crowd's approach. He was tearing up bunches of grass, beating them against his knees to clean them and stuffing them into his mouth.

I had halted on the road. As soon as I saw the elephant I knew with perfect certainty that I ought not to shoot him. It is a serious matter to shoot a working elephant—it is comparable to destroying a huge and costly piece of machinery—and obviously one ought not to do it if it can possibly be avoided. And at that distance, peacefully eating, the elephant looked no more dangerous than a cow. I thought then and I think now that his attack of "must" was already passing off; in which case he would merely wander harmlessly about until the mahout came back and caught him. Moreover, I did not in the least want to shoot him. I decided that I would watch him for a little while to make sure that he did not turn savage again, and then go home.

But at that moment I glanced round at the crowd that had followed me. It was an immense crowd, two thousand at the least and growing every minute. It blocked the road for a long distance on either side. I looked at the sea of yellow faces above the garish clothes—faces all happy and excited over this bit of fun, all certain that the elephant was going to be shot. They were watching me as they would watch a conjurer about to perform a trick. They did not like me, but with the magical rifle in my hands I was momentarily worth watching. And suddenly I realized that I should have to shoot the elephant after all. The people expected it of me and I had got to do it; I could feel their two thousand wills pressing me forward, irresistibly. And it was at this moment, as I stood there with the rifle in my hands, that I first grasped the hollowness, the futility of the white man's dominion in the East. Here was I, the white man with his gun, standing in front of the unarmed native crowd—seemingly the leading actor of the piece; but in reality I was only an absurd puppet pushed to and fro by the will of those yellow faces behind. I perceived in this moment that when the white man turns tyrant it is his own freedom that he destroys. He becomes a sort of hollow, posing dummy, the conventionalized figure of a sahib. For it is the condition of his rule that he shall spend his life in trying to impress the "natives," and so in every crisis he has got to do what the "natives" expect of him. He wears a mask, and his face grows to fit it. I had got to shoot the elephant. I had committed myself to doing it when I sent for the rifle. A sahib has got to act like a sahib; he has got to appear resolute, to know his own mind and do definite things. To come all that way, rifle in hand, with two thousand people marching at my heels, and then to trail feebly away, having done nothing—no, that was impossible. The crowd would laugh at me. And my whole life, every white man's life in the East, was one long struggle not to be laughed at.

But I did not want to shoot the elephant. I watched him beating his bunch of grass against his knees, with that preoccupied grandmotherly air that elephants have. It seemed to me that it would be murder to shoot him. At that age I was not squeamish about killing animals, but I had never shot an elephant and never wanted to. (Somehow it always seems worse to kill a *large* animal.) Besides, there was the beast's owner to be considered. Alive, the elephant was worth at least a hundred pounds; dead, he would only be worth the value of his tusks, five pounds, possibly. But I had got to act quickly. I turned to some experienced-looking Burmans who had been there when we arrived, and asked them how the elephant had been behaving. They all said the same thing: he took no notice of you if you left him alone, but he might charge if you went too close to him.

It was perfectly clear to me what I ought to do. I ought to walk up to within, say, twenty-five yards of the elephant and test his behavior. If he charged, I could shoot; if he took no notice of me, it would be safe to leave him until the mahout came back. But also I knew that I was going to do no such thing. I was a poor shot with a rifle and the ground was soft mud into which one would sink at every step. If the elephant charged and I missed him, I should have about as much chance as a toad under a steam-roller. But even then I was not thinking particularly of my own skin, only of the watchful yellow faces behind. For at that moment, with the crowd watching me, I was not afraid in the ordinary sense, as I would have been if I had been alone. A white man mustn't be frightened in front of "natives"; and so, in general, he isn't frightened. The sole thought in my mind was that if anything went wrong those two thousand Burmans would see me pursued, caught, trampled on and reduced to a grinning corpse like that Indian up the hill. And if that happened it was quite probable that some of them would laugh. That would never do. There was only one alternative. I shoved the cartridges into the magazine and lay down on the road to get a better aim.

The crowd grew very still, and a deep, low, happy sigh, as of people who see the theatre curtain go up at last, breathed from innumerable throats. They were going to have their bit of fun after all.

The rifle was a beautiful German thing with cross-hair sights. I did not then know that in shooting an elephant one would shoot to cut an imaginary bar running from ear-hole to ear-hole. I ought, therefore, as the elephant was sideways on, to have aimed straight at his ear-hole; actually I aimed several inches in front of this, thinking the brain would be further forward.

When I pulled the trigger I did not hear the bang or feel the kick—one never does when a shot goes home—but I heard the devilish roar of glee that went up from the crowd. In that instant, in too short a time, one would have thought, even for the bullet to get there, a mysterious, terrible change had come over the elephant. He neither stirred nor fell, but every line of his body had altered. He looked suddenly stricken, shrunken, immensely old, as though the frightful impact of the bullet had paralyzed him without knocking him down. At last, after what seemed a long time—it might have been five seconds, I dare say—he sagged flabbily to his knees. His mouth slobbered. An enormous senility seemed to have settled upon him. One could have imagined him thousands of years old. I fired again into the same spot. At the second shot he did not collapse but climbed with desperate slowness to his feet and stood weakly upright, with legs sagging and head drooping. I fired a third time. That was the shot that did for him. You could see the agony of it jolt his whole body and knock the last remnant of strength from his legs. But in falling he seemed for a moment to rise, for as his hind legs collapsed beneath him he seemed to tower upward like a huge rock toppling, his trunk reaching skywards like a tree. He trumpeted, for the first and only time. And then down he came, his belly towards me, with a crash that seemed to shake the ground even where I lay.

I got up. The Burman were already racing past me across the mud. It was obvious that the elephant would never rise again, but he was not dead. He was breathing very rhythmically with long rattling gasps, his great mound of a side painfully rising and falling. His mouth was wide open—I could see far down into caverns of pale pink throat. I waited a long time for him to die, but his breathing did not weaken. Finally I fired my two remaining shots into the spot where I thought his heart must be. The thick blood welled out of him like red velvet, but still he did not die. His body did not even jerk when the shots hit him, the tortured breathing continued without a pause. He was dying, very slowly and in great agony, but in some world remote from me where not even a bullet could damage him further. I felt that I had got to put an end to that dreadful noise. It seemed dreadful to see the great beast lying there, powerless to move and yet powerless to die, and not even to be able to finish him. I sent back for my small rifle and poured shot after shot into his heart and down his throat. They seemed to make no impression. The tortured gasps continued as steadily as the ticking of a clock.

In the end I could not stand it any longer and went away. I heard later that it took him half an hour to die. Burmans were bringing dahs and baskets even before I left, and I was told they had stripped his body almost to the bones by the afternoon.

Afterwards, of course, there were endless discussions about the shooting of the elephant. The owner was furious, but he was only an Indian and could do nothing. Besides, legally I had done the right thing, for a mad elephant has to be killed, like a mad dog, if its owner fails to control it. Among the Europeans opinion was divided. The older men said I was right, the younger men said it was a damn shame to shoot an elephant for killing a coolie, because an elephant was worth more than any damn Coringhee coolie. And afterwards I was very glad that the coolie had been killed; it put me legally in the right and it gave me a sufficient pretext for shooting the elephant. I often wondered whether any of the others grasped that I had done it solely to avoid looking a fool.

FROM THE SELF TO SOCIETY

There are any number of reasons for reading autobiography: an interest in the writer, such as wanting to learn how a person achieved fame or success; an interest in the history of the period during which the person lived; or even a general interest in human psychology, in learning why certain people do certain things. The best autobiography gratifies all of those desires and more. Good autobiographical writing connects the subject's life to some broader theme or meaning, some point about his or her life that has expanded significance. Writing about one incident, the killing of an elephant, Orwell also writes deeply about himself, his feelings, and his actions, and about the time and place in which the incident happened. He also connects his own story to the story of colonialism, and his actions become symbolic of the historic situation.

Keeping a journal is a useful technique for gathering the material that may later become part of an autobiographical essay. Journals and diaries are different from autobiographies mainly in that they are intensely personal, usually without the kind of broad significance and context attached to an autobiographical story, and generally written without the idea of being published. Most often, a writer keeps a journal to mine later for ideas and specific passages. Turning a journal entry into an autobiographical essay means, in part, translating "what I did and thought" into "what my experiences mean on the larger scale."

Study Questions

1. What is Orwell's attitude toward the Burmese people? What seems to be their attitude toward him as a police officer and as a member of the ruling classes? Why does he find this "perplexing and upsetting"? What other attitudes are expressed in the last paragraph?
2. Orwell writes, "A sahib has got to act like a sahib; he has got to appear resolute, to know his own mind and do definite things." In what way does this make the "master" a prisoner of his position? What other examples can you give of a person's being imprisoned by the expectations of others, by having to act and appear in one certain way and "do definite things"?
3. What makes the description of the elephant's death so horrifying? How do the details help the reader to picture the event? What specific details and sensory impressions are particularly effective?

Writing Topics

1. *Collaborative writing activity* (with the group members sharing and comparing early drafts of their pieces). Write about one of your ancestors or your family background, telling the story of that person or group as part of some larger historical movement. Explain, for example, what brought your family to America or impelled them to move from one place to another. (Did they come as a result of the Irish potato famine or the Spanish civil war? Did they travel from state to state to escape poor economic conditions? If they were Native Americans, what were the travels of their tribe or nation like?) Shape this material into either an imaginary autobiography, telling the story from the point of view of one of your ancestors, or an expository essay, looking back from the present.
2. Write an autobiographical essay about an incident in your own life during which you were forced by psychological pressure to do something you did not want to do. Describe the situation and also your feelings. Use appropriate details, following Orwell's style, to put your reader empathically in the picture.

Claiming the Self: The Cripple as American Man

LEONARD KRIEGEL

I am not a physician; I am not a psychologist; I am not a sociologist; indeed, I do not work in any aspect of health care. But I am a man who has lived all but eleven of his years here on earth as a cripple, a word I prefer to the euphemistic "handicapped" or "disabled," each of which does little more than further society's illusions about illness and accident and the effects of illness and accident. For to be "disabled" or "handicapped" is to deny oneself the rage, anger, and pride of having managed to survive as a cripple in America. If I know nothing else, I know that I have endured—and I know the price I have paid for that endurance.

As a writer and as a teacher of literature, I believe that the essence of what we like to call the human condition is each individual's struggle to claim a self, to create an *I* stamped with his own distinct individuality. This affirmation of the self is what we seek in biography and autobiography. It may exist beyond our capacity to create it, beyond our habits and virtues and will—but not beyond our need. I have never met a man or woman who did not want to stake a claim to an identifiable *I*.

Of course, it is a tentative claim, existing within the confines of a world in which we are never truly at home. Our capacities as individuals are always being tested. Everywhere we go, we seek to affirm the separate self, the identifiable *I* who possesses the strength and courage to withstand whatever tests lie in wait. Although it may be immodest to state it openly, the truth is that no one has a greater right to claim that *I* than a man who has wrested his sense of a separate identity from the very condition that threatened to declare his life as a man at an end. And however self-conscious and embarrassed I am about saying it, no one has a better right to claim that his sense of himself as a man has been seized from adversity than the cripple does.

Cripples are forced to affirm their existence and claim selfhood by pushing beyond those structures and categories their condition has created. On one level, this is what all men and women try to do. But in a culture that places such importance on the physical—however uncomfortable it may be with the actual body—the cripple's insistence on getting beyond the restrictions imposed by physical limitations is the kind of violent joining together of forces pulling in opposite directions that is characteristic of modern life.

It would be the most absurd nonsense to suggest that the cripple is envied by other Americans seeking to claim the *I*. No one *wants* to find himself the victim of disease or accident—no one, at least, who is rational. Anyone contemplating the prospect of spending the rest of his life in a wheelchair would exchange that fate for a normal pair of legs without a moment's hesitation. Ask me to give up the most visible symbols of being a cripple—in my case, the braces and crutches on which I walk—and I will jump at the chance. To insist on our capacity, to be willing to face the everyday risks that a cripple must confront simply to meet the world, to enjoy the sense of triumph that an *earned* mobility bestows—we can accept all this and yet hunger after what we lack. We can believe in our capacity to face whatever has to be faced; we can assume that we have paid a price for the existence we claim that others might not have been able to pay; we can think of ourselves as having confronted our fate even with such grandiose metaphors as Jacob wrestling with his angel. The one thing cripples cannot afford to do is to assume the luxury of lying to themselves.

Cripples are second-class citizens only because they are conscious of nothing so much as of the barriers the outside world places in their way. My hungers are invariably personal; the joys not tasted are joys not tasted *by me*. However simplistic my desires may seem to others, their significance is multiplied a thousand times by an imagination that knows what they are but has not been able to possess them. However absurd and childish they are as desires, I reach out and touch them in my imagination alone. And they are not abstract. They are available to any of those the distinguished social psychologist Erving Goffman labeled the "normals." That *they* should be able to touch them so easily, so unconsciously, infuriates me. For my life as a cripple tells me that a man should earn the self he claims. However successful I may be in the eyes of the world—and I certainly am, to use a phrase that should be burned out of the vocabulary, a man who has "overcome his handicap"—I am always measuring what I have against what I want. How do I tell the normals that I still dream about being able to run on the beach with my young sons (both of them long since grown adults), that I sometimes lie awake at night thinking about swinging a baseball bat again, that even as I visualize what I would do were I suddenly given the legs of a normal I know that what I want to do would seem stupid and banal in his normal eyes? I want to kick a football, jump rope, ride a bike, climb a mountain—not a mountain as metaphor but a real honest-to-god mountain—ride a horse. I want to make love differently; I want to drive differently; I want to know my sons differently. In short, I want to know the world as the normal is privileged to know it.

These are not great feats, not even for the imagination to conjure up. They do not call for special skills or training. But they are what *I* want—what I have never tasted or else tasted so long ago that the memories have become one with the desire, locked in a permanent embrace. And such memories frame all that is absent from my life.

People struggle not only to define themselves but to avoid being defined by others. But to be a cripple is to learn that one can be defined from outside. Our complaint against society is not that it ignores our presence but that it ignores our reality, our sense of ourselves as humans brave enough to capture our destinies against odds that are formidable. Here is where the cripple and society war with each other. If we were satisfied to be held up for compassion, to be infantilized on telethons, we would discover that this America has a great deal of time for us, a great deal of room for us in a heart open to praise for its own generosity. We are not, like Ellison's black man, invisible in America. But the outline of the shadow we cast has been created not by us but by those who will find a way to see what they want to see rather than what is there. In what we call literature, as well as in popular culture, we are what others make of us. In literature as demonic as Shakespeare's Richard III or as wooden as Lawrence's Clifford Chatterley, on television as bathetic as the stream of smiling children paraded before our eyes as if their palsy were Jerry Lewis's reason for living, what we invariably discover is that our true selves, our own inner lives, have been auctioned off so that we can be palatable rather than real. We can serve the world as victim or demon, the object of its charity or its terror. But the only thing we can be certain of is that the world would prefer to turn a blind eye and a deaf ear to our real selves—and that it will do precisely that until we impose those selves on the world.

Years ago, this recognition led me to write an essay entitled "Uncle Tom and Tiny Tim: Some Reflections on the Cripple as Negro." But the situation of the cripple in American society today seems to me considerably less grim than I described it in 1969. Tiny Tim is not the only image the cripple calls forth. The self wrested from adversity is a far more attractive image to be offered to society and ourselves.

And yet, society is more than a bit dubious about that image's validity. For if it honors what it sees as our suffering, it retreats before our need to define our inner lives, to speak of who and what we are. Society continues to need the ability to define us if it is to be comfortable with us. In its own eyes, it is society that defines our authenticity. I remember that when I returned at the age of thirteen from a two-year rehabilitation stay in a state home, my mother was immediately asked by the neighborhood chairman of the March of Dimes campaign (this was in 1946, before the introduction of the Salk vaccine) to go from door to door to collect in the campaign's annual fund drive. It seemed somehow natural: My mother possessed a kind of subaltern authenticity, for she was the mother of a cripple. Her presence at the door was supposed to remind our normal neighbors that their charity had been *earned.* Any other individual going from door to door would not have seemed as believable.

And the truth is that my mother *was* more effective, for she, along with our neighbors, assumed her authenticity. For the next forty years, long after the disease that had crippled me had been wiped out as a threat by the development of the Salk and Sabin vaccines, my mother made her annual door-to-door pilgrimage for the March of Dimes. Her "success" as a collector of charity was directly attributable to the sense our neighbors had that she was "the genuine article." Indeed, the kind of fund-raising she was doing mixes the comic and the bathetic, and it remains characteristic of efforts of such groups as the Shriners to support hospitals. The Shriners sponsor an annual all-star college football game that displays the salable talents of college athletes while giving everyone—sponsors, hospital executives, fans, professional football scouts, and players—a substantial charity fix. "Let strong legs run so that weak legs can walk" is the game's slogan. I can think of no better illustration of how society defines cripples as their condition. And it does this through the simple strategy of remaining purposely oblivious to the feelings it inspires in them. A child who thinks of himself or herself as an object for the charity of others has been defined as dependent. Only a considerable act of defiance can possibly save that child from the fate of being permanently dependent. In January, 1968, vacationing in Florida with my wife and two small children, I drove past a large shopping center. Strung out in huge black letters against a white marquee was a sign: "Help Crippled Kids! See Stalin's Limousine! Donation: $1.00."

Now, this is the kind of material Nathanael West or Woody Allen might have done justice to, for it is genuinely funny, a most human denial of the human. But it is also a definition of cripples from out-side, one that remains the most formidable obstacle in their path as they push toward defining the self. They want to realize all that they can make out of their situation. Society, in turn, wants them to make it feel good. Even the act of reaching out for a real self is a challenge to what society tells cripples is their proper due. Their task is not only to claim a self but also to refuse to allow their pain to be mar-keted. The authenticity they must insist on is one that each person alone can create—not the cripple's nurses, not the doctors, not the teachers, not the social workers. For no one knows what his exis-tence costs him as he does. No one has lived with the intimacy of his fears as he has. And no one understands better that the self's reality can be taken from the self's resistance. Better if Stalin's limo were laughed out of existence. Better if "Jerry's kids" forced Jerry to un-derstand the immense psychological destructiveness of his telethons. Better if hospitals were viewed as a right to be paid for, not by char-ity, but by a rational society.

Part of me still hungers to perform those banal tasks that define the normal for all of us. But another part of me—perhaps the braver part—insists that the mark of a man is to acknowledge that he has been formed by the very accidents that have made him what he is. Perhaps the task of those of us who are crippled is to face honestly what the normal can choose to ignore, to take a chance on a con-scious existence pulled from the remnants of disease or accident. Our condition is intense, our isolation massive. Society views us as both pariah and victim. We are pitied, shunned, labeled, classified, analyzed, and categorized. We are packed in the spiritual ice of a sanitized society in the hope that we can somehow be dealt with in some even more sanitized society of the future. Society will *permit* us anything, except the right to be what we can become. And yet with-out that right we cannot extricate ourselves from the role of suppli-cants for society's largesse.

If society is uncomfortable with us, it is not uncomfortable with what it can do for us. That shopping center sign was created for the same audience at whose doors my mother knocked. Those Jerry Lewis telethons are responded to by men and women who believe they are deeply concerned with "Jerry's kids." Those well-meaning Shriners in their silly hats interviewed at halftime do not intend to tamper with the cripple's need to establish a self. Accident and disease bring out the charitable in other men. They also bring out the sanctimonious and self-righteous in other men. What cripples discover they share is not a physical condition—the differences among them are far more pronounced than the differences between white and black, Jew and Gentile, German and Italian—so much as it is the experience of having been categorized by the normal world. For the normals, we possess a collective presence. For if cripples prove themselves capable of defining their own lives, then what excuse can normals offer for their failure? If cripples break with the restrictions placed upon their existence and insist that they will be what they have earned the right to be, then where does that leave the normals?

I do not wish to suggest that anyone is "better" for having suffered disease or disability. Nonsense does not cease being nonsense when it is cloaked in metaphysics or theology. All I mean is that cripples have no choice but to attempt to establish the terms and the boundaries of their existence, and that they should recognize that in choosing to do this they are going to offend those normals who have an interest in cripples remaining what they want to perceive. Only by turning stigma into strength can cripples avoid the categorization the normal world insists on thrusting upon them. "This is where I am because here is where I have placed myself." Only through scrupulous self-scrutiny can we hold up the ragged ends of our own existence and insist that the normals match our honesty with their own. In a mendacious time, during which what it really takes to become an authentic self has been buried beneath one or another variation on doing one's own thing, the cripple who chooses to be honest can at least keep faith with his wound.

Having already witnessed the power of chance and accident, cripples know that if the reconciliation of their needs with the world's actualities can lead to maturity, it can also lead to madness and despair and even suicide. Under the best of circumstances, maturity is not permanent. But when its necessity is dictated by disease or accident it is not only temporary, it is also what one is condemned to live with. Indeed, it can be said of cripples that they are condemned to adulthood. Every step one takes, every breath one draws, every time one makes love, crosses a street, drives a car, one lives out the terms of the adult's argument with responsibility for the self. The image of what one was or could have been smashes against the reality of what one is. And if one has accepted the rules of the game, then the sin of pride beckons—pride in performance, pride in one's capacity.

For there is a point at which the living on an everyday basis with that internal enemy who, as Ernest Becker wrote, unremittingly "threatens danger" leads to a certain haughtiness, perhaps even to a barely concealed sense of superiority to normals who have not been called upon to prove their selfhood. Our dirty little secret is the pride we may feel in a performance designed to impose the self on the world. For someone who has matched his or her will against possible destruction, the normal's frame of reference can seem comic, even banal, in the rhetoric it employs and the strategies it assumes. One who lives his daily life on intimate terms with pain can only listen in amazement to a sportscaster praising the courage of an athlete earning a great deal of money on enduring his "aching" knees.

But it is always within the power of the normals to diminish the cripples' sense of their own reality. We are, after all, trapped by the accoutrements of our existence. An individual may choose to create an authentic self out of defiance of accident or disease, but he cannot remake the truth of his condition. It is what it is. No matter what demands he makes upon himself, dead legs do not run and blind eyes do not see. The cripple can make of his injury an acquisition; he can transform his handicap into a symbol of endurance; he can formulate his very existence as an act of defiance. But he cannot change what has happened to him. He must recognize that his life is to be different in its essentials from the life of the normal person. He has learned to look on stigmatization itself as something he has earned. He comes to recognize that he has truly been set apart.

The process of recognition has been beautifully voiced in a poem by Karl Shapiro. The poem is about a soldier's loss of his leg during the Second World War. At first the soldier struggles to accept the loss of part of his body. The soldier discovers that he must learn to adapt to life without the leg even as the life he possesses is transformed into an act of defiance of the loss.

> Later, as if deliberately, his fingers
> Begin to explore the stump. He learns shape
> That is comfortable and tucked in like a sock.
> This has a sense of humor, this can despise
> The finest surgical limb, the dignity of limping,
> The nonsense of wheelchairs. Now he smiles to the wall:
> The Amputation becomes an acquisition.

But the soldier in "The Leg" will ultimately discover that even such hard-won acquisitions can be taken away by the society that insists on defining who he is, a society that will remain intent on shrinking his reality by insisting on its right to define the limits of his space, the boundaries of his quest for a self. And the effort to live honestly will pinch his sense of his own courage and test his ability to live on his own terms. For what we remember remains embedded in what we are—and in what we once were.

THE VIRTUAL WORLD OF LITERATURE

The most effective and most widely available method of virtual reality to date, literature constructs an imaginary world for the reader to enter—much like the world of dreams—except that the reader can exit by closing the book. In "Claiming the Self," Kriegel takes the reader into the world of physical disability. As the reader enters and views, an interesting thing happens: that spectator gets to not only share his experiences but also to share his emotional states, to feel—as he does—frustrated, hopeful, desperate, determined.

Notice how Kriegel leads the reader through his life as a crippled man and how he helps the reader to share his mental attitude. As the reader *identifies* with the author/narrator, the story becomes that of every disabled person, and the reader can both feel with Kriegel and stand apart as an observer.

The technical term for the way the reader participates in Kriegel's mental state is *empathy,* an identification of the reader (or listener, or audience) with the character. M. H. Abrams, in *A Glossary of Literary Terms* (San Diego: Harcourt, 1985), defines empathy as "an involuntary projection of ourselves into an object. . . . In thoroughly absorbed contemplation we seem empathically to pirouette with a ballet dancer, soar with a hawk, bend with the movements of a tree in the wind, and even share the strength, ease, and grace with which a well-proportioned arch appears to support a bridge." Sympathy, on the other hand, allows us to "feel along with" but not to "feel as." The difference between the reactions of empathy and sympathy may, of course, be more dependent on the reader or listener than on the writer. What kind of person might be able to empathize with Kriegel? Who might only sympathize?

Study Questions

1. At the beginning of the second paragraph, Kriegel writes, "I believe that the essence of what we like to call the human condition is each individual's struggle to claim a self, to create an *I* stamped with his own

distinct individuality." How, in the essay, does he show his own distinct individuality?

2. Why does Kriegel call himself a "cripple," rather than using some nicer term? Does he get to say this only because he himself is handicapped? Could someone else call him a "cripple"? Why would members of a minority group use words and jokes to describe themselves that would be offensive in the mouths of "outsiders"?

3. Kriegel speaks of his mother's having "authenticity" as "the mother of a cripple." Name other instances in which someone has "authenticity" by virtue of being who or what he or she is.

Writing Topics

1. Kriegel writes that "the mark of a man is to acknowledge that he has been formed by the very accidents that have made him what he is." Write a short essay about something in your life—an "accident" of birth (as in being who you are and not someone else) or something that happened later—that significantly formed you.

2. Is Kriegel right in objecting to the charity telethon? Write a response to his statement that it would be "better if hospitals were viewed as a right to be paid for, not by charity, but by a rational society."

Once More to the Lake

E. B. WHITE

One summer, along about 1904, my father rented a camp on a lake in Maine and took us all there for the month of August. We all got ringworm from some kittens and had to rub Pond's Extract on our arms and legs night and morning, and my father rolled over in a canoe with all his clothes on; but outside of that the vacation was a success and from then on none of us ever thought there was any place in the world like that lake in Maine. We returned summer after summer—always on August 1st for one month. I have since become a salt-water man, but sometimes in summer there are days when the restlessness of the tides and the fearful cold of the sea water and the incessant wind which blows across the afternoon and into the evening make me wish for the placidity of a lake in the woods. A few weeks ago this feeling got so strong I bought myself a couple of bass hooks and a spinner and returned to the lake where we used to go, for a week's fishing and to revisit old haunts.

I took along my son, who had never had any fresh water up his nose and who had seen lily pads only from train windows. On the journey over to the lake I began to wonder what it would be like. I wondered how time would have marred this unique, this holy spot—the coves and streams, the hills that the sun set behind, the camps and the paths behind the camps. I was sure that the tarred road would have found it out and I wondered in what other ways it would be desolated. It is strange how much you can remember about places like that once you allow your mind to return into the grooves which lead back. You remember one thing, and that suddenly reminds you of another thing. I guess I remembered clearest of all the early mornings, when the lake was cool and motionless, remembered how the bedroom smelled of the lumber it was made of and of the wet woods whose scent entered through the screen. The partitions in the camp were thin and did not extend clear to the top of the rooms, and as I was always the first up I would dress softly so as not to wake the others, and sneak out into the sweet outdoors and start out in the canoe, keeping close along the shore in the long shadows of the pines. I remembered being very careful never to rub my paddle against the gunwale for fear of disturbing the stillness of the cathedral.

The lake had never been what you would call a wild lake. There were cottages sprinkled around the shores, and it was in farming country although the shores of the lake were quite heavily wooded. Some of the cottages were owned by nearby farmers, and you would live at the shore and eat your meals at the farmhouse. That's what our family did. But although it wasn't wild, it was a fairly large and undisturbed lake and there were places in it which, to a child at least, seemed infinitely remote and primeval.

I was right about the tar: it led to within half a mile of the shore. But when I got back there, with my boy, and we settled into a camp near a farmhouse and into the kind of summertime I had known, I could tell that it was going to be pretty much the same as it had been before—I knew it, lying in bed the first morning, smelling the bedroom, and hearing the boy sneak quietly out and go off along the shore in a boat. I began to sustain the illusion that he was I, and therefore, by simple transposition, that I was my father. This sensation persisted, kept cropping up all the time we were there. It was not an entirely new feeling, but in this setting it grew much stronger. I seemed to be living a dual existence. I would be in the middle of some simple act, I would be picking up a bait box or laying down a table fork, or I would be saying something, and suddenly it would be not I but my father who was saying the words or making the gesture. It gave me a creepy sensation.

We went fishing the first morning. I felt the same damp moss covering the worms in the bait can, and saw the dragonfly alight on the tip of my rod as it hovered a few inches from the surface of the water. It was the arrival of this fly that convinced me beyond any doubt that everything was as it always had been, that the years were a mirage and there had been no years. The small waves were the same, chucking the rowboat under the chin as we fished at anchor, and the boat was the same boat, the same color green and the ribs broken in the same places, and under the floor-boards the same fresh-water leavings and débris—the dead helgramite, the wisps of moss, the rusty discarded fishhook, the dried blood from yesterday's catch. We stared silently at the tips of our rods, at the dragonflies that came and went. I lowered the tip of mine into the water, tentatively, pensively dislodging the fly, which darted two feet away, poised, darted two feet back, and came to rest again a little farther up the rod. There had been no years between the ducking of this dragonfly and the other one—the one that was part of memory. I looked at the boy, who was silently watching his fly, and it was my hands that held his rod, my eyes watching. I felt dizzy and didn't know which rod I was at the end of.

We caught two bass, hauling them in briskly as though they were mackerel, pulling them over the side of the boat in a businesslike manner without any landing net, and stunning them with a blow on the back of the head. When we got back for a swim before lunch, the lake was exactly where we had left it, the same number of inches from the dock, and there was only the merest suggestion of a breeze. This seemed an utterly enchanted sea, this lake you could leave to its own devices for a few hours and come back to, and find that it had not stirred, this constant and trustworthy body of water. In the shallows, the dark, watersoaked sticks and twigs, smooth and old, were undulating in clusters on the bottom against the clean ribbed sand, and the track of the mussel was plain. A school of minnows swam by, each minnow with its small individual shadow, doubling the attendance, so clear and sharp in the sunlight. Some of the other campers were in swimming, along the shore, one of them with a cake of soap, and the water felt thin and clear and unsubstantial. Over the years there had been this person with the cake of soap, this cultist, and here he was. There had been no years.

Up to the farmhouse to dinner through the teeming, dusty field, the road under our sneakers was only a two-track road. The middle track was missing, the one with the marks of the hooves and the splotches of dried, flaky manure. There had always been three tracks to choose from in choosing which track to walk in; now the choice was narrowed down to two. For a moment I missed terribly the middle alternative. But the way led past the tennis court, and something about the way it lay there in the sun reassured me; the tape had loosened along the backline, the alleys were green with plantains and other weeds, and the net (installed in June and removed in September) sagged in the dry noon, and the whole place steamed with midday heat and hunger and emptiness. There was a choice of pie for dessert, and one was blueberry and one was apple, and the waitresses were the same country girls, there having been no passage of time, only the illusion of it as in a dropped curtain—the waitresses were still fifteen; their hair had been washed, that was the only difference—they had been to the movies and seen the pretty girls with the clean hair.

Summertime, oh summertime, pattern of life indelible, the fadeproof lake, the woods unshatterable, the pasture with the sweetfern and the juniper forever and ever, summer without end; this was the background, and the life along the shore was the design, the cottagers with their innocent and tranquil design, their tiny docks with the flagpole and the American flag floating against the white clouds in the blue sky, the little paths over the roots of the trees leading from camp to camp and the paths leading back to the outhouses and the can of lime for sprinkling, and at the souvenir counters at the store the miniature birch-bark canoes and the post cards that showed things looking a little better than they looked. This was the American family at play, escaping the city heat, wondering whether the newcomers in the camp at the head of the cove were "common" or "nice," wondering whether it was true that the people who drove up for Sunday dinner at the farmhouse were turned away because there wasn't enough chicken.

It seemed to me, as I kept remembering all this, that those times and those summers had been infinitely precious and worth saving. There had been jollity and peace and goodness. The arriving (at the beginning of August) had been so big a business in itself, at the railway station the farm wagon drawn up, the first smell of the pine-laden air, the first glimpse of the smiling farmer, and the great importance of the trunks and your father's enormous authority in such matters, and the feel of the wagon under you for the long ten-mile haul, and at the top of the last long hill catching the first view of the lake after eleven months of not seeing this cherished body of water. The shouts and cries of the other campers when they saw you, and the trunks to be unpacked, to give up their rich burden. (Arriving was less exciting nowadays, when you sneaked up in your car and parked it under a tree near the camp and took out the bags and in five minutes it was all over, no fuss, no loud wonderful fuss about trunks.)

Peace and goodness and jollity. The only thing that was wrong now, really, was the sound of the place, an unfamiliar nervous sound of the outboard motors. This was the note that jarred, the one thing that would sometimes break the illusion and set the years moving. In those other summertimes all motors were inboard; and when they were at a little distance, the noise they made was a sedative, an ingredient of summer sleep. They were one-cylinder and two-cylinder engines, and some were make-and-break and some were jump-spark, but they all made a sleepy sound across the lake. The one-lungers throbbed and fluttered, and the twin-cylinder ones purred and purred, and that was a quiet sound too. But now the campers all had outboards. In the daytime, in the hot mornings, these motors made a petulant, irritable sound; at night, in the still evening when the afterglow lit the water, they whined about one's ears like mosquitoes. My boy loved our rented outboard, and his great desire was to achieve singlehanded mastery over it, and authority, and he soon learned the trick of choking it a little (but not too much), and the adjustment of the needle valve. Watching him I would remember the things you could do with the old one-cylinder engine with the heavy flywheel, how you could have it eating out of your hand if you got really close to it spiritually. Motor boats in those days didn't have clutches, and you would make a landing by shutting off the motor at the proper time and coasting in with a dead rudder. But there was a way of reversing them, if you learned the trick, by cutting the switch and putting it on again exactly on the final dying revolution of the flywheel, so that it would kick back against compression and begin reversing. Approaching a dock in a strong following breeze, it was difficult to show up sufficiently by the ordinary coasting method, and if a boy felt he had complete mastery over his motor, he was tempted to keep it running beyond its time and then reverse it a few feet from the dock. It took a cool nerve, because if you threw the switch a twentieth of a second too soon you would catch the flywheel when it still had speed enough to go up past center, and the boat would leap ahead, charging bull-fashion at the dock.

We had a good week at the camp. The bass were biting well and the sun shone endlessly, day after day. We would be tired at night and lie down in the accumulated heat of the little bedrooms after the long hot day and the breeze would stir almost imperceptibly outside and the smell of the swamp drift in through the rusty screens. Sleep would come easily and in the morning the red squirrel would be on the roof, tapping out his gay routine. I kept remembering everything, lying in bed in the mornings—the small steamboat that had a long rounded stern like the lip of a Ubangi, and how quietly she ran on the moonlight sails, when the older boys played their mandolins and the girls sang and we ate doughnuts dipped in sugar, and how sweet the music was on the water in the shining night, and what it had felt like to think about girls then. After breakfast we would go up to the store and the things were in the same place—the minnows in a bottle, the plugs and spinners disarranged and pawed over by the youngsters from the boys' camp, the fig newtons and the Beeman's gum. Outside, the road was tarred and cars stood in front of the store. Inside, all was just as it had always been, except there was more Coca Cola and not so much Moxie and root beer and birch beer and sarsaparilla. We would walk out with a bottle of pop apiece and sometimes the pop would backfire up our noses and hurt. We explored the streams, quietly, where the turtles slid off the sunny logs and dug their way into the soft bottom; and we lay on the town wharf and fed worms to the tame bass. Everywhere we went I had trouble making out which was I, the one walking at my side, the one walking in my pants.

One afternoon while we were there at that lake a thunderstorm came up. It was like the revival of an old melodrama that I had seen long ago with childish awe. The second-act climax of the drama of the electrical disturbance over a lake in America had not changed in any important respect. This was the big scene, still the big scene. The whole thing was so familiar, the first feeling of oppression and heat and a general air around camp of not wanting to go very far away. In midafternoon (it was all the same) a curious darkening of the sky, and a lull in everything that had made life tick; and then the way the boats suddenly swung the other way at their moorings with the coming of a breeze out of the new quarter, and the premonitory rumble. Then the kettle drum, then the snare, then the bass drum and cymbals, then crackling light against the dark, and the gods grinning and licking their chops in the hills. Afterward the calm, the rain steadily rustling in the calm lake, the return of light and hope and spirits, and the campers running out in joy and relief to go swimming in the rain, their bright cries perpetuating the deathless joke about how they were getting simply drenched, and the children screaming with delight at the new sensation of bathing in the rain, and the joke about getting drenched linking the generations in a strong indestructible chain. And the comedian who waded in carrying an umbrella.

When the others went swimming my son said he was going in too. He pulled his dripping trunks from the line where they had hung all through the shower, and wrung them out. Languidly, and with no thought of going in, I watched him, his hard little body, skinny and bare, saw him wince slightly as he pulled up around his vitals the small, soggy, icy garment. As he buckled the swollen belt suddenly my groin felt the chill of death.

IN FOCUS

THE APPEAL TO THE SENSES

One of the most powerful techniques White uses in this essay is the inclusion of *sensory images* showing the reader not only what things looked like but what they smelled, tasted, sounded like.

We tend to think of the word *image* as referring only to the visual, but *imagery* in writing refers to any kind of appeal to any sense. Thus, in addition to visual images, there are auditory images, tactile images, and so forth. Sensory images are the written forms of sense impressions.

Notice the various sensory images White uses to re-create his memories: the "pine-laden air" and the "smell of the swamp," the sounds of boat engines on the lake, the "fearful cold of the sea water." Locate other appeals to the senses in the essay. How does White convey what things looked like, sounded like, smelled like, tasted like, felt like? How do these images build up to create the illusory, dreamlike quality of the essay?

A writer can also use sensory images for their metaphoric quality, their meaning as symbols as well as their ability to convey physical characteristics. In this essay, various sensations emphasize White's illusion that "he was I, and therefore, by simple transposition, that I was my father." At the end, the child pulling on the cold wet bathing suit becomes an image of generations and also the process of generation, creation, as "my groin felt the chill of death."

Study Questions

1. Note the points at which White has the illusion that his son is really his younger self and that he is his own father. What forces are behind that illusion? How does he develop this theme through the essay?
2. Notice the language of the essay, the flow of the sentences. Read aloud to yourself the paragraph that begins "Summertime, oh summertime, pattern of life indelible." Try to feel the rhythm and pattern of the words. What kind of music could you connect to this rhythm?

Writing Topics

1. *Collaborative writing activity* (with the group sharing their memories and then each person writing an individual essay). Psychologists tell us that the senses of smell and taste are very closely connected to memory. Write a descriptive essay describing some of the smells and tastes from your childhood. Were there special foods cooked for special occasions? Describe the smells of those foods and the memories they bring back.
2. White writes, "It is strange how much you can remember about places

like that once you allow your mind to return into the grooves which lead back. You remember one thing, and that suddenly reminds you of another thing." Write a short essay about a place you remember, in which the memory of one thing leads to the memory of another.

To get started, write down the name of the place and begin jotting down the memories that come to mind. Then, choose two to four of those memories and write down the memories that these thoughts trigger. When you write the essay, try to show how one memory brings you into another.

The Looking-Glass Shame

JUDITH ORTIZ COFER

> "At any rate, the looking-glass
> shame has lasted all my life."
> —VIRGINIA WOOLF,
> *Moments of Being*

In her memoir, *Moments of Being,* Virginia Woolf tells of a frightening dream she had as a young girl in which, as she looked at herself in the mirror, she saw something moving in the background: ". . . a horrible face—the face of an animal . . ." over her shoulder. She never forgot that "other face in the glass" perhaps because it was both alien and familiar. It is not unusual for an adolescent to feel disconnected from her body—a stranger to herself and to her new developing needs—but I think that to a person living simultaneously in two cultures this phenomenon is intensified.

Even as I dealt with the trauma of leaving childhood, I saw that "cultural schizophrenia" was undoing many others around me at different stages of their lives. Society gives clues and provides rituals for the adolescent but withholds support. As I entered my freshman year of high school in a parochial school, I was given a new uniform to wear: a skirt and blouse as opposed to the severe blue jumper with straps, to accommodate for developing breasts, I suppose, although I would have little to accommodate for an excruciatingly long time—being a "skinny bones," as my classmates often called me, with no hips or breasts to speak of. But the warnings began, nevertheless. At home my mother constantly reminded me that I was now a "señorita" and needed to behave accordingly; but she never explained exactly what that entailed. She had said the same thing when I had started menstruating a couple of years before. At school the classrooms and the cafeteria were segregated into "boyside" and "girlside." The nuns kept a hawkeye on the length of the girls' skirts, which had to come to below the knee at a time when the mini-skirt was becoming the micro-skirt out in the streets.

After school, I would see several of the "popular" girls walk down to the corner out of sight from the school, and get into cars with public school boys. Many of the others went down to the drugstore to have a soda and talk loudly and irreverently about the school and the nuns. Most of them were middle class Italian and Irish kids. I was

the only Puerto Rican student, having gotten in after taking a rigorous academic test and after the priest visited our apartment to ascertain that we were a good Catholic family. I felt lost in the sea of
bright white faces and teased blond hair of the girls who were not
unkind to me, but did not, at least that crucial first year, include me
in their groups that traveled together to skating rinks, basketball
games, pizza parlors—those activities that they would talk about on
Monday in their rapid-fire English as we all awaited to be let into the
building.

   Not that I would have been allowed to go to these places. I lived
in the carefully constructed facsimile of a Puerto Rican home my
mother had created. Every day I crossed the border of two countries: I would spend the day in the pine-scented parochial school
building where exquisitely proper behavior was the rule strictly enforced by the soft spoken nuns, who could, upon observing an in-
fraction of their many rules, turn into despots—and never raise their
voices—as they destroyed your peace of mind with threats of shame-
ful exposure and/or expulsion. But there was order, quiet, respect for
logic, and there, also, I received the information I was always hungry for. I liked reading books, and I took immense pleasure in the
praise of the teachers for my attentiveness and my good grades. So
what, I thought to myself, if I was not invited to the homes of my
classmates who did not live in my neighborhood, anyway. I lived in
the city core, in an apartment that may have housed an Italian or
Irish family a generation before. Now they were prosperous and had
moved to the suburbs and the Puerto Ricans had moved into the
"immigrant" apartment buildings. That year I actually felt a sense of
burning shame at the fact that I did not have to take a bus or be
picked up in a car to go home. I lived only a few blocks away from
the church and the school which had been built in the heart of the
city by the original wave of Irish Catholics—for *their* convenience.
The Puerto Ricans had built no churches.

   I would walk home every day from school. I had fifteen minutes
to get home before my mother panicked and came after me. I did not
want that to happen. She was so different from my classmates' mothers that I was embarrassed to be seen with her. While most of the
other mothers were stoutly built women with dignified grey hair
who exuded motherliness, my mother was an exotic young beauty,
black hair down to her waist and a propensity for wearing bright
colors and spike heels. I would have died of shame if one of my classmates had seen her sensuous walk and the looks she elicited from the
men on our block. And she would have embraced me in public, too,

for she never learned moderation in her emotions, or restraint for her gesturing hands and loud laughter. She kept herself a "native" in that apartment she rarely left, except on my father's arm, or to get one of us from school. I had had to have a shouting match with her to convince her that I no longer needed to be escorted back and forth from school in the ninth grade.

My mother carried the island of Puerto Rico over her head like the mantilla she wore to church on Sunday. She was "doing time" in the U.S. She did not know how long her sentence would last, or why she was being punished with exile, but she was only doing it for her children. She kept herself "pure" for her eventual return to the island by denying herself a social life (which would have connected her too much with the place); by never learning but the most basic survival English; and by her ability to create an environment in our home that was a comfort to her, but a shock to my senses, and I suppose, to my younger brother's, both of us having to enter and exit this twilight zone of sights and smells that meant *casa* to her.

In our apartment we spoke Spanish, we ate rice and beans with meats prepared in *adobo,* that mouthwatering mixture of spices, and we listened to romantic ballads sung by Daniel Santos which my mother played on the record-player. She read letters from her family in Puerto Rico and from our father. Although she loved getting his letters, his descriptions of the Roman Coliseum or the Acropolis did not interest her as much as news from *casa*—her mother and her many brothers and sisters.

Most of my mother's sentences began with *En casa* . . . : at her Mama's house things were done like this and like that. At any place in the world other than her beloved *Isla* my mother would have been homesick: perpetual nostalgia, constant talk of return, that was my mother's chosen method of survival. When she looked into her looking-glass, what did she see? Another face, an old woman nagging, nagging, at her—*Don't bury me in foreign soil . . .*

> *A sailor went to see, sea, sea,*
> *To see what her could see, see, see,*
> *And all that her could see, see, see,*
> *Was the bottom of the deep, blue*
> *Sea, sea, sea.*

The black girls sang this jump-rope song faster and faster in the concrete play yard of the public school, perhaps not thinking of the words, landlocked in the city, never having seen the deep, blue sea. I thought of my father when I heard it.

The deep blue sea for my father was loneliness. He had joined the U.S. military service at eighteen, the very same year he had married, because for the young men of Puerto Rico who did not have money in 1951, it was the only promise of a future away from the cane fields of the island or the factories of New York City. He had been brought up to expect better things. My father had excelled in school and was president of his senior class. In my mother, whom he met when she was just fourteen, he must have seen the opposite of himself. He had forsaken his early dreams for her love, and later for the future of his children.

His absences from home seemed to be harder on him than on us. Whatever happened to him during those years, most of it, I will never know. Each time he came home he was a quieter man. It was as if he were drowning in silence and no one could save him. His main concern was our education, and I remember showing him my school papers, which he would pore over as if he were reading a fascinating book.

He would listen attentively while Mother recounted the ordinary routine of our days to him, taking it all in like nourishment. He asked endless questions. Nothing was too trivial for his ears. It was as if he were attempting to live vicariously each day he had missed with us. And he never talked about the past; unlike our mother, he had no yearning to return to the Island that held no promise for him. But he did not deprive her of her dream of home either. And her need to be with her family may have been what prompted him to devise the complex system of back-and-forth travel that I experienced most of my childhood. Every time he went to Europe for six months, we went back with Mother to her mother's *casa;* upon his return to Brooklyn Yard, he would wire us, and we would come back. Cold/hot, English/Spanish; that was our life.

I remember my father as a man who rarely looked into mirrors. He would even comb his hair looking down. What was he afraid of seeing? Perhaps the monster over his shoulder was his lost potential. He was a sensitive, intellectual man whose energies had to be entirely devoted to survival. And that is how many minds are wasted in the travails of immigrant life.

And so, life was difficult for my parents, and that means that it was no more and no less painful than for others like them: for the struggle, *la lucha,* goes on all around for people who want to be a piece that fits in the American puzzle, to get a share in the big picture; but, of course, I see that in retrospect. At fourteen and for a few years after, my concerns were mainly focused on the alarms going off in my body warning me of pain or pleasure ahead.

I fell in love, or my hormones awakened from their long slumber in my body, and suddenly the goal of my days was focused on one thing: to catch a glimpse of my secret love. And it had to remain secret, because I had, of course, in the great tradition of tragic romance, chosen to love a boy who was totally out of my reach. He was not Puerto Rican; he was Italian and rich. He was also an older man. He was a senior at the high school when I came in as a freshman. I first saw him in the hall, leaning casually on a wall that was the border line between girlside and boyside for underclassmen. He looked extraordinarily like a young Marlon Brando—down to the ironic little smile. The total of what I knew about the boy who starred in every one of my awkward fantasies was this: that he was the nephew of the man who owned the supermarket on my block; that he often had parties at his parents' beautiful home in the suburbs which I would hear about; that this family had money (which came to our school in many ways)—and this fact made my knees weak: and that he worked at the store near my apartment building on weekends and in the summer.

My mother could not understand why I became so eager to be the one sent out on her endless errands. I pounced on every opportunity from Friday to late Saturday afternoon to go after eggs, cigarettes, milk (I tried to drink as much of it as possible, although I hated the stuff)— the staple items that she would order from the "American" store.

Week after week I wandered up and down the aisles, taking furtive glances at the stock room in the back, breathlessly hoping to see my prince. Not that I had a plan. I felt like a pilgrim waiting for a glimpse of Mecca. I did not expect him to notice me. It was sweet agony.

One day I did see him. Dressed in a white outfit like a surgeon: white pants and shirt, white cap, and (gross sight, but not to my love-glazed eyes) blood-smeared butcher's apron. He was helping to drag a side of beef into the freezer storage area of the store. I must have stood there like an idiot, because I remember that he did see me, he even spoke to me! I could have died. I think he said, "Excuse me," and smiled vaguely in my direction.

After that, I *willed* occasions to go to the supermarket. I watched my mother's pack of cigarettes empty ever so slowly. I wanted her to smoke them fast. I drank milk and forced it on my brother (although a second glass for him had to be bought with my share of Fig Newton cookies which we both liked, but we were restricted to one row each). I gave my cookies up for love, and watched my mother smoke her L&M's with so little enthusiasm that I thought (God, no!) that she might be cutting down on her smoking or maybe even giving up the habit. At this crucial time!

I thought I had kept my lonely romance a secret. Often I cried hot tears on my pillow for the things that kept us apart. In my mind there was no doubt that he would never notice me (and that is why I felt free to stare at him—I was invisible). He could not see me because I was a skinny Puerto Rican girl, a freshman who did not belong to any group he associated with.

At the end of the year I found out that I had not been invisible. I learned one little lesson about human nature—adulation leaves a scent, one that we are all equipped to recognize, and no matter how insignificant the source, we seek it.

In June the nuns at our school would always arrange for some cultural extravaganza. In my freshman year it was a Roman banquet. We had been studying Greek drama (as a prelude to church history—it was at a fast clip that we galloped through Sophocles and Euripedes toward the early Christian martyrs), and our young, energetic Sister Agnes was in the mood for spectacle. She ordered the entire student body (it was a small group of under 300 students) to have our mothers make us togas out of sheets. She handed out a pattern on mimeo pages fresh out of the machine. I remember the intense smell of the alcohol on the sheets of paper, and how almost everyone in the auditorium brought theirs to their noses and inhaled deeply—mimeographed handouts were the school-day buzz that the new Xerox generation of kids is missing out on. Then, as the last couple of weeks of school dragged on, the city of Paterson becoming a concrete oven, and us wilting in our uncomfortable uniforms, we labored like frantic Roman slaves to build a splendid banquet hall in our small auditorium. Sister Agnes wanted a raised dais where the host and hostess would be regally enthroned.

She had already chosen our Senator and Lady from among our ranks. The Lady was to be a beautiful new student named Sophia, a recent Polish immigrant, whose English was still practically unintelligible, but whose features, classically perfect without a trace of makeup, enthralled us. Everyone talked about her gold hair cascading past her waist, and her voice which could carry a note right up to heaven in choir. The nuns wanted her for God. They kept saying that she had vocation. We just looked at her in awe, and the boys seemed afraid of her. She just smiled and did as she was told. I don't know what she thought of it all. The main privilege of beauty is that others will do almost everything for you, including thinking.

Her partner was to be our best basketball player, a tall, red-haired senior whose family sent its many offspring to our school. Together, Sophia and her senator looked like the best combination of immigrant genes our community could produce. It did not occur to me to ask then whether anything but their physical beauty qualified them for the starring roles in our production. I had the highest average in the church history class, but I was given the part of one of many "Roman Citizens." I was to sit in front of the plastic fruit and recite a greeting in Latin along with the rest of the school when our hosts came into the hall and took their places on their throne.

On the night of our banquet, my father escorted me in my toga to the door of our school. I felt foolish in my awkwardly draped sheet (blouse and skirt required underneath). My mother had no great skill as a seamstress. The best she could do was hem a skirt or a pair of pants. That night I would have traded her for a peasant woman with a golden needle. I saw other Roman ladies emerging from their parents' cars looking authentic in sheets of material that folded over their bodies like the garments on a statue by Michaelangelo. How did they do it? How was it that I always got it just slightly wrong, and worse, I believed that other people were just too polite to mention it. "The poor little Puerto Rican girl," I could hear them thinking. But in reality, I must have been my worst critic, self-conscious as I was.

Soon, we were all sitting at our circle of tables joined together around the dais. Sophia glittered like a golden statue. Her smile was beatific: a perfect, silent Roman lady. Her "senator" looked uncomfortable, glancing around at his buddies, perhaps waiting for the ridicule that he would surely get in the locker room later. The nuns in their black habits stood in the background watching us. What were they supposed to be, the Fates? Nubian slaves? The dancing girls did their modest little dance to tinny music from their finger cymbals, then the speeches were made. Then the grape juice "wine" was raised in a toast to the Roman Empire we all knew would fall within the week—before finals anyway.

All during the program I had been in a state of controlled hysteria. My secret love sat across the room from me looking supremely bored. I watched his every move, taking him in gluttonously. I relished the shadow of his eyelashes on his ruddy cheeks, his pouty lips smirking sarcastically at the ridiculous sight of our little play. Once he slumped down on his chair, and our sergeant-at-arms nun came over and tapped him sharply on his shoulder. He drew himself up slowly, with disdain. I loved his rebellious spirit. I believed myself still invisible to him in my "nothing" status as I looked upon my beloved. But toward the end of the evening, as we stood chanting our farewells in Latin, he looked straight across the room and into my eyes! How did I survive the killing power of those dark pupils? I trembled in a new way. I was not cold—I was burning! Yet I shook from the inside out, feeling light-headed, dizzy.

The room began to empty and I headed for the girls' lavatory. I wanted to relish the miracle in silence. I did not think for a minute that anything more would follow. I was satisfied with the enormous favor of a look from my beloved. I took my time, knowing that my father would be waiting outside for me, impatient, perhaps glowing in the dark in his phosphorescent white Navy uniform. The others would ride home. I would walk home with my father, both of us in costume. I wanted as few witnesses as possible. When I could no longer hear the crowds in the hallway, I emerged from the bathroom, still under the spell of those mesmerizing eyes.

The lights had been turned off in the hallway and all I could see was the lighted stairwell, at the bottom of which a nun would be stationed. My father would be waiting just outside. I nearly screamed when I felt someone grab me by the waist. But my mouth was quickly covered by someone else's mouth. I was being kissed. My first kiss and I could not even tell who it was. I pulled away to see that face not two inches away from mine. It was he. He smiled down at me. Did I have a silly expression on my face? My glasses felt crooked on my nose. I was unable to move or to speak. More gently, he lifted my chin and touched his lips to mine. This time I did not forget to enjoy it. Then, like the phantom lover that he was, he walked away into the darkened corridor and disappeared.

I don't know how long I stood there. My body was changing right there in the hallway of a Catholic school. My cells were tuning up like musicians in an orchestra, and my heart was a chorus. It was an opera I was composing, and I wanted to stand very still and just listen. But, of course, I heard my father's voice talking to the nun. I was in trouble if he had had to ask about me. I hurried down the stairs making up a story on the way about feeling sick. That would explain my flushed face and it would buy me a little privacy when I got home.

The next day Father announced at the breakfast table that he was leaving on a six-month tour of Europe with the Navy in a few weeks, and that at the end of the school year my mother, my brother, and I would be sent to Puerto Rico to stay for half a year at Mamá's (my mother's mother) house. I was devastated. This was the usual routine for us. We had always gone to Mamá's to stay when Father was away for long periods. But this year it was different for me. I was in love, and . . . my heart knocked against my bony chest at this thought . . . he loved me too? I broke into sobs and left the table.

In the next week I discovered the inexorable truth about parents. They can actually carry on with their plans right through tears, threats, and the awful spectacle of a teenager's broken heart. My father left me to my mother who impassively packed while I explained over and over that I was at a crucial time in my studies and that if I left my entire life would be ruined. All she would say was, "You are an intelligent girl, you'll catch up." Her head was filled with visions of *casa* and family reunions, long gossip sessions with her mamá and sisters. What did she care that I was losing my one chance at true love?

In the meantime I tried desperately to see him. I thought he would look for me too. But the few times I saw him in the hallway, he was always rushing away. It would be long weeks of confusion and pain before I realized that the kiss was nothing but a little trophy for his ego. He had no interest in me other than as his adorer. He was flattered by my silent worship of him, and he had *bestowed* a kiss on me to please himself, and to fan the flames. I learned a lesson about the battle of the sexes then that I have never forgotten: the object is not always to win, but most times simply to keep your opponent (synonymous at times with "the loved one") guessing.

But this is too cynical a view to sustain in the face of that overwhelming rush of emotion that is first love. And in thinking back about my own experience with it, I can be objective only to the point where I recall how sweet the anguish was, how caught up in the moment I felt, and how every nerve in my body was involved in this salute to life. Later, much later, after what seemed like an eternity of dragging the weight of unrequited love around with me, I learned to make myself visible and to relish the little battles required to win the greatest prize of all. And much later, I read and understood Camus' statement about the subject that concerns both adolescent and philosopher alike: if love were easy, life would be too simple.

OPENING WITH A QUOTATION

The *epigraph*, or quotation at the beginning, of this essay is the sentence by Virginia Woolf positioned above and indented to the right of the opening paragraph: "At any rate, the looking-glass shame has lasted all my life." Cofer begins with the epigraph, part of which she uses for the title, and then, in the opening paragraph, moves into a longer quotation from Woolf and then the point of her own essay.

Opening with a quotation is a useful way to begin an essay or research paper. For one thing, it helps the writer get away from the usual struggle of what to say at the beginning. It sets the stage nicely and, even in a personal essay, implies that the writer is a reading, thinking person. Once the quotation has established the theme, the writer can state the thesis at the end of the first paragraph or shortly after, usually in the second paragraph. (*Note:* Always give the full name and title of the piece being quoted. The titles of books are in italics or underlined, and the titles of essays or chapters are in quotation marks.)

Study Questions

1. What exactly is "the looking-glass shame"? Is Cofer ashamed of her Hispanic looks, or is she referring to some other self? Why do adolescents feel—justifiably or unjustifiably—ashamed of their families? Did you ever have such feelings as a teenager?
2. Cofer writes about how important and separate the family home was to her mother and father. Why did that place become so important and almost sacred to her parents? Why did her father "listen attentively while Mother recounted the ordinary routine of our days to him, taking it all in like nourishment"?

Writing Topics

Note: For each of the following assignments, use a quotation as your opening. You may, if you wish, take the quotation from the Cofer essay. An epigraph is optional.
1. In a short essay, describe the face you see in the mirror.
2. Have you, or has someone you know well, lived in two cultures as Cofer describes it? Write about some memorable aspects of the experience. Then widen the focus of your essay, discussing the difficulties, benefits, and kinds of adaptation required for groups (or a specific group) of people living in one culture within a larger, different culture.

From Notes
of a Native Son

JAMES BALDWIN

On the 29th of July, in 1943, my father died. On the same day, a few hours later, his last child was born. Over a month before this, while all our energies were concentrated in waiting for these events, there had been, in Detroit, one of the bloodiest race riots of the century. A few hours after my father's funeral, while he lay in state in the undertaker's chapel, a race riot broke out in Harlem. On the morning of the 3rd of August, we drove my father to the graveyard through a wilderness of smashed plate glass.

The day of my father's funeral had also been my nineteenth birthday. As we drove him to the graveyard, the spoils of injustice, anarchy, discontent, and hatred were all around us. It seemed to me that God himself had devised, to mark my father's end, the most sustained and brutally dissonant of codas. And it seemed to me, too, that the violence which rose all about us as my father left the world had been devised as a corrective for the pride of his eldest son. I had declined to believe in that apocalypse which had been central to my father's vision; very well, life seemed to be saying, here is something that will certainly pass for an apocalypse until the real thing comes along. I had inclined to be contemptuous of my father for the conditions of his life, for the conditions of our lives. When his life had ended I began to wonder about that life and also, in a new way, to be apprehensive about my own.

I had not known my father very well. We had got on badly, partly because we shared, in our different fashions, the vice of stubborn pride. When he was dead I realized that I had hardly ever spoken to him. When he had been dead a long time I began to wish I had. It seems to be typical of life in America, where opportunities, real and fancied, are thicker than anywhere else on the globe, that the second generation has no time to talk to the first. No one, including my father, seems to have known exactly how old he was, but his mother had been born during slavery. He was of the first generation of free men. He, along with thousands of other Negroes, came North after

1919 and I was part of that generation which had never seen the landscape of what Negroes sometimes call the Old Country.

He had been born in New Orleans and had been a quite young man there during the time that Louis Armstrong, a boy, was running errands for the dives and honky-tonks of what was always presented to me as one of the most wicked of cities—to this day, whenever I think of New Orleans, I also helplessly think of Sodom and Gomorrah. My father never mentioned Louis Armstrong, except to forbid us to play his records; but there was a picture of him on our wall for a long time. One of my father's strong-willed female relatives had placed it there and forbade my father to take it down. He never did, but he eventually maneuvered her out of the house and when, some years later, she was in trouble and near death, he refused to do anything to help her.

He was, I think, very handsome. I gather this from photographs and from my own memories of him, dressed in his Sunday best and on his way to preach a sermon somewhere, when I was little. Handsome, proud, and ingrown, "like a toe-nail," somebody said. But he looked to me, as I grew older, like pictures I had seen of African tribal chieftains: he really should have been naked, with war-paint on and barbaric mementos, standing among spears. He could be chilling in the pulpit and indescribably cruel in his personal life and he was certainly the most bitter man I have ever met; yet it must be said that there was something else in him, buried in him, which lent him his tremendous power and, even, a rather crushing charm. It had something to do with his blackness, I think—he was very black—with his blackness and his beauty, and with the fact that he knew that he was black but did not know that he was beautiful. He claimed to be proud of his blackness but it had also been the cause of much humiliation and it had fixed bleak boundaries to his life. He was not a young man when we were growing up and he had already suffered many kinds of ruin; in his outrageously demanding and protective way he loved his children, who were black like him and menaced, like him; and all these things sometimes showed in his face when he tried, never to my knowledge with any success, to establish contact with any of us. When he took one of his children on his knee to play, the child always became fretful and began to cry; when he tried to help one of us with our homework the absolutely unabating tension which emanated from him caused our minds and our tongues to become paralyzed, so that he, scarcely knowing why, flew into a rage and the child, not knowing why, was punished. If it ever entered his head to bring a surprise home for his children, it was, almost unfailingly, the wrong surprise and even the big watermelons he often brought home on his back in the summertime led to the most appalling scenes. I do not remember, in all those years, that one of his children was ever glad to see him come home. From what I was able to gather of his early life, it seemed that this inability to establish contact with other people had always marked him and had been one of the things which had driven him out of New Orleans. There was something in him, therefore, groping and tentative, which was never expressed and which was buried with him. One saw it most clearly when he was facing new people and hoping to impress them. But he never did, not for long. We went from church to smaller and more improbable church, he found himself in less and less demand as a minister, and by the time he died none of his friends had come to see him for a long time. He had lived and died in an intolerable bitterness of spirit and it frightened me, as we drove him to the graveyard through those unquiet, ruined streets, to see how powerful and overflowing this bitterness could be and to realize that this bitterness now was mine.

When he died I had been away from home for a little over a year. In that year I had had time to become aware of the meaning of all my father's bitter warnings, had discovered the secret of his proudly pursed lips and rigid carriage: I had discovered the weight of white people in the world. I saw that this had been for my ancestors and now would be for me an awful thing to live with and that the bitterness which had helped to kill my father could also kill me.

He had been ill a long time—in the mind, as we now realized, reliving instances of his fantastic intransigence in the new light of his affliction and endeavoring to feel a sorrow for him which never, quite, came true. We had not known that he was being eaten up by paranoia, and the discovery that his cruelty, to our bodies and our minds, had been one of the symptoms of his illness was not, then, enough to enable us to forgive him. The younger children felt, quite simply, relief that he would not be coming home anymore. My mother's observation that it was he, after all, who had kept them alive all these years meant nothing because the problems of keeping children alive are not real for children. The older children felt, with my father gone, that they could invite their friends to the house without fear that their friends would be insulted or, as had sometimes happened with me, being told that their friends were in league with the devil and intended to rob our family of everything we owned. (I didn't fail to wonder, and it made me hate him, what on earth we owned that anybody else would want.)

His illness was beyond all hope of healing before anyone realized that he was ill. He had always been so strange and had lived, like a prophet, in such unimaginably close communion with the Lord that his long silences which were punctuated by moans and hallelujahs and snatches of old songs while he sat at the living-room window never seemed odd to us. It was not until he refused to eat because, he said, his family was trying to poison him that my mother was forced to accept as a fact what had, until then, been only an unwilling suspicion. When he was committed, it was discovered that he had tuberculosis and, as it turned out, the disease of his mind allowed the disease of his body to destroy him. For the doctors could not force him to eat, either, and, though he was fed intravenously, it was clear from the beginning that there was no hope for him.

In my mind's eye I could see him, sitting at the window, locked up in his terrors; hating and fearing every living soul including his children who had betrayed him, too, by reaching towards the world which had despised him. There were nine of us. I began to wonder what it could have felt like for such a man to have had nine children whom he could barely feed. He used to make little jokes about our poverty, which never, of course, seemed very funny to us; they could not have seemed very funny to him, either, or else our all too feeble response to them would never have caused such rages. He spent great energy and achieved, to our chagrin, no small amount of success in keeping us away from the people who surrounded us, people who had all-night rent parties to which we listened when we should have been sleeping, people who cursed and drank and flashed razor blades on Lenox Avenue. He could not understand why, if they had so much energy to spare, they could not use it to make their lives better. He treated almost everybody on our block with a most uncharitable asperity and neither they, nor, of course, their children were slow to reciprocate.

The only white people who came to our house were welfare workers and bill collectors. It was almost always my mother who dealt with them, for my father's temper, which was at the mercy of his pride, was never to be trusted. It was clear that he felt their very presence in his home to be a violation: this was conveyed by his carriage, almost ludicrously stiff, and by his voice, harsh and vindictively polite. When I was around nine or ten I wrote a play which was directed by a young, white schoolteacher, a woman, who then took an interest in me, and gave me books to read and, in order to corroborate my theatrical bent, decided to take me to see what she somewhat tactlessly referred to as "real" plays. Theater-going was forbidden in our house, but, with the really cruel intuitiveness of a child, I suspected that the color of this woman's skin would carry the day for me. When, at school, she suggested taking me to the theater, I did not, as I might have done if she had been a Negro, find a way of discouraging her, but agreed that she should pick me up at my house one evening. I then, very cleverly, left all the rest to my mother, who suggested to my father, as I knew she would, that it would not be very nice to let such a kind woman make the trip for nothing. Also, since it was a schoolteacher, I imagine that my mother countered the idea of sin with the idea of "education," which word, even with my father, carried a kind of bitter weight.

Before the teacher came my father took me aside to ask *why* she was coming, what *interest* she could possibly have in our house, in a boy like me. I said I didn't know but I, too, suggested that it had something to do with education. And I understood that my father was waiting for me to say something—I didn't quite know what; perhaps that I wanted his protection against this teacher and her "education." I said none of these things and the teacher came and we went out. It was clear, during the brief interview in our living room, that my father was agreeing very much against his will and that he would have refused permission if he had dared. The fact that he did not dare caused me to despise him: I had no way of knowing that he was facing in that living room a wholly unprecedented and frightening situation.

Later, when my father had been laid off from his job, this woman became very important to us. She was really a very sweet and generous woman and went to a great deal of trouble to be of help to us, particularly during one awful winter. My mother called her by the highest name she knew: she said she was a "christian." My father could scarcely disagree but during the four or five years of our relatively close association he never trusted her and was always trying to surprise in her open, Midwestern face the genuine, cunningly hidden, and hideous motivation. In later years, particularly when it began to be clear that this "education" of mine was going to lead me to perdition, he became more explicit and warned me that my white friends in high school were not really my friends and that I would see, when I was older, how white people would do anything to keep a Negro down. Some of them could be nice, he admitted, but none of them were to be trusted and most of them were not even nice. The best thing was to have as little to do with them as possible. I did not feel this way and I was certain, in my innocence, that I never would.

But the year which preceded my father's death had made a great change in my life. I had been living in New Jersey, working in defense plants, working and living among southerners, white and black. I knew about the south, of course, and about how southerners treated Negroes and how they expected them to behave, but it had never entered my mind that anyone would look at me and expect *me* to behave that way. I learned in New Jersey that to be a Negro meant, precisely, that one was never looked at but was simply at the mercy of the reflexes the color of one's skin caused in other people. I acted in New Jersey as I had always acted, that is as though I thought a great deal of myself—I had to *act* that way—with results that were, simply, unbelievable. I had scarcely arrived before I had earned the enmity, which was extraordinarily ingenious, of all my superiors and nearly all my co-workers. In the beginning, to make matters worse, I simply did not know what was happening. I did not know what I had done, and I shortly began to wonder what *anyone* could possibly do, to bring about such unanimous, active, and unbearably vocal hostility. I knew about jim-crow but I had never experienced it. I went to the same self-service restaurant three times and stood with all the Princeton boys before the counter, waiting for a hamburger and coffee; it was always an extraordinarily long time before anything was set before me; but it was not until the fourth visit that I learned that, in fact, nothing had ever been set before me: I had simply picked something up. Negroes were not served there, I was told, and they had been waiting for me to realize that I was always the only Negro present. Once I was told this, I determined to go there all the time. But now they were ready for me and, though some dreadful scenes were subsequently enacted in that restaurant, I never ate there again.

It was the same story all over New Jersey, in bars, bowling alleys, diners, places to live. I was always being forced to leave, silently, or with mutual imprecations. I very shortly became notorious and children giggled behind me when I passed and their elders whispered or shouted—they really believed that I was mad. And it did begin to work on my mind, of course; I began to be afraid to go anywhere and to compensate for this I went places to which I really should not have gone and where, God knows, I had no desire to be. My reputation in town naturally enhanced my reputation at work and my working day became one long series of acrobatics designed to keep me out of trouble. I cannot say that these acrobatics succeeded. It began to seem that the machinery of the organization I worked for was turning over, day and night, with but one aim: to eject me. I was fired once, and contrived, with the aid of a friend from New York, to get back on the payroll; was fired again, and bounced back again. It took a while to fire me for the third time, but the third time took. There were no loopholes anywhere. There was not even any way of getting back inside the gates.

That year in New Jersey lives in my mind as though it were the year during which, having an unsuspected predilection for it, I first contracted some dread, chronic disease, the unfailing symptom of which is a kind of blind fever, a pounding in the skull and fire in the bowels. Once this disease is contracted, one can never be really care-free again, for the fever, without an instant's warning, can recur at any moment. It can wreck more important things than race rela-tions. There is not a Negro alive who does not have this rage in his blood—one has the choice, merely, of living with it consciously or surrendering to it. As for me, this fever has recurred in me, and does, and will until the day I die.

My last night in New Jersey, a white friend from New York took me to the nearest big town, Trenton, to go to the movies and have a few drinks. As it turned out, he also saved me from, at the very least, a violent whipping. Almost every detail of that night stands out very clearly in my memory. I even remember the name of the movie we saw because its title impressed me as being so patly ironical. It was a movie about the German occupation of France, starring Maureen O'Hara and Charles Laughton and called *This Land Is Mine*. I remem-ber the name of the diner we walked into when the movie ended: it was the "American Diner." When we walked in the counterman asked what we wanted and I remember answering with the casual sharpness which had become my habit: "We want a hamburger and a cup of coffee, what do you think we want?" I do not know why, after a year of such rebuffs, I so completely failed to anticipate his an-swer, which was, of course, "We don't serve Negroes here." This reply failed to discompose me, at least for the moment. I made some sardonic comment about the name of the diner and we walked out into the streets.

This was the time of what was called the "brown-out," when the lights in all American cities were very dim. When we re-entered the streets something happened to me which had the force of an optical illusion, or a nightmare. The streets were very crowded and I was fac-ing north. People were moving in every direction but it seemed to me, in that instant, that all of the people I could see, and many more than that, were moving toward me, against me, and that everyone was white. I remember how their faces gleamed. And I felt, like a physical sensation, a *click* at the nape of my neck as though some interior string connecting my head to my body had been cut. I began to walk. I heard my friend call after me, but I ignored him. Heaven only knows what was going on in his mind, but he had the good sense not to touch me—I don't know what would have happened if he had—and to keep me in sight. I don't know what was going on in my mind, either; I certainly had no conscious plan. I wanted to do something to crush these white faces, which were crushing me. I walked for perhaps a block or two until I came to an enormous, glittering, and fashionable restaurant in which I knew not even the intercession of the Virgin would cause me to be served. I pushed through the doors and took the first vacant seat I saw, at a table for two, and waited.

I do not know how long I waited and I rather wonder, until today, what I could possibly have looked like. Whatever I looked like, I frightened the waitress who shortly appeared, and the moment she appeared all of my fury flowed towards her. I hated her for her white face, and for her great, astounded, frightened eyes. I felt that if she found a black man so frightening I would make her fright worthwhile.

She did not ask me what I wanted, but repeated, as though she had learned it somewhere, "We don't serve Negroes here." She did not say it with the blunt, derisive hostility to which I had grown so accustomed, but, rather, with a note of apology in her voice, and fear. This made me colder and more murderous than ever. I felt I had to do something with my hands. I wanted her to come close enough for me to get her neck between my hands.

So I pretended not to have understood her, hoping to draw her closer. And she did step a very short step closer, with her pencil poised incongruously over her pad, and repeated the formula: ". . . don't serve Negroes here."

Somehow, with the repetition of that phrase, which was already ringing in my head like a thousand bells of a nightmare, I realized that she would never come any closer and that I would have to strike from a distance. There was nothing on the table but an ordinary water-mug half full of water, and I picked this up and hurled it with all my strength at her. She ducked and it missed her and shattered against the mirror behind the bar. And, with that sound, my frozen blood abruptly thawed, I returned from wherever I had been, I *saw*, for the first time, the restaurant, the people with their mouths open, already, as it seemed to me, rising as one man, and I realized what I had done, and where I was, and I was frightened. I rose and began running for the door. A round, potbellied man grabbed me by the nape of the neck just as I reached the doors and began to beat me about the face. I kicked him and got loose and ran into the streets. My friend whispered, *"Run!"* and I ran.

My friend stayed outside the restaurant long enough to misdirect my pursuers and the police, who arrived, he told me, at once. I do not know what I said to him when he came to my room that night. I could not have said much. I felt, in the oddest, most awful way, that I had somehow betrayed him. I lived it over and over and over again, the way one relives an automobile accident after it has happened and one finds oneself alone and safe. I could not get over two facts, both equally difficult for the imagination to grasp, and one was that I could have been murdered. But the other was that I had been ready to commit murder. I saw nothing very clearly but I did see this: that my life, my *real* life, was in danger, and not from anything other people might do but from the hatred I carried in my own heart.

OPENING WITH AN ANECDOTE

In the selection preceding this piece, Judith Ortiz Cofer uses a quotation opening, one of several effective methods of beginning any piece of writing. Here, James Baldwin uses an opening that *sets the scene.* He writes an *anecdote,* a very brief description, that in this case tells the reader when and where the action is happening and gives a context for what will follow.

Notice what Baldwin doesn't do: he doesn't begin the story in the beginning, with his own early memories of his father, or even with his father's family and earliest years. Instead, he describes the powerful scene of his father's funeral—the end of their physical relationship. An anecdotal opening such as this one should be chosen for its interest and for the way it supports the theme. For example, the ancient Greek poet Homer begins the *Iliad,* one of the greatest stories of war in Western literature, with an opening classical critics describe as *in medias res,* "beginning in the middle." Homer starts with the death of the hero Achilles, toward the end of the war, then tells the whole story.

An opening anecdote can describe a landscape or an environment, tell what is happening in the writer's personal or emotional life, signal the time period in some way (Baldwin simply gives the date), or generally put the reader into the picture. Whatever else it does, this kind of opening must signal the theme for what is to follow. The opening description should match the feeling and be connected to the point of the rest of the piece. For example, when Baldwin writes that "we drove my father to the graveyard through a wilderness of smashed plate glass," this image of death and violence both reflects on the author's relationship with his father and points to the rage running through society.

Study Questions

1. What happened to Baldwin during the year he lived in New Jersey? Why was he doing the things he was doing: getting fired, getting fired again, putting himself in danger going "to places to which I really should not have gone and where, God knows, I had no desire to be"?
2. Baldwin's essay works on two levels: the personal and the social. Who his father was and the relationship between father and son were deeply connected to the outer society, to the injustices of racial hatred. How does Baldwin weave these two themes together?

Writing Topics

1. Write a short essay on your relationship with your father or another parent (or a relationship you have observed between other people) that begins with a descriptive opening. The scene you describe should be a significant moment, something to establish the theme and feeling for the material to follow.
2. Write a short essay in the form of a letter to James Baldwin. Tell him what has changed and what hasn't changed about race relations in America since he first published *Notes of a Native Son,* in 1955.

Where
I Am

KATHLEEN NORRIS

> When you get the feeling that the whole world
> can see you but no one is watching, you have
> come to the grasslands of North America.
> —DAN O'BRIEN,
> *In the Center of the Nation*

Where I am is America's outback, the grasslands west of the 100th meridian that constitute the western half of North and South Dakota, Nebraska, Kansas, Oklahoma, and Texas. In all that vast space, extending all the way to the 107th meridian in eastern Montana and Wyoming, there are far more cattle than people. Only two cities (Lubbock and Amarillo) have populations of over 100,000, and there is only one large university, Texas A & M. Where I am is a town of 1,600 people that is by far the largest in northwestern South Dakota, an area encompassing nearly 15,000 square miles in seven counties, roughly the size of Delaware, New Jersey, Connecticut, and Rhode Island combined.

Where I am is a marginal place that is at the very center of North America, roughly 1,500 miles from the Atlantic and Pacific oceans, the Gulf of Mexico, and the Arctic Archipelago. It's a land of extremes, holding the absolute temperature range record for the Western Hemisphere, set in 1936 when a town in western North Dakota registered temperatures from 60 degrees below zero to 121 above within the same year.

Where I am is the West River of Dakota, a plateau that rises sharply out of the narrow valley of the Missouri River and extends to the Rocky Mountains. It's a high plains desert, full of sage and tumbleweed and hardy shortgrass, where it rains fifteen inches in a good year (New York City averages 44; Chicago, 33; San Francisco, 20) but is often as dry as Los Angeles, with an annual rainfall of only twelve inches. In a bad drought we register precipitation that is more like that of Phoenix, just seven inches a year.

It's a place where a pleasantly warm summer day with clear skies often means a violent thunderstorm with hail by late afternoon, where my enjoyment of the perennials in my garden is tempered by the knowledge that the ground they're in will be frozen hard for at least four months.

Where I am is a place that does not readily render its secrets or subtleties. Standing on a hillside near the Grand River in central Perkins
County, you realize suddenly that you are on the highest ground for
many miles around, and that the stones nearby are not random but
were placed there by human hands long ago. They are teepee rings,
and this is a lookout site for buffalo. You notice patches of deep green
in a shallow draw and realize that they are ruts from the old trail to
Seim, now drowned under a manmade lake, a former stop on the
stagecoach route between Fort Lincoln near Mandan, North Dakota,
and the Black Hills.

Where I am is a place where Native Americans and whites live
alone together, to paraphrase David Allen Evans, a South Dakota
poet. Many small towns are Indian or white, and in general there is
a deafening silence between the two worlds, a silence exacerbated by
ignorance and intolerance on both sides. Many in the dominant
white culture seem content with an indifference that amounts to
"live and let die," given the drastic unemployment and low life expectancy in the impoverished Indian community.

Signs of hope are few. Chuck Woodard, an English professor at
South Dakota State University, sees a possibility for change in a new
curriculum currently being developed for public school students in
grades K–12. "My hopes are based on the initially positive responses
from people to this new curriculum," he says. "My fears are based on
past history, a history of the short-term enthusiasms of American
society."

I find hope each year at Prairie Winds, a three-day writing workshop for high school students and their teachers held annually in the
Black Hills. A good third of the participants are Native American,
and this provides an unusual opportunity for Indians and whites to
meet in a reflective environment with no issues to contend with beyond the commitment to writing.

I'll never forget the year that my group consisted of six girls, three
Lakota and three white. At our first meeting the white girls, all pre-
cociously verbal, wouldn't shut up, and the Lakota girls wouldn't
speak. Everyone was nervous, including me. Knowing that silence is
typically Sioux—a virtue, as well as a common reaction to a new and
possibly threatening social situation dominated by whites—I decided
in desperation to have us "make silence," a trick I had learned from
the Benedictines.

We arranged our chairs in a circle and held hands. I had to resort
to counting to three in order to begin the silence, one girl literally
having to swallow the end of a sentence. And we kept the silence for

over a minute, during which time shy smiles began darting around the circle. By the time we finished we were relaxed enough to take turns speaking; we were better able to listen to one another. The shyest of the Lakota girls didn't say anything until the next day, but it was understood that this was all right.

We found that we liked our silence and kept coming back to it. We liked the way it made a space for us in the midst of noise—a teenager cursing a computer printer, construction workers hammering in an addition to the lodge—and the way it allowed friendships to develop. We began to talk about our real lives, and even talked about how unusual it was, in South Dakota, for whites and Indians to meet like this, to be human together.

Where I am is a place where the human fabric is worn thin, farms and ranches and little towns scattered over miles of seemingly endless, empty grassland. On a clear night you can see not only thousands of stars but the lights of towns fifty miles away. Scattered between you and the horizon, the lights of farmhouses look like ships at sea. The naturalist Loren Eiseley once commented on the way Plains people "have been strung out at nighttime under a vast solitude rather than linked to the old-world village with its adjoining plots. We were mad to settle the West in [this] fashion," he says. "You cannot fight the sky." But some have come to love living under its winds and storms. Some have come to prefer the treelessness and isolation, becoming monks of the land, knowing that its loneliness is an honest reflection of the essential human loneliness. The willingly embraced desert fosters realism, not despair.

I'm tempted to despair at times. For one thing, Dakota can be painfully lonely for the artist, and it's as hard for us to make a living here as it is for any farmer or rancher. Our difference stands out in an area where quiet conformity is the norm, and sometimes our local friends ask David and me, "Don't you ever miss having people to talk to about what you do?" The answer is yes, and no. A fledgling ascetic, I am learning to see loneliness as a seed that, when planted deep enough, can grow into writing that goes back out into the world. I'm also developing an ascetic's keen appreciation for the gifts of fast and feast. On the rare occasions when my writing engenders response and I'm invited to go play poet for a day or two at a college, it does seem like a feast.

And, on occasion, other artists come to me. Once a modern dance troupe came to Lemmon to work in the schools. They choreographed a witty dance about tilling the soil and got high school students to perform it. They held a workshop for the football team on avoiding

injury and working with damaged muscles. They asked me to participate in a collaboration of dance and poetry, something I'd never
done, although I know many dancers from my days at Bennington.

Best of all, the troupe managed to assault a number of racial and
social stereotypes held by the young people of Lemmon, whose
knowledge of the outer world is severely limited. Much of what they
know of other races they get from television cop shows. One dancer
was a black man who had been raised on a farm in Indiana and had
broken horses for a living. He'd been a bull rider on the rodeo circuit
and told the students he'd given it up because it wasn't good for his
body. "I'd rather dance," he said, and I felt he'd earned his fee right
there.

Out of gratitude I fed the dancers rich, carbohydrate-laden meals
for three nights running. One evening after supper was over and the
table had been cleared, we sat drinking coffee and began to talk
about feet. One dancer, to illustrate a point, took off her socks and
shoes and placed a foot on the table. Soon we had all followed suit,
and as we talked I realized that we had, by this odd gesture, stumbled into community. Dance, after all, is a communal affair, and we
had just made a community of those willing to bare the lowly foot.
It was hospitality, an exchange of gifts, that had brought this about;
the dancers' giving of themselves all week in teaching and performing, and my feeding them as they needed to be fed.

Hospitality is of primary importance in the desert. Bedouin hospitality is legendary, as is that of the Benedictines, who are instructed
by Saint Benedict in his *Rule* to "receive all guests as Christ." The people of the Great Plains can be hospitable as well, in the fashion of
people who have little and are willing to share what they have. The
poorest among us, in the Native American community, are exceptional in this regard, with a tradition of hospitality that has deep cultural roots in the giveaway, a sacred event that in application served
the purpose of providing for the entire tribe. Hunters brought their
surplus meat or buffalo robes, and those too old or infirm to hunt
brought handcrafted items like quillwork; and in the exchange
everyone received what was needed to survive the winter. Even
today the ceremonial giveaway, in the words of Arthur Amiotte, a
Lakota artist, remains an important and "reciprocal activity in which
we are reminded of sacred principles," an act of giving which "en-
nobles the human spirit."

Visitors from urban areas are often surprised by the easy friendli-
ness they encounter on the Plains. Even in Bismarck-Mandan (at
64,000, a major urban area by Dakota standards) strangers greet

travelers on the street and welcome them warmly. Recently a motel manager drove a woman nearly two hundred miles to the town where her husband had fallen ill, and stayed with her until family arrived. This could happen in a larger city, of course, but it's the expected thing on the Plains. Like all desert hospitality, this is in part a response to the severity of the climate; here, more demonstrably than in many other places, we need each other to survive.

But hospitality to the stranger does not necessarily translate into greater love for the people you live with every day, and the small town of both the heartland and the monastery are often stereotyped as either paradise on earth or backwaters full of provincial and self-righteous hypocrites. The truth, as is so often the case, lies somewhere in between.

I have observed that in the small town, the need to get along favors the passive aggressives, those for whom honest differences and disagreements pose such a threat that they are quickly submerged, left to fester in a complex web of resentments. This is why, when the tempests erupt in the small-town teapot, they are so violently destructive. This is why, when the comfortable fiction that we're all the same under the skin is exposed as a lie, those who are genuinely different so often feel ostracized and eventually leave.

The monasteries I am familiar with in Dakota also have their problems, the small-town problems of personality clashes at close quarters, of gossip, of pigeonholing people or taking them for granted. But overall they seem healthier than the towns. Benedictines live in such close proximity, and in his *Rule* Saint Benedict so clearly takes into account the different personalities and needs of individuals that one doesn't get far by pretending that everyone is the same; the monastery is far less likely than the small town to end up with conformity at the expense of community.

I'm not sure that Benedictines get along any better on average than small-town people do, but observation has led me to think that the fear of controversy that often paralyzes the small-town gathering, ensuring its dullness, is less a factor in the monastery, where scripture and the liturgy act as a leaven enabling (and sometimes forcing) people to be less defensive and fearful of one another. An example of how a monastic community and a small-town women's church group dealt with controversy will serve to illustrate this point.

A Benedictine sister from the Philippines once told me what her community did when some sisters took to the streets in the popular revolt against the Marcos regime. Some did not think it proper for nuns to demonstrate in public, let alone risk arrest. In a group meeting that began and ended with prayer, the sisters who wished to continue demonstrating explained that this was for them a religious obligation; those who disapproved also had their say. Everyone spoke; everyone heard and gave counsel.

It was eventually decided that the nuns who were demonstrating should continue to do so; those who wished to express solidarity but were unable to march would prepare food and provide medical assistance to the demonstrators, and those who disapproved would pray for everyone. The sister laughed and said, "If one of the conservative sisters was praying that we young, crazy ones would come to our senses and stay off the streets, that was O.K. We were still a community."

Things were different at a meeting of a church women's group in a small Dakota town, when a younger member distributed informational pamphlets about an upcoming election. Prepared by the county agricultural extension service, they explained in a nonpartisan manner several complicated constitutional issues on the state ballot. The woman was stunned to discover a few days later that another woman, a former teacher, had been criticizing her behind her back for bringing politics to the women's Bible circle. This is a story about fear, a fear so pervasive that even in a small group of people you've known most of your life you can't speak up, you can't risk talking about issues. That meeting had begun and ended with prayer, but no one had a say, no one was heard, and community was diminished.

Paradoxically, though monks are said to be "formed" into one way of life, monasteries are full of people who feel free to be themselves, often to the point of eccentricity. (An abbot once said to me, "if there is any such thing as a 'typical' monk, we sure don't have any here.") A monastery is cohesive; it is not a schismatic society that survives by expelling those who don't fit into a mold. This difference might be summed up in two versions of heaven I once heard from a Benedictine nun: in one, heaven is full of people you love, and in the other, heaven is where you love everyone who is there.

I once heard a woman in my church refuse outright to accept the help of another woman whose talents we could have used in presenting a musical program. It was rare to receive such an offer of help, and I thought it a shame to reject it and risk rejecting the woman in the process. But a personality clash or bad experience in the past had led this person to say, angrily and with grim finality: "I won't work with her." I couldn't help wishing we were in a monastery, where an abbot or prioress could command us under obedience to work with that woman, and maybe grow in our understanding of what Christian charity, and community, demand.

One thing that distinguishes the monastery from the small town is that the *Rule* of Saint Benedict, read aloud daily and constantly interpreted, provides definition of certain agreed-upon values that make for community. The small-town minister, expected to fill the role of such a rule by reminding people to love one another, is usually less effectual.

Benedict's admonishment to "bear with the greatest patience the infirmities of others," often acts like fresh air blowing into what could be the ultimate closed system, the smallest small town. Benedict was well aware that, as he put it, "thorns of contention are likely to spring up" in communal living, and he recommends as a remedy reciting the Lord's Prayer at both morning and evening office each day. "Thus warned by the pledge they make to one another in the very words of this prayer: *Forgive us as we forgive,*" he writes, the monks may "cleanse themselves of this kind of vice."

It seems to work. As one monk told me, "When someone in the community is driving me up the wall, we are still in church together four times a day. And that begins to make a difference. It takes the edge off." When I hear one monk complaining about another, however harsh the remark, however acute the exasperation or even rage, I sense that I am hearing an honest acknowledgment of differences grounded in love. Monks, after all, are conscious of moving, as Benedict says, "together unto life everlasting."

This might help explain the incredible expansiveness of Benedictine hospitality that on more than one occasion has turned my Dakota desert into a garden. One event could only have happened on the Plains, where monasteries are not besieged by many guests. I was visiting over Palm Sunday and the monk in charge of liturgy asked if I would take the part of one of the Gospel readers, the servant girl who nails Peter. I accepted, but scarcely felt I belonged; my being in church at all seemed unreal, either great folly or a miracle of hospitality on the part of both God and the monks. Later that day I read a vision of Mechtild of Magdeburg, a fiery and controversial mystic of the thirteenth century who was taken in by the Benedictines in her old age. I felt a twinge of recognition in her description of herself as someone who did not feel at home in church. As Mechtild was often in trouble with ecclesiastical authorities who frequently denied her the sacraments, this has a special poignancy. But in her vision the Blessed Virgin herself invites Mechtild into the choir, to "stand in front of Saint Catherine."

I sat in front of the abbey's farm manager, not Saint Catherine, but small difference. This is the power of desert hospitality: it transcends all our categories of division—male/female, Catholic/Protestant, celibate/married, monk/layperson—and changes us in the process.

Esther de Waal, a student of Benedictine spirituality, has described the Christian life as a series of open doors, and while I know that this is incomprehensible to many people, it is true of my experience in the monastery. After Mass that Palm Sunday, I wept for joy in my room, but I also laughed aloud when I read of Mechtild that "theology was not her strong point." To use a modern idiom, I could relate to that. For me, the greatest gift of the monastic tradition, beginning with the desert stories that contain some of the best theology I know, and continuing with my own experience of the Benedictines, is how easily and even beautifully theology converts into experience, and vice versa. It's a boon of the monastic liturgy, something I happen to have discovered in the desert of a monastery on the high plains desert of Dakota, and now no longer wish to live without.

The West River of Dakota encourages you to either make or find deserts for yourself. Sometimes it's a matter of adjusting to a harsh climate. (I'm writing this in a hermitage where the temperature by 11:30 A.M. is 92 degrees; the old air conditioner works, but drowns out the sound of birds and wind, so I don't use it.) Sometimes it means suffering in the constricted social atmosphere of a small town or seeking out the disciplined routine of a monastery. But in all of these places that couldn't be more deprived by worldly standards I also find an expansiveness, a giddy openness that has allowed me to discover gifts in myself and others that most likely would have remained hidden in more busy, sophisticated, or luxuriant surroundings.

In the small town on the Plains, as in the monastery, there are so few people for so many jobs that we tend to call on whoever seems the most likely to do the job well. This has its bad side, as capable people can find that they are doing too much. It can also lead to mediocrity. Many local events have made me think of what Minnesota writer Carol Bly has suggested as a motto for small towns: "If a thing is worth doing, it's worth doing badly."

But sometimes miracles occur. Sometimes people rise to the occasion and do well more than they believe they can do at all. The radical hope we must place in others on the Plains reminds me of Jesus, who called disciples from their ordinary work to change the world without once consulting a personnel manager to determine if they had the aptitude or credentials for the job.

When the pastor of our Presbyterian church in Lemmon moved away a few years ago, we were left with the task of filling the pulpit for an indeterminate period. The chair of the worship committee immediately commandeered me to preach, saying simply, "You're a writer, you can do it." And, to my surprise, I did. I had to confront some family ghosts, among them the fierce Methodist preachers in my blood. I had to contend with my own uncertain Christian faith. But the need was there, and I was able to answer it, preaching well enough so that in effect I became our half-time pastor for eight months, until other duties called me away.

There were other surprises in store for the congregation; we found that one of our elders, a housewife and proud of it, could lead a very dignified communion service. She also preached several fine devotional sermons, one on the subject of housework. What good is a desert? Well, I believe a desert is where such gifts appear. In a larger urban church with well-credentialed clergy, that woman and I would not have been asked to preach. We would never have discovered that we could preach. But on the Plains, as in the desert, book learning and training matters less than one's ability to draw from the well of one's experience, to learn by doing (a motto of John Dewey's). It's also a founding principle of Bennington College, and it amuses me to find that I'm finally living it nearly thirty years after graduation and a world away.

The aging congregations in small towns on the Plains may be an endangered species. But so are the family farmers of Dakota, and Benedictine monks, for that matter. All are generally viewed by the rest of the world as irrelevant or anachronistic. And yet we may find important lessons in these overlooked and undervalued lives. Despite their dwindling numbers, and despite the fact that they, like the rest of us, so often fail at caring for one another as they should, churchgoers are trying to keep alive both hope and community values.

Small-town churchgoers are often labeled hypocrites, and sometimes they are. But maybe they are also people who have learned to live with imperfection, what Archbishop Rembert Weakland, a Benedictine, recently described as "the new asceticism." Living with people at close range over many years, as both monastics and small-town people do, is much more difficult than wearing a hair shirt. More difficult, too, I would add, than holding to the pleasant but unrealistic ideal of human perfectibility that seems to permeate much New Age thinking.

And there is the land. Family farmers and monks cultivate living lightly on the land, the farmers because they love it and want to

preserve it for their children, the Benedictines because their communities put down permanent roots. Neither are frontier people in
the exploitative sense of the word—those who take all there is from
a place and then move on. As it becomes increasingly obvious that
the human race will eventually run out of places to move on to,
their wisdom and way of life may prove important to all of us.

Many people are just waking to the reality that unlimited expansion, what we call progress, is not possible in this world, and maybe
looking to monks (who seek to live within limitations) as well as
rural Dakotans (whose limitations are forced upon them by isolation
and a harsh climate) can teach us how to live more realistically.
These unlikely people might also help us overcome the pathological
fear of death and the inability to deal with sickness and old age that
plague American society.

Consumerism is fed by a desire to forget our mortality. But Benedict instructs his monks to remind themselves every day that they are
going to die, and in Dakota death has an undeniable day-to-day reality. The brutal massacres of Wounded Knee and the Killdeer Mountains (misnamed a "battle" to this day) are too recent to be comfortably relegated to history; they're still a living memory for the Native
American community. And for white settlers, the period since the
end of the "Indian Wars" has been marked by the slow death of their
towns, churches, schools, and way of life. We learn to live with a
hard reality: nothing lasts. As a pastor friend who has served in the
Dakotas for nearly thirty years recently wrote to me, "Dakota civilization does not support the idea that institutions will live on and we
with them . . . quite possibly what we value so highly might not
even outlast us."

Maybe the desert wisdom of the Dakotas can teach us to love anyway, to love what is dying, in the face of death, and not pretend that
things are other than they are. The irony and wonder of all this is
that it is the desert's grimness, its stillness and isolation, that bring us
back to love. Here we discover the paradox of the contemplative life,
that the desert of solitude can be the school where we learn to love
others.

In the monastic tradition, the desert of deprivation and solitude
has always been the well-spring of self-giving love. A scholar of the
early Christian church, Peter Brown, captured the essence of this
paradox in writing about Anthony, one of the earliest of the desert
ascetics, considered to have set the tone for the monastic movement
in Christendom. Brown points out that the battle for the heart is the
one that mattered to Anthony far more than the battle for control of

his bodily desires. He writes that the message of Anthony's life, that later monks made into a model of monasticism, was

> revealed (in Anthony's last years) ever more frequently in the quintessentially fourth-century gift of sociability. He came to radiate such magnetic charm, and openness to all, that any stranger who came upon him, surrounded by crowds of disciples, visiting monks, and lay pilgrims, would know at once, in that dense press of black-garbed figures, which one was the great Anthony. He was instantly recognizable as someone whose heart had achieved total transparency to others.

I have seen that transparency in a few old monks who over many years have come to incarnate hospitality. This doesn't seem like something one could aspire to, but it's inspiring to see how much ordinary human defensiveness can wear away in a well-lived and holy life. My own life has opened up more than I thought possible in the Dakota desert, the desert of the monastery and of the small town, the desert of a small and fairly conservative Presbyterian church.

I believe that it is because they so consciously and willingly live out the paradox of the desert that the monastic communities on the high Plains are more open to change than the small towns here, and are therefore more likely to survive. It is partly that monastic people value the leaven that outsiders can bring: as they're not easily suckered by the all-American myth of self-reliance and self-sufficiency, they're less likely to persist in thinking they can stand alone. Monks are also less likely to hide like mushrooms, like some small-town people I know who suffer in silent and obsessive despair as the inevitable happens, and another family moves out of town, eroding the tax base, putting on the market another house that won't find a buyer.

For one who has chosen the desert and truly embraced the forsaken ground it is not despair or fear or limitation that dictates how one lives. One finds instead an openness and hope that verges on the wild:

> Abbot Lot went to see Abbot Joseph and said: "Father, according as I am able, I keep my little rule, and my little fast, my prayer, meditation and contemplative silence; and according as I am able I strive to cleanse my heart of bad thoughts: now what more should I do?" The elder rose up in reply and stretched out his hands to heaven, and his fingers became like lamps of fire. He said: "why not become all flame?"

A Sense of Place

Being grounded in a subject means understanding its basic elements, and being grounded also means being firmly in position. The term refers essentially to the ground itself, the Earth, the place where we are rooted. Where on the planet does a person feel grounded, at home, belonging to a place as it belongs to that person? How is that sense of home fostered? When a person speaks of where he or she lives, is it really the place that gives life?

Marjorie Kinnan Rawlings expresses that sense of belonging to a place in *Cross Creek,* her book about the little town in Florida where she bought a run-down orange grove: "When I came to the Creek, and knew the old grove and farmhouse at once as home, there was some terror, such as one feels in the first recognition of a human love, for the joining of person to place, as of person to person, is a commitment to shared sorrow, even as to shared joy."

The sense of feeling one's own place in the world is not limited, however, to the country. A person's sense of home can be a city block, or an entire city, a tiny cottage, an ocean. Moreover, a writer can convey a sense of place even when the acquaintance is only casual and transitory. Travel writers describe places that they most definitely do not feel at home in, places that feel very strange and exotic, though the best kind of travel writing happens when the writer begins to come into close connection with even the most distant place. Wherever the place is, the work of effective description is to convey the feeling of what it is like to be there.

How is that sense of place achieved? Norris gives a good example of the kind of description that conveys a writer's feel for an area. She describes not only the physical landscape but also the way the physical characteristics of the Great Plains environment shape the people and the ways that people relate to one another. She reports conversations and events. She describes a series of small communities, the small towns of the region and the communities of the monasteries. From what she says, the reader gets a sense that she has seen and thought about events and people as well as landscape. By close, continual observation and participation, Norris shows herself deeply committed to her own particular place on the planet.

Study Questions

1. How does Norris show that the lives of the people are shaped by the landscape? What in the environment—the weather, the crops that can be grown, the way the land is laid out, among other things—affects the ways that people live and relate to one another?
2. Why is that particular region a good place for a monastery? Is one place as good as another for the religious lives the monks lead? Make a list of at least four reasons you can see from the essay that the aims of a monastery can be better carried out in that place rather than another, such as London or New York City. Alternately, argue that the choice of a location is immaterial and give your reasons.
3. "Many small towns are Indian or white," says Norris, "and in general there is a deafening silence between the two worlds." How does she try to bring those two worlds together? How does she compare the communication problems in the small towns with problems in the monasteries, and why can those problems be more easily solved in the religious communities?

Writing Topics

1. *Collaborative writing activity.* With a small group, try creating silence as Norris describes. Hold the silence for at least a minute, but make a rule that no one should look at his or her watch during that time. Then have each member of the group write a two-sentence description of what silence feels like. Put these short descriptions together into a group list.
2. Write your own essay on the topic of "Where I Am." Include your own sense of the surrounding countryside (or city) and the people you live among. What makes the place special to you? How do you relate to those people and that landscape? What makes it home?
3. Write a descriptive essay about a place in nature that you remember from your childhood, a place that is now very changed. Describe the place in your memories and as it is now.

    Consider the organization of your essay. You may wish to open with the present and then go back into your memories, or go from early years forward. Make the description as vivid and detailed as possible.

Textual Challenges

A Focus on Longer, More Difficult Prose

There is a moment in the sport of long-distance running when a tired runner "hits the wall." This is the point at which it becomes most difficult to continue. The wall is usually a mental as well as physical block, and in a marathon it frequently begins in the form of a hill. The runner, whose muscles by this time are urging "stop," suddenly comes to a rise in the course. It's not a high hill. Even higher hills may already have been run, and steeper ones might be ahead. But *this* hill is "the wall"; it feels enormous, impossible, insurmountable. It seems to expand as the runner approaches it, and looms larger and ever more difficult with each step.

If the runner can summon enough courage to keep from giving up, enough energy just to get past this one block, the rest of the race can be run. Here, it's not a matter of being first; just getting past the wall is triumph enough. The psychological secret is simply to *keep going*.

Complex passages and long reading assignments often seem like the same kind of wall to students, and the same kinds of methods—along with some good basic training—help to get past the challenge. The In Focus essays in this chapter will prepare students to deal with longer, more complex writing. "Active Reading" and "Pause and Consider" explain the importance of taking this material in small bites. "Texture," "Imagery," and "Irony" show how to perceive subtleties and meaning that might otherwise be missed. "Science and Philosophy" and "A Scientist Writes" emphasize that scientific writing—written for the average educated reader—provides important practice in dealing with advanced language and concepts. Finally, "Imaginary Worlds" paves the way for the even greater challenges of chapter 7.

The Readings in Focus

Each of the selections in this chapter represents a specific reading challenge, and each rewards the reader with some new insight, some intriguing description, some interesting conclusion. As the reader's abilities to concentrate, analyze, and interpret increase, the wide range of subjects in these pieces will become more and more attractive.

The lead essay, "Judge Hayden's Family Values" by Jan Hoffman, is not difficult reading, and the subject is interesting and important, but it's a long article. This piece runs over six thousand words and will require for most readers thirty to forty-five minutes of focused attention. Psychological studies tell us that many people raised in the television era, accustomed to thirty-second sound bites and two-minute television news stories, have trouble concentrating on anything for more than ten to twenty minutes at a time. Wandering minds need this kind of practice to help them stay on target.

Following the social analysis of "Judge Hayden's Family Values" is a historical analysis. In "An Inquiry into the Persistence of Unwisdom in Government," Barbara Tuchman asks the question "Why are governments so often so stupid?" Her inquiry demonstrates the use of extensive examples to drive home a point.

The next selection, Dennis Alan Mann's "Beams of Light: Looking at Architecture," is an academic paper that demonstrates how scholars use, and give credit to, other scholars' work.

Jonathan Marks's "Black White Other" is an introduction to scientific writing for a general audience, such as the educated readers of *Natural History* magazine, where this essay was first published. Later in the chapter, other selections written by scientists and mathematicians demonstrate different ways that logic, research, and experimental findings can be used to demonstrate points and argue positions: Stephen Hawking's thoughtful analysis (physics and mathematics) in "Is Everything Determined?", Mair Zamir's careful explanation (anatomy) in "Secrets of the Heart," and Douglas R. Hofstadter's vision in "Reductio Expansioque ad Absurdum."

The two other pieces in this chapter each present unique viewpoints and provide different stretching exercises for readers-in-training. Dylan Thomas's "The Force that Through the Green Fuse Drives the Flower" demands a loosening of linear thought in order to accept the elegant play of language in the poem. The selection from Jamaica Kincaid's *A Small Place* is not only a biting social commentary but also a brilliant example of the use of irony and sarcasm.

Judge Hayden's Family Values

It has taken almost four years to get to this afternoon in a muggy Newark courtroom. That's how long the parents have been duking it out over their son, each trying to win the judge over, each saying, Your Honor, *you* decide because we can't. Just let me be the one to keep the child. Yet no matter how she calls the custody fight, Judge Katharine Sweeney Hayden knows that one parent will bless her and the other will curse her. She shrugs. It's not my job to make happy endings, she thinks. If a couple is so anger-locked that they have to ask a stranger to make their most intimate decisions, well, too bad: I'm it, I'm what you've got.

Then she relents a little. She reminds herself that people so desperate that they must turn to an Essex County family court judge have no choice but to trust her. And that is why she often feels protective of them.

But today she's unusually edgy: she still has no idea how she is going to rule. It's already June and the case has a firm deadline, two months away.

During the years the parents have come before her, they have treated the boy like a shuttlecock—one month with the mother, first in Cleveland, more recently in Wilmington, Del.; the next month with the father in a New Jersey suburb. But now their son is 6. In September, he must start first grade in one state or another—and stay there.

The husband's lawyer is summing up. He makes a powerful claim for the father, Carl H., a 30-year-old airline supervisor. The court-appointed psychologist has favored the father—important, thinks the judge, but not a deal maker. A tall, quiet man with two years of college, Carl offers the boy not only his own love but also the love and caretaking of Carl's parents, with whom he lives, as well as the boisterous affection of an extended family.

399

Hayden, a slim, handsome woman of 53 with a passing resemblance to Sigourney Weaver, listens fixedly, chin cradled in her right palm, unconsciously inching an elbow forward across her desk until the upper half of her body is all but horizontal.

Carl's lawyer now turns on the mother, Amber H. It was she who had an affair and moved out, leaving her husband and son behind in 1991. She changed addresses half a dozen times in four years, landing briefly in a violent relationship.

The judge pauses from her note taking to flex a sore wrist. But why, she wonders, has Carl been driving with a revoked license for two years? And why is a 30-year-old man living with his parents?

Now Amber's lawyer gets to her feet. Sure, her 26-year-old client, an airline ticket agent, made some mistakes. But she's matured since she walked away from a marriage that left her emotionally and, she says, physically bruised. Amber has settled down. In Delaware she has a home, a school, a church ready for her boy.

But how, the judge worries, can Amber justify taking the boy to another state, away from his father and grandparents? This bothers her. A lot.

Finally the lawyer offers Amber's most provocative claim—biology is indeed destiny. Amber was adopted. Her only known blood relation is her son. That argument, thinks the judge, has an emotional pull but not a legal one. But the next point will send her to the law library: paternity tests have proved that Carl is not the boy's biological father.

The baby was born less than a year after they started dating. Carl says he always assumed the child was his. Amber says she told him the truth right away. The judge has to decide who's lying.

Hayden announces she will rule in a few weeks. Then she escapes to her chambers, where she tosses off her black robe and nervously runs her long fingers through her close-cropped hair.

This case is driving her nuts.

On most weekdays, the judge gets up at 5:30 A.M., pushes herself through three miles of race walking and makes a good-faith effort to pull into the court's parking lot by 8:26 A.M. She heads over to the Hall of Records, a gloomy, turn-of-the-century building in a downtown Newark neighborhood that empties out when darkness falls.

Today begins promisingly: one of the main entrance's six elevators is actually working. As she strides down a dimly lighted hallway to her chambers, she sees people of all races waiting for her. Aunts and grandmothers dandling babies. A skinny man with oozing scratches from ear to collarbone. An elderly couple. A couple looking prosperous and deeply annoyed, separated by lawyers. They are residents of Essex County, which includes Newark, one of the country's most ravaged cities, as well as the plush, Manhattan-commuter suburbs of South Orange, Livingston and Short Hills.

Hayden is acutely aware that the people who come before her have no buffer to protect them from how she, a white, affluent, divorced and remarried mother of two, views their case. She is their sole juror—there are no jury trials in family court. Many couples come before her without lawyers and cannot afford to challenge her rulings. A scant fistful of her cases have ever been appealed. So although she doesn't share the glamorous status of those who preside over lurid criminal cases or big-ticket lawsuits, the impact she has on litigants can often be more profound and longer lasting.

But her job, like that of her colleagues, is getting harder, at times seemingly impossible, as the definition of family keeps mutating. When Katharine Hayden was starting law school almost a quarter-century ago, in-vitro fertilization was still half a dozen years away, and the landmark New Jersey family court case about Baby M. and Mary Beth Whitehead, the child's surrogate mother, nearly 15. A father like Carl would almost never have challenged his wife over custody, regardles of blood ties. That gay and lesbian couples might adopt children was virtually unimaginable.

Bewildered and sometimes genuinely stumped by family dilemmas, she and her fellow judges have become society's gatekeepers, making decisions based on an uneasy mixture of inadequate laws and their own private values. The longer she sits on the bench, the more she realizes she's the interpreter of what society views as right and wrong.

Unlike those in many states, where different types of domestic cases are dispersed throughout the system, New Jersey's family court is a self-contained mini-mall of household horrors. Eventually, almost every modern family problem lands in Hayden's court. Her caseload includes child abuse, spousal violence, divorce, custody disputes among unmarried couples, deadbeat dads and termination of parental rights. (Adoptions and juvenile-delinquency cases are assigned to other judges.) She hears about 75 cases a week.

But in contrast to most of her colleagues around the country, who come to the despised, entry-level "kiddie court" with no background in family law, Hayden was a widely respected matrimonial lawyer. Even though she is to be rotated to the more high-profile criminal bench next year, when that stint is up she wants to return to family court. In a 1993 *New Jersey Law Journal* survey, for which lawyers rated Essex County's 56 family, equity, criminal and civil Superior Court trial judges on efficiency, knowledge and fairness, she was first overall.

While family court judges tend to cling tightly to confidentiality, Hayden spoke candidly about many of her cases to a reporter, whom she permitted to sit in on her court proceedings and chambers conferences for a month. (For privacy reasons, the parents have been identified in this article by first names or initials; the children's names have been omitted.) So it became possible to see how a family court judge, by questioning, scolding and listening to people for whom love has long since turned rancid and dull-eyed, performs a role that is far more complex than administrator of the law. From Hayden's wooden perch in her dingy four-row courtroom, she is mother, psychologist, preacher.

And to the families whose intimate lives she will reshape for years to come, she can seem like the hand of God. Or, occasionally, the Devil's.

This afternoon, the judge takes her first measure of a difficult domestic violence case. The husband presents his story and the judge hears his rough voice breaking; she particularly notices that as he leans toward his daughter and wife, they stiffen. Contact lenses corrected her poor eyesight years ago, but she noses around new cases like a mole, sensing shapes and body language.

Mr. and Mrs. B. have each filed a domestic violence complaint against the other. Each wants to evict the other from their home. Neither spouse has a lawyer. But Mr. B. has brought a witness— their shy, gangling 12-year-old daughter.

Smiling graciously, the judge immediately tells a court officer to escort the daughter outside. A child shouldn't have to hear her parents' ragged, recriminating tales of a 15-year marriage collapsing in infidelity and shattered pride.

At first, the father seems the more sympathetic figure of the two. Mr. B., a 49-year-old truck driver, says in a tear-soaked voice: "I love my wife. I've tried to do everything to keep our family together."

His story is ancient: he caught his wife with another man. At 2 A.M. their escalating fight culminated with Mrs. B.'s pulling a knife on her husband and locking him out of the house, barefoot. The daughter let him in and later confirmed his story to the police.

The judge squints at him. Something doesn't ring true here. Why didn't he kick her out or pack his things? He's a big guy—he can't possibly be physically afraid of her. So what does he want? To get me to evict her so he can get the house?

Mrs. B., a medical secretary, doesn't exactly deny what happened. But in a voice at once defiant and defensive, she explains that her husband, a recovering alcoholic, is insecure because the two have not had "an intimate relationship" in some time.

She locks eyes with the judge, scrupulously avoiding her husband. "He said he wanted to purchase a gun and blow my head off. He got my mink coat, along with my cellular phone."

The judge throws her arms in the air. Who's to blame? She will have to call the young witness. But first she cautions the parents: "The one who loses will think it's because your daughter pointed the finger one way or the other. I'm telling you on the record I've made up my mind, but I want to explain it to her first. You have to have faith in this judge that I'm not lying to you."

Warily, the daughter enters the courtroom, craning her neck to watch her parents leave, abandoning her to this stranger in a black robe. After they have gone, the judge speaks gently to the girl. "I want to ask your mom to leave the house because your dad's case fits the law better than hers. But how do you feel about living with him at home?"

The girl stares at her, dumbfounded. Then, to the judge's dismay, the child bursts into tears.

"I want to go with my mother," she says.

The judge pauses. Stay calm, she tells herself. "I could say I want you with your mother and I want you in the house. Do you mind if I tell your dad?"

The girl shakes her head. "He'll be real mad at me," she sobs. "When I was little, he used to beat me. My older sister told me that when they fought, to go to my room and turn the music up loud."

The judge's face is a mask of sympathetic anguish. "That must be a terrible thing for you."

The girl is warming up. "My sister said he used to hit my mother."

The judge scribbles notes and carefully asks, "When did he start up his drinking again?"

"Oct. 1, 1994," the child promptly replies.

"How do you know that date so well?"

"Because it was my birthday," says the girl. "He said he was happy I was turning 12, but I don't believe it, because he started drinking that day."

The judge massages her aching temples. So the family is in a far more precarious state than she had realized. Why did the father resume drinking? Given that his wife isn't sleeping with him, was he unnerved by his daughter's budding puberty?

The judge sighs and tells the girl that she will let her remain with her mother. "But I'm in a pickle," she adds. "I told your parents I wouldn't let you change my mind, but now you've gone and done it."

Then the judge telephones a lawyer who has a gift with child clients and asks her to represent the daughter. According to the law, Mrs. B. should have to leave because she threatened her husband with a dangerous weapon. But now that the daughter has raised new issues, the judge must consider which outcome will be in the child's best interest.

Meanwhile, the girl waits in the judge's chambers, looking almost chipper. Then she goes into the courtroom to whisper in the judge's ear: can Hayden now help the mother, who fears the father may damage their car, down in the court parking lot?

Damn it, the judge thinks irritably, I extended myself, and now she's taking advantage of me. I'm not going to micromanage their squabbles. Politely but firmly, she dusts the girl off.

The hearing resumes. The girl keeps her eyes on the table as her lawyer speaks. "She loves her dad and doesn't want to hurt him," says the lawyer, "but she would be happier if her dad moved and she could see him as much as possible."

The judge issues no-contact orders against both parents: "You are pushing each other's buttons. But if I say Mrs. B. leaves, then your daughter has to leave the house, too. So I'm asking Mr. B. to leave for two weeks."

The family walks tiredly, even peacefully out of court, wife smiling at husband, father wrapping his arm around his daughter. Hayden steps down from the bench. Good job, Katharine, she thinks.

Fifteen minutes later, Mrs. B. and her daughter race back into court, banging on the door of the judge's chambers. They say that in the elevator, Mr. B. swore he would mess up the house and his wife as well. Then he ran off. Mrs. B. speaks in gasps; her daughter looks crushed. When they got to the parking lot, Mrs. B. saw that her right front tire had been slashed and her antenna snapped. He had apparently attacked the car before he returned to court.

The judge's face goes taut with rage. She orders a sheriff's officer to accompany Mrs. B. and her daughter to a service station. Then, tremulously wishing the two of them the best of luck, the judge has another officer tell the local precinct to send a squad car to meet Mrs. B. at the house.

That night, Hayden sleeps fitfully. One of a family judge's worst

nightmares is to make a wrong call on a domestic violence case. At
4 A.M. she wakes herself, scolding: letting the daughter live with her
father would have been a stupid, dead-wrong decision.

She shouldn't have dismissed the girl when she asked for help.
And she had absolutely misread the couple's smiles. She had thought
that the wife was smiling in triumph for having got the house and
that the husband was smiling because he had just heard his daughter say she loved him.

But she now sees that Mrs. B. had the nervous smile of a very
frightened woman and that Mr. B. had been smiling because he
knew what was waiting for his wife in the parking lot. All the
while, the judge had had the arrogance to think that she had fixed
everything.

She can't go back to sleep. She has a strict rule about post-mortem
lashing. One good stinging self-beratement session, but that's it. As
dawn breaks, she forces herself out of bed and into her running
clothes. She cannot afford to let Mr. and Mrs. B. haunt her. Time to
cauterize the case, and move on.

Friday is divorce day. You can sniff the tension and the money in
the air. Not coincidentally, Friday is also the Day of the Lawyers.

Today Hayden wears her favorite earrings, dangling portraits of
moon-eyed cows. Too bad if people think they're completely silly. To
keep herself happy, a judge has to do what a judge has to do.

She takes the bench, sparring deftly with pin stripe after pin stripe
as they bring divorce motions before her, flexing her judicial muscle,
earrings swaying. She's almost having too much fun. Bearing down
on a battalion of lawyers, her face alight with the slyest of grins, she
says: "*I* don't know how you'll be ready for trial in two weeks either.
You'll have to cram and it will be horrible."

Who's next? One couple, unencumbered by counsel, raise their
hands. Like most family court judges, she hates to be the one to
divide up the spoils. "You've settled?" she sings out. "Be still, my
heart!"

But while 90 percent of divorce cases do settle, often the judge has
to bang heads in her chambers to get there. When tempers get too
short, she'll wind up the yellow Power Ranger she keeps on her desk
and let it stalk noisily across the floor before the embarrassed
lawyers.

One day she keeps stepping off the bench for updates from Howard
Danzig and Cary Cheifetz, who represent a suburban couple in their
mid-40's. The wife is a Wall Street lawyer who earns $165,000 a

year; the husband quit his job with the Internal Revenue Service 15 years ago and has since stayed home to raise their five children.

"We don't know what's happening, judge," says Danzig, looking hapless. "They sent us away and they're sitting in the cafeteria with their laptops."

By day's end, Hayden sets the trial for the following week. When they return on that date, Danzig, who represents the husband, announces that negotiations have broken down over alimony his client wants the wife to pay.

The judge is both indignant and trying not to laugh. The couple's youngest child is already in high school; the eldest is already out of the house. "Really, Howard! Your client has to go to work. He can't stay at home anymore!"

Danzig looks nearly apoplectic. "Reverse the sexes, Judge! Imagine he earns $165,000 and she stays home with the kids."

"But he's more employable than his analogue," says Hayden. "And I don't want to barter her future for his alimony."

Cheifetz points out that the wife has already offered to pay not only all child support but also all five college tuitions.

Hayden looks quizzical. "I smell a rat," she says. "Is the wife taking on extra responsibility for the children so she won't have to give him money?"

This piece of information is enough to turn her head around about the case. Ushering the two lawyers to the door, she says: "You're right, Howard. Tell them the judge agrees it's definitely an alimony case. I finally saw what a sexist pig I am."

The next week, the couple settle.

When the judge does have to hand out marital booty, she holds her nose. "Financial decisions are intrusive and awkward forays into how people spend their money," she sputters one Friday morning. She stares at a list of items. *"I hate TV's!"* she shouts. "Why can't people divide up their own toys?"

The judge's first marriage, to a professor of medieval literature, fell apart after nearly 20 years. The dissolution was slow, sad but civilized. Even so, she will never forget the one blowup in their Maplewood kitchen, when he shouted, "I'll get a lawyer!" She was by then a major league divorce lawyer, and yet she still felt as if an earthquake had shaken their home. Lawyers? Judges? Combing through *her* life?

All the trust between her and her husband, the father of her two sons, would have been ripped away by the legal system. Luckily, the two of them worked out an amicable settlement. But the memory of those 10 seconds of panic in a suburban kitchen stays with her still, and she recalls it every time she has to reach into a divorcing couple's private cupboard.

The next hearing is to give a couple in divorce litigation a temporary budget until a final ruling. In addition to the divorce case, the husband and wife have filed domestic violence charges against each other. Both matters are before Hayden. Suzanne Spina, 30, is a Verona homemaker with two little children; Robert Spina, 40, is Police Chief of West Orange, appointed last year by his father, the Mayor. In a few weeks, Hayden's finding that Robert Spina abused his wife will be local front-page news. But right now there are bills to be paid. And Suzanne wants Robert to keep right on paying them.

Like Suzanne's car phone.

"Go on the low monthly end—$50," Hayden says. "You can rob from the food bill if you talk too much. How about $55 for your home phone?"

Ellen Marshall, Suzanne's lawyer, leaps up. "Ma'am," she cries out, "this is a devastated lady! She needs the support of her family," who reside in long-distance area codes and whom Suzanne needs to telephone regularly. A piddling $105 a month?

The judge fixes the lawyer with a deadpan stare. "So put it on her family's dime," she says.

Propping her reading glasses on her nose, the judge marches down the list of operations at the Spina manse, revising expenses for lawn care, utilities, repairs on the Mercedes, the burglar alarm, karate and tennis lessons for the 4-year-old, cleaning woman, birthday parties. She informs the Spinas that she doesn't do TV's and VCR's. The couple snipe at each other but eventually strike an accord. Then the judge makes a ruling on the treadmill. She gives it to Robert.

She knows that every divorcing party, consciously or not, draws a line that cannot be crossed. Robert has testified extensively about his exercise routine, and she has a hunch that losing the treadmill would have been the deal killer for him.

Besides, she thinks, the Spina's health club is a good spot for Suzanne to meet people. Many hard bodies, many fancy treadmills— she laughs, shaking her head—and a regular Peyton Place.

Hayden hears hundreds of cases through June and July. But each dawn as she sets out to race walk through her riverfront town, the battle over Amber and Carl's boy hovers in her head. One morning, Amber wins. Carl, the next. While blocks of brownstones go by, details from the case pluck at her. Why hasn't Carl made getting back his driver's license a priority? What about Amber's overbearing mother back in Washington State? She had heedlessly told her grandson that his daddy wasn't his real father. Amber merely said in court that she couldn't control her. Worrisome?

The truth is, Hayden realizes, that even though state family law seems specific, in close cases she can stack the facts and find legal backing for her decision no matter which way she goes.

A week later, during lunch hour in chambers, she is thinking aloud between bites on a chicken sandwich from the corner truck. Amber's insistence on the paternity test is irking her. By saying to her son, "You're mine but not his," Amber is seeking to remove him from his grandparents and his father, as well as an uncle, aunts and cousins— all the family he grew up with. The judge can't buy that.

Yet today, she is starting to think that Carl should lose. The psychologist said Carl played beautifully with his son, but what does that mean? How much time does Carl spend with him, anyway, compared with the grandparents? By contrast, it is Amber who deals with doctors, sets up play dates, gets calls from school and, in the judge's view, edges out Carl because she does it on her own.

Still, is Amber getting her life together? No. During part of the litigation, Amber made some foolhardy choices that worry the judge: for one, she moved in briefly with a Cleveland boyfriend who beat her.

Hayden nibbles some potato chips. She remains unsure about the violence in Amber and Carl's marriage, a factor she must consider in a custody dispute. The testimony from witnesses was inconclusive. She thinks Carl is soft-pedaling the violence and Amber is over-describing. If Amber was so afraid of her husband, why did she leave their son with him for six months when she walked out?

All month long, the bulging Amber-and-Carl file sits, unexamined and accusing, on the judge's dining-room table at home, amid half a dozen glowering unpaid bills. The more she worries about a case, the longer she avoids it. She knows herself: she's Queen of the Last Minute and so must give herself a deadline.

Even so, the judge dithers away another week, obsessing now about geography. If only Amber had relocated within New Jersey, this case would be a no-brainer. Amber would win residential custody and Carl would get liberal visitation; the boy would not lose access to his extended family.

She asks her law clerk to search case law to see if she can give Amber custody on the condition that she move back to New Jersey.

Or construct a ruling that says Carl gets custody unless Amber returns.

But she's clutching at legal straws. A wasted week. And so another morning, another fast wobble-walk through the streets of her humid, somnolent town. It is now the third week of July. The first day of school is fast approaching and she has to make a decision.

At the end of the day—sometimes 6 P.M., occasionally 7—the judge droops out of the courthouse. The roughest days are those when she ignores her own rule: don't go out on a limb for people. Because every time you say, Follow me into the wilderness for I am the judge. . . . *Yeah, right.*

Sometimes a day closes just when she's in the exasperating middle of trying to solve someone's insoluble problem. Or just after somebody has yelled back and embarrassed her on the bench. Her face gets hot, her neck splotchy, her breathing choppy. She hates that. She hates for people in the courtroom to think she's vulnerable. She wants them to see Olympian perfection in a black robe.

She couldn't have done this job when her kids were small because once she got home, they made demands on her. In court, she lavishes all her maternal instincts on people. She is Judge Big Sister Katharine, eldest of three, who learned to take charge after her adored Wall Street lawyer father died when she was 17. But by the end of the court day, she has nothing left to give.

Her friends ask how she can stand it that her husband, Joe Hayden, a criminal lawyer, doesn't get home sometimes until 10:30 at night, but she thinks, thank God, that's the beauty of her marriage: no demands, the solitude at dusk, the freedom just to be quiet and rebuild herself. She returns to her lemon-yellow 19th-century brick behemoth with the twisting staircases and stained-glass windows, feeds the cats, settles back into her armchair and stares at the wall.

Once in a while her thoughts may stray over the cases she has heard in the last few days—in one July week, she terminated the parental rights of a formerly drug-addicted mother and sent a commodities broker to jail until he paid $15,000 in overdue support for his young son and wife. But mostly she tries to make her mind blank. Then she may read. Hardly the stuff of someone with a graduate degree in English literature: detective fiction and serial-murder mysteries.

In her first months on the bench, she'd sometimes nod off at the dinner table to stave off attacks of panic. She'd rip her cuticles, curl up in bed in a fetal position, then lie awake for hours, obsessing. This is fun? she would think.

Gradually the terror slid back into the corner and she took command of her court, her self. And she knows she couldn't do her job if this marriage weren't solid. When you're trying to salvage people from their emotional messes, you have to be in decent shape yourself. The Haydens are well known in a circle of New Jersey lawyers and Federal and state judges. A typical vacation for the couple begins in the car ride to a judicial conference, six hours together, the simple pleasures of talk.

To recharge herself, she goes to Mass every Sunday. She's a modern Catholic—she divorced and signs off on hundreds of divorces a year—but she's not entirely certain that God won't strike her dead if she misses a week at Mass. Sure, half the time she's sitting in church she's thinking up recipes. But she says that if she puts herself in the presence of God, when she needs to call upon Him, either shaking her fist or negotiating hard, she will already have paid her respects.

And it's usually on Sundays that she enters races. Her not-so-well-kept secret is that she is a lousy race walker. For a woman whose puckish sense of humor includes herself as fair game, she is unexpectedly earnest on the topic of her little races, as she calls them. She keeps at them to maintain her mental equilibrium. She is moved and bothered by the power she has over people as a judge. But every time she goes out for a race, she feels terror, the potential for humiliation, which may be something close to how the people who come before her feel.

Although the days wring her out, there has not been a morning yet when she hasn't looked forward to sitting in family court, which is still so much better than being a divorce lawyer. It was wrenching when your clients were so unhappy and all you could do was try to pave the way for less anarchy in their lives.

But as a judge, she can make things happen, in a glacial-pace sort of way. That's the thought that keeps her going, the optimism of being a Catholic: a judge can hold out legal absolution, the promise of a redeemed life.

Coming off the bench after a hearing one day, Hayden wants a reality check. "Miss Bert, what did you think of that methadone mother?" she asks Alberta Gregory, her court clerk.

Gregory, who has lived many of her 61 years in Newark, arches her brows. "Boss, she lies like a rug!"

Hayden looks taken aback but braces herself to hear more; she's quite aware that she's a white woman who was raised on Manhattan's Upper East Side and educated through college by nuns. She depends on Gregory, who is black, to clue her in about life in Newark's poor neighborhoods. "Judge," says Gregory with a sigh, "let me tell you how methadone goes down in this town."

Hayden's rulings are her own, but in addition to voraciously consulting legal, psychological and social tracts, she turns to a select few people to be her sounding board.

So today, she puts up her long legs and considers questions of great moment with Gregory and Patti Cassidy, her secretary: even though that couple have filed for divorce, are they still sleeping together? Is that why they are taking their sweet time to push the case? "Forbidden sex can be pretty hot," muses the judge.

She often speculates about the sexual dynamics of the couples who come before her. On another day, a suburban wife testified that as part of her husband's continuing emotional abuse, he made love to her one spring morning, then got out of bed and, without a word, packed and walked out. The judge, Cassidy and Gregory shriek, collectively appalled. "That's psychological rape!" says the judge.

"But you know the final insult? When he was asked on the stand about whether he had sex with her that morning, he said, 'I don't recall.' "

And Hayden regularly consults with the other "Cardinals," as the four judges in Essex County family court who hear divorce cases have been anointed by their sardonic boss, Judge Philip M. Freedman. ("More like the four Mouseketeers," mutters Gregory.) The Cardinals—Thomas P. Zampino, Richard C. Camp, Herbert S. Glickman and Hayden—sometimes handle multimillion-dollar divorces. Central to why so many matrimonial lawyers kiss their rings is that the Cardinals can order legal fees paid by the wealthier spouse.

The Cardinals often confer in Hayden's whimsical, who's-in-charge-here? chambers. Cat and cow memorabilia clutter the shelves, as do plastic monsters from the movie "Alien." A poster of her son's fledgling rock band hangs under her law diploma. As the Power Ranger looks on, the Cardinals frequently trade tales about litigants and lawyers. Their gallows humor may be indiscreet, but they say that because they preside daily over fraying lives, they need to blow off steam.

Sometimes the judges talk about how their own marriages affect their decision making. Hayden has her ear cocked for problems that face mothers struggling to re-enter the work force. Her own boys were toddlers and she was 30 when she entered Seton Hall University Law School. She would go on to become a Federal prosecutor, a formidable matrimonial lawyer and a county bar association president, dramatically outearning her first husband, the professor. To this day she credits his flexible schedule and willingness to share child care as critical to her success.

And she'll be sitting on the bench, trying to decide whether custody of a prison mother's newborn should be given to an aunt or to the state, when her own family comes knocking. One morning it's her 82-year-old mother, who is living with her this summer, phoning in a report on how the cats are handling the heat. Then her would-be-rock-star son calls. Then from Los Angeles, a call from the other musician son. Later it's her husband: dinner and a movie tonight? Now Patti Cassidy runs in with another scrawled message: does the judge remember where her mother put the house keys this morning?

On Thursdays, the judge wakes at 4 A.M., pads out to the big arm-chair in the living room and settles in with the two cats to read two dozen files of child abuse and neglect cases—the basic work of virtually every American family court. She pores over them like paperback mysteries, sometimes anxiously skipping to the end to find out what happened. Almost all the parties are Hispanic or black, yet what distinguishes them in her mind from other litigants is not their color but their poverty. Their life experiences couldn't be more different than hers; even so, she must decide which children must be saved from their parents, which struggling families should be saved from the intrusion of the state.

One morning in early July she opens a thick folder and smiles wearily. A mother known in court papers as M. W. is back: my all-star, thinks the judge, obdurate and durable, my Darryl Strawberry of the lot.

M. W., in her mid-20's, has been before Hayden many times over the past 18 months. She has a bad cocaine habit, four children under 6 in foster care and a 13-year-old son who until now has been staying with an uncle. She recently moved to a Southern state to live with a new boyfriend.

The latest issue involves the teen-ager. His uncle refuses to board him any longer. The Division for Youth and Family Services in New Jersey knows that placing the boy in a foster home is futile, because he will run away to find his mother. But M. W. refuses to undergo regular drug screens and enter treatment. The agency does not want to return the boy to her. But it feels it has no choice.

At the hearing later that morning, the judge's patience is sorely tried. (These proceedings are closed to observers. Hayden allowed a reporter to hear a tape of the case.) M. W. assumes that if she gets clean, all her children will be returned by September, a fantasy the judge struggles to dispel. Finally, the judge tells M. W. the unsweetened truth about the state's promises: "Let me make this clear. You will never, never, never get your kids back unless you kick your drug habit. If you kick your drug habit, you may still not get your kids back."

Hayden tells M. W. that she also has to set up a stable home for the children. "Does your fiancé know about the drug problem? Probably not, because I think one of the reasons you're not going to a program is because you're scared he'll find out."

The judge tells the agency's lawyers that she is inclined to deny the return of the son to his mother. Panicky, M. W. vows to enter a program, immediately go for drug screens, tell her boyfriend.

Hayden is dubious; she tries speaking mother to mother. She is about to make a risky decision, so she explains carefully for the record: "Anyone looking at this case will think I'm insane to send your boy to you. The division is telling me to do it anyway. But your son believes in you and he will walk all the way down South to be with you. If my firstborn felt that close to me, that would be an awfully good reason to try to clean up."

Then the judge talks to M. W.'s son. "I'm very concerned that your mom will have a problem licking her drug problem," she says. "In order to keep you with her, she's got to go into a program. I don't think it's right for me to lay on a kid the responsibility for his mother, but in a way, you've done it many times before." She tells him that his main job is to stay in school, that his mother has to come back to court with his attendance records.

"I think you and your mom are a good team," says the judge. "But I also want you to have a good life and be a kid and play sports and have fun."

But later that day, M. W. flunks her drug test: she is caught trying to dilute her urine sample by pouring toilet water into the cup. In the next two weeks, she doesn't head back to the South and doesn't begin treatment. The son briefly disappears.

At another Thursday hearing, the judge tells the boy that because M. W. has failed him, she is sending him to foster care; she tries to rile him so he will distance himself from his beautiful junkie mother. Hayden wants the boy to know that if he feels his mother is using him, she agrees. She says: if you run away, you run. It's up to you.

The system is powerless now, she thinks. What more can a judge do?

One Thursday, she gives herself a final deadline for Amber and Carl's case: next Wednesday, the last in July, 9 A.M., she tells the lawyers.

That Saturday, she opens the file on her dining-room table and puts in order nearly four years of narrative—events, motions, cross-motions, trial testimony, expert reports. On the Sunday afternoon before the decision is due, she dives into the file.

Who lied? Did Amber tell Carl during her pregnancy that the baby wasn't his, as she maintained, or didn't she? Did Carl beat her regularly or didn't he?

Late Sunday night the judge begins dictating notes for her secretary, Patti Cassidy. She's in court all day Monday; that night she continues scribbling thoughts. As a pattern emerges from the file, so does the decision. Tuesday she's back on the bench, and that night she works until 1 A.M., crashes and starts up again at 4 A.M. She sprawls on the living-room carpet, piles of legal pads around her.

On Wednesday morning she drives to work like an automaton, radio off. She silently chants, I just have to do this. She isn't dreading making the announcement, exactly; she's steeling herself.

When she takes the bench, she deliberately avoids eye contact with Amber and Carl, instead fixing her squint on the comfortable blur of the parking lot out the window. Then, walking them through her logic, she speaks for two and a half hours.

First she addresses Amber's claim that biology should trump in a custody dispute. She cites a 1984 New Jersey Supreme Court case, Miller v. Miller, which says that once you put something out there, you can't take it back if the repudiation helps you and hurts others. And that is Amber's problem. She had presented Carl as her boy's father for nearly six years and is now withdrawing the claim: it favors her and harms Carl and the boy.

Amber's lawyer glares at the judge. Amber flinches.

The judge plows on, now turning to the paternity question. State law permits a paternity test to establish a child's inheritance rights. But Amber, says the judge, has refused to contact the boy's biological father and so did not use the test for that purpose. Instead, she has stripped her son of one father, Carl; by not bringing in the unnamed one, she is eviscerating the boy's inheritance and rendering him fatherless.

And the judge concludes that because Carl helped raise the boy and held him out as his own, he stands in the shoes of a father. "How can Carl not be taken seriously as an equal parent?" she says.

So far, Carl has been sitting motionless, as if afraid to breathe. His father, whom the judge praises as a wise and loving grandparent, is in the row behind him, listening just as hard, taking notes, occasionally wiping a tear from under his bifocals.

The judge reviews the experts' evaluations. A psychologist said

Carl offered a more secure environment and that Amber tended to confuse her own needs with her sons' But both parents have strengths and weaknesses.

Finally she examines the question that propelled her hunt through the file: credibility. Amber, she concludes, has lied.

At one point Amber had testified that when she learned she was pregnant, she told Carl he wasn't the father. Another time she testified that she broke the news to him three months later after a sonogram showed a fetus too large to have been conceived when the couple starting having sex. Her early court papers, filed before she asked for the paternity tests, are evasive: instead of referring to the boy as "our child," she calls him "the child."

The judge concludes that Carl most likely did not know early on that he was not the father. "Why would he acquiesce only five months into their relationship to take on the public role of Dad?" Hayden says. "Probably because she kept it a secret."

Carl's shoulders lower a good inch; Amber is starting to weep.

From there the judge extrapolates about domestic violence, weighing the weak, contradictory testimony. She decides that Amber will say nearly anything to regain her child, her biological connection to the world, whom she believes to be her property right. Therefore, says the judge, "I do not believe that she was regularly abused by Carl."

Amber's lawyer looks fit to spit.

Finally, Hayden lists the 15 factors the state says she must consider to determine what is in the best interest of the child. Domestic violence, safety of the child, quality of education, fitness of the parent and so forth. The case is a close call, she says, but she has to decide whether it is better for the boy to stay with Carl and the grandparents in the home and the town with the friends, church and schools he has known from birth or to move in with his biological mother, who loves him dearly but whose life is still shaky.

Amber, she says, is a young woman still finding her way. She made choices that were in her best interest but not her son's. Carl, by contrast, put his son first, making the decision to move back in with his parents, who could help raise the child.

And although she says she believes Amber loves her son and so should spend substantial time with him, Hayden awards Carl residential custody. Then she stands and walks out.

Carl and his father rush from the courtroom, looking stunned. Amber's lawyer starts cursing furiously. Amber slumps, sobbing, saying over and over: "What trial was she at? What trial was she at?"

Meanwhile, Hayden is back in her chambers. She has taken off her black robe and is seated behind her desk, staring at her hands. It was her decision to place the boy, who is his mother's only known blood relative, with a man to whom the child has no biological connection. The judge looks completely drained.

Will Amber figure out that if she moves back to New Jersey, the custody issue could be reopened, perhaps with a differnet outcome? she wonders. The judge has a queasy feeling that Amber's loss is greater to her than Carl's win is to him. Amber, after all, is a reasonably good mother, she muses. Did she make a wrong ruling?

A poisonously seductive question, for that way lies judicial paralysis. No, the judge tells herself, she decided correctly; her responsibility was not to a sorrowful, desperate mother but to the son.

Patti Cassidy sticks her head in. Would the judge like her usual chicken sandwich? Ah, yes, the best way to put the case behind her: protein on rye, mayo on both slices.

But as Amber and Carl start to recede from her mind, she realizes that her impact on them is only beginning. In the years to come, they will have to struggle with the fallout from her decision, the very thing that they had wanted so badly from her. Hayden sighs. Doubt flickering across her face, the judge picks up the stack of papers her secretary has just dropped on her desk. On top is her calendar of cases. Looks like another busy afternoon.

IN FOCUS

ACTIVE READING

Sunday morning—a croissant, good coffee, and *The New York Times* scattered around the living room. The family dog snoozes in a corner, the television is blissfully silent, there is a quiet pause in the bustle of the week. Someone picks up the magazine section and begins to read "Judge Hayden's Family Values." The essay, while interesting, goes on and on, all six thousand words of it, and the reader follows, captured by the life of the judge and the decisions she is required to make. In the middle of the story, the coffee gets cold and needs to be reheated.

Not every family shares a quiet moment of reading every week, of course—and certainly not every family has (or even wants) access to fine pastries and expensive newspapers. Many families, in fact, spend Sunday mornings going to church. But managing to make space in one's life for reading brings the reward of putting priorities where they belong. Ideally, the time for reading should be open-ended—the telephone would never ring, children would never wail for dinner, the job would not start until the chapter was over. Unfortunately, a long, unbroken stretch for the sheer personal pleasure of enjoying a good book is seldom possible except on airplanes or late at night.

Taking notes on the materials one will later be responsible for, such as textbooks or business reports, becomes even more important when one's concentration is likely to be interrupted. Important facts, or passages one wants to remember later (even parts of novels), need to be marked for future reference. But many people who attended the public-school system in the United States, where books are loaned to the student rather than purchased by the parents, have been warned never to mark a book.

Books, however, *should* be marked—and owned, and read, loved, messed about with, commented on in the margins. A book so marked is one whose owner has entered into a working relationship with the text. Underlining, notes in margins, even coffee spots show that someone has worked with this book, taken it seriously, noted areas of importance and disagreement. Deliberate, uncaring, or stupid damage (never leave a good book in a closed car on a hot summer day) is one thing, but the markings that come from serious engagement with the text are marks of honor.

College students sometimes refrain from underlining or highlighting their textbooks in the hope that the books will bring more money back on resale. It's false economy, considering the overall cost of one's education (books are a tiny proportion) and the real help that comes from marking textbooks for later review. Besides—why sell your books? They are a record of your education. Many years later, even the texts for courses that never interested you might provide useful references.

The suggestions below will help you get the most out of your reading. Read with a pencil in your hand; mark this book freely.

- Mark words, sentences, or phrases that remind you of things you have already read.
- Mark passages that bring to mind personal experiences.
- Note passages that strike you as right or wrong.
- Circle unfamiliar words or terms. If not knowing what they mean makes it difficult for you to understand the text, look them up in a dictionary. Otherwise, keep reading and see if you can define them from the context (see "In Focus: Defining from Context," p. 59).
- Mark difficult sections that you need to return to and reread.
- Mark interesting examples that help you to understand what the author is saying.

Study Questions

1. At the beginning of the article, Judge Hayden has a decision to make, an almost impossible decision because the right thing to do is so unclear. Jan Hoffman also has a decision to make: what information to give first. Should the article open with the scene in the courtroom, the way it does? Should it instead begin with a description of the judge and her legal background? Or, perhaps, should it begin with a broad picture of the difficulties of divorce in modern society, with facts and figures, and then go on to discuss specific cases?

   Why did Hoffman begin "in the middle," as the article is written?
2. Choose one of the cases described in the article. Pretend you are a judge who would have ruled differently from the way Judge Hayden did. Give reasons for your alternate ruling.
3. Would you trade your life for Judge Hayden's? Why or why not?

Writing Topics

1. *Collaborative writing activity.* The article points out that "Hayden is acutely aware that the people who come before her have no buffer to protect them from how she, a white, affluent, divorced and remarried mother of two, views their case." As a group, think of and discuss other instances in current society in which people's lives are affected by a powerful person who comes from a completely different social class and situation. Then write individual essays on the issue.
2. Pretend you are one of the lawyers in Judge Hayden's court, on one of the cases described in the article. Write an essay in which you argue the best possible case for your client.
3. Here is Judge Hayden's way of dealing with her mistakes: "She has a strict rule about post-mortem lashing. One good stinging self-beratement session, but that's it." What are some good ways of dealing with guilt and errors? What is your own method of dealing with your mistakes? Is Judge Hayden's way any better? Write an essay on healthy and unhealthy ways of handling guilt.

BARBARA TUCHMAN

An Inquiry into the Persistence of Unwisdom in Government

A problem that strikes one in the study of history, regardless of period, is why man makes a poorer performance of government than of almost any other human activity. In this sphere, wisdom—meaning judgment acting on experience, common sense, available knowledge, and a decent appreciation of probability—is less operative and more frustrated than it should be. Why do men in high office so often act contrary to the way that reason points and enlightened self-interest suggests? Why does intelligent mental process so often seem to be paralyzed?

Why, to begin at the beginning, did the Trojan authorities drag that suspicious-looking wooden horse inside their gates? Why did successive ministries of George III—that "bundle of imbecility," as Dr. Johnson called them collectively—insist on coercing rather than conciliating the Colonies though strongly advised otherwise by many counselors? Why did Napoleon and Hitler invade Russia? Why did the kaiser's government resume unrestricted submarine warfare in 1917 although explicitly warned that this would bring in the United States and that American belligerency would mean Germany's defeat? Why did Chiang Kai-shek refuse to heed any voice of reform or alarm until he woke up to find that his country had slid from under him? Why did Lyndon Johnson, seconded by the best and the brightest, progressively involve this nation in a war both ruinous and half-hearted and from which nothing but bad for our side resulted? Why does the present Administration continue to avoid introducing effective measures to reduce the wasteful consumption of oil while members of OPEC follow a price policy that must bankrupt their customers? How is it possible that the Central Inteligence Agency, whose function it is to provide, at taxpayers' expense, the information necessary to conduct a realistic foreign policy, could remain unaware that discontent in a country crucial to our interests was boiling up to the point of insurrection and overthrow of the ruler upon whom our policy rested? It has been reported that the CIA was ordered *not* to investigate the opposition to the shah of Iran in order to spare him any indication that we took it seriously, but since this sounds more like the theater of the absurd than like responsible government, I cannot bring myself to believe it.

There was a king of Spain once, Philip III, who is said to have died of a fever he contracted from sitting too long near a hot brazier, helplessly overheating himself because the functionary whose duty it was to remove the brazier when summoned could not be found. In the late twentieth century, it begins to appear as if mankind may be approaching a similar stage of suicidal incompetence. The Italians have been sitting in Philip III's hot seat for some time. The British trade unions, in a lunatic spectacle, seem periodically bent on dragging their country toward paralysis, apparently under the impression that they are separate from the whole. Taiwan was thrown into a state of shock by the United States' recognition of the People's Republic of China because, according to one report, in the seven years since the Shanghai Communiqué, the Kuomintang rulers of Taiwan had "refused to accept the new trend as a reality."

Wooden-headedness is a factor that plays a remarkably large role in government. Wooden-headedness consists of assessing a situation in terms of preconceived, fixed notions while ignoring or rejecting any contrary signs. It is acting according to wish while not allowing oneself to be confused by the facts.

A classic case was the French war plan of 1914, which concentrated everything on a French offensive to the Rhine, leaving the French left flank from Belgium to the Channel virtually unguarded. This strategy was based on the belief that the Germans would not use reserves in the front line and, without them, could not deploy enough manpower to extend their invasion through the French left. Reports by intelligence agents in 1913 to the effect that the Germans were indeed preparing their reserves for the front line in case of war were resolutely ignored because the governing spirits in France, dreaming only of their own offensive, did not want to believe in any signals that would require them to strengthen their left at the expense of their march to the Rhine. In the event, the Germans could and did extend themselves around the French left with results that determined a long war and its fearful consequences for our country.

Wooden-headedness is also the refusal to learn from experience, a form in which fourteenth-century rulers were supreme. No matter how often and obviously devaluation of the currency disrupted the economy and angered the people, French monarchs continued to resort to it whenever they were desperate for cash until they provoked insurrection among the bourgeoisie. No matter how often a campaign that depended on living off a hostile country ran into want and even starvation, campaigns for which this fate was inevitable were regularly undertaken.

Still another form is identification of self with the state, as currently exhibited by the ayatollah Khomeini. No wooden-headedness is so impenetrable as that of a religious zealot. Because he is connected with a private wire to the Almighty, no idea coming in on a lesser channel can reach him, which leaves him ill equipped to guide his country in its own best interests.

Philosophers of government ever since Plato have devoted their thinking to the major issues of ethics, sovereignty, the social contract, the rights of man, the corruption of power, the balance between freedom and order. Few—except Machiavelli, who was concerned with government as it is, not as it should be—bothered with mere folly, although this has been a chronic and pervasive problem. "Know, my son," said a dying Swedish statesman in the seventeenth century, "with how little wisdom the world is governed." More recently, Woodrow Wilson warned, "In public affairs, stupidity is more dangerous than knavery."

Stupidity is not related to type of regime; monarchy, oligarchy, and democracy produce it equally. Nor is it peculiar to nation or class. The working class as represented by the Communist governments functions no more rationally or effectively in power than the aristocracy or the bourgeoisie, as has notably been demonstrated in recent history. Mao Tse-tung may be admired for many things, but the Great Leap Forward, with a steel plant in every backyard, and the Cultural Revolution were exercises in unwisdom that greatly damaged China's progress and stability, not to mention the chairman's reputation. The record of the Russian proletariat in power can hardly be called enlightened, although after sixty years of control it must be accorded a kind of brutal success. If the majority of Russians are better off now than before, the cost in cruelty and tyranny has been no less and probably greater than under the czars.

After the French Revolution, the new order was rescued only by Bonaparte's military campaigns, which brought the spoils of foreign wars to fill the treasury, and subsequently by his competence as an executive. He chose officials not on the basis of origin or ideology but on the principle of "la carrière ouverte aux talents"—the said talents being intelligence, energy, industry, and obedience. That worked until the day of his own fatal mistake.

I do not wish to give the impression that men in office are incapable of governing wisely and well. Occasionally, the exception appears, rising in heroic size above the rest, a tower visible down the centuries. Greece had her Pericles, who ruled with authority, moderation, sound judgment, and a certain nobility that imposes natural dominion over others. Rome had Caesar, a man of remarkable governing talents, although it must be said that a ruler who arouses opponents to resort to assassination is probably not as smart as he ought to be. Later, under Marcus Aurelius and the other Antonines, Roman citizens enjoyed good government, prosperity, and respect for about a century. Charlemagne was able to impose order upon a mass of contending elements, to foster the arts of civilization no less than those of war, and to earn a prestige supreme in the Middle Ages— probably not equaled in the eyes of contemporaries until the apperance of George Washington.

Possessor of an inner strength and perseverance that enabled him to prevail over a sea of obstacles, Washington was one of those critical figures but for whom history might well have taken a different course. He made possible the physical victory of American independence, while around him, in extraordinary fertility, political talent bloomed as if touched by some tropical sun. For all their flaws and quarrels, the Founding Fathers, who established our form of government, were, in the words of Arthur Schlesinger Sr., "the most remarkable generation of public men in the history of the United States or perhaps of any other nation." It is worth noting the qualities Schlesinger ascribes to them: They were fearless, high-principled, deeply versed in ancient and modern political thought, astute and pragmatic, unafraid of experiment, and—this is significant—"convinced of man's power to improve his condition through the use of intelligence." That was the mark of the Age of Reason that formed them, and though the eighteenth century had a tendency to regard men as more rational than they in fact were, it evoked the best in government from these men.

For our purposes, it would be invaluable if we could know what produced this burst of talent from a base of only two million inhabitants. Schlesinger suggests some contributing factors: wide diffusion of education, challenging economic opportunities, social mobility, training in self-government—all these encouraged citizens to cultivate their political aptitudes to the utmost. Also, he adds, with the Church declining in prestige and with business, science, and art not yet offering competing fields of endeavor, statecraft remained almost the only outlet for men of energy and purpose. Perhaps the need of the moment—the opportunity to create a new political system—is what brought out the best.

Not before or since, I believe, has so much careful and reasonable thinking been invested in the creation of a new political system. In the French, Russian, and Chinese revolutions, too much class hatred and bloodshed were involved to allow for fair results or permanent constitutions. The American experience was unique, and the system so far has always managed to right itself under pressure. In spite of accelerating incompetence, it still works better than most. We haven't had to discard the system and try another after every crisis, as have Italy and Germany, Spain and France. The founders of the United States are a phenomenon to keep in mind to encourage our estimate of human possibilities, but their example, as a political scientist has pointed out, is "too infrequent to be taken as a basis for normal expectations."

The English are considered to have enjoyed reasonably benign government during the eighteenth and nineteenth centuries, except for their Irish subjects, debtors, child laborers, and other unfortunates in various pockets of oppression. The folly that lost the American colonies reappeared now and then, notably in the treatment of the Irish and the Boers, but a social system can survive a good deal of folly when circumstances are historically favorable or when it is cushioned by large resources, as in the heyday of the British Empire, or absorbed by sheer size, as in this country during our period of expansion. Today there are no more cushions, which makes folly less affordable.

Elsewhere than in government, man has accomplished marvels: invented the means in our time to leave the world and voyage to the moon; in the past, harnessed wind and electricity, raised earthbound stone into soaring cathedrals, woven silk brocades out of the spinnings of a worm, composed the music of Mozart and the dramas of Shakespeare, classified the forms of nature, penetrated the mysteries of genetics. Why is he so much less accomplished in government? What frustrates, in that sphere, the operation of the intellect? Isaac Bashevis Singer, discoursing as a Nobel laureate on mankind, offers the opinion that God had been frugal in bestowing intellect but lavish with passions and emotions. "He gave us," Singer says, "so many emotions and such strong ones that every human being, even if he is an idiot, is a millionaire in emotions."

I think Singer has made a point that applies to our inquiry. What frustrates the workings of intellect is the passions and the emotions: ambition, greed, fear, facesaving, the instinct to dominate, the needs of the ego, the whole bundle of personal vanities and anxieties.

Reason is crushed by these forces. If the Athenians out of pride and overconfidence had not set out to crush Sparta for good but had been content with moderate victory, their ultimate fall might have been averted. If fourteenth-century knights had not been obsessed by the idea of glory and personal prowess, they might have defeated the Turks at Nicopolis with incalculable consequence for all of Eastern Europe. If the English, 200 years ago, had heeded Chatham's knocking on the door of what he called "this sleeping and confounded Ministry" and his urgent advice to repeal the Coercive Acts and withdraw the troops before the "inexpiable drop of blood is shed in an impious war with a people contending in the great cause of publick liberty," or, given a last chance, if they had heeded Edmund Burke's celebrated plea for conciliation and his warning that it would prove impossible to coerce a "fierce people" of their own pedigree, we might still be a united people bridging the Atlantic, with incalculable consequence for the history of the West. It did not happen that way, because king and Parliament felt it imperative to affirm sovereignty over arrogant colonials. The alternative choice, as in Athens and medieval Europe, was close to psychologically impossible.

In the case we know best—the American engagement in Vietnam—fixed notions, preconceptions, wooden-headed thinking, and emotions accumulated into a monumental mistake and classic humiliation. The original idea was that the lesson of the failure to halt fascist aggression during the appeasement era dictated the necessity of halting the so-called aggression by North Vietnam, conceived to be the spearhead of international communism. This was applying the wrong model to the wrong facts, which would have been obvious if our policy makers had taken into consideration the history of the people on the spot instead of charging forward wearing the blinders of the cold war.

The reality of Vietnamese nationalism, of which Ho Chi Minh had been the standard-bearer since long before the war, was certainly no secret. Indeed, Franklin Roosevelt had insisted that the French should not be allowed to return after the war, a policy that we instantly abandoned the moment the Japanese were out: Ignoring the Vietnamese demand for self-government, we first assisted the return of the French, and then, when incredibly, they had been put to rout by the native forces, we took their place, as if Dien Bien Phu had no significance whatever. Policy founded upon error multiplies, never retreats. The pretense that North versus South Vietnam represented foreign aggression was intensified. If Asian specialists with knowledge of the situation suggested a reassessment, they were not persuasive. As a Communist aggressor, Hanoi was presumed to be a threat to the United States, yet the vital national interest at stake, which alone may have justified belligerency, was never clear enough to sustain a declaration of war.

A further, more fundamental, error confounded our policy. This was the nature of the client. In war, as any military treatise or any soldier who has seen active service will tell you, it is essential to know the nature—that is, the capabilities *and* intentions—of the enemy and no less so of an ally who is the primary belligerent. We fatally underestimated the one and foolishly overestimated the other. Placing reliance on, or hope in, South Vietnam was an advanced case of wooden-headedness. Improving on the Bourbons, who forgot nothing and learned nothing, our policy makers forgot everything and learned nothing. The oldest lesson in history is the futility and, often, fatality of foreign interference to maintain in power a government unwanted or hated at home. As far back as 500 B.C., Confucius stated, "Without the confidence of the people, no government can stand," and political philosophers have echoed him down through the ages. What else was the lesson of our vain support of Chiang Kai-shek, within such recent experience? A corrupt or oppressive government may be maintained by despotic means but not for long, as the English occupiers of France learned in the fifteenth century. The human spirit protests and generates a Joan of Arc, for people will not passively endure a government that is in fact unendurable.

The deeper we became involved in Vietnam during the Johnson era, the greater grew the self-deception, the lies, the false body counts, the cheating on Tonkin Gulf, the military mess, domestic dissent, and all those defensive emotions in which, as a result, our leaders became fixed. Their concern for personal ego, public image, and government status determined policy. Johnson was not going to be the first President to preside over defeat; generals could not admit failure nor civilian advisers risk their jobs by giving unpalatable advice.

Males, who so far in history have managed government, are obsessed with potency, which is the reason, I suspect, why it is difficult for them to admit error. I have rarely known a man who, with a smile and a shrug, could easily acknowledge being wrong. Why not? *I* can, without any damage to self-respect. I can only suppose the difference is that deep in their psyches, men somehow equate being wrong with being impotent. For a Chief of State, it is almost out of the question, and especially so for Johnson and Nixon, who both seem to me to have had shaky self-images. Johnson's showed in his deliberate coarseness and compulsion to humiliate others in crude physical ways. No self-confident man would have needed to do that. Nixon was a bundle of inferiorities and sense of persecution. I do not pretend to be a psychohistorian, but in pursuit of this inquiry, the psychological factors must be taken into account. Having no special knowledge of Johnson and Nixon, I will not pursue the question other than to say that it was our misfortune during the Vietnam period to have had two Presidents who lacked the self-confidence for a change of course, much less for a grand withdrawal. "Magnanimity in politics," said Edmund Burke, "is not seldom the truest wisdom, and a great Empire and little minds go ill together."

An essential component of that "truest wisdom" is the self-confidence to reassess. Congressman Morris Udall made this point in the first few days after the nuclear accident at Three Mile Island. Cautioning against a hasty decision on the future of nuclear power, he said, "We have to go back and reassess. There is nothing wrong about being optimistic or making a mistake. The thing that is wrong, as in Vietnam, is *persisting* in a mistake when you see you are going down the wrong road and are caught in a bad situation."

The test comes in recognizing when persistence has become a fatal error. A prince, says Machiavelli, ought always to be a great asker and a patient hearer of truth about those things of which he has inquired, and he should be angry if he finds that anyone has scruples about telling him the truth. Johnson and Nixon, as far as an outsider can tell, were not great askers; they did not want to hear the truth or to face it. Chiang Kai-shek knew virtually nothing of real conditions in his domain because he lived a headquarters life amid an entourage all of whom were afraid to be messengers of ill report. When, in World War I, a general of the headquarters staff visited for the first time the ghastly landscape of the Somme, he broke into tears, saying, "If I had known we sent men to fight in that, I could not have done it." Evidently he was no great asker either.

Neither, we now know, was the shah of Iran. Like Chiang Kai-shek, he was isolated from actual conditions. He was educated abroad, took his vacations abroad, and toured his country, if at all, by helicopter.

Why is it that the major clients of the United States, a country founded on the principle that government derives its just powers from the consent of the governed, tend to be unpopular autocrats? A certain schizophrenia between our philosophy and our practice afflicts American policy, and this split will always make the policy based on it fall apart. On the day the shah left Iran, an article summarizing his reign said that "except for the generals, he has few friends or allies at home." How useful to us is a ruler without friends or allies at home? He is a kind of luftmensch, no matter how rich or how golden a customer for American business. To attach American foreign policy to a ruler who does not have the acceptance of his countrymen is hardly intelligent. By now, it seems to me, we might have learned that. We must understand conditions—and by conditions, I mean people and history—on the spot. Wise policy can only be made on the basis of *informed,* not automatic, judgments.

When it has become evident to those associated with it that a course of policy is pointed toward disaster, why does no one resign in protest or at least for the peace of his own soul? They never do. In 1917, the German chancellor Bethmann Hollweg pleaded desperately against the proposed resumption of unrestricted submarine warfare, since, by bringing in the United States, it would revive the Allies' resources, their confidence in victory, and their will to endure. When he was overruled by the military, he told a friend who found him sunk in despair that the decision meant "finis Germaniae." When the friend said simply, "You should resign," Bethmann said he could not, for that would sow dissension at home and let the world know he believed Germany would fail.

This is always the refuge. The officeholder tells himself he can do more from within and that he must not reveal division at the top to the public. In fact if there is to be any hope of change in a democratic society, that is exactly what he must do. No one of major influence in Johnson's circle resigned over our Vietnam policy although several, hoping to play it both ways, hinted their disagreement. Humphrey, waiting for the nod, never challenged the President's policy, although he campaigned afterward as an opponent of the war. Since then, I've always thought the adulation given to him misplaced.

Basically, what keeps officeholders attached to a policy they believe to be wrong is nothing more nor less, I believe, than the lure of office, or Potomac fever. It is the same whether the locus is the Thames or the Rhine or, no doubt, the Nile. When Herbert Lehman ran for a second term as senator from New York after previously serving four terms as governor, his brother asked him why on earth he wanted it.

"Arthur," replied the senator, "after you have once ridden behind a motorcycle escort, you are never the same again."

Here is a clue to the question of why our performance in government is worse than in other activities: because government offers power, excites that lust for power, which is subject to emotional drives—to narcissism, fantasies of omnipotence, and other sources of folly. The lust for power, according to Tacitus, "is the most flagrant of all the passions" and cannot really be satisfied except by power over others. Business offers a kind of power but only to the very successful at the very top, and even they, in our day, have to play it down. Fords and Du Ponts, Hearsts and Pulitzers, nowadays are subdued, and the Rockefeller who most conspicuously wanted power sought it in government. Other activities—in sports, science, the professions, and the creative and performing arts—offer various satisfactions but not the opportunity for power. They may appeal to status seeking and, in the form of celebrity, offer crowd worship and limousines and recognition by headwaiters, but these are the trappings of power, not the essence. Of course, mistakes and stupidities occur in nongovernmental activities too, but since these affect fewer people, they are less noticeable than they are in public affairs. Government remains the paramount field of unwisdom because it is there that men seek power over others—and lose it over themselves.

There are, of course, other factors that lower competence in public affairs, among them the pressure of overwork and overscheduling; bureaucracy, especially big bureaucracy; the contest for votes that gives exaggerated influence to special interests and an absurd tyranny to public opinion polls. Any hope of intelligent government would require that the persons entrusted with high office should formulate and execute policy according to their best judgment and the best knowledge available, not according to every breeze of public opinion. But reelection is on their minds, and that becomes the criterion. Moreover, given schedules broken down into fifteen-minute appointments and staffs numbering in the hundreds and briefing memos of never less than thirty pages, policy makers never have time to think. This leaves a rather important vacuum. Meanwhile, bureaucracy rolls on, impervious to any individual or cry for change, like some vast computer that when once penetrated by error goes on pumping it out forever.

Under the circumstances, what are the chances of improving the conduct of government? The idea of a class of professionals trained for the task has been around ever since Plato's Republic. Something of the sort animates, I imagine, the new Kennedy School of Government at Harvard. According to Plato, the ruling class in a just society should be men apprenticed to the art of ruling, drawn from the rational and the wise. Since he acknowledged that in natural distribution these are few, he believed they would have to be eugenically bred and nurtured. Government, he said, was a special art in which competence, as in any other profession, could be acquired only by study of the discipline and could not be acquired otherwise.

Without reference to Plato, the Mandarins of China were trained, if not bred, for the governing function. They had to pass through years of study and apprenticeship and weeding out by successive examinations, but they do not seem to have developed a form of government much superior to any other, and in the end, they petered out in decadence and incompetence.

In seventeenth-century Europe, after the devastation of the Thirty Years' War, the electors of Brandenburg, soon to be combined with Prussia, determined to create a strong state by means of a disciplined army and a trained civil service. Applicants for the civil positions, drawn from commoners in order to offset the nobles' control of the military, had to complete a course of study covering political theory, law and legal philosophy, economics, history, penology, and statutes. Only after passing through various stages of examination and probationary terms of office did they receive definitive appointments and tenure and opportunity for advancement. The higher civil service was a separate branch, not open to promotion from the middle and lower levels.

The Prussian system proved so effective that the state was able to survive both military defeat by Napoleon in 1807 and the revolutionary surge of 1848. By then it had begun to congeal, losing many of its most progressive citizens in emigration to America; nevertheless, Prussian energies succeeded in 1871 in uniting the German states in an empire under Prussian hegemony. Its very success contained the seed of ruin, for it nourished the arrogance and power hunger that from 1914 through 1918 was to bring it down.

In England, instead of responding in reactionary panic to the thunders from the Continent in 1848, as might have been expected, the authorities, with commendable enterprise, ordered an investigation of their own government practices, which were then the virtually private preserve of the propertied class. The result was a report on the need for a permanent civil service to be based on training and specialized skills and designed to provide continuity and maintenance of the long view as against transient issues and political passions. Though heavily resisted, the system was adopted in 1870. It has produced distinguished civil servants but also Burgess, Maclean, Philby, and the fourth man. The history of British government in the last 100 years suggests that factors other than the quality of its civil service determine a country's fate.

In the United States, civil service was established chiefly as a barrier to patronage and the pork barrel rather than in search of excellence. By 1937, a presidential commission, finding the system inadequate, urged the development of a "real career service . . . requiring personnel of the highest order, competent, highly trained, loyal, skilled in their duties by reason of long experience, and assured of continuity." After much effort and some progress, that goal is still not reached, but even if it were, it would not take care of elected officials and high appointments—that is, of government at the top.

I do not know if the prognosis is hopeful or, given the underlying emotional drives, whether professionalism is the cure. In the Age of Enlightenment, John Locke thought the emotions should be controlled by intellectual judgment and that it was the distinction and glory of man to be able to control them. As witnesses of the twentieth century's record, comparable to the worst in history, we have less confidence in our species. Although professionalism can help, I tend to think that fitness of character is what government chiefly requires. How that can be discovered, encouraged, and brought into office is the problem that besets us.

No society has yet managed to implement Plato's design. Now, with money and image-making manipulating our elective process, the chances are reduced. We are asked to choose by the packaging, yet the candidate seen in a studio-filmed spot, sincerely voicing lines from the Tele-PrompTer, is not the person who will have to meet the unrelenting problems and crucial decisions of the Oval Office. It might be a good idea if, without violating the First Amendment, we could ban all paid political commercials and require candidates (who accept federal subsidy for their campaigns) to be televised live only.

That is only a start. More profound change must come if we are to bring into office the kind of person our form of government needs if it is to survive the challenges of this era. Perhaps rather than educating officials according to Plato's design, we should concentrate on educating the electorate—that is, ourselves—to look for, recognize, and reward character in our representatives and to reject the ersatz.

Study Questions

1. What, according to Tuchman, are the primary reasons for the "wooden-headedness" that governments often display?
2. Tuchman analyzes the reasons that those in power persist in stupid and inevitably self-destructive activities, unwilling to change course or admit

they were wrong in the first place. Individuals also seem to do the same thing; very often, people keep repeating a mistake time and again, throwing more and more resources and energy into an ultimately disastrous course of action. What do you think are the reasons that individuals persist in this way?

3. On pp. 425–26, Tuchman writes: "Males, who so far in history have managed government, are obsessed with potency, which is the reason, I suspect, why it is difficult for them to admit error. I have rarely known a man who, with a smile and a shrug, could easily acknowledge being wrong. Why not? *I* can, without any damage to self-respect. I can only suppose the difference is that deep in their psyches, men somehow equate being wrong with being impotent."

Is Tuchman correct about sex differences in this area? Or is she simply indulging in "male-bashing"? Do many people, in your opinion, feel this way about the difference between men and women?

Writing Topics

1. After considering Study Question #2 above, write a descriptive essay about someone you know—or even yourself, or an imaginary person—who persistently kept doing more and more self-hurtful actions. What factors in the person's life led to that behavior? What could have helped, or did help, that person make a change?

Before you begin this assignment, give some thought to the outline of your essay, the pattern in which you want to present the material. Do you want to open with an anecdote, showing or describing some of that self-destructive behavior? Do you want to tell the person's story from the beginning and then give your opinion, or do you want to discuss "wooden-headed" behavior in general and then use your subject as a specific example?

2. *Collaborative writing activity.* Discuss, as a group, the kind of self-destructive behavior Tuchman describes. Each person should then choose an example, either historical or personal, of "wooden-headedness" and do some research. After each person has done preliminary work, the group should discuss different ways an essay of this type might be organized, considering the questions in Writing Topic #1 above. Each person should then write an expository essay explaining the factors that led to his or her example, and the result of the behavior involved in that example.

Beams of Light: Looking at Architecture

DENNIS ALAN MANN

"The church stands high on the summit of this granite rock, and on the west front is the platform, to which the tourist ought first to climb. From the edge of this platform, the eye plunges down, two hundred and thirty-five feet, to the wide sands or the wider ocean, as the tides recede or advance, under an infinite sky, over a restless sea, which even we tourists can understand and feel without books or guides; but when we turn from the western view, and look at the church door, thirty or forty yards from the parapet where we stand, one needs to know what this mass of encrusted architecture meant to its builders, and even then one must still learn to feel it. The man who wanders into the twelfth century is lost, unless he can grow prematurely young.

Mont-Saint-Michel and Chartres
HENRY ADAMS (1–2)

To know Mont-Saint-Michel as Henry Adams would wish us, we not only need to transport ourselves to eleventh-century France but we must also don the cloak of Norman sensibilities. As Ralph Adams Cram wrote in the preface to *Mont-Saint-Michel and Chartres* (1905), in order to fully understand these buildings we should merge ourselves in a long-dead time. Henry Adams would want us to "get our minds into the condition" to enter through the portals of the church and by doing so understand it in its own time, in its own unique locale and as its own citizens would have known it (Adams vii). His effort in writing this book which explores these two buildings in great depth is as heroic as its subjects and his masterwork treatise is as much of a cultural treasure as are Mt. St. Michel and Chartres Cathedral.

To develop the frame of mind to know these two buildings or, as a matter of fact, any building constructed in any time period in any part of the world would, following Adams' proviso, require an equally heroic effort. But is developing this frame of mind at all possible for the student of architecture? Or are there far too many buildings, far too many cultures and far too many understandings?

Since few of us are able to command both the patience and the in-tellectual rigor of a Henry Adams, could there be other ways that we can come to know a building? Certainly there are buildings that we regularly experience in our everyday comings and goings which ought to afford us similar opportunities. Although not as monu-mental or as revered as Mont-Saint-Michel or Chartres they are still buildings and, as ethnographer Clifford Geertz reminds us, "flecks of culture" in their own right (Geertz, "Thick Description" 6). And since most buildings that we might come into direct contact with lie around the corner, down the street or up the freeway they are much more accessible for our study.

There is little doubt that we each come to know buildings in our personal and unique ways. While these unique points of view might, to some degree, enlighten each and every one of us, these in-dividual experiences do little to add to the shared knowledge about those buildings in particular. One building will provide the stage for an infinite number of experiences and memories. Yet when we make the effort, we can gather some of these personal views into more generalizable views, views that, like the Normans of eleventh-century France, we momentarily share in common with others in our culture.

But what are some of the ways of looking at a building that we might share in common with others?

Most conventional techniques for studying a building center around its more concrete, measurable (and some might say, objec-tive) characteristics. For instance, we can analyze a building in order to reveal its structural system, that composition of columns, beams, walls and foundations which resists the variety of forces and loads to which a building is exposed. We can also observe how the spaces are organized and examine what kind of activities or functions occur in those spaces. We can compare the historic style of the building to other buildings in the same style in order to find commonalities as well as subtle innovations. We can even carry out a cost analysis of the income produced by the building and then correlate the income to the expenses incurred in constructing, maintaining and managing the building in order to determine if the building is a cost-effective investment. Should the building have been published in the press, we can undertake a text analysis of the writings and photographs in order to reveal the many readings or interpretations to which the building has been subjected. We can also perform post-occupancy evaluation studies and energy audits as well. These tests will give us more data still. These and other methods of studying a building are all teachable and, in fact, make up a large part of the curriculum of most schools of architecture today.

There are many additional ways of looking at buildings. All of these ways help us to understand some facet or other of the building. No one way is any better than another. While some are narrowly focused, others are more broad, sweeping and general. Each way simply serves to focus attention on one or another aspect of the building in question while pushing other ways into the background. Every looking-at-a-building experience is slightly different, and each experience adds to our repertoire of techniques as well as to our understandings of the building.

This paper is about two contrasting ways of coming to know buildings. One way examines how we are normally taught to look at buildings and the other challenges these conventional methods and dares us to ask different questions—to look, so to speak, through other sets of eyes. As a result of the questions that might crop up through this new way of looking, we might come to see a building in an entirely different light. Because these two ways are so fundamentally opposed in their approaches, they force us to pay more attention to many of the assumptions that we make about buildings.

The simplest technique for thinking about these two ways is to imagine yourself standing in front of a building, any building you choose, holding a flashlight in one hand and a piece of light-sensitive photographic paper in the other hand. For the moment, set the photographic paper aside and turn on the flashlight and let its beam of light play over the building. To slightly complicate this scenario, imagine that the batteries in the flashlight which are generating your beam of light contain all of the concepts that you have been taught or have ever learned about buildings. The beam then will be carrying within its light wave all of your culturally collected knowledge about buildings as it illuminates that particular building. All that you will see in the building, therefore, is what that beam of light exposes based on the knowledge that has already been stored in the batteries. As such, the beam can only reveal what you already know, albeit each time from a slightly different angle. Some aspects of the building undoubtedly will remain in the dark because your batteries do not contain the correct kind of knowledge-energy to seek them out.

In this first example, although you are enlarging your vocabulary of knowable buildings by shining the same light on a different building from the last time you carried out this exercise, you are still doing very little to recharge or replace the batteries, to increase their storage capacity or to add a different kind of energy to them. Even when you shine your light on a strange, new building, say a Dogon granary with cylindrical walls constructed of mud with a large face sculpted onto its surface and a conical roof built of grass, a granary that you may have come in contact with on a tour of the Niger River area near Timbuktu or in a picture book of West Africa, you are still aiming that same beam of light emanating from those same batteries onto the granary's surface. What you will see will again be carried on that light wave—*from you to the building.*

What you will see is what you already know, spiced up by your tour guide or by the description, if there is any, alongside the photograph.

You might ask at this stage then, how is it that we learn about buildings in the first place? And how is it that our knowledge about buildings never remains stagnant but always grows and changes? We learn about buildings in the traditional ways that other members of our society have always learned about buildings, first by experiencing them one by one and then by gradually constructing concepts about their significance to our own particular way of life—sweat lodges for the Navaho, mosques for the followers of Islam and shopping malls for American suburbanites.

Now, turn off your flashlight, lay it aside and pick up the piece of light-sensitive, photographic paper that you had set aside earlier. Imagine that the building is now emitting its own energy as a ray of light at you. As the building continues to vibrate energy, it is recording this energy/information about itself on your photographic paper. But what kind of information is that energy beam carrying? Does the beam of light coming from the building contain a different kind of information than the beam of light aimed from your flashlight? Could the building have its own set of batteries that generates its own light energy? Could it have its own memory of its coming-into-being? And if it does, what kind of knowledge is stored in *its* batteries? Now that's a more complicated question.

In the first example, you with your flashlight, the information (the basis for your seeing) was coming *from* you and being directed *at* the building. You were in charge of the data bank because the batteries were your own. They had been charged by your elders, by your imam or by your parents and peers. You were the youthful Navaho learning how to be cleansed in the sweat lodge before beginning a healing ceremony, you were the follower of Islam being taught the sequence of rituals before each prayer session or you were the suburbanite teen mimicking the behaviors of your parents in order to successfully shop at the mall and become a good consumer. To use

Michael Baxandall's term, you were seeing the building through your period eye. By period eye, Baxandall meant the kind of equipment, so to speak, that people bring to their encounters with buildings (Baxandall 107). This equipment, which, to be more scientific, is our culturally determined cognitive skills, causes us to order our encounters with buildings in very particular and knowable ways. Seeing, Baxandall suggests, is theory-laden and soaked in very specific cultural practices.

But in the second example, the building and the people who caused it to be built were the generators of the light beam. *It* was emitting light *at* you. You were just simply standing there holding up your light-sensitive paper patiently waiting for information to appear on it. Unlike your own batteries, the batteries housed in the building contain the motivations of the building's own builders, their own "period eye," not the knowledge about what you have learned buildings to be about. In this case, as Clifford Geertz has reminded us, the fundamental question that we should be asking ourselves as we study the image as it appears on the light-sensitive paper is what are the people who built this building trying to tell us? And as Geertz so aptly has put it, "the trick is to figure out what the devil they think they are up to" in their conceiving and constructing of the building (Geertz, "From the Native's Point of View" 58).

What was it that *they* were trying to tell *us?* Now that is a truly remarkable question if we are to understand what it is that makes buildings the way they are.

Understand the distinction between the two examples and you understand the complex nature of what is required in order to know buildings. In the first case we are doing the explicating; and in the second and much more difficult situation, we are trying to infer, construe, and interpret (or whatever other hermaneutic term you might want to use), *what the builders were trying to say about themselves with their building.*

Now from an outside observer's point of view, these two beams of light might appear to be the very same beam. But it doesn't take a quantum physicist to explain the difference in the beams. The difference is fundamental—fundamental to the very nature of how it is that we go about trying to understand buildings. The ultimate aim of the you-pointing-the-light example leads to a reductionist or universalist theory of architecture. This theory states that at the most basic level there are certain components of buildings that all human beings see and understand; columns *hold up* roofs which *shelter* spaces in which human beings *joyfully or tragically* carry on their lives both alone and as a community: Firmness, Commodity and Delight; or Form Follows Function; or Architecture as the Spirit of the Age Represented By Built Form; or the Primitive Hut or whatever other current, outdated or bankrupt theory you wish to apply to all buildings everywhere in the world.

But the ultimate end of the building-shining-a-light-on-your-paper scenario leads to a more disquieting conclusion. This conclusion would state that every time you study a building, every time you attempt to understand it, you must study it based on the terms of those who were responsible for bringing it about. As a result of coming to know a building in this manner, you must be prepared for radically different answers. In the second example, diversity most certainly will rule.

What is the point that *they* are trying to make with *their* building?

For a long, long time this kind of question made little sense to me because I had learned quite well to look at all buildings using my own flashlight, the one that had the batteries filled by my life experiences and by my architecture teachers—until recently. Not until two experiences that on first glance appear to be neither similar nor very consequential converged around this question. Both experiences were rather ordinary—events that I suppose many other people have had but to which they might not have paid much attention. The first was when I attended a Homefest of upper income new houses, all freshly landscaped and appropriately decorated to display an enviable lifestyle meant to appeal to the thousands who came searching either for their dream home or for some affordable, new design ideas. The second experience came close on the heels of the first. Perhaps that's what caused them to collide with one another and brought them to my attention. I went to a party at a similar country club development as the Homefest but in another part of the city. There, amid casual conversations, I overheard a remark about the host which made me wonder about my own misconceptions about what point people were trying to make with their buildings.

The remark went something like this: "He (the host) spent all day meticulously cleaning the house preparing for this party. It looks so good it seems as if nobody lives here." That's what struck me, ". . . it seems as if nobody lives here." As I wandered around the house and then later reflected on that comment, I realized how many other kinds of similar houses that I had been in over the past few years.

There was something about them, something about the way they all felt to me; but I couldn't quite put my finger on what I was feeling; that is, not until I was jolted out of my complacency by the it-seems-as-if-nobody-lives-here remark.

That comment made sense. All those other houses also did not look like people lived in them. In fact, they all appeared to be versions of Homefest model houses! There was nothing in those houses that told me anything about the lives of the people who lived there. Of course there was original art on the wall, ceramic vases with silk flowers on the coffee table, leather-covered books on the shelf, custom-made comforters on the bed, even Armani clothes in the closet. All the right things in the right places. But if I was trying to learn anything about the lives of the hosts in particular; that is, what made them unique people with unique stories to tell, I was having a difficult time. My problem, though, was not that my hosts didn't have a story to reveal but that I was the one who was holding the flashlight. I was looking for what *I* believed a house should contain (what Christopher Alexander has very appropriately called in the very last pattern of his book, *A Pattern Language*, "Things From Your Life"). That pattern reads:

> Do not be tricked into believing that modern decor must be slick or psychedelic, or 'natural' or 'modern art,' or 'plants' or anything else that current taste-makers claim. It is most beautiful when it comes *straight from your life* (my italics)—the things you care for, the things that tell your story. (Alexander 1166)

My flashlight's beam was trying to search out what I wanted to see, what I expected to see, what was contained in my batteries. I had hoped that I might see a woven tapestry brought back from a once-in-a-lifetime trip to Anatolia, an antique rolltop desk inherited from a grandparent, a leather sofa worn like a saddle from years of use by children who had now grown to adulthood, dog-eared books mixed in with family photo albums populating the bookshelves, maybe even a glass cabinet full of shells, foreign coins and small mementoes collected from past vacations. And where were the family portraits that seemingly would have had significance to the lives of the owners? I wanted to see things that told me about the unique lives of the home's inhabitants because I knew what that meant. I wanted to see things that told their story.

But what I saw (the beam of light aimed by me) was a model house looking as if no one in particular lived there. And what I overheard spoken *as a compliment* was that the house was so clean it didn't appear as if anyone lived there. So whose story was I seeing?

The question that I had to confront head on was what point were they (the hosts and complimenters) trying to make (the beam of light from them onto my light-sensitive paper) with that house, located in that development and landscaped, decorated and inhabited in that way? Were they saying that a good house, a well-done house, a desirable house—*a proper house*—should look similar to an unlived-in model home? And if so, what does that mean about conceptions that designers have about universal aesthetic standards, about form and function, about buildings reflecting the angst and fragmentation of our modern-day society or about other notions that they carry in their batteries about what it is that designers do for clients? And how do designers' conceptions stack up against what it is that hosts are saying about what they want other people to think about how it is that they are living? Is the projection of a life style in the most anonymous sense of that term more important than the telling of stories about the users? And what of the architect's self-appointed responsibility to reflect the conditions of our present age as *they* view those conditions—to explore ". . . the possibility of a truly horrific environment," as Peter Eisenman has described much of his recent work (Seabrook 77). Even Eisenman's early residential work, albeit only a handful of houses, but still houses that not only launched his career but also established a sensibility that remains important in some architectural circles today—even in this work he was exploring ways of building houses that were "against the traditional notion of how you occupy a house" (Seabrook 128). Of course, Eisenman was only following a tradition that had been established by early modernist projects like Le Corbusier's Villa Savoy, by Philip Johnson's own Glass House and by Charles and Ray Eames' house constructed entirely out of industrial materials. But architects are cut from a different cloth and have learned to see the world as if it were illuminated by a second sun. But what about the rest of us?

Now from the standpoint of the casual observer, these two beams of light might appear to be the same. But just as quantum physicists have learned to see both a wave and a particle when they look at light, we, as designers, must be able to adjust our vision to see beams of light traveling in both directions—from us to the building carrying all of our preconceived, architecturally determined ways of seeing and, when we study buildings, from those buildings to ourselves carrying the messages of what point the builders and the inhabiters are trying to make about what is important to them.

First, like physicists, we need to be able to accept the ambiguity that is present when we see a beam of light. Are we seeing a wave or are we seeing a particle? For as modern physicists have explained to us, the thing keeps changing from a wave to a particle and back again. In other words, observation, as they have taught us, is not a passive process (the detached observer model) but an active process, one in which what is being observed is affected by the process of observation. By analogy, my active involvement in seeing, in shining the light, causes things to appear *to me* in a certain way—my preconceived way.

Second, like the party-goer who overheard the comment on the cleanliness of the house, we have to learn to pay attention to what it is that we are hearing. Paying attention forces us to hear more than only what we want to hear.

Third, and most importantly, we have to learn to make inferences or interpretations from what it is that we hear. Be warned, though, that these inferences will not lead to grand theories, generalized insights or universal design strategies but simply what the host and everyone like him had in mind when he bought that house, furnished it the way he did and prepared for his party by giving the house an unlived-in appearance. Then each little inference added together might come to give us a new insight into what it is that we ought to be doing as designers.

Works Cited

Adams, Henry, *Mont-Saint-Michel and Chartres*. Boston: Houghton, 1905.

Alexander, Christopher, et al. *A Pattern Language*. New York: Oxford UP, 1977.

Baxandall, Michael. *Painting and Experience in Fifteenth-Century Italy*. Oxford UP, 1988.

Geertz, Clifford. "Thick Description: Toward an Interpretive Theory of Culture." *The Interpretation of Cultures: Selected Essays*. Boston: Basic Books, 1973.

———. "From the Native's Point of View: On the Nature of Anthropological Understanding." *Local Knowledge: Further Essays in Interpretive Anthropology*. Boston: Basic Books, 1983.

Seabrook, John. "The David Lynch of Architecture." *Vanity Fair* Jan. 1991: 73–127.

THE RESEARCH PAPER

Who hasn't at some time or other met a self-involved person who listens to nobody and appears convinced that his or her conclusions are unquestionable? Interestingly, those opinions often seem to have no basis in fact. Such a person will offer opinions about politicians and recent immigrants, but cannot accurately quote the daily news or current immigration law. He or she will happily carry on about the importance of taking certain vitamin doses, but be unable to give the correct names of the basic B-vitamins. And while the audience listens politely—or flees the room—the know-nothing babbles on in ignorance.

A person who wants to be taken seriously needs to demonstrate knowledge of the subject he or she is speaking or writing about. For most college writing assignments, that means a student will need to conduct research—to become better informed, to form opinions based on available knowledge, and to earn respect for his or her opinions by presenting them in writing. A student's research process follows the basic principles of academic scholarship. Like students, scholars share their findings by communicating with others in the field, using publications (print and now electronic) and interactions with other experts. There is a constant flow of information, and so to prevent confusion and streamline communication, scholars in each field have agreed upon consistent ways of presenting information. Scientists, for example, use specific formats to present their research findings while psychologists use different formats to present statistics. Humanists and social scientists use the research report as one way of demonstrating their research and ideas. Thus, college students are assigned research projects to broaden their knowledge, to learn how to find and present information as support for their conclusions, to write papers using the appropriate formats, and to cite their sources using an accepted documentation style. Research formats, such as the APA (American Psychological Association) or MLA (Modern Language Association) styles, are like grammars—those familiar with the method know how to correctly interpret the material.

As Mann's article from the *Journal of American Culture* demonstrates, it is possible to be creative, interesting, and academic at the same time. The quotations and references not only substantiate (i.e., "give substance to"—give weight to) his points, but other scholars can follow the Works Cited list to identify his sources. The research paper thus becomes a means of using information from various sources to lend support to and clarify ideas.

One issue that frequently plagues students and teachers is the question of "fair use" and plagiarism of sources. The difference between research and plagiarism is really quite simple: plagiarism is theft. The plagiarist takes someone else's wording or research without giving credit in the appropriate ways. Taking your cousin's research paper from a previous course and turning it in as your own is dishonest. Copying passages from other sources into your research paper without appropriate references is also dishonest because you have passed someone else's work off as your own—this is also plagiarism. Taking sentences or phrases, changing them slightly, and then slipping them into your paper is the same kind of theft—you have passed something (even if only a few words) off as your own. The scholar who is careful about giving credit and careful that every phrase not in quotation marks is his or her own is taking care not only to avoid plagiarism but to practice the best kind of scholarship.

Study Questions

1. Explain the two kinds of viewing (of perceiving) that Mann describes.
2. How might Mann's methods be applied in other areas, particularly an area with which you are familiar? Try applying his points to forms of art other than architecture, or even to human beings.
3. Trace Mann's use of sources to substantiate his assertions, listing his ideas and how the source supports what he says.

Writing Topics

1. Think of a situation in which you examined something by means of the "flashlight" method. Write an essay in which you describe how you might have seen the thing by using the other way Mann describes.
2. Do some library research on the topic of plagiarism. Write a brief research essay that includes quotations and information on the topic of honest academic scholarship.

Black
White
Other

JONATHAN MARKS

While reading the Sunday edition of the *New York Times* one morning last February, my attention was drawn by an editorial inconsistency. The article I was reading was written by attorney Lani Guinier. (Guinier, you may remember, had been President Clinton's nominee to head the civil rights division at the Department of Justice in 1993. Her name was hastily withdrawn amid a blast of criticism over her views on political representation of minorities.) What had distracted me from the main point of the story was a photo caption that described Guinier as being "half-black." In the text of the article, Guinier had described herself simply as "black."

How can a person be black and half black at the same time? In algebraic terms, this would seem to describe a situation where $x = 1/2x$, to which the only solution is $x = 0$.

The inconsistency in the *Times* was trivial, but revealing. It encapsulated a longstanding problem in our use of racial categories—namely, a confusion between biological and cultural heredity. When Guinier is described as "half-black," that is a statement of biological ancestry, for one of her two parents is black. And when Guinier describes herself as black, she is using a cultural category, according to which one can either be black or white, but not both.

Race—as the term is commonly used—is inherited, although not in a strictly biological fashion. It is passed down according to a system of folk heredity, an all-or-nothing system that is different from the quantifiable heredity of biology. But the incompatibility of the two notions of race is sometimes starkly evident—as when the state decides that racial differences are so important that interracial marriages must be regulated or outlawed entirely. Miscegenation laws in this country (which stayed on the books in many states through the 1960s) obliged the legal system to define who belonged in what category. The resulting formula stated that anyone with one-eighth or more black ancestry was a "negro." (A similar formula, defining

Jews, was promulgated by the Germans in the Nuremberg Laws of the 1930s.)

Applying such formulas led to the biological absurdity that having one black great-grandparent was sufficient to define a person as black, but having seven white great-grandparents was insufficient to define a person as white. Here, race and biology are demonstrably at odds. And the problem is not semantic but conceptual, for race is presented as a category of nature.

Human beings come in a wide variety of sizes, shapes, colors, and forms—or, because we are visually oriented primates, it certainly seems that way. We also come in larger packages called populations; and we are said to belong to even larger and more confusing units, which have long been known as races. The history of the study of human variation is to a large extent the pursuit of those human races—the attempt to identify the small number of fundamentally distinct kinds of people on earth.

This scientific goal stretches back two centuries, to Linnaeus, the father of biological systematics, who radically established *Homo sapiens* as one species within a group of animals he called Primates. Linnaeus's system of naming groups within groups logically implied further breakdown. He consequently sought to establish a number of subspecies within *Homo sapiens*. He identified five: four geographical species (from Europe, Asia, Africa, and America) and one grab-bag subspecies called *monstrosus*. This category was dropped by subsequent researchers (as was Linnaeus's use of criteria such as personality and dress to define his subspecies).

While Linnaeus was not the first to divide humans on the basis of the continents on which they lived, he had given the division a scientific stamp. But in attempting to determine the proper number of subspecies, the heirs of Linnaeus always seemed to find different answers, depending upon the criteria they applied. By the mid-twentieth century, scores of anthropologists—led by Harvard's Earnest Hooton—had expended enormous energy on the problem. But these scholars could not convince one another about the precise nature of the fundamental divisions of our species.

Part of the problem—as with the *Times*'s identification of Lani Guinier—was that we humans have two constantly intersecting ways of thinking about the divisions among us. On the one hand, we like to think of "race"—as Linnaeus did—as an objective, biological category. In this sense, being a member of a race is supposed to be the equivalent of being a member of a species or of a phylum—except that race, on the analogy of subspecies, is an even narrower (and presumably more exclusive and precise) biological category.

The other kind of category into which we humans allocate ourselves—when we say "Serb" or "Hutu" or "Jew" or "Chicano" or "Republican" or "Red Sox fan"—is cultural. The label refers to little or nothing in the natural attributes of its members. These members may not live in the same region and may not even know many others like themselves. What they share is neither strictly nature nor strictly community. The groupings are constructions of human social history.

Membership in these *un*biological groupings may mean the difference between life and death, for they are the categories that allow us to be identified (and accepted or vilified) socially. While membership in (or allegiance to) these categories may be assigned or adopted from birth, the differentia that mark members from nonmembers are symbolic and abstract; they serve to distinguish people who cannot be readily distinguished by nature. So important are these symbolic distinctions that some of the strongest animosities are often expressed between very similar-looking peoples. Obvious examples are Bosnian Serbs and Muslims, Irish and English, Huron and Iroquois.

Obvious natural variation is rarely so important as cultural difference. One simply does not hear of a slaughter of the short people at the hands of the tall, the glabrous at the hands of the hairy, the red-haired at the hands of the brown-haired. When we do encounter genocidal violence between different-looking peoples, the two groups are invariably socially or culturally distinct as well. Indeed, the tragic frequency of hatred and genocidal violence between biologically indistinguishable peoples implies that biological differences such as skin color are not motivations but, rather, excuses. They allow nature to be invoked to reinforce group identities and antagonisms that would exist without these physical distinctions. But are there any truly "racial" biological distinctions to be found in our species?

Obviously, if you compare two people from different parts of the world (or whose ancestors came from different parts of the world), they will differ physically, but one cannot therefore define three or four or five basically different kinds of people, as a biological notion of race would imply. The anatomical properties that distinguish people—such as pigmentation, eye form, body build—are not clumped in discrete groups, but distributed along geographical gradients, as are nearly all the genetically determined variants detectable in the human gene pool.

These gradients are produced by three forces. Natural selection adapts populations to local circumstances (like climate) and thereby differentiates them from other populations. Genetic drift (random fluctuations in a gene pool) also differentiates populations from one another, but in non-adaptive ways. And gene flow (via intermarriage and other child-producing unions) acts to homogenize neighboring populations.

In practice, the operations of these forces are difficult to discern. A few features, such as body build and the graduated distribution of the sickle cell anemia gene in populations from western Africa, southern Asia, and the Mediterranean can be plausibly related to the effects of selection. Others, such as the graduated distribution of a small deletion in the mitochondrial DNA of some East Asian, Oceanic, and Native American peoples, or the degree of flatness of the face, seem unlikely to be the result of selection and are probably the results of random biohistorical factors. The cause of the distribution of most features, from nose breadth to blood group, is simply unclear.

The overall result of these forces is evident, however. As Johann Friedrich Blumenbach noted in 1775, "you see that all do so run into one another, and that one variety of mankind does so sensibly pass into the other, that you cannot mark out the limits between them." (Posturing as an heir to Linnaeus, he nonetheless attempted to do so.) But from humanity's gradations in appearance, no defined groupings resembling races readily emerge. The racial categories with which we have become so familiar are the result of our imposing arbitrary cultural boundaries in order to partition gradual biological variation.

Unlike graduated biological distinctions, culturally constructed categories are ultrasharp. One can be French or German, but not both; Tutsi or Hutu, but not both; Jew or Catholic, but not both; Bosnian Muslim or Serb, but not both; black or white, but not both. Traditionally, people of "mixed race" have been obliged to choose one and thereby identify themselves unambiguously to census takers and administrative bookkeepers—a practice that is now being widely called into question.

A scientific definition of race would require considerable homogeneity within each group, and reasonably discrete differences between groups, but three kinds of data militate against this view: First, the groups traditionally described as races are not at all homogeneous. Africans and Europeans, for instance, are each a collection of biologically diverse populations. Anthropologists of the 1920s widely recognized *three* European races: Nordic, Alpine, and Mediterranean. This implied that races could exist within races. American anthropologist Carleton Coon identified *ten* European races in 1939. With such protean use, the term race came to have little value in describing actual biological entities within *Homo sapiens*. The scholars were not only grappling with a broad north–south gradient in human appearance across Europe, they were trying to bring the data into line with their belief in profound and fundamental constitutional differences between groups of people.

But there simply isn't one European race to contrast with an African race, nor three, nor ten: the question (as scientists long posed it) fails to recognize the actual patterning of diversity in the human species. Fieldwork revealed, and genetics later quantified, the existence of far more biological diversity within any group than between groups. Fatter and thinner people exist everywhere, as do people with type O and type A blood. What generally varies from one population to the next is the *proportion* of people in these groups expressing the trait or gene. Hair color varies strikingly among Europeans and native Australians, but little among other peoples. To focus on discovering differences between presumptive races, when the vast majority of detectable variants do not help differentiate them, was thus to define a very narrow—if not largely illusory—problem in human biology. (The fact that Africans are biologically more diverse than Europeans, but have rarely been split into so many races, attests to the cultural basis of these categorizations.)

Second, differences between human groups are only evident when contrasting geographical extremes. Noting these extremes, biologists of an earlier era sought to identify representatives of "pure," primordial races—presumably located in Norway, Senegal, and Thailand. At no time, however, was our species composed of a few populations within which everyone looked pretty much the same. Ever since some of our ancestors left Africa to spread out through the Old World, we humans have always lived in the "in-between" places. And human populations have also always been in genetic contact with one another. Indeed, for tens of thousands of years, humans have had trade networks; and where goods flow, so do genes. Consequently, we have no basis for considering *extreme* human forms the most pure, or most representative, of some ancient primordial populations. Instead, they represent populations adapted to the most disparate environments.

And third, between each presumptive "major" race are unclassifiable populations and people. Some populations of India, for example, are darkly pigmented (or "black"), have Europeanlike ("Caucasoid") facial features, but inhabit the continent of Asia (which should make them "Asian"). Americans might tend to ignore these "exceptions" to the racial categories, since immigrants to the United States from West Africa, Southeast Asia, and northwest Europe far outnumber those from India. The very existence of unclassifiable peoples undermines the idea that there are just three human biological groups in the Old World. Yet acknowledging the biological distinctiveness of such groups leads to a rapid proliferation of categories. What about Australians? Polynesians? The Ainu of Japan?

Categorizing people is important to any society. It is, at some basic psychological level, probably necessary to have group identity about who and what you are, in contrast to who and what you are not. The concept of race, however, specifically involves the recruitment of biology to validate those categories of self-identity.

Mice don't have to worry about that the way humans do. Consequently, classifying them into subspecies entails less of a responsibility for a scientist than classifying humans into subspecies does. And by the 1960s, most anthropologists realized they could not defend any classification of *Homo sapiens* into biological subspecies or races that could be considered reasonably objective. They therefore stopped doing it, and stopped identifying the endeavor as a central goal of the field. It was a biologically intractable problem—the old square-peg-in-a-round-hole enterprise; and people's lives, or welfares, could well depend on the ostensibly scientific pronouncement. Reflecting on the social history of the twentieth century, that was a burden anthropologists would no longer bear.

This conceptual divorce in anthropology—of cultural from biological phenomena—was one of the most fundamental scientific revolutions of our time. And since it affected assumptions so rooted in our everyday experience, and resulted in conclusions so counterintuitive—like the idea that the earth goes around the sun, and not vice-versa—it has been widely underappreciated.

Kurt Vonnegut, in *Slaughterhouse Five*, describes what he remembered being taught about human variation: "At that time, they were teaching that there was absolutely no difference between anybody. They may be teaching that still." Of course there are biological differences between people, and between populations. The question is: How are those differences patterned? And the answer seems to be: Not racially. Populations are the only readily identifiable units of humans, and even they are fairly fluid, biologically similar to populations nearby, and biologically different from populations far away.

In other words, the message of contemporary anthropology is: You may group humans into a small number of races if you want to, but you are denied biology as a support for it.

Texture

One thinks of *texture* in connection with fabrics and carpeting, as a measure of surface qualities: How does this feel? Is it thick or thin? Is it smooth, rough, or nubby? Is it heavy or light? The same term, *texture*, can be usefully applied to writing, as a quality: Is the texture of the writing dense and heavy, serious and thoughtful, complex? Is it light and easy, simply worded, without deep meaning or difficult phrasing? How does the prose or poetry *feel*, when it is first encountered?

Various literary critics have applied the term *texture* in different ways, but it is most useful in describing that initial feel of the work that a reader perceives in the first paragraph. The reader knows almost immediately, just as one person can gain a feel for another person in the first few moments of a conversation, whether the reading will be scientific or poetic; difficult, with many long and unfamiliar words or informal and quick-running; loaded with quotations and commentary; or a simple story line. Complex writing may have multiple textures, though usually one impression predominates.

The texture of Marks's essay reflects his awareness that he is writing for an educated audience that is not daunted by general scientific terminology. Clearly Marks is the kind of educated general reader who spends Sunday mornings with coffee and the *Times*—an intellectual leisure-time activity, even when followed by the Sunday afternoon football game. Marks is not afraid of using the passive voice, as academics often do: "my attention was drawn by . . ." Nor is he afraid of using terms like "editorial inconsistency," on the well-founded assumption that the reader will understand him immediately. The reader knows at the outset that the texture of this essay will be dense and thoughtful. If this essay were a carpet, it would be thick, high quality, and very expensive. Fortunately, it doesn't take a lot of money to enjoy high-quality prose.

Study Questions

1. The thesis of "Black White Other" is, essentially, the last sentence of the essay. Why would Marks place the thesis at the conclusion? Where else in the essay does he state this point?

2. How does the texture of this piece help Marks to be taken seriously and have his opinions accepted by educated readers? Would it have a different impact if it had a different texture? What other kinds of texture might be developed for an essay on the same subject?
3. Marks gives three major reasons that "racial" characteristics, differences among people, develop. Describe and explain each of those reasons. Give examples of how people can become differentiated—particularly if you can think of examples different from those in the essay.
4. Marks offers three "kinds of data" that oppose the idea of racial categories. List and explain, in your own words, these three arguments against the concept of completely separate racial categories.
5. Anyone who has studied algebra will understand that the equation in the second paragraph is a gentle joke. Explain the joke. (Or get a mathematician to explain it to you.)

Writing Topics

1. *Collaborative writing activity* (with the members of the group comparing their opinions on whether race is genetic or cultural). According to Marks, what we normally think of as race is a cultural concept, not a biological fact. Do you think most people today view race as biology or culture? How do you view those concepts? Write an essay in which you analyze the two sides, including a quotation from Marks to bolster your argument.
2. After reading the Marks essay, do you think we should eliminate the categories commonly found on college application forms, public documents, and so forth? (For example, one is often asked to check off one category: African-American, Native American, Hispanic, etc.) Why or why not? If you think those categories should be eliminated, what (if anything) would you put in their place? Write an essay in which you argue one side or the other. Use Marks's essay to bolster your argument, and be sure to cite it properly.

The Force That Through the Green Fuse Drives the Flower

DYLAN THOMAS

The force that through the green fuse drives the flower
Drives my green age; that blasts the roots of trees
Is my destroyer.
And I am dumb to tell the crooked rose
My youth is bent by the same wintry fever.

The force that drives the water through the rocks
Drives my red blood; that dries the mouthing streams
Turns mine to wax.
And I am dumb to mouth unto my veins
How at the mountain spring the same mouth sucks.

The hand that whirls the water in the pool
Stirs the quicksand; that ropes the blowing wind
Hauls my shroud sail.
And I am dumb to tell the hanging man
How of my clay is made the hangman's lime.

The lips of time leech to the fountain head;
Love drips and gathers, but the fallen blood
Shall calm her sores.
And I am dumb to tell a weather's wind
How time has ticked a heaven round the stars.

And I am dumb to tell the lover's tomb
How at my sheet goes the same crooked worm.

Study Questions

1. In what ways does Thomas's poem resist "logical" thinking? Which parts make sense on a feeling level, instead of a rational level? How does the poem use imagery to develop the emotional content?
2. If this poem were an essay, what kind of essay would it be—expository, descriptive, narrative, argumentative, or a mixture? (For a review, see the appropriate In Focus essays in chapter 3.) What, in your opinion, is the poet's primary purpose?
3. Notice how difficult it would be to write a thesis statement for this poem. A statement of the reader's general impression of the poet's idea is, however, possible. What general impression do you get from the poem? What is Thomas conveying? Support your answer with references to specific lines in the poem.
4. Notice the repetition of the phrase "And I am dumb" ("dumb" meaning "unable to speak"). Why is this phrase repeated so often? Can the inability to communicate actually be communicated in a poem?

Writing Topics

1. Find a different poem that somehow compares with "The Force That Through the Green Fuse Drives the Flower": another poem on a similar subject, another poem by Dylan Thomas, another modern or imagist poem, or some other appropriate choice. Write an essay in which you compare and contrast the two poems, showing the points of similarity and difference as you see them. Remember to support your ideas with specific references to the two poems.
2. As you examine the poem, notice the repeated connections between love and death. Find another work of literature or art that connects love and death (the story of Adam and Eve in the biblical book of Genesis is an example, as is the Robert D. Richardson Jr. piece on Ralph Waldo Emerson in chapter 3), then write an essay in which you examine the ways both works explore this theme. How can the understandings from one of the two works be applied to the other? (Alternately, find another theme in Thomas's poem, along with another comparable work of literature, and use that theme as the basis for your essay.)

Is Everything Determined?

STEPHEN HAWKING

In the play *Julius Caesar*, Cassius tells Brutus, "Men at some times are masters of their fate." But are we really masters of our fate? Or is everything we do determined and preordained? The argument for preordination used to be that God was omnipotent and outside time, so God would know what was going to happen. But how then could we have any free will? And if we don't have free will, how can we be responsible for our actions? It can hardly be one's fault if one has been preordained to rob a bank. So why should one be punished for it?

In recent times, the argument for determinism has been based on science. It seems that there are well-defined laws that govern how the universe and everything in it develops in time. Although we have not yet found the exact form of all these laws, we already know enough to determine what happens in all but the most extreme situations. Whether we will find the remaining laws in the fairly near future is a matter of opinion. I'm an optimist: I think there's a fifty-fifty chance that we will find them in the next twenty years. But even if we don't, it won't really make any difference to the argument. The important point is that there should exist a set of laws that completely determines the evolution of the universe from its initial state. These laws may have been ordained by God. But it seems that He (or She) does not intervene in the universe to break the laws.

The initial configuration of the universe may have been chosen by God, or it may itself have been determined by the laws of science. In either case, it would seem that everything in the universe would then be determined by evolution according to the laws of science, so it is difficult to see how we can be masters of our fate.

The idea that there is some grand unified theory that determines everything in the universe raises many difficulties. First of all, the grand unified theory is presumably compact and elegant in mathematical terms. There ought to be something special and simple about the theory of everything. Yet how can a certain number of equations account for the complexity and trivial detail that we see around us?

Can one really believe that the grand unified theory has determined that Sinead O'Connor will be the top of the hit parade this week, or that Madonna will be on the cover of *Cosmopolitan*?

A second problem with the idea that everything is determined by a grand unified theory is that anything we say is also determined by the theory. But why should it be determined to be correct? Isn't it more likely to be wrong, because there are many possible incorrect statements for every true one? Each week, my mail contains a number of theories that people have sent me. They are all different, and most are mutually inconsistent. Yet presumably the grand unified theory has determined that the authors think they were correct. So why should anything I say have any greater validity? Aren't I equally determined by the grand unified theory?

A third problem with the idea that everything is determined is that we feel that we have free will—that we have the freedom to choose whether to do something. But if everything is determined by the laws of science, then free will must be an illusion, and if we don't have free will, what is the basis for our responsibility for our actions? We don't punish people for crimes if they are insane, because we have decided that they can't help it. But if we are all determined by a grand unified theory, none of us can help what we do, so why should anyone be held responsible for what they do?

These problems of determinism have been discussed over the centuries. The discussion was somewhat academic, however, as we were far from a complete knowledge of the laws of science, and we didn't know how the initial state of the universe was determined. The problems are more urgent now because there is the possibility that we may find a complete unified theory in as little as twenty years. And we realize that the initial state may itself have been determined by the laws of science. What follows is my personal attempt to come to terms with these problems. I don't claim any great originality or depth, but it is the best I can do at the moment.

To start with the first problem: How can a relatively simple and compact theory give rise to a universe that is as complex as the one we observe, with all its trivial and unimportant details? The key to this is the uncertainty principle of quantum mechanics, which states that one cannot measure both the position and speed of a particle to great accuracy; the more accurately you measure the position, the less accurately you can measure the speed, and vice vera. This uncertainty is not so important at the present time, when things are far apart, so that a small uncertainty in position does not make much difference. But in the very early universe, everything was very close together, so there was quite a lot of uncertainty, and there were a number of possible states for the universe. These different possible early states would have evolved into a whole family of different histories for the universe. Most of these histories would be similar in their large-scale features. They would correspond to a universe that was uniform and smooth, and that was expanding. However, they would differ on details like the distribution of stars and, even more, on what was on the covers of their magazines. (That is, if those histories contained magazines.) Thus the complexity of the universe around us and its details arose from the uncertainty principle in the early stages. This gives a whole family of possible histories for the universe. There would be a history in which the Nazis won the Second World War, though the probability is low. But we just happen to live in a history in which the Allies won the war and Madonna was on the cover of *Cosmopolitan.*

I now turn to the second problem: If what we do is determined by some grand unified theory, why should the theory determine that we draw the right conclusions about the universe rather than the wrong ones? Why should anything we say have any validity? My answer to this is based on Darwin's idea of natural selection. I take it that some very primitive form of life arose spontaneously on earth from chance combinations of atoms. This early form of life was probably a large molecule. But it was probably not DNA, since the chances of forming a whole DNA molecule by random combinations are small.

The early form of life would have reproduced itself. The quantum uncertainty principle and the random thermal motions of the atoms would mean that there were a certain number of errors in the reproduction. Most of these errors would have been fatal to the survival of the organism or its ability to reproduce. Such errors would not be passed on to future generations but would die out. A very few errors would be beneficial, by pure chance. The organisms with these errors would be more likely to survive and reproduce. Thus they would tend to replace the original, unimproved organisms.

The development of the double helix structure of DNA may have been one such improvement in the early stages. This was probably such an advance that it completely replaced any earlier form of life, whatever that may have been. As evolution progressed, it would have led to the development of the central nervous system. Creatures that correctly recognized the implications of data gathered by their sense organs and took appropriate action would be more likely to survive and reproduce. The human race has carried this to another stage. We are very similar to higher apes, both in our bodies and in our DNA; but a slight variation in our DNA has enabled us to develop language. This has meant that we can hand down information and accumulated experience from generation to generation, in spoken and eventually in written form. Previously, the results of experience could be handed down only by the slow process of it being encoded into DNA through random errors in reproduction. The effect has been a dramatic speed-up of evolution. It took more than three billion years to evolve up to the human race. But in the course of the last ten thousand years, we have developed written language. This has enabled us to progress from cave dwellers to the point where we can ask about the ultimate theory of the universe.

There has been no significant biological evolution, or change in human DNA, in the last ten thousand years. Thus, our intelligence, our ability to draw the correct conclusions from the information provided by our sense organs, must date back to our cave dweller days or earlier. It would have been selected for on the basis of our ability to kill certain animals for food and to avoid being killed by other animals. It is remarkable that mental qualities that were selected for these purposes should have stood us in such good stead in the very different circumstances of the present day. There is probably not much survival advantage to be gained from discovering a grand unified theory or answering questions about determinism. Nevertheless, the intelligence that we have developed for other reasons may well ensure that we find the right answers to these questions.

I now turn to the third problem, the questions of free will and responsibility for our actions. We feel subjectively that we have the ability to choose who we are and what we do. But this may just be an illusion. Some people think they are Jesus Christ or Napoleon, but they can't all be right. What we need is an objective test that we can apply from the outside to distinguish whether an organism has free will. For example, suppose we were visited by a "little green person" from another star. How could we decide whether it had free will or was just a robot, programmed to respond as if it were like us?

The ultimate objective test of free will would seem to be: Can one predict the behavior of the organism? If one can, then it clearly doesn't have free will but is predetermined. On the other hand, if one cannot predict the behavior, one could take that as an operational definition that the organism has free will.

One might object to this definition of free will on the grounds that once we find a complete unified theory we will be able to predict what people will do. The human brain, however, is also subject to the uncertainty principle. Thus, there is an element of the randomness associated with quantum mechanics in human behavior. But the energies involved in the brain are low, so quantum mechanical uncertainty is only a small effect. The real reason why we cannot predict human behavior is that it is just too difficult. We already know the basic physical laws that govern the activity of the brain, and they are comparatively simple. But it is just too hard to solve the equations when there are more than a few particles involved. Even in the simpler Newtonian theory of gravity, one can solve the equations exactly only in the case of two particles. For three or more particles one has to resort to approximations, and the difficulty increases rapidly with the number of particles. The human brain contains about 10^{26} or a hundred million billion billion particles. This is far too many for us ever to be able to solve the equations and predict how the brain would behave, given its initial state and the nerve data coming into it. In fact, of course, we cannot even measure what the initial state was, because to do so we would have to take the brain apart. Even if we were prepared to do that, there would just be too many particles to record. Also, the brain is probably very sensitive to the initial state—a small change in the initial state can make a very large difference to subsequent behavior. So although we know the fundamental equations that govern the brain, we are quite unable to use them to predict human behavior.

This situation arises in science whenever we deal with the macroscopic system, because the number of particles is always too large for there to be any chance of solving the fundamental equations. What we do instead is use effective theories. These are approximations in which the very large number of particles are replaced by a few quantities. An example is fluid mechanics. A liquid such as water is made up of billions of billions of molecules that themselves are made up of electrons, protons, and neutrons. Yet it is a good approximation to treat the liquid as a continuous medium, characterized just by velocity, density, and temperature. The predictions of the effective theory of fluid mechanics are not exact—one only has to listen to the weather forecast to realize that—but they are good enough for the design of ships or oil pipelines.

I want to suggest that the concepts of free will and moral responsibility for our actions are really an effective theory in the sense of fluid mechanics. It may be that everything we do is determined by some grand unified theory. If that theory has determined that we shall die by hanging, then we shall not drown. But you would have to be awfully sure that you were destined for the gallows to put to sea in a small boat during a storm. I have noticed that even people who claim that everything is predestined and that we can do nothing to change it look before they cross the road. Maybe it's just that those who don't look don't survive to tell the tale.

One cannot base one's conduct on the idea that everything is determined, because one does not know what has been determined. Instead, one has to adopt the effective theory that one has free will and that one is responsible for one's actions. This theory is not very good at predicting human behavior, but we adopt it because there is no chance of solving the equations arising from the fundamental laws. There is also a Darwinian reason that we believe in free will: A society in which the individual feels responsible for his or her actions is more likely to work together and survive to spread its values. Of course, ants work well together. But such a society is static. It cannot respond to unfamiliar challenges or develop new opportunities. A collection of free individuals who share certain mutual aims, however, can collaborate on their common objectives and yet have the flexibility to make innovations. Thus, such a society is more likely to prosper and to spread its system of values.

The concept of free will belongs to a different arena from that of fundamental laws of science. If one tries to deduce human behavior from the laws of science, one gets caught in the logical paradox of self-referencing systems. If what one does could be predicted from the fundamental laws, then the fact of making that prediction could change what happens. It is like the problems one would get into if time travel were possible, which I don't think it ever will be. If you could see what is going to happen in the future, you could change it. If you knew which horse was going to win the Grand National, you could make a fortune by betting on it. But that action would change the odds. One only has to see *Back to the Future* to realize what problems could arise.

This paradox about being able to predict one's actions is closely related to the problem I mentioned earlier: Will the ultimate theory determine that we come to the right conclusions about the ultimate theory? In that case, I argued that Darwin's idea of natural selection would lead us to the correct answer. Maybe the correct answer is not the right way to describe it, but natural selection should at least lead us to a set of physical laws that work fairly well. However, we cannot apply those physical laws to deduce human behavior for two reasons. First, we cannot solve the equations. Second, even if we could, the fact of making a prediction would disturb the system. Instead, natural selection seems to lead to us adopting the effective theory of free will. If one accepts that a person's actions are freely chosen, one cannot then argue that in some cases they are determined by outside forces. The concept of "almost free will" doesn't make sense. But people tend to confuse the fact that one may be able to guess what an individual is likely to choose with the notion that the choice is not free. I would guess that most of you will have a meal this evening, but you are quite free to choose to go to bed hungry. One example of such confusion is the doctrine of diminished responsibility: the idea that persons should not be punished for their actions because they were under stress. It may be that someone is more likely to commit an antisocial act when under stress. But that does not mean that we should make it even more likely that he or she commit the act by reducing the punishment.

One has to keep the investigation of the fundamental laws of science and the study of human behavior in separate compartments. One cannot use the fundamental laws to deduce human behavior, for the reasons I have explained. But one might hope that we could employ both the intelligence and the powers of logical thought that we have developed through natural selection. Unfortunately, natural selection has also developed other characteristics, such as aggression. Aggression would have given a survival advantage in cave dweller days and earlier and so would have been favored by natural selection. The tremendous increase in our powers of destruction brought about by modern science and technology, however, has made aggression a very dangerous quality, one that threatens the survival of the whole human race. The trouble is, our aggressive instincts seem to be encoded in our DNA. DNA changes by biological evolution only on a time scale of millions of years, but our powers of destruction are increasing on a time scale for the evolution of information, which is now only twenty or thirty years. Unless we can use our intelligence to control our aggression, there is not much chance for the human race. Still, while there's life, there's hope. If we can survive the next hundred years or so, we will have spread to other planets and possibly to other stars. This will make it much less likely that the entire human race will be wiped out by a calamity such as a nuclear war.

To recapitulate: I have discussed some of the problems that arise if one believes that everything in the universe is determined. It doesn't make much difference whether this determination is due to an omnipotent God or to the laws of science. Indeed, one could always say that the laws of science are the expression of the will of God.

I considered three questions: First, how can the complexity of the universe and all its trivial details be determined by a simple set of equations? Alternatively, can one really believe that God chose all the trivial details, like who should be on the cover of *Cosmopolitan*?

The answer seems to be that the uncertainty principle of quantum mechanics means that there is not just a single history for the universe but a whole family of possible histories. These histories may be similar on very large scales, but they will differ greatly on normal, everyday scales. We happen to live on one particular history that has certain properties and details. But there are very similar intelligent beings who live on histories that differ in who won the war and who is Top of the Pops. Thus, the trivial details of our universe arise because the fundamental laws incorporate quantum mechanics with its element of uncertainty or randomness.

The second question was: If everything is determined by some fundamental theory, then what we say about the theory is also determined by the theory—and why should it be determined to be correct, rather than just plain wrong or irrelevant? My answer to this was to appeal to Darwin's theory of natural selection: Only those individuals who drew the appropriate conclusions about the world around them would be likely to survive and reproduce.

The third question was: If everything is determined, what becomes of free will and our responsibility for our actions? But the only objective test of whether an organism has free will is whether its behavior can be predicted. In the case of human beings, we are quite unable to use the fundamental laws to predict what people will do, for two reasons. First, we cannot solve the equations for the very large number of particles involved. Second, even if we could solve the equations, the fact of making a prediction would disturb the system and could lead to a different outcome. So as we cannot predict human behavior, we may as well adopt the effective theory that humans are free agents who can choose what to do. It seems that there are definite survival advantages to believing in free will and responsibility for one's actions. That means this belief should be reinforced by natural selection. Whether the language-transmitted sense of responsibility is sufficient to control the DNA-transmitted instinct of aggression remains to be seen. If it does not, the human race will have been one of natural selection's dead ends. Maybe some other race of intelligent beings elsewhere in the galaxy will achieve a better balance between responsibility and aggression. But if so, we might have expected to be contacted by them, or at least to detect their radio signals. Maybe they are aware of our existence but don't want to reveal themselves to us. That might be wise, given our record.

In summary, the title of this essay was a question: Is everything determined? The answer is yes, it is. But it might as well not be, because we can never know what is determined.

SCIENCE AND PHILOSOPHY

Predestination, determinism, and *unified theory* are concepts that have been considered for many centuries by great minds. Someone unfamiliar with these terms can always learn them and learn about them from reading this essay and the book from which it was taken because Hawking's writing is meant for general readers, not only specialized scientists. Knowing the terms before reading the essay is helpful, of course, because Hawking builds upon these basic ideas as he moves through the discussion. As a rule, having a good vocabulary helps a person read better and learn new words faster. In the same way, grasping general concepts makes one not only more knowledgeable but also more able to build expanded ideas on top of the concepts already in one's own possession. Opportunities for learning are always with us, but the universe is a complex place, and sometimes it takes complex reading and thinking to delve into its secrets. The more one knows, the more one is capable of learning.

We tend to think of scientists as they are portrayed in movies and television, as men and women in white coats who concentrate rigorously on facts and conclusions alone. Indeed, reliance on physical evidence and provable results is the bedrock of scientific thinking. But an entire area of science is the discipline of scientific philosophy: the known facts are presented, but what do they mean? What implications do those facts and conclusions carry? Some scientists meditate deeply on the meanings of facts and their relevance to our understandings of the nature of our world, and those scientists' thoughts join with those of artists and other thinkers. Slowly those ideas become part of the worldview of everyday society. It is not easy to work at the forefront of the intellectual universe, but Stephen Hawking is among those who have trained themselves to do it.

Study Questions

1. Illustrate the difference between free will and determinism by using specific examples. Take coming to class: Was it an act of choice? Or was it in various ways determined by your environment, your fears of failing the course, your background, your own desires, or some ultimate plan of God? If a leaf falls from a tree in your backyard, is the fall, and the

detachment from the branch, determined solely by physical forces? Does the leaf have, in any sense, free will? Does a dog chasing a cat have free will? Does a human eating a sandwich have free will? (Does the sandwich?)

2. Notice the organizational pattern of this essay: Hawking begins by setting up three problems with the existence of a "grand unified theory" of determinism. He spends the central part of the essay dealing with the various ramifications of the issue, then returns to his central focus: "To recapitulate: I have discussed some of the problems that arise if one believes that everything in the universe is determined." He then reexamines his first three questions. How does that pattern of organization help the reader through the essay?

3. According to Hawking, the mental abilities that have evolved in humans, such as language, were helpful for survival. Now, those mental abilities, encoded in our DNA, are used for other purposes. What are those other purposes?

Writing Topics

1. *Collaborative writing activity.* Stage a dialogue or debate between a supporter of free will and a supporter of determinism, using specific instances such as those in Study Question #1. Have one person represent one side and another person the other side, or divide the group into two halves. Make sure that each side remains consistent; avoid the tendency for both sides to move toward the middle ground and say that some things are determined while others are a matter of choice. Try, for the sake of this exercise, to avoid compromise, so that the two positions are consistently clear and separate.

2. Hawking draws on the work of contemporary evolutionary biologists when he writes, "There has been no significant biological evolution, or change in human DNA, in the last ten thousand years." Thus, all human beings are essentially biologically the same; the differences between modern people and prehistoric people are superficial. Write an essay in which you discuss the political or social implications of that idea.

From
A Small Place

JAMAICA KINCAID

If you go to Antigua as a tourist, this is what you will see. If you come by aeroplane, you will land at the V. C. Bird International Airport. Vere Cornwall (V. C.) Bird is the Prime Minister of Antigua. You may be the sort of tourist who would wonder why a Prime Minister would want an airport named after him—why not a school, why not a hospital, why not some great public monument? You are a tourist and you have not yet seen a school in Antigua, you have not yet seen the hospital in Antigua, you have not yet seen a public monument in Antigua. As your plane descends to land, you might say, What a beautiful island Antigua is—more beautiful than any of the other islands you have seen, and they were very beautiful, in their way, but they were much too green, much too lush with vegetation, which indicated to you, the tourist, that they got quite a bit of rainfall, and rain is the very thing that you, just now, do not want, for you are thinking of the hard and cold and dark and long days you spent working in North America (or, worse, Europe), earning some money so that you could stay in this place (Antigua) where the sun always shines and where the climate is deliciously hot and dry for the four to ten days you are going to be staying there; and since you are on your holiday, since you are a tourist, the thought of what it might be like for someone who had to live day in, day out in a place that suffers constantly from drought, and so has to watch carefully every drop of fresh water used (while at the same time surrounded by a sea and an ocean—the Caribbean Sea on one side, the Atlantic Ocean on the other), must never cross your mind.

You disembark from your plane. You go through customs. Since you are a tourist, a North American or European—to be frank, white—and not an Antiguan black returning to Antigua from Europe or North America with cardboard boxes of much needed cheap clothes and food for relatives, you move through customs swiftly, you move through customs with ease. Your bags are not searched. You emerge from customs into the hot, clean air: immediately you

463

feel cleansed, immediately you feel blessed (which is to say special); you feel free. You see a man, a taxi driver; you ask him to take you to your destination; he quotes you a price. You immediately think that the price is in the local currency, for you are a tourist and you are familiar with these things (rates of exchange) and you feel even more free, for things seem so cheap, but then your driver ends by saying, "In U.S. currency." You may say, "Hmmmm, do you have a formal sheet that lists official prices and destinations?" Your driver obeys the law and shows you the sheet, and he apologises for the incredible mistake he has made in quoting you a price off the top of his head which is so vastly different (favouring him) from the one listed. You are driven to your hotel by this taxi driver in his taxi, a brand-new Japanese-made vehicle. The road on which you are travelling is a very bad road, very much in need of repair. You are feeling wonderful, so you say, "Oh, what a marvellous change these bad roads are from the splendid highways I am used to in North America." (Or, worse, Europe.) Your driver is reckless; he is a dangerous man who drives in the middle of the road when he thinks no other cars are coming in the opposite direction, passes other cars on blind curves that run uphill, drives at sixty miles an hour on narrow, curving roads when the road sign, a rusting, beat-up thing left over from colonial days, says 40 MPH. This might frighten you (you are on your holiday; you are a tourist); this might excite you (you are on your holiday; you are a tourist), though if you are from New York and take taxis you are used to this style of driving: most of the taxi drivers in New York are from places in the world like this. You are looking out the window (because you want to get your money's worth); you notice that all the cars you see are brand-new, or almost brand-new, and that they are all Japanese-made. There are no American cars in Antigua—no new ones, at any rate; none that were manufactured in the last ten years. You continue to look at the cars and you say to yourself, Why, they look brand-new, but they have an awful sound, like an old car—a very old, dilapidated car. How to account for that? Well, possibly it's because they use leaded gasoline in these brand-new cars whose engines were built to use non-leaded gasoline, but you mustn't ask the person driving the car if this is so, because he or she has never heard of unleaded gasoline. You look closely at the car; you see that it's a model of a Japanese car that you might hesitate to buy; it's a model that's very expensive; it's a model that's quite impractical for a person who has to work as hard as you do and who watches every penny you earn so that you can afford this holiday you are on. How do they afford such a car? And do they live in a luxurious house to match such a car? Well, no. You will be surprised, then, to see that most likely the person driving this brand-new car filled with the wrong gas lives in a house that, in comparison, is far beneath the status of the car; and if you were to ask why you would be told that the banks are encouraged by the government to make loans available for cars, but loans for houses not so easily available; and if you ask again why, you will be told that the two main car dealerships in Antigua are owned in part or outright by ministers in government. Oh, but you are on holiday and the sight of these brand-new cars driven by people who may or may not have really passed their driving test (there was once a scandal about driving licences for sale) would not really stir up these thoughts in you. You pass a building sitting in a sea of dust and you think, It's some latrines for people just passing by, but when you look again you see the building has written on it PIGOTT'S SCHOOL. You pass the hospital, the Holberton Hospital, and how wrong you are not to think about this, for though you are a tourist on your holiday, what if your heart should miss a few beats? What if a blood vessel in your neck should break? What if one of those people driving those brand-new cars filled with the wrong gas fails to pass safely while going uphill on a curve and you are in the car going in the opposite direction? Will you be comforted to know that the hospital is staffed with doctors that no actual Antiguan trusts; that Antiguans always say about the doctors, "I don't want them near me"; that Antiguans refer to them not as doctors but as "the three men" (there are three of them); that when the Minister of Health himself doesn't feel well he takes the first plane to New York to see a real doctor; that if any one of the ministers in government needs medical care he flies to New York to get it?

It's a good thing that you brought your own books with you, for you couldn't just go to the library and borrow some. Antigua used to have a splendid library, but in The Earthquake (everyone talks about it that way—The Earthquake; we Antiguans, for I am one, have a great sense of things, and the more meaningful the thing, the more meaningless we make it) the library building was damaged. This was in 1974, and soon after that a sign was placed on the front of the building saying, THIS BUILDING WAS DAMAGED IN THE EARTHQUAKE OF 1974. REPAIRS ARE PENDING. The sign hangs there, and hangs there more than a decade later, with its unfulfilled promise of repair, and you might see this as a sort of quaintness on the part of these islanders, these people descended from slaves—what a strange, unusual perception of time they have. REPAIRS ARE PENDING, and here it is many years later, but perhaps in a world that is twelve miles long and nine miles wide (the size of Antigua) twelve years and twelve minutes and twelve days are all the same. The library is one of those splendid old buildings from colonial times, and the sign telling of the repairs is a splendid old sign from colonial times. Not very long after The Earthquake Antigua got its independence from Britain, making Antigua a state in its own right, and Antiguans are so proud of this that each year, to mark the day, they go to church and thank God, a British God, for this. But you should not think of the confusion that must lie in all that and you must not think of the damaged library. You have brought your own books with you, and among them is one of those new books about economic history, one of those books explaining how the West (meaning Europe and North America after its conquest and settlement by Europeans) got rich: the West got rich not from the free (free—in this case meaning got-for-nothing) and then undervalued labour, for generations, of the people like me you see walking around you in Antigua but from the ingenuity of small shopkeepers in Sheffield and Yorkshire and Lancashire, or wherever; and what a great part the invention of the wristwatch played in it, for there was nothing noble-minded men could not do when they discovered they could slap time on their wrists just like that (isn't that the last straw; for not only did we have to suffer the unspeakableness of slavery, but the satisfaction to be had from "We made you bastards rich" is taken away, too), and so you needn't let that slightly funny feeling you have from time to time about exploitation, oppression, domination develop into full-fledged unease, discomfort; you could ruin your holiday. They are not responsible for what you have; you owe them nothing; in fact, you did them a big favour, and you can provide one hundred examples. For here you are now, passing by Government House. And here you are now, passing by the Prime Minister's Office and the Parliament Building, and overlooking these, with a splendid view of St. John's Harbour, the American Embassy. If it were not for you, they would not have Government House, and Prime Minister's Office, and Parliament Building and embassy of powerful country. Now you are passing a mansion, an extraordinary house painted the colour of old cow dung, with more aerials and antennas attached to it than you will see even at the American Embassy. The people who live in this house are a merchant family who came to Antigua from the Middle East less than twenty years ago. When this family first came to Antigua, they sold dry goods door to door from suitcases they carried on their backs. Now they own a lot of Antigua; they regularly lend money to the government, they build enormous (for Antigua), ugly (for Antigua), concrete buildings in

Antigua's capital, St. John's, which the government then rents for huge sums of money; a member of their family is the Antiguan Ambassador to Syria; Antiguans hate them. Not far from this mansion is another mansion, the home of a drug smuggler. Everybody knows he's a drug smuggler, and if just as you were driving by he stepped out of his door your driver might point him out to you as the notorious person that he is, for this drug smuggler is so rich people say he buys cars in tens—ten of this one, ten of that one—and that he bought a house (another mansion) near Five Islands, contents included, with cash he carried in a suitcase: three hundred and fifty thousand American dollars, and, to the surprise of the seller of the house, lots of American dollars were left over. Overlooking the drug smuggler's mansion is yet another mansion, and leading up to it is the best paved road in all of Antigua—even better than the road that was paved for the Queen's visit in 1985 (when the Queen came, all the roads that she would travel on were paved anew, so that the Queen might have been left with the impression that riding in a car in Antigua was a pleasant experience). In this mansion lives a woman sophisticated people in Antigua call Evita. She is a notorious woman. She's young and beautiful and the girlfriend of somebody very high up in the government. Evita is notorious because her relationship with this high government official has made her the owner of boutiques and property and given her a say in cabinet meetings, and all sorts of other privileges such a relationship would bring a beautiful young woman.

Oh, but by now you are tired of all this looking, and you want to reach your destination—your hotel, your room. You long to refresh yourself; you long to eat some nice lobster, some nice local food. You take a bath, you brush your teeth. You get dressed again; as you get dressed, you look out the window. That water—have you ever seen anything like it? Far out, to the horizon, the colour of the water is navy-blue; nearer, the water is the colour of the North American sky. From there to the shore, the water is pale, silvery, clear, so clear that you can see its pinkish-white sand bottom. Oh, what beauty! Oh, what beauty! You have never seen anything like this. You are so excited. You breathe shallow. You breathe deep. You see a beautiful boy skimming the water, godlike, on a Windsurfer. You see an incredibly unattractive, fat, pastrylike-fleshed woman enjoying a walk on the beautiful sand, with a man, an incredibly unattractive, fat, pastrylike-fleshed man; you see the pleasure they're taking in their surroundings. Still standing, looking out the window, you see yourself lying on the beach, enjoying the amazing sun (a sun so powerful and yet so beautiful, the way it is always overhead as if on permanent guard, ready to stamp out any cloud that dares to darken and so empty rain on you and ruin your holiday; a sun that is your personal friend). You see yourself taking a walk on that beach, you see yourself meeting new people (only they are new in a very limited way, for they are people just like you). You see yourself eating some delicious, locally grown food. You see yourself, you see yourself . . . You must not wonder what exactly happened to the contents of your lavatory when you flushed it. You must not wonder where your bathwater went when you pulled out the stopper. You must not wonder what happened when you brushed your teeth. Oh, it might all end up in the water you are thinking of taking a swim in; the contents of your lavatory might, just might, graze gently against your ankle as you wade carefree in the water, for you see, in Antigua, there is no proper sewage-disposal system. But the Caribbean Sea is very big and the Atlantic Ocean is even bigger; it would amaze even you to know the number of black slaves this ocean has swallowed up. When you sit down to eat your delicious meal, it's better that you don't know that most of what you are eating came off a plane from Miami. And before it got on a plane in Miami, who knows where it came from? A good guess is that it came from a place like Antigua first, where it was grown dirt-cheap, went to Miami, and came back. There is a world of something in this, but I can't go into it right now.

The thing you have always suspected about yourself the minute you become a tourist is true: A tourist is an ugly human being. You are not an ugly person all the time; you are not an ugly person ordinarily; you are not an ugly person day to day. From day to day, you are a nice person. From day to day, all the people who are supposed to love you on the whole do. From day to day, as you walk down a busy street in the large and modern and prosperous city in which you work and live, dismayed, puzzled (a cliché, but only a cliché can explain you) at how alone you feel in this crowd, how awful it is to go unnoticed, how awful it is to go unloved, even as you are surrounded by more people than you could possibly get to know in a lifetime that lasted for millennia, and then out of the corner of your eye you see someone looking at you and absolute pleasure is written all over that person's face, and then you realise that you are not as revolting a presence as you think you are (for that look just told you so). And so, ordinarily, you are a nice person, an attractive person, a person capable of drawing to yourself the affection of other people (people just like you), a person at home in your own skin (sort of; I mean, in a way; I mean, your dismay and puzzlement are natural to you, because people like you just seem to be like that, and so many of the things people like you find admirable about yourselves—the things you think about, the things you think really define you—seem rooted in these feelings): a person at home in your own house (and all its nice house things), with its nice back yard (and its nice back-yard things), at home on your street, your church, in community activities, your job, at home with your family, your relatives, your friends—you are a whole person. But one day, when you are sitting somewhere, alone in that crowd, and that awful feeling of displacedness comes over you, and really, as an ordinary person you are not well equipped to look too far inward and set yourself aright, because being ordinary is already so taxing, and being ordinary takes all you have out of you, and though the words "I must get away" do not actually pass across your lips, you make a leap from being that nice blob just sitting like a boob in your amniotic sac of the modern experience to being a person visiting heaps of death and ruin and feeling alive and inspired at the sight of it; to being a person lying on some faraway beach, your stilled body stinking and glistening in the sand, looking like something first forgotten, then remembered, then not important enough to go back for; to being a person marvelling at the harmony (ordinarily, what you would say is the backwardness) and the union these other people (and they are other people) have with nature. And you look at the things they can do with a piece of ordinary cloth, the things they fashion out of cheap, vulgarly colored (to you) twine, the way they squat down over a hole they have made in the ground, the hole itself is something to marvel at, and since you are being an ugly person this ugly but joyful thought will swell inside you: their ancestors were not clever in the way yours were and not ruthless in the way yours were, for then would it not be you who would be in harmony with nature and backwards in that charming way? An ugly thing, that is what you are when you become a tourist, an ugly, empty thing, a stupid thing, a piece of rubbish pausing here and there to gaze at this and taste that, and it will never occur to you that the people who inhabit the place in which you have just paused cannot stand you, that behind their closed doors they laugh at your strangeness (you do not look the way they look); the physical sight of you does not please them; you have bad manners (it is their custom to eat their food with their hands; you try eating their way, you look silly; you try eating the way you always eat, you look silly); they do not like the way you speak (you have an accent); they collapse helpless from laughter, mimicking the way they imagine you must look as you carry out some everyday bodily function. They do not like you. *They do not like me!* That thought never actually occurs to you. Still, you feel a little uneasy. Still, you feel a little foolish. Still, you feel a little out of place. But the banality of your own life is very real to you; it drove you to this extreme, spending your days and your nights in the company of people who despise you, people you do not like really, people you would not want to have as your actual neighbour. And so you must devote yourself to puzzling out how much of what you are told is really, really true (Is ground-up bottle glass in peanut sauce really a delicacy around here, or will it do just what you think ground-up bottle glass will do? Is this rare, multicoloured, snout-mouthed fish really an aphrodisiac, or will it cause you to fall asleep permanently?). Oh, the hard work all of this is, and is it any wonder, then, that on your return home you feel the need of a long rest, so that you can recover from your life as a tourist?

That the native does not like the tourist is not hard to explain. For every native of every place is a potential tourist, and every tourist is a native of somewhere. Every native everywhere lives a life of overwhelming and crushing banality and boredom and desperation and depression, and every deed, good and bad, is an attempt to forget this. Every native would like to find a way out, every native would like a rest, every native would like a tour. But some natives—most natives in the world—cannot go anywhere. They are too poor. They are too poor to go anywhere. They are too poor to escape the reality of their lives; and they are too poor to live properly in the place where they live, which is the very place you, the tourist, want to go—so when the natives see you, the tourist, they envy you, they envy your ability to leave your own banality and boredom, they envy your ability to turn their own banality and boredom into a source of pleasure for yourself.

IN FOCUS

IRONY

Irony deliberately sets up a conflict or contrast, generally between what is and what ought to be. Irony happens when life is not what it ought to be, but people pretend it is; it happens when what a writer or speaker says is different from what is really meant. The perceptive reader understands the surface statement and, at the same time, picks up a wry or subtle suggestion.

In drama or fiction, the difference between what a character knows and what the audience knows is termed *dramatic irony*. At the beginning of Shakespeare's *King Lear,* for example, a proud king rejects his youngest daughter because she will not say she loves him more than her sisters do; ironically, it turns out that this daughter, Cordelia, is the only child who truly loves and stands by him.

Rhetorical irony is somewhat different from dramatic, though it maintains the element of contrast. Rhetorical irony, achieved by language and illustrated in Kincaid's essay, means that the writer is saying the opposite of what he or she really means. A classic example of rhetorical irony in English literature is the opening sentence to Jane Austen's *Pride and Prejudice:* "It is a truth universally acknowledged that a single man in possession of a good fortune must be in want of a wife." Since this is obviously not a "universal truth" (does every rich bachelor want to be married?), the sentence is an ironic comment on the social codes that Austen satirizes in her novel.

Jamaica Kincaid here carries irony to the extreme, often to the point of sarcasm, in her description of the contrasts between the rich, insulated tourists and the desperately poor natives of the Caribbean island. Even the first sentence, claiming that "this is what you will see," is ironic, because it becomes obvious as the description proceeds that the tourist will never see the reality of life on the island. Kincaid's anger at the injustice of the situation is the driving force behind her essay, yet anger alone would not be nearly as effective as the technique she uses. Just as a dark background becomes even darker when a lighter object is placed in front of it, irony works because the contrast between two things is intensified as they are viewed together.

Study Questions

1. Find examples of irony in the Kincaid essay. Where does she particularly express her anger at the contrast between the tourists and the natives and the injustice therein? What does she blame for the poverty the native people live in?

2. Travel brochures show a stereotype of smiling native people giving tourists a warm welcome, but Kincaid's satire of those brochures has a different message. Behind her smile is anger and hostility. In which parts of the essay is her anger most clearly expressed?

3. Would the islanders be better off if the tourists didn't come? What do you think Kincaid's answer to that question would be? What is your answer?

Writing Topics

1. *Collaborative writing activity.* As a group, discuss places in which the lives of rich people and poor people are markedly different. How do the members of the group feel about this disparity? Do they identify with one group or the other? How, for example, do they imagine homeless people feel about those who drive past in fancy cars? How do they think the people in those cars feel?

   Make a line down a sheet of paper. Imagine a wealthy person and a poor person in the same place at the same time. On one side of the page, list things that "The Rich Person Thinks." On the other side, balance this list with things that "The Poor Person Thinks." Then write individual essays giving one or two parallel items.

2. Write an essay in the form of a letter to Jamaica Kincaid, responding to this excerpt from *A Small Place.* If you wish, take the other side, challenging Kincaid's arguments and pointing out the benefits to Antigua's economy from tourism. Or you can agree with her and make some suggestions for improving the situation.

   A good way of preparing for this essay is to do some research on Antigua or similar tropical islands or resort destinations. Use your library's periodicals index (probably computerized) to find articles and commentaries. Also, check to see whether these destinations have Internet Web sites.

Secrets
of the Heart

MAIR ZAMIR

Early in *Pride and Prejudice* the heroine, Elizabeth Bennet, strides into her neighbors' breakfast parlor after a brisk three-mile country walk, with "weary ankles, dirty stockings, and a face glowing with the warmth of exercise." The unseemly display of physical vigor outrages Lizzy's high-society friends, but the brooding Mr. Darcy disarms them by remarking, to everyone's astonishment, that her bright eyes "were brightened [even further] by the exercise."

Darcy was in love, and Jane Austen, as usual, was ahead of her time. On the whole, however, subsequent generations have come down on the side of leisure. Mark Twain put it bluntly: "Exercise is loathsome." The American educator Robert Maynard Hutchins was similarly dismissive. "Whenever I feel like exercise," he is said to have remarked, "I lie down until the feeling passes." Only in the past twenty years or so, I think it is fair to say, has physical fitness emerged as a true mass movement, one of which I approve wholeheartedly. As far as I am concerned, the explosive growth in the popularity of physical exercise is one of the best things to befall humankind in recent memory—proof that, contrary to the conventional wisdom of this jaded decade, you *can* change human nature.

Yet the scientific justification for vigorous exercise is far from being intuitively obvious. Taken strictly at face value, why should subjecting your heart to avoidable stress be any better for you than, say, gulping down a five-pound steak to give your digestive tract a workout or guzzling whisky to exercise your liver?

Of course, the heart is special. Every cell in the body needs blood, flowing blood, in order to survive, and as the organ responsible for maintaining that flow, the heart bears both a crucial responsibility and a heavy, unrelenting burden. The heart, too, needs blood in order to continue functioning. Since all the blood in the body passes through its chambers, it would be convenient if the heart could nourish itself directly, by dipping into the gusher of blood (about a third of a cup each beat, or five quarts every minute) and simply absorbing

473

whatever it needs. Unfortunately, that is not the way it is designed. Instead the heart gets its blood from the outside, through the main coronary arteries, which curl off the body's main blood pipe, the aorta, like cloverleaf exits off an interstate highway, then enter the walls of the heart and branch and rebranch, forming an intricate web of blood vessels, the coronary network. Although the supply route is indirect, it still amounts to privileged access. For one thing, it is the first exit off the sanguinary freeway. For another, the heart consumes between 4 and 5 percent of the body's blood flow, yet on average it makes up only one-half of one percent of the body's weight. Of all the organs in the body, only the brain comes close to imbibing as much blood flow for every ounce of tissue.

The coronary network of every heart is bewilderingly complicated and, in its full geometric details, as unique as a fingerprint. Its sheer quirkiness, coupled with the paramount importance of the job it does, earns the network a deep fascination. With such a wide range of variation, how can anyone hope to say anything precise about the physics of blood flow through the system? What do coronary networks have in common? Which features are crucial to their functioning, and which are incidental? Why should the network of coronary vessels, far more than similar networks in other parts of the body, be so exceptionally prone to spectacular failure? Why are heart attacks so common? Why do people hardly ever have *hand* attacks? And again, what does exercise have to do with any of it?

It was with such questions in mind that, in 1984, I embarked on one of the most fruitful collaborations of my career. I spent the year on sabbatical leave at the University Hospital in London. Ontario, studying the coronary network with Malcolm D. Silver, a pathologist who has a deep passion for the coronary arteries. Silver (now at the University of Toronto) was interested in the role of coronary vessels in heart disease. I was more intrigued by how blood passes through them. For more than ten years I had conducted theoretical studies of flow with mathematical models of blood vessels. Now I was working on real blood vessels from real human hearts.

My specialty is fluid dynamics, the study of fluid flow. In this study fluids include gases as well as liquids. Air is a fluid. So is water. So, for most purposes, is blood. All three substances can be described by the same equations, suitably modified to take into account their different physical properties (such as viscosity, compressibility and, in the case of blood, the fact that it contains discreet corpuscles). Those are the equations with which one tackles the problem of flow through the arterial network.

In essence, the problem boils down to determining the relation between two opposing forces: the pressure driving the blood, and the resistance of the vessel walls. The simplest possible vessel for delivering a fluid is a fluid-filled tube with a circular cross section and perfectly rigid walls. If the pressure is higher at one end of the tube, the fluid will flow toward the other end, retarded only by viscous drag caused by friction between the fluid and the vessel walls.

Inside the body, however, things are rarely so simple. In a main coronary artery the bloodstream is so broad and deep, relatively speaking, that the resistance of the walls is slight. A capillary, in contrast, is so thin that the red blood cells must squeeze through it laboriously, one by one, like eggs passing through the oviduct of a hen. Yet the artery and the capillary are linked with a continuous chain of branching blood vessels, each finer than the one before. Somewhere in the twenty or thirty generations of vessels that link them, the force of friction and the graininess of blood at the cellular level start to play a critical role in constraining coronary blood flow. No one knows exactly at which level of the coronary tree the so-called resistance vessels are located, or how they play their role in the heart. To answer such questions it is necessary to dig deep into the structural complexities of the coronary network, a daunting task that has engaged the Italian pathologist Antonio L'Abbate and his coworkers at the National Research Council of the Institute of Clinical Physiology in Pisa.

Another complication in real blood vessels is that the driving pressure, far from remaining constant, is forever changing. It peaks after every beat of the left ventricle. The blood, retarded by its own inertia, surges to peak flow perhaps a tenth of a second later. Because of the lag between high pressure and flow, the peak blood flow is lower than it would be under constant pressure, an effect that intensifies the faster the pressure oscillates.

More complicated still, blood vessels are not rigid tubes. They have flexible walls, and a pulse of pressure can inflate them slightly, causing an increase in volume. That elastic property, called the capacitance, may have a small effect in a single vessel, but the cumulative effect from the entire coronary network can be significant. Because of capacitance, at any moment the amount of blood that is flowing into the coronary system need not be equal to the amount flowing out. Measuring the effects of capacitance was the aim of a set of ingenious experiments conducted in the late 1980s by the biomedical engineer Robert E. Mates and his coworkers at the State University of New York at Buffalo.

Furthermore, changes in pressure and flow can send waves rippling along the vessel walls the way the wake of a boat spreads across the surface of a lake. Where conditions change (for example, where a vessel suddenly widens, narrows, stiffens, branches or comes to a dead end), the waves give off reflections, further muddying the relation between pressure and flow. Add in the fact that the entire network of vessels is embedded in the tissue of an organ that is thrashing and churning as violently as a bucking bronco, and you can understand why mathematically modeling blood flow through coronary vessels is likely to keep investigators occupied for many years to come.

The biggest complication of all, of course, is that the coronary vessels form a bewilderingly intricate network. For almost a century the basic structure of that network was a contentious issue in the study of coronary blood flow. There were two possibilities. One was a tree structure, in which each vessel branched and rebranched so that the flow through any segment could be traced upstream in exactly one way. The second possibility was a mesh, in which vessels grew additional branches—so-called collateral vessels—"sideways" across the hierarchy, like cousin marriages in a family tree.

The distinction is important. In a tree structure, pressure at the upstream end of the network gives rise to flow everywhere downstream, just as it does in a single tube. A mesh, in contrast, can suffer from dead spots or gridlock. The price of the simplicity of the tree is that a single occluded vessel chokes off the flow to every vessel downstream of it. In a mesh the blood may be able to find a detour through a handy collateral branch. As far as safety is concerned, then, a tree structure is an all-or-nothing strategy, the coronary equivalent of a passenger jet aircraft with one engine.

While physiologists debated whether the body favors safety or efficiency, physicians continued making diagnoses. Advances in vascular imaging made it possible to return ever more precise verdicts: one-vessel disease, two-vessel disease, 50 percent stenosis of the left circumflex artery. Yet without knowing how the network as a whole is connected, there is no sound way of judging just how serious a particular occlusion might be or which part of the heart it might affect. It is as if the hydraulic engineers in New York City's water department possessed just one map, showing the spots where the major aqueducts enter Manhattan and where pipes feed into a few big hotels and office buildings, and nothing else. The engineers could be sure that a breakdown in a main pipe would cause problems somewhere, and over time they would learn that certain smaller pipes affect certain neighborhoods, but as for the master plan—the detailed linkages between aqueduct, pipe and neighborhood—they would be completely in the dark. Of course, any knowledge they did glean would be all but useless to hydraulic engineers in Toronto, London or Paris, because cities, like hearts, are unique.

Today investigators are still far from drafting a master map of the vasculature of the heart, but important progress has been made toward that goal. The major outlines have been drawn in, and sketching is proceeding apace. A useful tool in the work is a cast of the coronary network, made by injecting a specimen heart with a slow-hardening liquid plastic that fills the vasculature all the way down to the capillaries. The heart tissue can then be dissolved away with potassium-hydroxide solution, more commonly known as lye. The result is an accurate three-dimensional replica—a heart-shaped nest of vessels that reveals almost every twist, tangle and byway in the coronary network. In some places (such as the walls of the left ventricle, which does the heavy work of pumping blood through the body) the vasculature is so dense that it is hard to see where there was room for the muscle fibers it served.

Among other things, coronary casts played a central role in settling the mesh-versus-tree debate concerning the basic structure of the human coronary network. Early studies favored a mesh structure, mainly because the hearts of some other species, such as dogs, harbor a profusion of lateral branches. Examination of human hearts, however, gradually showed that, in general, the coronary network follows the safety-last structure of an open tree. Occasionally a few vessels forge collateral connections with other vessels; but those alternative routes are thought to play only minor roles in the scheme of things, and they are not a permanent feature of the coronary landscape. In 1967 an extensive study by the Italian pathologist Giorgio Baroldi and his coworkers, conducted at the University of Milan and at the Armed Forces Institute of Pathology in Washington, D.C., showed that collateral vasculature in the human heart is both transient and highly variable and that it occurs most frequently in networks afflicted with coronary disease.

Determining the underlying fluid-dynamic design of the coronary network was one objective of my work with Malcolm Silver. It would be stretching the truth to say that our collaboration got off to a roaring start. Silver's background is in pathology and medicine; mine is in engineering and applied mathematics. At first my questions of measure and quantity, angles and diameters, seemed as bizarre to him as his preoccupation with diagnostic symptoms of heart disease seemed to me. But our shared intense interest in the coronary network prevailed, and together we amassed a wealth of quantitative data that enabled us to tackle the design questions I had brought to the work.

The main result of our work was to add to the map of the coronary Manhattan the equivalent of a system of neighborhood mains. Silver and I proposed that the coronary network supplies the heart by dividing it into six zones. Each of the six major coronary arteries (the left and right main coronary arteries, the anterior and posterior descending arteries and the obtuse and acute marginal arteries) acts as a "distributing vessel," conveying blood to the borders of different zones. Offshoots of the artery then enter the zones as "delivering vessels" that branch profusely and carry the blood to the tissue cells within the zones.

Each zone is framed by two or three distributing vessels and is penetrated by the delivering vessels that arise from them. The sizes and shapes of the zones, and even the particular arteries that border a zone, may change from one heart to the next, but the relations between the zones and the distributing and delivering vessels remain the same. Those relations are important for assessing the true significance of a disease of a particular coronary artery in a particular heart. Having spotted a diseased artery, one must determine whether the artery is a distributing or a delivering vessel, which zone or zones of the heart it serves and which other coronary arteries serve the affected area. Only in that way is it possible to reach a meaningful assessment of the problem.

What especially impressed me about the coronary network is how extraordinarily adaptable it is. The vascular system, I came to realize, can adapt and shape itself to fit the needs of the body, and then readapt and reshape itself when those needs change. Investigators have not yet pinned down the precise molecular or cellular processes that trigger and sustain such vascular growth. The question is probably closely tied to the broader fundamental question of biological growth and development in general, and no doubt it will occupy investigators for years to come. From the perspective of fluid dynamics, however, the crucial point is that the vascular system can build new pathways for blood flow if it is triggered to do so, provided it has some local vasculature to build on and enough time to do the building.

The trigger is need. As long as an organism is growing, the need for new vasculature is clear and unrelenting, driven by the growth of the tissue that demands blood. Later the vascular system can still improvise new vasculature to fortify infected tissue, to rebuild or reroute blood flow around an injury or, more sinisterly, to feed the growth of a tumor. It appears that, whenever and wherever demand-driven growth takes place, it starts when body tissue soaks up oxygen from the interlaced capillaries. As the local concentration of oxygen in the blood drops, that of carbon dioxide rises. The vessels dilate to admit higher flow to the tissue. Over time the capillary bed thickens; the small vessels that feed the capillary mesh become larger and possibly start to grow new branches.

In the heart improvisatory growth is too slow to deal with sudden obstructions such as thromboembolisms. It copes better with the more slowly developing condition of atherosclerosis, in which lesions in the vessel wall gradually choke off the flow of blood. But even with years to work its magic, the rerouting mechanism often fails. The overwhelming majority of heart failures are associated with atherosclerosis. Indeed, the heart seems peculiarly prone to such failures. Atherosclerosis can strike blood vessels anywhere in the body, but nowhere else does it so often lead to dire consequences.

So what makes the vascular system of the heart so prone to failure? And why are you unlikely to suffer a hand attack?

It is not that the hand has a better blood-supply system. If anything, the coronary network ought to be more robust than the vasculature elsewhere in the body, because, as noted above, pound for pound it carries eight to ten times as much blood on average as the vasculature in the rest of the body does. It can easily handle higher volumes still. When the heart is suddenly called upon to work at maximum effort (for example, when a jogger hops out of bed and hits the pavement for a before-breakfast run), the flow through the coronary network can quintuple rapidly, possibly within a minute.

Paradoxically, that excess capacity may be the Achilles' heel of the coronary network. Because of it, when a coronary artery is slowly obstructed, the network can comfortably keep the blood flowing for some time without causing any heart tissue to feel needy, and thus without spurring the vascular system to deal with the obstruction. Only when the reserve capacity is exhausted—when the obstruction becomes so severe that the reserve can no longer cope with it—does some tissue become needy, triggering the improvisatory powers of the system. By that time the coronary network may have nothing extra left to give. If the heart is suddenly called upon to work at maximum effort, the network cannot deliver the blood flow needed to keep it working. One game of touch football with the grandchildren, and disaster strikes.

I like to illustrate that state of affairs with a financial analogy. Imagine I open a bank account with an initial deposit of $5,000. After I open the account, I deposit $1,000 a month to cover all my expenditures. The $5,000 is there as a cushion, enough to cover occasional spending binges; as long as my income and expenditures balance in the long run, the cushion will remain intact. But there is a catch: the bank does not issue regular statements. It will get in touch with me only if my account slips into the red.

That troubles me not a little, because I am hopeless at keeping track of my money. I know that as long as my overall balance stays high, the bank will consider me a valuable enough customer to shrug off an occasional bounced check. But I also know that, with my $5,000 cushion staving off overdrafts, I could inadvertently draw down my account for a long time without a word of warning from the bank. If I let it slide far enough, my tough-minded 1990s bank manager might decide that my account is marginal and seize the very next hint of red ink as an excuse to shut me down.

Although the analogy must not be pushed too far, such a bank account has some important points in common with the coronary network. Think of the $5,000 as the occasional large coronary output needed to engage in some heavy physical activity. The overdraft notices from the bank represent signals from cardiac tissue demanding more blood flow. A youthful coronary network can readily muster enough reserve flow to meet the demands of heavy activity. And like the valuable bank customer who occasionally bounces a check, such a healthy cardiovascular system can generally make an effective response to the occasional deficit.

As my vessels inevitably stiffen with age and fall prey to the ravages of atherosclerosis, the coronary reserve continues to make it easy to engage in moderate, everyday activity, supplying the blood my heart tissue needs. But in so doing the coronary reserve may be doing my heart no favors. For if tissue is not challenged by reduced blood flow, there is nothing to trigger the critical warning signals that stimulate vascular growth. Only when vascular disease and obstructions become so bad that the capacity of the existing network can barely get the blood through—when the reserve is exhausted and the account is on the verge of plunging into the red—does the improvising mechanism get the message that something is wrong. But by that time it may be too late: the diseased vessels may have deteriorated so far that even a moderate exertion will push heart tissue into a spiraling blood deficit from which the heart cannot recover. Like the response of the bank to a marginal customer who maintains a low balance and then writes a bad check, the response of a diseased heart to exertion may be a rapid shutdown.

Clearly, with money as with blood flow, I need some way of making sure that my reserve stays intact. In the case of the bank, the secret is to challenge my account. Every now and then, on a reasonably regular basis, I must write a check for $5,000, then sit tight and wait for a notice from the bank. If the notice does not come, I know the reserve is intact. If the notice comes, I know the reserve has been eroded and I must do something about it.

The same solution applies to my heart, except that the challenge it needs is physical activity. If I remain sedentary, never spending more than my normal $1,000 by taking a short walk from room to room inside my house, I can all too easily let myself slide into insolvency. But as long as I exercise—as long as I write the occasional check for $5,000 to test the reserve in my account—the coronary network receives the signals it needs to compensate for vascular insufficiency.

What about other parts of the body, such as the hands? In a hand the demand for blood flow varies over a much narrower range than it does in the heart. To extend the financial analogy, the hand's account has only a modest reserve. Any small monthly imbalances in the account get noticed, and dealt with, more promptly than they do in the heart. In any case, such imbalances are relatively rare: for reasons not fully understood, coronary arteries are particularly susceptible to the ravages of atherosclerosis. For better and for worse, it seems, the heart is special.

Evidently, what anyone who values a healthy heart should be concerned about is the ability of the coronary network to provide the heart with peak amounts of blood flow. The coronary network must be regularly challenged to maintain that ability, to maintain its reserve—continually spurred to seek new pathways and enlarge existing ones. Because such vascular growth is triggered by need, the growth will come about only if the heart works much harder than usual to meet an increased demand for blood flow in the body. And the key to creating that demand is physical activity—exercise.

A Scientist Writes

Mair Zamir's essay was written for a general educated audience, not a group of scientists. Had it been a scientific report, it would have been in a completely different form, accompanied by mathematical equations, charts, and graphs and structured in the format of an experimental report. Instead, this essay can be read by anyone—anyone, at least, with the basic background in science and mathematics that a high school education ought to have provided.

What about the people whose educational backgrounds, or lack thereof, have left them unable to read even simple scientific reports, such as those in newspapers? Most, of course, become victims— victims of ideologies that have no real basis in fact, victims of predators who sell crystals or peach pits as medicines, victims of whatever belief system happens along and seems attractive. This is not to say that the peach-pit cure won't, in fact, eventually be shown to have some validity. But the person who cannot understand and evaluate the methods of real science—serious, controlled experimentation with a healthy respect for reliable evidence—will never be able to distinguish the functional from the fake.

The key to effectively reading scientific writing is to be unafraid of the vocabulary. A reader of the Zamir article who learned the meaning of "fluid dynamics" in an elementary physics class is, of course, ahead (that is the advantage a good education confers), but the concept is not difficult. One good method of reading a scientific article is to skim it first for the general meaning, then go back and underline every unfamiliar word. Write the meanings of the specialized words in the margins. Finally, read the article again, noting how the terms are used. This method considerably slows down the reading, but the advantage is the tremendous increase not only in vocabulary but also in scientific understanding—understanding that can be put to very effective use in reading the next scientific article. Developing a good scientific vocabulary, as well as a knowledge of how experimentation and scientific thinking operate, is a process that pays back enormously—in the life of a person and of a nation.

Study Questions

1. Summarize Zamir's answer to the question of why exercise is good for the heart. Why would anyone think that it might *not* be (see the third paragraph)?

Notice that understanding how the cardiovascular system works is the key to accepting Zamir's argument. To test your understanding of the processes involved, trace the system as Zamir describes it.

2. What is the science of fluid dynamics, and how does it apply to anatomy? What other areas and natural studies might fluid dynamics apply to?

3. In what way is Zamir's use of fluid dynamics to explain the operation of the cardiovascular system an example of analogy?

3. The true scientist looks at phenomena that other people might simply accept, and asks the question "Why?" Most people do not question the idea that exercise is good for us, but Zamir begins with a challenge: Why should subjecting the heart to stress, when stress is normally a bad thing, be good for one's health?

Try the scientist's approach yourself. Think of at least three ideas that nearly everyone seems to accept without question, and apply the question "Why?" to each of those ideas.

Writing Topics

1. *Collaborative writing activity.* As a group, compare members' educations in science. Was the training adequate? Did it leave you with an understanding of and respect for the scientific method? How effective are the different ways that science is taught these days? Then write individual essays in which you evaluate contemporary science education, giving examples, and make some suggestions for improvement.

2. Does knowing how the body works, knowing that the heart is subject to mechanical forces that can be mathematically explained and described, make the human body seem more or less wonderful? How does this knowledge fit with whatever story of creation you were told as a child? Does religion have any place in a scientific world? Write an essay in which you discuss the conflicts between scientific knowledge and religious belief.

3. Most people know that exercise is good for them, yet many people get very little exercise. Probably you know people who don't have enough physical activity in their lives. Write an essay in which you analyze the reasons that people don't get the exercise they need, and offer some specific suggestions for improvement.

Reductio Expansioque ad Absurdum

DOUGLAS R. HOFSTADTER

In memory of Kees Boeke,
author of Cosmic View

I. REDUCTIO

Scale One

She swung around the bend—a little too fast, she knew, but she
needed to get there quickly. Her headlights bounced across the
snow, revealing corrugated mounds several feet high at the road's
edge, lining the fields. She stepped on the accelerator again and
gunned the car down a straight stretch. Ahead she saw a haystack
and realized another bend was coming. Timing it carefully, she put
on the brakes and careened around the bend to the left, almost but
not quite skidding out of control. Risky? She knew it was, yet it
was exhilarating at the same time—living at the edge of the abyss,
tempting fate.

Her headlights' glare caught something—something moving—
something darting ahead. What's that? She slammed on the brakes.
There was a loud noise as a deer smashed into her car's front end,
bumper then hood then windshield, all in a fraction of a second, all
blindingly fast, leaving her windshield a shattered web of white with
a large hole in it where the antlers and then the head had pierced.
The car was still going forty miles an hour when the deer's antlers entered her skull.

Scale Two

A piece of antler horn was moving slowly through the air, first
left, then right, then bobbing up and down a bit. A suddenly loud-
growing roar was accompanied by a freezing-in-place of the bit of
horn. Only half a second later, there was an enormously loud sound
and the piece of horn jerked wildly. Suddenly it was being dragged
along at forty miles an hour and in a strange path.

The piece of horn bounced down and slid across a cold, painted metal surface and in a tenth of a second encountered a thick sheet of glass. By itself, it would just have glanced off the glass, but it was part of a much larger piece of horn that was attached to a large massive object that was also being propelled in a strange, violent path toward the glass. So the horn, when it hit the glass, exerted much force on the sheet, and in a thousandth of a second, the sheet yielded and then cracked, with glassy splinters moving away in several directions at once from the hole the horn was opening up, while a little farther away, rays of white were shooting through the glass and forming an intricate, dense, crisscrossing web of fracture lines. The end of the piece of horn was now quite blunted, but it continued to move in approximately the same trajectory, as it was still attached to the larger body behind it, close on its heels, moving toward the glass, where it would soon open up a much larger gaping hole.

The horn fragment was now in open air, not too many inches from a suspended mirror. It was moving at about thirty-five miles an hour relative to the mirror, having been slightly slowed down by the collision with the glass. Now it quickly crossed a one-foot stretch of empty space, and then encountered a piece of softer material—a light-colored, warm membrane, which it instantaneously pierced. This membrane covered a heavier piece of bone a quarter of an inch thick, which offered as much resistance as the glass had. It was moving toward the mirror at about five miles an hour, so the horn entered the bone at nearly forty miles an hour. Again the large mass behind it impelled it forward and the bone gave way, splintering and cracking audibly.

Beyond the bone there was a very soft mass of sticky substance much warmer than the outside air. The piece of horn moved swiftly into that substance, which was so viscous that it soon impeded the horn's further motion after a couple of inches. The horn came to rest lodged in a hunk of red, oozing, spongy matter, warm and pulsing.

Scale Three

A packet of neurons was firing away rhythmically, receiving and sending pulses every few milliseconds. Its many thousands of neurons were all engaged in a collective mode, like birds in a flock, so that when one altered its activity, all the others were quickly affected and a ripple would pass through the many neurons, putting the team into a slightly different collective mode. Every eight milliseconds, roughly, the periodic pulsing of this particular mode took place. As regular as an oscilloscope trace of a slowly changing sound, the pattern repeated. Each cycle was just barely distinguishable from the preceding one—an adiabatically changing pattern.

Then an anomalous pulse train came in from another team of neurons that didn't usually communicate with this team. Its pulses were a little faster than normal, and they had an imperative quality to them. The pulse pattern was thus disrupted from its slowly drifting, adiabatically shifting periodic firing pattern, and it made a rather abrupt transition into a different mode.

In this mode it carried out about a dozen complete cycles when another disruptive event took place: several hundred of its neurons were severed from the main body (which contained around eight thousand neurons altogether), and no more influence from them was felt. Thus the firing pattern was again altered and became less periodic, for the usual stabilizing effect of the closed system was gone. The pulsing was a little irregular but continued for many thousands of periods longer. Then it slowly ebbed, and there was a gradual cessation of firing.

Scale Four

A retinal cell was firing away quite intensely. Its job was to respond to a brightness gradient oriented at about sixty degrees from the horizontal, relative to the straight-ahead gaze of the eye to which it belonged (although it knew nothing of eyes or their gazes). The cell was firing fairly rapidly because there was, in fact, just such a brightness gradient, a fairly strong one, at forty degrees, which was close enough to sixty degrees to induce a pretty strong firing rate.

A few milliseconds passed, and the intensity gradient shifted to the next cell. At the first cell, then, the intensity became zero and so the cell slowed up in its firing. A few more milliseconds passed, and then there was a new intensity gradient, this one at about fifty degrees from the horizontal. The cell obediently switched back to a high firing rate—slightly higher than before, in fact. It stayed this way for many thousands of cycles. In fact, it was an unusually constant stimulus, for generally such stimuli changed within a small fraction of a second. But this one just stayed at exactly the same spot for so many cycles that cellular fatigue set in and the cell fired less intensely.

The cell continued to fire sporadically but began to have less and less fuel to supply its energy for firing. Usually fuel was delivered regularly, allowing firing to go ahead without any trouble. But now, for some reason, fuel supplies were diminishing, and, like the clicks of a winding-down music box, each individual pulse threatened to be the very last one, and yet the next always just barely managed to occur.

And then one time it didn't. There wasn't enough energy to make it go one more time. The cell stopped firing altogether.

Scale Five

A ribosome was clicking away, codon by codon, down a very long strand of messenger RNA. This strand was exactly like the other strand that the ribosome had run down a while earlier, but it didn't know that. It simply chugged along, and codon by codon snapped a transfer-RNA molecule into place and fastened an amino acid onto a growing polypeptide chain.

Click-click-click-click . . . Over and over, repetitive work. This ribosome was inside a mitochondrion, inside a retinal cell, inside a— but that is hardly the point. It was doing its job. It had plenty of ATP floating nearby to power the reactions that snapped off the amino acids from the strangely shaped tRNAs. The ATP molecules were small and floated near the ribosome, where they were automatically attracted whenever tRNAs entered a certain channel and were guided into a special narrow chamber deep within the ribosome.

Usually the density of ATP molecules was such that several thousand of them clustered around the ribosome. Right now, however, there were only a couple of thousand, and so the ribosome's progress was slightly retarded. Consequently, this particular copy of this familiar enzyme came off the assembly line in about twice the time it usually took. As the protein grew, new ATPs floated into the vicinity of the ribosome to take the place of ones that had been used. However, there were slightly fewer, even, to replace the used ones, and the ribosome consequently worked a little more slowly. Still, it chugged smoothly down the irregularly winding strand of messenger RNA.

As the ATPs got sparser, the ribosome slowed down. After a while, there were too few ATPs around to make the ribosome really work. Every once in a while it clicked down one more codon, but eventually it stopped.

Scale Six

An electron was circling a phosphorus nucleus, fairly far out and therefore in a fairly classical orbit. It was an easily detachable electron and was attracted by ions of all sorts when they passed nearby. This kind of electron was sure to be pulled away from the phosphorus nucleus within a very short amount of time—at least statistics would have predicted so up till now—for all the other analogous electrons had been snatched away from their nuclei quickly.

But somehow, the proper ions were simply not passing by at the right distance. The phosphorus atom was not getting linked up with the proper partners. So this particular electron, instead of do-si-do-ing its way from one atom to another, continued to cycle rhythmically and periodically around its mother nucleus.

II. EXPANSIO

Scale One

The funeral was Friday morning, and her whole bridge club turned up to mourn the loss of their friend who had been so eager to join them that snowy Wednesday night in Oskaloosa. The minister uttered a moving prayer to the Lord, offering thanks for the time on earth that her soul had enjoyed, comfortingly reminding the gathered sorrowful ones that her soul had gone on to a place of peace and rest and joy. Amen.

Scale Zero

The Earth continued to spin and to revolve about the Sun. It did so many, many times in a row. After a few million such rotations, it was a bit closer in to the Sun than before, although not much. It was a little hotter, on average, partly because it was a little closer and partly because the Sun was burning its fuel differently.

After a while the Sun ballooned and its gases swallowed up the Earth and expanded far beyond it.

By this time the galaxy had rotated six times and was approaching another galaxy. Twenty rotations later, the two galaxies interpenetrated, and for a while they passed through each other like two ghosts or two ripples in water. A few million stars were destroyed, but most were unperturbed. Then after about two more rotations, the two galaxies came apart and went their separate ways.

Kees Boeke was a Dutch schoolteacher with a deep sense of wonder about the universe. In an attempt to share this sense with others, he wrote a classic little book called *Cosmic View: The Universe in Forty Jumps*. The book is based on a simple but powerful idea. It consists of two series of pictures: the first, beginning with a little girl sitting in a chair, zooms out over and over again, first revealing her schoolyard, then her town, then all of Holland, all of Europe, eventually engulfing the Earth, the Solar System, the Galaxy, and so on to the murky edge of the known universe. A second se-ries, starting again with the little girl, zooms inward, focusing first on a mosquito sit-ting on her hand, then on a nearby crystal of salt, a skin cell, a molecule, an atom, and eventually reaching the even murkier domain of elementary particles. Each of the forty jumps either increases or reduces the linear scale by an exact factor of ten, so both progressions are very smooth. The pictures are carefully drawn and clearly an-notated, resulting in a book that does a wonderful job of imparting a sense of profound humility and awe for the many-tiered and mysterious universe we inhabit. Boeke's *Cosmic View* inspired a short film bearing the same name, as well as several other books, most notably *Powers of Ten,* by Philip and Phylis Morrison and Charles and Ray Eames.

Study Questions

1. The Latin phrase *reductio ad absurdum,* in logic, refers to the method of pushing the opponent's argument to an extreme and obviously ab-surd conclusion. In the title of Hofstadter's article, the Latin phrase be-comes a pun. How does the title reflect the article's theme?
2. Douglas R. Hofstadter, a professor of cognitive science and computer science, pays homage to Kees Boeke for the idea. For what reasons, in your opinion, did Hofstadter feel it was necessary to give Boeke so much credit? Would you have done the same?
3. Does the "cosmic view" described in the article make you feel any dif-ferent about the woman's death than a simple description of her death and funeral would have? Does this viewpoint affect your feelings about the death of the deer?

Writing Topics

1. Try writing a "cosmic view" of an ordinary object in a *time zoom,* rather than a "space zoom." For example, take something like a paper clip. Where was the paper clip a hundred, or a million, years past? What and where will it be a hundred or a hundred million years in the future? In your essay, show transformations of the object in the past and in times to come.
2. Think of a natural process that is generally hidden from ordinary human sight: the changing of carbon into a diamond, for example, or the cir-culation of blood in the arteries and veins. Use the library or the Inter-net to research more about how the process works. Then, write a de-scription of the process in the same way Hofstadter did, as though the main elements were almost characters in a story.

Eloquence and Expertise

Elegant Writing in Focus

Sit back. Settle in. Provide yourself with an apple, a glass of iced tea; you are going to be here for a while. Here is reading that has weight and substance, by writers who have thought and felt deeply about their subjects and have spent many years polishing their craft. Here are readings that are among the best and most challenging works available for general readers.

The ideal readers for this kind of prose have, like the writers, spent a long time developing their own skills. They apprehend the meanings, enjoy the subtleties, are not discouraged by the vocabulary. These readers practice the art of reading on airplanes and buses, in the moments snatched from a busy day, in a well-lit corner of the house while everyone else is watching television, and late into the night when others are in bed. They read for the joy of it, and the people who write for those readers understand that they are engaging in a special relationship.

The best readers also cultivate understandings of literature that enrich the reading experience, and the In Focus essays in this chapter concentrate on a few of the more advanced points of literary studies. The first In Focus essay, following a selection by the critic Sven Birkerts about reading itself, is a brief introduction to "reader-response theory," closely allied to (though not the same as) the form of critical theory known as poststructuralism. Later in the chapter is a discussion of "literary language," followed soon after by a description of the uses of allusion. The last In Focus essay explains modernism as it derives from the work of James Joyce, connecting—as all fine literature makes connections—a contemporary Mexican-American essayist with an earlier Irish novelist. All of the In Focus essays here, like the selections themselves, offer the challenges and the rewards of reading at its most complex levels.

The Readings in Focus

Sven Birkerts's *The Gutenberg Elegies* is a book about reading itself: what it means, how it's done, and what the question "What are you reading?" really means. The section included here, the chapter "From the Window of a Train," speaks, appropriately enough, of the rhythmic relationship between reader and writer.

The essay following, Annie Dillard's "Total Eclipse," has become a modern classic both for its spiritual content and for its use of language and images. Cynthia Ozick's "Of Christian Heroism" exemplifies Ozick's description, in her foreword to *Art & Ardor* (New York: Dutton, 1984), of the way she proceeds as an essayist:

> Knowledge is not made out of knowledge. Knowledge swims up from invention and imagination—from ardor—and sometimes even an essay can invent, burn, guess, try out, dig up, hurtle forward, succumb to that flood of sign and nuance that adds up to intuition, disclosure, discovery.

Ozick's skill with lyrical language, her fluidity and precision, allow her work to stand beside Henry David Thoreau's *Walden,* a classic of American contemplative prose. In *Walden,* the conclusion of which is presented here, Thoreau balances his lively, epigrammatic descriptions with an analysis of the American social order that still applies today.

Richard Rodriguez, in "Mixed Blood: Columbus's Legacy. A World Made *Mestizo,"* digs deeply into his own background, and his own psyche, producing a series of sense impressions that form a mosaiclike figure of his divided consciousness. Finally, in "A Dangerous Literacy: The Legacy of Frederick Douglass," Henry Louis Gates Jr. elegantly and eloquently describes the process by which Frederick Douglass became the first African-American "public intellectual."

Each writer here has polished his or her individual technique and style until the surface seems almost invisible, but the perceptive reader sees the skill that has gone into the construction of the piece. These, too, are the pleasures of reading: to understand a writer's techniques and methods, the uses of language, pattern, and style, and then to go further and psychologically dissolve into the content. Ultimately, the most satisfactory kind of reading and writing happens for its own sake, for the pleasure as well as the profits, for knowledge and interest as well as for credit.

From the Window of a Train

I was traveling by train from Boston to New York. I make the trip several times a year, and I've found the five-hour run to be ideal for certain kinds of brooding and notetaking. I have never yet stepped out at Penn Station without a few pages of jumpy script packed away in my bag. On this occasion I had the beginnings of something in mind. I was going to try to work up a set of thoughts about a passage in Oscar Wilde's essay "The Decay of Lying" (the passage where his aesthete, Vivian, insists, "Life imitates Art far more than Art imitates Life"), and as we hurtled along toward Providence I tried to ease myself into the proper state of meditative focus, a receptive, associative casting about. But I was having no luck. Indeed, the harder I tried to get in the right place, the more obstructed I felt. All sorts of thoughts flashed through my mind, but none were the kind I was hoping for. Providence came and went. And as we began the long and exalting sweep along the Connecticut shoreline, I closed my eyes and tried to subdue my frustration.

It was soon after, somewhere in the vicinity of Old Mystic, that a single phrase set up its recursive beat in my head. "The reader and the writer . . ." There was no logic to it; it stuck like one of those songs we obsess on. I mouthed it silently half a hundred times, unsure of its origin or destination; I knew only that it soothed me to say the words. Before long, however, the packaging of sense fell away, leaving me with just the two thudding trochees: reader . . . writer . . . And these I repeated no less compulsively, aware as I did so that their beat fell in synch with the more extended dactyls of the train. And then, without warning, a string of sentences arrived and I hurried to record them in my notebook. But even as I wrote I had the sense that the words were going to be throwaways. They were too ripe, too purple. But I figured that they were just the locomotive for freight that would arrive later. And so they were. As soon as I got

back from New York I sat down and copied out the instigating passage and then the thoughts that had massed just behind them:

> Ree-durr-Rye-turr, Ree-durr-Rye-turr . . . A noise and a mo-
> tion like that of a galloping whirligig, a lone propeller whisper-
> ing over the meadows of history——something made of two
> parts conjoined, awkward in repose, but utterly married once
> set into motion; scarcely audible, certainly alongside the heavy
> creaking of the world's machinery, but passing along the very
> spirit breath itself, the long pneumatic hiss on which all mean-
> ing rides . . . Ree-durr—Rye-turr . . . The eerie, necessary
> interchange—a surge of animated air as the one breathes in
> and the other breathes out . . .

The writer writes and the reader reads—or so it appears. And there
the matter rests, for most. But in truth, this simple proposition is a
mask for a vast system of ambiguities and entanglements. For it is
also true, in a not so very farfetched way, that in writing the writer
reads and that in reading the reader writes. The activities are by no
means as clear-cut as appearances would lead us to believe.

To put it simply: Writing is not merely the action of moving the
pen or hitting the letters on the keyboard, any more than reading
is the straightforward ingesting of print through the eyes. Underneath these basic, seemingly definitive physical operations lie other
processes.

What the writer does while moving the pen is not invention; the
writer does not create the unknown and unforeseen whole cloth out
of nothing. Of course we recognize that. *That* is the unrepeatable,
paradigm act that we grant to our mythic gods alone. All subsequent
acts of creation—if they can be called "creation" at all—are finally an
arranging and interpreting of the given. Not so much a bringing-
into-being as a recovering of what is in some way already known.
The writer, then, places himself in a condition of silent receptivity. He
begins by repressing or pushing aside all impediments, tries to rid
himself of extraneous stimuli. Only then, when the way is clear, do
the fine hair-tip extensions of the inner senses begin their tracking
process.

The writer looks for the words that will best convey sensations
and ideas. These are known to us first as inklings, energy patterns
and traces of great distinctness that are inevitably bound up with
memories; anything we know is, after all, known through memory.
We do not find the units of our expression floating around in the interior space like so many colored balloons, each tethered to its own

meaning. More likely they lie embedded in the dense layers of our print memory. But don't imagine this as a dictionary or filing system. Our print memory is probably more like some indeterminate hyperspace filled with linked-up strands of coded matter, except that the matter is invisible—it is all impulse. The whole of our experience is there, disassembled, in saturated bits, ready for any of the myriad new formations that produce yet another version of the past.

Let us say that we are writers and that our aim is to describe a certain setting—an old wooden dock at a lake, for instance. We know, from some composite of our own experiences, the impressions that we are after: a morning silence, the air over the lake like a transparent membrane, the springy give and take of the boards as we walk toward the end of the dock, the sensations of peeling paint and damp, furred wood against our bare feet, the creaking sound, and so on.

To locate these images, these particular nuances, we research our sense memories, applying our attentiveness inward with the same diligence we would apply to the reading of a difficult text. And it's true, we are in some ways treating our experience as a text and setting about to work our way through it. We must, for we cannot have all of the images and sensations we need at our command at once; memory works by association, by accumulation, and by unconscious reconstruction.

First, we try to recall how it was—or, if we are translating experience, might have been—to walk down to the lake in the early morning. We move in sequence, very much as if we were following the logic of another writer's description. We see the dock from the distance, see the mist; we summon, in natural order, what must be the components of the experience. How cool the sand felt, how the boards first took the body's weight. We read ourselves, and then we report on that reading. We call it writing.

And when we do this reporting, we activate the relevant areas of our language memory which include not only all we know of words, but also all we know *through* words. The description we write will inevitably be a composite, a reworking of a hundred-odd descriptions that have dissolved together inside. For I don't think that we ever really forget what we read, any more than we forget what we experience. More likely, we break down the unity of the illusion, preserving the elements along with the mountains of other traces until they become virtually indistinguishable—until what we have read takes on the status of being something that once happened to us.

When we begin to write our description, then, we find that we already have a sense of the kind of shape we want, and some intuition of the pace. This is not because these are necessarily properties of the reality we would render; rather, because we have a very particular expectation built up from everything we have read and internalized. We know just the feeling—the effect—we want. In a sense we proceed toward our expression by trying to read in ourselves the very prose we are about to write. Writing, then, becomes a kind of matching up of the right words to the specific word-impulses that are lined up inside. This is all very Platonic—to see the act of discovery less as an inventing than a recovering, an *anamnesis.* In writing we grope toward what we think of as the inevitable wording, as though the prose were already finished in an inner place we can just barely reach. And when we do succeed, when from time to time we reach it, we know we are beyond revision.

This is where the subterranean influence of reading plays its part. The writers we read furnish us with expectations—they teach us how we like to see and feel and hear and think about things. So while it is true that we wrote the description of the dock, discovered it inside ourselves phrase by phrase, we will, if we are honest, share at least some part of the credit with E. B. White and Eudora Welty and Norman Maclean and Henry David Thoreau and the innumerable others whose words are packed like silt inside us.

We are not done. The other side of the picture—that reading is a kind of writing—is no less persuasive. Once again we locate ourselves in the cloudy zone where language and memory swirl together. The core question is: What do we do with words when we read? I would argue that we make another person's words our own not simply by looking at them but by apprehending, inhabiting, and reinscribing them. "The dock was old and ramshackle. The peeling boards were springy underfoot." We can only take possession of the words by filling them out with our own recollected experience. Once again, those saturated bits are set into motion, combined and recombined. The larger implications of this, bearing on our own sense of the personal past, are quite staggering. It may well be that we do not carry our memories in an existing archive of stored impressions. Isn't it just as likely that we create the past afresh from available components every time we remember? Each memory would then be a story we write for ourselves on the spot. Some of these, through a kind of narrative insistence (shaped, in turn, by obscure needs) become the authorized versions: This is how it *really* was.

In any case, when we read we bring the life—ultimately *our* life—to the words. In tapping our experience thus, reading becomes a steadily unfolding memory event. Which is not to say that we are actively reliving our pasts every time we read a story, but that our associative mechanisms are constantly operative—those "bits" are agitated like the molecules in a pot on the verge of boiling.

This is one of the great incentives and surprises of reading: that we are at all times so close to the subthreshold energies of the self. "The peeling boards were springy underfoot" means nothing much until we have produced the sensations in ourselves—*created* them. To do so we have had to brush against the original traces, whatever it is we carry inside that holds our knowledge of springy boards. In other words, we make the music indicated by the notes. But even more than the musician following a score, we invest ourselves in the act. This investment resembles closely what the writer does in putting words on the page.

Reading and writing—reader and writer. Could it be that at some level the two activities are not all that different, that they are just manifestations of the ebb and flow of our awareness, ways we have of breaking down and recombining the countless interlocking puzzle pieces inside? Every true reader, then, is a writer and every true writer is a reader, and every person engaged in the project of self-awareness is the reader and writer of himself. Writer and reader: They are the recto and verso of language, which is itself the medium of our deeper awareness.

THE RESPONSIVE READER

As Birkerts points out, reading and writing are active, not passive, processes. Just as a writer produces work in light of all that he or she has read and experienced before (how else would a writer know what to do?), the reader "produces" a story, essay, or poem in his or her own mind. What is in the reader's head is called forth by the words on the page, but is never—cannot ever be—exactly the same as the words on the page. A transformation takes place.

Scholars who study the ways that transformation happens, the ways that literature takes on meaning within the minds of the readers, are generally called *reader-response* critics. One of the most accessible books about reader-response literary theory is Louise M. Rosenblatt's *The Reader, the Text, the Poem: The Transactional Theory of the Literary Work* (Carbondale: Southern Illinois UP, 1978). The word *transaction* in the title is the key: readers, according to Rosenblatt, produce "texts" as a result of an interaction between the "poem" (by which she means any work of literature) and the work of the person who reads, a person who comes with an individual background and a set of special skills. The "poem," she explains, is an "event in time," created like a musical performance, which exists for a moment in the interaction between the musician and the score, the notes on the page and the person who wields the instrument. "The reader's creation of a poem out of a text," Rosenblatt writes, "must be an active, self-ordering and self-corrective process."

This concept puts a great deal of responsibility on the reader, of course. No longer is he or she regarded as a kind of sponge, soaking up and absorbing the words on the page; the better the reader's skills, the more technologies of understanding and interpretation that reader can employ, the better the "poem" that will emerge from the text. This idea goes back to the Greek philosopher and critic Aristotle, who noted that the person who perceives a work of art must be a kind of artist too, bringing skills and energy to bear upon the work so that it really takes life—inside the mind of the perceiver. In this way, as Birkerts lyrically reminds us, the acts of reading and writing are inextricably linked.

Study Questions

1. "We read ourselves, and then we report on that reading. We call it writing." Explain what Birkerts means by those two sentences (on p. 505).
2. What does Birkerts mean by the "subterranean influence of reading" (p. 506)? How do previous readings influence the reading we do now?
3. Birkerts symbolizes the interaction between writer and reader as the rhythmic rocking motion of a train. Where is the metaphoric train, the one that Birkerts creates on the page, going? (Hint: not New York!)

Writing Topics

1. Consider the "subterranean influence of reading" in your own life. Write a brief autobiography of yourself as a reader. Were you read to as a child, and do you remember any of those early books? How and what

did you read as an adolescent, a young adult, in the years following? Focus not on your life per se but on your reading activities and their effects on your life.

2. Choose any of the previous readings in this textbook. Write an essay in which you analyze the way you originally read that selection. What forces in your life, what parts of your background or circumstances in the present, influenced your understanding of and reaction to that selection?

Total Eclipse

ANNIE DILLARD

I

It had been like dying, that sliding down the mountain pass. It had been like the death of someone, irrational, that sliding down the mountain pass and into the region of dread. It was like slipping into fever, or falling down that hole in sleep from which you wake yourself whimpering. We had crossed the mountains that day, and now we were in a strange place—a hotel in central Washington, in a town near Yakima. The eclipse we had traveled here to see would occur early the next morning.

I lay in bed. My husband, Gary, was reading beside me. I lay in bed and looked at the painting on the hotel-room wall. It was a print of a detailed and lifelike painting of a smiling clown's head, made out of vegetables. It was a painting of the sort that you do not intend to look at and that, alas, you never forget. Some tasteless fate presses it upon you; it becomes part of the complex interior junk you carry with you wherever you go. Two years have passed since the total eclipse of which I write. During those years I have forgotten, I assume, a great many things I wanted to remember—but I have not forgotten that clown painting or its lunatic setting in the old hotel.

The clown was bald. Actually, he wore a clown's tight rubber wig, painted white; this stretched over the top of his skull, which was a cabbage. His hair was bunches of baby carrots. Inset in his white clown makeup, and in his cabbage skull, were his small and laughing human eyes. The clown's glance was like the glance of Rembrandt in some of the self-portraits: lively, knowing, deep, and loving. The crinkled shadows around his eyes were string beans. His eyebrows were parsley. Each of his ears was a broad bean. His thin, joyful lips were red chili peppers; between his lips were wet rows of human teeth and a suggestion of a real tongue. The clown print was framed in gilt and glassed.

To put ourselves in the path of the total eclipse, that day we had driven five hours inland from the Washington coast, where we lived. When we tried to cross the Cascades range, an avalanche had blocked the pass.

A slope's worth of snow blocked the road; traffic backed up. Had the avalanche buried any cars that morning? We could not learn. This highway was the only winter road over the mountains. We waited as highway crews bulldozed a passage through the avalanche. With two-by-fours and walls of plyboard, they erected a one-way, roofed tunnel through the avalanche. We drove through the avalanche tunnel, crossed the pass, and descended several thousand feet into central Washington and the broad Yakima valley, about which we knew only that it was orchard country. As we lost altitude, the snows disappeared; our ears popped; the trees changed, and in the trees were strange birds. I watched the landscape innocently, like a fool, like a diver in the rapture of the deep who plays on the bottom while his air runs out.

The hotel lobby was a dark, derelict room, narrow as a corridor, and seemingly without air. We waited on a couch while the manager vanished upstairs to do something unknown to our room. Beside us, on an overstuffed chair, absolutely motionless, was a platinum-blond woman in her forties, wearing a black silk dress and a strand of pearls. Her long legs were crossed; she supported her head on her fist. At the dim far end of the room, their backs toward us, sat six bald old men in their shirtsleeves, around a loud television. Two of them seemed asleep. They were drunks. "Number six!" cried the man on television, "Number six!"

On the broad lobby desk was a ten-gallon aquarium, lighted and bubbling, that contained one large fish; the fish tilted up and down in its water. Against the long opposite wall sang a live canary in its cage. Beneath the cage, among spilled millet seeds on the carpet, were a decorated child's sand bucket and matching sand shovel.

Now the alarm was set for six. I lay awake remembering an article I had read downstairs in the lobby, in an engineering magazine. The article was about gold mining.

In South Africa, in India, and in South Dakota, the gold mines extend so deeply into the earth's crust that they are hot. The rock walls burn the miners' hands. The companies have to air-condition the mines; if the air conditioners break, the miners die. The elevators in the mine shafts run very slowly, down, and up, so the miners' ears will not pop in their skulls. When the miners return to the surface, their faces are deathly pale.

Early the next morning we checked out. It was February 26, 1979, a Monday morning. We would drive out of town, find a hilltop, watch the eclipse, and then drive back over the mountains and home to the coast. How familiar things are here; how adept we are; how smoothly and professionally we check out! I had forgotten the clown's smiling head and the hotel lobby as if they had never existed. Gary put the car in gear and off we went, as off we have gone to a hundred other adventures.

It was before dawn when we found a highway out of town and drove into the unfamiliar countryside. By the growing light we could see a band of cirrostratus clouds in the sky. Later the rising sun would clear these clouds before the eclipse began. We drove at random until we came to a range of unfenced hills. We pulled off the highway, bundled up, and climbed one of these hills.

II

The hill was five hundred feet high. Long winter-killed grass covered it, as high as our knees. We climbed and rested, sweating in the cold; we passed clumps of bundled people on the hillside who were setting up telescopes and fiddling with cameras. The top of the hill stuck up in the middle of the sky. We tightened our scarves and looked around.

East of us rose another hill like ours. Between the hills, far below, was the highway that threaded south into the valley. This was the Yakima valley; I had never seen it before. It is justly famous for its beauty, like every planted valley. It extended south into the horizon, a distant dream of a valley, a Shangri-la. All its hundreds of low, golden slopes bore orchards. Among the orchards were towns, and roads, and plowed and fallow fields. Through the valley wandered a thin, shining river; from the river extended fine, frozen irrigation ditches. Distance blurred and blued the sight, so that the whole valley looked like a thickness or sediment at the bottom of the sky. Directly behind us was more sky, and empty lowlands blued by distance, and Mount Adams. Mount Adams was an enormous, snow-covered volcanic cone rising flat, like so much scenery.

Now the sun was up. We could not see it; but the sky behind the band of clouds was yellow, and, far down the valley, some hillside orchards had lighted up. More people were parking near the highway and climbing the hills. It was the West. All of us rugged individualists were wearing knit caps and blue nylon parkas. People were climbing the nearby hills and setting up shop in clumps among the dead grasses. It looked as though we had all gathered on hilltops to pray for the world on its last day. It looked as though we had all crawled out of spaceships and were preparing to assault the valley below. It looked as though we were scattered on hilltops at dawn to sacrifice virgins, make rain, set stone stelae in a ring. There was no place out of the wind. The straw grasses banged our legs.

Up in the sky where we stood, the air was lusterless yellow. To the west the sky was blue. Now the sun cleared the clouds. We cast rough shadows on the blowing grass; freezing, we waved our arms. Near the sun, the sky was bright and colorless. There was nothing to see.

It began with no ado. It was odd that such a well-advertised public event should have no starting gun, no overture, no introductory speaker. I should have known right then that I was out of my depth. Without pause or preamble, silent as orbits, a piece of the sun went away. We looked at it through welders' goggles. A piece of the sun was missing; in its place we saw empty sky.

I had seen a partial eclipse in 1970. A partial eclipse is very interesting. It bears almost no relation to a total eclipse. Seeing a partial eclipse bears the same relation to seeing a total eclipse as kissing a man does to marrying him, or as flying in an airplane does to falling out of an airplane. Although the one experience precedes the other, it in no way prepares you for it. During a partial eclipse the sky does not darken—not even when 94 percent of the sun is hidden. Nor does the sun, seen colorless through protective devices, seem terribly strange. We have all seen a sliver of light in the sky; we have all seen the crescent moon by day. However, during a partial eclipse the air does indeed get cold, precisely as if someone were standing between you and the fire. And blackbirds do fly back to their roosts. I had seen a partial eclipse before, and here was another.

What you see in an eclipse is entirely different from what you know. It is especially different for those of us whose grasp of astronomy is so frail that, given a flashlight, a grapefruit, two oranges, and fifteen years, we still could not figure out which way to set the clocks for daylight saving time. Usually it is a bit of a trick to keep your knowledge from blinding you. But during an eclipse it is easy. What you see is much more convincing than any wild-eyed theory you may know.

You may read that the moon has something to do with eclipses. I have never seen the moon yet. You do not see the moon. So near the sun, it is as completely invisible as the stars are by day. What you see before your eyes is the sun going through phases. It gets narrower and narrower, as the waning moon does, and, like the ordinary moon, it travels alone in the simple sky. The sky is of course background. It does not appear to eat the sun; it is far behind the sun. The sun simply shaves away; gradually, you see less sun and more sky.

The sky's blue was deepening, but there was no darkness. The sun was a wide crescent, like a segment of tangerine. The wind freshened and blew steadily over the hill. The eastern hill across the highway grew dusky and sharp. The towns and orchards in the valley to the south were dissolving into the blue light. Only the thin river held a trickle of sun.

Now the sky to the west deepened to indigo, a color never seen. A dark sky usually loses color. This was a saturated, deep indigo, up in the air. Stuck up into that unworldly sky was the cone of Mount Adams, and the alpenglow was upon it. The alpenglow is that red light of sunset which holds out on snowy mountaintops long after the valleys and tablelands are dimmed. "Look at Mount Adams," I said, and that was the last sane moment I remember.

I turned back to the sun. It was going. The sun was going, and the world was wrong. The grasses were wrong; they were platinum. Their every detail of stem, head, and blade shone lightless and artificially distinct as an art photographer's platinum print. This color has never been seen on earth. The hues were metallic; their finish was matte. The hillside was a nineteenth-century tinted photograph from which the tints had faded. All the people you see in the photograph, distinct and detailed as their faces look, are now dead. The sky was navy blue. My hands were silver. All the distant hills' grasses were finespun metal that the wind laid down. I was watching a faded color print of a movie filmed in the Middle Ages; I was standing in it, by some mistake. I was standing in a movie of hillside grasses filmed in the Middle Ages. I missed my own century, the people I knew, and the real light of day.

I looked at Gary. He was in the film. Everything was lost. He was a platinum print, a dead artist's version of life. I saw on his skull the darkness of night mixed with the colors of day. My mind was going out; my eyes were receding the way galaxies recede to the rim of space. Gary was light-years away, gesturing inside a circle of darkness, down the wrong end of a telescope. He smiled as if he saw me; the stringy crinkles around his eyes moved. The sight of him, familiar and wrong, was something I was remembering from centuries hence, from the other side of death: yes, *that* is the way he used to look, when we were living. When it was our generation's turn to be alive. I could not hear him; the wind was too loud. Behind him the sun was going. We had all started down a chute of time. At first it was pleasant; now there was no stopping it. Gary was chuting away across space, moving and talking and catching my eye, chuting down the long corridor of separation. The skin on his face moved like thin bronze plating that would peel.

The grass at our feet was wild barley. It was the wild einkorn wheat that grew on the hilly flanks of the Zagros Mountains, above the Euphrates valley, above the valley of the river we called *River.* We harvested the grass with stone sickles, I remember. We found the grasses on the hillsides; we built our shelter beside them and cut them down. That is how he used to look then, that one, moving and living and catching my eye, with the sky so dark behind him, and the wind blowing. God save our life.

From all the hills came screams. A piece of sky beside the crescent sun was detaching. It was a loosened circle of evening sky, suddenly lighted from the back. It was an abrupt black body out of nowhere; it was a flat disk; it was almost over the sun. That is when there were screams. At once this disk of sky slid over the sun like a lid. The sky snapped over the sun like a lens cover. The hatch in the brain slammed. Abruptly it was dark night, on the land and in the sky. In the night sky was a tiny ring of light. The hole where the sun belongs is very small. A thin ring of light marked its place. There was no sound. The eyes dried, the arteries drained, the lungs hushed. There was no world. We were the world's dead people rotating and orbiting around and around, embedded in the planet's crust, while the earth rolled down. Our minds were light-years distant, forgetful of almost everything. Only an extraordinary act of will could recall to us our former, living selves and our contexts in matter and time. We had, it seems, loved the planet and loved our lives, but could no longer remember the way of them. We got the light wrong. In the sky was something that should not be there. In the black sky was a ring of light. It was a thin ring, an old, thin silver wedding band, an old, worn ring. It was an old wedding band in the sky, or a morsel of bone. There were stars. It was all over.

III

It is now that the temptation is strongest to leave these regions. We have seen enough; let's go. Why burn our hands any more than we have to? But two years have passed; the price of gold has risen. I return to the same buried alluvial beds and pick through the strata again.

I saw, early in the morning, the sun diminish against a backdrop of sky. I saw a circular piece of that sky appear, suddenly detached, blackened, and backlighted; from nowhere it came and overlapped the sun. It did not look like the moon. It was enormous and black. If I had not read that it was the moon, I could have seen the sight a hundred times and never thought of the moon once. (If, however, I had not read that it was the moon—if, like most of the world's people throughout time, I had simply glanced up and seen this thing— then I doubtless would not have speculated much, but would have, like Emperor Louis of Bavaria in 840, simply died of fright on the spot.) It did not look like a dragon, although it looked more like a dragon than the moon. It looked like a lens cover, or the lid of a pot. It materialized out of thin air—black, and flat, and sliding, outlined in flame.

Seeing this black body was like seeing a mushroom cloud. The heart screeched. The meaning of the sight overwhelmed its fascination. It obliterated meaning itself. If you were to glance out one day and see a row of mushroom clouds rising on the horizon, you would know at once that what you were seeing, remarkable as it was, was intrinsically not worth remarking. No use running to tell anyone. Significant as it was, it did not matter a whit. For what is significance? It is significance for people. No people, no significance. This is all I have to tell you.

In the deeps are the violence and terror of which psychology has warned us. But if you ride these monsters deeper down, if you drop with them farther over the world's rim, you find what our sciences cannot locate or name, the substrate, the ocean or matrix or ether that buoys the rest, that gives goodness its power for good, and evil its power for evil, the unified field: our complex and inexplicable caring for each other, and for our life together here. This is given. It is not learned.

The world that lay under darkness and stillness following the closing of the lid was not the world we know. The event was over. Its devastation lay round about us. The clamoring mind and heart stilled, almost indifferent, certainly disembodied, frail, and exhausted. The hills were hushed, obliterated. Up in the sky, like a crater from some distant cataclysm, was a hollow ring.

You have seen photographs of the sun taken during a total eclipse. The corona fills the print. All of those photographs were taken through telescopes. The lenses of telescopes and cameras can no more cover the breadth and scale of the visual array than language can cover the breadth and simultaneity of internal experience. Lenses enlarge the sight, omit its context, and make of it a pretty and sensible picture, like something on a Christmas card. I assure you, if you send any shepherds a Christmas card on which is printed a three-by-three photograph of the angel of the Lord, the glory of the Lord, and a multitude of the heavenly host, they will not be sore afraid. More fearsome things can come in envelopes. More moving photographs than those of the sun's corona can appear in magazines. But I pray you will never see anything more awful in the sky.

You see the wide world swaddled in darkness; you see a vast breadth of hilly land, and an enormous, distant, blackened valley; you see towns' lights, a river's path, and blurred portions of your hat and scarf; you see your husband's face looking like an early black-and-white film; and you see a sprawl of black sky and blue sky together, with unfamiliar stars in it, some barely visible bands of cloud, and, over there, a small white ring. The ring is as small as one goose in a flock of migrating geese—if you happen to notice a flock of migrating geese. It is one 360th part of the visible sky. The sun we see is less than half the diameter of a dime held at arm's length.

The Ring Nebula, in the constellation Lyra, looks, through binoculars, like a smoke ring. It is a star in the process of exploding. Light from its explosion first reached the earth in 1054; it was a supernova then, and so bright it shone in the daytime. Now it is not so bright, but it is still exploding. It expands at the rate of seventy million miles a day. It is interesting to look through binoculars at something expanding seventy million miles a day. It does not budge. Its apparent size does not increase. Photographs of the Ring Nebula taken fifteen years ago seem identical to photographs of it taken yesterday. Some lichens are similar. Botanists have measured some ordinary lichens twice, at fifty-year intervals, without detecting any growth at all. And yet their cells divide; they live.

The small ring of light was like these things—like a ridiculous lichen up in the sky, like a perfectly still explosion 5,000 light-years away: it was interesting, and lovely, and in witless motion, and it had nothing to do with anything.

It had nothing to do with anything. The sun was too small, and too cold, and too far away, to keep the world alive. The white ring was not enough. It was feeble and worthless. It was as useless as a memory; it was as off kilter and hollow and wretched as a memory.

When you try your hardest to recall someone's face, or the look of a place, you see in your mind's eye some vague and terrible sight such as this. It is dark; it is insubstantial; it is all wrong.

The white ring and the saturated darkness made the earth and the sky look as they must look in the memories of the careless dead. What I saw, what I seemed to be standing in, was all the wrecked light that the memories of the dead could shed upon the living world. We had all died in our boots on the hilltops of Yakima and were alone in eternity. Empty space stoppered our eyes and mouths; we cared for nothing. We remembered our living days wrong. With great effort we had remembered some sort of circular light in he sky—but only the outline. Oh, and then the orchard trees withered, the ground froze, the glaciers slid down the valleys and overlapped the towns. If there had ever been people on earth, nobody knew it. The dead had forgotten those they had loved. The dead were parted one from the other and could no longer remember the faces and lands they had loved in the light. They seemed to stand on darkened hilltops, looking down.

IV

We teach our children one thing only, as we were taught: to wake up. We teach our children to look alive there, to join by words and activities the life of human culture on the planet's crust. As adults we are almost all adept at waking up. We have so mastered the transition, we have forgotten we ever learned it. Yet it is a transition we make a hundred times a day, as, like so many will-less dolphins, we plunge and surface, lapse and emerge. We live half our waking lives and all of our sleeping lives in some private, useless, and insensible waters we never mention or recall. Useless, I say. Valueless, I might add—until someone hauls the wealth up to the surface and into the wide-awake city, in a form that people can use.

I do not know how we got to the restaurant. Like Roethke, "I take my waking slow." Gradually I seemed more or less alive, and already forgetful. It was now almost nine in the morning. It was the day of a solar eclipse in central Washington, and a fine adventure for every-one. The sky was clear; there was a fresh breeze out of the north.

The restaurant was a roadside place with tables and booths. The other eclipse-watchers were there. From our booth we could see their cars' California license plates, their University of Washington parking stickers. Inside the restaurant we were all eating eggs or waf-fles; people were fairly shouting and exchanging enthusiasms, like fans after a World Series game. Did you see . . . ? Did you see . . . ? Then somebody said something that knocked me for a loop.

A college student, a boy in a blue parka who carried a Hasselblad, said to us, "Did you see that little white ring? It looked like a Life Saver. It looked like a Life Saver up in the sky."

And so it did. The boy spoke well. He was a walking alarm clock. I myself had at that time no access to such a term. He could write a sentence, and I could not. I grabbed that Life Saver and rode it to the surface. And I had to laugh. I had been dumbstruck on the Euphrates River, I had been dead and gone and grieving; all over the sight of something that, if you could claw your way up to that level, you would grant looked very much like a Life Saver. It was good to be back among people so clever; it was good to have all the world's words at the mind's disposal, so the mind could begin its task. All those things for which we have no words are lost. The mind—the culture—has two little tools, grammar and lexicon: a decorated sand bucket and a matching shovel. With these we bluster about the con-tinents and do all the world's work. With these we try to save our very lives.

There are a few more things to tell from this level, the level of the restaurant. One is the old joke about breakfast. "It can never be sat-isfied, the mind, never." Wallace Stevens wrote that, and in the long run he was right. The mind wants to live forever, or to learn a very good reason why not. The mind wants the world to return its love, or its awareness; the mind wants to know all the world, and all eter-nity, and God. The mind's sidekick, however, will settle for two eggs over easy.

The dear, stupid body is as easily satisfied as a spaniel. And, in-credibly, the simple spaniel can lure the brawling mind to its dish. It is everlastingly funny that the proud, metaphysically ambitious, clamoring mind will hush if you give it an egg.

Further: while the mind reels in deep space, while the mind grieves or fears or exults, the workaday senses, in ignorance or idiocy, like so many computer terminals printing out market prices while the world blows up, still transcribe their little data and transmit them to the warehouse in the skull. Later, under the tranquilizing influence of fried eggs, the mind can sort through these data. The restaurant was a halfway house, a decompression chamber. There I remembered a few things more.

The deepest, and most terrifying, was this: I have said that I heard screams. (I have since read that screaming, with hysteria, is a common reaction even to expected total eclipses.) People on all the hillsides, including, I think, myself, screamed when the black body of the moon detached from the sky and rolled over the sun. But something else was happening at that same instant, and it was this, I believe, that made us scream.

The second before the sun went out, we saw a wall of dark shadow come speeding at us. We no sooner saw it than it was upon us, like thunder. It roared up the valley. It slammed our hill and knocked us out. It was the monstrous swift shadow cone of the moon. I have since read that this wave of shadow moves 1,800 miles an hour. Language can give no sense of this sort of speed—1,800 miles an hour. It was 195 miles wide. No end was in sight—you saw only the edge. It rolled at you across the land at 1,800 miles an hour, hauling darkness like plague behind it. Seeing it, and knowing it was coming straight for you, was like feeling a slug of anesthetic shoot up your arm. If you think very fast, you may have time to think: Soon it will hit my brain. You can feel the deadness race up your arm; you can feel the appalling, inhuman speed of your own blood. We saw the wall of shadow coming, and screamed before it hit.

This was the universe about which we have read so much and never before felt: the universe as a clockwork of loose spheres flung at stupefying, unauthorized speeds. How could anything moving so fast not crash, not veer from its orbit amok like a car out of control on a turn?

Less than two minutes later, when the sun emerged, the trailing edge of the shadow cone sped away. It coursed down our hill and raced eastward over the plain, faster than the eye could believe; it swept over the plain and dropped over the planet's rim in a twinkling. It had clobbered us, and now it roared away. We blinked in the light. It was as though an enormous, loping god in the sky had reached down and slapped the earth's face.

Something else, something more ordinary, came back to me along about the third cup of coffee. During the moments of totality, it was so dark that drivers on the highway below turned on their cars' headlights. We could see the highway's route as a strand of lights. It was bumper-to-bumper down there. It was eight-fifteen in the morning, Monday morning, and people were driving into Yakima to work. That it was as dark as night, and eerie as hell, an hour after dawn apparently meant that in order to *see* to drive to work, people had to use their headlights. Four or five cars pulled off the road. The rest, in a line at least five miles long, drove to town. The highway ran between hills; the people could not have seen any of the eclipsed sun at all. Yakima will have another total eclipse in 2019. Perhaps, in 2019, businesses will give their employees an hour off.

From the restaurant we drove back to the coast. The highway crossing the Cascades range was open. We drove over the mountain like old pros. We joined our places on the planet's thin crust; it held. For the time being, we were home free.

Early that morning at six, when we had checked out, the six bald men were sitting on folding chairs in the dim hotel lobby. The television was on. Most of them were awake. You might drown in your own spittle, God knows, at any time; you might wake up dead in a small hotel, a cabbage head watching TV while snows pile up in the passes, watching TV while the chili peppers smile and the moon passes over the sun and nothing changes and nothing is learned because you have lost your bucket and shovel and no longer care. What if you regain the surface and open your sack and find, instead of treasure, a beast, which jumps at you? Or you may not come back at all. The winches may jam, the scaffolding buckle, the air-conditioning collapse. You may glance up one day and see by your headlamp the canary keeled over in its cage. You may reach into a cranny for pearls and touch a moray eel. You yank on your rope; it is too late.

Apparently people share a sense of these hazards, for when the total eclipse ended, an odd thing happened.

When the sun appeared as a blinding bead on the ring's side, the eclipse was over. The black lens cover appeared again, backlighted, and slid away. At once the yellow light made the sky blue again; the black lid dissolved and vanished. The real world began there. I remember now: we all hurried away. We were born and bored at a stroke. We rushed down the hill. We found our car; we saw the other people streaming down the hillsides; we joined the highway traffic and drove away.

We never looked back. It was a general vamoose, and an odd one, for when we left the hill, the sun was still partially eclipsed—a sight rare enough, and one that, in itself, we would probably have driven five hours to see. But enough is enough. One turns at last even from glory itself with a sigh of relief. From the depths of mystery, and even from the heights of splendor, we bounce back and hurry for the latitudes of home.

Study Questions

1. The first sentence of "Total Eclipse" demonstrates Dillard's writing style, characterized by deceptively simple wording, startling sentences, and extraordinary imagery (for example, in what way is driving down a mountainside like dying?). Point out some examples of her language, her "shock value" sentences, and her imagery. What other characteristics do you see in the way she writes?
2. "Total Eclipse" is not simply about a natural phenomenon; it is also about memory and forgetting. What passages deal with the processes of remembering and connecting events?
3. Locate passages that contain emotional content. How does Dillard convey those emotions? What sections best express her memory of feelings surrounding each experience?

Writing Topics

1. Choose an extreme emotion such as infatuation, fear, or grief. Describe a scene from the point of view of a person who is experiencing this emotion. Write your description in such a way that the reader understands what the narrator is feeling, but do not directly mention the emotion or the reason the person feels it.

   (Note that this topic can seem deceptively easy, but it requires considerable work in the writing process. The exercise is often used in creative-writing workshops and can teach a great deal about effective description.)
2. Pretend that you are Dillard's husband, Gary. Tell the story of the trip from his point of view. (Use the first person, "I.") In your imagination, does Gary share his wife's perceptions, or does he have concerns of his own? Show how he would respond to her and to the eclipse if he had written the essay.

Of Christian Heroism

CYNTHIA OZICK

There is a story about Clare Boothe Luce complaining that she was bored with hearing about the Holocaust. A Jewish friend of hers said he perfectly understood her sensitivity in the matter; in fact, he had the same sense of repetitiousness and fatigue, hearing so often about the Crucifixion.

—Herbert Gold,
"Selfish Like Me"

I

Of the great European murder of six million Jews, and the murderers themselves, there is little to say. The barbaric years when Jews were hunted down for sport in the middle of the twentieth century have their hellish immortality, their ineradicable infamy, and will inflame the nightmares—and (perhaps) harrow the conscience—of the human race until the sun burns out and takes our poor earth-speck with it. Of the murder and the murderers everything is known that needs to be known: how it was done, who did it, who helped, where it was done, and when, and why. Especially why: the hatred of a civilization that teaches us to say No to hatred.

Three "participant" categories of the Holocaust are commonly named: murderers, victims, bystanders.* Imagination demands a choosing. Which, of this entangled trio, are we? Which are we most likely to have become? Probably it is hardest of all to imagine ourselves victims. After all, we were here and not there. Or we were Gentiles and not Jews or Gypsies. Or we were not yet born. But if we had already been born, if we were there and not here, if we were Jews and not Gentiles . . .

"If" is the travail of historians and philosophers, not of the ordinary human article. What we can be sure of without contradiction—we can be sure of it because we *are* the ordinary human article—is that, difficult as it might be to imagine ourselves among the victims, it is not in us even to begin to think of ourselves as likely murderers. The

---

*We owe the perception of these categories to Raul Hilberg's *Perpetrators, Victims, Bystanders*.

"banality of evil" is a catchword of our generation; but no, it is an unusual, an exceptional, thing to volunteer for the S.S.; to force aged Jews to their knees to scrub the gutter with their beards; to empty Zyklon B canisters into the hole in the roof of the gas chamber; to enact those thousand atrocities that lead to the obliteration of a people and a culture.

The victims take our pity and our horror, and whatever else we can, in our shame, cede to their memory. But they do not puzzle us. It does not puzzle us that the blood of the innocent cries up from the ground—how could it be otherwise? Even if humanity refuses to go on remembering, the voices crushed in the woods and under the fresh pavements of Europe press upward. The new plants that cover the places where corpses were buried in mass pits carry blood in their dew. Basement-whispers trouble the new blocks of flats that cover the streets where the flaming Warsaw Ghetto fell. The heavy old sideboards of the Thirties that once stood in Jewish dining rooms in certain neighborhoods of Berlin and Vienna are in Catholic and Protestant dining rooms now, in neighborhoods where there are no longer any Jews; the great carved legs of these increasingly valued antiques groan and remember the looting. The books that were thrown onto bonfires in the central squares of every German city still send up their flocks of quivering phantom letters.

All that—the looting, the shooting, the herding, the forced marches, the gassing, the torching of synagogues, the cynicism, the mendacity, the shamelessness, the truncheons, the bloodthirstiness, the fanaticism, the opportunism, the Jews of Europe as prey, their dehumanization, the death factories, the obliteration of a civilization, the annihilation of a people—all that it is possible to study, if not to assimilate. Pious Jews, poor Jews, secular Jews, universalist Jews, baptized Jews, Jews who were storekeepers, or doctors, or carpenters, or professors, or teamsters, Jewish infants and children—all annihilated. Thousands upon thousands of Jewish libraries and schools looted and destroyed. Atrocity spawns an aftermath—perhaps an afterlife. In the last four decades the documents and the testimonies have been heaped higher and higher—yet a gash has been cut in the world's brain that cannot be healed by memorial conferences or monuments. Lamentation for the martyred belongs now to the history of cruelty and to the earth. There is no paucity of the means to remember; there may be a paucity of the will to remember. Still, we know what we think of the murders and the murderers. We are not at a loss to know how to regard them.

But what of the bystanders? They were not the criminals, after all.

For the bystanders we should feel at least the pale warmth of recognition—call it self-recognition. And nowadays it is the bystanders whom we most notice, though at the time, while the crimes were in progress, they seemed the least noticeable. We notice them now because they are the ones we can most readily identify with. They are the ones imagination can most readily accommodate. A bystander is like you and me, the ordinary human article—what normal man or woman or adolescent runs to commit public atrocities? The luck of the draw (the odds of finding oneself in the majority) saves the bystander from direct victimhood: the Nuremberg "racial" laws, let us say, are what exempt the bystander from deportation. The bystander is, by definition, not a Jew or a Gypsy. The bystander stays home, safe enough if compliant enough. The bystander cannot be charged with taking part in any evil act; the bystander only watches as the evil proceeds. One by one, and suddenly all at once, the Jewish families disappear from their apartments in building after building, in city after city. The neighbors watch them go. One by one, and suddenly all at once, the Jewish children disappear from school. Their classmates resume doing their sums.

The neighbors are decent people—decent enough for ordinary purposes. They cannot be blamed for not being heroes. A hero—like a murderer—is an exception and (to be coarsely direct) an abnormality, a kind of social freak. No one ought to be expected to become a hero. Not that the bystanders are, taken collectively, altogether blameless. In the Germany of the Thirties it was they—because there were so many of them—who created the norm. The conduct of the bystanders—again because there were so many of them—defined what was common and what was uncommon, what was exceptional and what was unexceptional, what was heroic and what was quotidian. If the bystanders in all their numbers had not been so docile, if they had not been so conciliatory, or, contrariwise, if they had not been so "inspired" (by slogans and rabble-rousers and uniforms and promises of national glory), if they had not acquiesced both through the ballot box and alongside the parades—if, in short, they had not been *so many*—the subject of heroism would never have had to arise.

When a whole population takes on the status of bystander, the victims are without allies; the criminals, unchecked, are strengthened; and only then do we need to speak of heroes. When a field is filled from end to end with sheep, a stag stands out. When a continent is filled from end to end with the compliant, we learn what heroism is. And alas for the society that requires heroes.

Most of us, looking back, and identifying as we mainly do with the bystanders—because it is the most numerous category, into which simple demographic likelihood thrusts us; or because surely it is the easiest category, the most recognizably human, if not the most humane—will admit to some perplexity, a perplexity brought on by hindsight. Taken collectively, as I dared to do a moment ago, the by-standers are culpable. But taking human beings collectively is pre-cisely what we are obliged not to do. Then consider the bystanders not as a group, not as a stereotype, but one by one. If the bystander is the ordinary human article, as we have agreed, what can there be to puzzle us? This one, let us say, is a good and zealous hater (no one can deny that hating belongs to the ordinary human article), en-couraged by epaulets, posters, flashy rhetoric, and pervasive dema-goguery. And this one is an envious malcontent, lustful for a change of leadership. And this one is a simple patriot. And this one, unem-ployed, is a dupe of the speechmakers. Such portraits, both credible and problematical, are common enough. But let us concede that most of the bystanders were quiet citizens who wanted nothing more than to get on with their private lives: a portrait entirely palatable to you and me. The ordinary human article seeks nothing more com-plex than the comforts of indifference to public clamor of any kind. Indifference is a way of sheltering oneself from evil; who would in-terpret such unaggressive sheltering as a contribution to evil? The or-dinary human article hardly looks to get mixed up in active and wholesale butchery of populations; what rational person would want to accuse the bystander—who has done no more than avert her eyes—of a hardness-of-heart in any way approaching that of the criminals? That would be a serious lie—a distortion both of fact and of psychological understanding.

Yet it is the nature of indifference itself that bewilders. How is it that indifference, which on its own does no apparent or immediate positive harm, ends by washing itself in the very horrors it means to have nothing to do with? Hoping to confer no hurt, indifference fi-nally grows lethal; why is that? Can it be that indifference, ostensi-bly passive, harbors an unsuspected robustness? The act of turning toward—while carrying a club—is an act of brutality; but the act of turning away, however empty-handed and harmlessly, remains nev-ertheless an *act*. The whole truth may be that the idea of human pas-sivity is nothing but the illusion of wistful mortals; and that waking into the exigencies of our own time—whichever way we turn, to-ward or away—implies action. To be born is to be compelled to act.

One of the most curious (and mephitic) powers of indifference is its retroactive capacity: it is possible to be indifferent *nunc pro tunc*. I am thinking of a few sentences I happened to be shown the other day: they were from the pen of a celebrated author who was commenting on a piece of so-called "Holocaust writing." "These old events," he complained, "can rake you over only so much, and then you long for a bit of satire on it all. Like so many others of my generation"—he was a young adult during the Forties—"who had nothing to do with any of it, I've swallowed all the guilt I can bear, and if I'm going to be lashed, I intend to save my skin for more recent troubles in the world."

Never mind the odd protestation of innocence where nothing has been charged—what secret unquiet lies within this fraying conscience? What is odder still is that a statement of retroactive indifference is represented as a commitment to present compassion. As for present compassion, does anyone doubt that there is enough contemporary suffering to merit one's full notice? Besides, a current indifference to "these old events" seems harmless enough now; the chimneys of Dachau and Birkenau and Belsen have been cold for fifty years. But does this distinguished figure—a voice of liberalism as well as noteworthy eloquence—suppose that indifference to "old events" frees one for attention to new ones? In fact, indifference to past suffering is a sure sign that there will be indifference to present suffering. Jaded feelings have little to do with the staleness of any event. To be "jaded" is to decline to feel at all.

And that is perhaps the central point about indifference, whether retroactive or current. Indifference is not so much a gesture of looking away—of choosing to be passive—as it is an active disinclination to feel. Indifference shuts down the humane, and does it deliberately, with all the strength deliberateness demands. Indifference is as determined—and as forcefully muscular—as any blow. For the victims on their way to the chimneys, there is scarcely anything to choose between a thug with an uplifted truncheon and the decent citizen who will not lift up his eyes.

II

We have spoken of three categories: criminal, victim, bystander. There is a fourth category—so minuscule that statistically it vanishes. Fortunately it is not a category that can be measured by number—its measure is metaphysical and belongs to the sublime. "Whoever saves a single life," says the Talmud, "is as one who has saved an entire world." This is the category of those astounding souls who refused to stand by as their neighbors were being hauled away to the killing sites. They were willing to see, to judge, to decide. Not only did they not avert their eyes—they set out to rescue. They are the heroes of Nazified Europe. They are Polish, Italian, Romanian, Russian, Hungarian, French, Yugoslavian, Swiss, Swedish, Dutch, Spanish, German. They are Catholic and Protestant. They are urban and rural; educated and uneducated; sophisticated and simple; they include nuns and socialists. And whatever they did, they did at the risk of their lives.

It is typical of all of them to deny any heroism. "It was only decent," they say. But no: most people are decent; the bystanders were decent. The rescuers are somehow raised above the merely decent. When the rescuers declare that heroism is beside the point, it is hard to agree with them.

There is, however, another view, one that takes the side of the rescuers. Under the steady Jerusalem sun stands a low and somber building known as Yad Vashem: a memorial to the Six Million, a place of mourning, a substitute for the missing headstones of the victims; there are no graveyards for human beings ground into bone meal and flown into evanescent smoke. But Yad Vashem is also a grove of celebration and honor: a grand row of trees, one for each savior, marks the valor of the Christian rescuers of Europe, called the Righteous Among the Nations. Mordechai Paldiel, the director of the Department for the Righteous at Yad Vashem, writing in *The Jerusalem Post* not long ago, offered some arresting reflections on the "normality" of goodness:

> We are somehow determined to view these benefactors as heroes: hence the search for underlying motives. The Righteous persons, however, consider themselves as anything but heroes, and regard their behavior during the Holocaust as quite normal. How to resolve this enigma?
>
> For centuries we have undergone a brain-washing process by philosophers who emphasized man's despicable character, highlighting his egotistic and evil disposition at the expense of other attributes. Wittingly or not, together with Hobbes and Freud, we accept the proposition that man is essentially an aggressive being, bent on destruction, involved principally with himself, and only marginally interested in the needs of others. . . .
>
> Goodness leaves us gasping, for we refuse to recognize it as a natural human attribute. So off we go on a long search for some hidden motivation, some extraordinary explanation, for such peculiar behavior.
>
> Evil is, by contrast, less painfully assimilated. There is no

comparable search for the reasons for its constant manifestation (although in earlier centuries theologians pondered this issue).

We have come to terms with evil. Television, movies and the printed word have made evil, aggression and egotism household terms and unconsciously acceptable to the extent of making us immune to displays of evil. There is a danger that the evil of the Holocaust will be absorbed in a similar manner; that is, explained away as further confirmation of man's inherent disposition to wrongdoing. It confirms our visceral feeling that man is an irredeemable beast, who needs to be constrained for his own good.

In searching for an explanation of the motivations of the Righteous Among the Nations, are we not really saying: what was wrong with them? Are we not, in a deeper sense, implying that their behavior was something other than normal? . . . Is acting benevolently and altruistically such an outlandish and unusual type of behavior, supposedly at odds with man's inherent character, as to justify a meticulous search for explanations? Or is it conceivable that such behavior is as natural to our psychological constitution as the egoistic one we accept so matter-of-factly?

It is Mr. Paldiel's own goodness that leaves me gasping. How I want to assent to his thesis! How alluring it is! His thesis asserts that it is the rescuers who are in possession of the reality of human nature, not the bystanders; it is the rescuers who are the ordinary human article. "In a place where there are no human beings, *be* one"—it is apparent that the rescuers were born to embody this rabbinic text. It is not, they say, that they are exceptions; it is that they are human. They are not to be considered "extraordinary," "above the merely decent."

Yet their conduct emphasizes—exemplifies—the exceptional.

For instance:

Giorgio Perlasca, an Italian from Padua, had a job in the Spanish Embassy in Budapest. When the Spanish envoy fled before the invading Russians, Perlasca substituted the Spanish "Jorge" for the Italian "Giorgio" and passed himself off as the Spanish chargé d'affaires. He carried food and powdered milk to safe houses under the Spanish flag, where several hundred Jews at a time found a haven. He issued protective documents that facilitated the escape of Jews with Spanish passes. "I began to feel like a fish in water," he said of his life as an impostor: the sole purpose of his masquerade was to save Jews. And he saved thousands.

Bert Berchove was a Dutch upholsterer who lived with his wife and two children in a large apartment over his shop, in a town not far from Amsterdam. At first he intended to help only his wife's best friend, who was Jewish; her parents had already been deported. Berchove constructed a hiding place in the attic, behind a false wall. Eventually thirty-seven Jews were hidden there.

In a Dominican convent near Vilna, seven nuns and their mother superior sheltered a number of Jews who had escaped from the ghetto, including some poets and writers. The fugitives were disguised in nuns' habits. The sisters did not stop at hiding Jews: they scoured the countryside for weapons to smuggle into the ghetto.

Who will say that the nuns, the upholsterer, and the impostor are not extraordinary in their altruism, their courage, the electrifying boldness of their imaginations? How many nuns have we met who would think of dressing Jewish poets in wimples? How many upholsterers do we know who would actually design and build a false wall? Who among us would dream of fabricating a fake diplomatic identity in order to save Jewish lives? Compassion, it is clear, sharpens intuition and augments imagination.

For me, the rescuers are *not* the ordinary human article. Nothing would have been easier than for each and every one of them to have remained a bystander, like all those millions of their countrymen in the nations of Europe. It goes without saying that the bystanders, especially in the occupied lands, had troubles enough of their own, and hardly needed to go out of their way to acquire new burdens and frights. I do not—cannot—believe that human beings are, without explicit teaching, naturally or intrinsically altruistic. I do not believe, either, that they are naturally vicious, though they can be trained to be. The truth (as with most truths) seems to be somewhere in the middle: most people are born bystanders. The ordinary human article does not want to be disturbed by extremes of any kind—not by risks, or adventures, or unusual responsibility.

And those who undertook the risks, those whose bravery steeped them in perilous contingencies, those whose moral strength urged them into heart-stopping responsibility—what (despite their demurrals) are they really, if not the heroes of our battered world? What other name can they possibly merit? In the Europe of the most savage decade of the twentieth century, not to be a bystander was the choice of an infinitesimal few. These few are more substantial than the multitudes from whom they distinguished themselves; and it is from these undeniably heroic and principled few that we can learn the full resonance of civilization.

LITERARY LANGUAGE

In the 1960s the great literary critic Northrop Frye pointed out the difference between two writing styles: the *demotic* style, which follows the patterns and diction of ordinary speech, and the *hieratic* style, which uses "elevated" or formal kinds of language and structure. Frye was following a method of analysis that has been used since the ancient Greeks to classify literature: the separation of speech and writing into categories of "common" (or "low," as the Greeks termed it) and "grand" (or "high") style. The idea is that a person adjusts his or her language and speech patterns to the occasion and the subject matter. The kind of language spoken publicly at a formal occasion, such as an elaborate wedding, is not that spoken at one A.M. on a Saturday night in a bikers' bar. In literature, the difference might be characterized as that between the "plain" and "fancy" styles, with room for gradations in the middle.

None of this analysis implies that one style is innately or automatically better than another (though the Greeks and the seventeenth-century British certainly thought so). Ernest Hemingway and many of the great American writers of the twentieth century followed Mark Twain in using demotic language, the language of ordinary speech, to create masterpieces. On the other hand, the works of Herman Melville or Henry James—or Cynthia Ozick, in the present case—put the reader in the presence of uncommon authority over language. Ozick's "Of Christian Heroism" represents the modern hieratic style, with its emotive vocabulary, its rolling, intricately constructed sentences, and expanded imagery. Ozick never "talks down" to the reader, but works toward the cumulative effect of resonant language.

The basic principle of judging literary style is *that style is best that best supports the aims of the author.* Appropriateness to the content and situation, to the reader who is being invited to join in the conversation—these are the determinations of effective literary language. A good reader can enjoy nearly every well-constructed situation, just as a good guest can enjoy nearly every kind of party.

Study Questions

1. Ozick defines three categories of "participants" in the Holocaust and then adds a fourth category. Notice the structural pattern of the essay, as the author identifies and describes each of those categories. Name and explain the categories.
2. Notice how Ozick is creating an argument, building toward her thesis point by point. Explain, in your own words, Mordecai Paldiel's point about the "normality of goodness." How is his idea different from our general view of whether human beings are basically good or bad?
3. "When a whole population takes on the status of bystander, the victims are without allies; the criminals, unchecked, are strengthened," Ozick writes. Can you name other examples in history or in personal experience (families, perhaps) that would fit this description? What about examples of hatred, war, even genocide and "ethnic cleansing," taking place today?

Writing Topics

1. In the second paragraph, Ozick asks intensely personal and pointed questions: "Which, of this entangled trio, are we? Which are we most likely to have become?" Perhaps we cannot even guess this about ourselves (does everyone secretly see himself or herself as a hero?)—but we might take a considered guess about other people. Describe a person who you think would be a bystander or a hero in a terrible situation such as the Holocaust. What qualities of character does that person exemplify? Explain your reasoning.
2. Is it possible for a horror such as the Holocaust to happen again, perhaps in the twenty-first century? Could it happen here? Write an essay in which you explain why or why not, under what conditions it could happen, or what has happened since that might prevent another such monstrous evil.

From Walden

CONCLUSION

To the sick the doctors wisely recommend a change of air and scenery. Thank Heaven, here is not all the world. The buck-eye does not grow in New England, and the mocking-bird is rarely heard here. The wild-goose is more of a cosmopolite than we; he breaks his fast in Canada, takes a luncheon in the Ohio, and plumes himself for the night in a southern bayou. Even the bison, to some extent, keeps pace with the seasons, cropping the pastures of the Colorado only till a greener and sweeter grass awaits him by the Yellowstone. Yet we think that if rail-fences are pulled down, and stone-walls piled up on our farms, bounds are henceforth set to our lives and our fates decided. If you are chosen town-clerk, forsooth, you cannot go to Tierra del Fuego this summer: but you may go to the land of infernal fire nevertheless. The universe is wider than our views of it.

Yet we should oftener look over the tafferel of our craft, like curious passengers, and not make the voyage like stupid sailors picking oakum. The other side of the globe is but the home of our correspondent. Our voyaging is only great-circle sailing, and the doctors prescribe for diseases of the skin merely. One hastens to Southern Africa to chase the giraffe; but surely that is not the game he would be after. How long, pray, would a man hunt giraffes if he could? Snipes and woodcocks also may afford rare sport; but I trust it would be nobler game to shoot one's self.—

> "Direct your eye sight inward, and you'll find
> A thousand regions in your mind
> Yet undiscovered. Travel them, and be
> Expert in home-cosmography."

What does Africa,—what does the West stand for? Is not our own interior white on the chart? black though it may prove, like the coast, when discovered. Is it the source of the Nile, or the Niger, or the

Mississippi, or a North-West Passage around this continent, that we would find? Are these the problems which most concern mankind? Is Franklin the only man who is lost, that his wife should be so earnest to find him? Does Mr. Grinnell know where he himself is? Be rather the Mungo Park, the Lewis and Clarke and Frobisher, of your own streams and oceans; explore your own higher latitudes,—with shiploads of preserved meats to support you, if they be necessary; and pile the empty cans sky-high for a sign. Were preserved meats invented to preserve meat merely? Nay, be a Columbus to whole new continents and worlds within you, opening new channels, not of trade, but of thought. Every man is the lord of a realm beside which the earthly empire of the Czar is but a petty state, a hummock left by the ice. Yet some can be patriotic who have no *self*-respect, and sacrifice the greater to the less. They love the soil which makes their graves, but have no sympathy with the spirit which may still animate their clay. Patriotism is a maggot in their heads. What was the meaning of that South-Sea Exploring Expedition, with all its parade and expense, but an indirect recognition of the fact, that there are continents and seas in the moral world, to which every man is an isthmus or an inlet, yet unexplored by him, but that it is easier to sail many thousand miles through cold and storm and cannibals, in a government ship, with five hundred men and boys to assist one, than it is to explore the private sea, the Atlantic and Pacific Ocean of one's being alone.—

> "Erret, et extremos alter scrutetur Iberos.
> Plus haber hic vitæ, plus habet ille viæ."

Let them wander and scrutinize the outlandish Australians.
I have more of God, they more of the road.

It is not worth the while to go round the world to count the cats in Zanzibar. Yet do this even till you can do better, and you may perhaps find some "Symmes' Hole" by which to get at the inside at last. England and France, Spain and Portugal, Gold Coast and Slave Coast, all front on this private sea; but no bark from them has ventured out of sight of land, though it is without doubt the direct way to India. If you would learn to speak all tongues and conform to the customs of all nations, if you would travel farther than all travellers, be naturalized in all climes, and cause the Sphinx to dash her head against a stone, even obey the precept of the old philosopher, and Explore thyself. Herein are demanded the eye and the nerve. Only the defeated and deserters go to the wars, cowards that run away and enlist. Start now on that farthest western way, which does not pause at the Mississippi or the Pacific, nor conduct toward a worn-out China or Japan, but leads on direct a tangent to this sphere, summer and winter, day and night, sun down, moon down, and at last earth down too.

It is said that Mirabeau took to highway robbery "to ascertain what degree of resolution was necessary in order to place one's self in formal opposition to the most sacred laws of society." He declared that "a soldier who fights in the ranks does not require half so much courage as a foot-pad,"—"that honor and religion have never stood in the way of a well-considered and a firm resolve." This was manly, as the world goes; and yet it was idle, if not desperate. A saner man would have found himself often enough "in formal opposition" to what are deemed "the most sacred laws of society," through obedience to yet more sacred laws, and so have tested his resolution without going out of his way. It is not for a man to put himself in such an attitude to society, but to maintain himself in whatever attitude he find himself through obedience to the laws of his being, which will never be one of opposition to a just government, if he should chance to meet with such.

I left the woods for as good a reason as I went there. Perhaps it seemed to me that I had several more lives to live, and could not spare any more time for that one. It is remarkable how easily and insensibly we fall into a particular route, and make a beaten track for ourselves. I had not lived there a week before my feet wore a path from my door to the pond-side; and though it is five or six years since I trod it, it is still quite distinct. It is true, I fear that others may have fallen into it, and so helped to keep it open. The surface of the earth is soft and impressible by the feet of men; and so with the paths which the mind travels. How worn and dusty, then, must be the highways of the world, how deep the ruts of tradition and conformity! I did not wish to take a cabin passage, but rather to go before the mast and on the deck of the world, for there I could best see the moonlight amid the mountains. I do not wish to go below now.

I learned this, at least, by my experiment; that if one advances confidently in the direction of his dreams, and endeavors to live the life which he has imagined, he will meet with a success unexpected in common hours. He will put some things behind, will pass an invisible boundary; new, universal, and more liberal laws will begin to establish themselves around and within him; or the old laws be expanded, and interpreted in his favor in a more liberal sense, and he will live with the license of a higher order of beings. In proportion as he simplifies his life, the laws of the universe will appear less complex, and solitude will not be solitude, nor poverty poverty, nor weakness weakness. If you have built castles in the air, your work need not be lost; that is where they should be. Now put the foundations under them.

It is a ridiculous demand which England and America make, that you shall speak so that they can understand you. Neither men nor toad-stools grow so. As if that were important, and there were not enough to understand you without them. As if Nature could support but one order of understandings, could not sustain birds as well as quadrupeds, flying as well as creeping things, and *hush* and *who*, which Bright can understand, were the best English. As if there were safety in stupidity alone. I fear chiefly lest my expression may not be *extra- vagant* enough, may not wander far enough beyond the narrow limits of my daily experience, so as to be adequate to the truth of which I have been convinced. *Extra vagance!* it depends on how you are yarded. The migrating buffalo, which seeks new pastures in another latitude, is not extravagant like the cow which kicks over the pail, leaps the cow-yard fence, and runs after her calf, in milking time. I desire to speak somewhere *without* bounds; like a man in a waking moment, to men in their waking moments; for I am convinced that I cannot exaggerate enough even to lay the foundation of a true expression. Who that has heard a strain of music feared then lest he should speak extravagantly any more forever? In view of the future or possible, we should live quite laxly and undefined in front, our outlines dim and misty on that side; as our shadows reveal an insensible perspiration toward the sun. The volatile truth of our words should continually betray the inadequacy of the residual statement. Their truth is instantly *translated;* its literal monument alone remains. The words which express our faith and piety are not definite; yet they are significant and fragrant like frankincense to superior natures.

Why level downward to our dullest perception always, and praise that as common sense? The commonest sense is the sense of men asleep, which they express by snoring. Sometimes we are inclined to class those who are once-and-a-half witted with the half-witted, because we appreciate only a third part of their wit. Some would find fault with the morning-red, if they ever got up early enough. "They pretend," as I hear, "that the verses of Kabir have four different senses; illusion, spirit, intellect, and the exoteric doctrine of the Vedas;" but in this part of the world it is considered a ground for complaint if a man's writings admit of more than one interpretation.

While England endeavors to cure the potato-rot, will not any endeavor to cure the brain-rot, which prevails so much more widely and fatally?

I do not suppose that I have attained to obscurity, but I should be proud if no more fatal fault were found with my pages on this score than was found with the Walden ice. Southern customers objected to its blue color, which is the evidence of its purity, as if it were muddy, and preferred the Cambridge ice, which is white, but tastes of weeds. The purity men love is like the mists which envelop the earth, and not like the azure ether beyond.

Some are dinning in our ears that we Americans, and moderns generally, are intellectual dwarfs compared with the ancients, or even the Elizabethan men. But what is that to the purpose? A living dog is better than a dead lion. Shall a man go and hang himself because he belongs to the race of pygmies, and not be the biggest pygmy that he can? Let every one mind his own business, and endeavor to be what he was made.

Why should we be in such desperate haste to succeed, and in such desperate enterprises? If a man does not keep pace with his companions, perhaps it is because he hears a different drummer. Let him step to the music which he hears, however measured or far away. It is not important that he should mature as soon as an apple-tree or an oak. Shall he turn his spring into summer? If the condition of things which we were made for is not yet, what were any reality which we can substitute? We will not be shipwrecked on a vain reality. Shall we with pains erect a heaven of blue glass over ourselves, though when it is done we shall be sure to gaze still at the true ethereal heaven far above, as if the former were not?

There was an artist in the city of Kouroo who was disposed to strive after perfection. One day it came into his mind to make a staff. Having considered that in an imperfect work time is an ingredient, but into a perfect work time does not enter, he said to himself, It shall be perfect in all respects, though I should do nothing else in my life. He proceeded instantly to the forest for wood, being resolved that it should not be made of unsuitable material; and as he searched for and rejected stick after stick, his friends gradually deserted him, for they grew old in their works and died, but he grew not older by a moment. His singleness of purpose and resolution, and his elevated piety, endowed him, without his knowledge, with perennial youth. As he made no compromise with Time, Time kept out of his way, and only sighed at a distance because he could not overcome him. Before he had found a stock in all respects suitable the city of Kouroo was a hoary ruin, and he sat on one of its mounds to peel the stick. Before he had given it the proper shape the dynasty of the Candahars was at an end, and with the point of the stick he wrote the name of the last of that race in the sand, and then resumed his work. By the time he had smoothed and polished the staff Kalpa was no longer the pole-star; and ere he had put on the ferule and the head adorned with precious stones, Brahma had awoke and slumbered many times. But why do I stay to mention these things? When the finishing stroke was put to his work, it suddenly expanded before the eyes of the astonished artist into the fairest of all the creations of Brahma. He had made a new system in making a staff, a world with full and fair proportions; in which, though the old cities and dynasties had passed away, fairer and more glorious ones had taken their places. And now he saw by the heap of shavings still fresh at his feet, that, for him and his work, the former lapse of time had been an illusion, and that no more time had elapsed than is required for a single scintillation from the brain of Brahma to fall on and inflame the tinder of a mortal brain. The material was pure, and his art was pure; how could the result be other than wonderful?

No face which we can give to a matter will stead us so well at last as the truth. This alone wears well. For the most part, we are not where we are, but in a false position. Through an infirmity of our natures, we suppose a case, and put ourselves into it, and hence are in two cases at the same time, and it is doubly difficult to get out. In sane moments we regard only the facts, the case that is. Say what you have to say, not what you ought. Any truth is better than make-believe. Tom Hyde, the tinker, standing on the gallows, was asked if he had any thing to say. "Tell the tailors," said he, "to remember to make a knot in their thread before they take the first stitch." His companion's prayer is forgotten.

However mean your life is, meet it and live it; do not shun it and call it hard names. It is not so bad as you are. It looks poorest when you are richest. The fault-finder will find faults even in paradise. Love your life, poor as it is. You may perhaps have some pleasant, thrilling, glorious hours, even in a poor-house. The setting sun is reflected from the windows of the alms-house as brightly as from the rich man's abode; the snow melts before its door as early in the spring. I do not see but a quiet mind may live as contentedly there, and have as cheering thoughts, as in a palace. The town's poor seem to me often to live the most independent lives of any. May be they are simply great enough to receive without misgiving. Most think that they are above being supported by the town; but it oftener happens that they are not above supporting themselves by dishonest means, which should be more disreputable. Cultivate poverty like a garden herb, like sage. Do not trouble yourself much to get new things, whether clothes or friends. Turn the old; return to them. Things do not change; we change. Sell your clothes and keep your thoughts. God will see that you do not want society. If I were confined to a corner of a garret all my days, like a spider, the world would be just as large to me while I had my thoughts about me. The philosopher said: "From an army of three divisions one can take away its general, and put it in disorder; from the man the most abject and vulgar one cannot take away his thought." Do not seek so anxiously to be developed, to subject yourself to many influences to be played on; it is all dissipation. Humility like darkness reveals the heavenly lights. The shadows of poverty and meanness gather around us, "and lo! creation widens to our view." We are often reminded that if there were bestowed on us the wealth of Crœsus, our aims must still be the same, and our means essentially the same. Moreover, if you are restricted in your range by poverty, if you cannot buy books and newspapers, for instance, you are but confined to the most significant and vital experiences; you are compelled to deal with the material which yields the most sugar and the most starch. It is life near the bone where it is sweetest. You are defended from being a trifler. No man loses ever on a lower level by magnanimity on a higher. Superfluous wealth can buy superfluities only. Money is not required to buy one necessary of the soul.

I live in the angle of a leaden wall, into whose composition was poured a little alloy of bell metal. Often, in the repose of my midday, there reaches my ears a confused *tintinnabulum* from without. It is the noise of my contemporaries. My neighbors tell me of their adventures with famous gentlemen and ladies, what notabilities they met at the dinner-table; but I am no more interested in such things than in the contents of the Daily Times. The interest and the conversation are about costume and manners chiefly; but a goose is a goose still, dress it as you will. They tell me of California and Texas, of England and the Indies, of the Hon. Mr. —— of Georgia or of Massachusetts, all transient and fleeting phenomena, till I am ready to leap from their court-yard like the Mameluke bey. I delight to come to my bearings,—not walk in procession with pomp and parade, in a conspicuous place, but to walk even with the Builder of the universe, if I may,—not to live in this restless, nervous, bustling, trivial Nineteenth Century, but stand or sit thoughtfully while it goes by. What are men celebrating? They are all on a committee of arrangements, and hourly expect a speech from somebody. God is only the president of the day, and Webster is his orator. I love to weigh, to settle, to gravitate toward that which most strongly and rightfully attracts me;—not hang by the beam of the scale and try to weigh less,—not suppose a case, but take the case that is; to travel the only path I can, and that on which no power can resist me. It affords me no satisfaction to commence to spring an arch before I have got a solid foundation. Let us not play at kittlybenders. There is a solid bottom every where. We read that the traveller asked the boy if the swamp before him had a hard bottom. The boy replied that it had. But presently the traveller's horse sank in up to the girths, and he observed to the boy, "I thought you said that this bog had a hard bottom." "So it has," answered the latter, "but you have not got half way to it yet." So it is with the bogs and quicksands of society; but he is an old boy that knows it. Only what is thought said or done at a certain rare coincidence is good. I would not be one of those who will foolishly drive a nail into mere lath and plastering; such a deed would keep me awake nights. Give me a hammer, and let me feel for the furrowing. Do not depend on the putty. Drive a nail home and clinch it so faithfully that you can wake up in the night and think of your work with satisfaction,—a work at which you would not be ashamed to invoke the Muse. So will help you God, and so only. Every nail driven should be as another rivet in the machine of the universe, you carrying on the work.

Rather than love, than money, than fame, give me truth. I sat at a table where were rich food and wine in abundance, and obsequious attendance, but sincerity and truth were not; and I went away hungry from the inhospitable board. The hospitality was as cold as the ices. I thought that there was no need of ice to freeze them. They talked to me of the age of the wine and the fame of the vintage; but I thought of an older, a newer, and purer wine, of a more glorious vintage, which they had not got, and could not buy. The style, the house and grounds and "entertainment" pass for nothing with me. I called on the king, but he made me wait in his hall, and conducted like a man incapacitated for hospitality. There was a man in my neighborhood who lived in a hollow tree. His manners were truly regal. I should have done better had I called on him.

How long shall we sit in our porticoes practising idle and musty virtues, which any work would make impertinent? As if one were to begin the day with long-suffering, and hire a man to hoe his potatoes; and in the afternoon go forth to practise Christian meekness and charity with goodness aforethought! Consider the China pride and stagnant self-complacency of mankind. This generation reclines a little to congratulate itself on being the last of an illustrious line; and in Boston and London and Paris and Rome, thinking of its long descent, it speaks of its progress in art and science and literature with satisfaction. There are the Records of the Philosophical Societies, and the public Eulogies of *Great Men!* It is the good Adam contemplating his own virtue. "Yes, we have done great deeds, and sung divine songs, which shall never die,"—that is, as long as *we* can remember them. The learned societies and great men of Assyria,—where are they? What youthful philosophers and experimentalists we are! There is not one of my readers who has yet lived a whole human life. These may be but the spring months in the life of the race. If we have had the seven-years' itch, we have not seen the seventeen-year locust yet in Concord. We are acquainted with a mere pellicle of the globe on which we live. Most have not delved six feet beneath the surface, nor leaped as many above it. We know not where we are. Beside, we are sound asleep nearly half our time. Yet we esteem ourselves wise, and have an established order on the surface. Truly, we are deep thinkers, we are ambitious spirits! As I stand over the insect crawling amid the pine needles on the forest floor, and endeavoring to conceal itself from my sight, and ask myself why it will cherish those humble thoughts, and hide its head from me who might perhaps be its benefactor, and impart to its race some cheering information, I am reminded of the greater Benefactor and Intelligence that stands over me the human insect.

There is an incessant influx of novelty into the world, and yet we tolerate incredible dulness. I need only suggest what kind of sermons are still listened to in the most enlightened countries. There are such words as joy and sorrow, but they are only the burden of a psalm, sung with a nasal twang, while we believe in the ordinary and mean. We think that we can change our clothes only. It is said that the British Empire is very large and respectable, and that the United States are a first-rate power. We do not believe that a tide rises and falls behind every man which can float the British Empire like a chip, if he should ever harbor it in his mind. Who knows what sort of seventeen-year locust will next come out of the ground? The government of the world I live in was not framed, like that of Britain, in after-dinner conversations over the wine.

The life in us is like the water in the river. It may rise this year higher than man has ever known it, and flood the parched uplands; even this may be the eventful year, which will drown out all our muskrats. It was not always dry land where we dwell. I see far inland the banks which the stream anciently washed, before science began to record its freshets. Every one has heard the story which has gone the rounds of New England, of a strong and beautiful bug which came out of the dry leaf of an old table of apple-tree wood, which had stood in a farmer's kitchen for sixty years, first in Connecticut, and afterward in Massachusetts,—from an egg deposited in the living tree many years earlier still, as appeared by counting the annual layers beyond it; which was heard gnawing out for several weeks, hatched perchance by the heat of an urn. Who does not feel his faith in a resurrection and immortality strengthened by hearing of this? Who knows what beautiful and winged life, whose egg has been buried for ages under many concentric layers of woodenness in the dead dry life of society, deposited at first in the alburnum of the green and living tree, which has been gradually converted into the semblance of its well-seasoned tomb,—heard perchance gnawing out now for years by the astonished family of man, as they sat round the festive board,—may unexpectedly come forth from amidst society's most trivial and handselled furniture, to enjoy its perfect summer life at last!

I do not say that John or Jonathan will realize all this; but such is the character of that morrow which mere lapse of time can never make to dawn. The light which puts out our eyes is darkness to us. Only that day dawns to which we are awake. There is more day to dawn. The sun is but a morning star.

ALLUSION

The language of *Walden* is well above common diction, but the selection's message—to turn inward and live simply—is accessible to any good reader. Some of the impressive quality of this work comes from Thoreau's use of *allusions,* or references to other works or writers.

An author who uses an allusion mentions another, separate work or idea in order to intensify or clarify what is being said. For example, in the second paragraph Thoreau alludes to a number of explorers, among them the Lewis and Clark expedition. The reader who knows about these expeditions gains understanding because with the mention of each name comes another little flood of ideas and understandings. An allusion is like a fine picture hung on the wall of a beautifully decorated room; the picture brings with it another view, a set of perceptions that increases the total effect.

An allusion works two ways: When a reader understands the allusion, it adds richness, depth, and detail to the reading. When a reader *doesn't* pick up on the allusion, he or she has the opportunity to learn something new.

The secret of reading heavily allusive prose without getting bogged down is to practice defining from context on a different level. (See "In Focus: Defining from Context," p. 59.) Instead of guessing briefly at the meaning of a word and then moving on quickly, guess at the content of a work being alluded to. If the allusion is clear immediately, all well and good. If not, mark the allusion for later reference. Of course, the more one reads and learns, the more allusions one will recognize and the less problematic Thoreau's level of writing becomes. Then the process of educating oneself by reading becomes an upward spiral.

Study Questions

1. Thoreau begins the chapter with a series of images of travel and exploration, pointing out that one can travel to foreign places but the best direction is inward. He himself never traveled very far from his home village of Concord, Massachusetts. The tiny cabin in the woods on the shores of Walden pond that Thoreau built and lived in for two years was a relatively easy walk from his family home in town (the countryside was easier to reach in the mid-nineteenth century). Yet Thoreau always considered himself a traveler, a voyager. "I have traveled much in Concord," he writes elsewhere. His journeying was of the mind, and he was not afraid of unknown territory.

   Compare Thoreau's kind of traveling, the kind he recommends, with the kind of traveling people normally do. What is ordinary traveling? What do people usually learn on a vacation trip? In what sense may traveling become a true challenge to the mind, an expansion of understanding?

2. "Let us consider the way in which we spend our lives," Thoreau writes. He spent his creative life challenging the ordinary thinking of his day, and of ours. He urged his readers to live life fully, with less concern for spending money than concern for spending life.

   Find, in the conclusion to *Walden*, three or four sentences or passages that challenge the way you (or others you know) spend life. What are you trading life for? When do you feel that you are living life (rather than spending it) most fully, and why aren't there more times like that? What could be done to bring your life more in accordance with the way that Thoreau recommends?

Writing Topics

1. Write an essay in which you describe the life of someone who "hears a different drummer." Give the reader an idea of what went into creating that person's individuality, and the joys and drawbacks of such a life. This can be fiction, but use details from real-life experiences to make it realistic.

   Alternately, do some research and describe Henry David Thoreau as a person who listened to a different drummer.
2. *Collaborative writing activity.* Thoreau writes, "I learned this, at least, by my experiment; that if one advances confidently in the direction of his dreams, and endeavors to live the life which he has imagined, he will meet with a success unexpected in common hours." Consider whether that statement is true in your experience, and what "advanc[ing] confidently in the direction of his dreams" really means, in light of the rest of the chapter. Write a description of one or two people you know who are "advanc[ing] confidently in the direction of" their own dreams. Then compare that description with those of others in your group or class. In what ways is "advanc[ing] confidently" similar and different for different people?

Mixed Blood: Columbus's Legacy: A World Made *Mestizo*

RICHARD RODRIGUEZ

I used to stare at the Indian in the mirror. The wide nostrils, the thick lips. Starring Paul Muni as Benito Juarez. Such a long face— such a long nose—sculpted by indifferent, blunt thumbs, and of such common clay. No one in my family had a face as dark or as Indian as mine. My face could not portray the ambition I brought to it. What could the United States of America say to me? I remember reading the ponderous conclusion of the Kerner Report in the Sixties: two Americas, one white, one black—the prophecy of an eclipse too simple to account for the complexity of my face.

Mestizo in Mexican Spanish means mixed, confused. Clotted with Indian, thinned by Spanish spume.

What could Mexico say to me?

Mexican philosophers powwow in their tony journals about Indian "fatalism" and "Whither Mexico?" *El fatalismo del indio* is an important Mexican philosophical theme; the phrase is trusted to conjure the quality of Indian passivity as well as to initiate debate about Mexico's reluctant progress toward modernization. Mexicans imagine their Indian part as dead weight: the Indian stunned by modernity, so overwhelmed by the loss of what is genuine to him—his language, his religion—that he sits weeping like a medieval lady at the crossroads; or else he resorts to occult powers and superstitions, choosing to consort with death because the purpose of the world has passed him by.

One night in Mexico City I ventured far from my hotel to a distant *colonia* to visit my aunt, my father's only sister. But she was not there. She had moved. For the past several years she has moved, this woman of eighty-odd years, from one of her children to another. She takes with her only her papers and books—she is a poetess—and an upright piano painted blue. My aunt writes love poems to her dead husband, Juan—keeping Juan up to date while watering her loss.

Last year she sent me her *obras completas,* an inch-thick block of bound onionskin. And with her poems she sent me a list of names, a genealogy braiding two centuries, two continents, to a common origin: eighteenth-century Salamanca. No explanation is attached to the list. Its implication is nonetheless clear: We are—my father's family is (despite the evidence of my face)—of Europe. We are not Indian.

On the other hand, at Berkeley, an undergraduate approached me cautiously one day, as if I were a stone totem, to say, "God, it must be cool to be related to Aztecs."

I sat down next to the journalist from Pakistan—the guest of honor. He had been making a tour of the United States under the auspices of the U.S. State Department. Nearing the end of his journey now, he was having dinner with several of us, American journalists, at a Chinese restaurant in San Francisco. He said he'd seen pretty much all he wanted to see in America. His wife, however, had asked him to bring back some Indian handicrafts. Blankets. Beaded stuff. He'd looked everywhere.

The table was momentarily captured by the novelty of his dilemma. You can't touch the stuff nowadays, somebody said. So rare, so expensive. Somebody else knew of a shop up on Sacramento Street that sells authentic Santa Fe. Several others remembered a store in Chinatown where moccasins, belts—"the works"—were to be found. All manufactured in Taiwan.

The Pakistani journalist looked incredulous. His dream of America had been shaped by American-export Westerns. Cowboys and Indians are the yin and yang of America. He had seen men dressed like cowboys on this trip. But (turning to me), Where are the Indians?

(Two Indians staring at each other. One asks where are all the Indians, the other shrugs.)

I grew up in Sacramento thinking of Indians as people who had disappeared. I was a Mexican in California; I would no more have thought of myself as an Aztec than you might imagine yourself a Viking or a Bantu. Mrs. Ferrucci up the block used to call us "Spanish." We knew she intended to ennoble us by that designation. We also knew she was ignorant.

I was ignorant.

In America, the Indian is relegated to the obligatory first chapter—the Once Great Nation chapter—after which the Indian is cleared away as easily as brush, using a very sharp rhetorical tool called an "alas." Thereafter, the Indian reappears only as a stunned remnant—Ishi, or the hundred-year-old hag blowing out her birth-day candle at a rest home in Tucson, or the teenager drunk on his ass in the park.

Here they come down Broadway in the Fourth of July parades of my childhood—middle-aged men wearing glasses, beating their tom-toms; *hey-ya-ya-yah; hey-ya-ya-yah.* They wore Bermuda shorts under their loincloths. High school kids could never refrain from the an-swering *woo-woo-woo,* stopping their mouths with the palms of their hands.

In the 1960s, Indians began to name themselves Native Americans, recalling themselves to life. That self-designation underestimated the ruthless idea Puritans had superimposed upon the landscape. Amer-ica is an idea to which natives are inimical. The Indian represented permanence and continuity to Americans who were determined to call this country new. Indians must be ghosts.

I collected conflicting evidence concerning Mexico, it's true, but I never felt myself the remnant of anything. Mexican magazines ar-rived in our mailbox from Mexico City, showed pedestrians strolling wide ocher boulevards beneath trees with lime-green leaves. My past was at least this coherent: Mexico was a real place with plenty of people walking around in it. My parents had come from some-where that went on without them.

When I was a graduate student at Berkeley, teaching remedial English, there were a few American Indians in my classroom. They were unlike any other "minority students" in the classes I taught. The Indians drifted in and out. When I summoned them to my office, they came and sat while I did all the talking.

I remember one tall man particularly, a near-somnambulist, beau-tiful in an off-putting way, but interesting too, because I never saw him without the current issue of *The New York Review of Books* under his arm, which I took as an advertisement of ambition. He eschewed my class for weeks at a time. Then, one morning, I saw him in a cafe on Telegraph Avenue across from Cody's. I did not fancy myself Sid-ney Poitier, but I was interested in this moody brave's lack of inter-est in me, for one, and then *The New York Review of Books.*

Do you mind if I sit here?

Nothing.

Blah. Blah. Blah . . . *N.Y.R.B.?*—entirely on my part—until, when I got up to leave:

You're not Indian, you're Mexican. You wouldn't understand.

He meant I was cut. Diluted.

Understand what?

He meant I was not an Indian in America. He meant he was an enemy of the history that had otherwise created me. And he was right, I didn't understand. I took his diffidence for chauvinism. I read his chauvinism as arrogance. He didn't see the Indian in my face? I saw his face—his refusal to consort with the living—as the face of a dead man.

As the landscape goes, so goes the Indian. In the public-service TV commercial the Indian sheds a tear at the sight of an America polluted beyond his recognition. Indian memory has become the measure against which America gauges corrupting history when it suits us. Gitchigoomeism—the habit of placing the Indian outside history—is a white sentimentality that relegates the Indian to death.

An obituary from the *New York Times* (September 1989, dateline Alaska): An oil freighter has spilled its load along the Alaskan coast. There is a billion-dollar cleanup, bringing jobs and dollars to Indian villages. "The modern world has been closing in on English Bay . . . with glacial slowness. The oil spill and the resulting sea of money have accelerated the process so that English Bay now seems caught on the cusp of history."

The omniscient reporter from the *New York Times* takes it upon himself to regret history on behalf of the Indians. "Instead of hanging salmon to dry this month, as Aleut natives have done for centuries . . . John Kvasnikoff was putting up a three thousand dollar television satellite dish on the bluff next to his home above the sea."

The reporter from the *New York Times* knows the price modernity will exact from an Indian who wants to plug himself in. Mind you, the reporter is confident of his own role in history, his freedom to lug a word processor to some remote Alaskan village. About the reporter's journey, the *Times* is not censorious. But let the Indian drop one bead from custom, or let his son straddle a snowmobile—as he does in the photo accompanying the article—and the *New York Times* cries *boo-hoo-hoo yah-yah-yah*.

Thus does the Indian become the mascot of an international ecology movement. The industrial countries of the world romanticize the Indian who no longer exists, ignoring the Indian who does—the Indian who is poised to chop down his rain forest, for example. Or the Indian who reads the *New York Times*.

Once more in San Francisco: I flattered myself that the woman staring at me all evening "knew my work." I considered myself an active agent, in other words. But after several passes around the buffet, the woman cornered me to say she recognized me as an "ancient soul."

Do I lure or am I just minding my own business?

Is it in the nature of Indians—not verifiable in nature, of course, but in the European description of Indians—that we wait around to be "discovered"?

Europe discovers. India beckons. Isn't that so? India sits atop her lily pad through centuries, lost in contemplation of the horizon. And from time to time India is discovered.

In the fifteenth century, sailing Spaniards were acting according to scientific conjecture as to the nature and as to the shape of the world. Most thinking men in Europe at the time of Columbus believed the world to be round. The voyage of Columbus was the test of a theory believed to be true. Brave, yes, but pedantic, therefore.

The Indian is forever implicated in the roundness of the world. America was the false India, the mistaken India, and yet the veritable India for all that. India—the clasp, the coupling mystery at the end of quest.

This is as true today as of yore. Where do the Beatles go when the world is too much with them? Where does Jerry Brown seek the fat farm of his soul? India, man, India!

India waits.

India has all the answers beneath her passive face or behind her veil or between her legs. The European has only questions, questions that are assertions turned inside out.

According to the European version—the stag version—of the pageant of the New World, the Indian plays a passive role. Europe has been accustomed to playing the swaggart in history—Europe striding through the Americas, overturning temples, spilling language, spilling seed, spilling blood.

And wasn't the Indian the female, the passive, the waiting aspect to the theorem—lewd and promiscuous in her embrace as she is indolent betimes? In European museums, she is idle, recumbent at the base of a silver pineapple tree or the pedestal of the Dresden urn or the Sèvres tureen—the muse of European adventure, at once wanderlust and bounty.

In Western civilization histories, the little honeymoon joke Europe tells on itself is of mistaking America for the extremities of India. But India was perhaps not so much a misnomer as was "discoverer" or "conquistador."

Many tribes of Indians were prescient enough, preserved memory enough, or were lonesome enough to predict the coming of a pale stranger from across the sea, a messianic twin of completing memory or skill.

None of this could the watery Europeans have known as they marveled at the sight of approaching land. Filled with the arrogance of discovery, the Europeans were not predisposed to imagine that they were being watched, awaited.

But the world was round. The entrance into the Indies was a reunion of peoples. The Indian awaited the long-separated European, the inevitable European, as the approaching horizon.

A friend of mine at Cambridge loses patience whenever I describe my face as *mestizo*. Look at my face. What do you see?

An Indian, he says.

Mestizo, I correct.

Mestizo, mestizo, he says.

Listen, he says. I went back to my mother's village in Mexico last summer and there was nothing *mestizo* about it. Dust, dogs, and Indians. People there don't even speak Spanish.

So I ask my friend at Cambridge what it means to him to be an Indian.

He hesitates. My friend has recently been taken up as amusing by a bunch of rich Pakistanis in London. But, facing me, he is vexed and in earnest. He describes a lonely search among his family for evidence of Indianness. He thinks he has found it in his mother, watching his mother in her garden.

Does she plant corn by the light of the moon?

She seems to have some relationship with the earth, he says quietly.

So there it is. The mystical tie to nature. How else to think of the Indian except in terms of some druidical green thumb? No one says of an English matron in her rose garden that she is behaving like a Celt. Because the Indian has no history—that is, because history books are the province of the descendants of Europeans—the Indian seems to belong only to the party of the first part, the first chapter. So that is where the son expects to find his mother, Daughter of the Moon.

Let's talk about something else. Let's talk about London. The last time I was in London I was walking toward an early evening at the Queen's Theatre when I passed that Christopher Wren church near Fortnum & Mason. The church was lit. I decided to stop, to savor the spectacle of what I expected would be a few Pymish men and women rolled into balls of fur at evensong. Imagine my surprise that the congregation was young—dressed in army fatigues and Laura Ashley. Within the chancel, cross-legged on a dais, was a South American shaman.

Now, who is the truer Indian in this picture? Me . . . me on my way to the Queen's Theatre? Or that guy on the altar with a Ph.D. in death?

We have hurled—like starlings, like Goths—through the castle of European memory. Our reflections have glanced upon the golden coach that carried Emperor Maximilian through the streets of Mexico City, thence onward through the sludge of a hundred varnished paintings.

I have come at last to Mexico, the country of my parents' birth. I do not expect to find anything that pertains to me.

We have strained the *rouge* cordon at the thresholds of imperial apartments; seen chairs low enough for dwarfs, commodious enough for angels.

We have imagined Empress Carlota standing in the shadows of an afternoon; we have followed her gaze down the Paseo de la Reforma toward the distant city. The Paseo was a nostalgic allusion to the Champs-Élysées, we learn, which Maximilian re-created for his tempestuous, crow-like bride.

Come this way, please . . .

European memory is not to be the point of our excursion. Señor Fuentes, our tour director, is already beginning to descend the hill from Chapultepec Castle. Señor Fuentes is consumed with contrition for time wasted this morning. Our "orientation tour" of Mexico City had started late, and so Señor Fuentes has been forced, regrettably— This way, please—to rush. He intends to uphold his schedule, as a way of upholding Mexico, against our expectation.

We had gathered at the appointed time at the limousine entrance to our hotel, beneath the banner welcoming contestants to the Señorita Mexico pageant. We—Japanese, Germans, Americans— were waiting promptly at nine. There was no bus. And as we waited, the Señorita Mexico contestants arrived. Drivers leaned into their cabs to pull out long-legged señoritas. The drivers then balanced the señoritas onto stiletto heels (the driveway was cobbled) before they passed the señoritas, *en pointe,* onto the waiting arms of officials.

Mexican men, meanwhile—doormen, bellhops, window washers, hotel guests—stopped dead in their tracks, wounded by the scent and spectacle of so many blond señoritas. The Mexican men assumed fierce expressions, nostrils flared, brows knit. Such expressions are masks—the men intend to convey their adoration of prey—as thoroughly ritualized as the smiles of beauty queens.

By now we can see the point of our excursion beyond the parched

trees of Chapultepec Park—the Museo Nacional de Antropología—
which is an air-conditioned repository for the artifacts of the Indian
civilizations of Mesoamerica, the finest anthropological museum in
the world.

"There will not be time to see everything," Señor Fuentes warns as
he ushers us into the grand salon, our first sight of the debris of the
Ancients. Señor Fuentes wants us in and out of here by noon.

Whereas the United States traditionally has rejoiced at the delivery of its landscape from "savagery," Mexico has taken its national
identity only from the Indian, the mother. Mexico measures all cultural bastardy against the Indian; equates civilization with India—Indian kingdoms of a golden age; cities as fabulous as Alexandria or
Benares or Constantinople; a court as hairless, as subtle as the
Pekingese. Mexico equates barbarism with Europe, beardedness with
Spain.

It is curious, therefore, that both modern nations should similarly
apostrophize the Indian, relegate the Indian to the past.

Come this way, please. Mrs. . . . Ah . . . this way, please.

Señor Fuentes wears an avocado green sports coat with gold buttons. He is short. He is rather elegant, with a fine small head, small
hands, small feet with his two rows of fine small teeth like a nut-
cracker's teeth, with which he curtails consonants as cleanly as bitten thread. Señor Fuentes is brittle, he is watchful, he is ironic, he is
metropolitan; his wit is quotational, literary, wasted on Mrs. Ah.

He is not our equal. His demeanor says he is not our equal. We
mistake his condescension for humility. He will not eat when we
eat. He will not spend when we shop. He will not have done with
Mexico when we have done with Mexico. He is Mexican.

Señor Fuentes is a mystery to us, for there is no American equivalent to him; for there is no American equivalent to the subtleties he
is paid to describe to us.

Mexico will not raise a public monument to Hernán Cortés, for example, the father of Mexico—the rapist. In the Diego Rivera murals
in the presidential palace, the Aztec city of Tenochtitlán is rendered—
its blood temples and blood canals—haughty as Troy, as vulnerable
as Pompeii. Any suggestion of the complicity of other tribes of Indians in overthrowing the Aztec empire is painted over. Spaniards appear on the horizons of Arcadia as syphilitic brigands and demon-
eyed priests.

The Spaniard entered the Indian by entering her city—the floating
city—first as a suitor, ceremoniously, later by force. How should
Mexico honor the rape?

In New England, the European and the Indian drew apart to regard each other with suspicion over centuries. Miscegenation was a sin against Protestant individualism. In Mexico, the European and the Indian consorted. The ravishment of fabulous Tenochtitlán ended in a marriage of blood and the generation of a "cosmic race," as the Mexican philosopher José Vasconcelos has called it.

Mexico's tragedy is that she has no political idea of herself as rich as her blood.

The rhetoric of Señor Fuentes, like the murals of Diego Rivera, resorts often to the dream of India—to Tenochtitlán, the capital of the world before conquest. "Pre-conquest" in the Mexican political lexicon is tantamount to "pre-lapsarian" in the Judeo-Christian scheme, and harkens to a time Mexico feels herself to have been whole, a time before the Indian was separated from India by the serpent Spain.

Three centuries after Cortés Mexico declared herself independent of Spain. If Mexico would have no yoke, then Mexico would have no crown, then Mexico would have no father. The denial of Spain has persisted into our century.

The priest and the landowner yet serve Señor Fuentes as symbols of the hated Spanish order. Though, in private, Mexico is Catholic; Mexican mothers may wish for light-skinned children; touch blond hair and good luck will be yours.

In private, in Mexican Spanish, *indio* is a seller of Chiclets, a sidewalk squatter. *Indio* means backward or lazy or lower-class. In the eyes of the world, Mexico raises a magnificent Museum of Anthropology—the finest in the world—to honor the Indian mother.

In the nave of the National Cathedral, we notice that the floor slopes dramatically. "The cathedral is sinking," Señor Fuentes explains as a hooded figure approaches our group from behind a column. She is an Indian woman. She wears a blue stole; her hands are cupped, beseeching; tear marks ream her cheeks. In spanish, Señor Fuentes forbids this apparition: "Go ask *padrecito* to pry some gold off the altar for you."

"Mexico City is built upon swamp," Señor Fuentes resumes in English. "Therefore, the cathedral is sinking." But it is clear that Señor Fuentes believes the sinkage is due to the oppressive weight of Spanish Catholicism; its masses of gold; its volumes of deluded suspiration.

Mexico blamed the ruin of the nineteenth century on the foreigner, and with reason. Once emptied of Spain, the palace of Mexico became the dollhouse of France. Mexico was overrun by imperial armies. The greed of Europe met the manifest destiny of the United States in Mexico. Austria sent an archduke to marry Mexico with full panoply of candles and bishops. The United States reached under Mexico's skirt every chance he got.

The Mexican habit of blaming the outsider persists. Mexicans call their civil war a "revolution"—"Mexico for Mexicans" was the cry. In fact, it was Mexican against Mexican. Whom now shall Señor Fuentes blame for a twentieth century that has become synonymous with corruption?

Well, as long as you stay out of the way of the police no one will bother you, is conventional Mexican wisdom, and Mexico continues to live her daily life. In the capital, the air is the color of the buildings of Siena. Telephone connections are an aspect of the will of God. Mexicans drive on the sidewalks.

A man on the street corner seizes the opportunity of stalled traffic to earn his living as a fire-eater. His ten children pass among the cars and among the honking horns to collect small coins.

Thank you. Thank you very much. A pleasure, Mrs. . . . Ah. Thank you very much.

Señor Fuentes bids each farewell. He accepts tips within a handshake. He bows slightly. We have no complaint with Señor Fuentes, after all. The bus was not his fault. Mexico City is not his fault. And Señor Fuentes will return to his unimaginable Mexico and we will return to our rooms to take aspirin and to initiate long-distance telephone calls. Señor Fuentes will remove his avocado green coat, and, having divested, Señor Fuentes will in some fashion partake of what he has successfully kept from us all day, which is the life and the drinking water of Mexico.

The Virgin of Guadalupe symbolizes the entire coherence of Mexico, body and soul. You will not find the story of the Virgin within hidebound secular histories of Mexico nor indeed within the credulous repertoire of Señor Fuentes—and the omission renders the history of Mexico incomprehensible.

One recent afternoon, within the winey bell jar of a very late lunch, I told the story of the Virgin of Guadalupe to Lynn, a sophisticated twentieth-century woman. The history of Mexico, I promised her, is neither mundane nor masculine, but it is a miracle play with trapdoors and sequins and jokes on the living.

In the sixteenth century, when Indians were demoralized by the routing of their gods, when Indians were dying by millions from the plague of Europe, the Virgin Mary appeared pacing on a hillside to an

Indian peasant named Juan Diego—his Christian name, for Juan was a convert. It was December 1531.

On his way to Mass, Juan passes the hill called Tepeyac just as the east is beginning to kindle to dawn. He hears there a cloud of bird-song bursting overhead, of whistles and flutes and beating wings, and look: a maiden dressed in the robes of an Aztec princess. She speaks Nahuatl, the Aztec tongue. Her complexion is brown as cinnamon. She is Maria, the Mother of God, the Christian Mary, she tells Juan Diego.

At the Lady's behest, this Prufrock Indian must go several times to the bishop of Mexico City, to ask that a chapel be built on Tepeyac where the Lady can share in the sorrows of her people.

The bishop wants proof.

Peering through the grille of her cigarette smoke, Lynn heard, and she seemed to approve the story.

The Virgin tells Juan Diego to climb the hill and gather a sheaf of roses as proof for the bishop, Castilian roses—impossible in Mexico in December of 1531. Juan carries the roses in the folds of his cloak, a pregnant messenger. Upon entering the bishop's presence, Juan parts his cloak and the roses tumble; the bishop falls to his knees.

The legend concludes with a concession to humanity, proof more durable than roses—the imprint of the Virgin's image upon the cloak of Juan Diego.

But in the end, with crumpled napkins, torn carbon, bitter dregs of coffee, Lynn gave the story over to the Spaniards. A recruitment poster for the new religion, no more, she said. An itinerant diva with a costume trunk. Birgit Nilsson as Aida.

Why do we assume Spain made up the story?

The importance of the story is that Indians believed it. The jokes, the vaudeville, the relegation of the Spanish bishop to the role of comic adversary, the Virgin's unlikely cavalier, and especially the brown-faced Mary—all elements spoke directly to Indians.

The result of the apparition and of the miraculous image of the Lady remaining upon the cloak of Juan Diego was a mass conversion of Indians to Catholicism.

The image of Our Lady of Guadalupe (privately, affectionately, Mexicans call her *"La Morenita"*—little darkling) has become the unofficial, the private flag of Mexicans. Unique possession of her image is a more wonderful election to Mexicans than any political call to nationhood. Perhaps Mexico's tragedy in our century, perhaps Mexico's abiding grace thus far, is that she has no political idea of herself as compelling as her icon.

The Virgin appears everywhere in Mexico. On dashboards and on calendars, on playing cards, on lamp shades and cigar boxes; within the loneliness and tattooed upon the very skins of Mexicans.

Nor is the image of Guadalupe a diminishing mirage of the sixteenth century. She has become more vivid with time, developing in her replication from earthy shades of melon and musk to bubblegum pink, Windex blue, to achieve the hard, literal focus of holy cards or baseball cards; of Krishna or St. Jude or the Atlanta Braves.

Mexico City stands today as the last medieval capital of the world. Mexico is the creation of a Spanish Catholicism that attempted to draw continents together as one flesh. The success of Spanish Catholicism in Mexico resulted in a kind of proof, a profound concession to humanity: the *mestizaje*.

What joke on the living? Lynn said.

The joke is that Spain arrived with missionary zeal at the shores of contemplation. But Spain had no idea of the absorbent strength of Indian spirituality. By the waters of baptism, the active European was entirely absorbed within the contemplation of the Indian. The faith that Europe imposed in the sixteenth century was, by virtue of the Guadalupe, embraced by the Indian. Catholicism has become an Indian religion. By the twenty-first century, the locus of the Catholic Church, by virtue of numbers, will be Latin America, by which time Catholicism itself will have assumed the aspect of the Virgin of Guadalupe.

Brown skin.

Time magazine dropped through the chute of my mailbox a few years ago with a cover story on Mexico headlined "The Population Curse." From the vantage point of Sixth Avenue, the editors of Time-Life peer down into the basin of Mexico City—like peering down into the skull of a pumpkin—to contemplate the nightmare of fecundity, the tangled mass of slime and seed and hair.

America sees death in all that life; sees rot. Life—not illness and poverty; not death—life becomes the curse of Mexico City in the opinion of *Time* magazine.

For a long time, I had my own fear of Mexico, an American fear. Mexico's history was death. Her stature was tragedy. A race of people that looked like me had disappeared.

I had a dream about Mexico City, a conquistador's dream. I was lost and late and twisted in my sheet. I dreamed streets narrower than they actually are—narrow as old Jerusalem. I dreamed sheets, entanglements, bunting, hanging larvae-like from open windows, distended from balconies and from lines thrown over the streets. These streets were not empty streets. I was among a crowd. The crowd was not a carnival crowd. This crowd was purposeful and ordinary, welling up from subways, ascending stairwells. And then the dream followed the course of all my dreams. I must find the airport—the American solution—I must somehow escape, fly over.

Each face looked like mine. But no one looked at me.

I have come at last to Mexico, to the place of my parents' birth. I have canceled this trip three times.

As the plane descends into the basin of Mexico City, I brace myself for some confrontation with death, with India, with confusion of purpose, that I do not know how to master.

"Do you speak Spanish?" the driver asks in English.

Andres, the driver employed by my hotel, is in his forties. He lives in the Colonia Roma, near the airport. There is nothing about the city he does not know. This is his city and he is its memory.

Andres's car is a dark blue Buick—about 1975. Windows slide up and down at the touch of his finger. There is the smell of disinfectant in Andres's car as there is in every bus or limousine or taxi I've ridden in Mexico—the smell of the glycerin crystals in urinals. Dangling from Andres's rearview mirror is the other appliance common to all public conveyance in Mexico—a rosary.

Andres is a man of the world, a man, like other working-class Mexican men, eager for the world. He speaks two languages. He knows several cities. He has been to the United States. His brother lives there still.

In the annals of the famous European discoverers there is invariably an Indian guide, a translator—willing or not—to facilitate, to preserve Europe's stride. These seem to have become fluent in pallor before Europe learned anything of them. How is that possible?

The most famous guide in Mexican history is also the most reviled by Mexican histories—the villainess Marina—"La Malinche." Marina became the lover of Cortés. So, of course, Mexicans say she betrayed India for Europe. In the end, she was herself betrayed, left behind when Cortés repaired to his Spanish wife.

Nonetheless, Marina's treachery anticipates the epic marriage of Mexico. La Malinche prefigures, as well, the other, the beloved female aspect of Mexico, the Virgin of Guadalupe.

Because Marina was the seducer of Spain, she challenges the boast Europe has always told about India.

I assure you Mexico has an Indian point of view as well, a female point of view:

> *I opened my little eye and the Spaniard disappeared.*
> *Imagine a dark pool; the Spaniard dissolved; the surface triumphantly*
>   *smooth.*
> *My eye!*
> *The spectacle of the Spaniard on the horizon, vainglorious—the shiny*
>   *surfaces, clanks of metal; the horses, the muskets, the jingling*
>   *bits.*
> *Cannot you imagine me curious? Didn't I draw near?*

European vocabularies do not have a silence rich enough to describe the force within Indian contemplation. Only Shakespeare understood that Indians have eyes. We took you in. Shakespeare saw Caliban eyeing his master's books—well, why not his master as well? The same dumb lust.

What dat? is a question philosophers ask. And Indians.

Shakespeare's comedy, of course, resolves itself to the European's applause. The play that Shakespeare did not write is Mexico City.

Now the great city swells under the moon; seems, now, to breathe of itself—the largest city in the world—a Globe, kind Will, not of your devising, not under your control.

The superstition persists in European travel literature that Indian Christianity is the thinnest veneer covering an ulterior altar. But there is a possibility still more frightening to the European imagination, so frightening that in 500 years such a possibility has scarcely found utterance.

What if the Indian were converted?

Then the Indian eye becomes a portal through which the entire pageant of European civilization has already passed, turned inside out.

Look once more at the city from La Malinche's point of view. Mexico is littered with the shells and skulls of Spain, cathedrals, poems, and the limbs of orange trees. But everywhere you look in this great museum of Spain, you see living Indians.

Where are the conquistadores?

Post-colonial Europe expresses pity or guilt behind its sleeve, pities the Indian the loss of her gods or her tongue. But let the Indian speak for herself. Spanish is now an Indian language. Mexico City has become the metropolitan see of the Spanish-speaking world. In something like the way New York won English from London after World War I, Mexico City has captured Spanish.

The Indian stands in the same relationship to modernity as she did to Spain—willing to marry, to breed, to disappear in order to ensure her inclusion in time; refusing to absent herself from the future. The Indian has chosen to survive, to consort with the living, to live in the city, to crawl on her hands and knees, if need be, to Mexico City or L.A.

I take it as an Indian achievement that I am alive, that I am Catholic, that I speak English, that I am an American. My life began, it did not end, in the sixteenth century.

The idea occurs to me on a weekday morning, at a crowded intersection in Mexico City: Europe's lie. Here I am in the capital of death. Life surges about me; wells up from subways, wave upon wave; descends from stairwells. Everywhere I look. Babies. Traffic. Food. Beggars. Life. Life coming upon me like sunstroke.

Each face looks like mine. No one looks at me.

Where, then, is the famous conquistador?

We have eaten him, the crowd tells me, *we have eaten him with our eyes.*

I run to the mirror to see if this is true.

It is true.

In the distance, at its depths, Mexico City stands as the prophetic example. Mexico City is modern in ways that "multi-racial," ethnically "diverse" New York City is not yet. Mexico City is centuries more modern than racially "pure," provincial Tokyo. Nothing to do with computers or skyscrapers.

Mexico City is the capital of modernity, for in the sixteenth century, under the tutelage of a curious Indian whore, under the patronage of the Queen of Heaven, Mexico initiated the task of the twenty-first century—the renewal of the old, the known world, through miscegenation. Mexico carries the idea of a round world to its biological conclusion.

For a time, when he was young, Andres, my driver, worked in Alpine County in northern California.

And then he worked at a Lake Tahoe resort. He remembers the snow. He remembers the weekends when blond California girls would arrive in their ski suits and sunglasses. Andres worked at the top of a ski lift. His job was to reach out over a little precipice to help the California girls out of their lift chairs. He would maintain his grasp until they were balanced upon the snow. And then he would release them, watch them descend the winter slope—how they laughed!—oblivious of his admiration, until they disappeared.

MODERNIST NONFICTION

Why is this story so complicated? A man who is Mexican-American by birth, whose family culture is the European culture that was brought to Central America from Spain but whose face reveals how much of his ancestry was Native American—this man is searching for his heritage. That may seem on the surface to be a relatively easy thing to do. But anyone who has seriously confronted the question "Who am I *really?*" will know at once that there aren't many easy or simple answers to that question. Finding one's true identity doesn't happen all in one easy slide from start to finish.

Thus, Rodriguez uses *discontinuous prose* to tell how he searches for his deep self and how he sees himself in his own and his people's history. His essay jumps around: the line spaces at various points in the text signal the start of related but new ideas and substories. Time jumps around, too; the reader doesn't get a sense that this search had a particular beginning or might ever have an end. Such gaps are deliberate, and the discontinuity they create suggests both Rodriguez's struggle to answer the question of who he is and the likelihood that he hasn't yet found any firm answers.

Rodriguez's nonfiction technique owes a great deal to the fiction of the early-twentieth-century Irish writer James Joyce, who in his masterpiece *Ulysses* (1922) used a method of writing called *stream of consciousness* to convey the thoughts of his characters. Joyce aimed to imitate the way the mind works, leaping from idea to idea to barely remembered memory in a steady flow. Here is an example from the first chapter of *Ulysses.*

> Woodshadows floated silently by through the morning peace from the stairhead seaward where he gazed. Inshore and farther out the mirror of water whitened, spurned by lightshod hurrying feet. White breast of the dim sea. The twining stresses, two by two. A hand plucking the harpstrings, merging their twining chords. Wavewhite wedded words shimmering on the dim tide.

Just as modern abstract painters are free from the stricture of making their work look "realistic," modern writers are free to experiment with different methods of communicating feelings and impressions. *Modernist* and *postmodernist* writing styles challenge readers' customary patterns and expectations, inviting the audience to take part in new ways of reading. There are many more ways than one to tell a story.

Study Questions

1. Rodriguez presents a whole series of myths and stories, some of them patent stereotypes and prejudices and others dealing straightforwardly with history and religion. He deliberately doesn't tell the reader what to believe and what to dismiss. Find an example of prejudice in the essay. Find a religious myth. Find an event described that many people take to be fact. Find a historic event. How does one tell the difference between history and story?
2. Rodriguez is looking for his heritage, but there are other searches in the story. What were the conquistadors looking for when they came to Mexico? What is the Pakistani journalist looking for? What is Señor Fuentes looking for?

Writing Topics

1. *Collaborative writing activity.* (If a group works on this topic, have each person relate an incident in some common group experience, then try putting them together.) Write an autobiographical essay in which you present three incidents from your experience in the same way Rodriguez does, with blank spaces between them. Make sure the three incidents are *related*—don't just tell three separate stories. A single theme, point, or feeling should be what gives this essay unity.
2. Take a long look at yourself in the mirror, as Rodriguez does in his first sentence. What do you see? What history is revealed in your face? Write an essay about the historical background of your face, the peoples who created it. (You may wish also to refer to Judith Ortiz Cofer's "The Looking-Glass Shame," p. 363.)

A Dangerous Literacy: The Legacy of Frederick Douglass

HENRY LOUIS GATES JR.

One hundred and fifty years ago, on May 28, Frederick Douglass published the first of his three autobiographies, "Narrative of the Life of Frederick Douglass, an American Slave, Written by Himself." He was barely 27 years old and already a popular figure on the abolition lecture circuit. Almost overnight he would become the most celebrated black author in history; his slender volume supplanted a book of verses by the 18th-century slave poet Phillis Wheatley as the abolitionists' favorite emblem of black eloquence and intelligence. By the time Douglass died, 100 years ago this past February, he had long been accustomed to being the most famous Negro in the world. Years before, he had been dubbed "the representative colored man of the United States"—a title that surely implied a confinement as well as a coronation, but that he wore proudly. The former slave, in so many ways the least representative of men, had become a great orator, abolitionist and—in a phrase much in favor these days—the first black "public intellectual."

Lionized in the 19th century, Douglass has been canonized in the 20th. The bibliography of the Modern Language Association bulges with critical treatises on his prose, and the centenary of his death has been marked by conferences and symposiums in his honor. Almost every aspect of his life has been laboriously interpreted and reinterpreted. We have been reintroduced to Douglass the slave, who painstakingly "stole" the secrets of literacy and who daringly made his escape in 1838 on the eastern shore of Maryland, by train and boat, disguised as a sailor; Douglass the statesman—he was appointed marshal for the District of Columbia by Rutherford B. Hayes in 1877, and minister and consul general to Haiti by Benjamin Harrison in 1889; Douglass the newspaper publisher—he founded the newspaper *North Star* in Rochester in 1847, and remained in some measure a newspaperman until 1874.

Moreover, Douglass is one of the very few black figures to have occasioned a steady flow of biographies, from those by Booker T. Washington and by Charles Chesnutt at the turn of the century to those by Waldo E. Martin Jr., by David W. Blight and, most recently, by William S. McFeely. Even W. E. B. Du Bois, Douglass's true heir as a public intellectual and a man given neither to magnanimity nor to sentimentality, was moved to write a poem in Douglass's honor on the night he heard of his death:

> *Then Douglass passed—his massive form*
> *Still quivering at unrighted Wrong.*
> *Live, warm and wondrous memory, my Douglass,*
> *Live, all men do love Thee.*

But it is his autobiographical work—and "Narrative of the Life" most of all—that has attracted the bulk of critical attention. No fewer that 12 editions are available, including an audio one and annotated editions by David Blight and the Library of America. Douglass's "Narrative" has been deconstructed, reconstructed, historicized, New Historicized, psychoanalyzed and otherwise subjected to every implement of textual torture my profession has been able to devise. Few black writers have so lent themselves to reinterpretation, and few have been so subject to it.

The book aroused excitement among critics and readers from the beginning. In a review in *The New York Tribune,* the transcendentalist Margaret Fuller, whose acceptance of the universe did not extend to its slaveholders, wrote: "Considered merely as narrative, we have never read one more simple, true, coherent and warm with genuine feeling. It is an excellent piece of writing, and on that score to be prized as a specimen of the power of the Black Race, which prejudice persists in disputing." The book was an overnight best-seller. By 1847, it had sold 11,000 copies, in nine editions. By 1850, 30,000 copies had been sold, including English, French and Irish editions.

And yet Douglass was scarcely alone in chronicling the experience of slavery; between 1760 and 1865, more than 100 book-length slave narratives were published. Some of them, it must be said, were not particularly persuasive; these were fabrications that, as the historian John Blassingame has noted, characteristically pitted demonic masters against angelic slaves. For example, the slave narrative of Francis Fedric turned out to be the creation of the Englishman Charles

Lee—who rather showed his hand, Mr. Blassingame observes, in the way he had the slaves "frequently shaking hands with their masters, using such expressions as 'fie' and 'bid you fare you well,' and offering high opinions of Great Britain and of Englishmen." Before the abolitionists published Douglass's "Narrative," they put him on the lecture circuit for four years: that way, his patrons would learn if his story could withstand public scrutiny, while Douglass himself could practice and improve the telling of his tale.

Part of what distinguished Douglass from others who testified to the experience of enslavement was his astounding command of oratory. Today his speeches, edited by Mr. Blassingame, fill five volumes. His verbal facility was matched by a resonant baritone and a "burning eloquence," as Elizabeth Cady Stanton put it. Even to those inclined to doubt a published account as a counterfeit, the fervor of his own speech might well seem self-authenticating. And yet the black abolitionist Charles Lenox Remond was said to be as great a speaker. The difference was that Remond, like a number of others, peaked on the lectern, never emerging as a writer of distinction. By contrast, Douglass's book was unrivaled in its eloquence, combining a certain severity of tone with a profound mastery of figurative language. Here, for example, is his famous apostrophe to the ships in Chesapeake Bay:

> You are loosened from your moorings, and are free; I am fast in my chains, and am a slave! You are merrily before the gentle gale, and I sadly before the bloody whip! You are freedom's swift-winged angels, that fly around the world; I am confined in bands of iron! O that I were free! O, that I were on one of the gallant decks, and under your protecting wing! Alas! betwixt me and you, the turbid waters roll. Go on, go on. O that I could also go! Could I but swim! If I could fly! O, why was I born a man, of whom to make a brute!

Ironically, Douglass's literary skill disquieted some of his abolitionist patrons, who worried that he might sound too polished to be the real thing. William Lloyd Garrison counseled him not to sound too "learned," or his listeners might not "believe you were ever a slave." And Parker Pillsbury said that it might be better for him to "have a little of the plantation" in his speech.

Such strictures would have been familiar enough to Douglass, who was expressly forbidden to read and write by his master, Thomas Auld. And the struggle to achieve the dangerous skills of literacy is a constant theme of Douglass's autobiographies. He writes, for example, that as a child he happened to learn four letters of the alphabet, and then tricked white boys into teaching him the rest (he would boast that he could write better than they could, copying down the few letters he knew: they would best him by writing others). To Douglass, literacy was "a new and special revelation, explaining dark and mysterious things, with which my youthful understanding had struggled, but struggled in vain." He added: "I now understood what had been to me almost perplexing difficulty—to wit, the white man's power to enslave the black man. It was a grand achievement, and I prized it highly. From that moment, I understood the pathway from slavery to freedom."

At the age of 12, he bought a copy of "The Columbian Orator" (1797) by Caleb Bingham for 50 cents in a Baltimore bookstore; here was an opportunity to read and to imitate the devices of rhetoricians like Cato and Socrates, Cicero and Sheridan. "Every opportunity I got," he writes in "Narrative of the Life," "I used to read this book." Douglass also tells of getting hold of a copybook belonging to his master's son and "copying what he had written" in the spaces between the lines.

For Douglass, the will to power was the will to write. Nowhere else among the slave narratives was the proverbial "leap to freedom" so inextricably intertwined with literacy. Using a remarkable range of tropes—chiasmus, irony, apostrophe and antithesis—with an astonishing comfort and ease, Douglass takes his reader on an anthropologist's voyage through the valley of the shadow of "social death" that is slavery, a phrase coined by his contemporary black abolitionist William Wells Brown.

And for Douglass, to write was always also to rewrite. Certainly this was so of his "Narrative," composed after several years of rehearsing his story on the hustings. And then he revised his story in his two later autobiographies, "My Bondage and My Freedom" (1855) and "Life and Times of Frederick Douglass" (1881, revised in 1892). Each of these was longer than the one before; but longer did not always mean more informative. Such significant personal details as the identity of his mother and father were changed. In his 1845 "Narrative," he repeats the rumor that "my master was my father," perhaps referring to Thomas Auld. By his 1881 account, he was telling his readers, "Of my father, I know nothing." Why the belated amnesia? As our Representative Colored Man, Douglass was meant to embody the excellence of the Negro race; it was a disadvantage to

have skeptics imputing his intellect to the circumstance of a white father. As the father went into an eclipse, Douglass's mother emerged
from the shadows. In 1845, Douglass claimed that he saw his mother
only four or five times, and then only at night; he greeted news of
her death, he wrote, as one would greet the news of "the death of a
stranger." In "My Bondage," he wrote that "her personal appearance
and bearing are ineffaceably stamped upon my memory," and went
on to describe her in striking detail.

As unlikely as it may seem, no one remarked on these inconsistencies until the historian Peter F. Walker did so in 1978. The fact is
that until relatively recently most of Douglass's biographers have
strayed little from the basic contours of Douglass's autobiographies,
as if caught in the grip of his powerful rhetoric. (A notable exception
is William S. McFeely's magisterial 1991 biography.) If his inconsistencies have often gone unremarked, so have his silences. Douglass,
chronicling the life of the Representative Colored Man, kept much of
his intimate life in shadow; his biographers have typically followed
suit. Douglass tells us almost nothing about his relation to either of
his two wives. His first wife, Anna, was a free black woman whom
he met while he was a member of a black "improvement society" in
Baltimore. She helped pay for the ticket that allowed him to escape,
and she worked as a domestic while he lectured abroad for almost
two years, supporting their family with her wages. But Douglass had
made of his life story a sort of political diorama in which she had no
role. Nor did his second wife, Helen Pitts, whom he quietly married
two years after Anna's death in 1882; she was 21 years his junior, a
white graduate of Mount Holyoke and formerly his secretary. Un-
surprisingly, the marriage to Helen Pitts was unpopular among many
of his black followers. His image had become a sort of collective property. A correspondent for the black Pittsburgh-based newspaper *The
Weekly News* wrote: "Fred Douglass has married a red-head white
girl. Good-bye black blood in that family. We have no further use for
him. His picture hangs in our parlor, we will hang it in the stables."
Never mind the correspondent's particular animus: consider merely
the hardship of living your life as the man whose image hangs in
black America's parlor.

And then there is Douglass's relationship with the German journalist Ottilie Assing, the nature of which has remained largely a matter of conjecture until recently. "How soon—and indeed, whether—
their friendship led to a sexual relationship is impossible to
determine," Mr. McFeely wrote in his biography. But new research
by Maria Diedrich, the chairman of the American studies depart-

ment at the University of Münster, confirms that Assing and Douglass had a passionate affair from 1856, when she traveled to Rochester to interview him, to 1881, when she returned to Germany for good. She translated "My Bondage" into German and kept her German readers abreast of Douglass's career for two decades. Assing spent all her summers with Douglass, at his homes in Rochester and in Washington; Douglass, for his part, frequented her home in Hoboken, where she had moved in 1852. Ms. Diedrich writes: "They moved openly as lovers in an elaborate social circle, entertaining friends in her home, visiting with them, attending dances, lectures, and theater productions together. To their acquaintances, their relationship was no secret."

The end of this affair was dramatic. When Douglass married Helen Pitts in 1884, Assing spent a few months traveling aimlessly across Europe and then swallowed a vial of poison in Paris. Her will left a trust fund of $13,000 that would pay a stipend semiannually to Frederick Douglass.

Ms. Diedrich bases her findings on a careful inspection of a cache of 91 letters, "written in difficult old German handwriting" from Ottilie to her sister between 1865 and 1877 and unavailable to scholars until the mid-1980's. "Portraying herself as Douglass's 'natural' wife of long standing," Assign wrote to her sister about her relationship with Douglass "as one sexually experienced woman to another," Ms. Diedrich observes.

Given that Douglass conceived his role, as he wrote in 1855, as that of a member of "a priesthood, occupying the highest moral eminence," he could ill afford the scandal of an affair. And he was especially sensitive to this risk because in the early 1850's he had been publicly accused of having an affair with Julia Griffiths, an English abolitionist and an editor at Douglass's newspaper, *The North Star*, and both had suffered gravely in the consequence.

Clearly, Assing was taken with Douglass; she considered him a member of the "true elite" and a writer "who confronts the reader in his unresistible attractiveness and distinction." Assing and Douglass exchanged letters once a week, in what she called "my weekly allowance." "When you are so intimately connected with *one* man as I am with Douglass, you will get to know men . . . from a perspective that would never be revealed to you otherwise," she wrote, "especially if it is a man who has seen so much of the world and was loved by so many women!" In 1874, Assing wrote her sister, Douglass asked her to "move in with him for good," but she had second thoughts: "You will imagine how happy it would make me to be always with him, yet I must consider seriously whether it would be prudent to live continually in proximity to his charming wife."

Assing was being ironic: she had little complimentary to say about Anna Douglass; she and Douglass refer to Anna as "the Border-State." More pointedly, Assing referred to Anna (who was illiterate to her death) as "this stupid old hag" and "the poor unfortunate piece of humanity." She and Douglass, she wrote her sister, were "united in a deeper love than many who were married, without the slightest perspective that it will ever be different." Moreover, they were "separated from each other by a true monster, who herself can neither give love nor appreciate it; what a terrible fate."

For much of Douglass's mature career, Assing was his principal intellectual consort; the two read widely together—Goethe, Fuerbach, Dickens, Shakespeare and Marx. Theirs was a salon for two. Assing wrote that her exchanges with Douglass made her feel as if she "had stepped back into the ages of magicians and fairies, when individual mortals sometimes got into a magic mountain, where the time they spent . . . passed with such mysterious speed that they, . . . convinced they had only spent a month inside the magic circle, discovered that a century had passed."

Ironically, the letters were originally part of the Varnhagen papers in Berlin, which, Ms. Diedrich notes, the Nazis used to "prove the Jewish lineage of German intellectuals." Hidden by the Nazis near the end of the war on a farm in Schlessingia, the papers were found by the Russians and donated to the Jagiellonian Library in Crakow, and only came to light just before the Iron Curtain fell. (Assing's relationship with Douglass was also observed by the Prussian secret service, which was eager to record the movements of the radical German intelligentsia after the revolution of 1848.)

Douglass's life is only enriched by findings like Ms. Diedrich's, however inopportune such public knowledge would have been in his day. The poet Robert Hayden has exhorted us to remember Douglass "not with statue's rhetoric, / not with legends and poems and wreaths of bronze alone / but with the lives grown out of his life, the lives fleshing his dram of the beautiful, needful thing." And, indeed, the life of Douglass has been important as an example of other lives. Yet in this era of tell-all biographies that somehow manage to tell us very little, Douglass is also important as a study in fame and self-creation. He belongs to the company of Victorian sages, but he was also a full-blown celebrity before the era of celebrity—someone who during the greatest moral struggle of modern times used the public presentation of his life as his chosen weapon.

The enterprise of biography, if it counts for anything, must be to restore humanity and complexity to someone so assiduously committed to the habit of self-invention and self-censorship. But Douglass's historical presence is unlikely to be fully contained by any latter-day interpretation. So much the better. We are impatient with heroes and sages these days, but we are as wedded to narrative as we ever were. And Frederick Douglass has left us a story of his life that will survive any of our own attempts to master it.

Study Questions

1. From what point of view is Gates writing? What is his stance? What are the tone and texture of his prose? What are his expected audience, his purpose, and his thesis?
2. What attitude does Gates take toward Douglass's relationships with women?
3. "For Douglass, the will to power was the will to write." In what ways does literacy convey power? Why was that power important to Douglass?

Writing Topics

1. Find a paragraph or sentence in Gates's essay that can serve as an essay topic. Quote it, explain the meaning of the quotation and its implications, and then use it as a starting point to develop your own ideas.
2. Write an essay in which you discuss the meaning of literacy in your own life, in Douglass's as you understand it from the reading, and in Gates's life, as you imagine it to be.

Authors

Anderson, David C. (19??–)

American writer. Anderson writes about criminal justice and other urban issues. In addition to articles written for such publications as *The American Prospect* and *The New York Times Magazine*, Anderson has written two books: *Crimes of Justice: Improving the Police, the Courts, the Prisons* and *Crime and the Politics of Hysteria: How the Willie Horton Story Changed American Justice*. He is a former member of the *New York Times* editorial board and a former editor of *Police Magazine* and *Corrections Magazine*.

Angelou, Maya (1928–)

American writer, poet, playwright, performer, producer, and director. Born Marguerita Johnson, Angelou is perhaps best known for her autobiographies (including *I Know Why the Caged Bird Sings, Gather Together in My Name*, and *All God's Children Need Travelling Shoes*) and her poetry (in addition to having published several volumes of poetry, she wrote and read the inaugural poem for President Bill Clinton's first inauguration). She also has performed both on and off Broadway; has written, produced, and directed her own plays; and has taken an active role in various civil rights movements.

Bader, Jenny Lyn (1972–)

American playwright and essayist. Bader has worked as a writer, theater director, and book editor. Author of the forthcoming book *The Male-Female Dictionary,* she has written for the *National Law Journal* and *The New York Times*, and her play *Shakespeare's Undiscovered One Act* premiered at New York City's Village Gate theater in 1992. In addition to working in print, Bader currently runs *The New York Times'* s electronic books and theater forums via America Online.

Baldwin, James (1924–1987)

American essayist, novelist, and playwright. The son of an African-American Pentacostal minister, Baldwin spent his formative years on the

American east coast, serving as a junior minister in a Pentacostal church during his teens, then spent most of his adult life in France. He produced novels (such as *Go Tell It on the Mountain* and *If Beale Street Could Talk*), plays (such as *Giovanni's Room*, which was adapted from a novel of the same name), and essays (such as *Notes of a Native Son*, *Nobody Knows My Name*, and *The Fire Next Time*). Much of his work focuses on the psychological impact of racism on both oppressors and the oppressed.

Birkerts, Sven (1951–)

American literary critic and writer. Although he holds a degree in English from the University of Michigan, Birkerts claims to be an "amateur" literary critic and rejects a detached, pedantic approach to criticism. Birkerts's essays, for which he has received a citation for excellence in reviewing from the National Book Critics Circle, have appeared in such publications as *The New Republic* and the *Boston Review*. Some of those reviews were collected in *An Artificial Wilderness: Essays on Twentieth-Century Literature* and *The Electric Life: Essays on Modern Poetry*. Birkerts has also written *The Gutenberg Elegies: The Fate of Reading in an Electronic Age*, in which he laments the present passing of "print literacy" in the face of new electronic media.

Bleecker, Marcus (1967–)

American musician and writer. Educated in jazz studies at the University of Wisconsin at Madison, Bleecker lives in Brooklyn, New York, where he plays drums for the music group Mosaic. He also writes screenplays and short fiction.

Broyard, Anatole (1920–1990)

American literary critic and writer. Broyard spent most of his working life as a book reviewer and feature writer for *The New York Times* and *The New York Times Book Review*. Many of those reviews appear in his collection *Aroused by Books*. His other works include *Men, Women and Other Anticlimaxes; Kafka Was the Rage: A Greenwich Village Memoir;* and *Intoxicated by My Illness: And Other Writings on Life and Death*. The latter book, published posthumously, includes essays written during Broyard's fourteen-month battle with prostate cancer.

Codrescu, Andrei (1946–)

Romanian-American writer, journalist, editor, translator, and educator. Born in Sibiu, Romania, Codrescu fled that country after being expelled from the University of Bucharest for criticizing the communist government. He lived in Rome and Paris before settling in the United States. Codrescu's award-winning work includes poetry (*License to Carry a Gun, Comrade Past and Mister Present,* and *Belligerence,* among other titles), novels (*The Blood Countess,* among others), and essays, many of which were first heard on National Public Radio and appear in *Zombification: Stories from NPR* and *The Dog with the Chip in His Neck: Essays from NPR and Elsewhere.* Codrescu also appeared in *Road Scholar,* a documentary film in which he and photographer David Graham cross the United States by car, commenting on various aspects of American culture.

Cofer, Judith Ortiz (1952–)

Hispanic-American poet, novelist, and essayist. Born in Hormigueros, Puerto Rico, Cofer immigrated to the United States as a child. She has studied at Augusta College, Florida Atlantic University, and Oxford University, and she began writing poetry while teaching at various south Florida colleges. In addition to numerous collections of poems (including *Latin Women Pray, Peregrina,* and *Terms of Survival*), Cofer has published a novel (*The Line of the Sun*), a collection of essays (*Silent Dancing*), and a collection of poetry and prose (*The Latin Deli*). She teaches creative writing at the University of Georgia.

Dillard, Annie (1945–)

American essayist, poet, and novelist. Dillard has written in numerous genres, but regardless of the genre, her work often examines the co-existence of beauty and violence in both nature and human civilization. Her books include *Tickets for a Prayer Wheel* (poetry), *Pilgrim at Tinker Creek* and *Teaching a Stone to Talk: Expeditions and Encounters* (essay collections, the former of which won the Pulitzer Prize in 1975), *An American Childhood* (a memoir), and *The Living* (a historical novel).

Duncan, David James (19??–)

American writer. Duncan, who has spent his entire life in Oregon, writes about the people and environment of the Pacific Northwest. In addition to his work for various periodicals, he has published *The River Why* (a meditation on fly fishing), *The Brothers K* (a chronicle of a family), and *River Teeth: Stories and Writings* (a collection of writings combining observations of such things as the environment, fly fishing, baseball, and spirituality).

Eco, Umberto (1932–)

Italian semiotician, medievalist, and novelist. A professor of semiotics at the University of Bologna, Eco writes in a number of styles, from the highly academic to the popular. Much of his work revolves around, as he put it in a 1986 interview, "a stubborn effort to understand the mechanisms by which we give meaning to the world around us." His books include texts on semiotics (including *A Theory of Semiotics* and *The Role of the Reader: Explorations in the Semiotics of Texts*), novels (including *The Name of the Rose, Foucault's Pendulum,* and *Island of the Day Before*), and collections of essays (including *Travels in Hyperreality* and *How to Travel with a Salmon and Other Essays*).

Ehrenfeld, David (1938–)

American writer and educator. Educated at Harvard University and the University of Florida, Ehrenfeld teaches ecology at Rutgers University. He is the author of *The Arrogance of Humanism* and the founding editor of the journal *Conservation Biology*. His latest book is *Beginning Again: People and Nature in the New Millennium*.

Ehrenreich, Barbara (1941–)

American socialist, feminist, and writer. Ehrenreich has pursued her quest for social justice in her work, her socialist party leadership, and her writing, in which she has critiqued American medicine (including *The American Health Empire: Power, Profits, and Politics—A Report from the Health Policy Advisory Center*, with John Ehrenreich), sexual politics (including *For Her Own Good: One Hundred Fifty Years of the Experts' Advice to Women*, with Deirdre English, and *The Hearts of Men: American Dreams and the Flight from Commitment*), and social class (*Fear of Falling: The Inner Life of the Middle Class*). Her latest work is *Blood Rites: Origins and History of the Passions of War*, in which she argues that human violence stems from a prehistoric need to defend against predators.

Endelman, Dee (1949–)

American businesswoman. A human-resources manager and organizational consultant for over twenty years, Endelman has kept journals since she was eleven years old. "Writing," she reports, "is very close to eating and breathing for me." She currently lives in Seattle, Washington.

Faulkner, William (1897–1962)

American writer. Faulkner (originally spelled Falkner) is considered one of the greatest American writers of the twentieth century. Born in New Albany, Mississippi, Faulkner remained near his native state for much of his life, and his finest work focuses on the land and characters of a fictional Mississippi county. His major novels (such as *Light in August, The*

Sound and the Fury, As I Lay Dying, and *Absalom, Absalom!*) as well as many of his short stories (including those collected in *Go Down, Moses*) are set there. The quality of this work won him the Nobel Prize for literature in 1949. Faulkner also occasionally worked on screenplays in Hollywood (including *The Big Sleep*), and another of his novels, *A Fable*, earned him the National Book Award and the Pulitzer Prize in 1955.

Fetsko Petrie, Kathye (1953–)

American writer and editor. Educated at Syracuse University, Fetsko Petrie is currently a freelance writer/editor and the author of *Flyin' Jack*, a children's book to be published in 1998. Her work has also been published in *The Philadelphia Inquirer* and *Parents Express*.

Frost, Robert (1874–1963)

American poet. Though he was born in San Francisco, spent his teen years in a Massachusetts mill town, and was educated at Dartmouth College and Harvard University, Frost is identified with rural New England, because he lived most of his adult life there and because his poetry tends to focus on rural life in that region. His poems often present that life through a first-person narrator—a narrator that should not be confused with Frost himself. Poems such as "Mending Wall," "Stopping by Woods on a Snowy Evening," and especially "The Road Not Taken" make him one of America's most widely recognized poets (that he read two poems at President John F. Kennedy's inauguration in 1961 signals the extent of that recognition). The poet's awards include four Pulitzer Prizes, awarded for *New Hampshire*, *Collected Poems*, *A Futher Range*, and *A Witness Tree*.

Fulghum, Robert (1937–)

American Unitarian minister, art teacher, and writer. Educated at Starr King Seminary, Fulghum has published several collections of essays on the experiences of everyday life. His essays, which cover such topics as laundry, crayons, and spiderwebs, have proven so popular that two of his books, *All I Really Need to Know I Learned in Kindergarten: Uncommon Thoughts on Common Things* and *It Was on Fire When I Lay Down on It*, were on the best-seller list at the same time. Fulghum has also published *Uh-Oh: Some Observations from Both Sides of the Refrigerator Door*.

Gates Jr., Henry Louis (1950–)

American literary critic, educator, and writer. Educated at Yale University and Clare College, Gates is one of the nation's most widely recognized scholars in African-American studies. His writings have developed theories of African-American literary criticism (*The Signifying Monkey: Towards a Theory of Afro-American Literary Criticism*), examined the need for diversity in American arts and letters (*Loose Canons: Notes on the Culture Wars*), and considered the responsibilities of the black middle class (*The Future of the Race*, with Cornel West). In addition to handling numerous editorial projects, Gates has also written a memoir of his youth in West Virginia (*Colored People*). He currently chairs the Afro-American Studies program at Harvard University.

Genz, Michelle (1954–)

American journalist. A graduate of Eckerd College, Genz began her journalism career as a television news anchor. In addition to feature stories and personal essays, she has written a column on family issues, called "Ties that Bind," for *Tropic* (the Sunday magazine of *The Miami Herald)*. Lately, she has focused on celebrity profiles.

George, Karen (1952–)

American library specialist. George was educated at New Mexico State University and works there in the Government Information Department.

Guinier, Lani (1950–)

American attorney. Since graduating from Yale Law School, Guinier has worked to improve civil rights. She has served as special assistant to then Assistant Attorney General Drew S. Days III and as assistant counsel of the NAACP Legal Defense Fund. Guinier was nominated by President Bill Clinton to the United States' top civil rights post, but her nomination was blocked because of her controversial writings on establishing a truly representative democracy. Many of those writings appear in her book *The Tyranny of the Majority: Fundamental Fairness in Democracy*. She also has written *Becoming Gentlemen: Women, Law School, and Institutional Change* and is a professor of law at the University of Pennsylvania.

Hawking, Stephen (1942–)

British theoretical physicist. Hawking, who was educated at Oxford and Cambridge Universities, has devoted his professional life to several issues in cosmology, including black holes, elementary particles, and the grand unification theory (an all-encompassing explanation of the universe). He has written numerous academic texts, but is most widely known for two works for lay audiences: *A Brief History of Time: From the Big Bang to Black Holes* and *Black Holes and Baby Universes and Other Essays.*

Hoffman, Jan (19??–)

American journalist. Hoffman, who was educated at Cornell University and received a Masters in the Study of Law from Yale University, is legal-affairs reporter for the Metro section of *The New York Times.*

Hofstadter, Douglas R. (1945–)

American scientist. Hofstadter has long had a combined interest in cognition, computer science, and artificial intelligence. His research and speculations on these issues appear in several books, including *Gödel, Escher, Bach: An Eternal Golden Braid* (which won the Pulitzer Prize), *The Mind's I: Fantasies and Reflections on Self and Soul* (which he coedited with Daniel C. Dennet), and *Fluid Concepts and Creative Analogies: Computer Models of the Fundamental Mechanisms of Thought.* Hofstadter currently directs the Center for Research on Concepts and Cognition at Indiana University, Bloomington.

Holloway, Connie (19??–)

American writer. In addition to training and exercising horses, Holloway writes short stories and treatments for movies. When not traveling, she lives in Seattle, Washington.

hooks, bell (1952–)

American essayist and educator. Born Gloria Watkins and educated at Stanford University, hooks (the name of her great-grandmother) writes about black womanhood, feminism, critical theory, and civil rights. Her early books (including *Ain't I a Woman: Black Women and Feminism* and *Talking Back: Thinking Feminist, Thinking Black*) focus on the efforts of black women to find a place in mainstream feminist movements. Later books have focused on the work of black intellectuals (*Breaking Bread: Insurgent Black Intellectual Life*, with Cornell West) and on depictions of blacks in the media (*Black Looks: Race and Representation*).

Hughes, (James) Langston (1902–1967)

American writer and lecturer. Born in Joplin, Missouri, and educated at Columbia and Lincoln Universities, Hughes most often wrote about the experiences of working-class African-Americans, and this focus earned him a significant popular following. His works include collections of poetry (such as *The Weary Blues* and *Montage of a Dream Deferred*), novels (*Not Without Laughter* and *Tambourines to Glory*), and collections of short stories (such as *Simple Speaks His Mind* and *Something in Common and Other Stories*), as well as nonfiction and stories for children.

Iggers, Jeremy (1951–)

American journalist. Born in Chicago, Illinois, and educated at Carleton College and the University of Minnesota, Iggers has focused much of his work on issues of community-based initiatives and food. His writing has appeared in newspapers such as the *Detroit Free Press* and in magazines such as the *Utne Reader, Bon Appetit*, and *Martha Stewart Living*. Iggers is currently a staff writer for the *Star Tribune* of Minneapolis–St. Paul and the author of *Garden of Eating: Food, Sex and the Hunger for Meaning*. His book *Good News, Bad News: Journalism, Ethics and the Public Interest*, is forthcoming.

Ivins, Molly (1944–)

American journalist. Ivins, who lives in Austin, Texas, is a regular columnist for the *Fort Worth Star-Telegram* and has also written for *Time, Newsweek, Dallas Times Herald*, and *Mother Jones*. She concentrates primarily on American politics. Many of her columns appear in two collections: *Molly Ivins Can't Say That, Can She?* and *Nothin' But Good Times Ahead*.

Kincaid, Jamaica (1949–)

West Indian–American writer. Born Elain Potter Richardson in St. John's, Antiqua, West Indies, and educated at the New School for Social Research and Fanconia College, Kincaid often writes about life in the West Indies and the experiences of adolescents. Her work includes a collection of short stories (*At the Bottom of the River*), novels (*Annie John* and *Lucy*) and essays (*A Small Place*). She currently writes for *The New Yorker* and lives in New York and Vermont.

King, Stephen (1947–)

American writer. King is one of the best-known contemporary writers of horror fiction. His books include novels (such as *Carrie, The Shining, Pet Sematary, Misery*, and *Rose Madder*) and collections of shorter fiction (including *Night Shift* and *Four Past Midnight*). Many of his works have been adapted for the screen, including *The Shining, The Shaw-shank Redemption, Stand by Me,* and *Dolores Claiborne.*

Kingsolver, Barbara (1955–)

American writer. Kingsolver often writes about people's struggles to form meaningful relationships and to come to terms with the communities in which they live. Her works include novels and short stories (*The Bean Trees, Homeland and Other Stories, Animal Dreams,* and *Pigs in Heaven*), poetry (*Another America*), and nonfiction (*Holding the Line: Women in the Great Arizona Mine Strike of 1983*).

Klawans, Harold (1937–)

American physician and writer. Educated at the Universities of Michigan and Illinois, Klawans has combined a life in medicine with work writing histories of medical issues, numerous scholarly books and articles on neuropharmacology, and several crime novels, including *Sins of Commission* and *The Third Temple.* These endeavors are more interrelated than one might think, Klawans explains, citing Arthur Conan Doyle's analogy between "medicine and classic detective work."

Klein, Marty (1950–)

American therapist. Klein has been a licensed marriage and family counselor and sex therapist for fifteen years. He is the author of several books, including *Ask Me Anything: A Sex Therapist Answers the Most Important Questions for the '90s,* and over one hundred articles on sex and relationships. He teaches human sexuality at Stanford University Medical School, and his book *Beyond Intercourse* will be published in 1998.

Kolata, Gina (1948–)

American journalist. Kolata, who studied molecular biology both as an undergraduate and as a graduate student at the University of Maryland, reports on science and health for *The New York Times.* Previously, she was a senior writer for *Science* and also has written for such periodicals as *Cosmopolitan, Smithsonian,* and *Seventeen.* The quality of her journalism has earned her three Pulitzer Prize nominations. Kolata also cowrote the book *Sex in America: A Definitive Survey* with Robert T. Michael, John H. Gagnon, and Edward O. Laumann.

Konner, Melvin (1946–)

American biologist, anthropologist, educator, and writer. Though Konner works as a biological anthropologist (he has written such books as

Why the Reckless Survive—and Other Secrets of Human Nature and *The Tangled Wing: Biological Constraints on the Human Spirit*, which was nominated for an American Book Award in 1982) he has also trained as a physician. He used his anthropological skills to write about his medical school experiences in *Becoming a Doctor: A Journey of Initiation in Medical School*, a critique of medical education in America. Konner has written a second critique of American medicine in *Medicine at the Crossroads: The Crisis in Healthcare*. He currently teaches biological anthropology at Harvard University.

Kriegel, Leonard (1933–)

American writer and educator. Educated at Hunter College, Columbia University, and New York University, Kriegel is the author of *Edmund Wilson* (a biography); *Working Through: An Autobiographical Journey in the Urban University; Of Man and Manhood* (a sociological study of America's views of manhood); and *Quitting Time* (a novel).

Laughlin, Meg (1947–)

American journalist. Educated in English literature at Louisiana State University and the University of Miami, Laughlin taught for fifteen years before becoming a journalist. She is now an award-winning writer on the staff of *Tropic* (the Sunday magazine of *The Miami Herald*) and recently completed a Knight Fellowship in journalism at Stanford University.

Lee, Andrea (1953–)

American writer. Educated at Harvard University, Lee has written on a number of subjects. Her first book, *Russian Journal*, recounts her experiences as an African-American woman in the Soviet Union during the late seventies. The quality of Lee's reporting and commentary earned the book a nomination for an American Book Award for general nonfiction in 1981. In addition to numerous articles for such periodicals as *The New Yorker* and *Vogue*, Lee has also written a novel, *Sarah Philips*.

Le Guin, Ursula K. (1929–)

American writer. Known primarily for her award-winning works of science fiction and fantasy, Le Guin has also published poetry, essays, and books for children. The quality of Le Guin's work has earned her the prestigious Nebula and Hugo Awards for short works (*The Word for*

World Is Forest and "The Ones Who Walk Away from Omelas") and for the novel *The Left Hand of Darkness*.

Lincoln, Abraham (1809–1865)

Sixteenth American president. Lincoln served as president of the Union during the American Civil War, and he is noted not only for preserving the United States but for the power of his oratory. Several of his speeches, including his "Gettysburg Address" and "Second Inaugural Address," continue to be cited as some of the best American political rhetoric ever written.

Logan, William Bryant (1952–)

American writer, playwright, poet, translator. Logan helped start the magazine *Garden Design* and frequently writes about landscapes and gardens of the West for *House and Garden* and other publications. Author of the Far West section of *The Literary Guide to the United States*, he also has written *Dirt: The Ecstatic Skin of the Earth*, *The Smithsonian Guide to Historic America: The Deep South* (with Vance Muse), *The Smithsonian Guide to Historic America: The Pacific States* (with Susan Ochshorn), *The Gardener's Book of Sources*, and *A Book of Roses*. With Angel Gil Orrios he has translated *Once Five Years Pass and Other Dramatic Works* by Federico García Lorca.

Lopez, Barry (1945–)

American writer. Educated at the Universities of Notre Dame and Oregon, Lopez often writes about humanity's interactions with nature. Whether writing nonfiction (such as the award-winning *Of Wolves and Men* and *Arctic Dreams: Imagination and Desire in a Northern Landscape*) or fiction (such as *River Notes: The Dance of Herons* and *Winter Count*), Lopez combines a rich understanding of natural history with a willingness to reflect upon metaphysical questions.

Mann, Dennis Alan (1940–)

American architect and educator. At the University of Pennsylvania, Mann studied under such prominent architects as Louis Kahn, Edmund Bacon, and Ian McHarg. In addition to his architectural work, he has published numerous articles and contributed chapters on the relationships between architecture and popular culture. He is a professor of architecture at the University of Cincinnati, and his current work focuses on the professional status of African-American architects.

Marks, Jonathan (1955–)

American anthropologist and educator. Having studied the natural sciences at Johns Hopkins University, anthropology at the University of Arizona, and genetics at the University of California at Davis, Marks is a professor of anthropology at Yale University. In his book *Human Biodiversity: Genes, Race, and History*, he argues that a high degree of genetic variability within a so-called "race" undermines the latter concept. Marks has also coauthored *Evolutionary Anthropology* with Edward Staski.

Martin, Rafe (1946–)

American writer, storyteller, and student of Zen. Martin has written a number of books on Zen in addition to traveling extensively as a storyteller and speaker. Among his books are *One Hand Clapping: Zen Stories for All Ages*, *Mysterious Tales of Japan*, *The Rough Face Girl*, and *The Hungry Tigress: Buddhist Myths, Tales and Legends*, and he also has edited *Awakening to Zen: The Teachings of Roshi Philip Kapleau*. He lives in Rochester, New York.

Maxwell, William (1908–)

American editor and writer. Educated at the University of Illinois and Harvard University, Maxwell has made his mark both through his work on *The New Yorker* and through his fiction. Much of Maxwell's fiction (including *They Came Like Swallows* and *Time Will Darken It*) offers historical accounts of life in Midwestern small towns. Maxwell has also written a geneological account of his family (*Ancestors: A Family History*), collections of essays (*The Outermost Dream: Essays and Reviews*), and numerous shorts stories, many of which appear in *All the Days and Nights: The Collected Stories of William Maxwell*.

Mead, Margaret (1901–1978)

American anthropologist. Mead, who was educated at DePauw University, Barnard College, and Columbia University, became not only one of the most influential figures in American anthropology but also a compelling voice on a variety of national issues. Much of her work (such as *Coming of Age in Samoa*, *Growing Up in New Guinea*, *Cooperation and Competition among Primitive Societies*, and *Culture and Commitment: The New Relationships between the Generations in the 1970s*) examines how individuals and cultures deal with various types of change. Among her many publications are a biography of fellow anthropologist Ruth Benedict, memoirs (such as *Blackberry Winter: My Earlier Years*), and a book on race relations (*A Rap on Race*, with James Baldwin). Mead and Rhoda Metraux produced a number of books together, including *Themes in French Culture, A Way of Seeing, An Interview with Santa Claus,* and *Aspects of the Present.*

Meadows, Donella H. (1941–)

American scientist. Meadows combines her training in biophysics with her interest in philosophy by using models (primarily computer models) to forecast environmental trends and to seek remedies for current problems. Two examples of this process appear in *The Limits of Growth: A Report for the Club of Rome's Project on the Predicament of Mankind* and *Beyond the Limits: Confronting Global Collapse, Envisioning a Sustainable Future* (cowritten with Dennis Meadows and Jorgen Randes). Meadows discusses the uses of models in *Groping in the Dark: The First Decade of Global Modelling* (which she coedited) and *The Electronic Oracle: Computer Models and Social Decisions.* She currently teaches at Dartmouth College.

Metraux, Rhoda (1914–)

American anthropologist. Educated at Vassar College and Yale and Columbia Universities, Metraux has devoted her work to the study of diverse cultures, ranging from European to South American and Pacific Island cultures. Metraux's work has appeared in a number of coauthored books, as well as in journals such as *Science* and *New Insights.* Metraux and Margaret Mead produced a number of books together, including *Themes in French Culture, A Way of Seeing, An Interview with Santa Claus,* and *Aspects of the Present.*

Morales, Aurora Levins (1954–)

Puerto Rican–American writer, poet, and activist. Morales's poetry and prose have appeared in a number of journals and collections, including *Puerto Rican Writers in the U.S.A.* In the book *Getting Home Alive,* she and her mother and coauthor, Rosario Morales, speak from multiple perspectives as feminists, Puerto Rican–Americans, and Jews. Morales is currently completing two books: *Medicine Stories: Writings on Cultural Activism,* about the healing power of stories, and *Remedios,* a prose-poetry narrative of the lives of Puerto Rican women in America, Africa, and Europe. She lives in New York City.

Nelson, Michael (1949–)

American political scientist. Nelson has devoted much of his professional life to the study of the American presidency. His works on the subject include *The Presidency and the Political System; Presidents, Politics, and Policy* (cowritten with Erwin Hargrove); and *The American President: Origins and Development, 1776–1990* (cowritten with Sidney M. Milkis), which earned the Benjamin Franklin Award for History, Politics, and Philosophy. Nelson also has written articles for such publications as *Newsweek* and *Washington Post Magazine,* and he has edited a series of books on contemporary presidential elections. He is currently a professor of political science at Rhodes College.

Norris, Kathleen (1947–)

American writer. Educated at Bennington College, Norris has published poetry (including *Falling Off, The Middle of the World,* and *Little Girls in Church*), but is perhaps best known for her two prose works, *Dakota: A Spiritual Geography* and *The Cloister Walk.* In her writings, Norris combines Christian reflection, observations of nature, and a keen eye for the spiritual in the mundane.

Orwell, George (1903–1950)

British writer. Born Eric Blair, in Bengal, and educated at Eton College, Orwell served in the Indian Imperial Police in Burma before returning to Europe. After that, he devoted himself to a career as a writer, and he has become known primarily for his political satires and commentaries. Orwell described himself as a socialist, and he spoke out regularly against communism and totalitarianism. His contempt for those two political orders is apparent in two of his novels: *Animal Farm* and *1984.*

Otetiani (c. 1758–1830)

Chief of the Seneca Nation. Born near what is now Branch Port, New York, Otetiani later took the name Sagoyewatha and is more commonly known to non-Native Americans as Red Jacket. Famed for his persuasive skills, he negotiated treaties with British and American forces during the Revolutionary War, and he represented his tribe in the Iroquois Confederacy and in white courts. Among his defenses in such courts were his arguments against the forcible conversion of his people to Christianity.

Ozick, Cynthia (1928–)

American writer. Though Ozick has written essays on a variety of subjects and has translated Yiddish verse, this New York City native is perhaps best known for her fiction, which often deals with Jewish identity and the discovery of the sacred rather than the merely idolatrous. These themes have appeared in novels such as *Trust* and *The Cannibal Galaxy* as well as in collections of short stories such as *The Pagan Rabbi and Other Stories, Bloodshed and Three Novellas*, and *Levitation: Five Fictions*.

Paulos, John Allen (1945–)

American mathematician and writer. Educated at the University of Wisconsin–Madison and a professor of mathematics at Temple University, Paulos has earned wide recognition for his accessible explanations of mathematical concepts for lay audiences. He has argued for the relevance of mathematics and has explained many of its critical concepts in books such as *Innumeracy: Mathematical Illiteracy and Its Consequences, Beyond Numeracy: Ruminations of a Numbers Man*, and *A Mathematician Reads the Newspaper*.

Pitts Jr., Leonard (1957–)

American journalist. Educated at the University of Southern California, Pitts has written for a number of media, including radio and print. He worked for "Casey Kasem's Top 40 Countdown" and wrote and syndicated the radio series "Who We Are: The Life and Times of Black America." Pitts also has written for such publications as *Parenting, TV Guide*, and *Entertainment Weekly* and is currently a syndicated columnist for *The Miami Herald*.

Quammen, David (1948–)

American writer. Educated in the liberal arts and literature at Yale and Oxford Universities, Quammen has written a number of political thrillers based on historical scenarios, among them *The Zolta Configuration* and *The Soul of Viktor Tronko*. In addition, Quammen has published several collections of essays on natural history, including *Natural Acts: A Sidelong View of Science and Nature* and *The Flight of the Iguana: A Sidelong View of Science and Nature*.

Quindlen, Anna (1953–)

American columnist, journalist, and writer. Quindlen took a job as a reporter before graduating from Barnard College, and she has been working in journalism for most of her time since then. She is perhaps best known for her *New York Times* columns "Life in the 30's" and "Public & Private," both of which have combined insight into her own experience with commentary on issues of national interest. The strength of her work won her a Pulitzer Prize for commentary in 1992. Quindlen also wrote a best-selling novel, *Object Lessons*.

Richardson Jr., Robert D. (1934–)

Educated at Harvard University, Richardson has devoted his professional life primarily to the study of American letters. He has published such works as *Literature and Film* and *Myth and Literature in the American Renaissance* and is best known for his two intellectual biographies: *Henry Thoreau: A Life of the Mind* and *Emerson: The Mind on Fire*.

Rodriguez, Richard (1944–)

American writer. Born in San Francisco to Mexican-American immigrants and educated at Stanford University, Columbia University, the University of California at Berkeley, and the Warburg Institute in London, Rodriguez examines the nature of racial and ethnic identity by combining biographical narrative with social and historical analysis. He uses this combination in *The Hunger of Memory: The Education of Richard Rodriguez* to examine his estrangement with his parents and to critique affirmative action and bilingual education. In *Days of Obligation: An Argument with My Mexican Father*, he writes about his own identities as well as political and social relations between California and Mexico.

Rogers, Pattiann (1940–)

American poet. Educated at the Universities of Missouri and Houston, Rogers has published six books of poetry, the most recent being *Firekeeper: New and Selected Poems*. She has received a Guggenheim Fellowship, two Pushcart Prizes (1984 and 1985) and a Poetry Fellowship from the Lannan Foundation. Her first book of poems, *The Expectations of Light*, explores the potential implications of modern science on humanity's sense of its place in the universe.

Ruskin, John (1819–1900)

British art and architecture critic, writer, and social commentator. The only child of a wealthy wine merchant and his wife, Ruskin was educated as a "gentleman-commoner" at Oxford University. This combination of "commoner" status and elite education is appropriate considering Ruskin's popularity as a writer for lay audiences. Through works such as *Modern Painters*, *The Stones of Venice*, and *Fors Clavigera*, he influenced Victorian tastes in art and architecture while arguing for social change in recently industrialized England.

Sandburg, Carl (1878–1967)

American writer. Born in Galesburg, Illinois, and educated at Lombard College, Sandburg infused early-twentieth-century American poetry with a gritty, urban sensibility drawn largely from the working class in the Midwest. Sandburg is perhaps best known for his Chicago poems (many of which appear in *Chicago Poems* and *Smoke and Steel*) and for his collection *The People, Yes!* In addition to his poetry, Sandburg produced a two-volume biography of Abraham Lincoln, a biography of Mary Todd Lincoln, and a number of children's books, including *Rootabaga Stories* and *Prairie-Town Boy*.

Santiago, Esmeralda (1948–)

Puerto Rican–American writer. Born in Puerto Rico, Santiago came with her mother to the United States when she was thirteen. She was educated at Harvard University and has published *When I Was Puerto Rican* and *America's Dream: El Sueno de America*. Her book *Becoming American* is forthcoming.

Selzer, Richard (1928–)

American writer. Selzer was a surgeon at Yale University's School of Medicine before turning to a career in writing. Since then, he has written a number of books on the medical profession, including memoirs of his own medical training (*Down from Troy: A Doctor Comes of Age*), descriptions of surgical practice (*Rituals of Surgery* and *Mortal Lessons: Notes on the Art of Surgery*), and a memoir of his own near-fatal battle with Legionnaire's Disease (*Raising the Dead: A Doctor's Encounter with His Own Mortality*).

Stein, Harry (1948–)

American columnist, journalist, and writer. A successful writer in several media, trained in journalism at Columbia University, Stein has earned wide recognition as a columnist, writing a regular column on ethics for *Esquire* in the early eighties and a syndicated column on family life entitled "Harry Stein's Homefront." Many of his ethics columns appear in *Ethics (and Other Liabilities): Trying to Live Right in an Amoral World*. Stein also has written *Hoopla*, a historical fiction based on the Black Sox scandal of 1919.

Swift, Jonathan (1667–1745)

British writer. Born in Dublin, Ireland, and educated at Trinity College, Swift is considered one of the greatest satirists to write in the

English language. His essays and books took aim at a number of issues, including the state of learning and religion (*A Tale of a Tub* and *The Battle of the Books*) and Irish political affairs (*Drapier's Letters* and "A Modest Proposal"). *Gulliver's Travels*, perhaps his most famous work, continues to be read and is regularly adapted for other media.

Thomas, Dylan (1914–1953)

British writer. Thomas is known primarily for his poetry, which appears in the collections *Eighteen Poems*, *Twenty-Five Poems*, *The Map of Love*, *The World I Breathe*, *New Poems*, and *Death and Entrances*. His poetry is distinctive for its frequent use of Celtic imagery (Thomas was born in Wales) and for its striking, sometimes difficult, syntax and metaphor. In addition to poetry, Thomas also produced plays for stage, screen, and radio; an autobiographical narrative entitled *Portrait of the Artist as a Young Dog;* and several prose tales.

Thoreau, Henry David (1817–1862)

American naturalist, philosopher, and writer. Thoreau most often wrote about two topics: the natural world and relations between the individual and civic government. He remains widely recognized for detailed observations of nature (much of it surrounding his native Concord, Massachusetts) and for the ways he mixed philosophy with such observations. His nature writings appeared in several books during his lifetime, including *A Week on the Concord and Merrimack Rivers*, *The Maine Woods*, and *Walden; or, Life in the Woods*.

Tuchman, Barbara (1912–1989)

American historian and journalist. Born in New York City to a prominent family (her grandfather had been ambassador to Mexico and Turkey under the Wilson Administration), Tuchman came to history through more journalistic than academic training. (She was educated at Radcliffe College, but held no advanced degrees in history.) She employed her literary approach to history in such books as *The Guns of August, Stillwell and the American Experience in China*, and *A Distant Mirror*, and the former two each won a Pulitzer Prize thanks to Tuchman's narrative skills and attention to historical detail.

Veciana-Suarez, Ana (1956–)

American journalist. Educated at the University of South Florida, Veciana-Suarez has been a staff writer for *The Miami Herald* for much of the eighties and nineties, and she currently writes a regular column, "Family Matters," which focuses on family and women's issues. She has published two books on Hispanic media and has recently completed a novel, *The Chin Kiss King*.

Walsh, Robb (1952–)

American writer. A freelance writer, Walsh is a columnist for *Natural History Magazine*, a contributing editor of *American Way* (the in-flight magazine of American Airlines), and a commentator for National Public Radio. He lives in Austin, Texas.

Welsch, Roger L. (1936–)

American folklorist, storyteller, and writer. Perhaps most widely known as "the guy in the bib overalls" who presents "Postcards from Nebraska" on the CBS weekly program *Sunday Morning*, Welsch most often writes about rural life and folklore in the American Plains states. Until 1988 a professor of anthropology and English, Welsch has written regular columns for a number of periodicals and has published numerous books, including *It's Not the End of the Earth, but You Can See It from Here*; *Touching the Fire: Buffalo Dancers, The Sky Bundle, and Other Tales*; *Uncle Smoke Stories* (tales for children); and, most recently, *Diggin' in and Piggin' out*, an examination of food and men.

White, E(lwyn) B(rooks) (1899–1985)

American writer and editor. Though he wrote in several genres, White is considered one of America's greatest essayists. In addition to his essays (many of which are collected in *One Man's Meat*, *The Second Tree from the Corner*, and *Essays of E. B. White*), he is known for *The Elements of Style* (a classic on prose style that White updated from William Strunk) and for two works of juvenile fiction: *Stuart Little* and *Charlotte's Web*. He is also credited for much of the success of *The New Yorker*.

Wiener, Jan (19??–)

Lecturer and historian. Wiener is the author of *The Assasination of Heydrich*.

Wolkomir, Richard (1943–)

American writer. A graduate of Syracuse University, Wolkomir is a contributing writer to *Smithsonian Magazine* and also writes for such magazines as *Reader's Digest*, *Omni*, *National Geographic*, and *Boy's Life*.

He is the author of chapters for a number of books, including *Robotics* and *Arthur C. Clarke's July 20, 2019*, and with his wife, Joyce Rogers Wolkomir, he coauthored the book *Junkyard Bandicoots and Other Tales of the World's Endangered Species*. The quality of many of Wolkomir's articles on science has earned him the American Association for the Advancement of Science/Westinghouse Award for Distinguished Science Writing in Magazines. He lives in Vermont.

Yamamoto, Luci (1966–)

American writer and editor. Educated at Occidental College (Los Angeles) and Boult Hall School of Law, Yamamoto currently edits a transportation magazine at the University of California at Berkeley. She lives in Berkeley and is working on a collection of essays about growing up as an identical twin in Hilo, Hawaii.

Yunus, Mohammad (1928–)

Bangladeshi reformer and business man. Yunus founded Grameen Bank (*grameen* means "village") in 1976 after failing to convince existing banks to make loans to the poor. (The World Bank at that time made only large loans to major organizations.) The Grameen Bank helps the working poor by making small loans (often called "microloans" or "microcredit"). Yunus's work is motivated by his belief that "we can remove poverty from the surface of the earth only if we can redesign our institutions."

Zamir, Mair (19??–)

Canadian applied mathematician. Educated at the University of London, Zamir studies viscous flow and fluid dynamics and teaches at the University of Western Ontario.

Zuger, Abigail (1955–)

American physician. Zuger is an infectious-diseases physician and the author of *Strong Shadows: Scenes from an Inner City AIDS Clinic*, an account of her experiences with a number of AIDS patients.

Zwinger, Ann H. (1925–)

American naturalist and writer. Much of Zwinger's work documents the natural life of the American Southwest while speculating on the place of humans in that region. In her book *Mysterious Lands: A Naturalist Explores the Four Great Deserts of the Southwest*, for example,

Zwinger speculates about the efforts of prehistoric peoples to learn which desert plants were poisonous, which edible, and which medicinal. Zwinger's other books of natural history include *Beyond the Aspen Grove, A Desert Country Near the Sea: A Natural History of the Cape Region of Baja California,* and *Downcanyon: A Naturalist Explores the Colorado River Through the Grand Canyon.*

Permissions Acknowledgments

ghum. Reprinted by permission of Villard Books, a division of Random House, Inc.

Henry Louis Gates Jr.: "A Dangerous Literacy: The Legacy of Frederick Douglass." Originally printed in *The New York Times Book Review,* May 28, 1995. Copyright © 1995 by Henry Louis Gates Jr. Reprinted with the permission of the author.

Michelle Genz: "Getting Pucked." From *Tropic* Magazine. Reprinted by permission of the author.

Lani Guinier: "The Tyranny of the Majority." From *The Tyranny of the Majority: Fundamental Fairness in Representative Democracy* by Lani Guinier. Copyright © 1994 by Lani Guinier. Reprinted by permission of The Free Press, a Division of Simon & Schuster.

Stephen Hawking: "Is Everything Determined?" From *Black Holes and Baby Universes and Other Essays* by Stephen W. Hawking. Copyright © 1993 by Stephen W. Hawking. Used by permission of Bantam Books, a division of Bantam Doubleday Dell Publishing Group, Inc.

Jan Hoffman: "Judge Hayden's Family Values." From *The New York Times,* October 15, 1995. Copyright © 1995 by The New York Times Co. Reprinted by permission.

Douglas R. Hofstadter: "Reductio Expansioque ad Absurdum" by Douglas R. Hofstadter. From *Mysteries of Life and the Universe* by William H. Shore. Copyright © 1992 by Share Our Strength, Inc. Reprinted by permission of Harcourt Brace & Company.

bell hooks: "Representing the Poor." From *Outlaw Culture: Resisting Representations* by bell hooks. Reprinted by permission of Routledge.

Langston Hughes: "The Animals Must Wonder." From *Langston Hughes and the Chicago Defender: Essays on Race, Politics and Culture 1942–62* edited by Christopher DeSantis. Reprinted by permission of the Chicago Daily Defender.

Jeremy Iggers: "Innocence Lost: Our Complicated Relationship with Food." Originally published in the *Utne Reader.* Reprinted by permission of the author.

Molly Ivins: "Get a Knife, Get a Dog, but Get Rid of Guns." From *Nothin' But Good Times Ahead* by Molly Ivins. Copyright © 1993 by Molly Ivins. Reprinted by permission of Random House, Inc.

Jamaica Kincaid: From *A Small Place* by Jamaica Kincaid. Copyright © 1988 by Jamaica Kincaid. Reprinted by permission of Farrar, Straus & Giroux.

Stephen King: "Why We Crave Horror Movies." Originally appeared in *Playboy* Magazine. Copyright © Stephen King. All rights reserved. Reprinted with permission.

Barbara Kingsolver: "Stone Soup." From *High Tide In Tucson* by Barbara Kingsolver. Copyright © 1995 by Barbara Kingsolver. Reprinted by permission of HarperCollins Publishers, Inc.

Harold Klawans: "The Mind of a Neurologist" by Harold Klawans. From *Mysteries of Life and the Universe* edited by William H. Shore. Copyright © 1992 by Share Our Strength, Inc. Reprinted by permission of Harcourt Brace & Company.

Marty Klein: "Erotophobia: The Cruelest Abuse of All." From *The Erotic Impulse*, edited by David Steinberg. Copyright © 1992 by David Steinberg. Reprinted by permission of Jeremy P. Tarcher, Inc., a division of The Putnam Publishing Group.

Gina Kolata: "Should Children Be Told If Genes Predict Illness?" From *The New York Times*, September 26, 1996. Copyright © 1994 by The New York Times Co. Reprinted by permission.

Melvin Konner: "Why the Reckless Survive." From *Why the Reckless Survive* by Melvin Konner. Copyright © 1990 by Melvin Konner. Used by permission of Viking Penguin, a division of Penguin Books USA Inc.

Leonard Kriegel: From *Claiming the Self: The Cripple as an American Man* (North Point Press). Reprinted by permission of the author.

Meg Laughlin: "The Test." Originally published in *Tropic* Magazine. Reprinted by permission of the author.

Andrea Lee: "Back to School." Originally published in *The New*

Yorker. Copyright © 1996 by Andrea Lee. Reprinted by permission of International Creative Management, Inc.

Ursula K. Le Guin: "The Creatures on My Mind." From *Unlocking the Air and Other Stories* by Ursula K. Le Guin. First appeared in *Harper's.* Copyright © 1990 by Ursula K. Le Guin. Reprinted by permission of the author and the author's agent, Virginia Kidd.

William Bryant Logan: "Clyde's Pick-Up." From *Parabola* Magazine. Reprinted by permission of the author.

Barry Lopez: "The Log Jam." From *River Notes: Dance of the Herons* by Barry Holstun Lopez. Copyright © 1978 by Barry Holstun Lopez. Used by permission of the author and Sterling Lord Literistic.

Dennis Alan Mann: "Beams of Light: Looking at Architecture." From *The Journal of American Culture.* Reprinted by permission of the author.

Jonathan Marks: "Black White Other." From *Natural History* Magazine, December 1994. Copyright © 1994 by the American Museum of Natural History. Reprinted with permission from *Natural History* Magazine.

Rafe Martin: "Zen Failure." From *The Sun.* Reprinted by permission of the author.

William Maxwell: "What He Was Like." From *All the Days and Nights* by William Maxwell. Copyright © 1996 by William Maxwell. Reprinted by permission of Alfred A. Knopf Inc.

Margaret Mead and Rhoda Metraux: "Time to Reflect, Time to Feel." From *A Way of Seeing.* Copyright © 1961, 1962, 1963, 1964, 1965, 1966, 1967, 1968, 1969, 1970 by Margaret Mead and Rhoda Metraux. Reprinted by permission of William Morrow & Co, Inc.

Donella H. Meadows: "Lines in the Mind, Not in the World." From *The Global Citizen* by Donella H. Meadows. Reprinted by permission of Alexander Hoyt and Associates.

Aurora Levins Morales: "Kitchens" by Aurora Levins Morales. From *Getting Home Alive* by Aurora Levins Morales and Rosario

Index